ORAL HISTORY

Second Edition

ORAL HISTORY

An Interdisciplinary Anthology

Second Edition

David K. Dunaway
Willa K. Baum
Editors

A Division of Sage Publications, Inc.
Walnut Creek • London • New Delhi

Published in cooperation with the American
Association for State and Local History and the Oral History Association

For information contact:

AltaMira Press
A Division of Sage Publications, Inc.
1630 North Main Street, Suite 367
Walnut Creek, California 94596 U.S.A.

Sage Publications Ltd.
6 Bonhill Street
London EC2A 4PU United Kingdom

Sage Publications India Pvt. Ltd.
M-32 Market
Greater Kailash 1
New Delhi 110 048 India

Printed in the United States of America

Library of Congress Cataloging-in-Publication Data

Oral History: an interdisciplinary anthology / David K. Dunaway, Willa K. Baum, editors. — 2nd ed.
    p. cm. — (American Association for State and Local History book series)
    Published in cooperation with the American Association for State and Local History and the Oral History Association.
    Includes bibliographical references and index.
    ISBN 0-7619-9188-3 (alk. paper). — ISBN 0-7619-9189-1 (pbk.: alk. paper)
    1. Oral History I. Dunaway, David King. II. Baum, Willa K. III. American Association for State and Local History. IV. Oral History Association. V. Series.
D16.14.O73   1996
907.2—dc20   96-25385
                                                                  CIP

            98   99   10   9   8   7   6   5   4   3   2

Interior Design and Production by Labrecque Publishing Services
Cover Design by Denise M. Santoro
Editorial Management by Denise M. Santoro and Barbara Richard

CONTENTS

PART THREE
ORAL HISTORY APPLIED:
LOCAL, ETHNIC, FAMILY, AND WOMEN'S HISTORY

PART FOUR
ORAL HISTORY AND RELATED DISCIPLINES:
FOLKLORE, ANTHROPOLOGY, MEDIA, AND LIBRARIANSHIP

PART FIVE
ORAL HISTORY AND REGIONAL STUDIES

INTRODUCTION

The Interdisciplinarity
of Oral History

David K. Dunaway

*I*n the original preface to this work, the editors speculated that three generations linked the founding of the first oral history center in the United States,
at Columbia University in 1948, with today's researchers.

In the last dozen years, a fourth generation of oral historians has emerged,
many trained in post-graduate institutions, with this anthology as a text, alongside the most sophisticated procedural guides. These are the children of the
1960s and 1970s, for whom cassette recorders, video cameras, and computers are
second-nature, unthreatening, technologies; for whom the oral (particularly the
media) presentation of recollection and reminiscence may seem more natural
than the written. The print culture of their grandparents has become a worldwide
technoculture based on new forms of aural information (music videos, advertis-
ing jingles, broadcast narratives), causing some to wonder if the bland cultural formulae of pop music and television will overwhelm our history-seeking,
identity-building instinct.

This new generation of oral historians has been influenced by postmodernist
critical movements, which have spilled over from literary theory into disciplines
such as anthropology, sociology, and history. Today, oral history faces intellectual
challenges posed by cultural critics who assert a previously unimagined complexity to its fundamental process, the recorded recollections of historically and culturally significant events or trends. Their audience-centered model of presenting
history has prompted a more process-oriented reading of history and culture.[1] As
a consequence, oral history has experienced a surge of interest in subjectivity and
in nontraditional sources.[2]

Since history is today widely viewed as a culture-specific construct, with the
historian only as important as the (present and future) audience who reads him
or her (and whose organization of facts and sources is idiosyncratic)—<u>what,
exactly, do we turn to history and oral history for?</u> The answer may lie in its past.

The first generation of professional oral historians, led by pioneering figures such as Allan Nevins and Louis Starr, to whom this volume is dedicated, conceived of oral history as a means to collect otherwise unwritten recollections of prominent individuals for future historians, for research, and as a tool for orally based biography.

A second generation, coming of age in the mid-1960s after the basic archives had been established, built upon this earlier work, by expanding the purposes of collectors and collections.[3] This group viewed oral history as more than a way to capture the accounts of important people for scholars; rather, it employed oral history techniques to describe and empower the nonliterate and the historically disenfranchised. Throughout the 1970s, many collectors of oral history used their research to document and promote community cohesion and ethnic diversity. In this period, oral history built a name for itself and a grassroots constituency based on efforts by educators, feminists, and activists as well as local, ethnic, and regional history campaigns. While collectors in the first generation continued to direct the principal archives, they found the younger group of social educators virtually beating on their doors to broaden the scope of collections beyond so-called elite interviews.

In the 1980s, a third generation emerged. Students and scholars learned the craft of oral historiography in an era removed from both the conservative 1950s and the socially radical 1960s. The principal oral history archives in the United States had set high standards for the maintenance and development of collections. New technologies such as computerized research aids and personal computers made professional oral history collections more capital-intensive. Many of the smaller, volunteer-oriented groups passed their first flush of collecting and considered how to focus and put their work to use. In this decade, the emergence of younger, academically trained oral historians raised issues of amateurism vs. professionalism (for the number of full-time posts in oral history is small, possibly as few as 500 in the United States).

Prior to the 1980s, the process of generating oral history was considered uncomplicated, with interviewers presumed to have recorded, from a neutral stance, whatever material of historical use they could glean for the good of the future. History would emerge at some later time, when writers and scholars used these oral sources. This notion was challenged by more theoretically oriented researchers (prompted by some of the authors represented in this volume, such as Ronald Grele, Paul Thompson, Alessandro Portelli, and others) who speculated that interviews—and their construction—*themselves* represent history: compiled within a historical frame negotiated by the interviewer and the narrator, within contemporary trends, within certain definable conventions of language and cultural interaction.[4] Now a debate emerged in the profession over the purpose of oral history: was it intended to be (1) a set of primary source documents or (2) a process for constructing history from oral sources?

Drawing upon a wealth of previous collecting experience, oral historians of this generation asked introspective, process-oriented questions of their colleagues. What is the effect, they wondered, of reducing a multilayered communication event (rich with gesture and intonation) to a printed page or a magnetic tape—what elements are lost or changed? What time period does such an interview represent: the time investigated or the time of the interview?

In similar fashion, the 1980s became the decade of the public program in the oral history profession. Museums increasingly incorporated oral materials into exhibits to add voices to the presentation of research and artifacts. Museologists turned to oral history as a central methodological procedure.[5] Libraries reached out beyond the stacks to establish educational programs with schools and community groups: some made the transition from depositories to collection centers generating new materials. Arts, humanities, and historical commissions funded projects involving public use of previously collected interviews: broadcasts, drama, multimedia exhibits, and popular publications of a broad range.

Oral history developed practical applications in administration and policy matters. The most prominent uses included historic preservation, land-use claims, litigation, environmental-cultural impact statements, and institutional and business history.

In the gradual shift within the historical profession from presenting facts as received wisdom to presenting theoretical analyses as specific to a given time and place and society, oral history has played a vital role. The generational distinctions mentioned above are more pronounced on this issue than on others. The young scholar may feel empowered by the deconstruction of history-making into a landscape of self-interest and subjectivism (and even by a rhetoric so internally referential that recent post-graduates have an edge over their elders in understanding it). On the other hand, a reaction may be setting in: as one senior oral historian commented after attending the 1993 International Conference on Oral History, in Siena/Lucca, Italy, "I hate subjectivism. That's not what I went into history to study." (This generation gap applies as well to the editors of this volume: Baum, trained in the 1950s, insists that oral history is a method and technique; Dunaway, trained in the 1970s, views oral history as progressing from a method of research into a distinct field of scholarly inquiry.)

Oral history in the 1990s is today characterized by a rising interest in interdisciplinarity. In folklore, linguistics, and ethnomusicology—to name just a few fields—oral history interviewing has long been a staple. In the last decade, however, as the fieldwork process of oral history has generated its own scholarly literature, more professors of these disciplines incorporate oral history practice into post-graduate programs. They are sending their students to the nearest oral history center or institute for specific methodological training to balance the content-area training from their home disciplines. As oral history becomes central to post-graduate and public history programs, its greatest effect may be its interdisciplinary applications.

The discussion which follows briefly surveys the interdisciplinarity of oral history, which this volume was designed to stimulate. No such reading of a field can pretend to be more than suggestive or avoid being outdated as soon as it is published; yet there may be value in charting the common ground of those relying on oral data collection and analysis. Each field relies on oral testimony collected in a particular manner; each uses that information in a unique fashion, according to disciplinary focus—yet each shares the difficulties and advantages in working with oral sources.

The discussion here omits a great deal more than it includes. The work of many is compressed or passed over for lack of space; thus the survey cannot be comprehensive, and its presentation concentrates on North American sources, yet in the book's section on European and Latin American oral history (Part Five), similar developments will be found.

Anthropology

At the meeting of anthropology and oral history, we find ethnographers using overlapping research techniques with historians, though seeking different data. Perhaps the principal difference is that the anthropologist records interviews not for historical fact but rather to learn the structure and variety of a society or culture, as manifested by a representative individual's world view, cultural traits, and traditions. Thus the ethnographic interview provides insights into individuals not as historical eyewitnesses but as culture- or tradition-bearers. As Sidney Mintz suggests in this volume, the ethnographer using oral history concentrates on intensive work with informants, rather than on documentary or survey data.[6] Such interviewing does not deemphasize individual uniqueness or personality, so much as it situates how individuality manifests itself in the systematic context of sociocultural forces.

Culture-seeking interviews were once considered to be transparent—a set of facts revealed to an interviewer by an interviewee, a text compiled without reference to the linguistic, cultural, gender, and performance factors in the interaction between narrator and interviewer. Yet in recent years, as attention has shifted from the content of the interview to the linguistic interaction which takes place there, and on to the functioning of humans' narrative instinct, both anthropologists and oral historians have explored the narrator–interviewer relationship reflexively.

One illustration of this crossing is a special issue of the *Journal of Narrative and Life History*, exploring the intersections of biography, oral history, and life history.[7] Instead of monolithic notions of culture, anthropologists working with oral sources are turning their attention to pluralistic models, including how interviewees (and groups) maintain traditions in changing societies.[8] The classic anthropologists included in this volume, Jan Vansina and Ruth Finnegan, are particularly concerned with oral tradition, as opposed to oral history: how narratives told either as history or as literature are affected by the presence (or absence) of a particular audience and performance context. Thus ethnographers have come to respect history-telling as a culture-bearing activity, subject to specific rules in a specific culture.

Education/Teaching

As the authors of a comprehensive guide on oral history for educators commented, oral history in the classroom bridges the gap between curriculum and community: "It brings history home by linking the world of textbook and classroom with the face-to-face social world of the student's home community."[9]

Oral history has served both as a means to preserve the contemporary history of education as a discipline and as a teaching strategy in social studies. Projects may record the history of instruction in a given field.[10] Others may focus on teaching, providing effective lesson plans for using oral history in the classroom—such as the work of Elliot Wigginton and Don Cavallini at the secondary level, and James Hoopes at the post-secondary level.[11]

Oral history works as a gateway to the rich cultural resources outside classrooms and textbooks. Teachers have found student interviewing to be an effective way for motivating learning in general, and community-based learning in particular. Oral history offers students a way to situate themselves in the history of their educational community.[12] (Because of the current wealth of articles and books on teaching and oral history, no readings in education are included in this volume.)

Beyond lessons in autobiography, biography, and validation techniques of history, teachers at the secondary and post-secondary levels use oral history to collect and study our aural landscape: the sounds which once surrounded us— the freight trains' moan, the streetcars' clang. (Teachers and historians alike sometimes ignore the historical context of sounds, smells, and sights, which may carry information as essential to the historical record as the words oral historians customarily preserve.)

Ethnic Studies/Ethnohistory/American Studies

Oral historians have long understood the value of oral testimony in creating a sense of community cohesion and of continuity across generations. This is particularly true for minority and ethnic groups as historically disenfranchised as African Americans, prohibited by law during slavery even to learn to read and write; or as Latin Americans in the southwestern United States, previously forbidden by law to speak their native language in schools. When such communities are denied the right to read and write—or to speak their native languages—scholars inevitably turn to oral history to reconstruct this history.

"Oral history is not only a tool or a method," Gary Okihiro writes in this volume, "it also is a theory of history which maintains that the common folk and the dispossessed have a history and that this history must be written."

In this way, the second generation of oral historian-activists used oral sources to right an imbalance in historical records, which have favored the literate and the formally educated over those whose culture has not left written records. In recent years, the study of intergenerational transmission has grown in importance to historians working from oral sources.[13]

Some oral historians working in ethnic history have enlarged research projects in the academy to use oral history techniques "to make history more accessible to its participants."[14] This orally based ethnic history has found a public via community history plays and radio programs based upon interviews.[15]

The field of American studies—the interdisciplinary approach to American cultural and intellectual life—has in recent years broadened its portfolio to include ethnically diverse sources. Scholars have pioneered new ways of reading oral testimony—in the case of Lawrence Levine's *Black Culture, Black Consciousness*, the Federal Writers' Project slave narratives—to balance minority and majority views.[16] (This trend is illustrated in this volume by the contributions of Alex Haley and Tamara Hareven.)

Folklore

Folklorists and ethnomusicologists collecting traditions (oral and otherwise) have long gathered historical and biographical context via oral history. Folklorists have made significant contributions to the methodology of oral history (see the discussion of oral history manuals, below), while membership rolls in oral history associations often cross with those in folklore societies. Sometimes the two fields hold joint conferences, such as the International Conference on Folklore and Oral History at the Centre for English Cultural Studies at the University of Sheffield (United Kingdom) in 1991.

One explanation for these crossings is the oral nature of many of the tradi-tions recorded by folklorists. Methods for collecting oral lore and oral history overlap, though the former tends to be more spontaneous in collecting approach. In this volume, Richard Dorson comments on the blending of personal and his-torical narratives and how episodes told as history can be traced to archetypal folktales, such as the labor of Hercules set in a small Illinois town, in the essay of Larry Danielson. Similarly, the degree to which history can be written from tradi-tional lore is a concern of Lynwood Montell, whose preface to the classic *The Saga of Coe Ridge* (an oral history of a geographically remote African-American com-munity in Kentucky) offers a typology of responses of historians to sources from traditional culture. Richard Dorson points out the different weights which folk-lorists and oral historians assign to factors in the formulation of a text: the histori-cal profession has traditionally ignored the role of performance, narrative, and audience, preferring to focus on factual content. One folklorist, in defining the narrative genre of the "life story"—as opposed to the life history, or the oral biog-raphy—asserts that the primary interest of the folklorist is *not* the historical accu-racy of life narratives, but rather the formulaic way in which they are expressed and represent motifs and tale-types of tradition.[17]

Gerontology

Prior to the 1980s, gerontologists were more inclined to study oral history than oral historians were to study gerontology. Therapists have long realized that the elderly are especially suitable for (and receive particular benefits from) oral his-tory interviews.[18] Gerontologists have used oral history techniques with success in taking medical histories, for example.[19]

For these studies, many researchers use what Robert Butler calls the "life review," a counseling technique for aging individuals who experience disassociation and depression.[20] Some researchers suggest that such therapeutic reminiscence has multiple functions: informative, evaluative, and, negatively, obsessive.[21] As the population of the western world ages, researchers will experience increased pres-sure to understand how our memory and history-telling instinct is affected by our aging; and oral historians, with their experience in eliciting narratives, will play an expanded role in gerontology. In the United Kingdom, oral history researchers are formulating a relationship between reminiscence among the elderly and the emergence of a social movement for the rights of the elderly.[22]

Legal Studies

The testimonies of oral history are often inadmissible in courts of law under the "hearsay" rule of evidence: one can testify only on what one has seen or experienced, rather than on what one has heard someone say. Nevertheless, in the last 15 years, oral history has entered into both litigation and the precedents which form the basis for legal decisions.[23] At the 1989 meetings of the American Society for Ethnohistory, one panel concerned the role of oral historical research in land- and water-use litigation. Just as anthropologists and archaeologists are increasingly involved in initial canvasses of sites for commercial development, so oral historians increasingly survey and testify on the oral tradition and oral history surrounding land and water tenure. (One difficulty here is the problem of obtaining "expert witness" status for oral historians.) While this field is too new and far too specialized for inclusion in this volume, studies of social history often involve the oral historian in legal thickets, when lawyers base litigation on their research.

Another application of oral history to legal history is the way in which law firms and legal history societies are turning to oral historians to document the history of their firm or branch of law, or the lives of outstanding jurists. Similarly, the complex of legal issues surrounding the creation, copyright, and "fair use" of an interview requires oral historians to pay progressively more attention to legal precedents.[24]

Literary History

For as long as there have been writers—indeed, *before* there were writers in the times when literature was exclusively oral—people have conducted interviews to document the literary process and its context. Oral history has influenced literary studies in primarily two categories: biography, both oral and written; and literary history, where interviews document the activities of the literary profession and publishing (as well as the work of specific writers).

Literary history or biography compiled primarily from oral sources differs significantly from that constructed primarily from written sources.[25] One interdisciplinary quarterly which examined this trend is *Biography*.[26] An orally sourced biography requires a researcher to evaluate the reliability and validity of his or her narrators, as does any book based on written sources. Yet the oral biographer may have certain advantages: interview sessions may expose new documents, letters, and photographs; interviews cover a full range of sources, not just those from the period of public activity (since the historical sources themselves are available for cross-examination); and the testimonies are depositories of living language with distinctive and exact phrasings.[27] (In this volume, Alex Haley comments on how oral history informed the creation of his classic, *Roots*.)

In 1990, the U.S. Oral History Association held its first panel on "oral literary history," that is, documenting via recorded interviews the literary culture of a period. This panel discussed everything from oral narratives of Vietnam survivors to the negotiation of a historical time frame between the interviewer and the interviewee.[28]

Oral literary history possesses certain key characteristics: (1) it focuses on works of contemporary literature where the researcher interactively probes the author's sources, creative process, and revisions, as well as his or her networks of influence; (2) works of interest to oral literary historians tend to be language-centered and concerned with the sociolinguistic dimension of the literary text; (3) oral literary historians are inclined to explore historical and social contexts to literature, as opposed to critics who view the text as internally referential, to the exclusion of the world outside; (4) texts studied via oral literary history reflect the fundamentally collaborative process of an interviewer and a narrator.

As George Held wrote in a review-essay on collections of interviews with contemporary writers, "the resulting harvest of critical and biographical information [gathered via interview] has become a subspecies of oral history."[29] Unfortunately, many such collections are not prepared by trained oral historians, which has often resulted in a blurring of the distinction between lived experience and created experience, the latter being a writer's stock-in-trade. Still, ranging from the early interviews on publishing in the Columbia University archives to those in Britain's National Sound Archives, the oral history branch of literary history is a growing and popular area of research. As new literary formats emerge, such as audio-books and "video-letters" (videotaped oral memoirs, illustrated with photographs and ephemera), their narrative voice will surely be influenced by the model of oral history.[30]

Media Studies and Media Production

For more than three-quarters of a century, since the dawn of radio broadcasting, producers have explored historical subjects in both documentary and fiction formats. In radio, television, and film, producers have sought to raise popular historical consciousness, to broadcast "to the man [and woman] in the street" in order to develop "historical mindedness," as a National Advisory Council on Radio and Education suggested more than 60 years ago.[31] Today, electronic and mass media are leading outlets for publicizing oral history's findings. Documentarians on radio and television—particularly on the sparsely funded public networks—are discovering the riches available in oral history archives. Local broadcasters are airing oral history interviews to fulfill their public-service obligations. Oral testimony has even been incorporated into full-length Hollywood feature films, such as *Reds* and *Zelig*.

In recent years, oral history organizations have held panels to promote an interchange of technical and artistic skills between media producers and oral historians. As discussed in "Radio and the Public Use of Oral History," in this volume, this collaboration has not been uncomplicated. Training in broadcasting and learning in content areas of the humanities are generally separated in post secondary and post-graduate education. The result of this mismatch leaves media producers with an acute knowledge of their medium's grammar but often without any knowledge of its potential content; and it leaves oral historians comfortable with their subject while lacking a plan for the use of their materials beyond archiving them.

In terms of the history of broadcasting, interviews at the Columbia University's oral history program covered the early, pioneering days of broadcasting in the United States; similarly in Canada, the Canadian Broadcasting Corporation has sponsored oral history interviews of its early staff.[32]

A separate trend has been a new, analytical treatment of broadcasting and oral history, including its representational strategies, its methodological implications, and its aesthetic. Typical of this approach was the 1993 conference of the Oral History Society in Britain, "Broadcasting and Oral History," which debated how documentaries based upon oral history represent (or possibly stereotype) regions and ethnicities. Documentarians discussed how their genre has been changed by including oral sources—and how today's historical sources anticipate media uses in their testimony. Researchers debated the implications of selection and editing procedures, including ethical and privacy issues affecting interviewees (such as those discussed in Amelia Fry's contribution for this volume).

Sociology And Community Studies

At issue in exploring how oral history is applied internationally is the way academic disciplines are defined differently in different countries. Much modern oral history research in Britain and Germany, for example, takes place as sociology (which includes what North Americans call social anthropology).[33] British sociologists are often involved in what psychologists call "depth interviewing," involving a deep, multilayered process of recounting individual experience. In Britain, this discipline includes more life history interviewing than in the United States, where sociologists conducting interviews are more apt to apply Robert Merton's notion of the "fixed-focus" interview, treating individual narrators as significant only as representatives of groups and subcultures. Thus American sociologists tend to receive training in survey-research methods and conduct "oral sociology" via structured questionnaires.

Oral history in the United States is more closely tied to the community history model.[34] Here, the localistic orientation of sociology tends toward the qualitative side of the profession, where individual experiences count as much as the statistical aggregate.[35] Recent arrivals at the juncture of sociology and oral history, such as the Institute of Sociology at the Russian Academy of Sciences, Moscow, tend to favor this combined life-history, life-story approach to inductive research in sociology.

In Britain, the community history/community studies movement has been particularly effective at finding local publishing outlets for its research. Whether community profiles, volumes of individual reminiscence, or documentation of acculturation, these works blend either single or collective narratives into works accessible to the community from which this history has come.[36]

Women and Gender Studies

Included in this volume is a pioneer essay in women's studies and oral history, "What's So Special About Women? Women's Oral History," by Sherna Gluck. Those interested in combining women's studies and oral history already confront questions which Gluck's essay raises: who is the appropriate interviewer for oral history projects on women—someone of the same gender? the same age? the same class? Are interviewing projects which dramatize and perhaps glorify women's domestic achievements perpetuating stereotypes of women's work?

As in the case of ethnic studies, oral historians interested in women's studies are harvesting recollections of groups and classes of people largely disenfranchised from the historical records.[37] "Historians attempted to offer modern women heroines and role models, characters in a single 'herstory' long ignored," Susan Strasser commented. "[Yet] housewives remained 'hidden from history'. . . . This 'history from the bottom up' produced articles in professional journals and local history projects. It used a variety of unconventional techniques to tell the tale of everyday life in the past."[38]

Where the majority of women are from working-class backgrounds, in which formal education was not a traditional priority, much of the data collected orally occurs in an anecdotal, narrative framework of autobiographies and memoirs.[39] Gluck and others have synthesized feminist concerns from fields related to oral history, such as gender-based styles in language, collaboration, and authority.[40]

Oral History Guides

Another way to examine how oral history has developed over the last two decades is to explore the variety and substance of its methodological guides.

Perhaps the first and most widely used guide to oral history practice was Willa K. Baum's *Oral History for the Local Historical Society,* which first appeared in 1966.[41] Previously, guides to fieldwork in interviewing were either drawn from sociology or from folklore, notably the 1964 work *A Guide for Fieldworkers in Folklore.*[42] Whereas Goldstein's work relies heavily on anthropology, including sections on rapport, observation, and collecting, Baum reached out to a nonprofessional audience, taking up such practical issues as preinterviewing and local history research and influencing other guides of this period.[43] In 1974, William

Moss's *Oral History Program Manual* approached oral history from an archivist's perspective, including sections on curating and conserving oral history collections. The publication of these two volumes documented the increasing popularity of oral history, particularly among those referred to above as the second generation of oral historians.[44] By this period, oral history guides were beginning to shift focus from how to make tape recordings and conduct interviews, in favor of exploring issues in collecting and circulating transcripts.

In 1976, William Langlois produced his *Guide to Aural History Research,*[45] a procedures manual from the Canadian perspective, which emphasizes listening to the tape recordings rather than reading transcripts of the interview; thus Canadians have perhaps explored the historical soundscape more fully than other nations. This work was followed in 1977 by another work from Baum, *Transcribing and Editing Oral History.*[46] Written by the co-editor of this volume and a key figure in the first generation of oral historians, *Transcribing and Editing* provided an overview of practical issues in processing interviews. One fieldworker with experience in folklore, oral history, and biography produced a guide specifically oriented toward recording procedure: Edward Ives's *The Tape Recorded Interview.*[47] Ives's work provided a basic technical orientation to fieldworkers using tape recorders alongside its sophisticated commentary on interviewing.

These works from the 1970s were eventually surpassed by guides to oral history procedure from major international archives in the 1980s. In 1984, the Provincial Archive of British Columbia published *Voices: A Guide to Oral History*; UNESCO published *Archives, Oral History, and Oral Tradition*; the British Broadcasting Company and the National Sound Archive Company produced *Telling It How It Was: A Guide to Recording Oral History.*[48] This generation of guides explored the creation of transcripts from a more theoretical perspective, constituting a practical oral historiography for the field.[49]

A continuation of this trend toward introspective methodology is the "Fieldwork in Oral History" issue of the *Oral History Review,* published in 1987. This explored such topics as the power relationship between the interviewer and the interviewee; the connections between ethnography and oral history; and sub-methodologies for oral history interviewing on political activism and feminism. Bruce Jackson's 1987 guide *Fieldwork* revisited the oral history-folklore juncture which Goldstein had analyzed nearly 25 years before—only now, the discussion of recording technology included both audio and video; and the analyses of fieldworker roles and recording technology show a dramatic leap in sophistication from oral history practice of the 1950s and 1960s. These and other, later, manuals and guides chart an increasingly reflexive dimension to oral history practice, in which the oral historian catalogues his or her background and ideology, as well as the performance and sociolinguistic context of the interview.[50]

For the new edition of *Oral History: An Interdisciplinary Anthology*, the editors have deleted a dozen articles on education and librarianship, and also eliminated the goals and guidelines of the Oral History Association (now available separately). We have added a section on oral history and regional studies to broaden the anthology's international scope. What was once an American text, used on hundreds of campuses from MIT to UCLA, is now more international.

We regret having to cut articles from the 1984 edition, for reasons of space, as much as we celebrate the diversity and range which our new essays offer to this edition. We similarly regret that we could not include many regions and individuals whose important work has not yet been represented in either edition. But a single volume could not contain such a range, and while debates remain unsettled, teachers of oral history still need a text.

As meetings of the International Oral History Association have shown in the 1980s and 1990s, oral history offers an entire world of opportunity. Today this world is challenged in several ways by incorporating emergent technologies—such as the Internet, plus computer-aided storage, processing, and retrieval. Oral historians have responded by finding ways of applying technology to create an international exchange of methods, approaches, and theory. If oral tradition is a river, at times flowing underground, tapped by successive generations, then oral history is its tributary, recycling history into story and sending story bubbling up into history by expanding the interdisciplinary boundaries of the field.

Notes

1. For an overview of postmodernism in cultural criticism, see George Lipsitz, "Popular Culture, Cultural Theory, and American Studies," *American Quarterly* 42 (December 1990), pp. 615–36.

2. See the discussion in the introduction to Raphael Samuel and Paul Thompson, eds., *The Myths We Live By* (London, New York: Routledge, 1990).

3. Perhaps the classic example of this period is Paul Thompson's *Voices of the Past* (Oxford: Oxford University Press, 1978), excerpted in the first edition of this work.

4. Examples of this trend include Barbara Allen, "Texture and Textuality in Orally Communicated History," *International Journal of Oral History* 6, (June 1985), pp. 92–103; David Hanige, *Oral Historiography* (London: Longman, 1982); Charles Briggs, "Historical Discourse," *Competence in Performance* (Philadelphia, Penn.: University of Pennsylvania Press, 1988); and Richard Baumann and Charles Briggs, "Poetics and Performance as Critical Perspectives on Language and Social Life," *Annual Review of Anthropology* 19 (1990), pp. 54–88.

5. See both the 1983 panel on "Oral History in Museum Work," at the 1983 Conference of the Canadian Oral History Association and a retrospective article in the British journal *Oral*

History, and Gareth Griffiths, "Museums and the Practice of Oral History" 17 (Autumn 1989), pp. 49–53. The Society of American Archivists' meetings throughout the 1980s also held panels on oral history.

6. Ethnography is not the only branch of anthropology interested in oral history; see, for example, the articles on ethnoarcheology and oral history in the *International Journal of Oral History* 20 (November 1983).

7. "The Afterlife of the Life History," Margaret Blackman, ed., *Journal of Narrative and Life History,* II:1 (Winter 1992).

8. See the commentaries in the "Historia Y Etnologia" issue of *Historia Y Fuente Oral* (no. 9, 1993), which in 1996 changed its title to include anthropology and folklore.

9. Barry Lanman and George Mahaffy, *Oral History in the Secondary School* (Los Angeles: Oral History Association Pamphlet Series, 1988); Thad Sitton, George Mehaffy, and O. L. Davis, eds., *Oral History: A Guide for Teachers* (Austin, Texas: University of Texas Press, 1983).

10. Another example is found in Allan Wieder, "Oral History and Questions of Interaction for Educational Historians," *International Journal of Oral History* 9 (June 1988), pp. 131–39.

11. Elliot Wigginton, *The Foxfire Book* (and its ten subsequent editions) (New York, N.Y.: Doubleday, 1972, et al.); Don Cavallini, "Oral/Aural History: In and Out of the Classroom," *Social Studies* 70 (May 1979), pp. 112–17; James Hoopes, *Oral History: An Introduction for Students* (Chapel Hill, N.C.: University of North Carolina Press, 1979); John Neuenschwander, *Oral History as a Teaching Approach* (Washington, D.C.: National Education Association, 1975).

12. William Cutler, "Oral History: Its Nature and Uses for Educational History," *History of Education Quarterly* 22 (Summer 1971), pp. 184–99.

13. One of the five strands of the 1993 International Conference on Oral History was devoted to intergenerational history; see the proceedings of the VIII International Conference, Siena/Lucca, Italy, pp. 1061–1143.

14. Laurie Serikaku, "Oral History in Ethnic Communities: Widening Focus," *Oral History Review* 17 (Spring 1989), p. 73; C. H. Bailey, "Precious Blood: Encountering Inter-Ethnic Issues in Oral History Research, Reconstruction, and Representation," *Oral History Review* 18 (Fall 1990), pp. 61–108.

15. One such project is "Writing the Southwest," an oral history radio documentary series funded by the National Endowment for the Humanities and state humanities endowments of Arizona, Colorado, and New Mexico, broadcast nationally in 1995–96 and produced at the University of New Mexico, Department of English; David Dunaway and Sara Spurgeon, *Writing the Southwest* (New York, N.Y.: Plume, 1995).

16. Lawrence Levine, *Black Culture, Black Consciousness* (New York, N.Y.: Oxford University Press, 1980). In American Studies, Michael Frisch has used his editorship of the *Oral History Review* to promote the interchange between ethnic studies and oral history; see the theme issue on Puerto Rican Women, *Oral History Review* 16 (Fall 1988).

17. Jeff Todd Titon, "The Life Story," *Journal of American Folklore* 93 (Summer 1980), pp. 276–92. See also David Braid, "Personal Narrative and Experiential Meaning," *Journal of American Folklore* 109 (Winter 1996), pp. 5–30.

18. An excellent bibliography of nonmedical applications of oral history is found in Paul Thompson, Catharine Itzin, and Michael Abendston, *I Don't Feel Old: The Experience of Later Life* (Oxford: Oxford University Press, 1990). See also Carl Ryant, "Comment: Oral History and Gerontology," *Gerontologist* 21 (February 1981), pp. 104–5; Robert Menninger, "Psychological Factors in Oral History Interviewing," *Oral History Review* (1975), pp. 68–75.

19. R. and S. Harris, "Therapeutic Uses of Oral History Techniques in Medicine," *International Journal of Aging and Human Development* 12 (1980), pp. 27–34.

20. Robert Butler, "The Life Review: An Unrecognized Bonanza," *International Journal of Aging and Human Development* 12 (1980), pp. 35–38.20.

21. Marianne Lo Gerfo, "Three Ways of Reminiscence in Theory and Practice," *International Journal of Aging and Human Development* 12 (1980), pp. 35–38; Barbara Meyerhoff, "Life History as Integration: An Essay on an Experiential Model," *Gerontologist* 15 (1975), pp. 541–43.

22. Joanna Bornat, "Oral History as a Social Movement" (and other articles in this special issue on aging), *Oral History* 17 (Autumn 1989).

23. Alessandro Portelli, "Oral Testimony, the Law, and the Making of History," *History Workshop Journal* 20 (Autumn 1985) pp. 5–35.

24. See, in particular, John Neuenschwander, *Oral History and the Law* (Los Angeles, Calif.: Oral History Association, Pamphlet Series, 1987, 1993). Neuenschwander may be the only oral history professor who simultaneously sits as a judge.

25. For an example of how oral history informs literary studies, see Alessandro Portelli, "Absalom, Absalom!: Oral History and Literature," in *The Death of Luigi Trastulli* (Albany, N.Y.: SUNY Press, 1991), and Stephen Arkin, "The Literary Interview as Form," *International Journal of Oral History* 4 (February 1983), pp. 12–18.

26. See David Mitchell, "Living Documents: Oral History and Biography," *Biography* 3 (1980), pp. 283–96; and David K. Dunaway, "Oral Biography and Memory," *Biography* 14 (Summer 1991), pp. 256–66.

27. David Mitchell, "Oral History and the Biography of Public Figures," *Canadian Oral History Association Journal* 6 (1983), pp. 33–37; David K. Dunaway, "Method and Theory in the Oral Biography," *Oral History* 20 (Autumn 1992), pp. 40–44.

28. Theories of narrativity, examining how history becomes configured into story, become important elements in current dialogues on the effect of performance on story-telling. See the review-essay "Storytelling as Experience," *Oral History Review* 22 (Winter 1995), pp. 87–91, and Simon Featherstone, "Narrative Form of Oral History," *Oral History* 19 (Autumn 1991), pp. 59–62.

29. George Held, "The Voice of the Writer Is Heard in the Land," *Oral History Review* 17 (Spring 1979), pp. 129; see also a review-essay by Maurice Maryanow, "Why Interview Writers," *International Journal of Oral History* 9 (February 1988), pp. 43–52.

30. Theresa Watkins, "A Video Letters Exchange," *Oral History* 20 (1992), pp. 45–46.

31. Tyson Levering, ed., *Proceedings of the Fourth Annual Assembly of the National Advisory Council on Radio in Education: Report of the History Committee* (Chicago, Ill.: University of Chicago Press, 1935).

32. See the comments of Dennis Duffy and others, pp. 49–61, and Jean Bruce, "Women in the CBC," *Canadian Oral History Journal* 5 (1982), pp. 7–18. For more recent examples of the role of history in broadcasting, see the articles on news-gathering in the *Oral History Review* 21 (Spring 1993).

33. Lucy Fischer, "Sociological Life History: Methodological Incongruence," *International Journal of Oral History* 20 (February 1983), pp. 29–40.

34. For examples, see Michael Frisch, "Town into City," *A Shared Authority* (Albany, N.Y.: SUNY Press, 1990), pp. 191–201, and Rickie Burman, "Oral History and Community History in the Work of Manchester Studies," *International Journal of Oral History* 5 (June 1984), pp. 114–24.

35. Typical of this perspective is Ingrid Scobie, "Family and Community History through Oral History," *Public Historian* 1 (Summer 1979).

36. See the detailed bibliography in Joanna Bornat, "The Communities of Community Publishing," *Oral History* 20 (Autumn 1992), pp. 23–31. See also a review-essay, Tom Woodin, "Recent British Community Histories," *Oral History* 20 (Autumn 1992), pp. 67–70.

37. One early symposium on the oral history of women is found in the *Canadian Oral History Association Journal* 6 (1983), pp. 7–20.

38. Susan Strasser, *Never Done: A History of American Housework* (New York, N.Y.: Pantheon, 1982), p. xii.

39. These reminiscences are often grouped by topic, such as women during wartime or women and settlement patterns, to cite but two articles in *Oral History* 19 (Autumn 1991).

40. Sherna Gluck and Daphne Patai, eds., *Women's Words: The Feminist Practice of Oral History* (New York and London: Routledge, 1991). This book has a comprehensive bibliography on oral history and gender studies.

41. Willa K. Baum, *Oral History for the Local Historical Society* (Nashville, Tenn.: American Association for State and Local History, 1967), 2d ed., 1974.

42. Kenneth Goldstein, *A Guide for Fieldworkers in Folklore* (Hatborough, Penn.: Folklore Associates/The American Folklore Society, 1964).

43. Gary Shumway and William Hartley, *An Oral History Primer* (Fullerton, Calif.: California State University, 1973). For a bibliography of early writings on oral history, see Gary Shumway, *Oral History in the United States: A Directory* (New York, N.Y.: Oral History Association, 1971).

44. The concerns of oral historians interested in prominent figures such as politicians were reflected in Anthony Seldon and Joanna Papausch, *By Word of Mouth: Elite Oral Histories* (London: Methuen, 1983).

45. William Langlois, *A Guide To Aural History Research* (Victoria, B.C.: Provincial Archives of British Columbia, 1976).

46. Willa Baum, *Transcribing and Editing Oral History* (Nashville, Tenn.: AASLH, 1977). For a theoretical discussion, see David Dunaway, "Transcription: Shadow of Reality," *Oral History Review* 12 (1984), pp. 113–19.

47. Edward (Sandy) Ives, *The Tape Recorded Interview*, (Knoxville, Tenn.: University of Tennessee Press, 1974, 1993).

48. Derek Reimer, David Mattison, and Allan Speckt, eds. *Voices: A Guide to Oral History* (Victoria, B.C.: Provincial Archives of British Columbia, 1984); William Moss and Peter Maziaana, *Archives, Oral History, and Oral Tradition*, (Paris: UNESCO, 1986), PGI-86/WS/2; Paul Thompson and Rob Perks, *Telling It How It Was: A Guide to Recording Oral History* (London: BBC Education, 1990).

49. These procedural guides benefited greatly from methodological studies in related professions, such as sociology (Michael Agar, *The Professional Stranger*, New York, N.Y.: Academic Press, 1980), folklore (Robert Georges and Michael Jones, *People Studying People*, Berkeley, Calif.: University of California Press, 1980), and Bruce Jackson, *Fieldwork*, Urbana, Ill.: University of Illinois Press, 1987).

50. Valerie Yow, *Recording Oral History: A Practical Guide for Social Scientists* (Thousand Oaks, Calif.: Sage, 1994) and Donald Ritchie, *Doing Oral History* (New York, N.Y.: Twayne, 1995).

51. See Rob Perks, *A Bibliography of Oral History* (London: National Sound Archives, 1990), and the *Directory of Recorded Sound Collection in the United Kingdom* (London: National Sound Archives, 1989).

From the Preface
to the First Edition

by Willa K. Baum

Writings about oral history began in the United States in 1938, with a paragraph in the introduction to Allan Nevins's *Gateway to History*. In the 1950s, there was a trickle of articles. Several appeared in the *American Archivist*, with others in less widely distributed journals. By 1971, the Oral History Association's *Bibliography on Oral History* listed 201 articles. From then on, innumerable articles and books on oral history—or on so-called oral history—flooded the United States and Europe. In Britain, a parallel explosion of oral history publications occurred, starting in the 1970s.[51] Yet for students of oral history and their teachers, finding the articles (which were often buried in specialized journals of limited distribution) posed a major task. The demand grew for a collection of readings to serve as a base on which teachers and researchers of oral history would expand into their own specialties. The editors of this volume, each faced with the need to compile readings for their respective seminars in oral history, first joined forces to select and assemble their own collections, and then agreed to work with the Oral History Association (OHA) and with the American Association for State and Local History to publish this material originally in 1984.

The first decision concerned the intended audience. At one time the greatest need was for basic procedural manuals for beginning practitioners, but as discussed above a growing body of how-to-do-it books, general and specific as to geographic area or topic, has met that need. The editors chose instead to aim at a broad spectrum of already initiated individuals: serious students and researchers of oral history as a methodology; practitioners of oral history, both amateur and professional; individual researchers of oral history materials; people who produce public and media programs that could incorporate oral history; teachers who could use oral history as an educational method; and librarians who must care for and dispense the tapes and transcripts that are the products of oral history.

Before this thoughtful audience we intended to display oral history in its many varieties, with some information as to how it began, who and what shaped the directions it has taken, and how it has been used by diverse scholars, writers, and producers of public programs. Our goal was the upgrading of the oral history process and end-product and the establishment of reasonable expectations for the authenticity and value of oral history by users and funders.

To widen the content and use of oral history, we chose articles from a variety of disciplines that collect oral data. To stimulate critical thinking, we included critiques of oral history. The selections represent the perspectives of both the archival collector, who collects for the use of others, and the historians and other professionals who collect for their own research.

Selecting the limited number of readings that could be included within the covers of an anthology was a difficult task. The editors solicited and received suggestions from many sources; we made the final decision ourselves. We tried to represent the major points of view in the oral history profession. In some cases, an adequate written presentation of an important school or scholar was not available or had not even been composed.

To broaden the spectrum of writers represented, we decided to publish only one article per writer; in the case of some prolific scholars the choice was difficult. In a few instances, we did not receive permission to reprint an article. More often, limitations of space made it necessary to excerpt the longest articles and to leave out many excellent pieces that had been recommended.

As far as possible, we have tried to include the entire reading in the form in which it first appeared. We felt the original format, whether a scholarly monograph or the printed version of an after-dinner speech, was essential to the integrity of the piece. Necessary cuts in lengthy articles are indicated by ellipsis points and were made with the permission of the authors. Full bibliographies and endnotes have been included as they appeared in the original (with minor editorial emendations). While some bibliographies duplicate entries, the attentive reader will find in the writers' footnotes a wealth of information and references for further reading.

In his introduction to the first edition of this work, Charles Morrissey suggested that this anthology should be read "with a questioning mind," just as oral history interviewing entails a questioning mind. Whether the interest in oral history that has brought the reader to this work stems from one of the many disciplines described above, or from others, we hope that you will find a resonance across specializations.

Acknowledgments

We would like to express our thanks to the many members of the U.S. Oral History Association who helped compile and evaluate articles for inclusion. In particular, Betty McKeever Key and Martha Ross, who first proposed an OHA-sponsored anthology; Richard Sweterlitsch, Thomas Charlton, and Samuel Hand, who helped William Moss and Enid Douglas, consecutive presidents of the Oral History Association, prepare a bibliography for the Wingspread conference on Evaluation of Oral History; the late Louis M. Starr, first editor of the anthology, whose untimely death halted the project for some years; and John Neuenschwander, Charles Morrissey, Juliette Cunico, and Will Schneider. Finally, thanks to the many unnamed students who, over the years, indicated rather clearly which readings they found the most stimulating.

PART ONE

*The Gateway
to Oral History*

1

Oral History:
How and Why It Was Born

Allan Nevins

Our first selections are from founders of the Oral History movement in the United States—Allen Nevins and Louis Starr. In 1938, Allan Nevins—biographer, historian, journalist—suggested two innovations, both of which came to pass. One was the popularization of history for the multitude, an idea soon realized in the publication American Heritage and subsequently in the many regional and topical lay-history books and journals. The other was "oral history," as it came to be called. In his introduction to The Gateway to History, Nevins suggested establishing "some organization which made a systematic attempt to obtain, from the lips and papers of living Americans who have led significant lives, a fuller record of their participation in the political, economic, and cultural life of the last sixty years." Ten years later, in 1948, Nevins presided at the opening of the country's first oral history project at Columbia University, which he labored to establish.

In the following two selections, Nevins outlines early milestones in the growth of the field of oral history. Because Nevins was an outspoken advocate of oral interviews as a base for "oral autobiographies," his comments on the varieties of autobiographical narratives are particularly important. Nevins's frank discussions of the difficulties of financing and providing interviewer comments on interviews reflect the combination of pragmatism and personal vision which made him the world-renowned "father of oral history."

Allan Nevins's career started in journalism: he wrote and edited for the New York Evening Post, the New York Sun, and the New York World. He worked as a professor at Cornell and Columbia universities and in the course of a brilliant career wrote or edited more than 60 volumes, including an eight-volume history of the Civil War and

"Oral History: How and Why It Was Born" by Allan Nevins is reprinted by permission from *Wilson Library Bulletin* 40 (March 1966), pp. 600–601. © by the H. W. Wilson Company.

seven biographies. His writing was twice awarded the Pulitzer Prize in biography and the Bancroft Prize in History.

"Oral History: How and Why It Was Born" originally appeared in the Wilson Library Bulletin *40 (March 1966). Nevins's remarks in "The Uses of Oral History" were made at Lake Arrowhead, California, at the First Colloquium of the Oral History Association in 1966.*

Oral History: How and Why It Was Born

"A curious thought has just occurred to me," Dr. Johnson once remarked. "In the grave we shall receive no letters." Despite such volumes as *Letters to Dead Authors,* that is indubitably true. It is equally true that from the grave no letters are sent out to the most anxious inquirers into old history or old mysteries. We can take a few precautions to prevent Time from putting too much as alms for oblivion into the monstrous wallet on his back; that is all. Oral history is one of the latest and most promising of these precautions, and already it has saved from death's dateless (and undatable) night much that the future will rejoice over and cherish.

In hardly less degree than space exploration, oral history was born of modern invention and technology. "Miss Secretary," says the President, "take a letter to the Prime Minister of —. No, stop! I'll just telephone him; quicker, easier, and above all safer. We know he has no recording device." What might have been a priceless document for the historian goes into the irrecoverable ether. The head of the great Detroit corporation, who wishes to get information on finance from several bankers, and important scientific facts from several laboratory experts, catches a plane to New York. The graphic letter that the student of social progress would prize is cut short—a telegram will do. The news-behind-the-news that a Wickham Steed once sent The (London) *Times* from Berlin or Bucharest does not even go on teletype; it is put on a confidential telephone wire.

All the while the hurry and complexity of modern politics, modern financial and business affairs, and even modern literary and artistic life slice away the time that men need for methodical, reflective writing. What wonderful letters Theodore Roosevelt gave the world, so full of his endless zest for life, his incredible energy, his enthusiasms and his hatreds. To go further back, what a shelf of delightful comments on a thousand subjects from the Western mastodons to the iniquities of European diplomacy, from decimal coinage to Watt's new steam engine, from slave management to Ossian's poetry, we find in the massive volumes of Jefferson's writings. No doubt great letter writers still exist. But their numbers are fewer, and the spirit of the times is hostile to them.

It was something more than a sense of these considerations that inspired the planners of oral history. It was natural that they should be rooted in the history department of the greatest university in the largest and busiest city of the continent. It was right that they should have some knowledge of what the California publisher H. H. Bancroft had done to preserve a picture of the life, lore, and legends of the youthful years of the Golden State by interviewing scores of pioneers, and getting their dictated reminiscences down on paper. The planners had a connection with journalism, and saw in the daily obituary columns proof that knowledge valuable to the historian, novelist, sociologist, and economist was daily perishing; memories perishing forever without yielding any part of their riches. They had enthusiasm, these planners. It was partly the enthusiasm of ignorance; the undertaking looked deceptively easy.

Anyway, they set to work, at first with pencil and pad, later with wire recorders, later still with early tape-recording machines. They found that the task needed a great deal of money, and money was hard to get. It needed system, planning, conscientiousness, the skill that comes with experience, and above all integrity. It was more complicated and laborious than they had dreamed. The results were sometimes poor, but hard effort sometimes made them dazzling.

And the work was adventurously entertaining. At every turn they met a new experience, a fresh view of history, a larger knowledge of human personality. They would never forget the eminent New York attorney who had once collected a million dollars in a single fee, and who interrupted the story of his career to exclaim, "This is the most delightful experience I have ever had, this reminiscing." They would always remember the labor leader who in the course of an engrossing story suddenly laid his head on the desk and burst into tears; he had come to the point where he had been sent to prison for alleged racketeering. They would always keep a picture of Norman Thomas singing a pathetic song composed by the harried tenant farmers of the Southwest, and of Charles C. Burlingham, still active at almost a hundred, recalling how as a mere urchin he had seen a Negro hanged in front of his father's parsonage in downtown Manhattan during the raging of the Draft Riots.

The original ventures had been modest, but they rapidly expanded into large national undertakings. With elation the managers watched Henry Wallace record for posterity about 2,000 typed pages of reminiscences, with large diary excerpts to illustrate them; with elation they heard Mrs. Frances Perkins, who possessed an approach to total recall, record what (with additional matter she contributed) came to a memoir of 5,000 typed pages. Governors, cabinet officers past and present, industrialists, and distinguished authors and editors lent themselves to the enterprise. Many of them had been badgered for years by their families to set down recollections that history would need; not infrequently they had long felt a desire to furnish their own account of an important transaction or controversial period, but had lacked time and opportunity until suddenly seated before a tape recorder with a well-equipped interviewer before them. This interviewer, upon whom half the value of the work depended, had prepared himself by reading files of newspapers, going through official reports, begging wives for old letters or diary notes, and talking with associates. Sometimes a subject possessed a fresh and copious memory, as did Secretary Stimson; sometimes his memory had merely to be jogged, as that of Governor Rockefeller; sometimes it had to be helped by extended work, as that of former Governor Herbert H. Lehman.

Now and then, too, the work originally done had to be revised and redone. This was true of the memoir prepared by that distinguished jurist and unforgettable personality, Learned Hand. His outspoken comment, his salty wit, made his original recollections remarkable. One or two sentences may be recalled. He commented on the reverence he felt for Brandeis: "I often scolded myself, when I was a young man. You eat too much, I told myself. You drink too much. Your thoughts about women are not of the most elevated character. Why can't you be like that great man Brandeis, who does nothing but read Interstate Commerce Reports?" Judge Hand's first version, however, lacked the depth and expertness supplied when a professor of law who had once been his clerk was induced to serve as a new interviewer.

Some of the anticipated obstacles never appeared. Even busy, important, and excessively modest men proved in many instances accessible; they entered into the spirit of the work. The mass of invaluable memoir material mounted. It proved possible to protect the reminiscences against intrusion; the integrity of oral history never came under suspicion, much less attack. Better and better equipment was purchased, better and better systems of interviewing, typing, and indexing were developed. About half of the memoirs were thrown open to students at once, the other half being kept under time restrictions. And the students appeared, first in scores, well accredited and watched; then in hundreds; then in more than a thousand, not a few of them writing important books.

One difficulty, however, always persisted: the difficulty of finance. It proved impossible to operate even a sternly economical but efficient office for less than $40,000 a year, and costs rose. Work had begun on funds supplied from a happy bequest to Columbia University by Frederic Bancroft of Washington, a bequest upon which the head of oral history had a special claim; and the University itself contributed quarters and money. As the project grew, certain foundations gave generous help. Other corporations made use of its skills, giving oral history not only valuable bodies of reminiscences, but a fee in addition.

Thus the material accumulated by oral history grew year by year, both in bulk and in quality. Thus the work it accomplished attracted wider and wider attention, raising up imitative agencies in various parts of the United States, and even abroad. Because New York City is an unapproachably effective seat for such work, because the office spent the utmost pains upon its methods, and because its personnel counted brilliant young men (some of whom have now made their mark elsewhere), the heads of the office on Morningside Heights believe that their accomplishment has not been equaled elsewhere. They are glad, however, to see the type of activity they began in the preservation of priceless memories for the instruction of posterity copied elsewhere, and the tree they planted, like a banyan, creating sister trees in surrounding ground. May the work flourish and spread!

The Uses of Oral History

Let us begin by disposing of the myth that I had anything to do with the founding of oral history. It founded itself. It had become a patent necessity, and would have sprung into life in a dozen places, under any circumstances. I'm in the position of a guide in Switzerland. A valley in the Alps that had previously been barren was filled by an avalanche with a great body of soil and became quite tillable. A poor guide in the village had stumbled over a rock as he came down the mountain, one wintry day, and had started this avalanche that filled the valley. People pointed to him and said, "There's Jacques, he made the valley fruitful!" Well, I stumbled over a rock [Laughter] and the avalanche came. It would have come anyway.

I listened this morning to the various discourses with the greatest interest. They seemed to me admirable. What I propose to do is to offer some general considerations, and to close with as spirited a defense of oral history as I can possibly present.

It struck me as curious this morning that nothing was said about what one would have ordinarily have expected a *great deal* to be said: The finances of oral history. We begin with finances and sometimes we end without finances. [Laughter] At any rate, we try to go on with finances.

This avalanche of which I spoke did begin with finances. Some of us at Columbia University were happy to know an old gentleman named Frederic Bancroft. He had been Librarian of the State Department. He had written valuable books of history. He had, more importantly, been the brother of a widower who was *Treasurer* of the International Harvester company, and this brother died while Frederic Bancroft was still very much alive, leaving his entire estate to Frederic. Frederic Bancroft grew old. He knew many of us at Columbia, for he had taken his doctoral degree there. I used often to go down to see him in Washington. He would talk about what he intended to do with the two million dollars he possessed. In the days of Franklin Roosevelt, he enjoyed pointing to the White House and saying, "My income is larger than *that man's!*" Well, as he talked about what he intended to do with those two millions, we made a few suggestions (which always centered around Columbia University). I would take him to dinner, or go to dinner at his house. He would chill my blood by saying, "I'm thinking now of giving the two million dollars to the Lowell Foundation for the Lowell

Lectureships in Boston." With chilled blood, I would then call my friend Henry Commager and say, "Henry, go take Mr. Bancroft out to dinner, and make some suggestions to counter this Lowell Lectureship idea." When I presently went to Washington again, he would say, "I've been thinking more about where I shall leave my money. It occurs to me that Knox College in Illinois [laughter] would be a very good place." My blood would run cold again, until I could get Commager, or someone else, to take him to dinner once more. Well, he finally did die, and we found that the two millions had been left to Columbia University for the advancement of historical studies. I had some ideas about how to use two millions, and one was in instituting our oral history office there. . . .

We always found it necessary to earn our own way, to a great extent. Columbia possessed itself of these two million dollars, but let us have only a tiny fraction of them, and we needed an annual budget of thirty-six thousand or forty thousand dollars a year. . . . We had to scratch for money, and it's no easy task to find it; but this necessity had the virtue of instilling in us a spirit of enterprise, and I think the spirit of enterprise is very important.

It was necessary to institute specific projects which had merit in themselves. For example, we began in a small way with a project in the petroleum industry which took us into Texas and realm of the great "wildcatter," Mike Benedum, just to earn money for oral history, and then we went on to the Book-of-the-Month Club, which had a history of great importance from the literary and cultural point of view; and then we went on to the Ford Motor Company, which was, of course, pivotal in the history of the whole automotive industry; and from that we went to the Weyerhaeuser Timber Company; and then we went to tracing certain government enterprises. We would not have gone into these projects if we had not been pricked by sheer necessity. If we had been given a great endowment, a few hundred thousand dollars, we might have been much more inert. . . .

It's hard to define the best interviewer. He must have a combination of traits of personality and of intellect that is hard to obtain. He must have the quality the Germans call gemütlichkeit, obvious sympathy with the person whom he interviews, friendliness and tact, as well as courage. He must work hard to prepare himself for every interview, and must have a great breadth of interests not often the possession of the candidate for the Ph.D. [Laughter], such candidates as appear in our universities.

There must also be an element of integrity in recording as well as in interviewing. We used to agree, and perhaps we still agree in theory, upon the value of accompanying every interview with a set of notes made by the interviewer upon the character of the man interviewed and the circumstances of the interview. These notes would indicate whether the person interviewed has or lacks intellectual power in the judgment of the interviewer. They would include a commentary upon the candor or lack of candor evinced by the man interviewed and comments upon the intensity of feeling exhibited during the interview, whether a man showed strong convictions upon a given subject or absolute fixity of opinions upon a given personality. There should be a pretty clear indication, if possible, of any point at which the interview passes into sarcasm or irony, because a record in cold type does not disclose the sarcasm evident only in an inflection of voice. We can't preserve enough tape to show where sarcasm is employed. For example, John W. Davis gave a very useful set of interviews upon his career, before and after he was nominated for the presidency. It included some comments upon Calvin Coolidge. My impression is that a note of sarcasm crept into some of his comments upon Calvin Coolidge. [Laughter] How far have we kept up our record, Louis?

LOUIS STARR (Columbia University): Well, that's a difficult problem for *us*, because we've always been haunted by the ghosts of the subject coming up and hoping to see and admire his memoir in the oral history collection, only to stumble upon an addendum that says that I don't think this man really leveled with us, or something to that effect—a critical comment; so that, I'm sorry to say, I've never resolved this riddle. We haven't done it as we should have, but it's something, perhaps, we can work out in the future. . . .

PHILIP BROOKS (Harry Truman Library): We have not done this in connection with our interviews. Suppose you interviewed somebody, and you had this set of notes commenting upon his candor, and then in the very near future some researcher comes along and uses that transcript. If he can't see the notes, then he's lost something that another researcher, coming along 20 years from now, may see. Well, what is your idea as to how and when these should be made available?

ALLAN NEVINS: Everything depends upon circumstances. It's an *ad hoc* question that has to be settled on an *ad hoc* basis, I should say.

WILLA BAUM (University of California, Berkeley): We write an introduction to each of our interviews, and we try to include a little bit of this, but it helps to make it a positive statement because the interviewee does get a copy and it's available to him and all his friends. So we try to word it in a positive way which the astute user can interpret. [Laughter] In other words, we say sometimes that he spoke very frankly. Now if it doesn't say that he spoke very frankly, we may say that he was circumspect about his comments on his close associates, or something which, phrased in a positive way, may alert the user; but we find writing our introductions very hard.

GOULD COLMAN (Cornell University): We have, in some ways, a rather difficult situation at Cornell. We share completely your feeling about the importance of the interviewer's record of process. We want to know whether the man was sober or drunk, senile or whatever. We save all of these statements; we bind them together under the title, "Interviewer Comments." They are available to any researcher who asks for them; however, we don't advertise that we have them. This is not an entirely happy solution but it's about all we have had the courage, thus far, to undertake. .

ALLAN NEVINS: That shows you have in mind the absolutely essential importance of integrity in the operation, so far as we can attain it. It must be honest. We at Columbia never felt our integrity threatened, did we, Louis? Once or twice threatened, but it was never infringed, never violated. Nobody ever went to a dinner party. . : .

LOUIS STARR: There are many problems, though, it seems to me, connected with this suggestion, and I don't know what the solution is. I think Mrs. Baum has come about as close as anyone I've heard—to write between the lines. It's sort of like reading the *AAA Guide* and trying to find out which are the places they don't think are quite so good.

ELIZABETH DIXON (University of California, Los Angeles): Maybe we could have a vocabulary which says, "Circumspect means he didn't say anything." [Laughter]

PHILIP BROOKS Professor Nevins, this is a real problem, and maybe I have the wrong impression when I said we didn't do this at the Truman Library. We do keep notes describing the circumstances of the interviews, but I'm not sure, in all cases, we've told how candid we thought that the interviewee was. I have in mind one particular interview that I did with a gentleman from another country on a subject of importance in international relations, and I don't believe what he said. I think he glossed it all over. This is very difficult to put down in writing, and, if you do, you're going to wonder who's to see it. I don't really know the answer.

ALBERT LYONS (Mt. Sinai Hospital, New York): Isn't it also true that those who hear the tapes later, for example, have to form their own conclusions, and their conclusions may be more accurate than the interviewer's because of greater retrospective knowledge, perhaps, or new information?

ALLAN NEVINS: That's certainly true. . . .

All history depends upon the great use of memoirs, autobiographies. Dependence often absolute, yet are they more trustworthy than oral history memoirs? Not a bit! Often much less trustworthy. We have been taught to enjoy Benvenuto Cellini, but do we believe all of Benvenuto Cellini's autobiography? I hope not! [Laughter] Or Casanova's? I'd much rather think that a great part of Casanova's was fiction, and I suspect that it was. We've been taught to regard J. J. Rousseau's *Confessions* as one of the frankest of autobiographies. We say, "Here's something in which a man absolutely bares his own soul; tells the full truth about himself."

Rousseau himself said, "This is the full truth about me. I've held nothing back." Actually we know, thanks to modern research, that Rousseau's *Confessions* comes close to pure invention. It's, in fact, one of the great works of fiction of that century. [Laughter] It's full of suppressions, distortions, evasions, and outright, unblushing lies.

Here is where one advantage of oral history lies. If Cellini and Rousseau had been set down before a keen-minded, well-informed interviewer, who looked these men straight in their eye and put to them one searching question after another, cross-examining as Sam Untermeyer used to cross-examine people on the witness stand, they would have stuck closer to the path of truth.

Or take St. Augustine's *Confessions,* a much-admired book. It is one of the immortal books of religious statement, a beautiful piece of art. But does it tell us what we really want to know about St. Augustine, and does St. Augustine, though obviously a man of great rectitude, tell the truth, the whole truth, and nothing but the truth about himself? He relates, at one point, how as a young man he repulsed and abandoned his mistress, keeping for himself, and depriving her of, their child. It was St. Augustine's, it was not hers; and how the poor girl wept bitterly and swore to God that she would never let another man touch her. Well, I should think she might, after that. He gives this occurrence, which was a brief episode to him, but was a terrible disaster to the poor girl, about three lines; that is, he glosses over it. A representative of oral history would have wrung from him a little more of the facts about that occurrence, I should think [Laughter]. . . .

It's true that autobiography and history have to be approached with highly critical minds, and that statements of an autobiographical character by a group producing a history of some particular development demand even more caution and a keener critical sense. To produce a truthful record of a man's acts, thoughts, and motives, two qualities are obviously essential: self-knowledge and a fair amount of candor. A great many people, however, never attain self-knowledge, but constantly deceive themselves as to their real motives and acts; they constantly dramatize themselves. Others are seriously deficient in candor. They don't like to tell the truth about themselves, sometimes for good reasons [Laughter]. . . .

But in the hands of an earnest, courageous interviewer who has mastered a background of facts and who has the nerve to press his scalpel tactfully and with some knowledge of psychology into delicate tissues and even bleeding wounds, deficiencies can be exposed; and oral history can get at more of the truth than a man will present about himself in a written autobiography. . . .

Another kind of candor we found in a man of much less freshness of memory, Herbert Lehman, who was 100 percent honest. He wouldn't lie to himself, under any circumstances, or lie to anybody else. He couldn't always remember what he should have remembered, but so far as memory went, it was absolutely trustworthy; when he was prompted by a good interviewer his memory went a long way, further than it otherwise might have gone. I think that people who pride themselves upon the accuracy of their recollections almost invariably find, on referring to diaries or other records of long-past occurrences, that their memories are, in essential points, confused or erroneous. . . .

Now for the third requirement. If a man's memory is keen and vivid, and if he does possess fairly full memoranda on his past, the array of facts upon his career is likely to be so immense that he needs a strong faculty of selection. In oral history, he finds useful aids to this process of selection among the multiplicity of facts locked into his past. The autobiographer, of course, possesses an endless array of facts about himself, if he can just remember them, far more than the biographer can ever find out. To use these facts well, to be his own Boswell or Lockhart, the memoirist requires an exceedingly just sense of proportion. When acumen of selection is wanting, we get a book as prodigious and as verbose as John Bigelow's five volumes. Volumes which nobody ever opens without a groan.

2

Oral History

Louis Starr

*Louis Starr's essay remains the best overall introduction to the practice and history of
oral history in the United States before 1977, when it was published.*

*Starr comments on the disappearance of traditional written sources for historical
writing and notes that the term "oral history" is actually a misnomer for the process of
oral data collection. His appreciation for the diverse moods and ends of oral history
research, and his firsthand account of the founding of the Oral History Association (he
was its first president), make this article required reading for anyone interested in the
field of oral history.*

*Louis Starr directed the Oral History Research Office at Columbia University for 24
years; during that time he was a ceaseless organizer and publicist for oral sources in
historical research. Starr began his career in journalism, after graduating from Yale; in
the 1940s he worked on newspapers in Tennessee and Chicago. Subsequently he studied at the graduate level under Allan Nevins at the time of Columbia's pioneering
efforts at oral history; his dissertation was published as "Bohemian Brigades: Civil War
Newsmen in Action" (1951). At the Oral History Research Office, his annual review of
Columbia's program stimulated scholarly interest in oral history; under his direction
the collection grew to more than half a million pages of oral memoirs. With his associate, Elizabeth Mason, he edited four editions of* The Oral History Collection of
Columbia University *and taught an annual seminar which helped educate the first
generation of oral history scholars.*

"Oral History" by Louis Starr is reprinted from the *Encyclopedia of Library and Information
Sciences,* vol. 20 (New York: Marcel Dekker, 1977), pp. 440–63. Reprinted by courtesy of
Marcel Dekker, Inc.

O ral history is primary source material obtained by recording the spoken words—generally by means of planned, tape-recorded interviews—of persons deemed to harbor hitherto unavailable information worth preserving.

Oral history as an organized activity dates only from 1948, when Professor Allan Nevins launched "The Oral History Project" at Columbia University. Yet the essence of the idea is as old as history itself. On the premise that it stems from the oral tradition (that body of lore by which one tribe or family knows of its past through stories repeated from one generation to the next), some scholars would argue, indeed, that it predates history. Herodotus, called by Cicero "the father of history," employed oral history in gathering information for his account of the Persian Wars in the fifth century B.C. Like most of his successors, however, Herodotus did not keep a verbatim record of what his informants told him, or if he did, it was lost. The purpose of oral history is to obtain and preserve such a record. Edmund Spenser expressed beautifully the thought that motivates the work when he wrote these lines in *The Ruines of Time* (A.D. 1591):

> For deeds do die, how ever nobile donne,
> And thoughts of men do as themselves decay,
> But wise wordes taught in numbers for to runne,
> Recorded by the Muses, live for ay.

The modern Muses, as oral historians would have it, are men and women armed with tape recorders, in quest of firsthand knowledge that would otherwise decay. This they would capture, not for their own benefit, but "for ay"—for libraries or other repositories to hold for the benefit of scholars of this and succeeding generations.

Oral History as Source Material

The verbatim record of what oral historians obtain is thus in one respect unique, in comparison with other forms of primary source materials. It is deliberately created solely for historical purposes. It can capture and preserve life stories that would otherwise be lost, by eliciting oral autobiographies that may run to a thousand or more pages. It can fill in the lacunae in one field of learning after another, by eliciting testimony from many on a single topic. It can convey personality, explain motivation, reveal inner thoughts and perceptions—serving scholars in much the same way as private letters and diaries. An oral history memoir is based on recall, and thus lacks the immediacy of these, but it can be fully as intimate, more reflective, and, if the questioner knows what to ask, quite as useful to the researcher. Obviously it is also quite as hazardous for the researcher, since memory is fallible, ego distorts, and contradictions sometimes go unresolved. Yet problems of evaluation are not markedly different from those inherent in the use of letters, diaries, and other primary sources. With caveat emptor ever in mind, the scholar must test the evidence in an oral history memoir for internal consistency and, whenever possible, by corroboration from other sources, often including the oral history memoirs of others on the same topic.

Inviting the comparison with private letters, diaries, and other intimate documents is doubly apropos, for it is the gradual disappearance of these in our own time that is most often advanced as the reason for the remarkable growth of oral history in the second half of this century. As early as 1950, Nevins pointed out that the telephone, the automobile, and the airliner, by enabling people to "contact" one another as readily as that expression suggests, were displacing the confidential letters of old, thereby robbing future historians of incalculable treasure.[1] Nevins was bold enough to suggest that oral history might help fill the void. If that seemed visionary at the time, the last quarter century has given it plausibility. The age of the holographic document has receded still further, jets and freeways and television have made further incursions on writing time, and oral history moves apace. The tape recorder has become omnipresent, there are oral history projects in all states of the Union and in many foreign lands, and professional associations flourish here and abroad. The oral history movement may be perceived as a conscious effort to utilize technology—not only the tape recorder, but (as we shall see) microforms [microfiche], the computer, and other tools of the age—to counter the inroads of technology that Nevins deplored.

Form and Substance

SUBSTANCE

In range of subject matter, particularly as it has been developing in the United States in recent years, oral history appears to know no bounds. Familiar published examples of the genre run from Theodore Rosengarten's moving evocation of a Black Alabama sharecropper's life story, *All God's Dangers,* to passages in Forrest Pogue's majestic four-volume life of General George Marshall; from Studs Terkel's interviewees talking about their jobs in *Working* to Merle Miller's version of his taped sessions with Harry Truman in *Plain Speaking;* from quotations in William Lynwood Montell's minor classic in folklore, *The Saga of Coe Ridge,* to Saul Benison's in polio research, *Tom Rivers: A Life in Science and Medicine.* If the oral history components of these books have a common bond, it is the authenticity of their firsthand testimony, delivered with spontaneity. Each, as the vernacular would have it, "tells it like it is" (or was) with a candor that is the forte of good oral history, a candor emanating from the rapport which the interlocutor, each in his way, was able to establish with the respondent.

More commonly, oral history remains unpublished, awaiting researchers in libraries. Its votaries range over terrain even more varied than these titles suggest. They include New Left scholars interviewing steel workers in Gary, Indiana; law students prodding the memories of eminent jurists in New York, or of those who knew Chief Justice Earl Warren in California; social historians exploring the Jewish community of Columbus, Ohio, or of mountain people in the piney woods of Georgia; musicologists on the trail of those who remember Charles Ives or Scott Joplin or Art Tatum; and historians pursuing institutional history, be it a study of the packaging industry, of unionism in the needle trades, of the development of the computer, or of NASA. Other projects focus upon an epoch, like the occupation of Japan; an episode, like the Memorial Day Massacre during the "Little Steel" strike of 1937; or a movement, like the suffragists, or the Civil Rights Movement of the 1960s. There are oral history projects on every branch of the armed services, and on each presidential administration beginning with Herbert Hoover's. . . .

In substance, then, oral history bids fair to reflect the myriad interests of a pluralistic society—its ethnic groups, its cultural pursuits, its political leadership, its institutions and occupational groups—so far as limited resources but apparently limitless enthusiasm permits.

FORM: TAPES VERSUS TRANSCRIPTS

Is the end product of oral history a tape or a transcript? For some local projects in the United States and Canada, and for most in Great Britain, the oral history process begins and ends with the tape. A written summary or some other finding aid may be prepared to guide listeners, and that is all. Some 70 percent of oral history centers in the United States, and many elsewhere, however, transcribe their tapes into typescript.[2] The prevailing practice is to persuade the oral author (a more precise designation than subject, respondent, narrator, memoirist, or interviewee, all of which are also employed) to verify the result, correcting the text for clarity and accuracy rather than for style. The edited transcript—completely retyped by some programs, by others left with its handwritten changes—then becomes the true end product. Indexed and cataloged, the final version takes its place in an oral history repository, subject to whatever restrictions upon access and use the oral author imposes.

Tapes versus transcripts has been a subject of lively debate among those engaged in oral history, one that is gradually moving toward resolution. Protagonists of the tape contend that this is the true primary source. Nuances of voice, they assert, must be heard rather than left to the reader to infer from a transcript, which cannot accurately convey accent, inflection, emphasis, or manner. Those who prefer the transcript emphasize the value to the scholar of knowing that the oral author has read and corrected what he said, a process that turns what might be dismissed as hearsay into a document that has much of the standing of a legal deposition. As to nuances·lost in the transcript, they hold this a small price to pay for the assurance of verification. One cannot read 20 pages of transcript, they contend, without comprehending the tone of the oral author, since this is conveyed by style, and in any case is frequently immaterial to the researcher's purpose.

The debate is subsiding in the United States largely because of the overwhelming preference of users for transcripts, calls for which exceed calls for tape in some of the larger oral history collections by ratios of a thousand to one and higher. This is not so much because those who favor the transcript have the better of the argument on theoretical grounds as because of practical convenience: to most researchers, a written document that carries page numbers, and an index to them, is vastly preferable. Whatever they wish to copy or paraphrase is before them in black and white. Tapes, no matter how carefully indexed, are awkward to use, particularly if the memoir is a massive one. Folklorists, linguists, and musicologists, nonetheless, find them indispensable.

A consensus emerges: tapes are more suitable for some purposes, transcripts for others; but so far as possible both should be preserved, allowing researchers to choose for themselves. Future generations may prove more aurally oriented.

The Oral History Movement

ANTECEDENTS

The modern roots of oral history antedate both the term itself and Allan Nevins's efforts. Several projects generated oral history (though the term was not applied) under New Deal auspices in the 1930s. One, the first of two endeavors to collect the reminiscences of former slaves, was launched by Lawrence D. Reddick under a Works Progress Administration grant in Kentucky, Indiana, and adjacent states, 1934–35. Others, done in the late 1930s for the Federal Writers Project in Georgia and other southern states, sought out Blacks and poor whites in rural areas for interviews that might enrich the state guides the agency was preparing, but this material was also perceived as having enduring archival value.[3] Like the slave narratives, these manually recorded interviews were largely forgotten in the National Archives until interest in Black studies combined with the oral history movement to resuscitate them decades later.

As for the term oral history, it appears to have been coined by a dissolute member of the Greenwich Village literati named Joe Gould, Harvard graduate, friend of the poet Maxwell Bodenheim and self-styled "Professor Sea Gull." Gould claimed to be compiling "an Oral History of Our Time," according to a *New Yorker* profile in 1942; a sequel proved this apocryphal.[4] Gould named an activity he may or may not have pursued, giving the world a misnomer now firmly embedded in the language. Suggested alternatives like oral documentation and living history have not survived the hour.

THE BEGINNINGS

The term may have slipped into Allan Nevins's vocabulary through the *New Yorker*, but his own thoughts about an ongoing interviewing effort for the benefit of future scholars germinated as far back as 1931. Engrossed in his biography of Grover Cleveland, he lamented that no one had had the wit to interview Cleveland or his associates, most of whom died without leaving historians a legacy of any kind. He discussed with friends, among them Adolf Berle and Dean Edwin F. Gay of the Harvard Business School, how the idea might be implemented, and in 1938 issued the first call for it in his preface to *The Gateway to History*:

> We have agencies aplenty to seek out the papers of men long dead. But we have only the most scattered and haphazard agencies for obtaining a little of the immense mass of information about the more recent American past—the past of the last half century—which might come fresh and direct from men once prominent in politics, in business, in the professions, and in other fields; information that every obituary column shows to be perishing.

A decade passed before Nevins found the means to implement such an agency. After years of gentle persuasion on his part, his wealthy friend Frederic Bancroft, a historian who held one of Columbia's earliest Ph.Ds (1885) left the university $1.5 million for the acquisition of new materials in American history.[5] A small portion of the income (initially but $3,000) helped start the work.

The beginnings were hardly auspicious. Nevins had no recording device. Limited by a skeptical faculty committee to New York City affairs, he took along a graduate student named Dean Albertson to help on the first interview, one of a series with a seasoned civic leader named George McAneny. On May 18, 1948, in the McAneny living room at 120 East 75th Street, Albertson took notes in longhand as Nevins evoked a stream of reminiscence from his subject. The young man then went home to type up a rough draft of the proceedings as best he could from his notes, and the experiment was suspended until fall.[6] Toward the end of 1948, three more memoirs had been obtained in this laborious fashion, when the pioneers of oral history got wind of an electronic device that would enable them to capture every word, the wire recorder. Judge Learned Hand was the first to speak in the presence of one of these, January 21, 1949. The process changed almost overnight. Transcribers were installed in a basement room of Butler Library, tape recorders replaced the awkward wire machines after a year or so, the horizon expanded to include national affairs, and production began in earnest.

Acquiring personal papers to complement an oral history memoir soon proved a fringe benefit, sometimes far more. Nevins's interviews with Herbert

Lehman led ultimately to the gift not only of his papers, but of a model facility to house them in Columbia's School of International Affairs Library, with its own curator, catalog, and seminar rooms.

Alongside the lengthy oral autobiographies Nevins favored from the first, there soon developed a second kind of oral history—the special project. It proved fruitful. The first of these bloomed when a national organization of radio pioneers called "The Twenty-Year Club" (later "Broadcast Pioneers") helped fund an effort, 1950–1952, on the early years of broadcasting. Nevins enlisted Frank Ernest Hill for work that generated over 4,000 pages of memoirs by radio's early announcers, program directors, technicians, and executives. A second one, launched a few months later, gave oral history its first foothold elsewhere—at the Ford Archives in Dearborn, Michigan. This was by way of preliminary research for the three-volume history Nevins and Hill ultimately produced on the Ford Motor Company, and it grew into the largest of industrial oral history projects. Owen Bombard, recruited from the Columbia office, saw to the interviewing of 434 persons who descanted some 26,000 pages about Henry Ford and his empire. A third special project, conducted by Nevins and Hill in 1951, produced a wealth of material on the history of oil wildcatting in Texas, and presumably was responsible for alerting scholars at the University of Texas to the potentialities. Their project on the oil industry, begun in 1952 by William Owens at the E. C. Barker Texas History Center, appears to have been the first such by another university. The Forest History Society, under Elwood Maunder, began its oral history program the same year. The first multipurpose project after Columbia's began two years later, in 1954, when the Regional Oral History Office of the University of California, Berkeley, was launched. UCLA began its own in 1959.[7]

Growth remained lethargic through the 1950s, as Figure 2.1 shows. In part this was because the early emphasis on the right of an oral author to close his entire memoir (rather than the sensitive parts only, as later) left oral history's pioneers with substantial holdings "in the deep freeze," as Albertson put it. Nevins, who retired in 1958, had been in no hurry to make them widely known in any case, for he conceived of the work as primarily for future generations. As for the other projects then in existence, most were wholly absorbed in creating: dissemination would come years later. (An exception was the Forest History project, which published excerpts of its oral histories in its journal, *Forest History*, from time to time.)

GROWTH IN THE 1960s

The explosive growth that ensued in the following decade cannot be wholly explained. A trickle of articles about oral history in learned journals and the popular press, which grew to a rivulet by the mid-1960s (Figure 2.2) undoubtedly helped. Nor was it lost on the academic world that such scholars as James

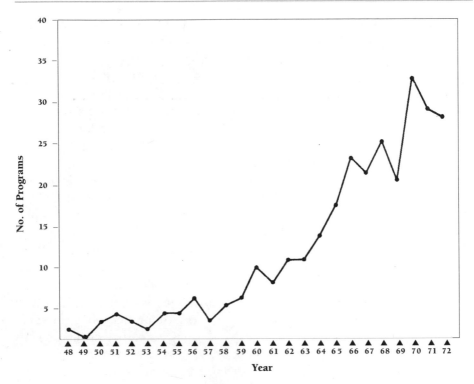

Figure 2.1 Oral history programs in the United States, by year of founding. *Source*: *Oral History Collections* (New York: Bowker, 1975).

MacGregor Burns, Frank Freidel, George F. Kerman, and Arthur M. Schlesinger, Jr., by the late 1950s were drawing upon oral history in their published work. Other factors include the phenomenal development of the portable tape recorder in the course of the 1960s, culminating in the cassette.

The appearance, in 1960, of the first published catalog may be noted: a slender volume titled *The Oral History Collection of Columbia University*, carrying brief descriptions of holdings then totaling 130,000 pages. Significantly, it was arranged like the catalog of a manuscript collection, a model that has been followed since. In 1961 came the first printed annual report, from the same office, both publications replacing multigraphed efforts of small circulation in the late 1950s. These reports, more widely circulated each year, served to spread the word. Scholarly traffic and inquiries from other institutions accelerated apace, and the Columbia office began a file on projects elsewhere. Its 1964 report provided brief information about oral history work in progress at the American Institute of Physics, Brandeis, Claremont Graduate School, Cornell University, Harvard (with which the JFK project was then affiliated), the Hollywood Museum, the George

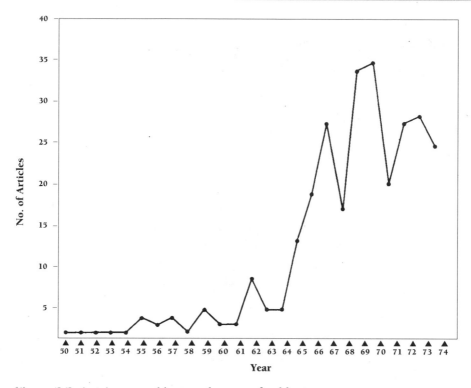

Figure 2.2 Articles on oral history, by year of publication.
Source: *Bibliography on Oral History,* ed. Manfred J. Waserman (New York: Oral History Association, 1975).

C. Marshall Research Library, Princeton (then beginning its project on John Foster Dulles), the University of Michigan (harboring the United Auto Workers project, begun in 1959 and shared with Wayne State), the Truman Library (first of the Presidential Libraries to enter the field, 1961), and Tuláne (where the New Orleans Jazz Archive began in 1958), in addition to projects already mentioned. A survey in the wake of this resulted in *Oral History in the United States,* a state-by-state listing of 89 projects, many still in embryo, as part of Columbia's 1965 report. The "veritable movement" cited in the second edition of its catalog (1964) had indeed materialized, but it was apparent from the data that growth was not along the lines the original office had anticipated. "Oral history holds potentialities that may well give an office like ours a place in most great universities of the future," its 1961 report had ventured. Instead, museums, historical societies, corporations, labor unions, church groups, and libraries were intermingled with colleges and universities large and small, most of them engaged in a single special project as opposed to the few (notably Cornell and several California institutions) making a broad acquisitions effort on the Columbia model (Table 1.1).

Was there sufficient common interest among these organizations to form a viable association? The collector of the information (and writer of this article) was doubtful. Nevins, then at the Huntington Library in San Marino, was convinced there was, and having failed to persuade the writer to call a meeting, he turned to James V. Mink, then in charge of oral history at UCLA. Mink had just such a meeting in mind.

THE ORAL HISTORY ASSOCIATION

With the promise of Allan Nevins as a speaker and the Columbia report as an invitation list, Mink attracted 77 persons to Lake Arrowhead, UCLA's conference facility in the San Bernardino mountains, in September 1966, for three days of wide-ranging discussion. It concluded with a resolve to meet again the following year and to form an association. Mink headed a steering committee which accomplished this at the Arden House meeting organized by the writer in 1967. The Oral History Association (OHA) has since published a quarterly newsletter; a *Bibliography on Oral History* (the fourth edition, edited by Manfred Waserman of the National Library of Medicine, appeared in 1975); a directory; and an annual, *The Oral History Review*. Its extraordinary growth in membership is charted in Figure 2.3.

Table 2.1 Oral History Centers in the United States, by Institutional Affiliation, 1973.

Type of Affiliation	No. of Centers
Universities (public, 75; independent, 33)	108
Public libraries (city, 26; county, 15; state, 7)	48
Colleges (independent, 31; public, 16)	47
Professional, ethnic, other special societies	29
Historical societies, local and state	25
Federal agencies	18
Museums, hospitals, church groups	12
Private collectors	5
Corporations	4
Medical centers	3
Alumni associations	2
Bookmobile	1
Unclassified	14
Total	**316**

Source: From *Oral History*, annual report (New York: Columbia University, 1975), p.4.

OHA has helped to alert the American Library Association, the Society of American Archivists, the Organization of American Historians, and other professional groups to the work, recruiting panel discussions on oral history for their meetings, staging exhibits at them, staffing workshops for them. Its own meetings, held in the fall in places remote from urban distraction—in 1974 at Jackson Hole, Wyoming; in 1975 near Asheville, North Carolina; in 1976 at Le Chateau Montebello in Quebec—from the first achieved an ambiance uncommon to academic gatherings, emanating in part from a sense of creative pioneering shared by all in the field, in part from a policy of enlisting speakers outside of academe (e.g., Barbara Tuchman, Walter Lord, Alden Whitman, Daniel Schorr) as well as within it to broaden perspectives, and in part from its attraction for younger scholars. Beginning with the Fifth National Colloquium at Asilomar, California, in 1970, OHA has run workshops for initiates each year prior to its colloquium. They deal with topics ranging from the ethics of oral history interviewing, as set forth in OHA's "Goals and Guidelines," to interviewing techniques, final processing, and control of access, generally interspersed with lively debate.

Toward Wider Dissemination

The rapidity of oral history's growth led to concern among its practitioners as to how all the riches gathered were to be made widely known and put at the

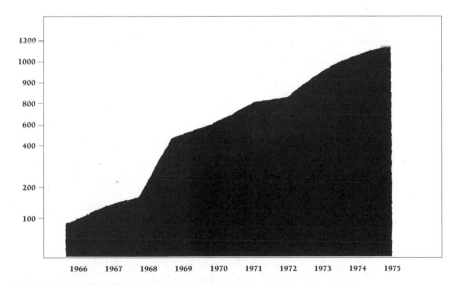

Figure 2.3 Membership of the Oral History Association, geometric scale.
Source: Oral History Newsletter, 1967–1974.

disposal of scholars. There has been significant progress in this direction in the 1970s. Through the OHA, the *National Union Catalogue of Manuscript Collections* (NUCMC), published by the Library of Congress, arranged to include oral history collections that met its criteria as to size, beginning with the 1970 edition. A directory of all known projects, *Oral History in the United States* (compiled by Gary Shumway of California State University at Fullerton and edited and published by Columbia in 1971 on behalf of OHA), provided a state-by-state guide to 230 collections, with notes on their contents and a name and subject index. It is in some 3,000 libraries in this country and abroad.

This was followed in 1975 by a far more ambitious directory, *Oral History Collections,* edited by Alan Meckler and Ruth McMullin and published by R. R. Bowker. It listed in a single name and subject index the individual memoirs held in many repositories, as well as many of the topics covered in subject collections. A centers section gave data about 316 oral history centers in the United States. Though far from complete, the guide broke a path toward comprehensive coverage in future editions.

A 1970 article on oral history observed that few projects had published descriptive lists of their holdings as yet.[8] Here, too, progress has been rapid. Study of the Bowker directory shows that by 1973 (when the data were collected) some 45 oral history centers had catalogs of their holdings (in a few instances in card rather than book form). Eight more were going to press. The third edition of Columbia's catalog, published the same year and set from computer tape to facilitate subsequent editions, carried subject and biographical indexes. Finding aids of this kind are, of course, indispensable to the researcher, for no union list can supply the detailed information they contain. The appearance of the Bowker directory is expected to stimulate such catalogs; without one, no oral history center can be properly represented in subsequent editions of this or of NUCMC.

ORAL HISTORY AND MICROFORMS

A development of potentially greater significance was signaled by the establishment of The New York Times Oral History Program in 1970, whereby selected "open" transcripts are made available to libraries in both microfilm and microfiche, and to individual scholars on fiches. This came in response to complaints that oral history was both inaccessible and difficult to use because of the prohibition against copying that most centers enforce, to protect the common-law copyright of their oral authors. By obtaining assignments of copyright from the authors or their executors, centers thenceforth could look to wider distribution of substantial parts of their collections by joining the program.

By 1976, 20 oral history collections in the United States and the largest one abroad, that at Hebrew University in Jerusalem, had done so. They are included in the annual *Guide to Microforms in Print* as well as in the Library of Congress

Cataloging in Publication program, making for a further increase in accessibility. Another advance was in the immediate offing: computerized name and topical indexes of some of these collections, following the general style of *The New York Times Index*. The first of these, covering the 200 memoirs in "Part One" of the Columbia collection on microfilm, was scheduled to appear in 1976.

Micropublication, of course, leaves "permission required" or "closed" memoirs untouched, but since all such restrictions end in due course, it appears likely that the most useful oral history transcripts in many fields will be available in microform in time for the next generation of scholars, accompanied by sophisticated finding aids.

MANUALS AND GUIDES

For all of the literature devoted to interviewing of various kinds, there was no suitable guide to the mysteries of oral history work for nearly two decades. The need was met partially, after the founding of OHA, by its printed proceedings, a series that provided hundreds of novices with their introduction to oral history. (Now out of print, the series has been micropublished by The New York Times Oral History Program. *The Oral History Review* took the place of these as the OHA's annual in 1973.)

Guides proliferated in due course. Credit for the first one belongs to William G. Tyrrell of the New York State Historical Commission, who in 1966 wrote *Tape Recording Local History,* a 12-page pamphlet issued by the American Association for State and Local History. This was followed in 1969 by *Oral History for the Local Historical Society,* by Willa K. Baum of the University of California's Regional Oral History Office, a work that has been called the Dr. Spock of its field. Concise and clearly written, its fourth edition (1974) met the need (title notwithstanding) well enough to have become assigned reading in graduate courses on the subject.

Both more elaborate and simpler guides have come since. An *Oral History Primer,* by Gary L. Shumway and William G. Hartley, published by the Oral History Program of the California State University at Fullerton in 1973, proved useful to schools and to programs that rely on volunteer interviewers. *A Guide for Oral History Programs,* published the same year under the same auspices, set forth in detail the oral history process from funding to cataloging, as practiced by that institution. A similar volume, into which is woven an interesting history of the John F. Kennedy Oral History project, was written by William W. Moss of its staff and published by Praeger, New York, in 1974. Cullom Davis, Kathryn Back, and Kay MacLean of Sangamon State University in Springfield, Illinois, produced *From Tape to Type* as a guide for small institutions in 1975; and Joseph H. Cash (of the University of South Dakota) and associates wrote yet another, *The Practice of Oral History,* published by The New York Times Oral History Program the same year. None is likely to displace Mrs. Baum's work, with its nice sensitivity to the interests of volunteers on the one hand and to the basic needs for attainment of professional competence on the other. All served to push back the walls of ignorance about oral history.

ORAL HISTORY IN THE CLASSROOM

Oral history has impinged on the learning process in one way or another since its early years. William E. Leuchtenburg, Eric McKitrick, and others in the Columbia history department took to immersing their students in the Oral History Collection as a means of exposing them to the problems peculiar to it. Columbia's Oral History office, as Henry Steele Commager recalled in addressing the Second National Colloquium on Oral History, became "a kind of Ecole des chartes for the training of oral historians and oral archivists," but it remained for many years a very informal école featuring private tutoring and learning-by-doing. At the Third National Colloquium the following year, attention was given to classroom applications, but the consensus was that these remained largely unexplored. Saul Benison of the University of Cincinnati told of using oral history in lectures and assignments in a course on historiography. Charles Morrissey involved students at the University of Vermont in demonstration interviews, and Gary Shumway of California State put them to work on specific projects he was conducting. Harry Kursh, a seventh and eighth grade teacher at Lakeland Middle School, New York, told of organizing his class to obtain an oral history interview, bringing history alive to students who had no interest in it hitherto. An OHA survey in 1974 showed sharply increasing use of all applications suggested in these models, on high school, college, and graduate levels.

Like archaeology, oral history is more than a tool and less than a discipline; yet one area in which significant progress has been made recently is in the teaching of oral history itself as a disciplined activity. Ground was broken by the University of California, Los Angeles, when it obtained a federal grant for a two-week session on oral history techniques for librarians in July 1968. Some 20 students went through the whole process, from preparing for interviews to processing and submitting them. An intensive course in every aspect of the work began at Columbia on the graduate level in 1973 and has been oversubscribed every year since. Wendell Wray, a student in the first class, transplanted it with his own embellishments to the University of Pittsburgh's Library School the same year. Jacquelyn Dowd Hall installed a similar course at the University of North Carolina, Chapel Hill, also in 1973. The école Commager alluded to thus spread to several campuses, suggesting that the first professionally trained interviewers and program directors presently will replace oral history's early practitioners.

A departure by William Chafe and Lawrence Goodwyn at Duke University sought to train graduate students to unearth specifics relating to Black disenfranchisement and other aspects of Black life in the South, on the premise that this buried history could be exhumed only by exhaustive digging in published sources, followed by pinpoint interviewing. While the program was a modest one, with seven students in 1974, development of this methodology for "history-from-the-bottom-up" projects attracted wide interest.[9]

Financing Oral History

"We begin with finances," Allan Nevins told the first OHA colloquium. "And sometimes we end without finances."[10] It was largely to help programs find funding that he urged they band together in the first place, yet in this area the OHA, up to 1976, had done little beyond promoting discussion. Oral history has been chronically underfinanced from the first. A survey by Adelaide Tusler of the UCLA office in 1967 showed only one-fifth of those responding had budgets of over $20,000.[11] Six years later data collected by Meckler and McMullin for *Oral History Collections* indicated a sharp increase in total expenditures for oral history, but the median for all centers providing figures fell in the $10,000–14,000 range. This was not enough to sustain an ongoing program without volunteer help. Volunteers, particularly as interviewers for local and regional projects, but also on occasion for some of the largest ones, have played an important role in the movement.

The cost of processing an hour of tape, from preliminary research through interviewing, transcribing, editing, indexing, and cataloging, runs from around $100 [$300] to as high as $500 [$1,200]. This is because of wide variations in processing the material, and also in paying interviewers and transcribers. Projects employing salaried staff for the whole process, particularly if this includes elaborate editing and final-typing, obviously incur the highest costs. Those employing specialists on a per-hour basis fall in the lower ranges.

Where does the money come from? In most cases from the parent institution, the Tusler survey reported: the college, society, or other body with which the program is affiliated. Major university programs, however, have been funded largely by outside sources, public and private. Special projects, according to one study, produced 43 percent of all income for one major university program over a decade. These were underwritten by foundations, corporations, and individuals, as well as by various federal agencies on a "cost plus" basis, the "plus" going toward support of unsubsidized work. General support came also from foundations and from university sources, each amounting to about half the percentage from special projects. The balance came from catalog sales, royalties, and services.[12] These proportions, derived from 1957–1967 data, have remained quite stable with the exception of income from royalties, which increased substantially after the introduction of microforms.

Oral History Abroad

A 1970 report on oral history suggested that the movement would become "worldwide in the 1970s."[13] "Worldwide" may prove too inclusive, but midway in the 1970s there are signs that, taken in sum, make it arguable.

In Britain, the Oral History Society took form in 1973, meets twice yearly, and issues its own journal. Limited largely to social historians—the government's Social Science Research Council funded its first conferences—it shows signs of broadening its base. Membership reached 300 by 1976. In Canada—where leadership has been provided by Leo La Clare of the Public Archives, together with William Langlois, head of an active regional project in Vancouver—an association was formed in 1974, bringing together programs of widely diverse interests. In Australia, Joan Campbell of La Trobe University drew 85 persons to a first oral history conference in 1974, saw to the publication of its proceedings, and held another that gave birth to an association in 1975. The National Library of Australia has had a full-scale oral history operation going since 1970.

In Latin America, leadership has come from Eugenia Meyer of the Instituto Naciónal de Antropologia e Historia in Mexico City. Her program has published some of its memoirs in pamphlet form, has attracted government funding, and has steadily expanded its interests. Argentina's Instituto Di Tella in Buenos Aires carried on a broad-scale economic, social, and political study of that country in an oral history effort begun in 1971, sharing its transcripts with Columbia [University]. In Brazil, interest was sufficient to mount a highly successful course in the subject in Rio de Janeiro in 1975 to prepare scholars from Brazil and Peru for a variety of planned projects.

A survey by Elizabeth B. Mason of Columbia University for the Oral History Association in 1974 turned up 165 projects outside the United States, on every continent. In addition to those mentioned, countries where oral history activity was found included Chile, Denmark, France, West Germany, Holland, India, Ireland, Israel, Jamaica, Kenya, Lebanon, the Philippines, Rhodesia, Singapore, South Africa, Sri Lanka, and Sweden. The 1976 *Oral History Review* included reports on oral history in Australia, Brazil, Mexico, and Great Britain, and OHA's Canadian meeting symbolized its awareness of international interest.

Long-Term Significance

Oral history, if it achieves the mission its votaries have set for it, will win universal acceptance as a form of primary source material, one that is quite as pervasive, and no more and no less valid, per se, than the holographic documents it purports to replace. Its most ardent champions would not contend that this is in the immediate offing, heartening as its progress has been.

The movement has weaknesses that have prevented it from having the impact upon the scholarly world that one might expect. The experience of Eugenia Meyer in Mexico has been all too common everywhere: difficulty in "convincing historians of the value of this new source material, which was initially received quite indifferently or as 'a waste of time' because of its inherent subjective and partisan qualities." Even after academic skeptics are converted, as she has pointed out, "few are willing to involve themselves in the task of producing this type of source," save when they have books of their own in mind.[14]

In consequence, oral history has failed to receive the critical attention it needs if it is to fulfill its potentialities. Its reception is the more striking if one contrasts it with the tumultuous one that greeted another ill-named child of the technology that burst into the house of learning on its heels—the child named quantitative history, or cliometrics. For a time, at least, its computer applications and their ramifications became a veritable obsession within the historical profession. Oral historians could argue that *All God's Dangers* was patently a more durable contribution to the history of the American South than *Time on the Cross,* the controversial attempt to apply cliometrics to the economics of slavery. They could insist that *Working,* or *By Myself, I'm a Book!,* an oral history of the immigrant Jewish experience in Pittsburgh, held values for urbanologists comparable to any that the quantifiers, or cliometricians, had given them. No matter. The critical attention accorded quantifiers, criticism that should serve to discipline their work, eluded oral history.

Should a transcript show changes made by the oral author when he reviewed it, for example, or should the final product be a smoothly edited, chaptered, completely retyped MS? Scholars worth their salt know the former is preferable. Yet they have been mute, with the result that some centers follow one procedure while others, more anxious to win the approval of their oral authors, follow another.

What of Barbara Tuchman's charge that oral history gathers trash and trivia with all the discrimination of a vacuum cleaner?[15] Defenders respond that what is trash to one researcher turns gold to another and that rapid development of finding aids will obviate her point by unearthing the nuggets. Yet they must own that standards of quality have been slow in developing, again for want of informed criticism by scholars for whom the work is intended.

What impact has the movement had upon historical literature? Manifestly, there has been an infusion of the spoken word into this tradition-bound branch of letters through the use of oral history, much of it so recent there are no studies, as yet, of the consequences. A single collection, Columbia's, has seen the number of books drawing upon it surge from 120 in its first 22 years (up to 1970) to nearly triple that total in the 6 years that followed. Notable books utilizing other collections in the same period included David Halberstam's *The Best and the Brightest* (John F. Kennedy Library oral histories); *The Devil and John Foster Dulles,* by Townsend Hoopes (Dulles oral history collection, Princeton); *Charles Ives Remembered,* by Vivian Perlis (Yale Music Library oral histories); Margaret Truman's biography of her father (Truman Library oral history collection); *Lyndon Johnson and the American Dream,* by Doris Kearns (LBJ Library oral history collection); and harbingers of more to come from these and other repositories, all of them still comparatively new.

In the same period there has been a parallel jump in the number of monographs, biographies, and studies of current affairs that rely wholly or in part upon their authors' own interviews. It is not journalists but academics who now account for the bulk of the interviewing that is carried out with books in view, the very academics who would have been loath to risk their reputations by so much as citing oral sources a decade or so back, assuming that interviews had occurred to them at all. It is a turnabout little noted. The impact of oral history extends beyond work drawing upon established collections, insofar as these have inspired individual scholars to sally forth and do it for themselves.

Are such books the better for it? The question defies a sweeping answer, but one would have to be churlish to deny that in innumerable cases they are. Some, like George Martin's life of Frances Perkins, *Madam Secretary,* would have been impossible without oral history, as the author has said. Others, like William H. Van Vorhis's *Violence in Ulster,* are "oral documentaries," distilled entirely from pools of oral history. Historical literature, then, is clearly the richer for it—richer in pungent quotation, in color, in anecdote, in personality, in insight—and beyond that there are now scores of authors to testify, as Walter Lord has, that intensive interviewing has enabled them to get to "the guts of the event, the heart of it," a point Lord has documented with examples from his own work.

Oral history's greatest growth to date has taken place in apparent defiance of the "Great Depression" engulfing the world of higher education in America (1967–). It would be a mistake to assume, however, that the movement was unaffected. Large institutions that normally could have been expected to respond to its challenge by committing themselves to the work, thereby endowing it with a stronger institutional footing, have held aloof. Oral history will continue to develop regardless. It draws vigor from a lively sense of mission, a strong professional association, and a future that excites imaginations in half a dozen disciplines. But until a better day, when more major universities and great research libraries perceive the work as central to their purpose—creating and disseminating by modern means "wise wordes taught in numbers for to runne," as Edmund Spenser put it, "for ay"—fuller assessment of its impact must wait.

Notes

1. Unpublished progress report, Oral History Research Office, Columbia University, 1950. The theme runs through oral history literature perhaps more strongly than any other.

2. *Oral History,* annual report (New York: Columbia University, 1975), 4.

3. Jerre Mangione, *The Dream and the Deal: The Federal Writers' Project, 1935–1943* (Boston: Little, Brown, 1972), pp. 257–58.

4. Joseph L. Mitchell, "Professor Sea Gull," *New Yorker,* December 12, 1942, pp. 28–37; "Joe Gould's Secret," *New Yorker,* September 19, 1964, pp. 61–125, and September 26, 1964, pp. 53–159.

5. Elizabeth Dixon and James V. Mink, eds., *Oral History at Arrowhead: Proceedings of the First National Colloquium on Oral History,* 2d ed. (New York: Oral History Association, 1967), pp 36–37.

6. In April 1948, just one month before the first oral history interview, the first two American-made tape recorders, modeled on a captured German Magnetophon, emerged from Ampex facilities in California. See John T. Mullin, "Creating the Craft of Tape Recording," *High Fidelity Magazine,* April 1976, pp. 62–67. Thus tape recorders existed before oral history was launched, but the launchers were unaware of them. (They did not become generally available until several years later.)

7. Much of the information on early years has been taken from file copies of unpublished reports of the Oral History Research Office, Columbia University. Other sources are given in Louis M. Starr, "Oral History: Problems and Prospects," in *Advances in Librarianship,* vol. 2, ed. Melvin G. Voigt (New York: Seminar Press, 1971).

8. Starr, "Oral History: Problems and Prospects," p. 296.

9. "Duke U. Students Learn Interviewing Techniques of 'Oral History' to Record Lives of Ordinary People," *New York Times,* May 6, 1974, p. 41

10. Allan Nevins, "The Uses of Oral History," in *The First National Oral History Colloquium,* ed. E. Dixon and J. Mink (New York: Oral History Association, 1967), p. 1. (See chapter 1 of the present volume.)

11. Adelaide Tusler, "Report on Survey of Oral History Programs," multilithed (Los Angeles: University of California, Los Angeles, 1967).

12. Louis M. Starr, ed., *The Second National Oral History Colloquium* (New York: Oral History Association, 1968), pp. 113–16.

13. *Oral History,* annual report (New York: Columbia University, 1970), p. 6.

14. Eugenia Meyer, "Oral History in Mexico and Latin America," *Oral History Review* 4 (1976), pp. 56–61.

15. Barbara Tuchman, "Research in Contemporary Events for the Writing of History," in *Proceedings of the American Academy of Arts and Letters and the National Institute of Arts and Letters,* 2d ser., no. 22 (New York, 1972), p. 62.

Bibliography

Albertson, Dean. "History in the Deep-freeze: The Story of Columbia's Oral History Project." *Columbia Library Columns* 2 (1953), pp. 2–11.

Allen, Richard B. "New Orleans Jazz Archive at Tulane." *Wilson Library Bulletin* 40 (March 1966), pp. 619–23.

Bartlett, Richard A. "Some Thoughts after the Third National Colloquium on Oral History." *Journal of Library History* 4 (April 1969), pp. 169–72.

Baum, Willa K. "Oral History: A Revived Tradition of the Bancroft Library." *Pacific Northwest Quarterly* 58 (1967), pp. 57–64.

——"Oral History, the Library, and the Genealogical Researcher." *Journal of Library History* 5 (October 1970), pp. 359–71.

——*Oral History for the Local Historical Society*, 2nd ed. rev. Nashville:, Tenn.: American Association for State and Local History, 1974.

Benison, Saul. "Reflections on Oral History." *American Archivist* 28 (January 1965), pp. 71–77.

Bombard, Owen W. "Speaking of Yesterday." Dearborn, Mich.: Ford Motor Company Archives, 1952.

——"A New Measure of Things Past." *American Archivist* 18 (April 1955), pp. 123–32.

Bornet, Vaughn Davis. "Oral History Can Be Worthwhile." *American Archivist* 18–19 (July 1955), pp. 241–53.

Campbell, Joan, ed. *Oral History 74*. Bundoora, Victoria, Australia: La Trobe University, 1974.

Catton, Bruce. "Talk Now, Play Later." Reprinted as "History-Making Idea." *Think* 31 (1965), pp. 20–23.

Challener, Richard D., and J. M. Fenton. "Recent Past Comes Alive in Dulles 'Oral History.'" *University: A Princeton Semiannual* 9 (1967), pp. 29–34.

Claremont Graduate School. "Oral History Program." Transcripts. Claremont, Calif., 1964.

Colman, Gould P. "Oral History—An Appeal for More Systematic Procedures." *American Archivist* 28 (1965), pp. 79–83.

"Oral History at Cornell." *Wilson Library Bulletin* 40 (1966), pp. 624–28.

Columbia University. Oral History Research Office. Annual Reports. New York: Columbia University, 1950.

——*Oral History in the United States*. New York: Columbia University, 1965.

Conference on Science Manuscripts, May 5–6, 1960. "Case Studies of Research Experience." *Isis* 53 (1962), pp. 39–51.

Cornell University. Oral History Project. "Reports." Ithaca: Cornell University, 1962–65.

Cornell University Libraries. *Bulletin of Cornell Program in Oral History*. Ithaca, N.Y.: Cornell University, 1966–72.

Crowl, Philip A. "The Dulles Oral History Project: Mission Accomplished." *American Historical Association Newsletter* 5 (1967), pp. 6–10.

Curtiss, Richard D., et al. *A Guide for Oral History Programs*. Fullerton, Calif.: California State University, 1973.

Dixon, Elizabeth I. "Oral History: A New Horizon." *Library Journal* 87 (April 1, 1962), pp. 1363–65.

——"The Implications of Oral History in Library History." *Journal of Library History* 1 (January 1966), pp. 59–62.

——"The Oral History Program at UCLA: A Bibliography." Los Angeles, Calif.: University of California Library, 1966.

————"Arrowhead in Retrospect." *Journal of Library History* 2 (April 1967), pp. 126–28.

Finnegan, Ruth. "A Note on Oral Tradition and Historical Evidence." *History and Theory* 9 (1970), pp. 195–201. (See chapter 9 of the present volume.)

Fontana, Bernard. "American Indian Oral History." *History and Theory* 8 (1969), pp. 366–70.

Forest History 16:3 (25th anniversary issue, 1972). Santa Cruz, Calif.: Forest History Society. (Contains editorial "Why Oral History?" and excerpts from 11 oral history interviews.)

Frank, Benis M. "Oral History: Columbia and USMC." *Fortitudine* 3 (Fall 1973), pp. 19–20.

Freese, Arthur S. "They All Made History." *Journal of the National Retired Teachers Association* 25 (May–June 1974), pp. 10–12.

Fry, Amelia R. "The Nine Commandments of Oral History." *Journal of Library History* 3 (January 1968), pp. 63–73.

————"Persistent Issues in Oral History." *Journal of Library History* 4 (July 1969), pp. 265–67.

Fry, Amelia R., and Willa K. Baum. "A Janus Look at Oral History." *American Archivist* 32 (October 1969), pp. 319–26.

Gilb, Corinne. "Tape Recorded Interviewing: Some Thoughts from California." *American Archivist* 20 (October 1957), pp. 335–44.

Glass, Mary. "The Oral History Project of the Center for Western North American Studies: A Bibliography." Mimeographed. Reno, Nev.: University of Nevada, Desert Research Institute, 1966.

Haley, Alex. "My Furthest-Back Person—The African." *New York Times Magazine,* July 16, 1972, pp. 12–16.

Harry S. Truman Library Institute. "Research Newsletter Number Ten." Independence, Mo., 1967.

Harry S. Truman Library Institute. Newsletter "Oral History: The Truman Library Approach" (Spring 1976).

Hart, Katherine. "Memories Become History." *Texas Library Journal* 45 (Spring 1969), pp. 33–34.

Hebrew University of Jerusalem. *Oral History Division, Catalogue No. 3.* Jerusalem: Institute of Contemporary Jewry, 1970.

Hewlett, R. G. "A Pilot Study in Contemporary Scientific History. *Isis* 53 (1962), pp. 31–38.

Hoyle, Norman. "Oral History." *Library Trends* 21 (July 1972), pp. 60–82.

Kielman, Chester V. "The Texas Oil Industry Project." *Wilson Library Bulletin* 40 (March 1966), pp. 616–18.

Krasean, Thomas K. "Oral History . . . Voices of the Past." *Library Occurrent* 22 (August 1968), pp. 297, 305.

Lieber, Joel. "The Tape Recorder as Historian." *Saturday Review* (June 11, 1966), pp. 98–99.

Lord, C. L., ed. "Ideas in Conflict: A Colloquium on Certain Problems in Historical Society Work in the United States and Canada." Harrisburg, Pa.: American Association for State and Local History, 1958.

McPherson, M. W., and J. A. Popplestone. "Problems and Procedures in Oral Histories." *Archives of the History of American Psychology* 23 (1967), p. 11.

Mason, Elizabeth B., and Louis M. Starr, eds. *The Oral History Collection of Columbia University.* 3d ed. New York: New York Times Company, 1973.

Mason, John T., Jr. "An Interview with John T. Mason, Jr." *U.S. Naval Institute Proceedings* 99 (July 1973), pp. 42–47.

Maunder, Elwood R. "Tape Recorded Interviews Provide Grass Roots History." *Forest History* 2 (1959), p. 1.

Meckler, Alan M., and Ruth McMullin, eds. *Oral History Collections.* New York: Bowker, 1975.

Meyer, Eugenia, and Alicia Olivera de Bonfil. "Oral History in Mexico." *Journal of Library History* 7 (October 1972), pp. 360–65.

Miles, Wyndham D. "Usefulness of Oral History in Writing the Story of a Large Scientific Project." *Ithaca* 26 (1962), pp. 351–53.

Morrissey, Charles T. "The Case for Oral History," *Vermont History* 31 (1963), pp. 145–55.

———"Truman and the Presidency—Records and Oral Recollections." *American Archivist* 28 (January 1965), pp. 53–61.

Moss, William W. *Oral History Program Manual.* New York: Praeger, 1974.

Nevins, Allan. *The Gateway to History.* Boston: Appleton-Century, 1938.

"Oral History: How and Why It Was Born." *Wilson Library Bulletin* 40 (March 1966), pp. 600–601. (See chapter 1 of the present volume).

Oral History: An Occasional News Sheet. Nos. 1–4. Colchester, Essex, England: University of Essex, 1969–74.

Oral History: The Journal of the Oral History Society. Colchester, Essex, England: University of Essex, 1973–. (Successor to *Oral History: An Occasional News Sheet.*)

Oral History Association. *Newsletter.* New York: Oral History Association, 1967–.

"Oral History Collection." *North Texas State University Bulletin* 420 (December 1970), p. 33.

Oral History Review. New York: Oral History Association, 1973–.

Perlis, Vivian. "Ives and Oral History." *Notes: Journal of the Music Library Association* 28 (June 1972), pp. 629–42.

Pogue, Forrest C. "History While It's Hot." *Kentucky Library Association Bulletin* 24 (April 1960), pp. 31–35.

———"The George C. Marshall Oral History Project." *Wilson Library Bulletin* 40 (March 1966), pp. 607–15.

Princeton University Library. *The John Foster Dulles Oral History Project: A Preliminary Catalogue.* Princeton, N.J.: Princeton University, 1966.

Regional Oral History Office. "Interviews Completed or In Process." Berkeley, Calif.: University of California, 1965.

Reynoldston Research and Studies. *Oral History Developments in British Columbia.* Vancouver, B.C., Canada, 1973.

Rollins, Alfred B., Jr. *Report on the Oral History Project of the John Fitzgerald Kennedy Library.* Cambridge, Mass.: Harvard University, 1965.

Rumics, Elizabeth. "Oral History: Defining the Term." *Wilson Library Bulletin* 40 (March 1966), pp. 602–605.

Schlesinger, Arthur M., Jr. "On the Writing of Contemporary History." *Atlantic Monthly* (March 1967), pp. 69–74.

Schruben, Francis W. "An Even Stranger Death of President Harding." *Southern California Quarterly* 48 (March 1966), pp. 57–84.

Shaughnessy, Donald F. "Labor in the Oral History Collection of Columbia University." *Labor History* 1–2 (Spring 1960), pp. 177–95.

Shockley, Ann Allen. *Manual for the Black Oral History Program.* Nashville, Tenn.: Fisk University Library, 1971.

Shumway, Gary L., and William G. Hartley. *An Oral History Primer.* Fullerton, Calif.: California State University, 1973.

Shurnway, Gary L. *Oral History in the United States: A Directory.* New York: Oral History Association, 1971.

Skeels, J. W. "Oral History Project on the Development of Unionism in the Automobile Industry." *Labor History* 5 (1964), pp. 209–12.

Starr, Louis M. "Columbia's Reservoir of Source Material." *Graduate Faculties Newsletter* (November 1959), pp. 1–3.

———"Oral History: Problems and Prospects." In *Advances in Librarianship,* vol. 2, ed. Melvin Voigt. New York: Seminar Press, 1971.

———"Studs Terkel and Oral History." *Chicago History* 3 (Fall 1974), pp. 123–26.

Stephens, A. Roy. "Oral History and Archives." *Texas Library* 29 (Fall 1967), pp. 203–14.

Swain, Donald C. "Problems for Practitioners of Oral History." *American Archivist* 28 (January 1965), pp. 63–69.

Teiser, Ruth. "Transcriber's Fancies." *Journal of Library* 5 (April 1970), pp. 182–83.

Van Dyne, Larry. "Oral History: Sharecroppers and Presidents, Jazz and Texas Oil." *Chronicle of Higher Education* 8 (December 24, 1973), pp. 9–10.

Waserman, Manfred. *Bibliography on Oral History.* Rev. ed. New York: Oral History Association, 1975.

White, Helen M. "Thoughts on Oral History." *American Archivist* 20 (January 1957), pp. 19–30.

Wilkie, James W. "Postulates for the Oral History Center for Latin America." *Journal of Library History* 2 (January 1967), pp. 45–54.

———*Elitelore.* Los Angeles: University of California, Latin American Center, 1973.

Wyatt, William. "Researching the South Dakota Frontier." *South Dakota Library Bulletin* 52 (October–December 1966), pp. 151–56.

Zachert, Martha Jane. "Implications of Oral History for Librarians." *College Research Libraries* 20 (March 1968), pp. 101–103.

———"The Second Oral History Colloquium." *Journal of Library History* 3 (April 1968), pp. 173–78.

———"Oral History Interviews." *Journal of Library History* 5 (January 1970), pp. 80–87.

3

Directions for Oral
History in the United States

Ronald J. Grele

*Ronald J. Grele's contribution to this anthology is not so much a history as an
annotation of recent methodological and theoretical debates within American oral history (and the Oral History Association). In the pages that follow, he comments on the
ideology of oral history in its formative years. He points out key trends—the interna-
tionalization of the field, the arrival and disappearance of journals, the use of contract
oral historians, the importance of reading the interview and its transcript reflexively
and as a sociolinguistic event. Many of these developments are very much in process
within the field; thus this essay is not only complementary to that of Grele's predeces-
sor, Louis Starr, but is suggestive of future trends.*

*Ronald J. Grele directs the Oral History Program of Columbia University (formerly,
he directed UCLA's program). He is the author of a pioneering exploration of oral history theory,* Envelopes of Sound, *and co-editor of a collection of oral history testimony, 1968. Portions of this essay appeared in* Bios *(1990), a German journal of oral
historical and biographical research.*

*O*ral history, the interviewing of eye-witness participants in the events of the past for the purposes of historical reconstruction, has a long patrimony in the United States. Many of the details of this legacy have been semi-humorously outlined by Charles T. Morrissey in his quest to discover the first usage of the term.[1] Among the early American oral historians mentioned by Morrissey are: Sheldon Dibble, missionary to the Hawaiian Islands, who in 1838 set out to collect "a true account" of the history of the islands by talking to "the oldest chiefs and people"; Mormon church historian Andrew Jensen [1850–1941] who in the mid-1890s began to interview the founders of the church in the United States; and Jonas Bergen, a Swedish-American utopian who in the 1880s devised his own recording device modeled upon that of Thomas Edison and set out to record the memories of the elders of his community. One of these recordings is reputed to be among the oldest still extant recordings of an interview. [2]

Morrissey also noted the contributions of more traditional historians and collectors such as: Lyman C. Draper [1815–1891] at the State Historical Society of Wisconsin and Hubert Howe Bancroft [1823–1918] at the University of California, both of whom gathered rather large collections of interviews from settlers of various parts of the American frontier; interviews which to this day are widely used by historians. More problematic in terms of a scholarly tradition is the legend of Joe Gould, a Greenwich Village roustabout and self-proclaimed "bohemian" who in the 1920s claimed that he was collecting an "oral history of the world," part of which he was gathering from seagulls with whom he supposedly talked. Although many Village writers and artists have recalled Gould's voluminous note books and his constant scribbling of their conversations, none of this oral history of the world has ever been found.[3]

As American academic historians attempted to professionalize themselves and make their study more "scientific" in the last decades of the nineteenth century, their view of their task was increasingly a view which limited them to the study of written records. This bias, as well as the research seminar and the definition of the historian as a holder of a Ph.D., they imported from Germany. Thus armed they set out to develop a new kind of history in which oral recollections would play no role. But old habits died hard. Herbert Baxter Adams is generally recognized as the father of the German method in American historiography. His seminars at Johns Hopkins became the model for the profession. Yet as one of his students, J. Franklin Jameson, noted somewhat contemptuously those seminars did not live up to the new model. They were, he argued, "tiresome. The staple of the meetings consists of outside attractions, now a Confederate general, now an elderly party exhumed to reminisce to us." While Adams still believed in the usefulness of personal testimony, Jameson obviously did not, and as Jameson and his peers assumed the direction of the profession, historical study was more and more limited to the examination of, and explication of, written documents. Interviewing, if it continued, was confined to amateur local historians or journalists.[4]

In the same years that interviewing became less and less a part of historical work, it found a new home in the developing social sciences, especially sociology. Following the pathbreaking work of W. I. Thomas and Florian Znaniecki in their study of the Polish peasant in Europe and the United States, sociologists, especially those at the University of Chicago, produced a number of life histories based upon intensive fieldwork and interviewing. In the process they also set forth a rationale for the use of the life history method, and a new way to view and use such evidence, especially in trying to understand social pathologies or to try to develop means to solve social problems. In the 1930s, with the enactment of New Deal legislation designed to put authors and journalists to work, and the growth of the field of folklore, the tradition of collecting interviews continued. One result was the recording of thousands of life history interviews with former slaves under the direction of the Federal Writers Project; interviews which, interestingly enough, went virtually unused by scholars until the 1960s.[6] Both the Chicago school of sociology and the various WPA projects, and those emulating them, had more or less frankly social agendas. In the case of the Chicago School it was the progressive ideology of applying knowledge to the solution of social problems. In the case of the WPA it was New Deal populism, the attempt to give a voice to the "people" and build a history from the bottom up—an early precursor of the new social history of the 1960s.[7]

In the post World War II era of the 1940s, as the influence of the Chicago School waned under the onslaught of the new quantitative sociology, interviewing made a renewed presence in historical study. During that decade, capitalizing upon the invention of new recording devices, several oral history programs were established at American universities and in some government agencies. The most notable of these was the Columbia University Oral History Research Office founded by Allan Nevins in 1948.[8] Nevins, although he was to become a president of the American Historical Association, was in many ways an outsider to the profession. He had begun his career as a journalist and was always considered a popularizer by many of his colleagues. He in turn was deeply disturbed by the development of a history that was divorced from the concerns of the society at large, which gloried heavily footnoted monographs unintelligible to the lay public. Mirroring Nevins' status in the profession, these early programs were not located within departments of history but usually within libraries or archival depositories. Thus they had little effect on the training of historians, or on historiographical practice. In addition, unlike the earlier, broadly based interviewing projects of the WPA, the emphasis of the new programs was upon the collection of memoirs from "movers and shakers" to fill in the gaps in existing archival or manuscript holdings. Thus, oral history in the United States was seen as an <u>archi-val practice</u>.

This early ideology was clearly articulated by Philip C. Brooks, then the Director of the Harry S. Truman Library, at the first organizing meeting of the Oral History Association in 1966. The Truman Library was one of the first governmental programs in oral history and Brooks, himself, was a staff member of the National Archives. Brooks claimed that "the fact that oral history is history . . . implies . . . that it should be done according to the traditional tenets of historical scholarship. This involves, primarily, objectivity; it involves accuracy; it involves thoroughness and a number of other things . . . —primarily objectivity." It is a "way of supplementing—not substituting for, but supplementing—the written record, the letters, the diaries, the records, whatever may exist, that were created in the period that we're dealing with." "Historians have been interviewing people for hundreds of years; there's nothing new about that, and I don't think they've been doing oral history. I think there's a *real* distinction between a researcher who interviews people for *his* own purpose to derive information for *his own* book, and that of what I sometimes call a 'pure' oral historian, who is accumulating a stock of evidence for the use of other researchers is almost by definition likely to be doing a more objective job than the one who is writing his own book, especially the one who has a case to prove."[9]

Based upon this model the <u>growth of oral history</u> in the United States from 1948 to the mid-1960s <u>was exponential</u>. Within three years of the organizing meeting of the Association there were almost 200 formal projects and hundreds of smaller community efforts.[10] Throughout this early history two major themes emerged. The first was the <u>marginal status of oral history</u> within the historical profession. The second was the <u>tension</u> between those who saw <u>interviewing as part of a defined social movement, and those who saw it as a historical practice in need of standards and respectability</u>; standards and respectability which would make oral history more <u>palatable</u> to academic historians, their clients and patrons. A sub theme of the second tension was the conflict between those who wished to concentrate their efforts on <u>interviewing the "movers and shakers"</u> who had left a body of documents upon which the interviews would be based, **vs** and those who sought to <u>use oral history as a way to give voice to the inarticulate</u>.

Until the 1970s, however, the <u>archival imperative</u> dominated the practice of oral history. Since most projects were located within archives or libraries, the assumption, often articulated, was that <u>oral history was a practice of gathering documents, not a practice of reflection upon those documents or speculation on how they might</u> be used to develop new ways to view and do history. The role of the oral historian was akin to that of the archivist. He or she was a collector who made materials available to others who produced the histories. The goal was to <u>produce ideologically neutral documents and leave interpretation to others</u>. Such

[margin note: objectivity]

a vision fell neatly into place as part of the dominant theme of "scientific" history. Thus for many years the major topics of discussion among oral historians within the Association and in journals devoted to the discussion of oral history were topics normally addressed by librarians and archivists, and the major intellectual effort was to define the nature of the document. How did one process an interview? Was the document the tape or the transcript? How should the interview be catalogued? What were one's legal responsibilities to the interviewee? What was the relationship between an oral history and other documents in the archive?[11]

But other impulses were not totally lacking. As early as 1957 Corrine Gilb warned that the concentration upon archival techniques in oral history threatened to obscure the larger issues presented by the ability of interviews to give us insight into questions of cultural construction.[12] At each meeting of the Oral History Association there were voices calling for a socially relevant practice of oral history. Indeed, the location of many projects in local libraries and historical societies, and the attempt of the Association to encourage local historians to join, often led to the founding of projects which had as their goals community pride, ethnic awareness, cultural preservation, and political mobilization rather than the production of ideologically neutral documents for the use of other historians.[13]

Even within the archival ethos there was room for debate. Saul Benison, in particular, expressed deep concern about the nature of the document and the fact that it was being created by the intervention of the historian and was therefore "a first interpretation." He also alerted American oral historians to the importance of the autobiographical uses of oral history and the literature on autobiographical narrative. Benison, who had been an interviewer for the Columbia Oral History Office and a close admirer of Nevins, took the discussion of the nature of the oral document to a new plane that was most useful to later oral historians in their insistence that the interview be seen as a joint creation and a cultural artifact with its own rules of creation and use.[14]

In the 1960s, oral historians, like many of their colleagues, were deeply affected by the upheavals of the New Left. History as a discipline was the object of scrutiny by many activists. The Black struggle for civil rights and the expression of Black identity (Black is Beautiful) spurred a new interest in the history of Afro-Americans, and a new way to view that past. Similar movements followed in other racial and ethnic communities, and were then initiated by women through the women's movement. In addition, the growth of the "new social history," based upon the work and writings of E. P. Thompson and Herbert Gutman, raised fundamental questions about the ways in which historians had looked at the past, and the consequences of such a view. The personal politics of the 1960s and the new social history combined to demand a new history, a history from the bottom up, a history not of movers and shakers but of members of the working class, of ethnic and racial minorities, of women. Within this new vision, oral history was seen as a way to recapture that history. It offered historians the opportunity to create documents where none existed and therefore rescue a hidden history, and to more sympathetically understand the viewpoint of the people they studied. In addition, oral history interviewing would also put one in direct contact with people, breaking through "false" social arrangements which kept intellect workers from other workers.[15] Elsewhere I have written about the auto-biographical and confessional urge of this generation of American activists and the ways in which it reflected their desire to merge the personal and the political.[16] This urge led many New Left scholars into oral history or into community history projects which used oral history as one way to gather documents of the past of the communities they studied and worked within. Oral history found a new home in these projects, many of them with an openly radical agenda.

Studs Terkel was, in many ways, a bridge from one generation to the next. A veteran of the Federal Writers Project, imbued with a Popular Front ideology derived from that experience, Terkel constructed very successful oral history books, based upon the testimonies of "the little people." They became models for many New Left publications and projects.

The archival impulse which had dominated American oral history with its demands for an "objective" history, and its positivist and empiricist view of that history, had left little room for discussion of the personal and social relationships between interviewer and interviewee, or for discussion of the nature of the interview itself. The new populist vision, while directing attention to these aspects of the practice of oral history, failed to articulate a view of history beyond its own populist enthusiasm. These two proposed agendas brought to the fore the lack of serious theory with the American oral history movement as well as its isolation from other social science disciplines. This contradiction was caught by Michael Frisch in his review of Terkel's *Hard Times*.[17] What Frisch found in the enthusiasm surrounding oral history was a contradictory set of views of history, neither of them very historical, and both deeply conservative in their implications. The first was the view that oral history was more history, simply piling on more and more data. The second was a populist drive to escape history embedded in the articulated mission to somehow go beyond professional historians and academic history to get a purer history from the voices of the folk. Neither posture, he argued, spoke to the potential of oral history to uncover the "rough beast of consciousness" or to raise the larger questions about the ways in which memory and historical construction guided the ways in which people made their histories and lived in history.

From a slightly different trajectory, the concerns of my own work merged with those of Frisch. Like many who had tried to come to grips with the collapse of the movement, I had turned to the work of Louis Althusser to explain the failure of a politics based upon the most spontaneous elements of the young Marx (an erroneous safari, I now realize). I found in Althusser not only a structured way to discuss ideology, but also a discussion of how one reads documents. Listening to my interviews in these ways, I tried to frame the old discussion of the nature of the documents in a somewhat different form. Rather than argue that it was either a recording or a transcript, I tried to argue that both were simply renditions of what was really a "conversational narrative." Working from that base, I tried to discern the ways in which that conversation was formed and expressed within an interview; its complex merger of a social situation, linguistic exercise, and historical dialogue. This analysis, I believed, would then allow one to talk with some more precision about the interview as cultural construct, relate it to the situation of its creation as well as the actual material world of the interviewee, and thereby <u>discern the ways in which consciousness was expressed</u>. This type of analysis was also, I felt, a way around the traditional debate about elitism since <u>elitism derived not from whom one interviewed, but from the ways in which one interviewed.</u>[18]

Whether or not that exercise fulfilled that promise, *Envelopes of Sound* seems to have become a useful work for many younger oral historians in looking at their work. I think one of its appeals was that it opened a kind of door to folklore, anthropology, and other fieldwork sciences which allowed us to talk in a different way about the experience of fieldwork.[19]

Between 1975 and 1985 a series of external events conspired to change the face of American oral history. The publication of Paul Thompson's *Voice of the Past* gave us a basic text heavily oriented to social history or history from the bottom up, which accented the nature of the historical enterprise, not the archival nature of the interview and interview processing.[20] The First International Conference on Oral History held in Essex, England, in 1978 brought a small but influential number of American oral historians into contact with their comrades in Europe, many of whom were expressing the same concerns about consciousness and subjectivity and experimenting with a wider variety of methods and theory to deal with those issues. Especially important was the work being done by Italian oral historians since it seemed so imbued with movement political concerns and had theoretical sophistication lacking in American efforts. The founding of the *International Journal of Oral History* in 1980 was an important turning point. It introduced European and Latin American oral historians to an American audience. It gave space to younger scholars in a wide variety of fields, such as sociology, folklore, and speech communications, an arena in which to speculate about the relationships between their concerns and what it was oral historians were doing. On a very basic level, the populist turn of the National Endowment for the Humanities during the presidency of Jimmy Carter funneled funds into a number of community history projects and local oral history projects which were thus able to test in the field their concern for a popular history.[21]

These events also affected the Oral History Association. Thompson's work gave a respectability to work in social history. The continuing international conferences have brought more and more American oral historians into contact with people beyond the borders of the United States, and these oral historians have, in turn, been instrumental in forming an International Committee within the Association and pressuring its officers for money to bring non-American oral historians to the organization's Annual Meetings.[22] *The International Journal of Oral History* was directly responsible for a change in the format and content of the Association's *Oral History Review*, first under Arthur Hansen and then under Michael Frisch. Although still running articles of a how-to nature, or show-and-tell, much more space in the *Review* is devoted to theoretical discussions and articles from around the world or from interdisciplinary perspectives. Recently the *Review* has ventured into the area of film and video reviewing and theory, much in advance of the *IJOH*.

The growth and growing sophistication of community history projects helped to create a new constituency for the Association.[23] Although the OHA had always welcomed local historians, it did not extend a general welcome to the more politicized community historians whose agenda was less archival and celebratory and more activist and populist. In the last few years, however, there has been a major effort devoted to this audience. The high point of that effort was an annual meeting of the Association (1989) which featured the work of over 30 community history projects, and the work of historians in nonwhite communities. The success of that program in terms of interest in the issues raised, participation of new members, and the commitment of the Association to continue to sponsor sessions devoted to the problems of community history in nonwhite communities marked a decided shift in orientation. This shift was, however, more programmatic than structural since the organization has had on its governing Council over the past several years members who had close links to the community history movement.[24]

The incremental transformation of the Oral History Association has not, however, been without struggle and tension, as evidenced in the angry exchange between Frisch and Benis Frank, Director of the Marine Corps Oral History Program, over Frank's report on his on-the-scene interviewing of Marines during the American invasion of Grenada. Frank's initial report was a glowing recitation of how he was able to go into the island with the landing forces, a privilege denied to newsmen or other observers, and his interviews with members of the invasion force. The publication of the report in the Association's *Newsletter* brought forth a commentary from Frisch pointing out this contradiction and raising questions about the political wisdom of committing one's research to efforts to offer an ideological prop to a questionable military operation. Frank replied with a vituperative attack accusing Frisch of political motives and of attacking his interviewing simply because Frisch opposed the invasion.[25]

The exchange was important not only because it reflected the ideological division within the Oral History Association, but also because Frisch in his commentary had raised fundamental questions about how neutral, indeed, were collecting projects which were so closely tied to established institutions. He raised in bald form a critique of the assumptions that had prevailed among a large number of Association members since the founding of the organization. It was a rebuttal to the vision of Brooks which has already been outlined above.

More important, perhaps, was the struggle of the Oral History Association to revise its *Evaluation Guidelines*, a struggle important enough to justify a somewhat extended discussion. In addition, the development, use, and role of the *Guidelines*, I think, presents an instance of one of the real cultural peculiarities of the American oral history movement. In no other nation in the world, as far as my knowledge goes, has the national organization of oral historians devised a set of guidelines for the practice of oral history, and had those guidelines accepted by sponsoring agencies, funding bodies, or the larger historical profession as the definitive guidelines for the practice of oral history.[26] The debate as it has so far been articulated reflects the historic tension with the Association and within American oral history more generally between those who view oral history as a practice and those who view it as a movement, and brings into stark contrast their differing perceptions of what the professional role of the oral historian is.

In 1978, the Association received a grant from the National Endowment for the Humanities to bring together a loosely knit group of evaluators (members who had been offering their services evaluating oral history programs and proposals) to devise a set of guidelines for the practice. In 1979, the guidelines adopted by this group were approved by the membership of the Association and they became the official policy of the Association. Their adoption by many granting agencies was one indication of the maturation of the Association and its increasingly important role in the field. The *Guidelines*, however, reflected a very heavy influence of archivists and archival practice. In addition, over the years as the field changed it became apparent that the *Guidelines* left whole areas unmentioned, such as, video or film interviewing, oral history in the classroom, community history, and the concern with the status of interviews done by academic historians and journalists, many of whom have been seeking to deposit their interviews in ongoing collections.

To speak to these issues, the Association established a number of committees, each of which was to prepare a report to the Association at its next Annual Meeting. The *Evaluation Guidelines*, as approved in 1979, contained a forward on "The Goals and Guidelines of the Association," which set forth a set of general principles for ethical and legal relations between interviewers and interviewees. The development of these *Guidelines* had been one of the most difficult and contentious tasks of the original designers of the document. Realizing the potentially divisive nature of a renewed discussion of these ethical guidelines, the Council directed each committee to commit its energies solely to the particular task ascribed, and not deal with the opening general statement. It did not take long for the Committee, which was to revise the more or less neutral set of legal and ethical guidelines contained in the body of the report, to realize that it could not revise these strictures without discussing the larger issues posed by the general ethical guidelines. This realization was natural for a committee which was, by and large, composed of community historians and social history activists who had flocked to that particular committee.

Two points immediately became points of issue. In their examination of the general guidelines, the committee urged a revision which would offer to individuals the choice of anonymity and the right to choose what to discuss within the interview. They also devised a statement urging historians to take steps to guard against potentially damaging effects of the publications of their research. Concerned by the fact that they generally interview people who have little recourse to the normal protections of society, such as lawyers, or who have been involved in activities, if not illegal, [at least] highly suspect or condemned by the culture at large, the committee members sought to protect their sources. This, of course, flew in the face of an "objective" history where all sources are properly noted. It also raised, in my mind at least, questions about the replicability of research results. Many historians in the United States have an aversion to so called "highly placed sources" or unnamed informants of the type that dominate so much of current American journalistic history and saw this protection as a step in that direction. Whether or not the Association will be able to develop a sort of situational ethics to resolve this conflict remains to be debated. In the meantime, it is clear that this tension is simply one of many which will arise over the years as the Association tries to bridge the gap between oral history as historical practice and oral history as movement.

Within the academic historical profession the status of oral history has never been higher. Each year the publication of historical works using oral history collections or based upon interviews conducted by the author increases. The Organization of American Historians recently awarded one of its most prestigious prizes to *Like a Family: The Making of a Southern Cotton Mill World*, written by a University of North Carolina collective and heavily based upon their interviews with Southern textile workers.[27] Issues raised by oral historians are more and more discussed within the profession, partly as a result of a growing interest in discourse analysis and deconstruction, but also because they raise fundamental questions about historical practice in general. A recent special issue of the *Journal of American History*, which contained an article by John Bodnar on his oral history interviewing of workers and managers at an automotive plant, opened with a frank admission of the key role of oral history in process of the study of historical memory. David Thelen, editor of the *Journal*, noted in his introduction to the issue that, "[T]he study of how people construct and narrate memories may encourage a greater sensitivity in historians to wider audiences who might listen to (and help shape) the narratives we want to construct and tell. Appreciation for the crucial participation of listener, interviewer, or audience in the creation of recollection represents a major contribution by oral historians to the historical study of memory." He then went on to claim, "[S]mall wonder, then, that three articles in this special issue on memory draw heavily from oral history." At a time when many historians believe that the narrative offers the most promising structure for solving interconnected problems of specialization and interpretation, the study of memory may provide the most promising entrance to the possibilities of narrative, and oral history may provide one of the most promising entries into memory, he remarked.[28]

In addition, many major history departments now offer or suggest that their graduate students take formal training in oral history methods and theory, and as social historians trained in the 1960s assume tenured positions within these departments, we now find ourselves with sympathetic allies on our own campuses, perceptive and willing consultants to local projects, and understanding reviewers for our published work.

All of this is gratifying to those oral historians who worked for many years on the fringes of the profession, but problems remain. Aside from the tension already noted between oral history as practice and oral history as movement, which will probably be with us forever and is understandable to those who view historical change as originating in contradictions, we face other obstacles. In Washington, D.C., under the Reagan administration, funding for community history programs came to an end. While some oral history programs are able to receive funding from the National Endowment for the Humanities, such funding is almost exclusively for archivally connected projects, or for the development of finding aids. Most oral historians in the United States continue to remain ignorant of the possibilities of filmed or videotaped interviewing, or, worse yet, ignorant of the reasons why, perhaps, they should not do such interviewing or waste large sums of money on such projects. It is a debate yet to happen. The *International Journal of Oral History* disappeared. Whether this is to be rued, or simply recognized as the result of the growing theoretical sophistication and international perspective of other mainstream journals, remains to be seen.

In the last 15 years, the public history movement has engaged the talents of hundreds of historians who seek to use their skills outside of the academy. Many of them work for agencies or corporations on a contract basis, and many of them are doing oral history, either on an individual basis or as part of their own corporations. While in the main this movement has been a boon to oral history, some aspects of this work raise fundamental questions for the practice. In particular, the willingness of oral historians working on contract to agree that the interviews they do will remain sealed forever in the vaults of the corporation gives a new meaning to secret research. While American oral history programs have always offered to seal interviews for a certain period of time, they have never agreed to close material forever. As the number of contract historians increases, they are bound to have an effect upon the movement and the practice. Exactly what that effect will be is yet to be discerned.

On another level, each year more and more books using oral histories are published, and each year more and more oral historians are publishing from their interviews. Many of these works are startling in their insight and originality.[29] We have only recently, however, begun to grapple with the issues raised by the editing of our interviews, and the subtle ways in which we transform them and the people we interview, in the editing process. Nor have we come face to face with the issues raised by Brooks about the fundamental differences between collecting oral histories and using them for publication. We have not been helped much by the counterclaim by Larry Goodwyn and his colleagues at Duke that we should take exactly the opposite posture and argue that the only reason for doing an interview is one's own research and publication agenda, and that the interview should not be a fishing expedition in the hopes of gathering useful material for others, or narratives, but a highly focused set of questions designed to elicit facts that the historian can use for his work.[30]

It is always difficult to stop in time and appraise a situation in flux and change. It seems clear that oral history in the United States has embarked upon a new era of growth and sophistication.[31] What direction it will take is undetermined. That it will continue to exhibit the characteristics which have defined it over the past 40 years is open to debate. Perhaps that is to be regretted, perhaps not. One thing seems clear: oral history will grow with more careful introspection among oral historians than it did in its early years. It will also grow in closer alignment with professional academic historians. The first instance is to be celebrated. The second is more ambiguous. It is all to the good that American oral historians have begun to develop a theoretical perspective on their work and have been able to integrate that theory into an ongoing dialogue about the way we study and practice history. In the process, however, were we to lose our base in the community, or among amateur historians, or local libraries and schools by too closely allying ourselves with the academy, we would lose a good deal of our inspiration and creativity.

Given the position of the oral history movement and the Oral History Association at the intersection of academic history and community history, it is clear that both will be torn by the tension over what oral history is and how it should develop. That is, perhaps, a healthy tension.

Afterword, 1996

When the editors of this anthology asked me to update this essay to include discussion of recent theoretical trends, I was reluctant to do so. The original essay was prepared for a seminar in Bad Homberg, Germany, on the state and practice of oral history in various areas of the world and published alongside others in *Bios* (in 1990 . . .). The extent and richness of recent work in oral historiography demands a full-scale and close examination. In these pages it can only be a superficial gloss. In addition, to add such a section requires that I try to assess my own work in relation to that of others, to situate it and at the same time consider some of the criticisms of that work.

ORGANIZATIONS

The number and extent of oral history projects has continued to increase, despite limited funding from both governmental and private sources. Many projects and programs continue to work against severe financial restraints and stringencies.[32] What is to be remarked upon is that this situation does not seem to mark a decline in the attraction of oral history or the sense of its importance. The Oral History Association continues to set directions for the field, and that is still rather unusual, although associations have been formed in other parts of the world such as Mexico, Argentina, and Southeast Asia, and revived in others such as Canada. Here, the services of the Association have expanded and, most significantly, its annual programs have come to include presentations of and the results of work that is both theoretically sophisticated and community-inspired. In particular there has been a yeoman effort to include work being done in nonwhite and non-Anglo communities.[33] Regional organizations, a footnote in 1989, have also prospered for community and academic historians, albeit on a limited basis since most meet, at best, only twice a year.[34]

Publications using oral history interviews, either those held in collections or collected by authors, and publications expressly oriented toward oral history continue to grow in number each year. Articles, monographs, and more popular work flood the field. When many of us began to work in oral history, it was quite common to be asked to justify the use of interviews as documentary sources. (One of the reasons for the defensive tone of much that was written about oral history). Now, it is usually the case that historians are asked to justify *not* using interviews or doing interviews.

Two publishers have initiated oral series. The most extensive is that of Twayne Publishers under the editorial direction of Donald Ritchie. To date 20 books have either been published or prepared for publication, and the hope is to produce four a year—some indication of the availability of material and the presence of a market. Subjects of the individual volumes vary from a study of one-room schoolhouses in Texas, to a study of Italian-American internment during the Second World War, to a study of 100-year-old Montenegran women.[35] In a break with standard formats each volume presents extended excerpts of oral history testimony with interpretative or methodological sections by the author either as an introduction or interspersed with the testimony.

The second series is less extensive but in some ways more ambitious. Undertaken by the State University of New York Press under the editorship of Michael Frisch, the series has published two works to date, both of which have become standards in the field: Frisch's *A Shared Authority* and Alessandro Portelli's *The Death of Luigi Trastulli and Other Stories*.[36] Other publishers, most notably Carlson Publishing, have issued books which reproduce oral histories from various archives, and a number of international anthologies have appeared.[37]

Perhaps the most explosive growth of the oral history has been in nonprint media. There is simply no way to begin to catalog the scope and variety of such productions. Interviews have, of course, been long used in radio and filmed presentations; what is new is the conscious effort to create and use oral history testimony in consultation with oral historians, and the increasing number of oral historians producing their own programs. Once a book-oriented practice where some projects actually destroyed tapes after creating written transcripts, oral history has become more and more the realm of orality. Perhaps, the best known oral history film or video project is that of Stephen Spielberg who has mounted an oral history project to collect memories of the Holocaust before those who survive pass from the scene. While this project has stirred debate, it should be noted that the producers did consult with various oral historians before embarking on the project and they do offer oral history training to their interviewers. We note the project here as an indication of the growing popularity of oral history.

As in 1989, bridging the gap between projects and programs remains a concern. One hopeful sign is the growth of public history and the interest of public historians in oral history. The recent *Guide to Graduate Programs* published by the National Council on Public History lists 57 projects, 22 of which offer training in oral history or internships in oral history projects. Ten others include oral history work in archives training or training in various forms of historical documentation.[38]

Yet the tensions persist, less ideological than in years past, partly as a result of the work of the Oral History Association and the regional associations, partly as a result of the general decline of politics, but still unresolved. Although the gap between projects and programs is now seen far more in practice, it still has repercussions for the ways in which we do our work.

It is still difficult for local projects to obtain on any long-term basis the kinds of training and expertise they so desperately need. And it is still the case that, for the most part, the work of community historians has not affected the practice of more established and academically oriented programs. While some programs do try, without being patronizing, to provide some help through workshops or even, perhaps, help in grant writing, this assistance is usually a one-time effort. The inability of local projects to develop or finance standard practices in the development of finding aids, tape or transcript storage, or bibliographic aids means that many worthwhile and exciting interviews remain unknown to a broader public. More importantly, many local projects tend to lapse into a sheltered antiquarianism because they have so little contact with a community of interested historians with some sense of how the local events being documented relate to larger historical processes. In earlier decades, projects such as the Brass Valley Workers Project or the Chinatown History Project provided one venue for such interaction, but cutbacks in funding have meant that such projects have not become models for growth. In worst-case scenarios many fine projects have simply stopped their efforts.

In some cases oral history programs have tried either to incorporate local projects into their programs or to assist these projects. Programs at the State University of New York at Buffalo, the University of North Carolina, the State University of California at Fullerton, and the University of New Mexico come to mind. But such work is rare.[39]

It would be interesting to document in what ways all of these efforts in public history and media programs, from-time-to-time advising, or direct relations with community projects have changed the practices of programs themselves. For the most part, oral history programs were founded at a time when our conceptions of history and our audience were quite different than they are today. If the field and the audience have changed, then we must ask whether or not our practices have.

For the most part, established programs, even many in public history or in universities extending themselves into the community, still see their audience as professional historians interested in using interviews to produce monographs. Interviews are often still conducted with an empiricist bent to garner detail about events or "facts," with questions of narrative or memory fitfully considered.

How different would our interviewing, transcription, editing, and processing be if we conceived our audience among non-historians, or local historians, or museum workers, or anyone interested in popular presentations? Are there ways in which we can combine our traditional practices for our traditional audiences with the demands of community history? Without stable long-term contacts between projects and programs, both fail to realize the inherent possibilities of the new history which oral history has always promised. Now that we have seen an abatement of the ideological tension between programs and projects, it is time to devise new practices.

No commentary on the present state of the field of oral history would be complete without some mention of the varied and exciting work that has been done uniting fieldwork and theory. While even in 1989 one could point to a serious lack of theoretical discussion of the issues raised about the nature of history and historical knowledge by oral history, that is no longer the case.

Several key texts—some published prior to 1989, most appearing after—have enriched oral history theory. First and most clearly there is Portelli's *The Death of Luigi Trastulli and Other Stories*, subtitled, interestingly, *Form and Meaning in Oral History*. *Trastulli* is an attempt to understand, through a close examination of narrative forms contained in oral testimony, how people formulate their histories and the ways in which those formulations both explain the past and inform the present and future. It is also a series of ruminations on the methodology of oral history and the relations between narrator and fieldworker as historical actors. A footnote in 1989, Eva McMahan's *Elite Oral History Interviewing*, has been another major contribution, an attempt to apply philosophical hermeneutics to the interview in order to understand both it as a speech act as well as the particular rules and codes of such speech acts. *Women's Words* edited by Sherna Gluck and Daphne Patai merits inclusion among the key texts because of the attempt of many of the authors of the essays collected in the volume to apply feminist theory to the issues of oral history fieldwork. Other works which were collected for a volume edited by McMahan and Kim Lacey Rogers in *Interactive Oral History Interviewing*, which appeared in the international journals previously mentioned and the *Oral History Review,* are also of note. Along with earlier works such as the work of Luisa Passerini, or the various authors whose articles appeared in the *International Journal of Oral History*, Frisch's *Shared Authority* and my own *Envelopes of Sound* have helped amplify this newer literature, to provide oral historians with a rich base for theorizing about their practice.[40]

Given the international scope of this work, and the fact that one of the leading authors, while Italian, is equally at home in Terni, Italy, and Appalachia, it would be absurd to talk about an American body of theory. If one were to make a note of any generic differences it would be to draw attention to a certain practicality noticeable in many of the American works noted here. The essays in *A Shared Authority* move easily from considerations of collective memory and a discussion of the narrative voices in television documentaries to issues of editing transcripts for publication and the presentation of oral history in museum exhibitions. In a similar vein many of the essays in *Women's Words* concern themselves with issues of the application of theory to fieldwork in the most practical sense.[41] It is not insignificant that one of the most interesting recent presentations of oral history theory, by Valerie Yow, appears as the opening section to a fieldwork manual.[42] While it is clear that works such as those by Portelli, Passerini, Isabel Bertaux-Wiame, and Isabel Hofmyer are deeply grounded in fieldwork, one would not look to those works for helpful hints on how to conduct an interview and how to process transcripts.[43] Obversely, it is quite clear that most oral historians in the United States do likewise.[44] The point here is that often when Americans sit down to talk about oral history it is not for theory alone. It is our bent, as the essays in this anthology show.

Crossing boundaries, there are several trends that one can discern in much of the theorizing about oral history. First, it seems obvious that we have been deeply affected by what has been called the "linguistic turn," the view that social reality is understood (perhaps can only be) through the discourse about that reality. Or, following and paraphrasing Stephen Jay Gould, the view that history is not so much a description of reality as it is a set of arguments that create knowledge about the past in a social context. It is clear why oral historians who deal with words so closely should be attracted to propositions that argue that what is said about an event is as interesting as the event itself; it may even be, as Richard Candida Smith has pointed out, that oral history is "an integral part" of the linguistic turn.[45] In any case, questions of language and language codes are integral to much recent work. They are central in Portellli's project which seeks to find in the language of daily life and self-presentation the narrative structures within the stories that people tell to keep their history alive. The concern with language also informs his discussion of popular memory, orality, and class relations. From a different perspective, McMahan's whole thrust is to understand the interview as a speech act. My own work has come to focus on the languages of history and how ideology is revealed in the structures of the interview. Kim Rogers' concern is again, narratives, as it is in the work of Elizabeth Tonkin.[46] Many of the authors in *Women's Words* (in this context a significant title) are concerned with the issues raised by Carol Gilligan about a women's language.[47]

Second, there is a concern for the relationship between the interviewer and interviewee. With some exceptions, most of our thinking about oral history fieldwork has been directed to issues that could be called "reflexive," a concern for how the interests, concerns, social attitudes, personal and collective ideologies of the interviewer affect the interview situation and the stories being told. Such interests are key to Portelli's discussion of methodology, to McMahan's hermeneutics, to Tonkin's concern for performance and audience, to my own speculation about the professional ideologies we bring to the interview, to Gluck's *Rosie the Riveter* and Martin Duberman's *Black Mountain*, among many other works. From whatever perspective recent work has viewed the interview, the older vision of the abstract and disinterested interviewer and the unaffected source is gone.[48]

The interest in narrative, language, and reflexivity is all a part of an interest in subjectivity, the ways in which desires, ideologies, visions, and above all memory formulate our histories as we construct them in the interview. Much of Passerini's work is directed to memory, as is that of Frisch and Portelli. More than one-fourth of all of the papers delivered at the last international conference on oral history were devoted to issues of memory, and the initial volume of the *Yearbook* series was devoted exclusively to "Memory and Totalitarianism." Other works of note would include Alistair Thomson's work with Australian war veterans, or David Shuldiner's study of aging political activists, as well as the investigation of "archival memory" by Alice and Howard Hoffman.[49]

Other trends can be discerned. Much of the work discussed here is deeply interdisciplinary and all of it is internationally embedded. Both topics deserve a full discussion but can only be noted here. What is of import now is to return briefly to the issue of subjectivity and note how work in oral history shares a set of interests with the larger scholarly community.

It is clear that much theorizing about oral history approaches a commonality with what is termed postmodernism, as briefly defined by Terry Eagleton. If we can agree that the postmodernist project is anti-essentialist, anti-totalizing, anti-reductionist, anti-naturalist, and anti-teleological,[50] then we can see the similarities.

We can also see how oral historians share with others many of the same contradictions that appear in recent work.[51] Questions of epistemology are far beyond our purview here, but we must be aware of the relativistic posture of our thinking about oral history. Perhaps the best we can do here is point to some of the complexities of the task we have set before us. To paraphrase one of Elizabeth Tonkin's most interesting points, to understand the testimony we are helping to bring into existence we must understand it as a literary mode, a narrative; to understand it as a literary mode, we must understand it as a part of the social action of the narrator; and to understand it as social action, we must understand it as history.[52]

Deeply embedded in that complexity is the contradiction between what we can know and how we know it, between history as process and history as commentary on that process. None of the works noted here would be termed "postmodernist" even though we share much with that project. Perhaps it is the nature of fieldwork, the close connectedness between interviewer and interviewee, that reins in the inherent impulse toward seeing social life as nothing but discourse. In the interview we are drawn back again and again to experience. While we watch people create their histories we see them struggle within and against codes, literary or social, just as we must do. We see the people we talk to dealing with these same contradictions between what they know and how they know it, and we realize that we are united in that struggle.

In his review of Tonkin's *Narrating Our Pasts*, Candida Smith, viewing this tension somewhat differently, tells us that the tension between the two halves of recent literary theory "sits like a time bomb, certain to force, sooner or later, a more fundamental revision of our current set of assumptions."[53] Until then, I think, we might find a less apocalyptic resolution by trying to develop a more discerning view of narrative, such as that propounded by David Carr; a view that sees the creation of narratives as inherent in the nature of experience itself, the way in which experience is lived, and the way in which experience continues to make those experiences meaningful and capable of being communicated to others.[54] Until we do so, we can only gasp in surprise as we review the efforts of oral historians to understand what we do and compare that to work of 20 years ago.[55]

Notes

1. Charles T. Morrissey, "Why Call It 'Oral History'? Searching for Early Usage of a Generic Term," *Oral History Review* (1980), pp. 20–48.

2. Morrissey, p.30.

3. Morrissey, pp. 30–31. See also Charles W. Conaway, "Lyman Copeland Draper, 'Father of American Oral History'," *Journal of Library History* (1966), pp. 234–41. Willa K. Baum, "Oral History: A Revived Tradition at the Bancroft Library," *Pacific Northwest Quarterly* 58 (1967), pp. 57–64.

4. As quoted in Peter Novick, *That Noble Dream: The 'Objectivity Question' and the American Historical Profession* (Cambridge, U.K., 1988), p.48. This discussion of the development of "scientific history" in the United States is derived from Novick's marvelous book.

5. There is an extensive bibliography on the Chicago School. See, for instance, Charles D. Kaplan, "An Exploration of the Methodological Grounds for the Study of Social Problems," *International Journal of Oral History* 3:1 (February 1982), pp. 31–51, and R. Angell, "A Critical Review of the Development of the Personal Document Method in Sociology: 1920–1940," in Louis Gottschalk et al., *The Use of Personal Documents in History, Anthropology and Sociology* (New York, 1945).

6. George P. Rawick, *From Sundown to Sunup: The Making of the Black Community* (Westport, Conn., 1972), introduction, pp. xiii–xxi. Paul D. Escot, *Slavery Remembered* (Chapel Hill, N.C., 1979).

7. Ann Banks, *First Person America* (New York, 1980), introduction, pp. 3–27. Kaplan, op. cit.

8. Louis M. Starr, "Oral History," in *Encyclopedia of Library and Information Services,* vol. 20 (1977), pp. 444–46.

9. *Oral History at Arrowhead: Proceedings of the First National Colloquium on Oral History* (Los Angeles, 1966), pp. 5–6. Brooks also noted that the Truman Library along with other oral history programs, notably Columbia, did not save tapes. This practice lasted until the 1960s. American oral history projects now, generally, save their tapes, although they still transcribe almost all of their interviews.

10. Gary Shumway, *Oral History in the United States: A Directory* (New York, 1970).

11. See for instance the various how-to manuals produced in the United States: Willa Baum, *Oral History for the Local Historical Society*, 2nd ed. rev. (Nashville, 1974), William W. Moss, *Oral History Program Manual* (New York, 1973), Cullom Davis et al. *From Tape to Type: Oral History* (Chicago, 1977).

12. Corrine L. Gilb, "Tape-Recorded Interviewing: Some Thoughts From California," *The American Archivist* 20 (October 1957), pp. 335–44.

13. See, in particular, Henry Glassie, "A Folkloristic Thought on the Promise of Oral History," *Selections from the Fifth and Sixth National Colloquia on Oral History* (New York, 1973), pp. 54–57, and in the same volume, Paul Bullock, "Oral History in the Ghetto," pp. 85–89.

14. Saul Benison, "Reflections on Oral History," *The American Archivist* 28 (January 1965), pp. 71–77. "Oral History: A Personal View," in *Modern Methods in the History of Medicine*, ed. Edwin Clarke (London, 1971), pp. 286–305. Benison was also particularly concerned that the tapes be saved since it was the tape that was the real document produced by the oral historian.

15. Robert Berendt, "History by Word of Mouth," *GW Times*, 3:4 (October–November, 1974), p. 8. Jacquelyn D. Hall, "Oral History Movement," *South Today*, vol. 4 (April 1973), pp. 1–3. Brass Workers History Project, *Brass Valley: The Story of Working People's Lives and Struggles in An American Industrial Region* (Philadelphia, 1982), pp. 275–77. For purposes of this paper I think it is necessary to draw a distinction between the terms local historians and community historians. There has always been a tradition of local history in the United States. Often those historians were intimately connected to local elites and worked on projects either approved by or glorifying those elites. In some cases, they mirrored academic historians by drawing hard-and-fast distinctions between themselves and others in the community. Community historians, on the other hand, most of them imbued with the organizing ethos of the New Left, argue that their work is an attempt to bring the people of the local community into the process of historical work, to develop within the community itself a historical ethos which, they hope, will serve as a counter to the hegemonic culture of the local elite.

16. Ronald Grele, "A Second Reading of Experience: Memoirs of the Sixties," *Radical History Review* 44 (Spring 1989), pp. 159–66.

17. Michael Frisch, "Oral History and *Hard Times*: A Review Essay," *Oral History Review* (1979), pp. 70–79. There were, of course, other manifestations of the tension, not all of them so concerned with the nature of history. The Eighth Annual Colloquium of the Oral History Association held at West Point in 1973 was marked by three days of intensive argument and sometimes accusations over the Vietnam War, and the role of military historians in building a justification for that war. The 1975 Colloquium in Asheville, North Carolina, was marked by a walkout of a sizeable portion of the attendance when the Association was addressed by former Secretary of State Dean Rusk, one of the architects of that war.

18. Ronald J. Grele, *Envelopes of Sound: Six Practitioners Discuss the Theory and Practice of Oral History* (Chicago, 1975), pp. 126–54.

19. See the review of *Envelopes of Sound* by Carl Ryant in *Oral History Review* (1986), pp. 98–100. A fuller discussion of the role of that work will be found in Virginia Yans, *Immigration Reconsidered: History, Sociology and Politics* (Oxford, 1990), introduction.

20. Paul Thompson, *The Voice of the Past: Oral History* (Oxford, 1978).

21. The most notable of these projects were The New York Chinatown History Project, The Brass Valley Workers History Project, The California Odyssey History Project, and Baltimore Voices. Other projects not NEH-funded include the Massachusetts History Workshop, The Center for Puerto Rican Studies, the Center for Southern Studies, and The Oral History of the Left. The latter is not technically a community history project.

22. In this context, the work of Carl Ryant of the University of Louisville should be noted.

23. James R. Green, "Engaging in People's History: The Massachusetts History Workshop," in *Presenting the Past: Essays on History and the Public*, ed. Susan Porter Benson, Stephen Brier, and Roy Rosenzweig (Philadelphia, 1986), pp. 339–59. See also Linda Shopes, "Oral History and Community Involvement: The Baltimore Neighborhood Heritage Project," in the same volume, pp. 249–66.

24. Since 1981 there has always been one, and often there have been two members, of the six-person Council who have their roots in either a local history project or a community history project.

25. Frank's initial article appeared in the Fall 1984 issue of the Oral History Association *Newsletter*. Frisch's letter was printed in the Spring 1985 issue, Frank's response in the summer 1985 issue.

26. Oral History Association, *Oral History: Evaluation Guidelines* (Lexington, Ky., 1988).

27. Jacquelyn Dowd Hall, James Leloudis, Robert Korstad, Mary Murphy, Lu Ann Jones, and Christopher Daly, *Like a Family: The Making of a Southern Cotton Mill World* (Chapel Hill, N.C., 1987).

28. David Thelin, "Memory and American History," *Journal of American History* 75:4, (March 1989), pp. 1118–19. John Bodnar, "Power and Memory in Oral History: Workers and Managers at Studebaker," in the same issue, pp. 1201–21.

29. See, for instance, Sherna B. Gluck, *Rosie the Riveter Revisited: Women, The War, and Social Change* (Boston, 1987); Gary Mormino and George E. Pozzetta, *The Immigrant World of Ybor City: Italians and Their Latin Neighbors in Tampa, 1885–1985* (Urbana, Ill., 1987); David Mas Masumoto, *Country Voices: The Oral History of a Japanese American Farm Family* (Del Ray, Calif., 1987). Listings of recent American publications can be found in the bibliography sections of the *Oral History Review*. A recent interesting publication seeking to analyze oral history interviews through speech communication theory is Eva M. McMahan, *Elite Oral History Discourse: A Study of Cooperation and Coherence* (Tuscaloosa, Ala., 1989).

30. The most thoroughgoing presentation of the Duke program is Alphine Jefferson, "Echoes from the South: The History and Methodology of the Duke University Oral History Program," *Oral History Review* (1984), pp. 43–62.

31. One of the most remarkable areas of growth of the oral history movement in the United Sates in the past ten years has been in the state and regional movement. There are now four major regional groups: the New England Association of Oral History, Oral History in the Mid-Atlantic Region, the Southwest Oral History Association, and the Northwest Oral History Association. In addition, there are at least 12 state organizations, several of which have more than 200 members. In total, these organizations have many more members than the national association. Most have their own programs and their own newsletters. The New England Association now publishes its own annual review.

32. For the purposes of this paper, "project" refers to local or community oral history, "programs" refers to ongoing academic or institutional oral history.

33. The various program announcements can be obtained through the office of the Executive Secretary of the Association.

34. Each of the regional oral history associations has its own history. The New England Association of Oral History became moribund for a number of years but is now being revived. The Southwest Oral History Association in the same period of time has flourished and has compiled a listing of holdings of all of its member institutions. New associations have been formed in the South and in Chicago.

35. Diane Manning, *Hill Country Teacher: Oral Histories from the One-Room School and Beyond* (Boston, 1990). Stephen Fox, *The Unknown Internment: An Oral History of the Relocation*

of *Italian-Americans During World War II* (Boston, 1990). Zorca Millich, *A Stranger's Supper: An Oral History of the Centenarian Women in Montenegro* (Boston, 1995).

36. Michael Frisch, *A Shared Authority: Essays on the Craft and Meaning of Oral History and Public History* (Albany, N.Y., 1990). Alessandro Portelli, *The Death of Luigi Trastulli and Other Stories: Form and Meaning in Oral History* (Albany, N.Y., 1991). Note the slight difference in the subtitles.

37. See Emily Stoper, *The Student Non-Violent Coordination Committee: The Growth of Radicalism in a Civil Rights Organization* (Brooklyn, N.Y., 1989). The international anthologies include the volumes in *The International Yearbook of Oral History and Life Stories* (hereafter, *Yearbook*) and one volume of *The International Annual of Oral History* (hereafter, *Annual*). The first volume of the *Yearbook* series is *Memory and Totalitarianism*, edited by Luisa Passerini. The *Annual* volume is *Subjectivity and Multiculturalism in Oral History*, edited by Ronald J. Grele (New York, 1992).

38. *A Guide to Graduate Programs in Public History*, compiled and edited by Parker Hubbard Cohen, National Council on Public History (Indianapolis, 1996).

39. These programs vary, of course. Some work closely with already existing local projects, some send students to work on projects, some mount their own projects. Contact individual programs to get a fuller description of their work.

40. Portelli, op. cit. McMahan, op. cit. Sherna Berger Gluck and Daphne Patai, eds, *Women's Words: The Feminist Practice of Oral History* (New York, 1991). Eva M. McMahan and Kim Lacy Rogers, eds., *Interactive Oral History Interviewing* (Hillsdale, N.J., 1994). Luisa Passerini, *Fascism in Popular Memory: The Cultural Experience of The Turin Working Class* (Cambridge, U.K. 1987). Frisch, op. cit. Grele, op. cit. Particular articles from journals and anthologies will be noted.

41. See for instance, chapters 2, 7, 4, 5, 13. Frisch, op. cit. Kathryn Anderson and Dana Jack, "Learning to Listen: Interview Techniques and Analysis," Gluck and Patai, op. cit., pp. 11–27. Daphne Patai, "U.S. Academics and Third World Women: Is Ethical Research Possible?," pp. 137–54, and Karen Olson and Linda Shopes, "Crossing Boundaries, Building Bridges: Doing Oral History Among Working Class Women and Men," pp. 189–204.

42. Valerie R. Yow, *Recording Oral History: A Practical Guide for Social Scientists* (Thousand Oaks, Calif., 1994).

43. Portelli, op. cit. Passerini, op. cit. Isabel Hofmyer, "Nterata/The Wire: Fences, Boundaries, Orality, Literacy," *Annual*, pp. 6991. Isabelle Bertaux-Wiame, "The Pull of Family Ties: Intergenerational Relationships and Life Paths, in *Between Generations*, vol. II, *Yearbook*, ed. Paul Thompson and Daniel Bertaux, pp. 39–50.

44. Kim Lacy Rogers, *Righteous Lives: Narratives of the New Orleans Civil Rights Struggle* (New York, 1993), and Tamara K. Hareven, "From Amoskeag to Nishijin: Reflections on Life History Interviewing in Two Cultures," *Annual*, op. cit., pp. 9–42, are two fine examples. See also Ronald Grele, "Useful Discoveries: Oral History, Public History and the Dialectics of Narrative." *The Public Historian*, 3:2 (Spring 1991), pp. 61–84.

45. This is actually a paraphrase of a paraphrase. See Jack Selzer, ed., *Understanding Scientific Prose*, "Introduction," (Madison, Wisc., 1993), p. 5. Richard Candida Smith, "Review Essay," *Oral History Review* 20:2 (Winter 1995), p. 90.

46. Portelli, op. cit. McMahan, op. cit. Grele, op. cit. Elizabeth Tonkin, *Narrating Our Pasts: The Social Construction of Oral History* (Cambridge, U.K. 1995).

47. Kristina Minister, "A Feminist Frame for the Oral History Interview," Gluck and Patai, op. cit., pp. 27–41.

48. Especially, Portelli, op cit., "Research as an Experiment in Equality," pp. 29–44. McMahan, op. cit. Tonkin, op. cit. Although a good deal of Tonkin's discussion focuses on the relations

between the fieldworker and the storyteller, her basic stance is somewhat more traditional. The term oral historian is reserved for the teller of the story; the interviewer is the "recordist." See also Ronald J. Grele, "History and the Languages of History in the Oral History Interview: Who Answers Whose Questions and Why?," McMahan and Rogers, op. cit., pp. 1–18. Gluck, op. cit. Martin B. Duberman, *Black Mountain: An Exploration in Community* (New York, 1972). Hareven, op. cit. For an interesting variation see Glen Adler, "The Politics of Research During a Liberation Struggle: Interviewing Black Workers in South Africa," *Annual*, op. cit., pp. 229–45.

49. Passerini, op. cit. Frisch, op. cit. Portelli, op. cit. *Yearbook*, 1992, op cit. Program, International Conference on Oral History, New York, 1994. Alistair Thomson, "Memory as a Battlefield: Personal and Political Investments in the National Military Past," *Oral History Review* 22:2 (Winter 1995), pp. 55–74. David P. Shuldner, *Aging Political Activists: Personal Narratives from the Old Left* (Westport, Conn., 1995). Alice M. Hoffman and Howard S. Hoffman, *Archives of Memory: A Soldier Recalls World War II* (Lexington, Ky., 1990). But not Grele, op. cit., a major weakness.

50. Terry Eagleton, "The Hippest," *London Review of Books* 18:5 (March 7, 1996), pp. 3–5.

51. Postodernism has produced an enormous literature. Five titles to start with are: Selzer, op. cit.; Peter Burke, editor, *New Perspectives on Historical Writing* (University Park, Pa., 1991); W. T. J. Mitchell, *The Politics of Interpretation* (Chicago, 1982); Greg Myers, ed., *Writing Biology: Texts in the Social Construction of Scientific Knowledge* (Madison, Wisc., 1990); and Alex Callinicos, *Against Post Modernism: A Marxist Critique* (New York, 1989). This is a very idiosyncratic listing covering my own interests in historiography. The Calincos critique is a cogent criticism from the left.

52. Tonkin, op. cit. This is my gloss on Tonkin's point. I trust it is true to the original intent.

53. Candida Smith, op. cit., p. 90.

54. David Carr, *Time, Narrative and History* (Bloomington, Ind., 1986). This very brief mention can only hint at the richness of Carr's work and its importance for the oral historian interested in narrative. It should be must reading. See also Jo Blatti, "Public History and Oral History," *Journal of American History*, vol. 77 (September 1990), pp. 615–25.

55. One concern must be voiced. Over the past ten years oral historians have produced a body of work startling in its sophistication. At the same time more and more historians are using oral history. Yet, the two do not seem to intersect. Very few books published by practicing historians show any interest in integrating oral history theory into their presentations. Recent works by Devra Weber (*Dark Sweat, White Gold: California Farm Workers, Cotton and the New Deal* [Berkeley, Calif., 1994]) and Deborah Levenson Estrada (*Trade Unionists Against Terror: Guatemala City, 1954–1985* [Chapel Hill, N.C., 1994]) do in some way reflect some of the issues we have noted here, but only mildly. For the most part historians remain remarkably sanguine about using interviews and interview materials.

PART TWO

Interpreting and Designing Oral History

4

Reliability and
Validity in Oral History
Alice Hoffman

In the second part of this book, we examine the strengths and limitations of oral history from a practical perspective: the problems of interpreting and designing oral history projects. Too often, as William Moss points out later in this part, researchers overlook the fact the all documents, written or oral, require scrutiny before use as historical sources. Many written documents upon which historians have depended for centuries—memoranda of conversations, dictated letters—are generated from oral sources, a fact which makes the debate over the "worth" of oral sources more complex.

Our first essay, by labor historian Alice Hoffman, introduces a theme of later selections: reliability and validity in oral history interviewing. While Barbara Tuchman and William Cutler criticize oral history procedures in the articles which follow, Hoffman provides a framework to understand their critiques. She defines "reliability" and "validity" and suggests that the oral historian should base interviews on a thorough analysis of available historical sources. Where inconsistencies emerge between the printed and the recollected records, the interviewer should have the living sources attempt to resolve these contradictions.

Alice Hoffman, was a Professor of Labor Studies at Pennsylvania State University, and directed the oral history program there. She retired from Bryn Mawr College. She has coordinated projects with a number of labor unions, including the United Steelworkers, Graphic Arts International, the Philadelphia Federation of Teachers, and the national AFL-CIO. Her publications include "Oral History in the United States" (1971) and "Using Oral History in the Classroom" (1982).

"Reliability and Validity in Oral History" by Alice Hoffman first appeared in *Today's Speech* 22 (Winter 1974), pp. 23–27, and is reprinted by permission of the author and *Communication Quarterly*.

*O*ral history may be defined as a process of collecting, usually by means of a tape-recorded interview, reminiscences, accounts, and interpretations of events from the recent past which are of historical significance. Critics of the process have usually focused on the fallibility of human memory and questioned both the reliability and the validity of data collected in this manner.

In order to deal with this problem, it will be necessary to describe in more detail the methods used by most practitioners of the art of "oral history." Allan Nevins is usually credited with having started oral history when he established the Oral Research Office at Columbia University in 1948. The Columbia project began to conduct tape-recorded interviews with men and women who had made significant contributions in various fields and who had been in a position to observe developments in them. A tape-recorded interview was conducted, transcribed, checked for accuracy by the interviewer and his respondent, indexed, and deposited for use by researchers in the oral history collection at Columbia University, subject, however, to whatever temporary restrictions the respondent might wish to impose. By 1967 there was enough interest in this method of preserving the past that an association of oral historians was formed. From the inception of the organization, the historians in the group have been somewhat surprised to find their ranks swelled by people from a variety of academic disciplines: medical doctors, anthropologists, sociologists, psychologists, librarians, archivists, educators, physicists, ethnographers, etc.

One of the most interesting forms of oral history projects which finds representation in the Association is the variety of medical projects. These came about when doctors recognized that the most significant developments in the history of medicine have occurred within the memory of individuals still alive today. While the scientific methodology was adequately spelled out, there was a lack of information about the specific details of how the specialties were developed, the great hospitals created, and the new techniques introduced into the practice of medicine. Therefore, a number of the specialties are conducting tape-recorded interviews with the pioneers in these fields; some of these interviews have been videotaped.

Another type of project which we have represented in the Association is what might be called "Famous People and Their Friends and Associates." There is, for example, a most significant project centered on the life and activities of General George C. Marshall. Since Franklin Roosevelt, each president, as he left office, has set up a library for the preservation and deposit of the materials associated with his presidency; and each of these libraries, beginning with the Truman Library, has an oral history office.

Then there are a large number of projects which deal with regional and cultural history. The project at the University of California in Berkeley is called the

Regional Oral History Project and is devoted to collecting and preserving information on a wide variety of topics from forestry to the development of the wine industry in California with all their attendant social, political, and economic ramifications. In this connection, a number of state archives have initiated governmental and social oral histories related to the development of their state.

Ethnic history finds significant representation in the Oral History Association, and there are oral history projects on the history of the Jewish people in the United States, and the history of various Indian tribes; and one very important recent development is a number of projects focused on black history. The development of oral history projects in these areas leads to one general observation about all of them. That is, oral history projects tend to come about where significant developments occur and where there is a paucity of archival or written records about them; black history serves as a case in point. We have been developing in the United States a new sense of racial pride among blacks, and they are desperate to recover their own past; but there is very little information. Black archives are largely nonexistent so that the only means of getting at the past is to interview people who were slaves or who were the children of slaves; with few exceptions, the only means of finding out what it was like to move into the northern ghettos in the twenties is to interview these people.

Finally, oral history offices are involved in organizational history. Organizations of a wide diversity, ranging from International Business Machines to the United Steelworkers of America, have become involved in oral history as a means to recovering and preserving their origins and development. One potential advantage of the organizational history approach—and one not to be dismissed as mundane inasmuch as it may involve the very survival of an oral history project—is that an organization or institution is often willing to provide funding for such a series of interviews. . . .

One of the persistent challenges presented by scholars to oral history regards the *reliability* and the *validity* of the interviews. In this connection reliability can be defined as the consistency with which an individual will tell the same story about the same events on a number of different occasions. Validity refers to the degree of conformity between the reports of the event and the event itself as recorded by other primary resource material such as documents, photographs, diaries, and letters. Now, while it is conceivable that an oral report might be a true description of an event, its validity cannot really be tested unless it can be measured against some body of evidence. Without such evidence, an isolated description of an event becomes a bit of esoterica whose worth cannot be properly evaluated.

When viewed in this fashion, an oral history informant is reliable if his or her reports of a given event are consistent with each other. For example, in 1966 the Pennsylvania State University Oral History Project conducted an interview with an employee of the Carnegie-Illinois Steel Company. An employers' organization had attempted to recruit him to provide undercover information on the union activities of his fellow employees. In the interview he described the means used to recruit him and the methods by which he was paid for his services. In 1935 Robert R. Brooks conducted research on the early organization of trade unions in the steel industry and published in his book, *As Steel Goes*,[1] an anonymous interview with the same individual. Both the published account in Brook's study and the transcribed interview done 30 years later read almost word for word the same.[2] Thus we are assured of the interview's reliability. Its validity, however, must be measured against other testimony and documents; for example, the accounts of industrial espionage uncovered by the LaFollette Senate Committee to investigate the Violation of Civil Liberties[3] and the accounts of other respondents in the Penn State Oral History Project. When compared with these accounts, this particular interview also appears to be essentially valid, but there are discrepancies between his testimony and the preponderance of other available sources. An informant can therefore be reliable (the same story emerges each time it is called for), but the story may or may not be a valid representation of the original events as judged by comparison with other sources. If, however, an informant is unreliable, the validity of the reports must be suspected. In short, in historical assessment, as in the area of psychological assessment, a data-gathering instrument can be valid only to the extent that it is also reliable.

David Musto at the Fourth National Colloquium of the Oral History Association presented a summary of research findings on the reliability over time of the information which parents gave with respect to the medical and training histories of their children. There was a common thread running through these studies: although many facets of the reports were found to be quite reliable, especially the "hard data" (for example, reports of the baby's birth weight), certain aspects of the reports, such as those dealing with the parents' attitudes and emotions, were less reliable.[4]

Moreover, in one study cited, a test of the validity of these oral reports was also made. At New York University there is a large and long-term study of child rearing, so that it is possible to compare parents' reports with clinical records over time. Again certain factual information was quite accurate; but where there was distortion, it tended to be in the direction of recommendations by child care experts.[5]

This tendency toward conformity with acceptable norms is probably characteristic of all human reports, and it both requires and receives special attention by the practitioners of oral history. When David Musto presented his data at the Fourth National Colloquium, the first question he was asked was as follows:

QUESTION: I would like to ask if, in any of these studies, the interviewee was faced with the apparent inconsistency in the record.

MUSTO: To my knowledge this was not done.[6]

Unlike the interviews which Musto reported where parents were not confronted with the inconsistencies in their reports, a well-trained oral historian will invariably familiarize himself with the available records on the matter under discussion and will raise the issue when inconsistencies arise. This practice was described by one of the Colloquium participants:

QUESTION: My experience indicates that, if you confront a person with a contradiction or inconsistency, he very often is able to resolve it. It will turn out that it had to do with a change over time in the understanding of the definition of a word, or it has to do with the context in which one event took place as opposed to another event. I think that in setting up an oral interview one of the basic motivations for agreeing to do this with you is to set the record straight. If you have a letter or a document which indicates that he was very angry at someone and he's now saying that he really thought he was a very nice fellow, if you challenge him or present him with these inconsistencies, he will often be very glad to have the opportunity to show you how his thinking changed. And that's very important material to record. If you have convinced him of your basic sensitivity and willingness to cooperate with him in the whole business of setting the record straight, I don't think he will be put off by making challenges to him.[7]

This, of course, reflects the difference in purpose of the studies Musto cites and the work of an oral historian. Those studies sought to assess the limits of reliability in the clinical reports made by parents uncontaminated by the corrections which would be induced if parents were faced with their inconsistencies. An oral historian, on the other hand, seeks a valid representation and hence uses the interview to enhance the opportunity to obtain a valid report.

It is unlikely, however, that in any given interview the oral historian will be entirely successful in this venture. Recognizing this, many oral historians assert that they are not historians at all but rather oral archivists and that the oral record is what the philosophers call a "memory claim"; that is, it is one person's claim as to what happened and, as such, is simply another primary resource to be stored by archivists along with the more traditional items in the archives to be evaluated and compared with documents, letters, etc., by future historians to assess its significance.

In this sense the oral record has certain advantages over the written document. One advantage is that there can be no doubt as to its authorship. In government circles in Washington it is standard operating procedure that an important letter may be the work of many individuals except the one who signs it. In that connection the journal *Science* recently [1973] reported that the letter written by Franklin Roosevelt suggesting the creation of the National Science

Foundation was not actually authored by Roosevelt but by two young Washington lawyers: Oscar Ruebhausen and Oscar S. Cox.[8]

Another advantage of the oral interview is that it is not a written document and often contains the freshness and candor which is more typical of direct conversation.

Its most important advantage in my view, however, is that it makes possible the preservation of the life experience of persons who do not have the literary talent or leisure to write their memoirs. In this way it facilitates a new kind of history—a history not of the captains, kings, and presidents but of farmers, workers, immigrants, and the like. Interviews with people who have been foot soldiers in various important movements of social change but have heretofore been unrecorded may now be preserved and hence their impact assessed. In that connection, it has been interesting to observe the frequency with which we have collected evidence that many policies developed by the United Steelworkers of America have been the result of the experience, knowledge, and suggestion of a much lower level of leadership than is commonly reported in historical studies of the Union or in contemporary journalistic accounts.

In sum, then, one might say that oral history is simply one among several primary resources. It is no worse than written documents. Archives are replete with self-serving documents, with edited and doctored diaries and memoranda written "for the record." In fact, when undertaken in the most professional way, oral histories may be superior to many written records in that there is always a knowledgeable interviewer present actively seeking to promote the best record obtainable. Norman Hoyle in an article on oral history has defined the interview as "a kind of social transaction in which each party has a direct, though perhaps indeterminate, effect upon the other. The whole array of stimuli emitted by the interviewer—his age, his appearance, his manner of speech, his actions, his preparations, his credentials—will determine how he is perceived by the person being interviewed. And the way he is perceived will in certain measure determine the content, style, and quality of the response he elicits."[9] While the presence of the trained interviewer provides certain advantages, it also obviously colors the results in somewhat unpredictable ways. In this connection oral historians stand to benefit greatly from contact with professionals in the area of speech communication. Our colleagues in this area understand the parameters of the kind of communication represented by an oral interview, and they could provide insights which would greatly enhance the reliability and validity of oral histories.

Notes

1. Robert R. Brooks, *As Steel Goes . . . Unionism in a Basic Industry* (New Haven: Yale University Press, 1940), p. 9.

2. John Mullen, oral interview conducted by Alice M. Hoffman, February 1966, PSUUSWA Archives, pp. 8–10.

3. U.S. Senate, Committee on Education and Labor, *Violations of Free Speech and Rights of Labor, Hearings,* 75th Cong., lst sess., pt. 14 (Washington, D.C.: U.S. Government Printing Office, 1937).

4. David F. Musto and Saul Benison, "Studies on the Accuracy of Oral Interviews," in Gould P. Colman, ed., *The Fourth National Colloquium on Oral History* (Warrenton, Va.: Oral History Association, 1970), pp. 167–72.

5. Fourth National Colloquium, p. 173.

6. *Fourth National Colloquium,* p. 176.

7. Fourth National Colloquium, p. 180.

8. "Historical Footnote," *Science* 182 (October 12, 1973), p. 116.

9. Quoted in James E. Sargent, "Oral History, Franklin D. Roosevelt, and the New Deal," *Oral History Review* 1 (1973), p. 93.

5

Distinguishing the
Significant from
the Insignificant

Barbara Tuchman

A major problem in using oral sources for history is the public misconception that recording reminiscences is the same as sifting and melding them into a work of history. The late Barbara Tuchman, Pulitzer Prize–winning historical writer, underlines the point by sharply criticizing those who collect oral data indiscriminately, thus confusing history gathering with history making.

Tuchman writes as a historian who conducts interviews for her own research; whereas many oral historians collect information not for their own work, but for future scholars working after the narrator is gone. For this reason, the archival oral historian must cast a broader net than the thesis-minded historian.

The author fears that tape recording will mean "a downgrading both of source material and what is made from it" and considers that in early oral history work, thanks to the apparent ease of tape recording, "a few veins of gold and a vast mass of trash are being preserved." On the other hand, Tuchman acknowledges that some of her best sources have been "verbal interviews" conducted by historians. Thus she validates the field while at the same time criticizing it for a lack of selectivity and self-discipline. Ultimately, she makes the same point that William Moss and Gary Okihiro do in later selections: oral history must be based firmly on research.

Barbara Tuchman was one of the most vivid and successful writers of history in the United States. Educated at Radcliffe College, she has achieved prominence through

"Distinguishing the Significant from the Insignificant" by Barbara Tuchman appeared in *Radcliffe Quarterly* 56 (October 1972), pp. 9–10. © 1972 by Barbara W. Tuchman. Reprinted with the permission of the author and *Radcliffe Quarterly*.

a series of historically astute, popularly written books, including The Guns of August *(1962),* Stilwell and the American Experience in China *(1971); both received the Pulitzer Prize. A collection of her essays on the craft of history is* Practicing History *(New York: Alfred Knopf, 1981).*

*H*ow does research in contemporary history differ from research into past history? My own opinion is, that apart from the obvious physical difference of interviewing live people instead of reading their published memoirs or unpublished papers, the difference in *research* is not very great. The real difference is in the stance and the intent of the historian. Where does he stand in relation to the events? Is he writing from inside or out, as participant or as observer? Is his intent basically apologia, or an attempt to collect the whole story and stand back from it so that he can see it in the round? The answer determines the research, or rather what is done with it, for what finally counts is not the research *per se* but what you do with it after you've got it.

I am not concerned here with diaries and memoirs which are the *stuff of* history, that is, primary source material, but with the *ex post facto* account, that is, the work of the conscious historian. As told by a participant, these accounts belong in a great tradition from Flavius Josephus to the Earl of Clarendon to Winston Churchill, but they are all apologia; some more, some less but all special pleading, as history by a participant is bound to be. Research in such cases, especially if the author played a central role in the events, is usually designed to fit a desired result as for example in the account of 1914 by General Joffre, or the latest entry in the field of contemporary history by the Texas historian Mr. Lyndon Johnson, two works, incidentally, that closely resemble each other. Both are based on the work of teams of researchers and both come up with an equally fanciful result: a never-never hero, idealized beyond recognition.

The participant's advantage in research is his special access to sources. The normal historian, of course, does not have the whole staff of the General Staff or a federally subsidized 12-story library at his personal disposal, which is perhaps just as well—Thucydides, too, like the rest of us, did his own work. I have had no experience in the research of special advantage, that is, the insider's research, because I have never written as a participant—except perhaps once, as an emotional participant, so to speak. My first book *Bible and Sword,* which, to give you an idea of the subject, was subtitled, *Britain and Palestine from the Bronze Age to Balfour,* came to an end at 1918. Since it was written after the achievement of statehood by Israel in 1948, the publisher was insistent on an epilogue bringing it up to date. I spent six months on research in the period of the Mandate, the

White Papers, Ernest Bevin, and the barring of the refugees and all that, but when I came to write it, the result was a disaster. Even I could see that. I was too angry to write history, so I tore it up, and the book came out without an epilogue. Since then, whenever someone, about once a year, proposes that I must write the history of modern Israel or the Six-Day War, I am not tempted because I know that an emotional participant is no historian.

I have never come nearer to contemporary history than a perspective of 25 years. The book on Stilwell concerned events of my own time and research involving people still alive, but except for the technique of interviewing, I did not find the problems of research very different for this book than for the others. The memories of the living, one soon discovers, are no more reliable or free of wishful recollection and the adjustments of hindsight than the memoirs of the dead.

The chief difficulty in contemporary history is over-documentation or what has been called, less charitably, the multiplication of rubbish. Ever since the advent of mechanical means of duplication there has been an explosion of material that cannot be dealt with by less than teams of researchers. The twentieth century is likely to be the doom of the individual historian. (Actually I do not really believe that. Though the doom seems logical, I believe somehow the historian will illogically survive.)

With the appearance of the tape recorder, a monster with the appetite of a tapeworm, we now have, through its creature oral history, an artificial survival of trivia of appalling proportions. To sit down and write a book, even of memoirs, requires at least *some* effort, discipline, and perseverance which until now imposed a certain natural selection on what survived in print. But with all sorts of people being invited merely to open their mouths, and ramble effortlessly and endlessly into a tape recorder, prodded daily by an acolyte of oral history, a few veins of gold and a vast mass of trash are being preserved which would otherwise have gone to dust. We are drowning ourselves in unneeded information. I should hastily add here that among the most useful and scintillating sources I found were two verbal interviews with General Marshall tape recorded by Army historians in 1949. Marshall, however, was a summit figure worth recording, which is more than can be said for all those shelves and stacks of oral transcripts piling up in recent years.

In my interviews I failed to take advantage of technology and did not use a tape recorder, chiefly, I suppose, because a machine makes me quail. This may have something to do with being female. A woman is accustomed to entering upon a conversation as a personal thing, even with a stranger—perhaps more so with a stranger—and I can't imagine myself plunking a machine down in front of someone and saying, "Now, talk." Besides I am quite certain I would not know how to make it work. So I took along a notebook instead, one that fitted into my purse and so was always handy for planned or unplanned need. The loose-leaf pages, being the same size as my index cards, could be filed conveniently along with the other research material.

Taking notes of an interview, like taking notes on reading, is a crystallizing process which is part of the writer's business. You are practicing the essential function of the historian—distinguishing the significant from the insignificant—as you go along. It is true you miss a lot by not having the taped transcript. In skilled hands and in needful circumstance, the tape recorder is unquestionably useful, but its effect in the long run, as it proliferates, will I think be a downgrading both of source material and what is made from it.

Technology has made two additions to historical method: oral history via the tape recorder and quantitative history via the computer. Quantification in history is the business of feeding vast multiples of data into a computer which sorts it, packages it, and returns it gift-wrapped, as it were, in a suitable historical generalization, usually one that the unassisted human would have no difficulty in arriving at by ordinary deduction or intuition. An interesting moment in my career was a visit some years ago by two quantitative historians from California and, I think, Wisconsin who had been working for several years in a group spread over two universities on a project dealing with the origins of World War I. They had collected all—and I mean all—the diplomatic messages of the crisis period of June–July 1914 between sovereigns, ambassadors, foreign offices, etc.; had classified them according to various decimal-point degrees of friendship, suspicion, concealed or overt antagonism; and had fed these into the computer, and tabulated the result in three or four mimeographed bound volumes. The conclusion reached by the study was this: that the likelihood of war increases in direct proportion to the increase in expressed hostility.

Actually I do not wish to discount the contributions that may be made by the quantitative method in some more useful study than the 1914 endeavor. In a field susceptible of quantification—wage and price levels, migrations, demography, anything that can be counted—they may discover principles not known before or cause a revision of accepted theories—like the professor at a recent conference I attended who, by quantitatively comparing the price movement of cotton and of slaves, discovered something very significant about the cause of the Civil War, though I forget what.

An incomparable and, I think, indispensable source for contemporary historians is film, both for the physical realities of places and people that one cannot get any other way, and for flashes of insight and understanding through visual means. I think I learned more about Chinese propaganda from a film of the military parade staged for Wendell Willkie in Chungking, and more about Stilwell from a film showing him lying in the dust next to a Chinese soldier at the Ramgarh training ground and demonstrating how to handle a rifle, than I could have in any other way.

In the research for the Stilwell book, among the most valuable insights I gained were one from a verbal interview, one from unpublished letters, and one from published but obscure material found almost by accident.

Of course the most vivid and difficult to deal with were the diaries—difficult because they bring events down to too small a scale. It was as if I had been a cartographer trying to draw a map on a scale 100 miles to the inch and working from surveys detailed down to one mile to the inch. I might almost advise a putative biographer to find a subject who did *not* keep a diary.

6

Accuracy in Oral
History Interviewing

William Cutler III

*Critiques of oral documentation come both from writers, such as Tuchman, and profes-
sional academic historians, such as the author of this next essay, William Cutler. This
article, published in 1970, was one of the earliest critiques of oral history interviewing.
Cutler suggests that factors inherent in the interview process—forgetfulness, self-
delusion, and reticence of narrators; the biases of interviewers; the inaccuracy of
human memory—all make the creation of history from oral sources a questionable
proposition.*

*In later selections, professional oral historians answer Cutler's arguments through a
self-evaluation of the oral interviewing process. Yet Cutler's critique raises questions
worthy of consideration; many individuals in the historical profession publicly (or privately) profess a suspicion of oral sources and share Cutler's reservations.*

*While some practitioners felt Cutler's article depended on marginally
relevant studies, others found his arguments provocative. This essay inspired a healthy
debate about the importance of historical standards (and better public relations) within
the oral history profession.*

*William Cutler III is Professor of History and Education at Temple University. His
writings include* The Divided Metropolis: Social and Spatial Dimensions of Philadelphia: 1800–1975 *(1980) and "Oral History in the Study of Education in the
1980s," in* Historical Inquiry in Education: A Research Agenda, *ed.*

"Accuracy in Oral History Interviewing" by William Cutler III, from *Historical Methods
Newsletter* 3 (June 1970), pp 1–7, is reprinted by permission of the author.

*S*ince 1948, when the technique of oral history originated at Columbia through the work of Allan Nevins, its practitioners have searched for ways to make the memoirs which they produce as accurate as possible. The chief obstacles, of course, have been the human failings of the people interviewed. Forgetfulness, dishonesty, or reticence have frequently introduced errors of fact or emphasis into oral history tapes.[1] Interviewers, too, have not been faultless, and misunderstandings have undoubtedly resulted in many distortions by confused respondents. But unlike those librarians and scholars who collect and use documents from the past with no guarantee of their accuracy, the oral historian can exert at least some control over his primary resource, the respondent, and strive to minimize the number of errors in the memoir which is produced.

Recent work in such fields as medicine, psychology, and sociology suggests that accuracy in interviewing is not easy to achieve. In one disquieting study of conservationists done a decade ago, researchers interested in the reliability of the human memory found that when asked the same seven questions one year apart, fifty-nine respondents showed an overall consistency in their responses of only 63.6 percent. Three of the questions were factual, and logically enough, they were answered more consistently than the other four, which tested attitudes.[2]

Likewise, other investigators at New York University and the University of Pennsylvania discovered that after several years parents recalled the facts concerning their children's infancies more reliably than their own attitudes as new parents.[3] But the evidence is not conclusive that attitudes are remembered better than facts; nor were Wenar and Coulter at Pennsylvania convinced by their data that time always dulls the memory. Because most of the mothers they questioned knew the details of their children's illnesses but had forgotten the facts of their own health during pregnancy, it was hypothesized that, regardless of its affective content, a brief and completed activity, like a child's one-time bout with the mumps or measles, might be "more reliably recalled than one which is continuously present over long periods of time."[4]

That time is not the oral historian's only enemy is further borne out by psychological findings of an important connection between the culture and values of an era and human perception and memory. In the study done at NYU by Lillian C. Robbins, mothers tended to remember having practiced demand feeding as advocated by Dr. Spock when, in fact, many had not fed on demand, for scheduled feeding was still in vogue at the time of their children's infancies.[5] Researchers interested in the past might still conclude from this study that respondents ought to be interviewed as soon as possible after an event in question, but even that view must be qualified by some findings reported in 1961 on the powerful and enduring cultural stereotype of the ideal American family. Among a matching group of parents, half the couples and their children were observed for nearly six years, while half were merely questioned once about the chief characteristics of their family life. While their observations told them otherwise, the researchers, Joan and William McCord, learned from those they asked that in their family everyone loved each other, and father was a "decent" man who provided faithful leadership.[6] Similarly, other psychologists have found a close relationship between the social desirability of a given trait as seen by a group of respondents and the probability of its later being highly rated by them as one of their own characteristics.[7]

The cultural milieu is not the only bad influence on the accuracy of perception and recall. The spurious features of a research situation can damage the validity of any study, as Roethlisberger and Dickson demonstrated in analyzing the now famous Hawthorne experiments. Published in 1939, their book, *Management and the Worker*, stressed the importance of social relations to worker performance and hypothesized that the synthetic nature of the experimental work group was primarily responsible for the increases in output of the laborers studied.[8] Because the interviewing milieu is fundamentally unnatural, comparable distortions are entirely possible in oral history, resulting in unintentional exaggerations or timidity. The potential for such errors in oral history can hardly be eliminated, since interviewers and respondents must interact at least somewhat, but measures can be taken to neutralize or diminish their effect. Interviewers can diversify their inquiries into a given subject to expose unconscious distortions or ask indirect questions to bypass sources of accidental error. Knowing the difficulties of extensive self-awareness, the oral historian might, for example, inquire about a person's feelings on an issue and hope to infer his beliefs from these. And yet making the interviewing situation as natural as possible may be the simplest and surest way of suppressing this elusive kind of error. Oral historians are great believers in personal rapport with respondents and often try to interview them in their homes or offices where the setting is familiar and the tape recorder may be less menacing. But caution is advised, for too much good fellowship can distract attention from the serious work at hand and even encourage respondents, who might otherwise be honest, to disrespect the occasion and twist their answers deliberately in their own favor. Enough will try this anyway when interviewed for posterity, and the oral historian must be watchful and prepared to minimize it.[9]

The research milieu can also cause intentional distortions in the opposite direction. A respondent may deflate his role in an event or even refuse to discuss it to avoid embarrassment should his recollections ever become known to friends or associates. The same man might also bend the truth in an interview for fear of reprisal, as industrial sociologists have learned from questioning workers who will not always be honest or complete without assurances of privacy from management.[10] The best defense against all dishonesty by respondents is the well-informed interviewer. Poll takers know the value of removing threatening questions or surroundings, while balanced questions which allow respondents to praise as well as criticize can sometimes loosen fearful tongues.[11] In oral history interviewing legal options guaranteeing confidentiality have often persuaded the apprehensive. To be able to restrict the use of a memoir for a stated number of years is to be able to discuss openly and truthfully what otherwise might be too controversial or revealing at the time of recording. In 1968 approximately 20 percent of Columbia's oral history transcripts were partially or totally closed; and while most of these probably contained little or nothing earthshaking, such limitations undoubtedly have saved much important information for the historian.[12]

Because it is commonly assumed that a warm and friendly atmosphere is conducive to frank conversation, rapport is often cited as another key to accuracy in touchy interviewing. By increasing a respondent's confidence, it can discourage dishonesty or reticence, even when an interviewer must eventually ask a threatening question. Public opinion takers believe that good rapport can also neutralize the biasing effects of wide social distance between the participants in an interview. However, if the social distance is too great, an interviewer is hard-pressed to hide obvious distinctions and to prevent distortion. Oral historians do not normally face this problem since they and their respondents are usually well-educated, but they ought to know about it and remember as well that too much rapport can easily become interviewer bias and have damaging effects, especially where social distance is a factor.[13]

Interviewers should always try to know their biases and conceal them as far as possible. Prejudiced remarks, emphatic intonations, or even a simple affirmation, if consistently applied, can distort a respondent's account of the past. Interviewers themselves are vulnerable to error because of their own biases since a strong point of view, if unrecognized, can induce a narrow plan of questioning accidentally tailored to suit private principles and assumptions.[14] Those same prejudices can also cause an interviewer to make hasty judgments about respondents, branding them with a stereotype which can then wrongly guide the rest of an interview. Poll takers know that canvassers sometimes mark their ballots on the basis of what a respondent is supposed to say and not in accord with what is actually said. In oral history the use of tape recorders eliminates this kind of clerical error, but interviewer expectations can still mean overlooked opportunities and an incomplete, invalid memoir. When social or ideological differences are readily apparent, it is all too easy to neglect to probe unusual responses or fail to ask questions for which the stereotype provides an answer. Such expectations may even rub off on respondents and influence them to falsely match the interviewer's stereotype.[15]

There are then many internal sources of error in oral history interviewing, but ultimately accuracy begins before the tape recorder is turned on, with foresight in the selection of topics and respondents. Ideally, a project should be pursued only when there are knowledgeable people to interview as well as existing manuscripts or corroborating witnesses to provide checks on what respondents say. Nor should hearings be sought with those whose obvious biases would surely overpower their ability to "tell it like it was." But ideal conditions seldom prevail, and the oral historian should be capable of hard work and ingenuity. Before an interview he ought to have a clear idea of his purposes and learn as much as he can about his prospective respondent. If there is to be a run of interviews with the same person, he should first discuss them with the respondent, without a tape recorder. Respondents should be encouraged to use their files to refresh their memories, although such conscious preparation can tempt dishonesty. Therefore, in extended projects it is important to include further research and reevaluation between taping sessions.[16]

With such groundwork the oral historian can more effectively bring out the fullest amount of accurate recall and reporting. In actual interviewing, broad-based questions are initially preferable to ensure a common understanding of fundamental concepts and prevent the bypassing of unanticipated essentials. But later on the well-prepared interviewer is better able to avoid enticing his respondent with questions which he cannot answer. He has the background to probe sensitive areas with precision and knows which questions to repeat for the amplification or verification of previous responses. If done with tact or a reasoned explanation of its importance, such repetition can catch and clarify deliberate errors or accidental inconsistencies and even rescue information first given off the record. It can connect related topics, separately discussed, and above all promote greater respondent enthusiasm and participation by attesting to the interviewer's interest and involvement.[17]

If backed by research and reevaluation, the leading question is yet another technique to improve the accuracy of any interview, including those done by oral historians. Traditionally interviewers have shied away from such questions for fear of prejudicing responses. But in a recent study by three public opinion experts, the same people in a test group gave a comparably small number of distorted answers to both leading and straightforward inquiries. Furthermore, correct premises or assumptions in questions can increase honesty and candor by convincing respondents that only a frank answer will satisfy the interviewer.[18] The particular reluctance of the aged to discuss matters of peripheral importance to their lives can be overcome by insightful leading questions, but should they miss their mark, the reverse can occur, especially if the respondent is old, impatient, or too eager to please. Oral historians, who often interview the aged, must be conscientious and bear the burden to be well-informed.[19] What other qualifications good interviewers share are moot among the experts, who seem able to agree only on the value of some experience. People from a variety of backgrounds have produced good results as oral history interviewers, and this without the

benefit of standardized interviewing techniques. The resulting problems of comparison of oral history interviews have not troubled most oral historians, perhaps
because historians as a group have let the special nature of their evidence preclude concern for the statistical accuracy of their generalizations. Recently,
though, some oral historians have become concerned with their inability to compare responses in different interviews. To overcome this difficulty, one Cornell
oral history project is subjecting the same respondents to both open-ended interviews for depth and penetration and standardized questionnaire-type interviews
for comparability.[20] But there is room for much improvement. Oral historians
must become more familiar with proper sampling techniques to ensure that in
any project dealing with broad ranges of opinion the respondents selected represent the population under study as closely as possible.

With so many special ways for oral historians to increase accuracy, it seems a
shame that both careless typing and overzealous editing can diminish the credibility of oral history manuscripts. Most oral history programs in the United States
today transcribe their interviews to ease the process of editing by respondents
and handling by scholars. The average typist needs careful supervision, and editing should be minimal and done in ink on the original transcript to show
researchers what was said on the tape and what was not. Elaborate or concealed revisions give a distorted picture of an interview and may even lead the
researcher to unwarranted conclusions.[21]

Despite the merit of these criteria, few oral historians ever meet them all, and
probably many often meet very few, indeed. Inaccuracies are common in oral history interviews, but if the researcher can identify them, especially those resulting
from dishonesty or reticence, he can profit handsomely, for sometimes they provide an important avenue of insight into a respondent's state of mind. In fact,
some claim that oral history is valuable chiefly because of the light it can shed on
a respondent's past state of mind and thereby on the milieu of an era in history,
and not because of any facts which might be derived.[22] But as has been noted,
recent work in sociology and psychology suggests that attitudes may be forgotten
even faster than facts, and thus the researcher must constantly beware. He must
always remember that oral history transcripts are raw material to be treated with
the same care as any other primary source. Extra wariness may even be in order
because of the potentially biasing effects of the research situation. Yet oral historians will not cease to refine their craft, and meanwhile, despite its imperfections,
oral history must continue to be done if our increasingly electronic society is to
supply the future with both a full and human account of itself.

Notes

1. See, for example, Francis W. Schruben, "An Even Stranger Death of President Harding," *Southern California Quarterly* 48 (March 1966), pp. 57–84; "Is Oral History Really Worthwhile?" *Ideas in Conflict: A Colloquium on Certain Problems in Historical Society Work in the United States and Canada,* ed.; Clifford L. Lord (Harrisburg, Pa.: American Association for State and Local History, 1958), pp. 17–57; R. G. Hewlett, "A Pilot Study in Contemporary Scientific History," *Isis* 53 (March 1962), pp. 35–36.

2. In this study the authors defined "consistency" as "an identical response to identically or highly similarly worded questions asking for the same information, of the same respondent, on different occasions" (Ralph Dakin and Donald Tennant, "Consistency of Response by Event-Recall Intervals and Characteristics of Respondents," *Sociological Quarterly* 9 [Winter 1968], pp. 73–84). See also R. J. Van Zooneveld, "An Orientation Study of the Memory of Old People," *Geriatrics* 13 (1958), pp. 532–34; Gladys Palmer, "Factors in the Variability of Response in Enumeration Studies," *Journal of the American Statistical Association* 38 (June 1943), pp. 143–52.

3. In the study done at NYU the time elapsed was three years, while at the University of Pennsylvania the differential was three to six years (Lillian C. Robbins, "The Accuracy of Parental Recall of Aspects of Child Development and of Child Rearing Practices," *Journal of Abnormal and Social Psychology* 66 [March 1963], pp. 261, 264–67; Charles Wenar and Jane B. Coulter, "A Reliability Study of Developmental Histories," *Child Development* 33 [1962], pp. 453–62). See also Ernest Haggard, Arne Brekstad, and A. G. Skard, "On the Reliability of the Anamnestic Interview," *Journal of Abnormal and Social Psychology* 61 (November 1960), pp. 311–18.

4. Wenar and Coulter, "A Reliability Study of Developmental Histories," *Child Development,* pp. 460–61.

5. Robbins, "The Accuracy of Parental Recall," *Journal of Abnormal and Social Psychology,* p. 261.

6. Joan McCord and William McCord, "Cultural Stereotypes and the Validity of Interviews for Research in Child Development," *Child Development* 32 (1961), pp. 171–86.

7. See, for example, Allen L. Edwards, "The Relationship Between the Judged Desirability of a Trait and the Probability That the Trait Will Be Endorsed," *Journal of Applied Psychology* 37 (1953), pp. 90–93. See also Bernard S. Phillips, *Social Research: Strategy and Tactics* (New York, 1966), pp. 108, 112; Stephen A. Richardson, Barbara S. Dohrenwend, and David Klein, *Interviewing: Its Forms and Functions* (New York, 1965), p. 132.

8. Marie Jahoda, Morton Deutsch, and Stuart W. Cook, *Research Methods in Social Relations* (New York, 1958), p. 60; Fritz J. Roethlisberger and William J. Dickson, *Management and the Worker* (Cambridge, Mass., 1939), pp. 183–84, 575. Recently, critics have argued with the conclusions of Roethlisberger and Dickson, one claiming that economic factors and not the dynamics of the social situation caused the changes in production discovered in the Hawthorne experiments. See Alex Carey, "The Hawthorne Studies: A Radical Criticism," *American Sociological Review* 32 (June 1967), pp. 403–16. Whether Carey is right or not, however, oral historians would be unwise to ignore the artificialities of the research milieu and their possible effects on accuracy in interviewing.

9. Jahoda, Deutsch, and Cook, *Research Methods,* pp. 154–55, 160–64.

10. *The Third International Colloquium on Oral History* (New York, 1969), pp. 25–26. See also Herbert H. Hyman, *Interviewing in Social Research* (Chicago, 1954), pp. 311–13.

11. Phillips, *Social Research,* p. 119.

12. Oral History Research Office: Columbia University, *The Oral History Collection* (New York, 1964); OHRO: Columbia University, *The Oral History Collection: Recent Acquisitions and a Report for 1966* (New York, 1966); OHRO: Columbia University, *Oral History: The First Twenty Years* (New York, 1968); Louis M. Starr "History Warm," *Columbia University Forum* 5 (Fall 1962), pp. 27–30.

13. Hyman, *Interviewing in Social Research,* pp. 22, 258, 308–10; J. Allen Williams, Jr., "Interviewer Role Performance: A Further Note on Bias in the Information Interview," *Public Opinion Quarterly* 32 (Summer 1968), pp. 287–88; Barbara S. Dohrenwend, John Colombotos, and Bruce P. Dohrenwend, "Social Distance and Interviewer Effects," *Public Opinion Quarterly* 32 (fall 1968), pp. 419–22.

14. Richardson, Dohrenwend, and Klein, *Interviewing: Its Forms and Functions,* pp. 132, 201–03, 227, 232, 242.

15. Harry L. Smith and Herbert H. Hyman, "The Biasing Effect of Interviewer Expectations on Survey Results," *Public Opinion Quarterly* 14 (Fall 1950), pp. 491–506; J. J. Feldman, Herbert H. Hyman, and C. W. Hart, "A Field Study of Interviewer Effects on the Quality of Survey Data," *Public Opinion Quarterly* 15 (Winter 1951–52), p. 761.

16. See, for example, Owen W. Bombard, "A New Measure of Things Past," *American Archivist* 18 (April 1955), p. 128. Elwood R. Maunder, "Tape-Recorded Interviews Provide Grass Roots History," *Forest History* 2 (Winter 1959), pp. 1, 15. For further references, see Donald J. Schippers and Adelaide G. Tusler, *A Bibliography on Oral History* (Los Angeles: Oral History Association, 1978).

17. Richardson, Dohrenwend, and Klein, *Interviewing: Its Forms and Functions,* pp. 57–58. Sociologists call interviews which begin on a general level and gradually close in on a specific top "funneled," or "focused," interviews, as first described by Robert K. Merton and Patricia Kendall in "The Focused Interview," *American Journal of Sociology* 51 (May 1946), pp. 541–57. See also Phillips, *Social Research,* p. 118.

18. Richardson, Dohrenwend, and Klein, *Interviewing: Its Forms and Functions,* pp. 55–91, 196, 214, 240–42.

19. See Kenneth J. Gergen and Kurt W. Back, "Communication in the Interview and the Disengaged Respondent," *Public Opinion Quarterly* 30 (Fall 1966), pp. 385–98.

20. Hyman, *Interviewing in Social Research,* pp. 291, 300–301; Feldman, Hyman, and Hart, "A Field Study of Interviewer Effects," pp. 749–51, 758–59; *Bulletin of the Cornell Program in Oral History* 2 (December 1969), pp. 3–4.

21. Some oral history programs, most notably Berkeley's, entirely retype all of their transcripts but alert researchers to the extent of the editing in a preface to every interview. Since the Berkeley program also reorganizes many of its interviews to coordinate their content, such warnings are, in my view, minimal at best.

22. Saul Benison, "Oral History and Manuscript Collecting," *Isis* 53 (March 1962), pp. 13–17; Corinne L. Gilb, "Tape-Recorded Interviewing: Some Thoughts from California," *American Archivist* 20 (October 1957), pp. 335–44; Doyce B. Nunis, Jr., ed., "Recollections of the Early History of Naval Aviation: Session in Oral History," *Technology and Culture* 4 (Spring 1963), pp. 149–76; Donald C. Swain, "Problems for Practitioners of Oral History," *American Archivist* 28 (January 1965), pp. 63–69.

7

Oral History:
An Appreciation
William Moss

In response to charges of inaccuracy in oral history interviewing, this next article on oral historiography spells out the need for evidentiary standards for oral history and for a more precise documentation on the conduct of the interviews.

William Moss, chief archivist for a distinguished oral history project at a presidential library, suggests five principal types of historical records: transactional (contracts, licenses, written instructions); selective records (notes, memoranda, audio and visual recordings); recollections (the stuff of oral history, short- and long-term); and reflections (self-evaluations of the past, which oral historians should avoid because of their subjectivity) and analyses. He goes on to propose a method whereby historians can evaluate the content and conduct of an interview.

Moss's article, published in 1977, summarizes many of the concerns of archivists since the First Colloquium of the Oral History Association in 1966 and a survey made not long after by the Society of American Archivists. The present article helped prompt the OHA to convene a meeting of experienced professionals to develop its evaluation guidelines.

William Moss was for many years chief archivist of the John F. Kennedy Library in Boston; he is now affiliated with the Smithsonian Institution. His Oral History Program Manual (1974) remains one of the best guides to organizing a large-scale project. His extensive lectures on oral history, delivered in the United States and abroad, have resulted in surveys such as "Archives in the People's Republic of China" (1974) in the American Archivist.

"Oral History: An Appreciation" by William Moss appeared in *American Archivist* 40 (October 1977), pp. 429–39. It is reprinted by permission of the author and the Society of American Archivists.

*I*n the generation since Allan Nevins demonstrated the great potential of personal narratives as sources for writing history, much time and effort have been spent, and much money, in the activity that has come to be called "oral history." But the product of all this effort and expense remains largely untested in terms of its promise. Broad and undiscriminating charges of wasteful triviality or of biased and self-serving narrations do little to improve or clarify the situation. Nor do naive and enthusiastic praises of its potential serve to prove its worth. Even the occasional use of oral history information by biographers does not establish its validity as an important source. The promise remains impressive in the abstract, but the product is still untested. Yet, if oral history is to be a reliable research tool, if it is to be respected historical evidence, and if it is to justify a national association in its name, then those who produce oral history, the scholars who use its product, and the institutions that finance its projects must have some means of understanding its proper role and of evaluating what is being done in the field. We need to know more about the place of oral history in the system of historical analysis, and we need to understand better the contribution that oral history can make to the writing of history. Clues are scattered in the literature on oral history. This essay attempts to bring them together and to place oral history in its proper context, to give it a proper value as historical evidence, and to offer some ideas for critical testing in order that the product may justify the promise.

The Evidentiary Value of Oral History

To understand its proper place in the system of historical analysis, we must examine oral history in relation to other kinds of historical evidence. For purposes of this thesis, it is suggested that there are five types, or levels, of source material that go into the writing of history: transactional records, selective records, recollections, reflections, and the analyses that are written by one's predecessors.

From the usual meanings of these five terms we can recognize an ascending scale of sophistication and abstraction. There is also a counterscale of evidentiary value. As abstraction increases and we get farther away from the immediate reality, the evidentiary value of the information decreases. The simple thesis that evidence and abstraction are in an inverse relation to one another often is forgotten because it is so elementary; but it is crucial to an understanding of the value of oral history.

The historian is engaged in the task of mastering the past. The discipline of history is a means by which we may keep from kidding ourselves about what has happened. It is axiomatic that such discipline is essential to coping with the present and planning for the future. If the discipline of history in general and the tool of oral history in particular are to be employed successfully, then we must have some systematic means of relating evidentiary and abstract values and of distinguishing them from each other. An examination of the five levels of sources is necessary to achieve this understanding.

TRANSACTIONAL RECORDS

Transactional records are not so much abstractions of human actions and interactions as they are the actions themselves. They may be abstract in the sense that they are symbolic representations of agreements or communications, but the documents produced are the transactions as well as their records or reports. Any document that embodies in its text the substance of the action it represents is a transactional record and is the authoritative basis for any action arising from or dependent upon the transaction recorded. Constitutions, laws, contracts, deeds, wills, treaties, diplomas, certificates, licenses, patents, proclamations, orders, instructions, advertisements, and similar documents are transactional records. They are primary evidence. An order never obeyed and an advertisement never responded to are nevertheless actions that occurred. Unless they are forged, we may accept the documents at face value, as primary evidence. There is no interpretive or selective process between the document and the reality it represents, beyond that inherent to the transaction itself. No interpretive element intrudes between the document and the observer other than the observer's own bias and perception.

SELECTIVE RECORDS

Selective records are attempts to preserve and to communicate to others descriptions of what is happening at a given time. Concurrency is important in order to distinguish this level of evidence from recollections, discussed below. Audio, video, or cinematic recordings of actions as they unfold, stenographic notes of conversations as they are taking place, still photographs, and even recorded running descriptions (such as that of a sports broadcaster) may be included in the category of selective records. They are selective in that there is a selective or interpretive process between the reality and the record. We are so accustomed to accepting electronic or film recordings as substitutes for reality that we tend to confuse them with reality. In fact, the technical limitations of the camera and tape recorder are not unlike those of human perception. The human observer records in his memory not exactly what is happening, but rather what his predisposition toward people and events make him capable of recording. The mechanical or photographic or electronic device records only so much as its technical range and capacity will allow. There is not a truly one-to-one relationship between the reality and the record. Some interpretation through selection, decision, or translation is unavoidable.

Selective records, because of their contemporary nature, are highly valued as historical evidence, but their evidentiary value must always be somewhat less than that of transactional records. The very interpretive nature of the selective class of records, however, produces commensurate value for the historian. Selective records are, after all, primary evidence of what someone decided to record or was capable of recording. If we further suppose that such recordings are generally more deliberate or purposeful than whimsical or random, then we may infer some contemporary value to what is recorded. What is recorded is what someone contemporary to the events believed to be important or worth recording. The first step away from primary evidence and into abstraction has been taken. Selective records are abstracts of reality. In the next category we take a much larger step away from reality and into abstraction.

RECOLLECTIONS

If the human memory is a selective record, then recollections are still further selective and selection is compounded to a second degree. It might be fairer to subdivide recollections into those emerging soon after the events recalled, and those emerging later. The distinction is one of degree rather than kind, and it begs the question of where to draw the line between sooner and later. Nor is it important to this thesis. Into the category of recollections we may place any accounts that are firsthand and yet are not concurrent to the subject or event described. Recollections include diaries, information solicited from eyewitnesses by investigators, tales told by grandfathers to little children, and information supplied by oral history narrators.

Recollections are clearly another step removed from reality into abstraction. As evidence they must be considered less reliable than either transactional or selective records. They may perhaps be all a historian has, and therefore a sine qua non to his research; but this value must not be confused with the relative evidentiary value. For too often a recollection is used as the basis for a historical thesis simply because it is the only evidence available. Because it is the only evidence available does not mean that we may rely on it as we would a transactional record or a selective record. The distinction is an important one in terms of mastering the past, and the values are far too often confused.

Several factors contribute to the decreased evidentiary value of recollections vis-à-vis transactional or selective records. Recollections may, and often do, include secondhand accounts and hearsay, or will at least be colored by the impact of such information on the witness/narrator recounting a description from memory. Furthermore, intervening events in the experience of the witness/narrator, or his prior receptivity to certain ideas and not to others, may induce him to diminish the importance of some evidence and perhaps to enhance beyond proper proportion the importance of other evidence. We also have in the process of recollection an intrusion of purposes that may affect the evidence: to inform a group; to secure one's own dignified position in history; to prosecute or defend a case; to sell a newspaper or book; to instruct a grandchild; or even to enhance the collection of a library. All are purposes that may overtly or subtly affect the character and nature of the evidence presented.

Historians clearly must be careful about using recollections as evidence. They must understand that a recollection is itself a complex piece of evidence. Three levels are included. There is the initial event or reality, there is the memory which is a selective record at least one step removed from reality, and there is the further selective and interpretive account recalled from memory by the witness/narrator. Furthermore, when an interviewer deliberately questions a person to solicit information as evidence, a fourth level of selection and potential for intrusion enters the process. The questions that an interviewer asks and the apparent purpose of his interviewing have a direct bearing on what is being called up from memory, and why.

Crucial to a sound understanding of oral history is that the record produced by an interview should never be confused with the original events, nor even with the memory of that event. The record is a selective one that itself selects information from the selective record of the witness/narrator's memory of past events and subjects. Whatever other values oral history may have for journalists, novelists, dramatists, educators, and propagandists (and these values may be many), the historian must understand and respect the evidentiary limitations of recollections if he is to use them honestly in his attempts to master the past. He must understand that the evidence has been refracted several times before he confronts it in an oral history recording.

Yet, even as we move further from reality, recollections provide the historian with a corresponding abstractive value of fascinating richness. We may infer from what is recalled what it is that people believe to be significant enough to remember and to recount about the past. One of the historian's tasks in analysis is to assess the importance of past events in terms of subsequent developments. The selective recollections of others may contribute insight and understanding to the task. Even when erroneous or misguided, recollections may in their very errors provoke understanding and insight. Furthermore, the aggregate recollections of many people can provide a rough means for approximating historical truth where no transactional records or selective records exist. But it requires many accounts from a good cross-section sample of witnesses to endow this kind of evidence with a reliability even approaching that of transactional or selective records.

REFLECTIONS

It is necessary to distinguish reflections from both recollections and analysis. Reflections go beyond simple recollections of facts in that they are what an individual person thinks spontaneously about the past, the values and affective impressions with which he characterizes the past and makes it relevant to his own present situation. Although deliberate, reflections are subjective and emotional and are not usually characterized by the thorough and systematic weighing of evidence required by historical analysis.

Reflections are usually recorded along with recollections in an oral history interview or diary; but, like recollections, they must not be confused with the past on which they focus. A reflection is a contemporary event of contemplating and evaluating the past, but it is not the past which is the subject of the evaluation. The historian must use reflections with the same caution that he uses recollections, as clues to the significance and meaning that past events have for people in the present. Reflections are hardly to be classed as evidence about the past at all, and thus they must be separated from recollections as a level of historical evidence. They may certainly provoke insight and understanding, and usually do so more directly than recollections. The significance attributed to past events in reflections does not mean that the events had that particular importance when they occurred, nor does it mean that they necessarily ought to have such meaning for us now or in the future. They are useful to analysis as a record of what people have thought about the past, and they may be the basis for inferences about the meanings of events. As with recollections, isolated reflections make poor foundations for analysis, and an aggregate of many concurring values is necessary before a historian may rely on the interpretation with any confidence.

ANALYSIS

Analysis is the process by which form and order are brought to the chaos of evidence about the past, to bring meaning and understanding not only to the individual historian but to many people with differing subjective views of reality. Analysis requires a rigorous accounting of all the evidence, of all levels and kinds, available to the historian. It requires the making of hypotheses about how and why things happened as they did and why they occurred in the sequence that they did. Analysis may be good or bad, sound or weak, honest or biased, depending on how good the evidence is, whether or not all the available evidence has been accounted for, whether or not all possible hypotheses have been tested against the evidence, and whether or not the analyst's own private interests intrude unfairly to distort the evidence and analysis.

Analysis goes far beyond the simple collection, preservation, and retrieval of information. It goes beyond the mere description of events, people, places, and things. Nor is analysis merely the repetition or aggregate of notions that have occurred to others about what might be personally or universally significant about the past. Analysis requires the comparing and testing of different records against each other, weighing the relative values of insight and evidence that they contribute in fair proportion, forming theoretical structures from the information (both evidence and insights), and then testing these new hypotheses against the evidence again and again to see if it can survive critical examination.

Analysis is performed not only by historians but by journalists, writers of government reports, and others. Analysis inevitably has a limited perspective based on the purposes for which the analysis was performed and the subjective interests of those performing the analysis. But analysis can be fair and honest if all the evidence has been accounted for, the hypotheses rigorously tested, and the author's bias well defined and accounted for in the process. It is true that not only journalists and government report writers but also historians can misuse and have misused analysis to serve subjective prejudices and ideologies. But, when they do, they are no longer masters of the past but rather creators of new mythologies in the present. Such efforts may have value in documenting present prejudices and interpretations, but they cannot properly be called good history that masters the past. Enhancing or suppressing particular bits of evidence not on the basis of relative evidentiary or insight value but rather in the service of a subjective purpose is inimical to mastering the past with the integrity that must be demanded by the discipline of history. Moreover, because of the authoritative pretensions of historical analysis to mastering the past, its conclusions, when erroneous, may compound the illusion every time they are quoted or relied upon uncritically by subsequent scholars. The stronger the analysis and the more it rests on comprehensive accounting of all the evidence and on proper evaluation of evidence and insight, the more likely it is to produce a more reliable and more enduring mastery of the past.

The Lesson for Oral History

Oral history has a proper place in the system of evidence, experience, and analysis that produces good history, and properly used it can make an important contribution. Improperly used it can be mischievous and destructive. Oral history, to be most effective, must itself be well-grounded in sound analysis and in a thorough knowledge and understanding of all the other available and pertinent sources, if it is to produce the best and most reliable oral documentation. Figure 7.1 illustrates the place of the oral history interview in the system and its relationship to the other component elements. Each arrow in the diagram indicates not only the direction of influence and effect, but also the intrusion of a selective or interpretive factor between reality and analysis.

Systematic Evaluation of Oral History

In order to evaluate oral history properly we must first distinguish it from other forms of oral documentation. Essentially, there are three classes of oral documentation. The first is the recording of performances in which the participants are following a prepared script (which provides additional documentation about the event). Performances include political speeches as well as dramatic presentations.

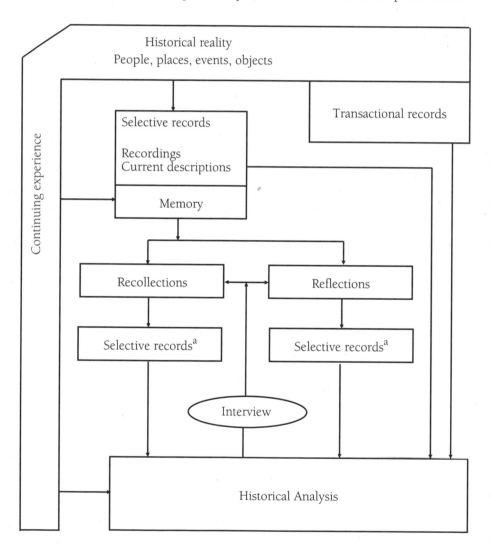

Figure 7.1 Components of historical analysis: Levels of evidence and the place of oral history interviewing in the process.
[a]Includes diaries and retrospective writings as well as tape recordings of oral history.

The second class of oral documentation is the recording, sometimes surreptitiously, of unrehearsed events in which the speaking of the participants is spontaneous and dynamic and entirely concerned with immediate purposes or plans. Finally, there is the oral documentation that has come to be called oral history: the recording of a special kind of event, the interview, in which historical information, insight, and opinion are sought deliberately and are deliberately preserved as a historical source. The third category must be evaluated somewhat differently from the other two.

There are two steps in the evaluation of any record: determining its genuineness, authenticity, and integrity as a record; and determining the value of its content information against known and previously established facts.

Evaluation of the record itself is the same for all three categories of oral documentation. The historian needs to know a number of things to establish that the recording is just what it purports to be, is complete, and has not been altered or changed. He must know when the recording was made, and under what circumstances. He should know why it was made. He should know, if possible, what kind of equipment was used to make the recording. If the tape or film of an event is a second, third, or fourth generation copy of the original recording, then the historian should know something of the equipment, procedures, and conditions involved in making the copies. The historian needs to know if the voices on the tape are indeed those of the people they are represented to be. (We may find a growing role for the electronic voice-analysis devices for authenticating oral documents.) In order for the historian to have full confidence in the recording being offered as evidence, he must have a full and authenticated record of its creation, preservation, processing, and custody. He needs assurances that the recording was not tampered with, falsified, or edited—or if it was, then by whom, under what circumstances, to what extent, and why? In this the tape recording is no different from traditional written documents, for which the historian needs similar kinds of information and assurances about its provenance. In many cases a full record of provenance is not available, and the historian must perforce rely on the reputation of the producing or custodial institution for integrity.

Once the integrity and authenticity of the recording have been established, the historian's evaluation turns to the contents. Once a performance has been identified as a performance, the historian's task is a relatively simple one. The value is clearly that of a contemporary selective record and ranks very high on the scale of evidence. With the unrehearsed event, the historian does have a very important first question to ask. Even if the record is fully authenticated, is this truly an unrehearsed event and not a performance? In our current age of dramatized history and electronic simulations on television, the historian must truly ask himself if the creation of the recording was not somehow deliberately

manipulated to leave a biased record. He must find reassurances that the participants were indeed acting spontaneously and not with half a mind on the tape
recorder. He must find reassurances that the whole thing was not prepared in
advance and stage managed for the sake of producing a distorted historical
record. But, the same can be said for written minutes of meetings, on which historians have traditionally relied, so there is really nothing new here.

The oral document produced by an oral history interview, however, presents
the historian with a far more complex problem of evaluation. Its effective and
proper use in historical analysis requires special understanding and a lot of hard
work. It cannot be accepted quite as readily as the first two categories of oral
documentation. Interviews depend on memories, and we know memories to be
tricky with respect to reality. The historian, faced with the information content of
a recorded interview, really has no way of knowing, from the record itself,
whether the record is faulty or true, distorted or accurate, deliberately falsified or
spontaneously candid. The historian is at the mercy of the witness who is testifying, and the historian does not have the opportunity to stop the testimony to
cross-examine. He must rely on the interviewer to do that for him.

Faced with such risky evidence, the historian must approach oral history
documentation warily and with great skepticism. He must find means to determine if the witnesses are reliable. A particular problem with the modern process
of recording oral testimony for historical use is that so many of the narrators are
unknown, are of unproven reliability, and there exists little with which to test
their evidence. So much of the evidence is personal and unique that there is not a
body of data against which to cross-check the information. In some published
works relying on personal interviews the contributing witnesses are anonymous.
Nor, in his assessment, should the historian neglect the need to evaluate the
interviewer. Although the interviewer may seek to be objective and unobtrusive,
he must inevitably play a dynamic role in the creation of the interview record,
and the way he plays his role often determines not only the tone and character
of the record produced but also the substance of the record content. Narrators requently respond with what they think the interviewer wants to hear. The
apparent aims and objectives of the interview may have much to do with the way
the interviewee perceives his role and therefore with the way he responds to the
interview as a whole and to individual questions in particular.

Further, the historian must compare the content information, both questions
and answers, with other sources on the same subjects to see if both participants
know what they are talking about. He must not impute authority to a statement
or an assertion in an interviewer's question (even if the respondent does) simply
on the assumption that the interviewer must know what he is talking about.
Interviewers often test hearsay, and its repetition in a question should not be con-
strued as corroboration unless it is supported by adequate responses from the

interviewee. Interviewers, too, like interviewees, may on occasion be whimsical or frivolous. The historian must discover discrepancies in the accounts presented and must try to account for them or (perhaps reluctantly) discard those accounts. He must identify unique information and attempt to obtain corroboration from additional sources. Ultimately, in the case of truly unique information, he may have to make a leap of faith; but it should be an informed leap, based on an accumulated sense of the reliability of the witnesses as proven by their testimony on other and related subjects.

In order for the historian to develop such confidence about any given interview or any collection as may permit him to make these leaps of faith in the absence of corroborating evidence, we require a regular and continuing process of systematic and critical evaluation and review of the oral history documentation that is being produced, not only of published books directly or loosely based on interviews, but of interviews. Since it is the deliberate interview that makes oral history unique as a historical source, it is proper that critical examination should focus primarily on the content and conduct of the interview. There are a series of questions that can be asked and must be answered in any thorough evaluation of the content or conduct of an oral history interview.

EVALUATING CONTENT

Evaluating content focuses on three groups of questions familiar to most historians. These questions may be applied either to a single interview or to a group of interviews dealing with a common theme.

1. How sound is the evidence presented? Are several sources in corroboration? Is the evidence presented at variance with previous evidence, and if so, why? Does the testimony ring true not only in the subjective judgment of the reviewer but also with the whole pattern of evidence? Does the testimony seem contrary and out of place, and if so, why? To what extent are the facts presented credible in the light of the known consequences of the actions and events recounted? In the light of subsequent events, does the story make sense?

2. Is the interview a thorough one? Does it cover all possible relevant themes? Are all topics probed in depth for detail, amplification, and appreciation? Do both interviewer and interviewee seem to be aware of gaps in recorded history and conventional wisdom? Do they deal with the topics and the omissions candidly? What has been omitted from the interview that ought to have been included, and why was it left out? Does the interview work on both the rational or logical level of facts and conclusions and also on the affective, emotional level of opinions, with clear indications of the value of each?

3. Is the information provided really needed, or is it superfluous and redundant? In what ways does the interview provide a unique contribution to history? Is there unique information? Is there a unique perspective on the past? Does the interview provide the historian with a unique arrangement or concentration of information that is enlightening or at least helpful? Does the interview provide corroboration or challenges to previously held notions, and how should these be valued? Does the interview contribute richness of detail and description, or perhaps a richness of affective response and commentary that aids insight?

EVALUATING CONDUCT

The interview is not a passive document that merely accepts evidence. It is a dynamic process in which the observer/collector (interviewer) has a marked effect on what the witness/narrator (interviewee) produces in the way of information and opinion. The historian must ask a number of questions about the way in which any given interview or any given group of interviews was conducted, and the first of these questions shakes the practice of oral history to its very roots.

1. Is an interview, after all, the best means of acquiring the evidence produced? Is it, perhaps, the only means? If not, what other means exist and have they been used? If not, why not?

2. Does the interview get the most possible out of the interviewee; or does much appear to have been held back, omitted, suppressed, or distorted? How effectively did the interviewer exercise the opportunity for critical challenge within the interview?

3. Do both interviewer and interviewee appear to understand, to be committed to, and to be able to pursue the inquiry for the sake of historical integrity and truth, or are other purposes being served? Why? To what effect? How does history suffer or benefit from either?

4. Do both interviewer and interviewee appear to be knowledgeable about the subject under discussion? Are they in command of the information? If they are guessing, then to what effect?

5. Do both interviewer and interviewee use a variety of approaches to the subjects and bring to bear a variety of perspectives, or do they seem to be limited to rigid, one-dimensional discussions? Do they both seize upon and appreciate the clues provided by associating ideas? Do they pursue trains of thought thoroughly, or is the inquiry essentially a lazy one?

6. Does the narrator seem to have been an appropriate one for the subjects discussed? What were his strengths and weaknesses? What about the interviewer with respect to the same questions?

7. Do the interviewer and interviewee seem to be well-matched so that they excite each other to produce the best and most complete possible record? Do they bring to bear the most productive combination of empathy and critical judgment?

8. Is either participant really a disinterested party? If not, what personal interests or biases are apparent and why? What effect do they produce and how must the historian handle it?

EVALUATING PROJECTS

Of less immediate concern to the historian's research topic but nonetheless important is the evaluation of and the confidence the historian may have in the project that produced the interviews. A rather different approach must be taken to evaluating projects. Even when the individual interviews and the aggregate collection can pass critical inspection, there are still additional questions about the project that the historian must find satisfactory answers to before he can have full faith and confidence in the material.

1. Does the project have a well-defined set of purposes and objectives? What are they? Are they compatible with and do they contribute to honest historical inquiry or are they distorted by bias? What are the real objectives of collecting the information and how do they affect the information collected? What other influences may tend to tilt the information produced toward a particular attitude or character over the whole aggregate collection?

2. Are the interviews and interviewers that have been chosen to produce the records appropriate to the purposes of the collecting agency? Are they the best available, or were compromises made and, if so, why? Where could the choices have been improved? Which significant narrator/witnesses were omitted, and why?

3. Are the policies and procedures of the program consistent with providing accurate information on the provenance of the material produced? Are the procedures designed to produce the most accurate and undistorted record of the interviews for use by the historian? If not, to what effect, for the purposes of historical analysis, were the procedures designed?

4. What is the availability of the interviews collected, and what restrictions on access (if any) are there? How do these affect the aggregate picture presented by the material that is available? Who may use the material? Is the researcher population limited? By what criteria? What effect does the limitation have on the critical reception of the material to date? How have the interviews been used by researchers, and what contributions have they made thus far to historical writing?

5. What kinds of finding aids are provided to the researcher? Are these adequate to the purposes of most researchers or only to a few? How could they be improved and why?

6. What other kinds of information resources does the collecting agency or institution provide that the researcher can use to test and corroborate or refute the information found in the oral history interviews?

7. Does the project provide information about both the interviewees and the interviewers in sufficient detail to help the researcher make judgments about reliability?

Summary and Conclusion

Oral history interviewing and the documentation that it produces are a logical part of the system and process by which we transform the evidence of reality into the composition of history that masters the past. As evidence, oral history is less than transactional or selective records; but it makes a significant contribution to insight and understanding, and in the absence of primary evidence an aggregate of testimony may serve to approximate historical certainty. To be effective, oral history interviewing must proceed from a base of primary evidence and sound analysis. Producers and users of oral history must be critical when they deal with this source. Only when they can provide or obtain the answers to a large number of questions about the character of the material can the kind of confidence in it needed for good history be developed.

A continual and regular process of critical review, not only by institutions that sponsor oral history projects but also by the historians who use the material, is essential to the continued improvement of oral history sources. Oral history can be done well, and it can make an important contribution to history; but in order to do so it must be properly understood and rigorously tested, and those who produce it must measure their efforts against, and strive to meet, the highest standards of evidentiary value.

8

Oral Tradition and Historical Methodology

Jan Vansina

Though few practitioners of oral history work with oral tradition (unwritten knowledge passed verbally through successive generations), the next two sections discuss the histori-cal worth and reliability of oral sources from nonliterate societies. The traditional nature of much orally elicited data tends to be overlooked by students of oral history, for narrators are themselves often unable to distinguish between accounts of witnesses to historic events and accounts based upon generalized knowledge or anecdotes and folklore told within a community.

Oral history is in a number of ways similar to oral tradition: error or falsification can be introduced in the same ways as in oral narratives; differing oral documents need to be evaluated for veracity by comparison with each other or with written documents, where available; and many interviews show the performance associated with oral tradi-tion, as a result of the narrator's wish to create an explainable experience.

This excerpt from Jan Vansina's classic Oral Tradition: A Study in Historical Methodology *provides criteria useful to historians distinguishing between community story-telling and historical fact. Based on field research in Africa, where oral tradition remains a living force, Vansina's insights into the types and functions of oral narrative can be applied to the survivals and new creations of tradition in an electrified, post-literate society. His comments on interpreting history on the basis of oral sources may apply equally to interviewers working on Wall Street or along the Amazon.*

"Oral Tradition and Historical Methodology" by Jan Vansina appeared in *Oral Tradition: A Study in Historical Methodology* [De la tradition orale (1961)], trans. H. M. Wright (Chicago: Aldine, 1965). © Jan Vansina. Reprinted by permission of the author.

Jan Vansina's writings about oral tradition have been translated from French into English, Spanish, Italian, and Arabic. He is the author of a dozen books on African history, and his Children of Woot (1978) tested oral tradition against other historical sources in Africa. A member of the Royal Academy of Overseas Sciences and a consultant to UNESCO, Vansina is Vilas Research Professor of History at the University of Wisconsin.

O ral traditions are historical sources of a special nature. Their special nature derives from the fact that they are "unwritten" sources couched in a form suitable for oral transmission, and that their preservation depends on the powers of memory of successive generations of human beings. These special features pose a problem for the historian. Do they *a priori* deprive oral tradition of all validity as a historical source? If not, are there means for testing its reliability? These are precisely the questions to which the present study seeks to find an answer, and I hope to show that oral tradition is not necessarily untrustworthy as a historical source, but, on the contrary, merits a certain amount of credence within certain limits.

In those parts of the world inhabited by peoples without writing, oral tradition forms the main available source for a reconstruction of the past, and even among peoples who have writing, many historical sources, including the most ancient ones, are based on oral traditions. Thus a claim for the practical utility of research on the specific characteristics of oral tradition, and on the methods for examining its trustworthiness, is doubly substantiated. . . .

I should like to make it clear that my examination of the topic is primarily based on traditions still alive among peoples without writing, since sources of this kind preserve the essential nature of oral tradition better than traditions found in literate societies. Among peoples without writing, oral tradition continues to exist at the very heart of the environment that gave rise to it. It has not yet been supplanted, nor had its main functions taken over, by written documents, as is the case in a society where writing has taken pride of place. Nor has it yet been torn from its natural context, as happens once traditions have been committed to writing. For these reasons, and also because of the opportunities open to me, I have based this study mainly on the oral traditions of the Kuba, the Rundi, and the Rwanda, among whom I carried out field researches from 1955 to 1956, and from 1957 to 1960. . . .

The first thing to note about the historical information that can be obtained from oral traditions is that it varies according to the type of tradition. A survey of the typology of traditions and an outline of the characteristics of each type show that the types vary widely, and that all have a given historical bias which imposes certain limitations, but which gives each type its own particular usefulness in providing information about certain particular aspects of the past. Next, oral tradition as a whole can be shown to have its limitations, as well as certain tendencies towards bias due to the influence of the political system—which accounts for the very existence of many traditions—and also due, to a lesser extent, to cultural factors. The limitations of the information that can be derived from oral traditions are real, and must be accepted by the historian; but he can attempt to make up for them by using data supplied by other historical sources, such as written documents, and the disciplines of archaeology, cultural history, linguistics, and physical anthropology. Each of these disciplines furnish data which in themselves are limited; but by putting together all the available information, the area of the past about which we can acquire some knowledge is greatly extended. Nevertheless, even if all these techniques are used, we can never arrive at a complete knowledge of all the events of the past. We can never do more than touch upon a small part of past history—namely, that part which has been preserved in the various surviving historical documents. But this statement must not be taken as an excuse for abandoning the study of history on the grounds that perfection can never be attained.

The Interpretation of History

. . . [O]ral traditions are historical sources which can provide reliable information about the past if they are used with all the circumspection demanded by the application of historical methodology to any kind of source whatsoever. This means that study of the oral traditions of a culture cannot be carried out unless a thorough knowledge of the culture and of the language has previously been acquired. This is something which is taken for granted by all historians who work on written sources, but it is too often apt to be forgotten by those who undertake research into the past of preliterate peoples.

In these final remarks I shall make several observations about the interpretation of the facts obtained. The layman is too often inclined to entertain a completely false idea as to the powers of the historian, and is apt to regard any historical reconstructions offered as absolutely valid. He fondly imagines that written sources reveal events of the past which can be accepted as fact, but considers that oral sources tell of things about which there is no certainty—things which may or may not have happened. He forgets that any historical synthesis comprises an interpretation of the facts, and is thus founded upon probabilities.

I must apologize in advance to those historians who are only too familiar with the reflections which are here offered for their perusal. I make them in order to refute a prejudice which is commonly found among all those who have raised objections to the use of oral traditions as a historical source.

There is no great difficulty in accepting the proposition that history is always an interpretation. An example will prove the point better than abstract argument. If a Rwandese source tells us that a certain king conquered a certain country, what does this statement mean? It may mean that a cattle raid was carried out in enemy territory and was highly successful; or that the chief or king of the enemy country was deposed or killed, and his territory annexed, in theory, by Rwanda, while local government was left as it was; or it may mean that the conquered chief remained in power, but recognized the suzerainty of the king of Rwanda. Or yet again, it may mean that the king of Rwanda occupied the country, incorporated it as part of the states over which he ruled, and replaced the administration from top to bottom. Any one of these possibilities could be inferred from the statement, and this is still leaving out of account the subsidiary question as to whether the measures taken were temporary or final. That stating the problem in this way is not merely the sign of a Byzantine finicalness is shown by the following factual example from Rwanda. A certain King Ndabarasa conquered Gisaka, a country bordering on Rwanda. This meant in effect that he carried out several raids there with the intention not only of bringing back cattle, but also of weakening the military power of the enemy and disorganizing the government's project in which he succeeded. His great grandson, Mutara Rwogera, also "conquered" the same country, and succeeded in killing or exiling all the various chiefs who ruled there, thus ending the country's existence as an autonomous state. But it was his successor Rwabugiri who first founded administrative centers there of the kind found in Rwanda, and who appointed Rwandese to high government posts. In 1901, Rwabugiri's son was faced with a rebellion there, and it was not until this ended in 1903 that all the native chiefs and subchiefs were deprived of their rights, and the entire administration was taken over.

Thus every historian is obliged to interpret the sources he is dealing with. He does not and cannot have an unlimited knowledge of history, and there is usually more than one interpretation possible of the facts at his disposal. In addition, the historian adds something of his own to these facts, namely, his own particular flair, which is something more akin to art than to science. The only concession to history as a scientific discipline he can make here is to ensure that he discloses what his sources are, so that his readers will be informed as to the reasons for the choice he has made in his interpretations of the texts.

Interpretation is a choice between several possible hypotheses, and the good historian is the one who chooses the hypothesis that is most likely to be true. In practice it can never have more than a likelihood of truth, because the past has gone for good and all, and the possibility of firsthand observation of past events is forever excluded. History is no more than a calculation of probabilities. This is true not only as far as the interpretation of documents is concerned, but for all the operations of historical methodology, and above all for the most important ones. How shall one decide whether a statement is an error, or a lie, or is "veracious"? Each of the three hypotheses has a varying degree of probability, and the historian will choose the most probable one. Or if, in comparing two texts, resemblances between them are found, the historian must judge whether the resemblances imply that the texts have a common origin or not. Here again what he does is to assess possibilities and weigh probabilities. Historical science is a science of probabilities. Nor is it the only science of this kind. A large number of present-day scientific disciplines make use of the concept of chance and of probability.

From what has been said, it follows that there is no such thing as "absolute historical truth," and no one can formulate an "unchanging law of history" on the basis of our knowledge of the past. The truth always remains beyond our grasp, and we can only arrive at some approximation to it. We can refine our interpretations, accumulate so many probabilities that they almost amount to certainty, and yet still not arrive at "the truth." We can never hope to understand everything, and indeed do not even understand all that we experience personally. We cannot arrive at a full understanding of the past because the past is something outside our experience, something that is other. It has been said that it is possible to describe historical events because history is a science which deals with mankind, to which we ourselves belong, whereas a scientific description of bees does not make sense, since we cannot imagine what it is like to be a bee. This is true. But is also true that we cannot understand the past because the men who lived then were different from us, and however great an effort we make, we cannot ever completely enter into the mentality of someone else. We can never understand his motivations, and thus we can never pass judgment on them.

What the historian can do is to arrive at some approximation to the ultimate historical truth. He does this by using calculations of probability, by interpreting the facts and by evaluating them in an attempt to recreate for himself the circumstances which existed at certain given moments of the past. And here the historian using oral traditions finds himself on exactly the same level as historians using any other kind of historical source material. No doubt he will arrive at a lower degree of probability than would otherwise be attained, but that does not rule out the fact that what he is doing is valid, and that it is history.

9

A Note on Oral
Tradition and
Historical Evidence

Ruth Finnegan

This selection continues our exploration of oral tradition as historical evidence. Ruth Finnegan, one of the foremost experts on oral literature, suggests that a given oral tradition should be analyzed for its function as either literature or history before historical generalizations are drawn. She also notes the impact of what the folklorist calls the performance context of oral tradition: how the audience's (and the performer's) desires influence the ways in which a tradition is told—which, in turn, influence an oral historian's or ethnohistorian's interpretation of a given text in reconstructing history when few print sources exist.

Historians reading transcripts face a similar task in determining how an interview's sociolinguistic elements (pauses, verbal emphases, gestures not included in the transcript) affected the "performance" of the narrator. While there is clearly a distinction between oral literature and the authorized, formalized accounts produced by oral historians in developed nations, Finnegan's study opens up useful avenues for comparing the two forms.

Ruth Finnegan was trained at Oxford University and has taught in Rhodesia, Nigeria, Fiji, and England at the Open University (since 1969). She has written widely on ethnography, anthropology, and oral tradition, including Oral Literature in Africa *(1967),* Oral Poetry: its Nature, Significance, and Social Context *(1977), and* Conceptions of Inquiry *(1981).*

"A Note on Oral Tradition and Historical Evidence" by Ruth Finnegan appeared in *History and Theory* 9 (October 1970), pp. 195–201. © 1970 Wesleyan University. Reprinted by permission of the author and *History and Theory*.

*T*here are a number of assumptions about the nature of oral tradition in Africa which are sometimes made by historians and others. Two of these will be discussed in this Note—the assumption that "oral tradition" is something unitary and self-evident and that it is somehow impervious to many of the factors which historians usually take account of in critical assessment of sources. These (and other) assumptions about the nature of oral tradition are generally unconscious, but—perhaps because of that—they have often seriously affected its use as a source in African history. Of course not all historians make the assumptions discussed here, but they are common enough to warrant some general comment.

The common assumption that "oral tradition" is something uniform, something that can be treated as an undifferentiated and self-evident entity, leads to the tendency of some historians and others to speak of "oral tradition" generally as a source, without apparently feeling the need—which would be obvious in the case of documentary sources—to describe and analyze the detailed source material.[1] In practice a number of very disparate sources have often been lumped together under the name "oral tradition." Broadly one can list three main classes of oral tradition: recognized literary forms, generalized historical knowledge, and personal recollections.

First there is what has been called "oral literature." Though hard to define precisely, this class is composed of various types of both prose and poetry which correspond to literature in literate societies. Oral literature is relatively formalized, in the sense not of verbal accuracy but of genres clearly recognized in the society, and is sometimes—poetry especially—regarded as the product of specialist activity. A brief survey of the forms of oral literature follows.[2]

Praise poetry is one of the best-known forms, occurring in most of the traditional centralized states of Africa. Since its main theme is eulogy (most often of the ruler) it is political propaganda, and we cannot expect any very direct historical information, in the sense of exact description or narration. Nevertheless, praise poetry can lead to insight into the values and ideals of the society, or of one group, at least. Religious poetry, particularly if by highly trained specialists, can be conservative and thus potentially a good source; for the history of earlier times the problem, of course, is to sort out not only which are the older poems but which parts of these preserve earlier references and which not—which is difficult to do without knowing a lot about the earlier history already. Lyrics—songs for weddings, dance, work, love, and so forth—can throw light on values and personal preoccupations in a society at a particular time, but of course tend to be ephemeral. Topical and political poems can be an excellent source if they are recorded at the time they spring up; essentially short-lived, they are seldom or never feasible sources for arguing back to an earlier period.[3]

All in all, poetry in nonliterate as in literate societies can be illuminating for the historian—of direct relevance for the intellectual history of the time and indirectly useful for other aspects of society, provided the historian avoids literalistic interpretations and proceeds circumspectly, bearing in mind all the elements of propaganda, idealization, personal whim, exaggeration, artistry, and desire to please that variously characterize different kinds of poetry. In nonliterate societies there is the additional and often overwhelming difficulty that unless a poem is recorded at the actual time being studied—which few have been—there is usually no way of knowing from a later poem whether it is the same as or even slightly similar to versions in the earlier period. Normally the safest assumption can only be that it is not.

It will have been noticed that I have said nothing about "historical poetry" or about "epic." Surely these provide the best and most relevant source for the historian? The truth is that this type of poetry seems surprisingly uncommon in Africa. Certainly there are some exceptions, and there are of course a number of well-known instances of written historical poems under Arabic influence. But in general terms specifically "historical poetry" seems rare as an oral form, and even apparent instances turn out to be basically more like panegyric, the element of narration being subordinate to that of eulogy. True "epic," in spite of widespread assumptions about its being the natural form in many nonliterate societies, is hard to find.[4]

Prose literature can be discussed more briefly. It tends to less specialization than poetry in African oral literature. Unlike poets, the performer/composer of prose is seldom an expert, and often genres are not recognized. The outside analyst could list several main categories. First there are obviously fictional narratives concerned with people, imaginary beings, or animals. These clearly give little clue to the historian, though scholars still steeped in the idea that they date from the immemorial past purport to find traces of earlier ages and ideas in them. "Myths," or narrations about creations, deities, and so on, do not occur in the wide-ranging sense in which they appear among, say, the Polynesians or American Indians, but have nevertheless been spoken of by a number of writers. These narratives are admitted to be of little direct historical relevance: they tend to reflect present realities and preoccupations rather than those of earlier periods.[5] If recorded at the time, however, they can be useful for a later historian by throwing light on local attitudes rather than as literal statements.

The narrations often termed "legends" or historical narratives again are unfortunately rather less promising as sources than they might seem at first mention. The common picture of formalized historical accounts being passed down from generation to generation by specialists whose duty is to recite and transmit them accurately turns out to be not so widely applicable as one might expect; in fact it appears that the concept of historical narrative as a definite literary form distinct from other genres is relatively rare, except in societies much influenced by Arabic culture. This exception is of course not an unimportant one, as it affects many of the societies in the huge Sudan area across Africa and on the East African coast. Here historical accounts not infrequently took a written form and there was mutual interchange between oral and written versions.[6] There are also perhaps some other exceptions in states where, like Dahomey, Kuba, or Rwanda, the king kept close control over a centralized and authoritative version of the history.

Even these exceptions, however, involve their own difficulties. Were they really handed down "word for word"? There is almost no way of checking this (for even if one earlier version coincides closely, this cannot prove that still earlier ones did too); the fact that unfortunately local people believe that accounts are given accurately is not necessarily evidence. Again, the fact that such accounts are often the versions authorized by those currently holding political and/or religious power and, furthermore, are often mingled with praise of the ruling house and its ancestors, means that one must treat them with caution as an historical source.[7] In addition one has to be chary of taking such accounts literalistically. A narrative about first arrival in an area—a common topic—need not necessarily be interpreted as the migration of a whole people. Even if the account of actual arrival is accurate it may really only refer to one influential family coming to an already populated area. One good example of this is in Gabon oral tradition. If the traditions of specific "migrations" were taken literally "the history of Gabon would begin with an empty forest only 300 years ago, into which various peoples penetrated abruptly"; in fact it is clear from documentary and archaeological evidence that the area was inhabited long before this.[8] Travels, conquests, and arrivals are in any case common themes in stories, even among long-settled peoples, and one must always be cautious about accepting them literally as the record of either wholesale migrations or specific military engagements.[9] Nevertheless, these professed historical narratives can be useful for the relatively recent periods when the description is usually less steeped in supernatural elements than the early portions of such accounts.

However—to return to the main point—there seem in fact to be relatively few specifically historical formal narratives in Africa. Some of the apparent exceptions rest on a misunderstanding. Many of the texts presented as "local historical accounts" are in fact elicited rather than spontaneous narratives. In other words, an answer is being given to a particular researcher which would not be naturally given in other circumstances and therefore does not form part of the formal transmission of traditions in that society. An elicited narrative of this kind is of course particularly subject to current preoccupations and conflicts, the status of an attitude to the inquirer, the present political situation and so on. This is not to say that such narrations are useless. But they are clearly a different kind of account from one formally handed down and authorized by the society or a dominant group in it. Too often we are not told by the researcher which type of "historical narrative" he is relying on; we may thus be given the impression that what was in fact an elicited version is really an authoritative and formalized account.

So far we have been concentrating on the first broad category of oral tradition—recognized literary forms. The second category is rather different. This is the general historical knowledge in a particular society which is not normally crystallized into actual recitations.[10] This knowledge may consist of beliefs about recent events or may include references to the more remote past. In each case such beliefs or references are less subject to formal requirements than the "oral literature" type, and are perhaps particularly subject to modification or embroidery in the light of current fashions, interests, events, or the availability of written accounts.

Informal historical knowledge includes not only general notions of what happened in the past, but also a few elements which, though not eligible for the term "oral literature," can take a somewhat formalized shape. These include items like place names, praise names, or genealogies. Again, such sources have both uses and limitations.

Genealogies are a good case in point. There are a few instances in which genealogies are formally recited in, say, prayers or praises, but most often they merely form part of the general knowledge of a society or group. As such, they might seem an excellent source as far as they go. Some of their drawbacks, however, are well known.[11] There is the tendency to telescope, i.e., for links to fall out and be forgotten; there may be grafting on of extraneous links—as in Koranko genealogies going back to Noah and Adam, Fung pedigrees claiming descent from the Prophet,[12] or others from locally well-known but equally unrelated personages; or early ancestors may be rationalized in terms of current ideas or claims so that, say, early chieflets or village heads are presented as equally paramount chiefs or kings with their descendants. All these points arise from the inherent changeability of oral forms.

Perhaps less well known are the dangers of the way apparently objective genealogies are in fact closely tied to current—and ephemeral—political or social realities. An example can illustrate this.[13] The Tiv of Nigeria are a people who have traditionally had an uncentralized political system largely based on lineages and for whom, therefore, genealogies are of the utmost importance. They believe that they are all descended from one man (Tiv) through 14 to 17 generations of known ancestors. Yet these genealogies are constantly in dispute, and one even finds the same person citing different and contradictory genealogies on different occasions. These changes are not dependent on lapses of memory or on what Vansina would call "distortions," but arise merely because their actual use is always tied to some practical issue; there is never recitation or learning of genealogies as a whole for their own sake. Genealogies are thus used to fit particular facts and are constantly being modified in the light of the current situation. One incident illustrates this very clearly. A certain law case involved a question of genealogies. The details do not concern us, but roughly, the question of whether a certain man (X) received compensation or not turned on the exact position of one of his ancestors, Amena, possibly his great-grandfather. But it was not agreed by the elders whether Amena was in fact one man, two men, or even perhaps a woman. It was first decided on a priori grounds that he was not a woman, but the issue still remained: if he was one man, then X was not due compensation; if two, then he was due it. In the event, he was not compensated, because none of the relevant property happened to be currently available. Two days later, however— and this is the point—the elders all agreed that Amena was only one person on the grounds that the compensation had not been paid. The genealogy was thus directly dependent on the result of the law case. This is a particularly striking example of the variability of genealogies, but many similar cases could be mentioned.[14]

Leaving the discussion of this flexible type of general historical knowledge, we come to the third broad category of oral tradition—personal recollections. In many ways these are the best sources of all. Of course, there are still obvious safeguards to be observed—exactly the same kind as for similar recollections in literate societies. There is the need to cross-check and to allow for personal prejudices, romantic memories, special interests, lack of direct involvement, exaggeration, and so on. But clearly this kind of source is much nearer the primary facts than similar accounts which have been handed down through several generations.

In using oral tradition as an historical source, it is important to make clear in each instance under which of these three broad categories a particular item falls: formalized oral literature, informal historical knowledge, or personal recollections. The reason for this is an obvious one. Each type has its own particular dangers or limitations, and critical use of sources involves making these explicit—something which it is impossible to do without differentiating between the categories. The idea that "oral tradition" is something unitary and can be treated as such runs counter to all the normally accepted historical procedures of assessing each type of source on its own merits.

The notion that when using "oral tradition" one can suspend many of the normal critical canons of historical research is, despite the caution of more experienced historians, surprisingly prevalent.[15] Perhaps this is because the various assumptions about oral tradition coming down word for word, about its unitary nature, or about its supposed freedom from individual originality or artistry seem to add up to the conclusion that oral tradition is somehow impervious to the kinds of factors of which historians are so aware with other sources—the effects of, say, prejudice or propaganda, personal interests or fantasies, aesthetic forms, or just the variations between different types of sources.

I would suggest that the opposite of this assumption is in fact true. Oral sources are in many ways even more open to such factors than written ones. A written document is certainly liable to many influences as it is written down, but once written it can be taken as permanent. Oral forms, on the other hand, are open to all these influences, not only on the occasion of the first formulation and delivery, but on every single occasion of delivery afterward. Because they are oral, and thus can exist only as and when they are rendered by word of mouth, obviously they are closely affected by a number of additional factors that do not apply to documentary sources.

First there is the whole aspect of performance. The oral speaker is by definition a performer, and all the arts of drama, rhetoric, display, and verbal facility may be relevant in his performance. Furthermore, since speakers vary in these arts, so too will the style, structure, even content of what he says. Unlike the author of a written document, the author of an oral historical account does not always remain the same; in the case of traditions handed down over long periods he is necessarily different; and different individuals have different ways of presenting the facts, different prejudices, different interpretations. Over any length of time at all this is likely to lead to many changes and in a very complicated way.

Oral forms, are, secondly, deeply affected by the kinds of audiences to which they are addressed on any particular occasion. The audience is there, face to face, inescapable; it may be members of the family, friends, the king, children, a government official, a foreign researcher—and in each case the version may be different. Those whom local people rightly or wrongly associate with the government are particularly likely to have special versions given to them. In parts of Nigeria local people gather the evening before to prepare a version for delivery to the researcher the next day, and government officials frequently find that different accounts of history are being given by contending families or areas to bolster their own claims to some desired benefit. This is a consideration which makes one doubtful about the value of hasty recording of oral traditions. One example that springs to mind is Meyerowitz's research in Ghana; she visited over 130 towns and villages within nine months to record their traditions of origin—and this at a period when European visitors were associated with the government and regarded with suspicion.[16]

Oral tradition is also more constantly subject to outside influences because of its close connection with the current social situation. Each performance is on a specific occasion, and each occasion is in turn subject to the whole changing social background. This means that there is constant interpretation and reinterpretation in terms of the current situation. One example of this is provided by the Tiv genealogies already mentioned. Another is the story of the founding of the kingdom of Gonja in northern Ghana. One version of this was recorded around 1900, a period at which Gonja was divided into seven administrative divisions. The story tells how the state was first founded by a certain Jakpa who came to the area in search of gold, conquered the local inhabitants and became king by right of conquest; his seven sons and their descendants became the seven divisional chiefs. About 1960 the "same" story was recorded again. By that date two of the old divisions had disappeared, leaving only five; and the tale speaks of only five sons, with no mention at all of the other two.[17] A narrative like this is obviously influenced as much by present realities and power relationships as by historical considerations.[18]

The idea therefore that oral tradition is somehow impervious to all the kinds of influences of which historians must take cognizance in other sources is far from the truth. Oral tradition, being inherently variable and unfixed, is in certain ways peculiarly susceptible to such factors, and this is something of which an historian using these sources must take special account.

Notes

1. Not some of the more rigorous analysts, however, like J. Vansina, *Oral Tradition: A Study in Historical Methodology,* trans. H. Wright (London: Routledge and Kegan Paul, 1965; see chapter 8 of the present volume); P. D. Curfin, "Field Techniques for Collecting and Processing Oral Data," *Journal of African History* 9 (1968), pp. 367–85; E. J. Alagoa, "Oral Tradition among the Ijo of the Niger Delta," *Journal of African History* 7 (1966), pp. 405–19; G. S. Were, *A History of the Abaluyia of Western Kenya* (Nairobi: Uniafric House, 1967).

2. The list makes no attempt to be comprehensive. Further types are discussed in Vansina, *Oral Tradition,* and R. Finnegan, *Oral Literature in Africa* (London: Oxford University Press, 1970).

3. The Mau Mau political songs, for instance, were thus recorded and should prove extremely useful to the historian of this period.

4. For a further discussion of this problem, see Finnegan, *Oral Literature,* note to chap. 4, pp. 108–10.

5. For an instance of this, see below on the "myth" about the founding of Gonja.

6. With the corollary that some of these written chronicles must be subject to the same cautious treatment as oral accounts.

7. A point well discussed in Vansina, *Oral Tradition,* p. 155, but often neglected (see, for instance, M. Southwold's acceptance at their face value of claims in official Ganda king lists that those who succeeded to the kingship by rebellion were all in any case highly qualified to succeed (*History and Social Anthropology,* ed. I. M. Lewis [London: Tavistock Publications, 1968], p. 130).

8. H. Deschamps, "Traditions orales au Gabon," in *The Historian in Tropical Africa,* ed. J. Vansina (London: International African Institute, 1964), p. 175.

9. For a critique of the concept of migration as an explanatory device, see H. S. Lewis, "Ethnology and Culture History," in *Reconstructing African Culture History,* ed. C. Gabel and N. R. Bennett (Boston: Boston University Press, 1967), pp. 32–33, and references given there.

10. The "elicited narrations" just mentioned properly fit into this category.

11. See the account in Vansina, *Oral Tradition,* pp. 153–54.

12. E. F. Sayers, "The Funeral of a Koranko Chief," *Sierra Leone Studies,* o.s., 7 (1925), p. 24; B. A. Ogot, "The Impact of the Nilotes," in *The Middle Ages of African History,* ed. R. Oliver (London: Oxford University Press, 1967), p. 51.

13. This account is based on L. Bohannan, "A Genealogical Charter," *Africa* 22 (1952), pp. 301–15.

14. For some further examples of changes in genealogies, see E. E. Evans-Pritchard, *The Nuer* (Oxford: Clarendon Press, 1940), pp. 199–200; *Tribes without Rulers,* ed. J. Middleton and D. Tait (London: Routledge and Kegan Paul, 1958), pp. 10, 42ff, 198ff, 218; J. Middleton, *Lugbara Religion* (London: International African Institute, 1960), pp. 8, 235–36, 265; J. van Velsen, *The Politics of Kinship* (Manchester, England: University Press of Manchester, 1964), pp. 268–69; and the references given in J. A. Barnes, "Genealogies," in *The Craft of Social Anthropology,* ed. L. Epstein (London: Pergamon Press, 1967), pp. 118–21.

15. See the warnings in, for example, Vansina, *Oral Tradition*, and Curtin, "Field Techniques."

16. E. Meyerowitz, *Akan Traditions of Origin* (London: Faber Press, 1952), pp. 15, 17.

17. J. Goody and I. Watt, "The Consequences of Literacy," *Comparative Studies in Society and History 5 (1963), p. 310.*

18. An aspect brought out by the common point in social anthropological writings that such accounts are "mythical charters" for the existing social and political situation.

10

Oral History Project Design
David Lance

The design and evaluation of the research goals of an oral history project are subjects often slighted in how-to manuals. As a result, many beginning interviewers overlook the need for a balanced collection of sources and ignore relevant earlier work in their area, leaping with their microphones before looking at previous collections. The next four articles provide guidance on practical and theoretical considerations in designating (and attaining) realistic project goals.

Archivist David Lance dissects one English oral history project to demonstrate the research which necessarily precedes and informs the interviews. He indicates the necessity for a thoughtful analysis of potential research problems before beginning interviews and provides a matrix design to assure a balanced sample of narrators. Novices to oral history, as Charles Morrissey has written, frequently confuse the tape recorder with the vacuum cleaner. David Lance's article, however, explores an area which even experienced interviewers occasionally neglect. Lance offers compelling suggestions on research procedures and topic selection.

David Lance is the Assistant Director of the National Museum of Australia in Canaberra. For 15 years he worked as the keeper of sound records at the Imperial War Museum in London; there he not only established a department of sound records but also helped produce documentaries for the British Broadcasting Corporation and the Canadian Broadcasting Corporation, using oral sources. Some of his writings are "Oral History: Legal Considerations" (1976) and "Oral History: Perceptions and Practice" (1980), published in the British journal Oral History.

"Oral History Project Design" by David Lance is excerpted and reprinted from *An Archive Approach to Oral History* (London: the Imperial War Museum and the International Association of Sound Archives, 1978) by permission of the author and the publishers.

*T*he organizational methods on which this section is based have been applied across a wide subject and chronological range. They can be adapted for much oral history research which is concerned with the history of particular social and occupational groups. To allow readers to relate the various phases of project management to specific examples, however, it is convenient to concentrate on a single project. The project used for illustrative purposes was concerned with the experiences and conditions of the service of sailors who served on the lower deck of the Royal Navy between the years 1910 and 1922.

1. Preparation

The organisation of any project should be set within realistic research goals. Since oral history recording is dependent for worthwhile results on human memory, this fallible faculty must be accommodated by careful preparation. The planning of the project should, therefore, be based on as thorough an understanding of the subject field (and of the availability of informants) as the existing records permit.

It is prudent, first, to fix a research period which is historically identifiable as being self-contained. In the lower deck project, for example, the so-called Fisher Reforms of 1906 altered several important aspects of naval life; the First World War stimulated further changes during the early 1920s; and the Invergordon Mutiny in 1931 was another watershed for Royal Naval seamen. The combination of these three distinct periods in a recording project would have made it extremely difficult for sailors who served throughout them to avoid confusion on many details of routine life which, for research purposes, might be of critical importance. Three distinct periods of social change within a single career of professional experience are clearly difficult for informants to separate with few points of reference beyond their own memories. By setting the general limits of the lower deck project at 1910 to 1922, a reasonably distinct period of naval life was isolated as appropriate for oral history research.

The research problems which are created by rapid social change can seldom be eliminated entirely from oral history recording. It is for this reason that historically unsophisticated interviewing can result in information of uncertain reliability. Therefore, the project organiser's responsibility is to minimise the dangers implicit in such situations by his own common sense and historical sensitivity, and he should always apply the question "Is this reasonable?" to the goals which he sets. Some practical examples of the application of this principle in oral history research are given on page 140.

The chronological scope of an oral history project should be fixed before any recording begins, bearing in mind the age of the likely informants as well as the historical character of the subject field. By the time the lower deck project began in 1975, men who saw service in the Navy as early as 1910 were in their eighties, and thus the opportunities for preceding this date were limited. This basic consideration affects all oral history recording. The informants who are actually available to be interviewed also predetermine many of the topics which may be sensibly raised. Thus, owing to the slowness of promotion in the Royal Navy there was little point in introducing questions about, for example, conditions in petty officers' messes in 1910. Only informants into their nineties would have had the necessary experiences to be able to answer them. The chances of locating a sufficient number of interviewees of this great age were sufficiently slight to preclude this—and many similar topics—from being a practical aim within a systematic research project.

Similarly, the project organiser must take into account the structure of the particular group of people he is concerned with. For example, a battleship of the Dreadnought era—with a complement of some 700 men—might carry one writer (i.e. accounts clerk) and one sailmaker. The odds against tracing such rare individuals more than fifty years after the events eliminated some aspects of financial administration and some trade skills aboard ship from the range of what it was likely to be able to achieve.

The selection of and possible bias among informants are related factors which have to be appreciated. Between 1914 and 1918 the total size of the Navy increased threefold owing to the needs of war. A substantial proportion of those who served for hostilities only may not have accepted the traditional mores of regular lower deck life. At the end of a carefully organised and conducted project, the organiser had no clear idea of whether wartime personnel generally adopted the attitudes of those who had been in the service since they were boys, because the original selection of informants simply did not permit systematic investigation of their particular prejudices. An appropriate selection of sailors to be interviewed would have produced a representative sample of these kinds of informants and thereby provided suitable evidence from which conclusions about this particular question could be drawn. This obviously does not devalue the information for the purposes for which it was recorded, but it does eliminate the range of hypotheses to which this body of data is open. Thus, the project organiser must take into account the relationship between the subject matter of the project and his selection of informants and—at one stage yet farther removed from recording—this involves being clear about the kind of research evidence he is actually seeking to collect.

2. Specification

The list of topics which guided the interviewers' work in the lower deck project is given below, as one example of subject delineation in oral history research. The field of study was first broken down into the following main areas:

a. Background and enlistment
b. Training
c. Dress
d. Ships
e. Work
f. Mess room life
g. Rations and victualling
h. Discipline
i. Religion
j. Traditions and customs
k. Foreign service
l. Home ports
m. Pay and benefits
n. Naval operations
o. Effects of the war
p. Family life
q. Post service experience

Each of these topics was examined in some detail, the extent and nature of which may be demonstrated by one example. Thus, in dealing with the subject of "Discipline," the following questions influenced the interviewers' approach:

a. What was the standard and nature of discipline on the lower deck? Who influenced it? Did it vary much?

b. What were the most common offenses? What were the most extreme? How were they punished?

c. Was the discipline fair? Was it possible to appeal effectively against any unfair treatment, if it occurred?

d. What was the lower deck's attitude to naval police? How much and what sort of power did they have? Did they ever abuse their authority?

e. What were relations like between the lower deck and commissioned officers, "ranker" officers, NCOs, and the Marines?

f. Was there any code of informal discipline or constraint on the lower deck? What kind of behavior was considered unacceptable and how would it be dealt with?

g. Who were the most influential members of the lower deck? Was their influence based on any factors other than rank?

3. Application

While there can be no question that the purposes of oral history research need to be very carefully defined, the way in which project papers should be used is open to variation. Some important work has been done in which listed questions are much more numerous and refined than in the above example and the resultant paper used in the form of a social research questionnaire. While such methods may serve the purposes of some historians, for the wider aims of collecting centres . . . formal questionnaires have not been found suitable. Partly this is because no questionnaire is sufficiently flexible to accommodate, in itself, the unexpected and valuable twists and turns of an informant's memory; and partly it is due to the fact that a questionnaire can become an obstacle to achieving the natural and spontaneous dialogue that is the aim of most oral historians.

But, short of a questionnaire, lists of topics can provide useful guidelines for interviewers to work to. The more interviewers there are engaged on a particular project, the greater becomes the need to ensure consistency of approach. As a device for obtaining such consistency, topic lists have a practical value throughout a recording project. Even with a project which is in the custody of one historian, the construction of a formal research paper is still valuable for reference purposes, because consistency is no less important and only somewhat more certain with one interviewer than with many, in the course of a recording project of any significant scale.

4. Monitoring

It is possible, simply by drawing the interviewers together and taking their reactions, to get an impression of the progress that has been achieved at various stages of the recording programme. However, for the effective monitoring of the project, more systematic aids should be introduced. These are needed because the creation of oral history recordings usually far outstrips that of processing the recorded interviews. Cataloguing, indexing, and transcribing generally lag so far behind recording that the customary aids which give access to the material are not available when they would be most useful for project control.

As an intermediate means of registering the project information as it is being recorded, simple visual aids can be designed which are appropriate to the work being carried out. In the case of the lower deck project the chart reproduced on page 140 was useful as such a tool. When projects are geared to preparatory research papers and control charts of the kind reproduced in Figure 10.1, oral history recording can be effectively monitored and sensibly controlled. At the beginning of the project, the research paper represents the academic definition of the project goals. By careful application in the field, academic prescription and practical possibility can begin to be reconciled. Thus, in the light of early interviewing experience, the list can be altered after some initial application. Certain questions may be modified, some removed, or new questions may be introduced into the initial scheme, until a more refined and useful document emerges.

Informant	Clarke	Ashley	Holt	Boin	Maloney	Burke	Boughton	Clarkson	Basford	Ford	Pullen	Heron	Lazenby	Hutchings	Cox	Leary	Halter	Masters	Adshead	Roberts
Port division	A	B	C	A	A	B	C	B	C	B	A	A	B	B	A	A	C	C	B	C
Branch	B	E	A	C	E	D	C	C	E	F	B	A	B	E	D	A	D	C	F	B
Service: from 19	09	13	17	17	16	08	17	15	08	11	11	18	17	13	18	13	11	12	03	13
to 19	25	19	30	20	19	10	32	37	32	23	24	40	31	22	33	19	24	36	26	25
Interview period	B-C	A-C	B-C	A-B	A-C	C	B-C	B-C	C	B-C	A-C	A-C	B-C	A-C	A-A	B-C	A-C	A-C	C	A-B
Motivation	✔	✔		✔	✔	✔	✔	✔		✔		✔	✔	✔	✔	✔	✔		✔	✔
Boy training	✔	✔	✔	✔	✔	✔		✔	✔	✔		✔	✔	✔	✔	✔	✔		✔	✔
Man training	✔		✔		✔	✔		✔	✔	✔			✔		✔		✔	✔		✔
Dress	✔	✔	✔		✔	✔	✔	✔	✔	✔	✔		✔		✔		✔		✔	
Work		✔		✔		✔	✔			✔				✔	✔	✔			✔	✔
Mess room life		✔			✔	✔	✔			✔	✔	✔	✔		✔		✔			
Food		✔						✔		✔					✔	✔	✔	✔	✔	✔
Discipline	✔	✔	✔	✔	✔	✔		✔	✔			✔	✔	✔	✔			✔		
Religion	✔							✔		✔									✔	✔
Traditions and customs			✔				✔		✔				✔	✔						✔
Foreign stations	AD	AC	CE	AD	A	AC	C	CE	AC	B	C	AD	CE	DE	A	C	AC	D	A	AD
Home ports	✔	✔	✔	✔	✔			✔	✔		✔	✔	✔	✔	✔	✔				
Operations	✔		✔	✔			✔	✔		✔					✔		✔		✔	✔
Effects of war	✔							✔							✔	✔		✔	✔	✔
Pay			✔	✔	✔	✔	✔	✔			✔							✔		
Family life			✔								✔	✔	✔	✔		✔			✔	✔
Port service experience	✔	✔	✔				✔	✔	✔	✔		✔		✔		✔	✔		✔	✔

1. Port division		2. Branch		3. Interview period		4. Foreign stations	
Portsmouth	A	Signals	A	Pre-war	A	China	A
Devonport	B	Torpedo	B	Wartime	B	Cape	B
Chatham	C	Engine room	C	Post-war	C	Mediterranean	C
		Gunnery	D			N. America	D
		Artisan	E			S.E. America	E
		Other	F				

Figure 10.1 Sample control chart

Sensible alterations to the scope of a project cannot be made without a systematic approach of the kind that is implied in the formulation of a project paper.

As recording progresses, a chart of the information being collected permits the monitoring of the project's interim results. The value of the original topics—and their various divisions—should not be treated as inviolate until the work has run its full course. A common experience is that the collection of information in some subject areas reaches a point of saturation before many of the others. Such lines of questioning may be discontinued when there is reasonable certainty that their continuation would be unlikely to add significantly to the information that has already been recorded. The converse is also facilitated by a framework which permits the interim analysis of results. That is to say, areas in which the collection of information has proceeded less satisfactorily can more easily be singled out for greater attention.

Devices of the kind described above are usually essential in the effective management of oral history research. Unless the resources of the collecting centre are untypically lavish, there is usually no other means by which it can be established that the interviewing and recording is achieving the results which were originally sought. It is obviously necessary, through such methods, to be able to control the course of the project and to judge when it may be terminated.

5. Documentation

For the proper assessment and use of oral evidence, the collecting centre should systematically record the project methodology. Without this background information the scholar may not be able to use appropriately the information which has been recorded. What were the aims of the project organiser? By what means were informants selected for interview? What was their individual background? How were the interviews conducted? How was the work as a whole controlled? The more information there is available to answer such questions as these, the more valuable oral history materials will be to the researcher and the more securely he can make use of them in his work.

A formal paper, of the kind recommended earlier, can tell the user a great deal about how the project was structured. A working file will be even more useful, if it reveals the way in which the work evolved (recording what changes were introduced at what stage in the development of the project). Such files should be maintained and regarded as an integral part of the research materials which may be needed by historians.

Individual informant files should also be accessible for research. They should contain biographical details of the informant and also be organised in such a way that the user can correlate tapes or transcripts with places and dates which are covered by the interview. In this respect, interviewers are in a uniquely valuable position to secure a documentary basis of the information they record. Often the informant's memory, photographic and documentary materials in his possession, reference sources, and the interviewer's own subject expertise can be combined to formulate quite a detailed chronology. This will support and give background to the recorded interview.[1]

Similarly, the interview itself should be used as a means of establishing the kind of background information that will give additional significance to the information the informant provides. Thus, in addition to the specific project information the interviewer is seeking, he can with advantage also record details of the informant's place of birth and upbringing, his family background, economic circumstances, educational attainments, occupational experiences, and so on.

Much that an informant says during the course of an interview he may wish to correct, amend, or amplify subsequently. No documentation system would be complete without providing him with the means so to do. The opportunity to listen to or read the completed interview often provides the informant with a considerable stimulus to add to the information which has already been recorded. Once committed to an oral history interview, most informants feel the need for historical exactitude. Collecting centres can maintain their transcripts in pristine condition, whilst also giving informants full opportunity to supplement with written notes the information they have already given, and filing such notes along with the final tapes and transcript.

Notes

1. The outstanding British example of this kind of approach is Dr. Paul Thompson's (University of Essex) study of family life and social history in Edwardian Britain.

11

Introduction to *Tom Rivers*
Saul Benison

An oral history project would ideally engage as a researcher and interviewer someone trained both as a professional oral historian and as an expert in the subject being examined. Our next selection shows what can be realized under these conditions, given substantial financial support.

Saul Benison's biography of Tom Rivers demonstrates the results possible when a specialist designs a closely researched agenda of questions. Benison's approach requires an exactingly prepared interviewer who not only shapes the reminiscence with background facts but also annotates it by including footnoted material which contradicts or explains his narrator's comments. The reader should observe the ways in which the author's notes stand in an unusual counterpoint to Dr. Rivers' recollections.

This introduction affords an example of a carefully executed interview history, describing the circumstances of the interview and both the character and mood of the interviewee as they relate to the interview context, and indicating the approach taken to editing.

Saul Benison is Professor of the History of Science and Environmental Health at the University of Cincinnati. He has written an oral history memoir of Dr. Albert Sabin and the first volume of a biography of Dr. Walter Bradford.

Saul Benison's introduction to *Tom Rivers: Reflections on a Life in Medicine and Science* (Cambridge, Mass.: MIT Press, 1967) is reprinted by permission of the author and MIT Press.

Whoever elects to study history, as far as I am concerned, may bring to bear the most pathetic and childish belief in the classifying power of our spirit and methods, but apart from this and in spite of it he should have respect for the incomprehensible truth, reality, and singularity of events. To deal with history, my friend, is no jest and no irresponsible game.

Hermann Hesse, *Magister Ludi*

Historyans is like doctors. They are always looking f'r symptoms. Those iv them that writes about their own times examines th'tongue an' feels th' pulse an' makes a wrong dygnosis. Th' other kind iv histhry is a post mortem examination. It tells ye what a counthry died iv. But I'd like to know what it lived iv.

Peter Finley Dunne, *Observations by Mr. Dooley*

O n February 5, 1962, 100 distinguished microbiologists, virologists, and biochemists, including four Nobel laureates, met in a New York hotel to pay tribute to Dr. Thomas Rivers, a member emeritus of the Rockefeller Institute for Medical Research. A fifth Nobel laureate, Dr. John Enders, ill in Boston and unable to attend the festivities, telegraphed the following message to Dr. Rivers: "We the members of the church salute the apostolic father."

The recognition that Dr. Enders and others accorded Dr. Rivers that day was singularly appropriate. For a period of almost 40 years, Dr. Rivers had been a dominant figure both as an investigator and as an administrator in virus research in the United States. Three months later, at the age of 73, he was dead. Dr. Rivers' death did not mark the end of one era in virology or the beginning of another. His career in essence spanned the development of virology from its status at the beginning of the twentieth century as an adjunct to bacteriological study to its current position as an independent discipline, as much concerned with the fundamental problems posed by molecular biology as with the diseases caused by viral agents.

This oral history memoir is an attempt to chart the evolution of Dr. Rivers' career. Oral history is a relatively new phenomenon in American historiography, and a note as to its development, purpose, and procedures may serve to put Dr. Rivers' memoir in perspective. In 1938 Professor Allan Nevins, in his handbook of historiography, *The Gateway to History,* urged his fellow historians to establish an organization which would make a systematic attempt to obtain from the lips and papers of living Americans an expansive personal record of their participation in the political, economic, and cultural life of the nation. It was his hope that in this way a unique archive of autobiographical material might be prepared for the use of future historians. There was precedence for Professor Nevins' proposal. Autobiography was an old and vital tradition in western historiography. Further, during the 1920s several notable projects had been organized for the collection of autobiographies to elucidate the history of psychology and medicine. Equally important, other social scientists, in particular anthropologists and folklorists, had long demonstrated the usefulness of oral traditions for historical research.

Professor Nevins' proposals, however, elicited little enthusiasm from his contemporaries. Some voiced reservations about the wisdom of having historians gather memoirs from the living. They felt that such a procedure would of necessity compromise the historians' objectivity and in the end lead to the production of self-serving, partisan accounts of recent events. Others argued that historians had neither the skills nor funds necessary to capture autobiographical interviews verbatim. In spite of these and other objections, Professor Nevins continued to proselytize for his idea. In 1948, soon after the tape recorder was perfected for commercial use, he secured funds from several foundations and established an oral history research office at Columbia University to carry out the plans he had projected a decade before. Professor Nevins' persistence not only showed a belief in his own original vision and purpose, it also reflected the growing need of those who worked in contemporary history to find a way of coping with some of the complexities created for historical research by modern technology.

Historians are agreed that modern society rests in part on foundations created by printing and paper making. These are important not only because they rank among the oldest of modern industrial processes but because they also serve as catalysts of human thought. Newspapers, magazines, books, and a vast mechanically produced correspondence can testify to the pervasiveness of print and paper communication in all facets of our daily public and private life. Indeed the one constant result of both business and government seems to be the production of new records. It is a condition which has provoked some archivists to make the irreverent suggestion that the best possible thing that could happen to modern historical records was a good fire.

Paradoxically, the industrial process which has created this superabundance of records has also produced a technology which threatens to deprive the historian in future of a great deal of the substance, detail, and variety usually found in the process of human events. This technology, of which the automobile, airliner, radio, television, and telephone are but a part, has created a revolution in communication that has made the world smaller, changed the tempo of living, and transformed the nature and uses of time. Its hallmark is talk. As a result of new sound and visual communication, much of the detail of human experience, which was previously put to paper because of the exclusive nature of print and writing communication, has today been sapped from the record and become fleeting and ephemeral. Such experience, if preserved at all, is only to be found in the memory of living men. It is this paradox of simultaneous plenty and scarcity in contemporary records that in large measures defines the tasks of those who work in oral history.

In an important sense oral history is misnamed. While it is true that the oral historian helps gather an oral memoir, it is equally true that such an account is based on a written record. It is precisely this record which ultimately determines the course and substance of his work. That work may be divided into four parts. Once a subject has been chosen to be interviewed, the oral historian, like any other historian, must prepare himself in extant primary and secondary source material so as to see and define relevant historical relationships and problems. Second, armed with a tape recorder, he must so handle himself and his preparation as to spur the chosen subject's memory of past events. Third, he must gather from his subjects, and other people, supporting documents of contemporary demonstration, both as a check on the tenuousness of memory and to supplement the account gathered. Fourth, he must edit or aid the subject in editing the final preparation of the memoir so that it says what the subject wants it to say.

The memoir that emerges as a result of this process is a new kind of historical document. Although it has been created by a participant in past events, it is also the creation of the historian-interviewer who has in fact determined the historical problems and relationships to be examined. This mutual creation contributes to both the strength and weakness inherent in oral history memoirs. And it is for this reason that the circumstances surrounding the production of any given memoir must be clearly set forth. The events leading to the creation of Dr. Rivers' memoir were these.

In the spring of 1961, soon after beginning research on a projected history of poliomyelitis and The National Foundation, I asked Dr. Rivers, then Vice President for Medical Affairs of The National Foundation, to allow me to record his memoirs. This was not the first such request I had made of Dr. Rivers. Five years before, while gathering medical and other scientific memoirs for the Oral History Research Office at Columbia University, I had presented a similar petition and was refused. This time he consented. I was helped in obtaining that decision by an untoward circumstance. A short time before I had approached Dr. Rivers, he was operated on for a malignancy in one of his lungs. It so happened that on the day I met with him he was more than usually bored by the inactivity that convalescence had forced on him, and he seized on my request as a way of escaping the confinement of recovery. Dr. Rivers' consent was not without restrictions. Although he agreed to talk with me about his career in science, he stipulated that under no circumstances would he speak to me of his family or his private life. When I remonstrated that posterity would never believe that he had appeared, fully grown and armed, from Zeus' forehead, he agreed to tell me a little about his father and mother, but nothing more. Both the circumstance of Dr. Rivers' illness and the restrictions he placed on our talks are important because they serve to explain some of the content of his memoirs.

By nature Dr. Rivers was a curmudgeon.[1] He had a keen critical mind, possessed a waspish tongue, and loved a good fight. His illness accented some of these characteristics. Further, from the beginning of his illness he knew he was suffering from a malignancy. While he initially hoped that the operation he had undergone might stem its development, by the end of the summer of 1961 he knew he did not have long to live. These circumstances not only contributed to his candor about himself and his work, they also encouraged him to make uninhibited comments and judgments about people he knew in science—comments that in ordinary circumstances might have been more discreet. His illness affected the conduct of the interviews as well. Although on several occasions I saw Dr. Rivers socially in his home, at no time would he permit interviews to be held there. All interviews were held in his office at The National Foundation or his offices and sickroom at the Rockefeller Hospital. I felt that he insisted on this for two reasons. First, it allowed him to keep the interviews on a formal plane, and second, by arranging interviews in his office he created an added incentive for himself to carry on his daily activities as he had before his operation. In the last seven months of his life he came into his office at The National Foundation five days a week until his illness required hospitalization two weeks before his death.

I particularly regretted Dr. Rivers' decision not to speak about his family and private life, because it meant that I was unable to examine with him his home environment and the larger social environment of the New South in which he came of age. More important, it prevented me from discussing with him his social beliefs or examining the impact of his scientific career on those beliefs.

As a result of both Dr. Rivers' restrictions and my ultimate purpose in writing a history of poliomyelitis and The National Foundation, I concentrated my interviews on four basic subjects or problems: the development of Dr. Rivers' medical and scientific education, the evolution of his virus research, an examination of those scientific institutions and organizations in which he had played a singular or important role, and finally an examination of problems in the administration of scientific research, as exemplified by the development of polio research during the 1940s and '50s.

My preparation for the interviews began several months before the first interview actually took place and was continued throughout the course of the interviews, a period of approximately 15 months. Interviews were so arranged as to facilitate research and were usually held at the beginning and end of each week. In general, the interviews ran for no longer than an hour, though an occasional one ran for an hour and a half or an hour and three-quarters.

At the end of each interview I would not only outline for Dr. Rivers the subject matter or problems that the next interview would cover, I would also supply him with copies of letters, documents, and scientific papers that might serve to refresh his memory. For his part, Dr. Rivers would frequently direct my attention to material that he thought might be useful to me in my preparation. In this sense the interviews were "prepared." At every interview I came armed with relevant books and documentary material so that if the need to look at or quote from such material arose it was immediately to hand. On several occasions Dr. Rivers quoted passages from such documents or books or asked that such material be inserted later in the memoir. Once an interview was completed, it was immediately transcribed.

While the end product of oral history often looks neat and logical, the process itself isn't, because man's memory and the course of conversation are frequently untidy. Although I tried to examine all subjects and problems with Dr. Rivers chronologically, so as to establish a rudimentary outline of development, I was not always successful. Often during the pursuit of a subject, both Dr. Rivers and I were led by the nature of conversation and subject matter into making digressions. At times Dr. Rivers would repeat himself. On other occasions he would forget a precise date or name of a person. At such times he would ask me to find the date or name and insert it in the memoir. Such forgetfulness is common at any age and was in no sense characteristic of Dr. Rivers' memory. His recall of substantive matters was prodigious—so much so that it was often a conversation piece among his long-time colleagues at the Rockefeller Institute and his associates at The National Foundation.

When interviews on a given subject were completed, I edited that portion of the transcript and submitted it to Dr. Rivers for his approval. My editing chores in the main consisted in arranging the material in chronological and chapter order, eliminating repetitious material, and inserting blank dates and names. No attempt was made to alter Dr. Rivers' language, or to make him grammatical, nor were the expletives and other expressions he was fond of eliminated. Errors of fact and interpretation, even when known to be errors, were kept because such mistakes were often revealing of the man and his thought. These I have footnoted *passim*.

In the end my method of proceeding chronologically and editing the transcript while the interviews were still in progress worked against me, because Dr. Rivers died before I could carry my investigations and interviews much beyond 1958. I was unable therefore to examine with Dr. Rivers at least two important subjects, the development of the Sabin vaccine after 1958 and the scientific background of the decision of The National Foundation to enter the field of birth defects and arthritis.

After Dr. Rivers' death, I sent portions of his memoir to several of his former colleagues and friends mentioned in the text for critical comment. Among those who commented on the manuscript were Dr. Peter Olitsky, Dr. Peyton Rous, Dr.

John Enders, Dr. Joseph Stokes, Jr., Dr. Albert Sabin, Dr. David Bodian, Dr. Hilary Koprowski, Dr. Thomas Turner, Dr. Jonas Salk, Dr. Joseph Smadel, Dr. Harry Weaver, and Dr. Walter Schlesinger. They sent valuable critical material which is appended in various footnotes throughout the text.

It is an impertinence to tell a reader how to read a book. The nature of a book, however, must be understood. Dr. Rivers' oral history memoir is an account of some aspects of the recent history of American virology from a particular moment in time filtered by individual experience. In no sense is it presented as an exclusive historical source. It is rather a corroborative source and guide. As such it is a beginning of interpretation, not an end.

Notes

1. Dr. Richard Shope, a long-time associate of Dr. Rivers at the Rockefeller Institute, characterized him as follows in a biographical notice he wrote soon after Dr. Rivers' death. "Although Dr. Rivers was by nature a friendly person, he had the capacity of being irascible and pugnacious. He was a difficult and formidable person to oppose and could be stubbornly inflexible in maintaining a position. His discussion at scientific meetings of findings with which he disagreed could on occasion be so stinging that the audience, even though realizing the correctness of Rivers' position, often had their personal sympathies entirely with Rivers' opponent. Many of those who have known Dr. Rivers best have felt the sting that he could so picturesquely deliver in an argument. Few of us have had the nerve openly to side with his opposition in one of these 'knock down' and 'drag out' discussions" (R. E. Shope, "Tom Rivers," *Journal of Bacteriology* 84 [1962], pp. 385–88).

12

Theory, Method, and Oral History

Peter Friedlander

Our third approach to oral history project design is a theoretical essay from The Emergence of a UAW Local *by historian Peter Friedlander. The author challenges the prevailing view of the oral history interviewer as the miner of facts from an interviewee's memory. Instead, Friedlander suggests, we should rethink the process: the interviewer (by his or her questions) and the interviewee (by his or her answers) participate jointly in the manufacture of a historical fact—"The problem of the interpretation of facts is bound up with the manner of their production: they arise out of a matrix of meaning."*

In this complex work of oral historiography, Friedlander borrows insights from linguistic and anthropological theory to pose some tough questions for oral historians: what is the significance of the collaboration between interviewer and interviewee in generating history? Does the structure of human memory affect history made of reminiscence? The following text represents only a small portion of the introduction to this important book, which has attracted attention among the more theoretically inclined researchers studying oral history.

Peter Friedlander's research crosses the boundaries of anthropology and history, such as in his article, "The Origins of the Welfare State, 1910–1937." He has taught at the Weekend College of Wayne State University in Detroit, Michigan.

*T*his account of the emergence of Local 229 of the United Automobile Workers is based on a lengthy and detailed collaboration with Edmund Kord, the president of the local during most of its first 18 years, since the 1930s. Because there is little documentary evidence bearing directly on the history of this local,[1] I have had to rely almost entirely on Kord's memory. For this reason I think I owe the reader an explanation of the nature and extent of these discussions and communications with Kord, so that the limitations of this study will be clear.

In December 1972 Kord and I spent eight days together on the east side of Detroit. At that time I took notes of our discussions, and Kord showed me the plant and the surrounding neighborhood in Hamtramck, pointed out the important bars, and described such details as the configuration of workers in front of the gate during strikes. I wrote a draft based on this material and on [Constance] Tonat's dissertation. I sent this to Kord, along with a set of questions, for comments and criticism. On the basis of his response to these I constructed a further set of questions and sent them to him. Later, in late June of 1973, we spent a week together. This time I recorded our conversations on about eight hours of tapes. These were then transcribed and reordered in a rough narrative sequence and in this form became the basis for the major series of communications: an extensive correspondence occupying 75 pages. A draft of the first three chapters was then drawn up and submitted to Kord for comments and corrections. Following this we met for a week in January 1974 and two days in March 1974. Again the conversations were recorded. Finally, to fill some gaps which became apparent in the course of drawing up the final draft, Kord and I had six recorded telephone conversations totaling about four hours. What follows, therefore, is the outcome of a lengthy collaboration extending from December 1972 to March 1974.

The extent of Kord's knowledge of events in the plant varied in relation to the location of those events. Kord, who was a grinder in the torchwelding department, had an intimate knowledge of his own department and a substantial, but less intimate, knowledge of the adjacent press departments, based on direct contact and close observation. His knowledge of the front of the shop—frontwelding and departments 16 and 18—was gained mainly through discussions at the time with activists and leaders in that part of the shop, although he possessed a good deal of direct knowledge even there. However, Kord's knowledge of both the toolroom and the inspection department in the early period of the union's history, with which the first chapters of this book are concerned, was limited not only by their physical distance from his own department, but also by the resistance to unionization exhibited by these two departments.

Nevertheless, because of the nature of the questions which I sought to answer in this study, the limitations imposed by the character of the evidence have little significance: not only is the necessary information unavailable except in the form of the memories of participants; it emerges only through a critical dialogue.[2] Therefore I did not simply ask questions of Kord or solicit his reminiscences. On the contrary, I sought to bring to bear on Kord's experience a number of theoretical and historical conceptions which I thought critical to an understanding of the CIO [Congress of Industrial Organizations]—conceptions which I found myself forced to alter as my increasingly concrete information obstinately refused to fall into some of my prefabricated categories.

Even if, for example, a certain amount of "hard" evidence were available, say in the form of census data for the plant, it would be of almost no use. The census would only distinguish between foreign-born and native-born of foreign or mixed parentage. Yet among the latter, it turns out, there were at least three distinct groups of young, unskilled second generation Polish workers: (1) those who were helpers in front—welding and who expected to be promoted to welders (the most highly skilled production work in the plant), (2) those unskilled press operators who were in their middle 20s, who had left their parental homes, and who were married or planning to get married, and (3) those who were just out of high school (or who had dropped out) and who were members of neighborhood gangs and barroom cliques. Obviously, this kind of information cannot be gleaned from available documentary evidence.

The same problems emerge in regard to other major questions. What was the subjective, psychological content of relationships to authority, and how did this change in the course of the organizing effort? Who were the leaders: what was the inner structure of leadership, conceived of as a social formation, and how did it emerge from the matrix of social relations in the plant? What was the role of leadership, and to what extent did the leaders act or seem to act independently of their followers? How did the various groups of workers conceive of their struggle for power, and what impact did that struggle have on their personal lives and social outlooks? Until recently, the major current in labor historiography has been frankly institutional in orientation, yet the emergence of institutions is only an aspect of a more complex social process. What are the sources of institutionalization, and what is its relationship to the broader social process out of which institutions emerge? . . .

The foregoing briefly summarizes the theoretical intent of this study. Because of the nature of this investigation, however, the problem of methodology is intimately connected with the pursuit of these theoretical purposes. Since this work is almost entirely dependent on oral sources and on memory, questions emerge about the structure and reliability of memory and about the nature of the interview process itself—a problem which occupies the middle (and perhaps hybrid) ground between epistemology and linguistic philosophy, on the one hand, and more orthodox historiography on the other. For the problem which we face arises not so much out of the interpretation of data as in its creation. And because the interview process is above all linguistic, language itself becomes a methodological problem.

Superficially, of course, Kord and I shared the same language: everyday English. Moreover, Kord's cultural and social background is fairly close to that of my own family, so that, even if the results of this study might be called ethnographic, the environment I chose to study was familiar. Thus, in the collaboration which we undertook, I brought my own curiosity, informed and disciplined by a specific body of knowledge, a theoretical framework, and a rudimentary method of investigation. To these Kord added his own background in history and theory, the consequences of his father's Socialist culture, his mother's broad intellectual and cultural interests, his own schooling, his intellectual experience in the Socialist party, and, above all, his experience not merely as a participant but as the architect of Local 229. Because of Kord's cosmopolitan, rationalist background, we were able to establish a theoretical framework within which to discuss and interpret such cultural phenomena as the differences between Polish immigrants and their children. Such a theoretical framework is a vital necessity if a discussion is to get beyond the primitive stage of collecting anecdotes.

Yet in spite of this common ground, we initially had considerable difficulty with language and meaning: for history as a discipline has its own language, its canon of interpretation, its collection of problems occupying the forefront of contemporary inquiry. And my approach, a Hegelian Marxism greatly influenced by phenomenology, linguistic philosophy, and structuralism, at first only intensified this problem. Yet if the work of generating a theoretically meaningful account of the development of Kord's local union was to progress, a common language had to emerge out of our collaboration, one whose logic and terms of description would be clear and unambiguous to each of us, and within the framework of which our discussion could proceed with precision. While explicit discussion of theory would help to clarify the problems which I was concerned with, the actual emergence of our common language, and its verification, came only after months of "practice."[3] If at first our discussions seemed unclear and unfocused— if we had difficulty understanding each other—by the mid-point of our collaboration we had arrived at a sufficiently clear language and had eliminated a number of extraneous or irrelevant avenues of investigation, so that both question and answer seemed increasingly to be complementary moments in a more integrated historical discourse involving the two of us. The clarity of theoretical focus which developed, in fact, was an important part of the development of our common language.

It was within the framework of linguistic interaction that "data" was produced: since few facts existed, we had to create them. This is less arbitrary than it seems. A census enumerator, for example, does not merely collect data. Rather, standing behind him are not only the census bureau and its staff of statisticians, but also a cultural matrix and an administrative purpose which give a specific shape to certain perceptions of family structure, nationality, education, etc. Likewise, a newspaper account is hardly "factual"; it is a reporter's impression, which is itself the outcome of his predisposition to view people and situations in a certain way. Even the "obvious" fact that there were a certain number of paid-up members in the union at a particular time is a fact only because someone looked at the situation in a certain way and made an observation. (Even such hard observations can dissolve into a welter of complex, uncertain shadings and contradictory meanings when one begins to focus more closely on the phenomenology of social processes.) If, for example, the designer of the census was oblivious to the fact that Lutheran Slovaks lived in a different cultural, political, and social world than Catholic Slovaks, and that Bohemian Freethinkers were quite unlike both, the resulting category, Czechoslovak, is not only limited in its historical usefulness, but is misleading and mythological.

Thus, the historian who deals with artifacts is restricted to bringing his own intellectual apparatus to bear, not on the object itself (an epistemological fantasy at any rate), but on another object: the result of a previous process of abstraction. The limitations of depending on traditional sources are therefore obvious. . . .

How reliable is Kord's memory? This is a problem which encompasses any oral history project, and it must be dealt with forthrightly. [John] Kruchko has observed that, in his interviews with veterans of the struggle to organize UAW Local 674 in Norwood, Ohio, "the memories of the men . . . even down to small details, were surprisingly accurate."[4] I found the same to be true of Kord. The depth and intensity of his involvement was such that even now, 36 years later, his remembrances are both vivid and detailed.

Nevertheless, memory does not provide us with the kind of pinpoint accuracy found in documentary evidence. Kord's margin of error in the precontract period, he estimates, is of the order of several days to two weeks. Thus, I refer to a meeting which was held during the last part of February, for example. How important such a margin of error is depends upon how well Kord could recall the dramatic sequence of events not only in terms of order, but also in terms of the tempo and dynamic of development. In this regard Kord's memory was generally clear and unambiguous, and he was quite certain of all but a handful of minor points. Nevertheless, in addition to the external verification, which was found in the few sources which relate to Local 229 and which appears in the footnotes, a system of internal checking was also used. As the broad picture began to emerge in the course of our discussions and correspondence, I in effect "cross-examined" Kord. In general, the contradictions which I found were relatively minor, more often than not based on misunderstandings. In addition, these contradictions were ironed out early in the course of our work: Kord, having become deeply involved in this endeavor, began to do his own checking. Wherever any uncertainty has remained, it is indicated.

Yet if the contents of memory are simply "facts" as discussed above, we would find ourselves in the same situation which obtains when dealing with more orthodox sources. But while the structure of memory is related to the structure of perception and the latter is itself rooted in culture, education, and experience (native American informants, for example, are extraordinarily unperceptive about Slavs), memory itself is a vast welter of impressions and feelings, as well as a more structured, rational schemata. Many impressions either were not important to Kord in 1937 or did not appear to make any sense; yet, as we brought them to the foreground their possible interconnectedness and meaning emerged. Furthermore, the elaboration of this matrix of meaning and the gradual construction of the history of the local reacted back upon the original source, Kord's memory. As a consequence, Kord's recollections became richer and more precise, and the elaboration of a number of hypotheses gave a critical focus to his effort to recall. And precisely because memory is richer than the rational narrative superstructure to which it is often reduced, the whole enterprise remained openended: there were numerous ways of structuring the material. What it would become depended on how we approached our work, what leads we followed, and what problems concerned us. For example, I continued to press for cultural and psychological data on as many workers as Kord could remember, especially the primary and secondary leadership. Certain Freudian and Weberian concerns led me to ask particular kinds of questions (e.g., about personal habits such as drinking). These questions themselves emerged in my own thought only over a period of many months, and the responses to them were by no means immediately intelligible. I was looking for patterns and relationships. At first, however, the material was necessarily fragmentary; then, after more such questions and answers had accumulated, the material became less fragmentary, but it was still difficult to penetrate. Only gradually did patterns emerge relating some characteristics of personality with certain aspects of the history of the local.

Two further examples help clarify the relationship between memory and theory. In the course of our first series of discussions in December 1972, Kord made a remark about "new hires" in department 19 (in the spring of 1937). The remark registered, but I let it go by. Later, as we continued to discuss the situation in the plant, "new hires" came up again. What gave the department where these employees worked its peculiar character was the fact that they were members of neighborhood gangs. Yet what I had at this point was not a concept of a social group, but rather the understanding that very likely these gang kids were in fact a group, that they had to be studied further, and that out of all this a concept might emerge. In the next series of discussions and in the 75 pages of letters which I sent to Kord, whenever relevant I brought up questions relating to these young workers. What did they say to the foreman under certain circumstances? What forms of recreation did they engage in? Where did they live, and under what circumstances? What were their attitudes toward the union effort at specific times? How did they react to the five-cent raise? The results of such inquiry are contained in the body of the book.

Another determination I sought out more purposefully. I was convinced that there were significant ethical or moral differences between the Appalachian migrants, the first-generation Slavs, and the wildcatters among the second generation. Twice in the course of our second series of discussions (July 1973) I raised this question. Twice Kord replied negatively. The third time, however, something clicked. Kord briefly but cogently described actual confrontations, quoted typical statements made by representative members of the three groups, and described the interrelationship of these groups within the union and their different relationships to the leadership in confrontation situations. Further, he discussed their varying attitudes toward authority, both that of the management and that of the union leaders, and their conceptions of society, of the individual, and of standards of behavior.

This example illustrates both the obstacles to and the immense potential of this kind of investigation. The process of searching, guessing, hypothesizing, and probing which the historian must undertake depends for its success on the degree to which his collaborator is willing to get involved in these questions. Often the relevance of what I asked was not obvious, and some of the more exciting questions were obscure and even ambiguous. To make sense out of some of my questions required that Kord search his memory for any evidence which might have had a bearing on the question, sort it out, and verbalize it. If these cultural differences were not clear at the time, then Kord's cognitive processes did not organize his perceptions along such lines. Such an organization of perceptions, drawn from the complex welter of memory, was precisely what I asked of Kord. And it was here that a real dialectic unfolded, in the course of which we collectively shaped both concept and perception, batting ideas and observations around, exploring their significance, and conceiving of new questions as material developed.

From the foregoing, it is obvious that, if certain problems are to be explored at all, they must be investigated through the use of oral history techniques: the usual sources which historians traditionally rely upon simply fail to throw any light on some of the most fundamental historical processes. Yet even in those areas of data collection where the census is thought to excel, oral history techniques are far more accurate than any but the most accurate hypothetical census. For example, we have already seen one of the problems with the census—its tendency to amalgamate under a single category (such as Czechoslovak) several distinct and often contradictory social groups. Beyond this, however, even if the ethnic composition of a factory were known to a high degree of precision, its relevance would remain dubious. Of what value would be the knowledge that 30 percent of the workers in a particular plant were Polish, if we knew from previous investigations that this geographical unit was far too large to be meaningful? On the other hand, the response of an informant that a single department, say metal-finishing, possessed a work force which was 90 percent Polish might be off by a few points, or even by as much as 10 or 15 percent, but it would be far closer to the truth than the census estimate, which would be unable to go any farther than specifying that 30 percent of the workers *in the plant* were Polish. When one realizes that each department possessed a very specialized ethnic structure, it becomes obvious that if one is to write the social history of the organization of a factory, one must have this information; and from the standpoint of the historian, such data, regardless of the greater margin of error of this technique, is far more useful and indeed, from a historiographical standpoint, far more accurate than the results of a hypothetical census based on plant-wide surveys.[5]

To meaningfully describe patterns of behavior or to analyze the structure of an event are objectives which often lie beyond the reach of orthodox uses of data, particularly when one's interest shifts from the various intellectual, social, and political elites to the industrial working class. In the present study, for example, a critical union action inside the plant is met with strikingly different positive responses on the part of the first and the second-generation Poles. Such occurrences provide invaluable materials out of which to develop a sense of the interaction of the various political cultures within the plant—or they even permit one to define such cultures in the first place.

Nevertheless, in the conduct of a series of interviews it is important to maintain a critical attitude. Failure to cross-examine can lead to astonishing reversals of fact. For example, in an interview by Jack Skeels of Frank Fagan, a unionist active in the Murray Body plant during the formative years of the UAW, an entirely different story emerges from that found in my own interviews with Fagan.[6] In the Skeels version, an incident in 1933 in which Fagan organized a petition campaign among 30 welders asking for company-supplied leather armlets to protect their clothing and arms from red-hot sparks resulted in the firing of Fagan and another worker. This event, according to Fagan, "broke the back of the men." In this section of the interview, Skeels himself intervened very infrequently, resulting in long periods of unbroken reminiscences which were left to stand as they were, with no effort made at cross-examination or elicitation of detail.

Unprepared for what was to follow, I reopened the question of the leather armlet incident with Fagan, mainly in order to investigate the ethnic background of the workers involved and the structure of the event. This 18-minute section of the interview began with a discussion of the year. Fagan thought that it was 1935. I told him that in his previous interview he had said 1933. He was unable to remember that interview, but began to fix the leather armlet incident in relation to other events, finally settling on 1935 as the most likely year. The story then unfolded in great detail; I constantly asked for more bits of information—the names of people, descriptions of the welding process and the problem it posed in terms of burning holes in the welders' shirts, etc. Then I asked Fagan to remember as many individuals as he could who were working on the same line and who got involved in the petition incident. At this point the interview makes for poor reading: long periods of silence, punctuated first by one name—about whom I asked such details as ethnic background and union experience—then by another name, the whole liberally sprinkled with remarks by Fagan that this was a long time back and was hard to remember, yet at the same time that he could visualize all of the welders involved in the incident. Nevertheless, he succeeded in remembering eight others besides himself. He described the incident itself: the misgivings of many of the workers about signing the petition, its delivery, and the response of the personnel manager to Fagan and his co-worker Udata as he politely threw them out onto the street. From this point on, however, the story directly contradicts the earlier version told to Skeels. Following the firing of Fagan and Udata, some of the welders began a job action, letting the arcs of flame get too big and burning holes in the automobile bodies, as a result of which production of the entire plant was piling up in the repair shop. The foreman told all the welders to go home and to behave themselves when they returned the next day. Alex Faulkner replied (as was reported to Fagan a few days later) that Fagan and Udata both better be at work too. Within a couple of days the company had gotten in touch with Fagan and rehired him. When Fagan returned to work, however, the other workers wanted to know where Udata was, and Fagan, after a visit to Udata's home, ascertained that Udata had gotten another job, not wanting to return to Murray Body. Only then did the tension subside.

The point of retelling this story is to illustrate some of the pitfalls of writing oral history. Memory is a treacherous thing, as more than one of my informants has remarked. The necessity for cross-examination, digging for details, and even confronting an interviewee with contradictory evidence, is critical. It is important *before* the interview to get deeply into the documentary materials relevant to an interviewee's experience, to anticipate several strategies of questioning, and to be prepared with a battery of questions which are derived from the historian's special understanding of social phenomena. It is equally necessary to be alert to the possibility that an offhand remark may contain an important clue, the consequences of which may be totally unexpected and even contrary to some basic assumptions. In general, the historian must counterpose his *intensive* approach to the *extensive* narrative which tends to be the spontaneous response of most informants. Thus, in the Skeels interviews, there are numerous junctures in which an informant reveals something of critical significance. Instead of interceding and sharpening the focus of the discussion, Skeels let these things go by. In fairness to Skeels, of course, we should remember that many of these theoretical concerns are of recent origin. Nevertheless, as the leather armlet incident indicates, there may be some question about the accuracy of interviews conducted in an expansive narrative style, rather than through intensive cross-examination.

Notes

1. This evidence includes Constance S. Tonat, "A Case Study of a Local Union: Participation, Loyalty and Attitudes of Local Union Members" (master's thesis, Wayne State University, Detroit, 1956), which is based on a study of Local 229; a few brief notices which appeared in the *United Automobile Worker* between 1938 and 1940; and a collection of correspondence found in the George F. Addes Papers on deposit at the Archives of Labor History and Urban Affairs at Wayne State University (henceforth cited as Archives).

2. The material contained in the Archives pertaining to Local 229 is sparse. Even in regard to two of the most thoroughly documented locals—Local 51 (Plymouth) and Local 3 (Dodge)—the materials available are of such character as to render impossible any attempt at answering the questions posed in the present study.

3. The problem of language as practice in this sense is one of the central points of Ludwig Wittgenstein, *Philosophical Investigations* (Oxford: Basil Blackwell, 1963).

4. John G. Kruchko, *The Birth of a Union Local: The History of UAW Local 674, Norwood, Ohio, 1933–1940* (Ithaca, N.Y.: New York State School of Industrial and Labor Relations, Cornell University, 1972), p. iii.

5. The following is an example of the generation of data. The excerpts are from my interview with Frank Fagan of August 9, 1974. Fagan was active in Murray Body during the formative years of the UAW.

FAGAN: In Murray there was a predominance of Polish people. And I always had the feeling that they—although I don't know this to be a fact—they're all pretty close. Nearly all lived in Hamtramck, which was nearby. . . . There seemed to be a predominance of Polish—I realized that when I first got active in the union when we actually got recognized and I had to keep book as a steward.

FRIEDLANDER: Steward in the welding department?

FAGAN: I covered quite a large building. I'm talking now about after we organized the union . . . later 1937, late '36. I know I had a predominance of Polish there, because I had trouble with the names. . . .

FRIEDLANDER: When you shouldered union responsibilities and you were going around and checking up on people, how widely did you travel in body in white?

FAGAN: The whole thing.

FRIEDLANDER: I assume you know that best then?

FAGAN: Yeah. . . .

FRIEDLANDER: I find that there's a lot of Hungarians floating around metal-finishing. Now is that true here?

FAGAN: I, I don't . . . I'm sitting here thinking about the metal-finishing gang, all the guys on the different floors that I knew. I don't recall a metal finisher that wasn't a great big strong Polish fella in Murray Body.

FRIEDLANDER: So they're all Polish in Murray Body?

FAGAN: Yeah. Come to think of it . . . I'm just thinking about all the lists of names of the metal finishers, because I used to list them for wage negotiations, always trying to get them up higher.

FRIEDLANDER: I just want to double-check something. There's no chance of your confusing a Polish name with some other Slavic nationality?

FAGAN: There's that possibility, but not very great possibility. I knew everyone.

FRIEDLANDER: Between Yugoslav on the one hand, and Rumanian and Hungarian on the other hand. . . .

FAGAN: No, I don't think I could have made that mistake. There might have been some, but I doubt it very much. It just seems to me they were nearly all Polish. Even the foremen. . . . I don't think—I can't recall anyone that I don't know—because we had a lot of affairs going where we needed their names and that sort of thing.

   6. Interview with Frank Fagan, February 19, 1963, Archives, pp. 10–11.

13

Reflections on Ethics
Amelia Fry

The final essay on designing oral history discusses ethics, a part of project design often overlooked in the initial stages of planning. The national scandal concerning Richard Nixon's presidency provides the backdrop for this statement by Amelia Fry, veteran interviewer.

Taking in turn the rights and responsibilities of interviewees, interviewers, and institutions, Fry discusses the dilemmas which arise daily during efforts to work within the principled guidelines of the profession, the Goals and Guidelines of the Oral History Association. The author sets up a dialogue with the reader, posing real-life difficulties which bedevil professional oral historians. Like Friedlander, Fry recognizes the collaborative nature of the oral history process, which requires interviewers—as the more experienced partners—to educate narrators as to the implications of their accounts. Just as doctors try to obtain an "informed consent" before operations, so oral historians should be sensitive to the danger of victimizing or harming interviewees in the quest for historical fact.

Amelia Fry has conducted interviews and directed projects for the Regional Oral History Office at the University of California, Berkeley, since 1959. She has taught oral history institutes and workshops for the Oral History Association and the University of Vermont and has contributed articles on oral history to a wide variety of professional journals. She wrote a biography of Alice Paul, a spin-off from her oral history project on the Suffragists.

"Reflections on Ethics" by Amelia Fry first appeared in *Oral History Review* 3 (1975), pp. 17–28. It is reprinted by permission of the author and the Oral History Association.

*Reflection: an action of the mind whereby we obtain a clearer view of our rela-
tion to the things of yesterday and are able to avoid the perils that we shall not
again encounter.*

Ambrose Bierce, *The Devil's Dictionary*

Watergate made us question anew the ethics governing American life. Oral history, too, has received its share of scrutiny. Although stemming partially from Watergate, it has also sprung from an accumulation of questions oral historians have evolved from years of collective experience.

Uncertainty about fair practices was a recurring theme of the 1974 Oral History Workshop and Colloquium at Jackson Lake Lodge. Discussions ranged from lively rump sessions in the lobby to hushed debates in hallways outside the meetings, to the formal sessions themselves. One of the first acts of the new president, Samuel Proctor, was to appoint a committee to revise, and, if necessary, augment the OHA's present one-page statement of ethics called *Goals and Guidelines*.

A concrete ethical question related to the Nixon tapes has confronted some individual oral historians. They have been called upon to provide affidavits verifying that inaccuracies are inherent in interpretation when the transcriptions cannot be checked against their tapes—the one precept which probably would receive unanimous agreement by all OHA members who have ever checked a transcript with its tape. The underlying issue here is whether the question of public access to the Nixon tapes is relevant to oral history. Consider the facts that the tapes are conversations recorded with knowledge of the President (the person in charge of taping) but kept secret from others being taped; that the conversations were released only by the person who taped, in disregard of any wishes of those unknowingly recorded. Should an oral historian allow himself to be called upon, *as an oral historian,* for an opinion which will facilitate the public release of tape recordings produced in a manner which violates the code passed unanimously by the OHA? Does OHA's *Goals and Guidelines* give him, in fact, any relevant goals and guides for this question? Should it?

Part of the confusion is voiced in the guidelines' initial statement (a sort of preamble) as a fact of life: oral historians have a dual nature as both producers and users of the tapes. To quote in full:

> The Oral History Association recognizes Oral History for what it is—a method of gathering a body of historical information in oral form usually on tape. Because the scholarly community is involved in both the production and use of oral history, the Association recognizes an opportunity and an obligation on the part of all concerned to make this type of historical source as authentic and as useful as possible.

It is this inherent schizophrenia that gives us two views of the Nixon tapes. As users, we want them made available to the public. As producers, we can never approve of the methods used by the White House.

The main body of the ethics document is organized around a sort of trinity: the researcher, the interviewee, and the sponsoring institution. The fact that there is a set of guidelines for each of the three implies reciprocal do's and don'ts. A basic question is, Are they a delineation of principles precise enough to apply to concrete situations, and broad enough to cover all varieties of oral history and changing techniques?

Saith Guideline Number One, on behalf of the interviewee:

> The person who is interviewed should be selected carefully and his wishes must govern the conduct of the interview.

This guideline was written in the belief that it takes two to produce an interview and that they should have equal rights. In addition to the philosophical underpinnings, this one has a practical base, too: you are not likely to have a good session if your interview is not conducted in agreement with the basic arrangements. In addition, it stands also as a reminder to those of us who come to feel that it is my interview, my skillful technique which elicits the answers—a point of view which results from our abiding concern with interviewing techniques. However, the information we are after is the interviewee's. It is in her memory cells and frequently in her private files. If she wants something sealed for five years, that is her prerogative and your responsibility. And, as William Manchester will sadly attest, her prerogatives and desires should be agreed upon beforehand, lest tremors of disagreements and even litigation fall upon your head afterward.

Number Two says as much:

> Before undertaking a taped interview for the purpose stated above, the interviewee (or narrator) should be clear in his mind regarding mutual rights with respect to tapes and transcripts made from them. This includes such things as: seal privileges, royalties, literary rights, prior use, fiduciary relationships, the right to edit the tape transcriptions, and the right to determine whether the tape is to be disposed of or preserved.

One might note that if our former President had followed that procedure, the taped evidence in the Watergate cover-up would have been quite different, or—more likely—not created in the first place.

Many oral history offices now send to the prospective interviewee an informal agreement letter, which is signed by each party and which spells out these rights and conditions for each reference by each party during the course of the interview; others simply tape record the agreement at the first session.

If the interviewee wants a passage sealed, this means you have to remove the sealed passage from your transcription to locked storage with the opening date noted, then, if you wish to keep one available for public access, erase that portion from a tape which you have copied. The original tape you lock up with the sealed pages of the transcript. True, precious staff time is required for searching out the place and going through this process. In addition, the sealed passage presumably resides in your memory cells and must be held there with no leaks.

However clear-cut this guideline appears, a "yes, but" (hereafter called a *yes-but*) arises when the material on the tape is likely to backfire on the interviewee, or to damage your project or your institution—and she does not want it sealed. An example (partly fictitious):

> When you interview Professor Curt, recently deposed from the deanship, she criticizes another professor with an eloquence which is born only of a person wronged. The controversy is still warm; you can see that these transcripts would create history right on the spot if the interview is released, and you envision a sudden escalation of the strife, with a spin-off of secondary charges that the oral history office is doing at least one portion of the faculty no good. Or, even if the oral history office survives the controversy, a certain sector on campus will view the transcript as a collection of unsubstantiated accusations and will demand to tape its side—which disrupts the office budget for the year. In addition, future narrators in other subjects would be more inhibited, less candid, after witnessing this spectacle.

> So, are you being irresponsible if you leave the material open for anyone to use: the opposition, the campus newspaper, or the local *Daily Bugle*?

> You point out to Professor Curt that she could be dismissed, that jobs are hard to find, that she should seal it for a couple of years. She says absolutely not, that this is the way she was railroaded and she wants the world to know—now.

Is it ethical to press for sealing, as your part of the mutual right? You could seal it unilaterally, of course, but that would be an open disregard of her privilege as a coauthor with equal rights. Although in many projects, like the Berkeley office, either party has the *legal* right to seal, the question here concerns ethics, not legalities.

If it comes to a choice, would you risk sacrificing your project on the altar of that first guideline—*her* wishes "governing the conduct of the interview"? Should this guideline be softened, perhaps, to read wishes "*mutually arrived at* governing the use of the interview"?

A stickier yesbut is, What do you do when she gives you information which is confidential and which she refuses to put on tape? It is presumably for your ears only and important as background. You probably make a note of it, mark it confidential, and stick it in your own private files. *Should* you write it down? Can you keep it in your private papers which are then sealed for your lifetime—or a time specified far enough in the future that the reasons for the confidentiality will no longer exist? In the meantime, should you use it as a source on which to base a line of questions when interviewing someone else? Off-tape information is not specifically dealt with in the guidelines. Perhaps it should be.

Probably most of the infractions of guideline number two issue from the oral historian's chronic disease of insufficient time: we are in a hurry and neglect to schedule a period with the narrator in which we make clear to her what her options are and negotiate the agreement before interviewing. Sometimes the legal agreements are themselves cause for quandaries. For example:

> Shortly after completing the taping, your interviewee has a stroke and is too debilitated to sign the final agreement. The transcript and the agreement fall into the hands of a conservator who is either incompetent, over-protective, or suspicious. You realize he is never going to sign. You are caught between two commitments: one to the interviewee to finish processing her interview and deposit it as she expected you to do (a responsibility which may also extend to a granting foundation which underwrote the project); on the other hand you are legally committed not to release it until she or her conservator sign.

> And there is the now-classic oral history nightmare in projects that transcribe: What happens when the interviewee dies and the agreement is there on her desk awaiting her signature? You have, again, a responsibility to her to finish it and make it available, but you are legally restrained from doing so.

The third guideline for the memoirist can be evoked to help her distinguish between an oral history interview for an archive or serious research as opposed to a television-type interview for entertainment:

> It is important that the interviewee fully understand the project, and that in view of costs and effort involved he assumes a willingness to give useful information on the subject being pursued.

Underlying this is the recognition that your own preparation alone can never achieve the rich tapestry of overtones, the warp and woof of interrelationships, the unexpected leads which you can get only if you have a serious and well-prepared narrator.

The second section of the trinity—the guidelines for the interviewer—is also riddled with yesbuts. It begins by providing a procedural goal rather than an ethical guideline:

> It should be the objective of the interviewer to gather information that will be of scholarly usefulness in the present and the future.

Then follows an attempt to reconcile the dual and sometimes conflicting nature of the oral historian as both creator and consumer of his product:

> The interviewer who is collecting oral history materials for his own individual research should always bear in mind this broader objective.

All of us are depressingly familiar with the limitations of time and funding which most researchers have to accept. Visualize an interviewer who is teaching half-time, doing faculty committee work half-time, and supposedly using another half to write a book on the migratory farm workers in the Imperial Valley of California. She tape records Cesar Chavez. She may not have the time to expand the interview to include the childhood of Chavez or the broader story of Chavez's efforts nationwide. Again, the interviewer's commitments conflict: guideline number one is pitted against her obligations to her institution and publisher to use her time efficiently and keep her research to the point. Yet the archives will be the poorer in that collection of transcripts or tapes which she will eventually donate.[1] Dealing as it does with a basically irreconcilable dichotomy produced by one researcher wearing two hats, this guideline is probably as precise as is realistically possible. To "always *bear in mind* this broader objective" is as much as anyone can demand from the harassed interviewer-writer.

Number two stems from the perennial question, "How much research is enough?" and also from the recognition that broad variations in interview preparation exist among the diversity of projects, each embodying different goals. The statement reads:

> In order to obtain a tape of maximum worth as a historical document, it is incumbent upon the interviewer to be thoroughly grounded in the background and experiences of the person being interviewed, to select the interviewee carefully, and, where appropriate and if at all feasible, to review the papers of the interviewee before conducting the interview. In conducting the interview, an effort should be made to provide enough information to the interviewee to assist his recall.

If you are funded with a sufficient grant over several years and a staff of graduate students, you may research every scrap of relevant paper and produce an unsurpassable oral history memoir, as has been done in *Tom Rivers: Reflections on a Life in Medicine and Science.*[2] It is a magnificent use of oral history. Forrest Pogue from his intensive research and years of interviewing is producing a multivolume biography of General George Marshall which is the ultimate in scholarship.[3]

Most of us, however, dig down in our pockets and realize that we have to settle for less grant money, fewer staff, shorter time, and pressures for greater quantitative output. This number two guideline was meant to discourage those unfortunate interviews which result from someone buying a $60 tape recorder and then calling on his favorite community character. Or what about the interviewer who goes to his senator armed only with blank tapes and background research similarly blank except for the *Who's Who* vaguely in his memory? Those who developed the guidelines believed it is not fair either to the interviewee or to future scholars to tape with only slight preparation. This makes a victim of the memoirist, it clutters libraries with superficial and usually redundant material, and it creates difficulties when a serious interviewer tries to get an appointment with the victimized memoirist.

Nor is it *fair* to put the burden of the interview on the narrator. She is giving her time and brain power to this; you, the interviewer, are doing the research, which you then share with her to help her recall those far-off dates and names. Such a joint effort will more likely produce a document of which both of you will be proud. And, on the purely practical side, you will more likely avoid difficulties getting a release signed.

Yesbuts lurk here, too. For instance, what do you do when you want to interview a public official who has just gone out of office, and her papers have been sealed until her death? She feels that she cannot give one person special access to those papers; you feel you must use them or you cannot be adequately prepared. Is your alternative not to interview her at all? That would be a loss to history. So what do you do? You might compromise; you can dig around in collections of her contemporaries, where you may find letters and references to her. You can talk to her old friends, and enemies, and of course to her, to help you prepare topical outlines. Sometimes you can confer with a scholar who has researched areas relating to her career and who will contribute questions for the interview.

Yesbut two: What if her papers *are* open, but they fill 350 unorganized filing cabinets in a warehouse? Are you going to go through these? They are not even catalogued yet. Here it is pertinent to bring up a point in reference to interviewer's guideline number two: there is a difference in preparation when your objective is to draw up *questions,* as distinguished from a scholar's research for dependable answers for his book. In oral history, you are not aiming at making final judgments; the historian who later uses your interview is the one who has to assess the evidence and draw conclusions. Your task is to provide evidence. In fact, you will probably produce more useful interviews if you cannot reach the finality of clear answers. Defining puzzles is the focus of your research.

The final guideline for the interviewer, although the shortest, occasions more ethical dilemmas than any of the others:

> It is important that all interviews be conducted in a spirit of objectivity and scholarly integrity and in accordance with stipulations agreed upon.

This is partially an attempt to prevent the creation of oral history myths, innuendoes, and fictions not unlike those fashioned from unevaluated FBI files; its principal aim is to discourage tapes which are primarily entertainments that either fascinate with intrigue or tickle the funnybone, but which are unhampered by accuracy. Outside of collections for folklore, the quality of oral history suffers from such amusements.

Once in a while a single word expresses a coalition of meanings more adequately than a torrent of prose. *Heuristic,* "helping to discover and learn," "serving to guide, discover or reveal" is such a word.[4] Although not specifically stated in the guidelines, be heuristic is what this final guideline means to say. When, after reading an oral history interview, a researching historian can lay it down with the comment, "Now that's a solid, heuristic effort," he has paid the oral historian the highest possible compliment.

Even with the best preparation, however, you sometimes find yourself on the other side of the microphone from a skilled and witty raconteur who, although amusing and delightful, does not share your commitment for heuristic interviews. Actually, you can develop some techniques to discourage exaggerations and distortions by using your research to pin her down with specific names and facts. And you can show her you are simply turned off by the exaggerated story or the colorful scandal which she may be telling you for the immediate reward of the look of relish on your face. Or you can always say, "Well, we'd better leave that out. It might be slanderous, you know, unless you can document it." If she persists in going through with it and leaving it in the transcript, your remaining recourse is to point out in her introduction to the tape or transcript that her charges are worth noting as an example of the perceptions of persons who hold her point of view in that particular group.

The truly heuristic approach is to choose memoirists for a series of interviews designed around a central core of inquiry, so that when one interviewee makes a charge or tells an unlikely story, you have a chance to tape others on the same topic. The result will be a series of different views which explore ambiguities and offer counter-weights to each other. However, even with the series technique, difficulties may arise. Example:

> You interview Mr. Wiley. He insists on taping a serious charge against Mrs. Goldfarb. In a series, the logical follow-up is to make a note to include a question on this charge when you interview Mrs. Goldfarb. However, both interviews are still in process, so you are not free to quote Mr. Wiley to her and disclose your source if she should ask you, since the final agreement has not been signed. Besides, by quoting him to her, you may be starting a new controversy with possible chain reactions.

So you have a responsibility both ways: Goldfarb can insist she has a right to know her accuser. But your prior source, Wiley, retains quoting privileges. So getting a balance and counterbalance in a series sometimes places you in a moral morass.

But that is the good news. The bad news is that a virtuous, heuristic attitude can lead you into even a more difficult situation. Are you game for another example?

> Interview transcripts are continually coming and going out of your office—being transcribed, being sent to the memoirists, being returned to the office with their corrections and additions. In an interview, Interviewee A gives you a clear, running account of an event which started with a corruption scandal, moved into the state administration for investigation, and finally landed in the courts for resolution. Her account is not detailed: it is the sequential outline with valuable information on who acted as catalyst in each stage. Such a comprehensive picture is not available in print, so it is important.
>
> Armed with this scenario, you then tape Interviewee B on his recollection of the administration investigation. He does not request your source because he sees you have only the general idea of what happened, and he cooperatively fills in part B for you. Then you go to Interviewee C, who fills in the litigation section and wraps up the story. With all three interviews, you have the story put together from first-hand informants.
>
> Put together, that is, until about two weeks later, when Interviewee A calls and says, "I've decided to cull that story out of the transcript because I want to run for office this year. It might be too controversial."

What is right for you to do in such a case? Is it fair to keep her information in the other two interviews, where it appears as a major reference? It is still her story, although Interviewees B and C have covered their respective chapters with more detail and much more vividly than she had done.

Should you protect her confidentiality by removing those sections in B's and C's interviews too? This action could throw you in conflict with guideline number one (the interviewee's wishes should govern the conduct of the interview) because neither man wants that section disturbed. You are back in the conundrum mentioned earlier, when you want something closed and *he* wants it left open.

It is unlikely that any additions to the present guides and goals can protect the conscientious oral historian from perplexities like these. As with other dilemmas in life, some just have to be negotiated and muddled through. In the example above, you could wait to see if she loses the election. If she does, she will likely open that story again and all is well; if she does not, then you either negotiate to close all three, or you put all three in that office drawer labeled "temporary limbo" and try to explain the delay to B and C.

The third part of the trinity—"Guidelines for Sponsoring Institutions"—is actually only one guideline as it stands now:

> Subject to meeting the conditions as prescribed by interviewees, it will be the obligation of sponsoring institutions to prepare easily usable tapes and/or accurate typed transcriptions, and properly to identify, index, and preserve such oral history records for use by the scholarly community, and to state clearly the provisions that govern their use.

In practice this means that the sponsoring institution must serve as a vehicle for carrying out long-term obligations incurred through the other two parts of the trinity. And this requires continuity and longevity of the institution. A library or historical society whose permanence is not reasonably assured can investigate allying itself on a cooperative basis with another more permanent institution.

Since that guideline was written, the number of institutions sponsoring oral history projects has soared, and many of the older sponsoring institutions have developed oral history research specialties. Perhaps it is time to consider a second guideline here: one for *relations* between oral history offices. It has become increasingly important for institutions to cooperate so that their oral history offices develop specialties which complement those in other institutions while reflecting their own particular strengths. This will help prevent overlap of effort, competition for outside funds, and redundancy in the total pool of oral history tapes and transcripts.

Before we leave the *Goals and Guidelines*, let us consider a few which are not touched upon at all and which do not logically fit under any of the three headings.

It appears now that we might add "Guidelines for the Relations Between Oral History Projects"—and thereby become the first in history to create a four-part trinity. This guideline springs from the phenomenon that more than one project frequently interviews the same memoirists. Horace Albright, who spoke briefly at the 1974 colloquium, has been interviewed by many major oral history projects in this country because he was the number two man in creating the national parks and was around to run them through several presidential administrations. His popularity is also due to his excellent memory.

Such overkill of interviewees indicates the need for agreement among oral historians not to interview a big-name person with a short, low-research interview which contributes little more than the aggrandizement of a project. Such an interview can make it appear that this major figure has already done his memoir, and when another project applies for a grant to do a thorough biography, it can be turned down on the grounds he has already been interviewed. Second, short topical interviews should be carefully noted as such in an appropriate catalog, with a notation of the subjects covered if possible. It also means making clear to the interviewee that history still lacks a full memoir from him; otherwise he might refuse subsequent requests to be interviewed since he's already done that. Sometimes a second interview request is rejected because his first was so superficial that he wants none of that again.

This problem also implies that each project should give priority to disseminating regular reports on what it has produced, through mailing its catalog (as Columbia and a few others do), notifying relevant journals, and turning in its listing to NUCMUC and other centralized cataloging services.

Another problem: the Grand Tetons colloquium seemed to be marked by much discussion and questioning of ethics involved in the commercial use of oral history. Parts of the present code relate to this question, such as agreeing beforehand with the memoirist on who will hold prior use rights and the literary rights. Royalties should be a part of this agreement, also. (In a number of projects, if an interview is published, the interviewee gets royalties automatically once the expenses for the interview are reimbursed to the project.)

In England, the law requires that anyone be paid whose interview is aired on BBC, and most oral history produced in Great Britain is for this purpose. This has led to problems in paying interviewees because their whereabouts are not known: they are not public figures and many were taped five or ten years before.

Unlike England, our country has a tradition of writers and researchers "exploiting" public figures for interviews. Similar exploitation of private citizens who belong to a special group such as core city dwellers, women, Native Americans, and Chicanos is occurring with increasing frequency. The question repeatedly raised is, Should oral history be made available for commercial publication with no remuneration to such interviewees?

In the United States the legal answer is often yes. But we need to examine this question further, or research in the several fields of ethnic studies could be badly undercut. One consideration which often balances the researcher's exploitation of an interviewee is the nonmonetary benefits of publication to the group being studied. If the researcher cooperates, for example, with a tribal council (or perhaps its opposition group) when planning the interviews, or with an urban coalition committee, the end product could be useful for them too, perhaps for textbook material or for community consciousness raising.

Similarly, today's public figure is generally loath to keep a diary and rarely has time in her schedule, even when "retired," to approach her memoir without the help of a highly-paid researcher and ghost writer. An oral historian furnishes her with background research, organizes and outlines interview sessions, guides her through with questions, and finally presents her with her own copy of the transcript. For her, it is a fortuitous way to leave a memoir for posterity, a free service which could otherwise have cost her untold dollars and hours. With publishing rights and royalties clearly spelled out beforehand, perhaps there is a fair balance of "exploitation" between the person of distinction who gets her memoir and the interviewer who gets a career credit for a heuristic piece of research.

Those of you who have wrestled the angels down to this last paragraph probably see little relevance now between the taping of oral history *properly done* and the processes indulged in by the former President. Anguished objections to Nixon-as-historian are based on his violations of every tenet in *Goals and Guidelines,* with the exception of number one for the interviewer: ". . . to gather information that will be of scholarly usefulness in the present and the future." As we reject any classification of the Nixon tapes as "oral history," do we base that rejection on the definition of oral history which was offered at the First Colloquium? (It has to be oral and it has to be history.) Surely the Nixon tapes meet both those qualifications. Try the definition in the first sentence in the preamble of *Goals and Guidelines:* "The OHA recognizes oral history for what it is—a method of gathering a body of historical information in oral form usually on tape." Nixon's efforts fit that description, too.

So we conclude with a larger question for our ethical code: Should we seek a less-inclusive definition of oral history, in an effort to disassociate ourselves from surreptitious, noninterview taping? This requires further thought because there are, to mention only one related aspect, those members of OHA who tape speeches, riots, and current happenings, without infringing on anyone's rights. That is a fitting dilemma on which to end this set of reflections.

Notes

1. This is, of course, one argument for oral history offices which interview for the entire scholarly community.

2. Saul Benison, *Tom Rivers: Reflections on a Life in Medicine and Science* (Cambridge, Mass.: MIT Press, 1967). See chapter 11 of the present volume.

3. Forrest C. Pogue, *George C. Marshall,* 3 vols. (New York: Viking, 1963–73).

4. *American Heritage Dictionary of the English Language* (New York and Boston: American Heritage and Houghton Mifflin, 1969). See also *The Random House Dictionary*, 2nd Edition (New York, N.Y.: Random House, 1987).

PART THREE

Oral History Applied:
Local, Ethnic,
Family, and Women's History

14

Preface to
The Saga of Coe Ridge
Lynwood Montell

In Part Three we explore the ways in which oral documentation can be applied to the varieties of history: folk, local, regional; then ethnic, women's, and family history. Many of these overlapping fields can be viewed together as the emergent discipline of ethnohistory, the frame of historical reference that a community uses to understand its traditions.

Our introductory selection comes from a recognized classic, The Saga of Coe Ridge by Lynwood Montell of Western Kentucky University. The author compiled the history of an isolated African-American community in rural Kentucky; of necessity he found himself writing folk history, "a body of oral traditional narratives told by a people about themselves." His preface, which appears below, successfully resolves the confusion surrounding history based on local legends and tales.

The subject here is not oral history, as it is commonly understood, as much as oral traditional history, based not on interviews with witnesses of history but on accounts passed on among generations—the sort of materials which Jan Vansina and Ruth Finnegan discuss in their essays earlier in this book. Montell's approach is, in effect, that which any oral historian might adopt if called upon to explore an event which happened a century before without benefit of written sources. The community Montell studied left few documents such as birth records or tax rolls, and most interviewees were two and three generations removed from the events they described. Thus the author worked from the community's storehouse of self-knowledge, and he concentrated as much on the legendary growth which surrounded century-old events as on the solid kernel of fact.

Lynwood Montell has written and lectured extensively on the use of oral materials in historical research. He has published Monroe County History (1970), Ghosts Along the Cumberland (1975), and From Memory to History (with Barbara Allen Montell) (1981).

Coe Ridge is the name of a tiny Negro colony that was nestled in the foot-hills of the Cumberland Mountains in Cumberland County, Kentucky, near the Tennessee line. Placed on the ridge as a result of Negro emancipation following the Civil War, the settlement withstood for almost a century the attempts of neighboring whites to remove this "scar" from the cultural landscape of an otherwise homogeneous white society. During its existence, the Coe colony, sometimes called Coetown and Zeketown, produced a belligerent group of people who became a legend before the community died in the late 1950s. It became a place of refuge for white women rejected by their own society and the breeding ground for a race of mulattoes. Additionally, Coe Ridge had ranked first among the moonshiners of southern Kentucky and, consequently, became the chief concern of federal revenue agents. It was this occupation, this livelihood of the outcasts that eventually was to bring about their downfall. After years of raids, arrests, and skirmishes, the revenuers succeeded in driving the Negroes from Coe Ridge into the industrial centers north of the Ohio River. Thus the colony died.

Historical events in the life of this Negro colony provide the basis for this book. *The Saga of Coe Ridge* is not an ordinary reconstruction of local history, however, for only a very few written records pertaining to this settlement remain. The major source materials are the inveterate oral traditions collected from former members of the colony and their white neighbors. A work of this type is founded on the premise that the story of any local group, as viewed by its people, is worthy of being recorded, for it can serve as a historical record in those areas where written accounts have not been preserved. One must be prepared to defend a thesis which holds that folk history can complement historical literature. This study proposes such a defense.

The Controversy over Oral Traditions

The utilization of oral traditions as undertaken here represents an area of open controversy and is severely attacked by some scholars who are accustomed to more conventional methods of documentation. A less hostile attitude claims that oral traditions can be utilized in historical writings, provided that these recollections are approached with proper caution. Still another line of thought holds that folklore is a mirror of history. That is to say, history can be viewed through folklore. A fourth position contends that the tales and songs of a people are grounded in historical fact. Inasmuch as *The Saga of Coe Ridge* is patently built upon the utilization of oral tradition, these various positions are worth examining in some detail. Let us look, therefore, at the thinking behind all four positions, beginning with the totally negative approach.

FOLK TRADITION AS HISTORICAL FALLACY

Legends and traditions of the people should be avoided, according to Homer C. Hockett, who claimed in 1938 that "the historian can make nothing of them of any positive value, in the absence of corroboratory evidence of a documentary, archaeological, or other kind, for the simple reason that they cannot be traced to their origins. And without knowledge of origins the ordinary critical tests cannot be applied."[1] Hockett renewed his attack on oral tradition in 1955 when he defined history as "the written record of past or current events"; he gave some credence, however, to certain devices such as utensils, structures, weapons, and artifacts as items that the historian could use to supplement the absence of written records.[2] Hockett saw no potential in myths, legends, or traditions as informative channels which might be utilized as aids to the historian. Yet in a chapter on "New Trends," Hockett recognized a recent rapprochement between local history and folklore.

Allen Johnson, writing in 1926, also enumerated a list of "remains," some three dozen in number, which could be included as source materials for historical research. Oral tradition was not listed because it was "handed on from generation to generation by word of mouth without being committed to writing." Johnson immediately contradicted his attack on oral tradition, however, by attaching some weight to the Icelandic sagas. "Under certain conditions," he stated, "where the professional raconteur has a pride in keeping the conventional tradition intact, the tale may have a fixed content and a stereotyped form, and eventually may be set down in writing substantially unchanged. On these grounds, the essential historicity of the Icelandic sagas is defended."[3]

Robert H. Lowie, an anthropologist, criticized the veracity of oral tradition a few years earlier than either Hockett or Johnson. He made what has been termed "the strongest statement against traditional history on this side of the Atlantic."[4] In 1915, Lowie published a short comment in the *American Anthropologist* on "Oral Tradition and History," objecting to the prohistorical position taken in that journal the previous year by John R. Swanton and Roland B. Dixon. Lowie's most biting comments were issued two years later to the American Folklore Society on the occasion of his presidential address, which was published in the *Journal of American Folklore*. He illustrated his thesis by using the traditions of North American Indians. "Indian tradition is historically worthless," he charged, "because the occurrences, possibly real, which it retains, are of no historical significance; and because it fails to record, or to record accurately, the most momentous happenings."[5] He further stated that stories of war and quarrels are not records of actual occurrences but are folklore, as attested to by their geographical distribution. Lowie conceded the point that traditional narratives are significant in the understanding of psychological, social, and religious phenomena associated with a tribal culture, but he categorically refused to allow any historical credence to the details of the narratives.

Lord Raglan, a recent student of comparative folklore and a clamorous champion of the skeptics of oral traditional history, studied both the classical and medieval bodies of traditional narrative and concluded that the great folk epics, the cherished sagas, the heroic legends and ballads, even the Christ story itself were ultimately drawn from ritual drama, not from historical fact.[6] The heroes of tradition, Raglan contended, were originally not men but gods, and the whole body of folk legend is a detritus of mythical accounts connected with ritualistic rites. After the rites ceased, the narratives remained and entered the realm of folk tradition where they were perpetuated as accounts of historical experiences. Raglan felt that a nonliterate people could not orally preserve the record of a historical event for more than 150 years and that any belief in the historicity of tradition stemmed from the desire to believe rather than from a critical analysis of the facts.

Edwin Sidney Hartland and Alfred Nutt, both talented Victorian folklorists, displayed negative attitudes toward the authenticity of oral historical narratives at an earlier date than Lord Raglan. Hartland studied *The Legend of Perseus* and was able to contend persuasively that certain African traditions are basically void of trustworthy history. Like Raglan, Hartland could allow only a brief time span to the limits of historical reliability in oral tradition. Among African peoples, he would concede 100, or at the most, 200 years. In an article, Nutt attacked Sir William Ridgeway's *Early Age of Greece*, which contained a strong plea for the acceptance of the Homeric poems as history. Nutt posed the question whether historic myths ever existed among barbaric peoples living in an oral-traditional mythopoetic stage of culture.[7] To Nutt's credit he at least called for an accumulation of more evidence before the thorny problems on the relationships of heroic legend and historic fact could be properly attacked.

FOLKLORE AS EMBELLISHED HISTORY

Joan Wake, a British historian, deemed folklore to be embellished history. She noted that although the old English village traditions are "liable to fluctuations and variations without end . . . there is much that is valuable in them. . . ."[8] And Américo Paredes wrote that "folklore does not always make a complete wreck of historical facts." He further stated, "Where documents are available for comparison, one may actually trace the process—the reshaping of history to conform with the folk group's own world view, the embellishment of bare historical detail with universal motifs." At that point in the accumulation of historical data, the historian should be familiar with the research methods of the folklorist, Paredes continued, for "some knowledge of the frequency with which motifs of this kind occur in folk narratives would put the historian on guard."[9] Merle W. Wells, historian and archivist, similarly wrote, "Historians who are not interested in folklore ought to have their work examined regularly by good folklorists. . . . Only a skilled folklorist, thoroughly familiar with several hundred folklore types and several thousand folklore motifs, has the competence necessary to distinguish folklore from history in scholarly historical accounts."[10]

Louis R. Gottschalk conceded that oral tradition, when utilized with proper caution, can supplement the efforts of the formal historian. He wrote that the legendary stories of William Tell, the imaginary hero of the Swiss war for independence, and Dr. Faustus, the sixteenth-century necromancer, "are good examples of folklore that may tell about the aspirations, superstitions, and customs of the peoples among whom the stories developed, provided the historian (or folklorist) is able to distinguish between the legendary embroideries and their authentic foundations."[11]

Despite occasional deviations from fact, Russian historical songs have been excellent sources of history when approached by the discerning scholar. Y. M. Sokolov described how the tendency of the people to idealize Ivan the Terrible led to a departure from historical truth in one of their songs. In the year 1581 Ivan the Terrible, in a fit of wrath, murdered his son Ivan, but in the historical song describing the incident, the anger of Ivan was vented on another son who had been accused of treachery. Other than this one radical departure from reality, Sokolov contended, the song preserved a great many of the real circumstances surrounding the event.[12]

FOLKLORE AS A MIRROR OF HISTORY

Allan Nevins, the founder of Columbia University's oral history program in 1948,[13] is among those who feel that folklore mirrors history, and he points out that folksongs and legends should be considered in the study of American history. After first challenging historians to record systematically the personal reminiscences "from the lips and papers of living Americans who have led significant lives," Nevins notes that "in our more recent history the legends of pioneer settlements, mining camps, lumbermen, and the cowboys of the western range, whether in prose or ballad, are by no means devoid of light upon social and cultural history."[14] Nevins advocates oral history as a means of documenting decisions in recent history that otherwise would be unrecorded. He uses oral testimonies narrated by members of the Ford family and household servants in *Ford: The Man, The Times, and The Company*, and praises their testimonies as "pure gold for the historian."[15] M. Gorky, an authority on Russian literature, also writes that the oral creations of the people provide excellent material for ascertaining the popular historical opinions on the phenomena of history. "From remote antiquity," Gorky states, "folklore persistently and with originality attends upon history. It has its own opinion of the doings of Louis XI, of Ivan the Terrible, and this opinion differs sharply from the evaluation made by history, which is written by specialists who are not very much interested in the question of what the conflict between the monarchs and the feudal lords actually contributed to the life of the laboring people."[16]

Certain American historians have directed their efforts toward producing works that point out the need for genuine cultural histories as a background for historical syntheses. One historian holding this view is Theodore C. Blegen, who feels that in order to understand the American people, historians should utilize folk documents, such as letters and diaries, which are the genuine indicators of history. In the past, our failure to define the American culture has been caused by what Blegen called "inverted provincialism"—that is to say, historians have scorned the simple and steered clear of the near-at-hand.[17] Philip D. Jordan, another cultural historian, writes that unless social stimuli are investigated, the contributions of the common man to historical movements cannot be articulated. American history has been written, he continues, but the full story is not to be found by a study of population statistics and historical documents; such channels of research are available to anyone, but the folklorist can bring to the formal historian knowledge of deep-lying cultural patterns. Folklore grows out of the national experience, Jordan states, and an understanding of oral traditions would greatly contribute to those who wish more clearly to understand the historical narrative.[18]

Research Opportunities in American Cultural History, a collection of 12 essays, sounded the clarion call to historians. Leading cultural historians and folklorists pointed out that too much stress can be placed on our nation's political and religious institutions, thus jeopardizing consideration of the human element in history. A more rounded approach, the contributors felt, would be to focus attention on the people who lived during the major movements in American history. Among the more common words used throughout the book were "grass roots," "everyday life," and "folkways."[19]

FOLK TRADITIONS AS HISTORICAL FACT

The fourth view, that "traditions often have a basis in historical fact," is supported by an article which appeared in the *Journal of American Folklore*. In reporting the investigations of a historical tradition among the Southern Paiute Indians of southern Utah, David M. Pendergast and Clement W. Meighan disclosed that casual comments made by the Paiute revealed history that was consistent with archaeological evidence some 800 years old.[20] The traditions, which dealt with a prehistoric people, the Puebloids, were specific and generally accurate concerning the Puebloids' economic institutions, physical appearance, material culture, and Paiute-Puebloid relationships. The authors concluded that "archaeologists in particular should explore the possibilities of correlating historical traditions with archaeological data, since the historical information may substantiate, and in some cases broaden, inferences based solely on archaeological materials."[21]

The Southern Paiute example of the persistency of oral traditions was one of many emphatic rejoinders against the anti-historical pronouncements of Lowie and others who held to his school of relentless dogmatism. Frederica de Laguna, for example, issued a strong positive statement in 1958, writing that when a 1957 geological survey team reported habitable periods of the Icy Yakutat Bay area, the team was thereby confirming by means of radiocarbon tests native traditions dating from 1400. De Laguna concluded by saying, "Other natives' statements about the stages in the retreat of the ice in the Yakutat Bay during the late 18th and 19th centuries are in complete accord with geological evidence."[22]

The English folklorist George Laurence Gomme approached the question of the validity of oral tradition with what can be termed the extreme approach. He asserted that every folk custom and belief has roots in a historical event.[23] Closely akin to this stand, but not as dogmatically so, were the positions taken by the Chadwicks and Knut Liestøl. Hector M. and Nora K. Chadwick totally differed with the Raglan thesis by maintaining that folk heroes are rooted in history. During the process of cultural evolution experienced by a people, there was a historical Heroic Age characterized by a semi-nomadic, warring, raiding type of existence. At this stage of phylogeny, a great hero rose up to assume the leadership of his people. In some instances, the hero's exploits then entered the printed page and were thus perpetuated, but prior to that a great deal of fiction had already crept into the oral recountal. The painstaking scholar can winnow the historical from the unhistorical elements in that event, and this was one of the tasks undertaken by the Chadwicks.[24] If, for some reason, the hero's feats did not reach print, then the legends about him devolved into a cycle of songs or tales carried on in oral tradition. But historical traditions, whether oral or written, are authentic records of history, and the recurrent thesis postulated by the Chadwicks looks upon many of the persons and events described in the Teutonic, British, and Irish Heroic Ages as historical actualities.

The folklorist Knut Liestøl studied the origin of the Icelandic sagas and persuasively argued that under favoring conditions oral history can preserve its core of reality over long periods of time.[25] By a close analysis of oral traditions that originated during the period 930 to 1030 and later were written down in the period from 1120 to 1230, he showed that oral traditions could serve as a form of record-keeping, distinct from written historical accounts. Liestøl tested the reliability of the episodes recorded in the sagas by (1) comparing variant examples of the same incident in different sagas, to ascertain the original content and form of the oral tradition; (2) analyzing stylistic devices of oral narration, to see which of the written pages reveal the marks of oral style; (3) evaluating the amount of recognizable folklore material in the sagas, and (4) assessing the social milieu and the common historical background from which the sagas stemmed. In a society of more advanced peoples unshaken by wanderings and uprootings, according to Liestøl, historical recollections and folklore elements mingle to a considerable extent, but these two channels can be positively identified. The more advanced peoples utilize oral traditional history as a form of historical record-keeping that is separate and distinct from written historical records. Students of history, Liestøl contended, should not apply the rules of evidence belonging to documentary history in their evaluation of oral history.[26]

This was virtually the same stand taken by many Folklore Society members who could not agree with Hartland and Nutt. Lach-Szyrma felt that the basic historicity of oral traditions in the West of England could be ascribed to the selective process of folk memory; David MacRitchie pointed out that archaeological findings in Wigtownshire verified local traditions which claimed that a cave in the vicinity had been occupied 14 centuries earlier by Saint Ninias; and John Myres gave much credence to folkmemory in such isolated, stable, homogeneous, and preliterate societies as the Icelandic and the Polynesian, where family, community, and even regional history were matters of practical concern and common knowledge.[27] When a people share a common historical experience, according to Myres, the events in this experience become a tenacious part of folkmemory and may be perpetuated for centuries.

The Nature of Oral Traditions

Through the years the American continent has witnessed the birth and flowering of an immense body of local historical legends arising in response to actual occurrences, usually of a sensational nature. These traditions may vex the historian of the articulate classes, and he may continue to have nothing to do with something as elusive as folk tradition. Yet, no historian who is aware of the ways of the people on a local level, especially in rural areas where ties with the land are strong, will question the importance played by oral traditions in the lives of the people. Accuracy of local historical legends is not the most important question to be faced by the person who gathers and analyzes them, but rather the essential fact is that these folk narratives are believed by the people who perpetuate them. Even in the more literate societies, folklore records the joy, humor, pathos, and indestructible spirit of the local group. In the preface to their book on Mormon folklore, Austin and Alta Fife state that "we have sought the authenticity not of history but of folklore. . . . We have tried to view the materials less as historical data than as legend—not as they actually were, but as they have been viewed by the folk."[28]

Richard M. Dorson made a similar point in his concluding comments on the trustworthiness of oral traditional history. He noted that blanket judgments regarding the historicity of oral traditions should be avoided, and added, "It is not a matter of fact versus fiction so much as the social acceptance of traditional history."[29] And in another article Dorson astutely wrote, "If the event is historically false, it is psychologically true, and its incorporation into tribal histories is something for the American historian to note."[30]

Ethnohistorians specializing in African history have approached the idea of historical truth from a perspective which stresses a periodical or cyclical rhythm of eternal repetition within the life-cycle of the individual. They note a direct correlation between the time perspective recognized by the society and the social structure.[31] One ethnohistorian, Paul Bohannan, writes in "Concepts of Time Among the Tiv of Nigeria" that repetitive natural or social events recorded in Tiv myths and legends explain the social process, not the historical past. Specifically, he remarks that "The most common incidents all cluster about a standard situation which arises time and again in the dynamic Tiv social process: particularly fission and fusion of lineage territories, which are the modal points in Tiv political process."[32]

Jan Vansina, pursuing these ideas in a book-length historiographical outline on nonliterate African societies, examined in depth the processes and functions of oral traditions in African societies. He pointed out the contrast in attitudes toward historical knowledge displayed by societies even in the same culture area. Because of a coherent political structure, the Rwanda were rich in family and local historical traditions, Vansina explained, but the Burundi were restricted in their oral communication because of an incohesive political framework. In conclusion Vansina stated, "Each type of society has in fact chosen to preserve the kind of historical traditions suited to its particular type of structure, and the historical information to be obtained by studying these traditions is restricted by the framework of reference constructed by the society in question."[33] Vansina's statement may well summarize the case for African ethnohistory.[34]

American folklorists, on the other hand, are concerned with a literate people who have produced bodies of oral traditional narratives which may reflect social conditions but certainly not reflect political organization. By utilizing methods of research peculiar to his discipline, the comparative folklorist can study these narratives in societal context and thus function as a cultural historian. In addition, he can come to the aid of the formal historian, whose analysis of statistical data and historical documents seldom permits conclusions regarding the ways of life on a local level.

In the interests of formal history, therefore, a summary of the history of the immediate area surrounding Coe Ridge is presented in the Prologue of *The Saga of Coe Ridge* as a complement to the oral traditions of the people themselves. Data for this summary are drawn almost exclusively from the federal census and from other sources which in turn were based on generalized data. The use of data,

however, does not' make it possible to take a personal approach to history—that
is, to consider the people as a living force. This is the critical distinction between
folk history and history written by orthodox methods of research.

Folk history, as applied in this book, can be defined as a body of oral traditional
narratives that are told by a people about themselves, and, therefore, the narratives articulate the feelings of a group toward the events and persons described.[35]
Folk attitudes are included as a part of this definition because they are an integral
part of almost every narrative recorded from the informants. In this account of
Coe Ridge, these attitudes occasionally become the primary consideration, for
local history is often intricately tied with the subjectivity of the people. . . .[36]

Notes

1. Homer C. Hockett, *Introduction to Research in American History* (New York: Macmillan,
1938), p. 90.

2. Homer C. Hockett, *The Critical Method in Historical Research and Writing,* 3d ed. (New
York: Macmillan, 1955).

3. A. Johnson, *The Historian and Historical Evidence* (New York: Scribner's, 1926), p. 5.

4. Richard M. Dorson, "The Debate over the Trustworthiness of Oral Traditional History," Volksüberlieferung: *Festschrift für Kurt Ranke,* ed. Fritz Harkort (Göttingen: O. Schwartz,
1968), p. 21.

5. Robert H. Lowie, "Oral Tradition and History," *Journal of American Folklore* 30 (April–
June 1917), p. 165.

6. F. R. Raglan, *The Hero: A Study in Tradition, Myth, and Drama* (New York: Vintage, 1956).

7. Alfred Nutt, "History, Tradition, and Historic Myth," *Folk-Lore* 12 (1901), pp. 336–39.

8. Joan Wake, *How to Compile a History and Present-Day Record of Village Life,* cited in Donald D. Parker, *Local History: How to Gather It, Write It, and Publish It* (New York: Social Science
Research Council, 1944), p. 25.

9. Américo Paredes, "Folklore and History," in *Singers and Storytellers,* ed. Mody C. Boatright (Pallas: Southern Methodist University Press, 1961), pp. 58, 61.

10. M. W. Wells, "History and Folklore: A Suggestion for Cooperation," *Journal of the West*
4 (January 1965), pp. 95–96.

11. L. Gottschalk, *Understanding History: A Primer of Historical Method* (New York: Knopf,
1950), p. 114.

12. J. M. Sokolov, *Russian Folklore,* trans. Catherine Ruth Smith (New York: Macmillan,
1950), pp. 350–51 and passim. The basic historicity of the Russian historical songs has com-
manded the attention of Carl Stief, *Studies in the Russian Historical Song* (1953; reprint ed.,
Westport, Conn.: Hyperion Press, 1981).

13. The increasing popularity of both university and private oral history projects is
especially pleasing to folklorists, for the private interview is thus recognized as the basic unit of

transmission in oral history. And, again in the mold of the folklorist, the oral historian uses the same tools and methodologies in field collecting. Some typical methodological descriptions would include the following works: Elizabeth I. Dixon, "Oral History: A New Horizon," *Library Journal* 87 (April 1, 1962), pp. 1363–65; Charles T. Morrissey, "The Case for Oral History," *Vermont History* 21 (July 1963), pp. 145–55; and Helen McCann White, "Thoughts on Oral History," *American Archivist* 20 (January 1957), pp. 19–30. Charles T. Morrissey's "Oral History and the Mythmakers," *Historic Preservation* 16 (November–December 1964), pp. 232–37, contains a brief but workable bibliography of the subject.

14. Allan Nevins, *The Gateway to History* (Boston: Appleton-Century, 1938), pp. iv, 66; Wyman D. Walker, "Western Folklore and History," *American West* 1 (Winter 1964), pp. 45–51, noted the strong relationship between folklore and the history of the American West, especially in the beliefs held by the pioneers concerning water, weather, and animals and in their stories of Indian fighting and in the lore of miners, cowboys, and sheepherders.

15. Cited in Morrissey, "Case for Oral History," p. 151.

16. M. Gorky, *On Literature*, cited in Sokolov, *Russian Folklore*, p. 347.

17. Theodore Blegen, *Grass Roots History* (Minneapolis: University of Minnesota Press, 1947).

18. P. O. Jordan, "The Folkorist as Social Historian," *Western Folklore* 12 (July 1953), pp. 194–201.

19. John F. McDermott, ed., *Research Opportunities in American Cultural History* (Lexington: University of Kentucky Press, 1961).

20. D. M. Pendergast and C. W. Meighan, "Folk Traditions as Historical Fact: A Paiute Example," *Journal of American Folklore* 72 (April–June 1959), pp. 128–133.

21. Pendergast and Meighan, "Folk Traditions," p. 132.

22. F. de Laguna, "Geological Confirmation of Native Traditions, Yakutat, Alaska," *American Antiquity* 23 (1958), p. 434, also cited in Dorson, "The Debate," pp. 23–24.

23. G. C. Gomme, *Folklore as an Historical Science* (London: Methuen, 1908). See especially chapter 1, "History and Folklore," pp. 1–122.

24. H. M. Chadwick and N. K. Chadwick, *The Heroic Age* (Cambridge: Cambridge University Press, 1912). The comments about this work were drawn from Richard M. Dorson, *American Folklore* (Chicago: University of Chicago Press, 1958), p. 209; the Chadwicks' three-volume study of *The Growth of Literature* is summarized by Dorson in "The Debate," pp. 20–21.

25. Knot Liestøl, *Origin of the Icelandic Family Sagas* (Oslo: H. Aschebourg, 1930). Dorson presents a brief but succinct summary of Liestøl's work in "The Debate," pp. 26–30.

26. Liestøl's persuasive arguments met with strong opposition in the analyses of Sigurdur Nordal, *The Historical Element in the Icelandic Family Sagas* (Glasgow: Jackson, 1957); Peter Hallberg, *The Icelandic Saga*, trans. Paul Schach (Lincoln: University of Nebraska Press, 1962); and Theodore M. Andersson, *The Problem of Icelandic Saga Origins* (New Haven: Yale University Press, 1964).

27. W. S. Lach-Szyrma, "Folk-Lore Traditions of Historical Events," *Folk-Lore* 3 (1881), pp. 157–68; David MacRitchie, "The Historical Aspect of Folk-Lore," in *The International Folk-Lore Congress 1891, Papers and Transactions,* ed. Joseph Jacobs and Alfred Nutt (London: D. Nutt, 1892), pp. 105–106; and John L. Myres, "Folkmemory," *Folk-Lore* 37 (1926), pp. 12–34 but especially p. 28.

28. A. E. Fife and A. S. Fife, *Saints of Sage and Saddle: Folklore among the Mormons* (Bloomington: Indiana University Press, 1956), p. xi.

29. Dorson, "The Debate," p. 34.

30. R. M. Dorson, "Oral Tradition and Written History: The Case for the United States," *Journal of the Folklore Institute* 1 (December 1964), p. 230.

31. See, e.g., Meyer Fortes, *The Dynamics of Clanship among the Tallensi* (New York: Oxford University Press, 1945), p. xi; G. I. Jones, "Oral Tradition and History," *African Notes* 2 (January 1965), pp. 7–11, uses narratives from eastern Nigeria and, in particular, origin myths of the Kalabari of the eastern Delta to show how oral traditions change in response to different social requirements and attitudes.

32. Paul Bohannan, *Southwestern Journal of Anthropology* 9 (1953), pp. 260–61.

33. J. Vansina, *Oral Tradition: A Study in Historical Methodology,* trans. H. M. Wright (London: Routledge and Kegan Paul, 1965), pp. 170–71 (see chapter 8 of the present volume); also quoted by Dorson in "The Debate," p. 35.

34. The theme of a conference on oral history in Africa, held at Northwestern University in 1965, was methodology as attested by the papers published in the *African Studies Bulletin* 8 (September 1965): Aristide R. Zolberg, "A Preliminary Guide for Interviews, " pp. 3–8; Jan Vansina, "The Documentary Interview," pp. 8–14; Ronald Cohen, "Quantification," pp. 16–19; and Raoul Naroul, "Data Quality Control," pp. 19–23.

35. Benjamin A. Botkin, *Lay My Burden Down: A Folk History of Slavery* (Chicago: University of Chicago Press, 1945), p. xiii, defines folk history as "history from the bottom up, in which the people become their own historians." From the study of folk history, Botkin contends, one is able to consider "the inarticulate many as well as the articulate few."

36. In chapter 1, for example, it is demonstrated that oral tradition offers rich insight into Negro attitudes toward the insecure status on the plantation experienced by slave ancestors. Additionally, these narratives provide ample documentation of the socioeconomic aspects of plantations located along the upper Cumberland River. ⁀

15

The Folklorist, the Oral Historian, and Local History

Larry Danielson

Beginning where Lynwood Montell left off, the author of the next selection discusses local history from the perspective of folklore. Because folklorists have specialized training, they can help explain how local legends, folk beliefs, and customs interrelate; how traditional motifs crop up in oral narratives; and how local history can be "personalized" by specialized collecting. Selections later in this volume, particularly that of Richard Dorson, also explore the relation between oral history and folklore. While researchers in the two fields have often speculated on their differences, few of their narrators debate such matters. One key difference, however, is whether material collected orally is used for historical reconstruction or to understand the role and weight of oral tradition within a community. Larry Danielson's essay is a case study of cooperation between the two fields.

Danielson is a Professor of Modern Languages and Folklore at Western Kentucky University. Danielson has written articles on topics in American folklore as wide-ranging as transmuted spirits and Swedish-American mothers. He is the author of a two-part series on folklore and film in Western Folklore *(1980, 1981).*

"The Folklorist, the Oral Historian, and Local History" by Larry Danielson originally appeared in *Oral History Review* 8 (1980), pp. 62–72, and is reprinted by permission of the author and the Oral History Association.

*R*ichard M. Dorson is one of the most vocal and active matchmakers in the courtship of folklore and oral history. Over a decade ago, in his presidential address to the American Folklore Society, he exhorted: "If the folklorist moves outside genre collecting and the oral historian moves beyond interviews with the political and business elite, the two can meet in the recording of folk prejudices, rumors, biases, awes, hatreds, loyalties, phobias, stereotypes, obsessions, and fantasies."[1] Since then many folklorists have made the journey beyond the boundaries of genre restriction and item collection. Simultaneously, oral historians have often defined their purposes with the commonplace and ordinary men and women in mind, in contrast to the elitist orientation of their earlier research. The courtship between the two groups is under way, although no marriage announcement is forthcoming. It cannot be denied, however, that one of the parties—folklore—sometimes sulks when academicians enthusiastically commend the advent of oral history into their scholarly circles, or harbors surly suspicions that the new companion does not adequately understand how to undertake the task at hand.

On occasion students of folk history and the oral record become so immersed in their research they forget that the truisms about their topic are not common knowledge in the outside world. I recently interviewed an insightful and eloquent Finnish-American who grew up on the Minnesota Iron Range, worked in the mines as a young man, and eventually became a Lutheran pastor on the Michigan Upper Peninsula and the Iron Range. We talked a full afternoon, mostly about his Finnish-American childhood, his experiences on the farmstead and in the underground mines, and his ministry to tradition-directed Finnish-Americans. As we parted, he said to me: "I guess I didn't understand what you wanted to know from me. I thought you were going to ask me about history." The puzzled comment forcefully reminded me that even though the folklorist and the oral historian are beginning to cooperate more fully in their mutual concerns about the local past and its expression in the oral testimony, we should not assume that what we have said to one another has been heard or understood by all those outside our academic communities. History for many continues to be spelled in capital letters and describes "important events" in the national past. The life history and community history, which most of us accept as legitimate historical topics, still bear explanation to many as important subject matter, in spite of Alex Haley's *Roots* and by the easy availability of genealogy handbooks on the paperback stands.

Complications in such explanations will arise, sometimes because we have not adequately conceptualized the terms we use so casually. For example, how have we distinguished folk history from oral history? A common definition of oral history among oral historians focuses on the reminiscence about direct personal experience. According to Willa Baum, oral history "involves the tape recording of an interview with a knowledgeable person, someone who knows whereof he or she speaks from personal participation or observation, about a subject of historical interest."[2] Cullom Davis stresses that oral history is no longer exclusively concerned with the elite and reflects "the trend toward 'people's history'. . . . evident throughout the historical profession." He distinguishes between "genuine oral history (first-hand recollections) and oral hearsay (second-hand [recollections])," and notes "this is not to say that [oral hearsay] is of no value. It also is important to acknowledge that human memory is a fragile historical source; it is subject to lapses, errors, fabrications, and distortions."[3] Charles Hudson separates folk history from ethnohistory in order, it appears, to distinguish what is studied from how it is studied. Folk history, according to this ethnohistorian, "denotes the historical beliefs of other societies and cultures," but the aim of ethnohistory is "to reconstruct, using all available materials, 'what really happened' in terms that agree with our sense of credibility and our sense of relevance. . . . In a folk history we attempt to find what people in another society believe 'really happened,' as judged by their sense of credibility and relevance." Finally he uses the magic words: "Thus, the methodology of ethnohistory is essentially 'etic,' while the methodology of folk history is essentially 'emic.' "[4]

Richard M. Dorson wishes to create a new designation that will once and for all separate the folklorist's interest in the oral record from that of the orthodox oral historian: "Oral traditional history . . . seeks out the topics and themes that the folk wish to talk about, the personal and immediate history with which they are concerned." He distinguishes the recollections of first-hand experience as oral personal history in contrast to oral traditional history ("hearsay" in Davis's terminology) and calls both types of accounts species of oral folk history.[5] The eavesdropper must regard these discriminations concerning what is and is not oral history and folk history as pointless hair-splitting. Edward D. Ives has solved the issue easily. He suggests that oral history is a technique that may be used for a variety of purposes. It involves collecting different types of oral material about the past. The data can be used in the reconstruction of historic occurrences, or it can be used in the analysis of popular conceptions of past event and behavior.[6] Therefore folk history, unlike the methodology of oral history, is a substantive, particular subject matter. If we are interested in folk history, we are interested in a native view of the past, whether it is in the form of a collective tradition or a personal reminiscence. In order to gather data necessary in describing and interpreting that perception of the past, we use the techniques of oral history, among others.

Personal history, indeed, may be more reliable than collective "hearsay" in historical reconstructions. The folklorist, however, has long been sensitized to recognize the possibilities of tabulation in first-person accounts and fact in third-person accounts.[7] Sometimes, I think, folklorists sell themselves short in communicating to nonfolklorists this special sensitivity. Mody Boatright's discussion of the family saga, for example, deserves a wider recognition than it has thus far received. In it he examines the clusters of traditional narratives and motifs that appear and reappear as descriptions of actual occurrence in oral family history and printed accounts based on that oral record.[8] The folklorist does not ignore them as unwelcome falsities, even though the cooperating family member may resent the classification of the stories as versions of widespread folk traditions. Instead the folklorist wonders why and how such narratives were created and maintained over the generations. Boatright's observations are insightful, but historians are not often interested in examining such materials for what they indicate about a community's perception of the past. It is difficult to convince many critics that it is as important to analyze the "inaccurate" account as it is to reconstruct the "objective reality." Folklorists perhaps respond more empathetically than do historians to Pontius Pilate's existential query, "What is truth?"

In addition to reminding others that the investigation of subjective reality is an important goal in oral local history research, folklorists need to share their knowledge of traditional patterns of behavior in past contexts. Sometimes folk arts and actions of the past, although verifiable as realities, are interpreted as so much hokum, either grotesque fictions or conscious prevarications. I once discovered a curious nineteenth century manuscript in the archive of a well-known ethnic community in the Midwest. The dozen or so handwritten pages were filled with detailed folk remedies, so I asked a resident authority about the manuscript. "It looks like a put-on to me," he replied, pointing to such remedy ingredients as urine and mouse droppings. The fragile document was irrelevant to the settlement's cultural history, in his opinion. It was a revelation to him that the bizarre prescriptions were indeed legitimate folk medicine practices, often described in ethnographic accounts of nineteenth century European peasant life, but ignored by scholars more interested in kinship structure and patterns of religious dissent. Sensitivity to tradition and an understanding of its specific expression in behavior are important contributions to the descriptions of the local past. In such cases either the oral record or the printed document and artifact, or all three, may communicate confused messages that require specialized interpretation by the folklorist.

I will not belabor other justifications for the folklorist's involvement in historical research that relies on the oral testimony because they are so familiar. Acquaintance with certain tendencies and tropisms in oral literature, for instance traditional patterning and repetition devices, an understanding of oral transmission processes and their possible consequences in matters of continuity and change, recognition of the mercurial relocations and transpositions that float a traditional story from one vivid personality to another years and miles apart, and fieldwork experience that requires observation and passive listening as well as asking questions—these are other well-known contributions the folklorist can make in cooperation with the oral historian in local history studies. The folklorist recognizes the oral narrative as an art form and is sensitive to the ways in which it reshapes the past. As history finds expression in story, the oral testimony communicates a variety of truths.

History is made up largely of stories and tradition, and the folklorist is, or should be, an expert on that relationship.[9]

At this point it would be helpful to describe a specific venture of the folklorist into local history research that makes use of the oral record and the analysis of artifacts and printed sources. In 1977 community leaders in Homer, Illinois, a rural community of some 1,400 residents, became interested in renovating a turn-of-the-century opera house located in a Main Street commercial building, now used as a city services center. As the renovation movement developed, it became clear that information about the original appearance of the opera house and its uses in the past was not available in printed sources. Few state or county histories had paid much attention to Homer, and its newspaper, the reliable, standard source for many community historians, was represented in official state archives by but a few scattered issues. The oral record, along with family memorabilia—photographs and old programs stored in attic boxes—became major sources of information about the opera house and its role in community life.

Soon, however, the local historical society began to expand its research goal, and, with a grant from the state humanities and arts council and aid from an area community college, an organized effort to retrieve Homer's past took shape. I was asked to direct the local history workshop that would effect that retrieval. In it I attempted to consider the uses of the oral testimony and the different kinds of truth it can yield up to us. The first session dealt with the rationale of local history research and its worth; the second, with field interview methodology and the types of information that can be extracted from oral sources; the third, with gaps in the record of Homer's history and the use of artifacts, photographs, and memorabilia in filling those gaps; and the fourth, with the preservation of the materials collected by the historical society and their organization into a usable Homer history archives. By mid-winter a number of active society members were at work with their cassette tape-recorders, notebooks, and cameras. The participants hoped to gather information about the community's past unavailable in the few official histories of Homer, to make these new historical materials available to the public, and to use them in a community presentation, "The Living History of Homer." Mostly middle-aged and elderly, they embarked their efforts in a spring program on the opera house stage.

The project was a successful one. Workshop participants became experienced in the collection and analysis of local history narratives, photographs, and the ephemeral documents some people, fortunately, cannot bear to consign to the trash can. Their research retrieved valuable information about public and private experience in Homer's past that is of interest to the serious student of small-town life in the turn-of-the-century Midwest. As their studies progressed, the work of the local historical society gained impetus. The group now plans to relocate its materials from members' homes into an archive in the old city hall, which it is renovating with funds collected through an opera house series, a varied group of entertainments, including a recital of American parlor music and a Victorian melodrama, presented in the renovated opera house. Individual members continue their interviewing and data collection, even though the official project has concluded. (One enterprising fieldworker brought her elderly informant and her tape recorder out to a local cemetery in order to question him about the past generation as the two walked among the gravestones—an imaginative innovation in the field interview.) The culmination of the project, the "Living History of Homer" program, was lengthy, elaborate, and detailed, and it proved to be a satisfying community experience.

The project was certainly not flawless. There were problems with tape quality, both in terms of sound reproduction and, on occasion, interview responses. A historical society crisis occurred because a local resident withdrew his donation of early twentieth century photographs, thereby denying a rich source of information about Homer's everyday life usable in the public program. The opera house presentation, a multimedia event using slides, tapes, and film, proved to be a difficult task. And, of course, there were frustrations about the organization of the tape materials for the program, "The Living History of Homer," and for classification and retrieval purposes in the new archives.

The positive consequences of the project, however, were persuasive in demonstrating that the folklorist's involvement in local oral history research is justified. A remarkable collection of data about significant events, social behavior, and personal concerns in Homer's past was amassed: traditional medical remedies, burial and funeral traditions, descriptions of butchering and smoking meat, putting up ice, and threshing, information about Ku Klux Klan activities in the community during the 1920s, the functions of the opera house in past decades, commercial and political life over the years, everyday and holiday foodways, attitudes toward Gypsies and itinerants, and even a few stories about the sledding of community homes over the snow in 1855 from a river location, Old Homer, to a railroad location, New Homer. It is apparent that a folklorist's interests are reflected in the array of information. The materials are strongest in their description of daily and customary activities that many historians have paid little attention to—what old Homerites ate, what they did when they got sick, how they celebrated important occasions, and what traditional methods they put to use in their daily labors. Here, then, we have an illustration of oral history methods used to locate information about the past that is difficult to obtain in other sources. It is information that is ignored in many historical studies, even though most people, today and years ago, probably spend more time wondering about their health or the chores at hand than contemplating abstract, intellectual issues. In future decades information about living in Homer in the early to mid-1900s, data easily lost with the death of each generation, will be available to students of small-town life, whether they are historians, folklorists, anthropologists, or sociologists.

Another kind of information is also present. The stories were collected by Homer residents from Homer residents and they often reflect their own historical concerns and satisfactions. An elderly woman recalled that her father feared the widespread use of tractors would ruin the rich Illinois farmland because of their weight. Several interviewees excitedly described a local parrot and its salty vocabulary. (The bird still lives, but its communication is impaired, though not so much as to discourage one fieldworker from taping its squawks.) A simple request for information about old-time washdays prompted a lengthy and detailed description of the lye-making and soap-making. The interviewee, enlivened by the memory, reminisced that once a farmyard turkey flew into the lye kettle and "just got eaten up." Ephemera perhaps, curious local-color footnotes to some, but for community members sharing such stories, they are satisfying narratives about the past that make it come alive in personal ways. The emic categories expressed in stories about the town drunk, how a family managed to eat well during the 1930s depression, and what grandma did when one of her children stepped on a barnyard nail, are more meaningful to community members than those etic categories we are tempted to use in local history research, "history" in capital letters. Many of the tapes are made up of conversations among the residents themselves in which they talk about their community and personal past. The outsider plays no direct role in the transaction, and the folk history of Homer comes alive. The reconstruction of a meaningful past becomes less artificial and self-conscious when community members talk with one another rather than for an interested, though alien visitor.

As usual in reminiscences and anecdotes about the rural American past, snake stories, for example frightening encounters with poisonous snakes and serpentine visitors in unexpected places, were shared in some of the liveliest exchanges. One elderly woman recalled seeing black snakes attached to the cows' udders as the animals were herded home for milking. And, sure enough, there appeared the story about a child innocently sharing her bowl of milk with a backyard snake. In this case, the informant herself recalled taking her bowl of milk to the well where she fed it to a large black snake each evening. The secret was eventually discovered by her father, who threatened to kill the serpent. A farmhand intervened, however, warning that if the snake were killed the child would also die.

What is the historian to make of such narratives? In many cases convincing details merge with bizarre motifs that confound the separation of fact and fiction. According to zoological expertise it is impossible for a snake to attach itself to a cow's udder, but the Homer interviewee asserts that she witnessed such an odd union. Her anecdote expresses a common folk belief concerning milk-sucking serpents. Harry M. Hyatt, for example, cites four instances of the belief and includes a third-person narrative concerning the phenomenon in his detailed collection, *Folk-Lore from Adams County, Illinois*. The fact that snakes can lap liquid from a saucer or cup does not necessarily validate the second traditional narrative as historical incident. "The Child and the Snake" is a widespread folktale plot, categorized in *Types of the Folktale* as number 285. It is found in the Grimm Brothers' *Kinder-und Hausmdrchen* as the first narrative in tale number 105 and has been collected in Northern Europe, England, France, Spain, Hungary, Czechoslovakia, Russia, India, and the New World. It appears in the WPA slave narrative collection, a number of American folktale collections, and occasionally in publications of pioneer reminiscences. The traditional tale is also the subject of an early nineteenth century literary poem for children, probably written by Charles Lamb. As might be expected, the Hyatt collection of Adams County, Illinois, lore includes the full narrative (remarkably similar to the story collected as personal reminiscence in Champaign County, Illinois) as well as a related folk belief: "If you find a snake drinking milk from a cup out of which some of the milk was previously drunk by a child, always let the snake escape; for if the snake is killed, the child will not live long."[10]

The folklorist is delighted to find such traditional motifs imbedded in talk about the past, but both the folklorist and the historian must be perplexed about further evaluation of these stories, especially when they are narrated as personal experiences. We can probably assume that the Homer interviewee was not prevaricating, even though her anecdotes can be classified as accounts of traditional belief and legend rather than as descriptions of historical occurrence. The fusion of traditional motif and personal experience is not unusual in reminiscence (just as dream and reality occasionally become confused in recall). This incorporation of legend and hearsay into one's personal history is a complex problem, demanding the cooperative effort of folklorist and historian. Localized, personalized versions of a widely diffused traditional narrative are not useless or unimportant. The fact that the snake stories cited here are compelling to both interviewee and interviewer is significant and indicates the potency of the quasi-historical narratives for raconteur and audience. That the tales have been transmuted into first-person experience stories suggests that they constitute a meaningful perception of the rural past, a view of the prairie world remarkable for a strange and sometimes dangerous fauna. To dismiss oral traditional narrative because it cannot be used in the reconstruction of objective history is to ignore the community's perception of its past and to disregard the complex interaction between human psychology, narrative function, and historicity in oral history research.

The opera house program, "The Living History of Homer," crystallized the importance of the project for its participants, interviewer and interviewee, performers and audience. Not only did it provide some answers to interesting questions about Homer's past; it also reminded townspeople of their unique as well as representative location in time and space, how their town's history is similar to, yet different from, the histories of countless Midwestern villages. A few years ago Sam Bass Warner, Jr., urged his colleagues to re-evaluate their roles as professional historians: ". . . history is a natural act, a universal behavior. . . . I see the key to the reform of our historical profession to be freeing it from its artificial university constraints so that it may be turned to its multiplicity of useful tasks. The proper role of the professional historian, thus, should be to act as the facilitator of others' historical consciousness."[11] The folklorist and the oral historian can play crucial roles in this facilitation. The Homer project expanded the historical consciousness of many, and I include myself in that number. It did so, in part, because it allowed the contemplation of the oral record on the community's terms. It also accepted a conception of history as nourished, like literature, in Constance Rourke's words, by "the slow accretions of folk elements . . . the humble influences of place and kinship and common emotion that accumulate through generations to shape and condition a distinctive native consciousness."[12]

It is easy at this point to slip into a sentimental golden-glow about the folk doing their own folk history: let them collect what they wish and let them be content and self-satisfied in their forays into historic consciousness-raising. Such a patronizing attitude allows no efforts in the more official, scholarly analysis and interpretation of the local past. It is my experience, both personally and in working with various community history projects, that pleasurable appreciation and critical evaluation are not mutually exclusive. Around the workshop table we can soberly piece together the outlines of a past event from a dozen different interviews, and we can suggest that all the stories we have collected about a colorful settler may be more important for what the narratives say about community response to the eccentric than about the individual in question. A few hours later, perhaps, we may exchange some of the same stories that both entertain us and communicate some sort of historical information. We may share the tales as "true" even though we half-consciously question their veracity. We share them as history, nevertheless, because they satisfy a complicated need to talk about the past and to do so with some verbal artistry.

Richard M. Dorson has suggested that in "literate civilizations the personal sense of history has all but vanished—save in the local community" and that it is at this level that folk history plays a paramount role in the historical record.[13] The need for cooperation between the folklorist and the oral historian in local history research is obvious. We may reach some agreement that the collective oral record and the personal oral testimony can provide us data with which to construct a quasi-objective past as well as valuable insights into the way in which that past is perceived by community members. And these materials amassed may be studied for a variety of purposes. They are a significant contribution to the understanding of the local past, historically, sociologically, even psychologically. The personalization of history—that complicated nexus of art, tradition, comprehension of the past, and human psychology—which is crucial in the maintenance of historic consciousness, is a more difficult matter to assess. That it can most easily be studied within the contexts of local oral history, whether community, neighborhood, or family, is clear. That the folklorist and the oral historian be involved in its consideration is a necessity. Our contributions to understanding that process of personalization may be more consequential than anything else we have to say about folklore-oral history relations.

Notes

1. "A Theory for American Folklore Reviewed," reprinted from the *Journal of American Folklore* 72 (1969), pp. 197–242, in Richard M. Dorson, *American Folklore and the Historian* (Chicago: University of Chicago Press, 1971), p. 58.

2. *Transcribing and Editing Oral History* (Nashville: American Association for State and Local History, 1977), p. 5. See also Willa Baum, *Oral History for the Local Historical Society* (Nashville: American Association for State and Local History, 1971), p. 7.

3. *History with a Tape Recorder: An Oral History Handbook* (Springfield, Ill.: Sangamon State University, Oral History Office, n.d.), inside cover.

4. Charles Hudson, "Folk History and Ethnohistory," *Ethnohistory* 13 (Winter–Spring 1966), pp. 53–54. The terms "etic" and "emic" often appear in contemporary folklore studies. In informal academic usage "etic" has come to designate an outsider's point of view and system of classification and "emic" the insider's conception of cultural categories and their order. The terms were borrowed from Kenneth Pike's linguistic theory. Writes Pike, "An emic approach must deal with particular events as parts of larger wholes to which they are related and from which they obtain their ultimate significance, whereas an etic approach may abstract events, for particular purposes, from their context or local system of events, in order to group them on a world-wide scale without essential reference to the structure of any one language or culture," in *Language in Relation to a Unified Theory of the Structure of Human Behavior,* 3 pts. (Glendale, Calif.: Summer Institute of Linguistics, 1954–60), p. 10. Alan Dundes discusses the relevance of the terms to folk narrative analysis in "From Etic to Emic Units in the Structural Study of Folktales," reprinted from the *Journal of American Folklore* 75 (1962), pp. 92–105, in Alan Dundes, *Analytic Essays in Folklore* (The Hague: Mouton, 1975), pp. 61–72.

5. Richard M. Dorson, "The Oral Historian and the Folklorist," in *Selections from the Fifth and Sixth National Colloquia on Oral History,* ed. Peter D. Olch and Forrest C. Pogue (New York: Oral History Association, 1972), pp. 44–46, passim.

6. Personal conversation, October 11, 1978. Edward D. Ives edits *Northeast Folklore,* an annual publication of special interest to the folklorist-oral historian, and directs the Northeast Archives of Folklore and Oral History, Department of Anthropology, University of Maine, Orono, Maine.

7. See, for example, Lynwood Montell, "The Oral Historian as Folklorist," in *Selections from the Fifth and Sixth National Colloquia on Oral History,* p. 52.

8. Mody C. Boatright, "The Family Saga as a Form of Folklore," in *The Family Saga and Other Phases of American Folklore,* ed. Mody C. Boatright, Robert B. Downs, and John T. Flanagan (Urbana: University of Illinois Press, 1958), pp. 1–19.

9. Specific studies by folklorists that address the historical event include Gladys-Marie Fry, *Night Riders in Black Folk History* (Knoxville: University of Tennessee Press, 1975); Edward D. Ives, "Argyle Boom," *Northeast Folklore* 17 (1976), pp. 24–100; William Ivey, "The 1913 Disaster: Michigan Local Legend," *Folklore Forum* 3 (1970), pp. 100–14; and Lynwood Montell, *The Saga of Coe Ridge: A Study in Oral History* (Knoxville: University of Tennessee Press, 1970; see chapter 14 of the present volume). These studies are heavily indebted to the oral testimony. Bruce A. Rosenberg's *Custer and the Epic of Defeat* (University Park: Pennsylvania State University Press, 1974) is an intriguing analysis of the Custer legend in terms of traditional heroic epic patterns.

10. See items 1567, 1568, 1569, 1570, 1571, 1572, and 1578 in Harry Middleton Hyatt, *Folk-Lore from Adams County, Illinois* (Hannibal, Mo.: Western, 1965). See also George Lyman Kittredge, *Witchcraft in Old and New England* (New York: Russell and Russell, 1956), p. 166, for a brief discussion of the belief in milk-sucking snakes.

The distribution of the tale type is found under no. 285, "The Child and the Snake," in Antti Aarne and Stith Thompson, *The Types of the Folktale: A Classification and Bibliography,* FF Communications no. 184 (Helsinki: Academia Scientiarum Fennica, 1964). See also Butler Waugh, "The Child and the Snake, A Comparative Folktale Study" (Ph.D. diss., Indiana University, 1959), and "The Child and the Snake," *Norveg* 7 (1958), pp. 153ff., and the bibliographic citations under tale type 285, "The Child and the Snake," in Ernest W. Baughman, *Type and Motif-Index of the Folktales of England and North America,* Indiana University Folklore Series No. 20 (The Hague: Mouton, 1966).

Easily available versions of the story appear in B. A. Botkin, ed., *Lay My Burden Down: A Folk History of Slavery* (Chicago: University of Chicago Press, 1965), p. 128; "The Little Girl Who Fed the Snake," in the Frank C. Brown *Collection of North Carolina Folklore,* vol. 1, *Games, Speech, Customs, Proverbs, Riddles, Tales,* ed. Paul G. Brewster, Archer Taylor, Bartlett Jere Whiting, George P. Wilson, and Stith Thompson (Durham: Duke University Press, 1952), p. 638. "The Snake and the Baby" (three texts), in Richard M. Dorson, *American Negro Folktales* (Greenwich: Fawcett, 1967), pp. 174–75; "The Little Boy and the Snake," in Vance Randolph, *Who Blowed Up the Church House? and Other Ozark Folk Tales* (New York: Columbia University Press, 1952), pp. 87–89; and the *Foxfire Book,* ed. Eliot Wigginton (Garden City, N.Y.: Doubleday, 1972), p. 290. It appears as part of a Swedish-American pioneer's reminiscence in an unidentified newspaper story by Karolina Falk Miller in the *Salina Journal* (Salina, Kansas), 1932, reprinted in *The Smoky Valley in the After Years,* ed. Ruth Bergin Billdt and Elizabeth Jaderborg (Lindsborg, Kans.: Lindsborg News-Record, 1969), pp. 191–92. The children's poem "The Child and the Snake" appears in Charles and Mary Lamb, *Poetry for Children* (Freeport, N.Y.: Books for Libraries Press, 1970), pp. 21–23.

11. Sam Bass Warner, Jr., "An Urban Historian's Agenda for the Profession," *Indiana Historical Society Lectures, 1971–1972: History and the Role of the City in American Life* (Indianapolis: Indiana Historical Society, 1972), pp. 52–53.

12. Constance Rourke, "The Significance of Sections," *New Republic,* September 20, 1933, p. 149, quoted in Benjamin Botkin, "Folklore as a Neglected Source of Social History," in *The Cultural Approach to History,* ed. Carolina F. Ware (Port Washington, N.Y.: Kennikat Press, 1940), pp. 314–15.

13. Richard M. Dorson, "Local History and Folklore," reprinted from the *Detroit Historical Society Bulletin* 18 (1961), in Dorson, *American Folklore and the Historian,* p. 148.

16

Oral History and the
Writing of Ethnic History

Gary Y. Okihiro

When the methods of oral history are applied to research on ethnic and minority groups, the history which emerges frequently has a populist or self-consciously democratic cast. Ethnic communities tell their history among themselves, and textbook writers have rarely listened. As a result such groups have lacked a nationally recognized identity. Efforts to redress the balance suggest a key problem in doing oral history: the impact of differences in world view between the interviewer and the interviewee differences in setting, communication styles, dress, even in the reasons why narrators respond.

In our next selection, a professor of ethnic studies, Gary Okihiro, traces the place of ethnic history in the mainstream of the historical profession. Okihiro advocates oral sources as a means of enfranchising and empowering people whose lives have previously been shaped by "colonized history" written from the standpoint of outsiders, not cultural insiders.

Okihiro foresees an oral-based ethnic history which could help ethnic groups understand their true condition and could help devise the means for their liberation from economic and social constraints. His essay reflects a recent trend toward increasingly theoretical and introspective writings on oral history.

Gary Y. Okihiro teaches at Cornell University. He has done field work in Africa and among Japanese-Americans; he has edited a collection of essays, Resistance in America's Concentration Camps *(19).*

"Oral History and the Writing of Ethnic History" by Gary Y. Okihiro was first published in *Oral History Review* 9 (1981), pp. 27–46, and is reprinted by permission of the author and the Oral History Association.

While ethnic historians have utilized oral history for a number of years, in varying degrees of sophistication, few have addressed themselves to the methodological problem of oral history as a tool for recovering history or the theoretical problem of what constitutes history which oral history proposes to answer. The intent of this paper is a modest one. It synthesizes the scattered body of literature on oral history method and seeks to show that oral history is not only method, but also is theory, in the loose sense of the word, and a way of conceptualizing history. The paper, therefore, is mainly concerned with the writing of history—particularly ethnic history—and is neither a primer on how to set up an ethnic oral history program nor a critical analysis of existing ones or the extant literature in ethnic studies. It is an essay on the writing of history and oral history as method and theory and is a reminder of oral history's significance to ethnic history.

The Writing of History

History is the knowledge of human beings in time. Marc Bloch argued that even if history were indifferent to political man/woman and were unable to promote social change, it would be justified by its necessity for the full development of human beings.[1] Still, history would be incomplete if it did not eventually help us to lead better lives. Historical explanation derives, in the first instance, from our need for explanation but thereafter enables us to act reasonably. Accordingly, this humanistic history advocated by Bloch springs from a desire to satisfy human intellectual needs/curiosity through an explanation of human lives—the human condition—for the guidance of human action.

Both of these aims in history—the needs for explanation and human guidance—require that historians reconstruct and explicate historical reality freed from the oppression of myths and lies. That objective reality, however, is independent of the historian's consciousness and may not even be approached. In his well-known 1932 presidential address to the American Historical Association, Carl Becker expressed an extreme position on that subject. According to Becker, history (which is past reality complete and unchanging) is distinct from our knowledge of history which is merely our conception of that historical reality incomplete and subject to change. Thus, he concluded, every man was his own historian.[2]

Two decades later, C. Vann Woodward objected to Becker's relativism. While conceding that myths may influence human activity and constitute a part of intellectual history, Woodward nonetheless maintained that they must be separated from historical reality, the object toward which historians strive.[3] As his own work on segregation in the South underscored,[4] individuals may well behave on the basis of misconceptions or myths; these may constitute reality for them, but it was Woodward's contention that the historian must distinguish between those subjective perceptions and objective reality.

While in accord with Woodward's strictures on the subject, I share the sentiments voiced by those like Arthur Schlesinger, Jr., Jan Vansina, Studs Terkel, and Staughton Lynd to the effect that the historian must shed intellectual arrogance which presumes that s/he knows better than the historical actors themselves or that nonliterate people have no conception of history.[5]

Still, a revival of the old extreme relativism in the form of what Gene Wise has labeled as "perspectivist history" is ill-conceived if the distinction is blurred between historical reality and individual reality.[6] Stanley Elkins's Sambo might have been reality to some southern whites who only saw that profile of black people,[7] but it was not historical reality to blacks in their accounts of plantation life. What blacks emphasize are the subjects of slave rebellions and the deceptions played on white masters. Sambo was not, then, an internalized image, as proposed by Elkins, but was merely a mask for survival.[8] The contract here is elucidating. Elkins's thesis was derived from the traditional plantation sources—records, diaries, letters, et cetera—while the refutation came from the people themselves, the oral traditions or black folk. Further, the distinction between individual or group reality and historical reality is a necessary and liberating one.

Historians generally agree that historical explanations are really only propositions placed within a general interpretive framework postulated by the historian. "The history of societies," observed E. J. Hobsbawm, requires us to apply, if not a formalized and elaborate model of such structures, then at least an approximate order of research priorities and a working assumption about what constitutes the central nexus or complex of connections of our subject, though of course these things imply a model. Every social historian does in fact make such assumptions and holds such priorities."[9] At the very first, therefore, historical research presumes that there is direction and purpose and that it is not value-free.

The apparent paradox is that historians argue for the reconstruction of historical reality while, at the same time, they also admit that historical research begins with assumptions; and, in fact, they advocate the construction of models and theories to explain reality. If, however, one agrees that historical reality behaves in a systematic fashion, then theory which most closely resembles that reality best explains it; this is because theory provides boundaries for the system; identifies its elements, structure, and function; proposes explanations; poses questions; and provides a test of logical consistency for explanations. Even if the theory is divorced from reality, it at least provides expectations, things for the historian to look for; and if these are not found, the model can be modified accordingly.[10] The historian must, therefore, be sensitive and receptive to whatever the historical evidence may reveal.

A diagram of the process by which history is written is displayed in Figure 16.1.

The Nature of Historical Evidence

While maintaining a receptive mind, the historian must also view the historical evidence critically. Apart from cultural and physical artifacts such as pottery, bones, and so forth, there are two broad categories of historical evidence—written documents and oral documents. Both of these varieties share common elements which are of concern to the historian. Historical documents derive from humans who have biases and prejudices, selective perceptions and memories, incomplete and limited powers of observation, and fallible memories. Further, people undergo changes over time and are subject to external influences and manipulation and, as such, are mirrors of their time and environment.

Besides these common human qualities which pervade historical documents, there is the question of audience to which the document is addressed. This assumes that historical documents are purposeful and that those purposes may determine, in a deliberate or unconscious way, the final shape of the document in which facts may be altered, emphases misplaced, or information suppressed. The historian must, therefore, distinguish between the behavioral or apparent meaning of the document and the ideational or internal, and thus hidden, meaning.[11]

Because of these characteristics of historical documents, they cannot stand alone nor can they "speak for themselves." They are, in fact, parts of a human-communications system which consists of a network of elements within a pervasive environment over time. Thus, in historical documents, the critical historian must identify the author of the document in an identified position or vantage point at an identified moment.[12] The task, therefore, is a mapping of the terrain through a sociology of the systems or network to identify its elements and

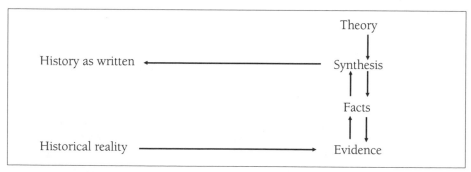

Figure 16.1 The writing of history.
Source: Robert F. Berkhofer, Jr., A Behavioral Approach to Historical Analysis (New York: Macmillan, 1969), pp. 20–23.

determine their relationships at a particular moment in time. That process, termed internal textual criticism, enables the historian to make a more valid evaluation of the reliability of the historical evidence.

When several historical documents are compared with each other, we say that the historian is engaged in external textual criticism. The comparative method of documentary evaluation is indispensable in reconstructing historical reality; for by comparing several texts, one is able to see variation, contradictions, and similarities. From that comparison, then, and through internal textual criticism and theory, the historian is better able to approach historical reality.

The reliance on theory increases as the quantity of historical documents diminishes because the less the number of witnesses to support, contradict, or modify a particular version, the greater the degree of uncertainty. Besides quantity, the quality or nature of the evidence may determine the extent for the need for theory. Thus, for example, one objective and perceptive witness is usually more valuable than three witnesses who had a particular ax to grind although that in itself could be illuminating;[13] and if the weight of the evidence supports a point of view which does not correspond with the historian's view of reality, the evidence may be used selectively to make it conform to the historian's theory of historical reality.

The end product of that process, history as written, may in an extreme case not even resemble the documents from which it was drawn; but the historian may claim that the interpretation is a closer approximation of historical reality because the theory more closely conforms to that reality. Some may see that claim as intellectual arrogance while others may view it as a breakthrough in interpretation; it depends on their world view or theory of history. Historical debate is fueled by the scarcity of reliable evidence—the lesser the amount of reliable evidence, the greater the dependence on theory; and the greater the dependence on theory, the greater the opportunity for debate.

Types of Oral Documents

While sharing certain common features, oral documents are not identical to written ones. There is an important distinction which is of concern to the oral historian. The author of a written document is usually no longer living when the document is used by a historian—a feature of various privacy and ethical codes. In contrast, oral documents are derived from living persons; at least the initial recording of any such document on tape or paper is a product of living persons in conversation. Thus, whereas written documents are often referred to as dead letters, oral documents are generally styled living testimonies.

The difference here can be an important one if, as is commonly the case, a historian generates oral documents which s/he subsequently uses for historical interpretation. This is because the archival historian is limited to the written word and cannot go beyond what the author of a given document thought, what s/he thought happened or ought to happen, or what s/he wanted others to think happened; in other words, the distinction between the behavioral and ideational is blurred; and the historian is uncertain of the historicity of the evidence. On the other hand, the oral historian who employs a document which s/he has created with an interviewee is able to observe human behavior firsthand in all its complexity and under varying circumstances; and s/he is able to engage in dialogue with the historical actor.

Of course, this interaction between historian and historical actor can both illuminate and obscure historical reality. While a greater degree of precision may be obtained by direct observation and communication, greater uncertainty may also arise from the historian's role in altering behavior or in predetermining the responses by the nature of the questions or from the historian's diminished capacity to be objective because of any friendship so cultivated.[14]

There are several varieties of oral documents. Personal reminiscence or oral history is the most elemental of these. Oral history is the recollections of a single individual who participated in or was an observer of the events to which s/he testifies. The document, therefore, derives from the historical actor him/herself or from an eyewitness. When oral history is passed on to another person, usually of a succeeding generation in that family or lineage, it becomes oral tradition.[15] Thus, oral tradition is derived from a transmission of testimony vertically. If that tradition spreads horizontally to a wider, definable group of people, it is referred to as folklore or elitelore, depending on the social class of the group.[16]

As indicated at the outset, this paper is limited to a discussion of oral history, and the distinction between that type of oral evidence and the other varieties such as oral tradition, folklore/elitelore, legend, epic, fable, and myth should be kept in mind.[17]

Oral History

Despite the claim that oral history is history, no more, no less, the distinctions remain between individual perceptions of historical reality and historical reality and between the process by which archival history is written and by which history derived from oral documents is written. The latter process is more complex than archival history, as is evident by contrasting Figure 16.2 with Figure 16.1.

The program director is the person who conceptualizes the oral history program, its purposes and direction. The director's world view or idea of history helps determine the linguistic community selected. ("Linguistic community" herein refers to those who share linguistic symbols and patterns of articulation, and a common world view and experiences.) Thus, for example, Joe Grant

Masaoka, the director of the oral history collection of the Japanese American Research Project housed at the University of California, Los Angeles, generally chose to interview those who reflected his point of view about such controversial issues as the causes and conduct of the World War II evacuation and incarceration of West Coast Japanese Americans.[18] In that way, the collection to a large extent mirrored Masaoka's perceptions.

The selected individuals, however, need not be comprehensive nor statistically representative of the wider linguistic community from which they originate. Oral historians realize that the interview is a limited document. At the same time, they maintain that a given individual has as much right to be heard as anyone else and that his/her history is worthy of being recorded.[19] The difference is in one's conception of what constitutes history.

On the other hand, the oral historian (i.e., one who is a consumer of the interviews s/he has conducted) does not merely regurgitate the contents of the interview. As noted above, the historian must examine the oral document critically, both internally and externally, and place that document within his/her theoretical framework. Thus, the oral historian must keep clearly in mind the distinction between an individual's right to be heard and the writing of history. The individual's perception of history need not necessarily coincide with historical reality. The oral historian is not a mere publicist of individual perceptions; the ultimate goal is the reconstruction of historical reality.

The second step in oral history, the interview, involves at least two different world views, that of the linguistic community and that of the interviewer or oral historian. A concern, therefore, is with these world views. Are they parallel, or do

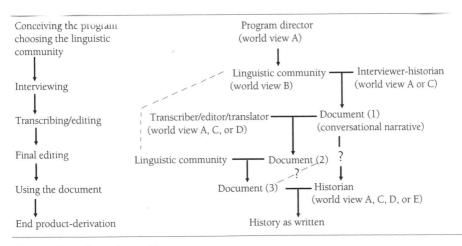

Figure 16.2 Steps in oral history.

they clash, and what are the implications if they do not correspond? These questions are of particular relevance in cross-cultural situations in which the conceptions of what constitutes history differ.

When I did my fieldwork in Botswana, Africa, in 1974–75, at first, hoping not to bias the response, I invariably began with an open-ended question like "Tell me about the history of the Bakwena (the people I was studying)." The responses to that question were always very general and vague and indicated that the interviewees had little knowledge of Bakwena history. After numerous such disappointing interviews, I became discouraged and began to think that no one in the community had a deep and clear understanding of history. Because I was getting nowhere with that question, I began to pursue a different tack by asking more localized questions about the interviewee, his/her family, lineage, and clan. And as the information gushed forth, it became apparent to me that our conceptions of what constituted history did not correspond. The people's view was limited to one's family, lineage, and kin while my conception was one of nation or "tribe"; and because of our different world views, there was a restricted flow of information, and I labored under false impressions.

A second concern arising from the interview situation is the extent to which external factors influence the responses. It is a recognized fact that the setting in which the interview is held, the nature of the questions, and even the appearance of the interviewer may bias responses and restrict the flow of information. Various authors have noted how a setting unfamiliar to the interviewee or a highly formalized list of questions tends to inhibit communication and how class- or culture-bound assumptions, mode of speech, or dress has a similarly stultifying effect.[20] In addition, the oral historian must concern him/herself with the motives of the interviewee in agreeing to be interviewed. Studs Terkel, for instance, pays his interviewees; the question then arises, to what extent does reimbursement or the promise of publication influence the nature of the responses?

Certain bands of Bushmen (San) in southern Africa, frequently sought out by anthropologists, have grown astute in handling their visitors, giving them answers which the anthropologists want to hear in return for gifts.

One proposed solution to the problems of cross-cultural research has been participant observation. Oscar Lewis, in his studies of poverty and families, proposes that to understand the culture of the poor it is necessary to live with them, learn the language and customs, and identify oneself with their frustrations and aspirations.[21] That method stands in marked contrast to those studies done by Nathan Glazer and Daniel P. Moynihan, who relied on census data rather than engaging in ethnographic field research among the people themselves.[22] Then, too, there is the case of Victor and Brett Nee whose 1972 publication *Longtime Californ'* represents the most notable Asian-American book to date using oral history. While claiming that it was an advantage to be outsiders because they could stand above local partisan conflict, the Nees nonetheless found that not being residents of Chinatown and not knowing Cantonese or other dialects restricted their full entry into the community and, no doubt, resulted in a less-than-complete picture of San Francisco Chinatown.[23]

Because of the many opportunities for distortions to arise in the interview, oral historians are cautioned to familiarize themselves with the extensive literature on interviewing techniques and to be aware of the various external factors which may influence the responses.[24] Further, they are urged to make thorough research preparations concerning the interviewee and subject matter before each session to provide the basis for a productive and meaningful conversation.[25] Oral historians maintain that the knowledge derived from those background researches, coupled with the empathy and sensitivity developed through participant observation, enables them to elicit significant and valid historical documents and to reconstruct historical reality.

As noted by Ronald Grele, the primary theoretical concern in writings on oral history has been the possibility for distortion in the interview while little discussion has focused on the exact nature of the oral document which is the end product of that interview. The document, observed Grele, is not simply a transcript or tape; nor is it an autobiography, biography, or memory; rather, it is a conversational narrative—conversational because it is a dialogue between interviewer and interviewee and narrative because it is a form of exposition. There are three sets of relationships in this conversational narrative: (1) internal to the interview, consisting of its linguistic and literary structure; (2) external to the text, the relationship created by interaction of interviewer and interviewee; and (3) external to the text, the relationship between the interviewee and the wider community which is both his/her audience and molder of his/her historical consciousness.[26]

All three relationships are enormously complex, but by untangling them invaluable insights can be gained. A linguistic analysis of the text, for example, may contribute toward a cultural definition of class; for, as demonstrated by William Labov, among ethnic groups and social classes there is a tendency of speakers to conform to certain unique patterns of speech.[27] In that way, those groups maintain their ethnic and class identity.

The relationship between interviewer and interviewee involves a reflexive process by which the interviewee's view of history is developed in relation to the historian's view, while the historian's questions, in turn, are developed in response to the interviewee's answers. Thus, *The Autobiography of Malcolm X* is not an autobiography; rather it is the mutual creation of two men, Malcolm X and Alex Haley.[28] The task of the oral historian is to analyze carefully that relationship between interviewer and interviewee to understand what kind of communication is taking place, what meaning is being conveyed, and what mutual influences are at work in the shaping of the conversation.

The relationship between the interviewee and the wider community involves the ideological or theoretical context within which words or phrases are placed, the presence or absence of concepts, and the individual's vision of history. To extricate the interviewee from both the interviewer and his/her wider community, then, is an exceedingly complex and commanding task. But by being able to direct questions at the interviewee's conceptions of history and historical change, the oral historian, unlike the archival historian, is able to arrive at a deeper understanding of the people and their history.[29]

The end product of the interaction between interviewer-historian and linguistic community-interviewee is oral document 1 (see Figure 16.2) defined as a conversational narrative and normally in the form of a tape recording. Next come the transcription, editing, and sometimes translating of that recording onto paper.

When Allan Nevins, considered to be the founder of oral history in the United States, set up the Oral History Research Office at Columbia University in 1948, he at first conceived his task to be a simple one. He interviewed well-known individuals about significant events, had the tapes transcribed onto paper, and saw the transcription as the raw stuff of which history would be written. The tapes were then erased, keeping only a small segment to give the flavor of the interview. During the transcription phase, there was free editing of the text which included the striking out of words and phrases.[30]

Later, on reflection, Nevins's procedure was seen to have posed serious methodological problems. The historian's intervention in transcribing and editing effectively altered the text so that entire meanings could be lost or changed. Thus, oral historians were cautioned to make certain that the transcriber faithfully recorded what was on the tape, including pauses, laughter, and coughs. In addition, the interviewer must be sure that everything which took place during the interview was recorded because oftentimes in the course of the interview the participants took a break, the duration for which the recorder was turned off. But a number of important things may transpire or be said during that period of relaxation. Thus, the interviewer was advised to keep the recorder on at all times.[31] And finally, the original tape recording must be kept intact for future reference.

Despite these cautions, there still remains the possibility of distortions in the transcribed text which may be the result of fatigue, hearing impairment, or mis-perceptions caused by divergent world views. This last factor is even more pro-nounced if the text is being translated as well as transcribed; translation, of course, introduces a whole new set of opportunities for distortion.

The end result of this interaction between transcriber and document 1 (see Figure 16.2) is document 2 which is, ideally, an exact replica of the voices on the tape recording in written form. The usual procedure is then to give document 2 back to the interviewee for final editing. This is normally done because of the interviewee's ethical right to see the text before final release and out of courtesy to him/her who can if s/he so wishes delete or retract words, phrases, or expressions made during the interview. In effect, the interviewee acts as his/her own censor. Document 3 (see Figure 16.2) is the end product of this interaction between interviewee and document 2, and the documents may or may not be the same.

Document 3 is used by the historian in the same way as other historical documents are used, as diagrammed in Figure 16.1; the text is critically examined both internally and externally, and the final outcome of that interaction is history as written.[32] There is little doubt, from the process outlined above, that oral documents are qualitatively different from written ones; there exist more possibilities for distortions to arise, and they are more complex and hazardous to use. At the same time, however, oral history provides a unique opportunity for the writing of Bloch's humanistic vision of history, a people's history.

Oral History and the Writing of Ethnic History

This work is an impression and the search for a silenced voice, a crucial part in the chorus of American voices.

Black woman, silent, almost invisible in America, has been speaking for 300 years in pantomime or at least in a borrowed voice. She has moved silently through the mythological roles forced upon her—from chattel to Mammy to Matriarch. She has solaced and fortified the entire South of the United States, black and white, male and female, a South which reveres and heeds her in secret, which confides in her and trusts her to rear its children, black and white, yet which—like the rest of America—has never asked her to speak, to reveal her private history, her knowledge, her imaginings, never asked her participation in anything but maintenance of humanity by way of the back door.[33]

The writing of ethnic history is both necessary and possible. It need neither be justified nor defended. The collective voice of the people, once silenced, has a right to be heard. Oral history is not only a tool or method for recovering history; it also is a theory of history which maintains that the common folk and the dispossessed have a history and that this history must be written. At the same time, however, this is not to ignore the importance of elitelore and the history of the ruling class, nor does it intend to equate oral history with the working class and written documents with the ruling class. Instead, the point is that there has been an overemphasis on the elite at the expense of the masses and that this imbalance has resulted in the writing of mythical histories.

Ethnic history does not deny the political importance of focusing on the dominant (oppressor) group in society and those institutions through which the majority represses and exploits the minority. Rather, ethnic history is the first step toward ultimate emancipation; for by freeing themselves from the bonds of a colonized history, they will be able to see their true condition, their own history.

From that realization and from an understanding of the majority group and their institutions, minorities can proceed to devise means for their total liberation.

Oral history has been shown to be an invaluable means by which to recover the past of the inarticulate—women, the working class, ethnic and racial minorities, and people in nonliterate societies[34]—because these groups rarely leave written records of their lives; the meager documentary evidence about them is usually biased against them and rarely penetrates to the ideational, and they have largely been ignored by historians who view history in terms of "big men" and "important" events.[35] Besides being a tool for recovering history, oral history forges a link between the academy and the community through ethnographic field techniques and participant observation; and it has a potential for raising social consciousness and can provide strategies for social change.[36]

Terkel noted that the absence of knowledge about the past perpetuates myths about it and contributes to maintaining of the status quo.[37] A graphic illustration of that is the Republic of South Africa, where the official version of history is used to justify the repressive system of apartheid. Staughton Lynd, in his studies of American labor history, observed that rank-and-file unionists wanted to know the history of the 1930s so they could respond to the present upsurge of labor militancy in the CIO.[38] That knowledge was obtained by interviewing old-time activists; and, armed with those insights, the militants were able to understand how CIO unions had so rapidly grown bureaucratic and conservative and thereupon to devise effective tactics in seeking change. Socialist historians, though, like historians and intellectuals in general, must strive for maximum objectivity. Myths, both ideologically and radically inspired, must not be permitted to distort the historical landscape.[39]

The historiographical development in African history is of particular significance and relevance.[40] African history was first written by Europeans who saw Africans, in the words of the distinguished British historian Sir Reginald Coupland, as having no history and as having "stayed, for untold centuries, sunk in barbarism . . . [so that] the heart of Africa was scarcely beating."[41] African history, accordingly, was derived exclusively from European archives and the reminiscences and accounts of white colonialists, missionaries, and travelers. This variety of history portrayed Africa as being dark and peopled by primitive, faceless hordes; African history began with the arrival of the Europeans who brought Christianity, enlightenment, and civilization. The focus, therefore, was on the white man who was the historical actor; and the African was merely a docile object to be manipulated.

During the 1950s, a new generation of historians broke away from that European tradition, pointing out that, besides its mythical qualities, the interpretation was not truly African history but merely the history of Europeans in Africa. Further, the official version was used to justify the colonization of Africa by Europeans. The revisionist historians sought to rewrite the history of Africa by seeing Africans as historical actors and as human beings; but the traditional archival and published sources provided only brief, superficial, and biased glimpses of African society. That impasse was finally broken when the historians went into the field to record the oral traditions of the African people themselves; new insights were gained and a more humane variety of African history was written.

The primary characteristic of "colonized" history is that it is the view of outsiders and not the people themselves. The historical evidence upon which that variety of history draws is from the colonizer. Usually this is in the form of written documents—letters, diaries, and reminiscences of visitors—which describe the author's position among the people and his/her perceptions of that people. For various reasons, from the resumption of the primacy of written documents over oral ones to the assumption that the elite are the only ones who matter historically, the people themselves are ignored and are not asked about their perceptions of history. As a consequence, the actions of the colonizers are magnified so they become the central figures in the narrative; they are portrayed as the historical actors while the people are rendered as passive, powerless objects.

What, then, are the implications for American ethnic history? To varying degrees, the written history of ethnic minorities in our country has suffered under the yoke of colonial oppression. Our collective histories have long been colonized, and our self-perceptions have been distorted by historical documents written by strangers who have sojourned among us but who have little knowledge of us. Oral history offers an alternative way of conceptualizing history and a means by which to recover that past. And while oral history does not maintain that each individual's view of history is equally legitimate or that every voice must be heard, it does argue that by going directly to the people for historical documents, a more valid variety of history can be written. Oral history proposes that we rewrite our history to capture the human spirit of the people, to see how ethnic minorities solved or failed to solve particular problems, how they advanced or resisted change, and how they made or failed to make better lives for themselves and their children. In short, oral history proposes nothing less than the writing of a people's history, liberated from myths and imbued with humanity.

Notes

1. Marc Bloch, *The Historian's Craft* (New York: Vintage, 1953), pp. 9–10. See also Karl R. Popper, *The Poverty of Historicism* (London: Routledge and Kegan Paul, 1957). Cf. Staughton Lynd, "Guerilla History in Gary," *Liberation* 14 (October 1969), pp. 17–20, who argues that the reason for "guerilla history," or history from the bottom up, is to raise political consciousness and to promote action.

2. Carl Becker, "Everyman His Own Historian," *American Historical Review* 37 (January 1932), pp. 221–36.

3. C. Vann Woodward, *American Attitudes toward History* (London: Oxford University Press, 1955).

4. C. Vann Woodward, *The Strange Career of Jim Crow* (London: Oxford University Press, 1955), demonstrates that point by showing how widely believed lies of the past have shaped Southern opinions of the future.

5. Arthur Schlesinger, Jr., "The Historian as Participant," in *Historical Studies Today,* ed. Felix Gilbert and Stephen R. Graubard (New York: Norton, 1972), pp. 393–412; Jan Vansina, "Once upon a Time: Oral Traditions as History in Africa," *Daedalus* 100 (Spring 1971), pp. 442–68; Studs Terkel, *Hard Times: An Oral History of the Great Depression* (New York: Pantheon, 1970); and Staughton Lynd, ed., "Personal Histories of the Early CIO," *Radical America* 5 (May–June 1971), pp. 49–76.

6. Gene Wise, *American Historical Explanations: A Strategy for Grounded Inquiry* (Homewood, Ill.: Dorsey Press, 1973); Arthur A. Hansen and David A. Hacker, "The Manzanar Riot: An Ethnic Perspective," *Amerasia Journal* 2 (fall 1974), pp. 112–57.

7. Stanley M. Elkins, *Slavery: A Problem in American Institutional and Intellectual Life* (Chicago: University of Chicago Press, 1959).

8. Gladys-Marie Fry, *Night Riders in Black Folk History* (Knoxville: University of Tennessee Press, 1975), pp. 5–6; Ann Lane, ed., *The Debate over Slavery* (Urbana: University of Illinois Press, 1971).

9. E. J. Hobsbawm, "From Social History to the History of Society," *Daedalus* 100 (Winter 1971), p. 31.

10. John Habakkuk, "Economic History and Economic Theory," in *Historical Studies,* ed. Gilbert and Graubard, pp. 42–43; and Robert P. Baker, "Labor History, Social Science, and the Concept of Working Class," *Labor History* 14 (Winter 1973), pp. 98–105.

11. Robert F. Berkhofer, Jr., *A Behavioral Approach to Historical Analysis* (New York: Macmillan, 1969), pp. 9–10.

12 Jurgen Ruesch, "The Observer and the Observed: Human Communication Theory," in *Toward a Unified Theory of Human Behavior,* ed. Roy R. Grinker (New York: Basic, 1956), pp. 36–54.

13. James W. Wilkie and Edna Monzon de Wilkie, "Dimensions of Elitelore: An Oral History Questionnaire," *Journal of Latin American Lore* 1 (Summer 1975), p. 83; Saul Benison, "Oral History and Manuscript Collecting," *Isis* 53 (1963), pp. 113–17.

14. Berkhofer, *Behavioral Approach,* pp. 10–11, 14–17; Daniel Aaron, "The Treachery of Recollection: The Inner and Outer History," in *Essays on History and Literature,* ed. Robert H. Bremner (Columbus: Ohio State University Press, 1966), pp. 7–10, 16–17.

15. For definitions of oral tradition, see Jan Vansina, *Oral Tradition: A Study in Historical Methodology,* trans. H. M. Wright (London: Routledge and Kegan Paul, 1965; also see chapter 8 of the present volume).

16. Wilkie and Monzon de Wilkie, "Dimensions of Elitelore," pp. 82–83; Richard M. Dorson, "Oral Tradition and Written History," in *American Folklore and the Historian,* ed. Richard M. Dorson (Chicago: University of Chicago Press, 1971), pp. 129–44.

17. See Vansina, *Oral Tradition,* pp. 157–60, for definitions of legend, epic, fable, and myth.

18. Gary Y. Okihiro, *The Oral History Tapes of the Japanese American Research Project, Tapes 1–112: A Survey* (Los Angeles: Asian American Studies Center, 1974), pp. iv–vi. The collection reflects a point of view characterized as a JACL–WRA interpretation. See Gary Y. Okihiro, "Japanese Resistance in America's Concentration Camps: A Reevaluation," *Amerasia Journal* 2 (Fall 1973), pp. 20–34; and Hansen and Hacker, "Manzanar Riot."

19. See, for example, Studs Terkel, *Working: People Talk about What They Do All Day and How They Feel about What They Do* (New York: Pantheon, 1974); and Louis Starr, "Studs Terkel and Oral History," *Chicago History* 3 (Fall 1974), pp. 123–26.

20. Donald C. Swain, "Problems for Practitioners of Oral History," *American Archivist* 28 (January 1965), pp. 66–67; William W. Cutler III, "Accuracy in Oral History Interviewing," *Historical Methods Newsletter* 3 (June 1970), pp. 3–4 (see chapter 6 of the present volume); Alice Kessler-Harris, introduction, *Envelopes of Sound,* ed. Ronald J. Grele (Chicago: Precedent Publishing, 1975), pp. 2–3; and Victor Nee and Brett Nee, *Longtime Californ': A Documentary Study of an American Chinatown* (New York: Pantheon, 1972), p. xiv.

21. Oscar Lewis, *Five Families: Mexican Case Studies in the Culture of Poverty* (New York: Basic, 1959); Lewis, *The Children of Sanchez: Autobiography of a Mexican Family* (New York: Random House, 1961); and Lewis, *La Vida: A Puerto-Rican Family in the Culture of Poverty—San Juan and New York* (New York: Random House, 1966). Still, there are obvious limits to the efficacy of participant observation. For instance, it can never transform the researcher into the observed.

22. Charles A. Valentine, *Culture and Poverty: Critique and Counter-Proposals* (Chicago: University of Chicago Press, 1968), p. 101.

23. Nee and Nee, *Longtime Californ',* pp. xiv–xv, xx.

24. See, for example, Lewis Anthony Dexter, *Elite and Specialized Interviewing* (Evanston: Northwestern University Press, 1970); William H. Banaka, *Training in Depth Interviewing* (New York: Harper and Row, 1970); Alfred Benjamin, *The Helping Interview* (Boston: Houghton Mifflin, 1969); and Robert K. Merton, Patricia Kendall, and Marjorie Fiske, *The Focused Interview* (Glencoe, Ill.: Free Press, 1956).

25. Saul Benison, "Reflections on Oral History," *American Archivist* 28 (January 1965), p. 73; Cutler, "Accuracy in Oral History," p. 4; and Ronald J. Grele, "Movement without Aim: Methodological and Theoretical Problems in Oral History," in *Envelopes of Sound,* ed. Grele, pp. 130–31.

26. Grele, "Movement without Aim," pp. 131–33, 135–37; Cutler, "Accuracy in Oral History," p. 7; Saul Benison, "Oral History: A Personal View," in *Modern Methods in the History of Medicine,* ed. Edwin Clark (London: Athlone Press, 1971), p. 291; and Lynd, "Personal Histories," pp. 50–51; all touch upon this subject, but they do not deal with its theoretical implications.

27. William Labov, "Phonological Correlates of Social Stratification," *American Anthropologist* 66 (December 1964), pp. 164–76; and *The Social Stratification of English in New York City* (Washington, D.C.: Center for Applied Linguistics, 1966). See also, Baker, "Labor History," pp. 98–105.

28. Malcolm X, *The Autobiography of Malcolm X,* with the assistance of Alex Haley (New York: Grove Press, 1965).

29. Grele, "Movement without Aim," pp. 135–42.

30. Kessler-Harris, introduction, pp. 1–2.

31. Gould P. Colman, "Oral History—An Appeal for More Systematic Procedures," *American Archivist* 28 (January 1965), pp. 79–83.

32. See Hansen and Hacker, "Manzanar Riot"; Charles T. Morrissey, "Truman and the Presidency—Records and Oral Recollections," *American Archivist* 28 (January 1965), pp. 53–61; and Gould Colman, "Theoretical Models and Oral History Interviews," *Agricultural History* 41 (July 1967), pp. 255–56, for examples of how oral documents can complement written documents in the writing of history.

33. Joseph Carson, *Silent Voices: The Southern Negro Woman Today* (New York: Delacorte Press, 1969), p. 1.

34. Richard M. Dorson, "Ethnohistory and Ethnic Folklore," *Ethnohistory* 8 (Winter 1961), pp. 12–30; Gerda Lerner, ed., *Black Women in White America: A Documentary History* (New York: Pantheon, 1972); Lee Rainwater, Richard P. Coleman, and Gerald Handel, *Workingman's Wife: Her Personality, World, and Life Style* (New York: Oceana, 1959); Lynd, "Guerilla History"; Ronald Blythe, *Akenfield: Portrait of an English Village* (New York: Pantheon, 1969); William Lynwood Montell, *The Saga of Coe Ridge: A Study in Oral History* (Knoxville: University of Tennessee Press, 1970; and see chapter 14 of the present volume); Theodore Rosengarten, *All God's Dangers: The Life of Nate Shaw* (New York: Knopf, 1974); Fry, *Night Riders;* John Stands in Timber and Margot Liberty, *Cheyenne Memories* (New Haven: Yale University Press, 1967); and Daniel Francis McCall, *Africa in Time Perspective: A Discussion of Historical Reconstruction from Unwritten Sources* (Boston: Boston University Press, 1964).

35. Alice M. Hoffman, "Who Are the Elite, and What is a Non–Elitist?" *Oral History Review* 4 (1976), pp. 1–5.

36. Arthur J. Vidich, Joseph Bensman, and Maurice R. Stein, eds., *Reflections on Community Studies* (New York: Wiley, 1964); Lynd, "Guerilla History"; Kessler-Harris, introduction, *The Writing of Ethnic History,* p. 4; and Willa K. Baum, "Building Community Identity Through Oral History—A New Role for the Local Library," *California Librarian* 31 (October 1970), pp. 271–84.

37. Kessler–Harris, introduction, p. 4.

38. Lynd, "Guerilla History," pp. 17–29.

39. Eugene D. Genovese, *In Red and Black: Marxian Explorations in Southern and Afro-American History* (New York: Vintage, 1971).

40. For a similar development in Afro-American historiography, see Fry, *Night Riders,* pp. 3–29.

41. Basil Davidson, *The African Past* (Boston: Little, Brown, 1964).

17

What's So
Special About Women?
Women's Oral History

Sherna Gluck

In this next essay, we review the efforts of feminists to apply oral historical methods to the history of women. The approach of Sherna Gluck, researcher and social activist, is to seek out "everywoman," whose story can illustrate the "common threads that link all women"; the writing of history thus becomes a validation of women's experiences and "a feminist encounter."

Gluck explores the problems of a mismatch between interviewer and interviewee and suggests that race (and particularly sex) differences can inhibit the success of interviews. She also discusses the practicalities of interviews that deal with women's-only issues, such as sex, contraception, and menstruation. The author writes with great sympathy about the difficulty of interviewing women unaccustomed to expressing themselves publicly, particularly members of the working class. When it was originally published in the women's studies journal of the University of Colorado, this article was a landmark survey of women's oral history. In describing her methods, Gluck touches on one of the by-products of oral history, the increase in self-esteem of the interviewee, and on one of its crucial functions in uniting social groups, the search for a collective memory and identity.

Sherna Gluck teaches women's studies at California State University, Long Beach, and directs the oral history program there. She has worked on several oral history projects on women, including one on women who worked in the Los Angeles aircraft industry during World War II. She is the editor of From Parlor to Prison: Five American Suffragists Talk about Their Lives (1976) *and the author of numerous articles which utilize oral history.*

"What's So Special about Women? Women's Oral History" by Sherna Gluck is excerpted from *FRONTIERS: A Journal of Women Studies* 2 (summer 1977 Special Issue on Women's Oral History), pp. 3–13, with the permission of the author and *FRONTIERS*.

*R*efusing to be rendered historically voiceless any longer, women are creating a new history—using our own voices and experiences. We are challenging the traditional concepts of history, of what is "historically important," and we are affirming that our everyday lives are history. Using an oral tradition, as old as human memory, we are reconstructing our own past.

When women historians first began the task of creating and expanding the field of women's history, we relied on traditional historical concepts and methods. We busily searched for hidden clues to direct us to "lost heroines," and, whenever possible, we sought out those who were still alive in order to record their past experiences. Because so little documentation was available on the lives and activities of these women, we found ourselves in a situation similar to that of Allan Nevins, who "developed" the method of oral history in 1948.[1] With the advent of the telephone and the decline in the practice of journal writing and lengthy correspondence, historians were faced with a "drying up" of many of the sources on which they traditionally depended. Oral history, emerging then as the sound recording of the reminiscences of public figures, was hailed as a method which could create alternative sources.

Fitting women into this new scheme of things was essential and not very difficult. There were and are women who have been "important" figures in public life, both those who have functioned in the public eye and those who have worked behind the scenes. Some women achieved recognition as a result of their struggle for women's rights, while others who participated in that struggle remain unrecognized. But the majority of women did not lead public lives. Most women were not women's rights activists or union leaders or public participants in social movements. Until relatively recently, most women in the United States did not engage in wage-earning labor. By virtue of acculturation and socialization in a sexist society, women's lives were and are different from most men's. Whether women have played out public roles or adopted the traditional female role in the private realm, their lives have been governed by what Gerda Lerner has called a special rhythm.[2] In tracing this rhythm, it is important to document the lives and experiences of all of these women: to pore over newspaper accounts and organization papers, to seek out their living associates, to research fully their lives and activities, and to record their stories, for only then can we see the whole picture of women's lives, and how their rhythm has affected our lives.

Women all over the country have been using oral history to explore this rhythm of women's lives. In doing so, we are harking back to an oral tradition much older than that developed by white male historians in the United States in the 1940s. We are part of the tradition in which the life and experiences of "everywoman/man" was considered worthy of remembering and passing on to others—because it was history. It was this tradition, brought from Africa, which black historians tapped in the 1920s when they started to record the stories of former slaves.[3] It was this same tradition which both inspired Alex Haley to trace his roots and helped him to reconstruct the kidnap of his ancestors from West Africa.[4]

For women, using this model of oral history not only leads us to "any-woman," but it also raises a different set of questions to be explored. We thus ask about clothing and physical activity, menstruation, knowledge and attitudes about sex and birth control, childbirth, economic functions in the household, household work, the nature of relationships among women, the magazines and books they read, menopausal experience, and the relationship of the private life to the public life. Thus, not only is the political base of women's oral history different from the Nevins model, but also, and, just as important, the content is special. No matter what women we choose to interview, regardless of how typical or atypical their life experiences have been, there are certain common threads which link all women.

It is the recognition that women's oral history is so special, and significantly, that it has developed as a field unto itself—primarily through the work of women outside the major university oral history centers—which inspired us to devote an entire issue of a women studies journal to the subject. . . .

The [oral history] process is a significant experience not only for the interviewer or those who might use the product, but also for the interviewee. As those of us collecting oral histories from women well know, there is invariably a reciprocal affirmation between interviewer and interviewee of the worth of the women being interviewed. The fact that someone is interested in learning about her life—a life the interviewee may see as "unexciting" and "uninteresting"—increases her self-esteem. In fact, the oral history process can serve a positive function in the aging process by helping to integrate past life experiences, cope with reduced life activity and loss of close relationships, and ultimately, prepare for death.

Women's oral history, then, is a feminist encounter, even if the interviewee is not herself a feminist. It is the creation of a new type of material on women; it is the validation of women's experiences; it is the communication among women of different generations; it is the discovery of our own roots and the development of a continuity which has been denied us in traditional historical accounts.

Oral history, the creation of a new "document" through the tape-recorded interview, traditionally has been divided into three types: topical, biographical, and autobiographical. Each type is represented in this issue. The topical interview is, in many ways, most akin to the open-ended sociological interview; the interviewer brings in a specific focus in order to gather information about a particular event. It might center on something which applies to both women and men, like Yung's interviews with Chinese immigrants about their detention on Angel Island, or it might focus on those experiences particular to women only, such as hysterectomy.[5] The biographical oral history is characterized by this same kind of specificity, but the focus is, instead, on a specific individual usually a public figure. . . .

In the autobiographical interview, the course of the individual interviewee's life is what determines both the form and content of the oral history. Even when one interviews a group of women who participated in the same kind of activity, the questions will be tailor-made to each individual's experience and the information will be recorded as part of a total memoir. In other words, in biographical and topical interviews, a slice of the interviewee's life is explored; in the autobiographical interview, the total life history is recorded.

In reality, there is a great deal of overlapping among the three forms. In both the topical and biographical interview, enough autobiographical material must be recorded to establish the specific relationships of the interviewee to the event of the individual being researched. On the other hand, when autobiographical interviews are collected from a group of women who shared a similar activity, for example, participation in the labor movement, some common questions would be explored with all. . . . Further, in our efforts to revise women's historiography, there are certain areas which should be explored with all women as part of their autobiographical accounts, such as their reactions to the onset of menses.

The distinction between the autobiographical and topical interviews is further blurred by the fact that, ultimately, specific materials might be extracted from several different autobiographical interviews and clustered together around a specific topic. . . .

In fact, the so-called autobiographical oral history should be as complete a document as possible so that a variety of uses can be made of it. Much like the anthropological life history, it should reflect the experiences, values, attitudes, and relationships of the interviewee—the patterns and rhythms of her life and times. It can stand on its own, as an autobiography of an individual, or sections can be extracted from it for analysis or use in documentation.

As with any source, questions about the validity of the material must be raised. Despite their awareness of the obvious bias of contemporary newspaper reports, historians traditionally have relied on journalistic accounts as primary sources. The same criteria should be used to assess the validity of any source, written or oral: how does it "fit" with what we know about the subject? The usual questions about the reliability of memory and the problem of retrospective interpretation must also be raised, as they would be for any autobiographical account.

The autobiographical oral history, however, is a rather strange hybrid, not like conventional autobiography, which is usually characterized by a certain amount of studied reconsideration by the "author" and by her self-selection of both form and content. The so-called autobiographical oral history is a collaborative effort of the interviewer (archivist/historian) and the interviewee (source/history). This very collaboration makes the oral history memoir unique. Based on face-to-face interaction, during which the source can be both questioned and evaluated, it becomes more than the sound of one voice.

Based on the background research and the historical perspective which the interviewer brings to the process, the life of the interviewee is reconstructed within a broader social context—a context not ordinarily provided by the self-recorded memoirist. An understanding of this context guides the interviewer in deciding which spontaneous material should be elaborated on more fully. Though the best interviewer will encourage spontaneity and self-direction, it is intellectually dishonest to discount the interviewer's role in creating the oral history. The advantages derived from her knowledge and perspective can, ideally, sensitize her to personal and cultural inconsistencies in the content of the interview. Such inconsistencies might be indicative of a highly idiosyncratic woman; they might be an important source of information about the complex patterns in women's lives; or they might raise questions about memory and candor.

Besides subtle nuances in the content of the interview and voice inflections—which are captured on tape—there are nonverbal gestures which only the sensitive interviewer (or—if the interview is being filmed or video taped—the sensitive photographer) will observe. These nonverbal cues reveal the emotional tone of the interview and should be carefully noted afterwards; they will become part of the record used by both the interviewee and others to evaluate the validity and reliability of the material recorded.

Despite the obvious advantages of the collaborative reconstruction of the interviewee's life, there are, of course, drawbacks. The perspective of the interviewer cannot help but influence, even subtly, the content of the material—particularly what the interviewee will judge as "important." After we completed an interview, one woman commented that she could tell by the way my eyes sparkled at various times that I was particularly interested in the problems she faced as a woman in the male world of science. Although we can console ourselves with the knowledge that there is no such thing as "objective" reporting, we must recognize our own influence in the interview process and make a concerted effort to maintain a balance between what we, as feminist historians, think is important and what the women we are interviewing think was important about their own lives.

The collaboration between interviewer and interviewee results in more than new "historical" documents. It allows for the creation of a new literature, a literature which can tap the language and experiences of those who do not ordinarily have access to such public expression except perhaps through the more anonymous form of folk culture.

Oral history is not, nor should it be, the province of experts. On the contrary, some of the best work today is being done by individuals and groups outside "the groves of academe" and often by those without any formal training in history or journalism. Anyone who can listen to the women who are speaking can do oral history. It is not enough, however, to rush off to the nearest Senior Citizen Center with a tape recorder. It is important to be prepared.

Reading about interviewing technique is a helpful first step. Discretion and common sense must be used in evaluating recommendations for interviewing technique. Patently absurd suggestions are sometimes made, for example, the edict not to laugh when the interviewee says something funny. The oral history interview is a human interaction and the same kind of warm, human responses expected in other interactions should govern our behavior. Reading the instructional articles will heighten awareness of the interview process, but nothing will contribute to this awareness more than the actual interview experience. The best training for conducting an oral history interview is actual practice; practice interviews which are carefully listened to and evaluated and analyzed. These "mock" interviews should be conducted with persons other than the intended subject.

The more practice the interviewer has, and the more experience she gains, the more partisan she becomes to her own methods. Although there is widespread agreement among oral history practitioners on some points, there is also disagreement. The oral history interview, above all, is specialized, and therefore highly variable; it is tailored to the experiences and style of the individual interviewee. Keeping in mind the proviso that there is no *one* perfect method of collecting oral histories, I offer the following ideas based on my own experiences over the past five years in personally interviewing an enormous number and wide range of women, and in training students to gather in-depth women's oral history. The methods of making contact, choosing equipment, adopting an interview style, and processing the interviews have all worked successfully for me. Although these suggestions are based on autobiographical oral history interviews with women in their 70s, 80s, 90s, and even 100s, many of the points are equally valid for the topical and biographical interviews and for women of almost any age group.

Making Contact

Whom we select to interview obviously will be governed by our own specific interest. In my classes for the past three years, randomly selected women have been contacted and "everywoman" interviews were conducted. Fully exploring the life of each individual woman became the basis for a study of women's lives in the early twentieth century. To locate women who have had a particular kind of experience, such as involvement in the labor movement, or defense industry work during World War II, different methods might be used. I have successfully located union women through the retiree groups of various unions, through widespread advertisement of my work among older radicals, and through public speaking. Other oral historians and interviewers have placed ads in local and national newspapers.

In selecting the women to interview, the question of cultural likeness—including gender, race, class, ethnic, and even regional identification—immediately arises. The combined forces of racism and sexism have also limited the number of "minority" women in the United States who have had access to the skills and equipment which would enable them to record their own past. Until these skills are learned—and each of us must do everything in her power to share these skills—the role of the "outsider" will remain crucial. Otherwise, the history of Black, Hispanic, Asian, and Native American women will be lost, not only to them, but also to us.

Besides being governed by necessity, the outsider can sometimes delve into certain kinds of experiences that insiders cannot.[6] There might be specific topics that are more easily discussed with "outsiders." Also, because outsiders are less conversant with the culture or subculture, they may take less for granted and ask for more clarification than insiders. On the whole, though, my experience has been that cultural likeness can greatly promote trust and openness, whereas dissimilarity reinforces cultural and social distance.

Because of my own light complexion and hair, the Jewish immigrant women I have interviewed have assumed that I was not Jewish. As soon as I dropped a clue for them, both the content of the interview (particularly about their childhood in the shtetls of Europe or the ghettos of America) and the nature of our relationship changed. On the other hand, because of my appearance and my socialization into the larger Anglo culture I have "passed" when I have conducted interviews with Anglo-Saxon women. A very light-skinned black student of mine from Texas was politely treated and her interview with a black 92-year-old woman and her 70-year-old daughter progressed uneventfully until, during the third session, the interviewees realized that she was "one of us." The nature of the interview changed dramatically. Similarly, the few male students I have had in my women's oral history classes, despite their efforts, never overcame the barriers of gender difference.

It is not only a matter of trust; the subtle cues to which culturally similar women can respond might mean the difference between a good and bad interview. Though these nuances cannot be thoroughly learned by an outsider, the interviewer must prepare as best she can so that she can understand the attitudes, vocabulary, and body language of the group or subgroup with which the interviewee identifies.

No matter whom we choose to interview or how we have located her, the first contact with our interviewee is crucial, particularly since she might be subtly influenced by the way in which we located her. One of the activists whom I found through her union was convinced, despite all my explanations and protestations, that I was from the "union office." She was, therefore, guarded in her description of the difficulties she had faced as a woman in her union. On the other hand, when a particularly respected or loved friend was the source of my contact, the door was opened wide and the interviews were quite candid.

It is important in contacting the person to make clear how her name was obtained and to explain to her, in advance, what the interest in her is. For most women, especially those who did not participate in "important" events or in organizations outside of the home, there is tremendous initial reluctance to being interviewed; it is the reluctance which comes from being socialized female in this society. It is important to establish for her, at the very outset, why we feel her life and experiences are important. This might mean not only an explanation about our specific project, but also a discussion of how we view the daily life experiences of all women to be a part of history.

The interviewer's own credibility must also be established; this can be accomplished by reference to a relationship with someone the interviewer knows and/or by the use of letterhead stationery or a brochure which describes her work. (Though a letter from the instructor might be helpful for students, I have found that the "grandmother role" which the elderly so often adopt towards the student makes their entree relatively easy.)

Because it is often difficult for the elderly to hear well on the telephone, it is best to try to communicate this essential introductory material first by mail. Then, when contact is made, she will be clear about who is calling and what is wanted, and an appointment can be made. It is important to determine what time of day is best for her; her stamina and memory will vary. All the women I have interviewed have been sufficiently in tune with their own body rhythms to tell me *exactly* what was the best time to interview; then I adjusted my schedule accordingly.

It is still that initial face-to-face meeting which will make or break the oral history. Rather personal and intimate details about the woman's life will be openly discussed, and to do so means that there must be an attitude of trust. She will, rightfully, want to know how the material will be used. Although it is important to be open about both the purpose of the interview and the use of the material, I usually wait until after some sort of trusting relationship has developed before asking her to sign any releases or agreements; there is no subterfuge here, but even the simplest agreement forms can raise specters and create suspicions. . . . I have had only two woman refuse to sign an agreement once the interviews were completed; in both cases their oral histories were made anonymous and all identifiable references were deleted.

Open communication is crucial to establishing trust with an interviewee. Since we are asking a stranger to be self-revealing, we, in turn, must be willing to divulge information about ourselves. I have had some interviewees question me at length about my own background and life, whereas others have asked nothing. It is with the former that I have developed the most intimate mutual relationships and with whom I have probably created the richest oral histories. I do not mean to imply that the interviewer should insert her own life story into the actual interview. However, before beginning the first interview or while chatting over coffee, tea, or juice after the interview, the interviewer may talk about herself—to whatever extent is natural and the interviewee seems to expect. The interviewer's sharing her own feelings about the interview (her nervousness, for example), encourages the interviewee to talk about *her* feelings, and both parties can be placed at ease.

The first interview is not "just to get acquainted." The expectations and relationship which develop during the first encounter can determine the course of the other interviews. For this reason, the practice interviews, during training, should be done with others than those to be actually interviewed for a project. That first interview might be the only one conducted with a woman or, on the other hand, it might represent the first of some 20 sessions. The decision about how many interviews will be recorded can best be made on the basis of the outline developed and the research undertaken *after* the initial interview. Though it is best not to make a definite commitment to the interviewee until you can be more precise, she should be prepared for the eventuality that more than one interview may be recorded.

How much preparation is done before the first interview will depend largely on who the woman is. For a prominent individual, a "local figure," or someone involved in a well-documented activity, it is possible to research existing sources such as newspapers, organization records, and histories ahead of time. However, many of those we will interview are women about whom a great deal is not recorded; they are the "voiceless" unknown women who worked in the home, the women who worked at office jobs pushing the huge carriages of old typewriters, the women who rose at five in the morning to chop cotton, the women who bore three, four, five, and more children, the women who panicked at their frequent pregnancies and performed abortions on themselves. The best preparation for a first interview with these women is a familiarity with the time period, especially the living conditions and tenor of life in both rural and urban settings.

Familiarity with the texture of life allows us to explore fully her family history and her early years. The same principles will guide us as in later interviews; her own experiences and style of reminiscing provide the framework, while our general topical outline sensitizes us to certain areas and provides suggestions for probing. . . . After covering the early years, usually to adolescence (which might require more than one interview), a general biographical sketch is recorded in roughly chronological sequence. It is this sketch which will then be used as the basis for both structuring the subsequent interviews and directing us to the areas which should be researched.

Though most of the women whom we will interview probably do not have "papers," almost all do have photographs and various objects which they have kept from their past. Looking over these helps to inform the interviewer and to jog the memory of the interviewee.

I thought I had fully exhausted the recollections of a union woman about the various strikes in which she had participated until we looked over her photographs, late in the interview series. A picture of an ILGWU (International Ladies Garment Workers Union) picnic reminded her that this was a victory celebration; she was then able to recount her activities in yet another strike. It is best to look over these records early in the project, ideally during the first interview. Furthermore, it is a good idea to let the tape recorder run as she comments on her photo album or a newspaper clipping or displays her yellowed wedding dress. Although the material should be recorded again later, in the context of the period in which it took place, the second version of the story might be quite different from that first rendition—which could become a lost gem were we not to record it when the memory spontaneously surfaced.

The Interview Process

The interview is a transaction between the interviewer and the interviewee, and their responses to each other form the basis for the creation of the oral history. Each woman has her own style of recollecting, as well as her own specific experiences. As sensitive interviewers, we respond to each individually, and the interview process will therefore vary. This variability is one of the most distinctive features of the oral history interview and is what makes it different from the standardized interviews used by social scientists.

Despite experience and careful planning by the interviewer, there are several common tendencies which can mar any interview. These are a function of our own impatience and (in our eagerness to use our background research) a dependency on our prepared outlines or guides. We fear lapses of silence. We squirm at what appear to be long, irrelevant digressions. We become impatient at the chaotic manner in which memory divulges the past. In our fear and impatience, and also in our enthusiasm for the material we are uncovering, we succumb to talking too much, asking too many questions too soon.

The best oral history is a quasi-monologue on the part of the interviewee which is encouraged by approving nods, appreciative smiles, and enraptured listening and stimulated by understanding comments and intelligent questions. Though the ideal interviewer is there primarily to provide a broad leeway in which to help the interviewee structure her recollections, sensitivity to both individual idiosyncrasies and class or culturally determined characteristics might lead to more direct questioning in some cases and total silence in others.

For example, despite her protestations that she would not be able to talk without a lot of questions, an old Jewish immigrant woman whom I interviewed would embark on an hour-long monologue at the beginning of each session. She had self-selected that material which was important to her, or which she thought was of general interest. I quickly learned that asking questions—except for points of clarification—was an intrusion. She demanded total eye contact at all times! During her spontaneous reminiscing, I remained virtually silent. Then, towards the end of the session, or at the beginning of the next one, I would ask some additional questions relating to the material she had provided or to my own outline.

In planning for the interview, I review the types of questions I wish to ask, and the order in which I want to ask them, but I also try to avoid too much "pre-ordering" of the material. The principle which I generally use is to ask the most general question first, waiting to see where that question leads. It might lead to a detailed description, to what appears to be a digression, or to a blank. My own reaction, then, is tailored to the woman's response. If the general question, for example about living conditions during her childhood, yields detailed information, I can sit back, keeping a sharp ear for unexpected information, new directions to explore, and confusing material. If, on the other hand, the general question leads to a vague or general response, then the questions can be recast or phrased more specifically. If we are clear in our own minds what it is we are looking for, this is not difficult to do. For instance, when I ask about living conditions during the woman's youth, what I am seeking is sufficient information to re-create the basic social setting as well as the financial circumstances of the family. A general response such as "we were very poor," or "we lived in a tenement" does not tell me much. Asking more specific questions (for example, how many slept in a room, a bed; was there water/plumbing in the living space, in the corridor, outside) can yield sufficiently rich descriptions so that no further questioning is necessary.

A general or vague response might indicate that the interviewee did not consider the subject very important. If we have touched upon an area that is not part of her basic self-definition, but is important to us as feminist archivists, then we must devise a way to get the information without letting our questions over-determine the interview. It might mean that we wait until the very end of the oral history recording sessions to ask some of our questions, even though they may be out of context. Otherwise, we can easily end up with an oral history that is defined not by the values and rhythm of the individual's life, but by the perspective that *we* bring about women, about class, about race.

If our general questions lead to a lengthy digression, then we must be prepared to follow that line until it is exhausted. It is imperative that we learn to let the train of memory association run its course; that we be able to scrap totally the direction in which we were originally headed; that we know when to ignore our outlines and pick up new avenues of inquiry. If, at the end of this new track, we still do not have the information we were initially seeking, then we can return to our original line of inquiry, perhaps asking for the same content in a different way.

Sometimes, though, the interviewee truly cannot recall the information we are seeking. As little as we know about memory function, we do know that it is related to blood flow and that it will vary at different times of the day and on different occasions during the week. Thus, sensitivity to the health and stamina of the interviewee is important; it is also a basic sign of human respect. This generally means determining what time of day is best to interview her; being prepared to cancel an interview if, when you arrive, she seems tired, upset, or "under the weather"; and, knowing when to cut the session short. During the course of the interview, as she tires, there will be noticeable memory loss and increased difficulty in remembering words. That should signal that it is time to end the interview for the day. (I have found that the 90-minute interview is about the right length for most elderly women, though for some, one hour is the maximum. I openly discuss this with the interviewee.) When a question draws a blank or a line of inquiry is not productive, we have to be willing to give up. If it is important, we might want to make a mental note of it and try again on another occasion.

How do we keep track of our own line of thought during the various passages into the by-ways of memory? With attentive listening we can easily forget our own questions. How do we quickly note a new line of inquiry that was triggered by a comment of the interviewee; how do we keep some chronological sense when an interviewee's style is to rush headlong from one anecdote to another? There is as much diversity of opinion on note-taking during the interview as there is on sharing the outline or guide with the interviewee. My own experiences vary from one interviewee to the next, though invariably I do not share with her my outline or specific questions. My fear is that this outline, which is really just a guide for myself, will determine the course of the interview too much. I will suggest at the end of each session the *general areas* we might want to cover at the following session.

As for note-taking during the interviews, I usually try to avoid making notations of more than a single word or phrase—just enough to keep my memory intact. Stopping to take notes signifies to her either that what she is saying is not very important and that you do not have to listen, or that it is very important and you are taking notes in order to ask her more about it. In any event, the loss of eye contact, even for a brief moment, the break in the pattern of concentrated listening, can be very disruptive. In reviewing the tape later, the interviewer can note names, places, and dates, and can then ask for clarification of confusing material at the next session.

Perhaps the most difficult and frustrating task is to keep clear in our own minds some sense of chronology and the order of events. Some women, particularly less educated working-class women, are not accustomed to reflecting about themselves, to viewing their lives as important. The stories they are used to repeating are those which recount a courageous act, a funny episode, or a tragic event in their families. Consequently, the interview might be a string of anecdotes with little connecting material or insufficient descriptions to place these anecdotes in a context adequately understandable to outsiders. This is her style and rather than interfere (which would be useless anyway) the interviewer has to develop some systematic way of keeping time references clear and to ask questions *in relation to* the anecdote which helps to provide the total context. I have found it helpful to actually develop a chronological chart, based on the first contact interview, which clearly outlines the various stages in the woman's life. In this way, it becomes easier to keep straight which anecdote fits where.

The interview with the more educated, middle-class woman usually is quite a different process. She is more accustomed to reflecting about life, and also to articulating ideas. As a result the interview is more "orderly"; thoughts are more often completed, and sentences hang together. This is not to say that one interview is better or worse than another, but rather that we have to be aware of the ways in which class, particularly, affect thought processes and speaking patterns, and to adapt ourselves to these variations.

In addition to those differences related to class origins there are certain cultural characteristics which are a function of both ethnicity and generation. Though older and/or immigrant women might talk without much hesitation about "female concerns," they often find it difficult to be very explicit. For instances, most women will freely talk about the onset of menses. However, they might find it more difficult to describe the "pads" they used, where they were collected, washed, and so on. By the same token, though women might be willing to talk about birth control, they might be embarrassed to describe specific techniques and might speak in euphemisms, such as, "My husband took precautions." She might be referring to his using condoms, or to coitus interruptus. It will be up to the interviewer to then phrase questions which elicit the information without requiring the interviewee to use words with which she has difficulty or which embarrass her. Faced with the timidity of some older women, the interviewer must have sufficient knowledge about birth control practices in the earlier part of the century to step in and provide words as well as to ask for more details. This is part of the preparation that any good interviewer will have done, and these cultural differences may have important implications for the editing process.

Processing the Interview

Once we have successfully recorded one or a series of interviews, the initial product (and perhaps, the final one) is the raw tape recording. Since an important primary document has been created, it is important to take measures both to protect it and, at the same time, to make it accessible to others.[7] Minimally, this requires some summarizing and indexing of the contents of the tapes and either depositing them in archives or making their existence known to those who would have an interest in the materials. By using either extensive funding or a willingness to put in countless unpaid hours, we can next transcribe and edit the interviews, perhaps ultimately into a continuous narrative. The way in which the recordings are further processed depends on both the resources available and the use to which the material will be put.

The easiest and least expensive method is to develop a running summary of *each* tape. As a matter of course, if more than one interview is recorded with a single individual, it is a good idea to listen and to take notes on each interview before proceeding with the next. This is both to make sure that nothing has been missed—particularly new avenues hinted at—and to continually appraise our methods and sharpen our skills. Since the tapes should be reviewed anyway, it does not require much more time to keep a running summary while listening to them. Properly done, this summary can then be used as a basis for indexing the entire group of interviews with a single individual. . . .

This simple system allows the use of the material for any of several purposes, including extraction of specific segments for presentation as evidence, and development of audio or audio-visual presentations. In other words, this system allows for easy retrieval of the material which can then be selectively transcribed as needed. Though it might take a bit longer to locate the material on a tape and listen to it than it would to scan quickly the printed page, the material is *available* for scholarly use, nevertheless. Furthermore, because of subtle communication patterns that cannot be captured on the printed page, listening to the segments might be considerably more revealing than merely reading a passage.

This is not to argue against transcribing the tapes if it is possible to do so, and if the resources are available. However, we should bear in mind that the enormous amounts of time and money required to transcribe an interview (an average of five to eight hours per interview hour) might be better utilized in collecting more oral histories from those older women whose numbers are rapidly diminishing.

If the tapes are transcribed, there are then several different methods of treating the literal transcription. Minimally, it is edited for clarity, punctuation, and correct spelling of names and places. The resulting "edited transcript" is usually placed on a library shelf, to be used primarily by scholars. More extensive editing of the transcripts might be done, when sufficient funds are available, as is the practice of the Regional Oral History Office of the Bancroft Library (University of California, Berkeley). The transcript is edited for smooth flow and continuity, which means that similar material from different portions of the interview is pulled together and organized into coherent sections with headings and subheadings. After a review of the transcript by the interviewee, the interviewer/editor writes an introduction and indexes the volume. Photographs and other documents might be included selectively in the final bound volume, which is deposited at Berkeley and UCLA and is available for purchase by other libraries. The resulting volume is more readable and certainly more accessible and usable than a simple, minimally edited transcript. However, it is quite costly to produce.

Another form of editing, usually in preparation for wider publication, involves all the other prior steps discussed above *and* editing the question/answer format into a continuous narrative, removing the interviewer's questions and comments. Once the questions are removed, transitional passages might be missing. We don't want to put words into the interviewee's mouth, yet we want the materials to flow smoothly and to preserve her unique syntax. We must work the material in ways that will render the written form the most authentic rendition of her oral account. This does not necessarily mean the most literal. When the spoken word is translated into the printed word, a great deal is lost particularly when we are interviewing women unaccustomed to articulating their ideas or to revealing themselves publicly, especially working-class women. The subtle nuances of the spoken word, or the posturing and gesturing which accompany it often more effectively communicate emotional tone than do the words themselves. The sensitivity of the interviewer to the interviewee will largely determine many of the editorial choices that will be made. Ultimately, this kind of editing entails what can only be described as literary judgment, though it certainly does not require a writer to make these judgments.

No matter how we process the recorded interview, we must remember that we have created a unique "document," one which above all is oral/aural. There is no one method for best creating this new source or for best processing the raw materials. Each of us must develop the style that best suits her and the women she interviews. With our foremothers we are creating a new kind of women's history, a new kind of women's literature. To this task we should bring the sensitivity, respect, tremendous joy, and excitement that come from the awareness that we are not only creating new materials, but that we are also validating the lives of the women who preceded us and are forging direct links with our own past.

Notes

1. Allan Nevins, "Oral History: How and Why It Was Born," *Wilson Library Bulletin* 40 (March 1966), pp. 600–601 (see chapter 1 of the present volume).

2. Gerda Lerner, *The Female Experience: An American Documentary* (Indianapolis: Bobbs-Merrill, 1977), pp. xvi–xviii.

3. A good account of the use of oral history in the study of slavery, beginning with the work at Southern and Fisk Universities in the 1920s, is to be found in Ken Lawrence, "Oral History of Slavery," *Southern Exposure* 1 (Winter 1974), pp. 84–86.

4. Alex Haley, "Black History, Oral History, and Genealogy," *Oral History Review* 2 (1973), pp. 1–25. (See chapter 20 of the present volume.)

5. Judy Yung, "A Bowlfull of Tears: Chinese Women Immigrants on Angel Island," *FRONTIERS* 2 (Summer 1977), pp. 52–55.

6. Yvonne Tixier y Vigil and Nan Elsasser (contributors to "Grandmother's Stories" in this issue [*FRONTIERS* 2 (1977)] found that in interviews with Hispanic women there was a greater willingness to discuss sex with the Anglo interviewer than with the Chicana interviewer. On the other hand, topics associated with discrimination were more likely to be discussed openly with the Chicana than with the Anglo. See Tixier y Vigil and Elsasser, "The Effects of the Ethnicity of the Interviewer on Conversation: A Study of Chicana Women," in *Sociology of the Language of American Women, ed. Betty L. DuBois and Isabel Crouch (San Antonio: Trinity University Press, 1976), pp. 161–70.

7. There are several free booklets on the care of tapes which are available from 3M Company, St. Paul, Minnesota 55101. Generally it is a good idea to make duplicate copies of your tapes, preferably on a high-speed copier (which is available at the audio-visual centers of most schools). To avoid accidentally recording over your taped interview, the tabs at the back of the cassette should be punched out. Should you, for some reason, later wish to record on the tape, it is possible to do so by taping over the empty space created where the tab was punched out. For storage of tapes, a moderate temperature is recommended. Some sources recommend rewinding and winding the tapes at least once a year.

18

Using Oral History
for a Family History Project
Linda Shopes

Our section on the applications of oral history concludes with three articles that con-
sider the growing field of family history. In the first, Linda Shopes, a community histo-
rian, describes the basic oral historical techniques used by the family researcher. The
approach that she advocates helps develop a comprehensive context to an individual's
life, a sense of where one stands among generations on the road of life. Without a his-
torical frame of reference, an individual family's record hangs suspended, out of time
and place.

Shopes offers useful advice on searching family records before interviewing and on
creating a historical setting from personal and public documents. The author insists on
the value—often overlooked among those researching their family's history—of index-
ing and organizing the project results with an eye to adding information to the public
record.

Linda Shopes has taught American Studies at the University of Maryland, Baltimore
County. Her interests lie in labor, community, and family history, and she has done
extensive research in the Baltimore area.

Linda Shopes now works at the Pennsylvania Historical and Museums Commission
in Harrisburg, Pennsylvania.

"Using Oral History for a Family History Project" by Linda Shopes originally appeared as
Technical Leaflet 123 (Nashville: American Association for State and Local History, 1980). It is
reprinted by permission of the author and the American Association for State and Local History.

Introduction

Imagine listening to an elderly relative tell of her journey to America as an immigrant, her arrival at Ellis Island, and her first job in a clothing factory. Or imagine another family member describing how he worked on the family farm, learned to read in a one-room school house, and courted his wife at church socials. Such are the opportunities available to the family historian who draws upon the method of oral history.

Traditionally, family history has been equated with genealogy, the reconstruction of a person's lineage through the use of written records. However, the stories family members tell about their past are also a rich source of information on a family's history. In particular, they can yield information about motives and attitudes and the "feeling tone" of life that even the most extensive genealogical reconstruction lacks. Enlarging the notion of family history to include information gathered from oral sources also encourages people to investigate their pasts even though extensive genealogical records are not available.

The personal benefits of such an investigation are numerous. For subsequent generations of the family, who frequently lack significant contact with extended relatives and so have little knowledge of "where they came from," a collection of taped interviews is a rich inheritance. For people who are interviewed, particularly older people, reviewing their life experiences and trying to order them and articulate their significance can be a rewarding experience.

But it is for the family researcher that such a project perhaps has the greatest value. It can be the impetus for developing or deepening relationships with other family members. Even more important, it can enhance one's own sense of identity. By tying together the strands of the family history and trying to understand the meaning of individual lives in relation to the social and historical context within which they were lived, family historians can gain perspective on the context of their own lives.

This notion of family history as moving beyond the domain of the genealogist is supported by several recent developments in historical study. Since the 1960s, historians increasingly have sought to understand the daily life experiences of ordinary people. They have paid particular attention to the history of the family since it is so fundamental a social institution and shapes so much of people's daily lives. Oral history, too, has emerged in recent years as a method of historical research. Though by no means limited to the study of ordinary people, oral history interviews are especially valuable as a source of information about those individuals and groups for whom the written record is both scant and misleading.

Doing Background Research

Although oral history interviews may lie at the heart of a family history research project, they must be preceded by careful preparation if they are to be of much value. Before doing any interviewing, the family historian needs to assemble basic data on individual family members and then locate those individual lives within their broader historical context. This background information will give the researcher some idea what to interview family members about and will enable the interviewer to ask more thoughtful and searching questions during the interview itself.

Though the researcher may know some of this information already, especially about immediate family members, a good deal more can be gathered by research into both primary and secondary written sources. A good place to begin this research is the family Bible. In addition, in almost every family there is someone who has an old shoe box full of miscellaneous family papers such as school diplomas, old letters, and tax records. These need to be located and examined for information. Family photographs and material objects are especially interesting. Sensitively interpreted, they can suggest much about "what life was like" years ago. Also available to the family researcher are the kinds of public documents used by genealogists—birth, marriage, and death records; wills; censuses; immigrant passenger lists.

By drawing upon a number of these personal and public documents, the family researcher can begin to understand the basic pattern of events in family members' lives—when and where they were born, educated, and married, residential and occupational histories, the children born to them. It is useful to assemble this data on a single form for each family member being researched; a sample form is illustrated (Figure 18.1). It also should be noted that background data might fruitfully be gathered for deceased relatives. Not only will it make the family history more complete, but also it can help stimulate recollections about these people during interviews with their relatives and close friends.

Once some background information about family members has been gathered, the next step for the family researcher is to try to understand these individual lives in relation to the social circumstances that affected them. This kind of understanding will add depth to the interview and may help the researcher perceive the family's history as something more than a collection of individual biographies. Thus, an afternoon spent in the local historical society or the local history section of the library might yield not only specific information about individual ancestors, but also a clearer sense of the historical setting within which these ancestors lived. Also useful are general accounts of American history and specific studies of historical events and processes like immigration or the Depression that may have affected family members. Biographies, particularly some of the more recent biographies of ordinary Americans based largely on oral sources, are yet another possible source of insight. The number of such works is enormous, but a local librarian or college history instructor might be able to make some useful suggestions for background reading relevant to individual families.

Determining a Focus

After gathering biographical data on family members and researching the general background of the family history, the family historian then needs to decide what direction the interviews will take. Possible areas of inquiry fall within three broad categories: the impact of major historical events and trends such as racial segregation, technological developments, or the post–World War II housing boom on the family; the relationship of various aspects of social life such as work, religion, community life, or class status and mobility to individuals within the family; and the structure and dynamics of family life itself, including household membership, relationships among family members, and family values. A fourth area of inquiry is suggested by family folklorists who are concerned not so much with the content of a family's history as with the forms a family uses to preserve its experiences. Thus, the family researcher also might collect family stories, traditions, customs, and beliefs.

Since the number of possible topics and subtopics within each of these broad categories is enormous, it is advisable to focus on a few main themes that seem most relevant to the family's experience; otherwise, the information gathered will be a random collection of unrelated facts, anecdotes, and insights. These themes, however, should only be tentative. The family historian needs to be aware that interviewees themselves may open up new areas of inquiry, new ways of understanding the family history.

Conducting the Interviews

Once some background research is done and a general focus for the investigation is determined, the family researcher is ready to begin interviewing. Choose for first interviews those family members with whom you feel most comfortable and who seem to enjoy talking about the past. If these interviews are successful, less enthusiastic family members might be encouraged to participate. In addition, the interviewer will have acquired skill in interview techniques before dealing with more difficult situations. Of course, common sense dictates that the oldest family members be interviewed first.

After selecting persons to interview, the family historian needs to consider very carefully how to encourage extensive and thoughtful recall from the interviewees. An interview is above all a social interaction; if it is awkward and tense,

Name: _____

Date of Birth: _____ Place of Birth: _____

Mother's Name (include maiden name): _____

Father's Name: _____

Siblings' Names (include birthdates if known): _____

_____

_____

Spouse's Name (include wife's maiden name): _____

Date of Marriage: _____ Place of Marriage: _____

Children's Names (include dates and places of birth): _____

_____

Date of Death: _____ Place of Death and Burial: _____

Religion and Church Membership: _____

Schooling and/or Other Training (list all schools attended, the dates of attendance, and the level of education completed at each):_____

_____

Residential History (list all residences chronologically, noting the dates lived at each): _____

_____

Occupational History (list all occupations chronologically, noting the place of work, the type of work done there, and the approximate salary):_____

_____

Membership in Clubs and Organizations (note dates of memberships and offices held): ___

_____

Figure 18.1 A sample form for recording family data. A separate form should be completed for each member of the family.

no matter how carefully researched, it will be intellectually and personally unrewarding.

The interviewer needs to contact the interviewees and explain the purpose of the interview, acquire additional biographical data if necessary, explore possible topics for the interviews, and in general encourage the subjects to begin thinking about their own and the family's history. A good technique is to review old photographs and documents with the interviewees for they are often valuable memory jogs. It also might be interesting to take the people back to scenes from their earlier years—former homes, schools, churches, places of employment—as a way of stimulating additional memories.

Based on this pre-interview conversation, as well as the background research and the general focus determined for the project, the family historian next needs to prepare an outline of topics to pursue during the interviews. Interviews can be structured autobiographically, so that the interviewees are guided into giving a chronological account of their lives, or topically, so that only certain aspects of their experiences are probed. The best family history interviews are probably a combination of autobiographical and topical narratives, though the individual researcher needs to decide which method best suits the previously established purposes.

The outline for the interviews should facilitate recall, not inhibit it. It is not a list of "20 questions" to which the interviewer rigidly adheres, but a list of topics and subtopics to give direction to the interviews. It is important to emphasize, however, that the interviewer needs to have a clear sense of the categories of information to be sought; otherwise, it is easy to become overwhelmed by a welter of disparate facts and wandering recollections. Trying to compress the highlights of some 50, 70, or even 90 years of living into a few hours of a taped interview is, after all, a difficult task and demands considerable forethought.

During the interviews, the interviewer needs to encourage a mood of expansiveness in the subjects so that they are stimulated to recount life experiences openly and on their own terms. The best way to do this is to ask open-ended questions that can be developed at length by the interviewees. However, questions should not be so broad or complex that the interviewees do not know where to begin an answer. For example, suppose the interviewer wants to learn about the interviewee's childhood. A closed question like "When and where were you born?" does not allow room for elaboration upon experiences. Yet a too open statement like "Tell me about your childhood—your family, your school experiences, what your community was like—anything that you can remember" might simply elicit a few bits and pieces of information with no real focus. A better way to probe childhood experiences would be to say, "I understand you were born in Baltimore in 1905 to parents who had recently immigrated to this country [all this information having been learned from the background research done before the interview]. Tell me something about this family that you were born into."

Follow-up questions on what an interviewee has just said can encourage additional recall. Thus, to refer to the example above, depending upon how the interviewee has answered the question about the family, the interviewer can dig for details about the economic circumstances, emotional climate, the roles and responsibilities of each parent, the children's place in the family, and so forth. Then the researcher can go on to ask questions about other aspects of the interviewee's childhood such as school experiences and the community lived in. In all cases, each topic should be explored as completely as possible before moving on to another. If the interviewee wanders off the track, the interviewer can simply return to the subject by saying something like, "Before getting into the subject of your school experiences, I'd like to learn some more about your family. Tell me something about what your mother did in the home."

Throughout the interviews, the interviewer should play the role of "active listener," gently guiding and encouraging the interviewees' recollections but never intruding upon them. Thus, questions should be unbiased; they should be phrased in such a way that no particular answer seems expected. "Tell me more about . . . ," "Why do you think that . . . ," and "Give me an example of . . ." are all good ways to draw out an interviewee even on fairly sensitive or controversial topics. On the other hand, phrases like "Don't you agree that . . ." or "Isn't it true that . . . " are likely to inhibit all but the most assertive interviewees. Interviewers also should refrain from commenting favorably or unfavorably on what the interviewees say. Good rapport can be maintained nonverbally by eye contact, nods and smiles, an intent expression, and a relaxed body position and verbally by an occasional noncommittal "I understand" or "I see."

It is important also not to inhibit interviewees by interrupting once they have started to answer questions. Let them unfold the logic of their lives as they choose. Clarification and examples can be elicited after the original question is answered. It is a good idea to have a pad and pencil handy during interviews to jot down notes for these follow-up questions.

The interviewer should also be certain that the interviewees actually have finished answering a question before asking another. Pauses in narration, though uncomfortable for an eager interviewer, often signal efforts to gather additional thoughts on a topic, not the end of thought on it. The interviewer should keep in mind that generally the best interviews are those in which the interviewer says the least.

The setting of interviews can help nurture recall, and the interviewer should pay attention to this detail of the interview process also. Interviews should take place where those being questioned are most comfortable and used to talking informally; usually this means their own home—perhaps in the living room, but more often in the den, kitchen, or back yard. Wherever the interviews take place, they should be free of interruptions and distractions that might break the interviewees' concentration. They should also be free of background noise—nothing makes a tape harder to understand than the regular creaking of a rocking chair or the steady hum of an air conditioner. Interviewer and interviewee should sit close enough to one another to maintain eye contact easily. The tape recorder microphone should be directed toward the interviewee, and the recorder itself, which the interviewer is completely at ease with operating, should be near the interviewer so that tapes can be changed unobtrusively as necessary.

Though oral historians generally agree that maximum rapport is gained by interviewing only one person at a time, sometimes talking with a small group of family members about old times is an especially enjoyable and valuable experience that provides considerable information as individuals trigger each other's memories and spur one another on. A group interview also may provide insight into patterns of interaction among family members and may highlight differences and similarities among family members' individual experiences. A group session is perhaps best used in conjunction with more extensive individual interviews.

Because interviews are often exhilarating experiences for both interviewer and interviewee, the interviewer should take care not to end abruptly, but rather ask one or two deflationary questions at the end of the interview and then spend a few minutes visiting with the interviewee once it is over. They are also tiring, and two hours generally seems to be the limit for a single productive session.

A Word of Caution

Although interviewing family members is usually a mutually rewarding experience, sometimes certain problems arise. Some potential interviewees, schooled in the great-men-and-events version of history, have difficulty understanding that the story of their life experiences is of particular interest to anyone and so have little enthusiasm for a family history project. Others are simply unwilling to speak candidly about what they feel is personal and, therefore, private. Other difficulties can arise. Pain over a deceased relative, embarrassment at a youthful indiscretion, efforts by estranged relatives to get the interviewer "on their side," and attempts by an interviewee to present only "the good side" of the family history have all been encountered by family historians. There is no single solution to handling any of these problems, but tact, persistence, and a sensitivity to this human dimension of family history research are the best guides.

The very human quality of oral testimony raises particularly complex questions about its validity as a historical document. Memories do fade over the years, and it is difficult for most people to be objective about their own experiences. However, the mood the interviewer creates during the interview itself and the creativity of questions can affect significantly the candor of the interviewee's recollections. It is also important for the interviewer to do background research and interview several family members about the family history in order to judge the veracity of any single account. But what is most important is to accept all interviewees' interpretations of their lives as their interpretation. Oral testimony, like any other historical source, needs to be evaluated both for its factual accuracy and for what it reveals about the attitudes and values of the interviewee.

After the Interview

The family historian may well feel that a collection of documents and taped interviews is an adequate record of the family history. This material, however, should be organized in some way to facilitate access. A filing system, with individual files containing all pertinent information for each relative, coupled with a carefully labeled set of tapes, is perhaps the simplest way to organize a collection. A more complex filing system, by theme or by time period, may be necessary for more ambitious projects. It should be noted, however, that transcribing the tapes or making a running index of what is discussed on each tape makes retrieval of information considerably easier.

The family historian also may wish to organize and interpret more completely the data collected, write up a family history, and circulate it among family members. It might be well also to consider placing a copy of the completed paper in the local historical society or library so that future researchers may have the benefit of the work. If a written family history goes outside the hands of the immediate family, the family historian is advised to secure written permission from the interviewees for researchers to draw upon information contained in their tapes.

Conclusion

A family history project may seem to be enormously ambitious. Certainly, the methods outlined in this pamphlet can be adapted to fit specific situations. Considerable background research and a pre-interview conversation may not always be possible before each interview. Interviewing itself becomes easier as the interviewer gains experience. Careful organization of data, too, can wait for a later date. In the end, perhaps the best advice is simply to START.

Bibliography

Daum, Willa K. *Oral History for the Local Historical Society.* 2d ed. Nashville: American Association for State and Local History, 1974. (An excellent introduction to the hows and whys of an oral history project)

———*Transcribing and Editing Oral History.* Nashville: American Association for State and Local History, 1977.

Blyth, Ronald. *Akenfield: Portrait of an English Village.* New York: Grove Press, 1969. (An eloquent description of the hardness of a rural way of life in the words of the people who have lived it.)

Doane, Gilbert H. *Searching for Your Ancestors: The How and Why of Genealogy.* 4th ed. Minneapolis: University of Minnesota Press, 1973. (An excellent introduction to the methods and sources of genealogical research.)

Epstein, Ellen Robinson, and Rona Mendelsohn. *Record and Remember: Tracing Your Roots through Oral History.* New York: Monarch, 1978. (A guide to the use of oral history techniques for personal family history research; emphasizes the mechanics of conducting and processing interviews.)

Gordon, Michael, ed. *The American Family in Social-Historical Perspective.* 2d ed. New York: St. Martin's Press, 1978. (A collection of scholarly articles on various aspects of the history of the American family.)

Hartley, William G. *Preparing a Personal History*. Salt Lake City: Primer, 1976. (A brief guide to preparing an autobiography; includes a list of hundreds of interview topics.)

Hoopes, James. *Oral History: An Introduction for Students*. Chapel Hill: University of North Carolina Press, 1979. (A comprehensive guide to oral history as a research technique; includes an excellent bibliography.)

Jeffrey, Kirk. "Varieties of Family History." *American Archivist* 38 (October 1975), pp. 521–32. (An overview of recent scholarship in the field of family history.)

Kramer, Sydelle, and Jenny Masur. *Jewish Grandmothers*. Boston: Beacon Press, 1975. (An oral history of the immigrant experience of 12 Jewish women.)

Kyvig, David E., and Myron A. Marty. *Your Family History: A Handbook for Research and Writing*. Arlington Heights, Ill.: AHM, 1978. (Another guide to doing a personal family history; includes many excerpts from student-written family histories.)

Lichtman, Allan J. *Your Family History*. New York: Vintage, 1978. (The best available guide to the kind of family history research described in this article; includes chapters on oral history, written records, photographs, and methods of research, also an excellent bibliography.)

Rosengarten, Theodore. *All God's Dangers: The Life of Nate Shaw*. New York: Knopf, 1974. (The oral biography of a black Alabama sharecropper.)

Shumway, Gary L., and William G. Hartley. *An Oral History Primer*. Salt Lake City: Deseret, 1974. (A brief guide to oral history with particular emphasis on biographical interviews.)

Starr, Louis. s.v. "Oral History." Vol. 20. lst ed. *Encyclopedia of Library and Information Science*, New York: Marcel Dekker, 1977. (A brief overview of developments in oral history over the last three decades; see chapter 2 of the present volume.)

Tyrrell, William G. *Tape-Recording Local History*. Technical Leaflet 35. rev. ed. Nashville: American Association for State and Local History, 1978.

Watts, Jim, and Allen F. Davis. *Generations: Your Family in Modern American History*. 2d ed. New York: Knopf, 1978. (A manual for doing a family history project that stresses locating one's individual history in its broader social context; includes several essays on aspects of twentieth century American history.)

Zeitlin, Steven, et al., eds. *Family Folklore*. Washington, D.C.: Smithsonian Institution, 1976. (An explanation of family folklore with many examples culled from visitors to the Smithsonian's Festival of American Folklife.)

19

The Search for
Generational Memory

Tamara Hareven

*Of the many possible explanations for the current interest in oral and family history,
our next selection offers one of the most thoughtful: the widespread need to link our individual existences to a place in time—to understand where we came from and where we
may be going.*

*Tamara Hareven, one of the best-known researchers in family history, here analyzes
how oral history can fire a collective historical consciousness through discovery of how a
common past. She traces the present movement to New Deal efforts to collect "living history" and to the vast popularity of Alex Haley's epic Roots. Hareven's work has shown how
people previously involved in organized social or political activity can overcome their feelings of powerlessness through participation in a community history project.*

*The rising interest in ethnic identity and nationalism, Hareven suggests, can be
attributed to the increasing assimilation of ethnic subcultures within America. At times
when a group's unique customs, traditions, and history falter, a drive for preservation
and celebration often surfaces. The author presents her arguments in the context of family history and generational memory, which she defines as "memories which individuals
leave of their own families' history, as well as more general collective, memories about
the past."*

*Tamara Hareven taught for many years at Clark University and at the Center for
Population Studies at Harvard University; she currently teaches at the University of
Delaware. She is the author, with Randolph Langenbach, of* Amoskeag: Life and
Work in an American Factory City *(1978) and* Family Time and Industrial Time
(1982). She has edited two volumes on family history research, Transitions: The Family and the Life Course in Historical Perspective *and* Aging and Family Transitions in Interdisciplinary Perspective *(1982).*

"The Search for Generational Memory" by Tamara Hareven, from *Daedalus* 106 (Fall 1978),
pp. 137–19, is reprinted by permission of the author.

*I*n 1958 Claude Cockburn recalled a meeting with three Ladino-speaking Jews in Sofia shortly after the Second World War. They explained that they were not Spaniards, but one of them added, "Our family used to live in Spain before they moved to Turkey. Now we are moving to Bulgaria." When Cockburn asked him how long it had been since his family lived in Spain, he responded that it had been approximately 500 years. The man spoke of these events as though they had occurred "a couple of years ago."[1] This famous incident has been cited frequently as an example of the relativity of historical memory. It also suggests the lengthy time over which individuals associate themselves with events which occurred generations earlier.

By comparison to other cultures, for most Americans generational memory spans a relatively brief period. The term generational memory is employed here broadly to encompass the memories which individuals have of their own families' history, as well as more general collective memories about the past. Most people do not even remember, or never knew, their grandfathers' occupation or place of birth. For a small proportion of the American population memory reaches back to the American Revolution, or to pre-Mayflower England or Europe. For descendants of later immigrations, memory extends mostly to the first generation in America, or, in fewer instances, to the last generation in the "old country." A sense of history does not depend on the depth of generational memory, but identity and consciousness do, because they rest on the linkage of the individual's life history and family history with specific historical moments.

Recently, efforts in American society to stretch generational memory, namely, the search for roots, through the tracing of genealogies and through oral history, have gained considerable popularity. A touch of magic has been attached to the process since the Bicentennial, and, in the aftermath of *Roots*,[2] a number of efforts to commercialize the search have emerged as well. More traditional scholars and foundations have also begun to encourage oral history, both as a means of retrieving or salvaging vanishing historical information and as a way to spark community identity. The success of *Roots* has publicly dramatized the symbolic significance of such efforts.

Genealogies originally functioned to provide pedigrees and legitimization for status, claims for property, inheritance, or access to skills or political positions. Such real and symbolic functions of genealogies have survived in American society, especially in the South, despite an increasing democratization of society. Even the Daughters of the American Revolution, whose genealogical efforts were initially directed towards the inclusion of common people into the nation's ancestry (providing they were present in America in the colonial and revolutionary period), eventually turned their pedigree into an exclusive status grouping justified by a genealogy.

When it was founded in 1890, the DAR was reacting against the heraldic genealogical movements of the earlier period, which tried to link Americans with the English nobility. Applicants for membership were required to have an ancestor who was alive during the American Revolution, regardless of rank or status. "Lineage tracing," writes Margaret Gibbs, "was as much the rage in this decade— and in the early 1900s as Mah-jong and crossword puzzles in the 'roaring twenties.' "[3] Along with numerous other patriotic societies which were founded in that period, the DAR was dedicated to the preservation and protection of patriotic ideals. Partly, the movement developed as an expression of anxiety in face of expansive foreign immigration, a fear of "race suicide," and a fear of loss of status for native-born middle and upper classes.

On the other hand, the recent genealogical movements, especially the search for roots and the reconstruction of family histories, involve a different constituency and fulfill an entirely different function. They encourage individuals to locate their own life histories in the context of activities and historical settings of family members in earlier generations. Rather than concentrating on lineages as such, they encourage detailed knowledge of those relatives and of the historical events and the social context surrounding their activities. In this respect, family histories represent a recent popular version of an older generation of autobiographies or traditional biographies of great families. Whereas, in the past, formal family histories were limited primarily to the upper classes, the uniqueness of our time lies in the democratization of the process and in the inclusion of large segments of the population in the search. The tapestry has thus broadened from those claiming descent from the Mayflower or from Southern aristocrats, to include the descendants of African slaves and immigrants.

The emphasis on individual identification with genealogy has thus shifted from the search for legitimization of exclusive status to a concern with emergent identity. [Erik] Erikson defines "identity" as the meeting between individual life history and the historical movement.[4] The process involved in the current reconstruction of individual family histories goes beyond individual identity in Eriksonian terms. It encompasses the linkage of one's family background with the larger historical experience, which is recognized and accepted as part of a collective heritage. Earlier, and even today in some circles, the search for a genealogy was considered successful only if it led to high-status ancestry, but the current populist mood encourages the search for one's origin, regardless of the social status of one's ancestry. The discovery of ancestors who were mere commoners, poor immigrants, or slaves is now considered as legitimate as linkage to nobility and great heroes. The recent acceptance of slavery as part of America's heritage by whites as well as blacks is indicative of this change.

This is precisely why *Roots* had the impact on the American public which it did. Its most compelling aspect was not the book's rendition of the story of slavery in a humane and moving way, but rather, the successful trace of the connection between a contemporary man and the origins of slavery through an individual line of descent. In itself *Roots* offers few new insights into the history of slavery. Its key message is the resilience and survival of African traditions, demonstrated in the effort of Chicken George and his descendants to transmit their family history from generation to generation. Its uniqueness lies in the *process* of search and trace of the history of one family, whose odyssey fits closely the contours of the collective experience of American slavery. Although most reviews have praised Haley's book as a great epic of slavery, they underestimated the significance of the final chapter recounting Haley's journey into the past in his effort to trace his family history back to its African origin, prompted by several fragments of an aging grandmother's narrative.

Significant here are both the process of the historical search itself and its successful outcome, which offered thousands of people the opportunity of a vicarious linkage with the historical group experience. (This is one of the rare occasions when the painstaking and tedious process of historical research has been acclaimed in the popular culture as a heroic act.) To understand fully the role which *Roots* has fulfilled in American culture it is important to realize that Haley's search *had* to be successful. The process of search would not have been recognized as important in its own right.

What if Haley had failed? Consider two hypothetical alternative outcomes. The first alternative could have been a break in the chain of evidence. This is, in fact, what happens to the majority of people attempting to trace their family histories beyond two generations. Most people embarking on such efforts without Haley's ingenuity, commitment of time, networks of scholarly support, and financial resources, could never dream to travel a similar road. Had he failed, Haley's story of the search itself, without the final linkage to Africa, would not have electrified the public. Alternatively, suppose Haley had been successful in tracing his ancestry, but the tracks did not lead back to the kind of ancestor he found. Suppose the story diverged, and Haley discovered an ancestor, who, rather than being an innocent victim captured and sold as a slave, had himself been a collaborator in the buying and selling of slaves. The search itself would still have been historically meaningful and personally satisfying, but it would not have had the same impact on the American public, because it would have lacked the direct link with collective experience of slavery. In short, the significance of Haley's book for American culture of the 1970s lies not merely in the successful tracing of a line of ancestry back to Africa, but rather in the fact that this ancestor's history was characteristic of the mainstream of the slave route to North America and of the slave experience.

It is no coincidence that Haley is also the author of the *Autobiography of Malcolm X*.[5] Both the *Autobiography* and *Roots* are American success stories. In both, the hero follows a progression which he views as destined to culminate in the ultimate triumph. Earlier life events lead in an almost linear sequence to the moment of triumph and redemption. In Malcolm X's biography, as in the *Confessions of St. Augustine*, the entire life sequence leading to the moment of conversion is viewed as providential. Even Malcolm's devastating life experiences, his "sins" and suffering, were justified as steps toward the final redemption. Similarly, in Haley's story, the memory of the suffering of Kinte and that of his descendants in slavery were redeemed in the historical moment of rediscovery and linkage between past and present.

Both individual stories fulfilled significant public functions: at the height of the Black Power movement, Malcolm X's story and conversion performed a symbolic function, purging Black Americans from repressed anger reaching back into several generations. Haley's story provided a symbolic route for rediscovery of a past and, with it, a historic identity for Black Americans. The two had to occur in this sequence. First, the anger had to be purged in order to reverse a negative into a positive identity. Then came the search for roots, the discovery of a past, and the acceptance of this past as a significant part of America's heritage. Appropriately, the subtitle of Haley's book is *The Saga of an American Family*.

Roots also represents another important historical linkage, namely, that of the informal family narrative transmitted from generation to generation, which is not intended as a formal source of history, with the formal oral tradition of Gambian society—the official chronicle recited by the Griot. In Africa and in other nonliterate societies both types of oral traditions coexist, each performing a different function. The oral history genre which has survived in the United States, especially in black culture, is personal and informal. One of the most remarkable of Haley's discoveries was the survival of fragments of an oral tradition in his grandmother's memory in 1950s America. By that time, these fragments had lost their specific significance, but they were still being transmitted with a purpose; so that one's children and children's children would remember.

In modern American society, archives and formal histories have long replaced oral chronicles as official history. As the rich collection of folklore in Appalachia, or the very moving account of *All God's Dangers* suggests, generational memory and real traditions have persisted as historical sources in islands of local folk culture throughout the United States, though most prominently in black culture.[6] There is, however, a significant difference between the informal oral tradition which has survived in the United States and the official oral tradition in nonliterate societies. In such societies, the oral tradition has an institutionally recognized place and purpose in the culture, and whether it constitutes an official chronicle, a family narrative, a fable, or other types of memories, it is structured and presented in specific formulae. The function of oral testimony may range from myths aimed at providing an explanation of the creation of the world and of society as it exists, to those providing a pedigree for tribal rulers or to a justification of the political structure. The oral testimony can be legalistic, didactic, or explanatory, and its structure and mode of presentation may vary accordingly. Whatever its function, its social purpose is officially valued in these cultures.

In modern American society, though, in the absence of such a well-defined tradition as in nonliterate societies, it is difficult to find a formal place for oral history. Informal oral history as a historical source is not a new phenomenon. It has been utilized systematically as an archival and research tool especially to record the memories of public figures who have been active in political and social life, as evidenced in projects of Columbia University and the Kennedy Library. Such projects have been carried out with historical scrupulousness, where the process of interviewing itself was preceded by research in written documents. Informal oral history has been employed effectively also in more modest historical projects, where the oral evidence was linked with written records and interpreted in conjunction with them.

Oral history also has an important social science heritage, which has developed since the 1930s, namely, the use of the individual life history for the "study of lives," which [John] Dollard and subsequently [Gordon] Allport and [Robert] White had developed as a major research method in psychology.[7] More recently, Oscar Lewis and Robert Coles have demonstrated the power of this method when applied to the urban poor, to Puerto Ricans and Mexicans, and the children of migrant workers and sharecroppers.[8] Inspired by this approach, radical historians have utilized oral history as a means to record the experiences of workers, activists, and participants in social protest movements, not only to retrieve and record information, but also as a way to form group consciousness through the process of interviewing itself.

More recently, oral history has been used on the community level for a similar purpose, namely, that of firing collective historical consciousness through the discovery of a common past. Some oral history efforts which emerged in recent years are filiopietistic and attach a mystique to the process because of the encounter with the living past which it represents.

The Bicentennial, in particular, gave an impetus to oral history projects which are intended to stimulate "community awareness" and "identity." Such undefined slogans, which have been used rather indiscriminately, do not explain how community consciousness would be raised through such projects and *whose* history is actually being recovered. The widespread use of the cassette tape recording machine over the past decade has contributed considerably to the popularization of oral history interviewing. Like the computer, the recorder has not only facilitated the gathering and preservation of data; it has also generated a mystique of authenticity which is conveyed through the magic of technology. Oscar Lewis somewhat glorified its role: "The tape recorder used in taking down the life stories in this book has made possible the beginning of a new kind of literature of social realism. With the aid of the tape recorder, unskilled, uneducated and even illiterate persons can talk about themselves and relate their observations and experiences in an uninhibited, spontaneous and natural manner."[9] People using the tape recorder, like those using the computer, discover quickly, however, that it does not have intrinsic magic. Without the historical and sociological imagination shaping the interview, one can end up recording miles of meaningless information.

Little attention has been paid to two aspects of oral history which are central to its role, namely, the nature of the interview process itself and the function of oral traditions in a modern, literate society.

First, the interview process. During an extensive oral history project in a large New England industrial community,[10] we became acutely aware of the fact that oral history is not strictly a means of retrieval of information, but rather one involving the generation of knowledge. Essentially, an oral history narrative is the product of an interaction between interviewer and interviewee. By its very nature such a process determines what is going to be recalled and how it will be recalled. The interviewer is like a medium, whose own presence, interests, and questions conjure corresponding memories. Even if the interviewer tries to remain inconspicuous, the very process is intrusive.

Oral history is therefore a subjective process. It provides insight into how people think about certain events and what they perceive their own role to have been in the historical process. "A testimony is no more than a mirage of the reality it describes," writes Jan Vansina, the leading scholar of oral tradition in Africa. "The initial informant in an oral tradition gives either consciously or unconsciously a distorted account of what has really happened, because he sees only what he has seen."[11]

Oral history is an expression of the personality of the interviewees, of their cultural values, and of the particular historical circumstances which shaped their point of view. This is precisely its great value, rather than its limitation. Similar arguments could be made about written documents; diaries and personal letters are also highly subjective, though their subjectivity is of a different origin. A diary reflects a person's individual experiences or observations, whereas an oral history is the individual's experience as evoked by an interviewer who has an intentional or unintentional influence on what is remembered and the way in which it is remembered. Oral histories are also distinguished from diaries or letters in their retrospective construction of reality. Like autobiographies, oral histories are past experiences presented from the perspective of the present.

The dynamic interplay between past and present in an individual's reminiscences can take different forms. At times, interviewees temporarily immerse themselves into a past episode as they recount it. This is especially true for childhood memories. On such occasions, the individual reminiscing slips back into the past, and recounts vibrant memories without any consciousness of the present. The interviewee becomes like an actor fully playing the role in his or her own past. On most occasions, the person remembering maintains a conscious separation between the account of the past and the present, though hindsight provides a contemporary perspective on past experience.

On many other occasions, interviewees find it difficult to distinguish past from present, or earlier from subsequent events. Interviewees also misrepresent or reinterpret actual events or situations through faulty memory or repression of difficult experiences. Traumatic experiences also lead to the reinterpretation of events. For example, when we interviewed former workers of the Amoskeag Mills, some of them said they had finished working in the Amoskeag in 1922. When we pointed out to them that their work records in the corporation files indicated they had worked until 1930 or later, the typical reply was "Oh yes, but that was after the strike. Things were not the same anymore." The strike of 1922 represented to the majority of the people who worked there at the time the destruction of the world to which they had become accustomed. Even though they returned to work after the strike, they associated the strike with the end of their career.

Sometimes people just forget experiences; other times they *care to* forget, or, if they remember them, they do not want to talk about them. As Gunhild Hagestadt points out, in many families there are prohibited zones, which most family members choose not to tread in, as if by unspoken agreement. An interviewer can sense the invisible electrified fences when approaching such areas, but can do very little about them.

Oral history is a record of perceptions, rather than a re-creation of historical events. It can be employed as a factual source only if corroborated. The difficulty of cross-checking information does not detract, however, from its value for understanding perceptions and recovering levels of experiences which are not normally available to historians. It offers almost the only feasible route for the retrieval of perceptions and experiences of whole groups who did not normally leave a written record. The major contribution of *Akenfield* and of *Hard Times* is not in their historical accuracy, but rather in their contribution to an understanding of human experiences and social conditions.[12] As long as one understands this, rather than assumes, as some do, that oral history is the closest to "unadulterated human memory" we can approach, it can be valued for what it is and utilized creatively.[13]

The second major feature of oral history involves its very significance in modern industrial society. In the absence of an established oral history tradition in American society, it is difficult to define its place and to justify its meaning to individual interviewees. It is almost impossible to *stimulate spontaneous reminiscing* as many community identity projects suggests one should. To make oral history meaningful, one has to find a link between an individual life and a broader historical context. Such links are exceedingly difficult to identify unless the individuals participated in a common distinct cultural activity, organization, or group with a shared interest or if their lives were affected directly by a common dramatic event.

Even in the black community, where the oral tradition is alive, particularly in the South, it is often difficult to link informal experiences and memories to a larger picture, unless the interviewees themselves are aware of a common focus.

Without such linkages, in most instances in the United States, oral history interviewing remains a private exercise. In Africa, by contrast, Vansina points out, "Every testimony and every tradition has a purpose and fulfills a function. It is because of this function that they exist at all."[14] In nonliterate societies the functions of an oral tradition are socially defined and are recognized by all members. In modern America there is no such established tradition, except in regional oral traditions which survive in isolated localities. Within the larger community, the public role and social significance of oral history are not automatically understood.

People who have not been "famous" or who have not participated jointly in a specific movement, such as a labor movement, or a strike, or in an organized political or social activity, would find it difficult to achieve such an identification. Such people experience great difficulty in making the connection between their own lives and the historical process. Community organizers who expect the emergence of "instant identity" through the interview process face an instant disappointment.

In societies where the oral narrative is part of the formal culture, no explanation is needed as to why a certain story is significant. The very time-honored practice and the setting within which the oral tradition takes place lend it strength and meaning. In modern America, except for historically conscious individuals or groups and unusually articulate and interested individuals, most people do not see an immediate significance in being interviewed. Although they might be inclined to reminiscence privately, telling stories to their own grandchildren or sharing memories of past experiences, most people are rather bewildered when requested to tell their life histories to strangers.

When approaching the former workers of the Amoskeag Mills in Manchester, New Hampshire, for interviews, we frequently encountered the questions: "Why ask me? My story is not special," or "What is so important about my life?" Except for a few people, those who consented to be interviewed did so, not because of their understanding of the importance of this process, but because, prompted by their own work ethic, they wanted to help us do "our job."

Attitudes changed drastically after the exhibit "Amoskeag: A Sense of Place, A Way Of Life" opened in Manchester.[15] Although this exhibit was primarily architectural and was aimed at professionals and preservationists rather than at the larger public, it evoked an unexpected response from former and current textile workers in the community. It provided the setting for the former workers' public and collective identification with their old work place and it symbolized the historical significance of their work lives. Thousands of people, mostly former mill workers and their families, came to see the exhibit. Most striking were recurring scenes where old former workers searched for their relatives in huge historic group portraits of the workers, and where grandparents led their grandchildren through the exhibit, often describing their work process of 30 to 40 years earlier. Even though they had privately cherished many memories associated with their work experience, they felt that industrial work, especially textile work, was generally looked down upon. The sudden opportunity to view their own lives as part of a significant historical experience provided a setting for collective identification. Under these circumstances, interviewing ceased to be an isolated individual experience. It turned, instead, into a common community event. Former mill workers recognized each other at the exhibit, some not having seen each other for 30 years. Although the exhibit was not designed to serve this purpose, it turned into a catalyst.

The oral histories which followed were of an entirely different character from the earlier ones: people we approached were willing to be interviewed. They related their work and life histories with a sense of pride. Many individuals who had heard about the project volunteered to be interviewed. Identification with the work place and with the buildings thus provided a more direct and immediate stimulation of memory and interest in the process than isolated interviewing. The exhibit established our credibility as interviewers and laid the foundation for a continuing series of interviews with the same individuals. This is not to suggest that every successful oral history requires an exhibit or some other external device to engender identification. It suggests, however, how tenuous oral history is among those elements of the population who do not have an oral tradition. It is also becoming clear that, except for the search for roots through the reconstruction of one's own family history, the quest for oral history is more common among the educated, the professional, and the semiprofessional, especially among second- or third-generation ethnics, than as a "folk movement."

Why this exercise of "tribal rites" in an advanced technological society? Today, when the printing and circulation of information have reached an all-time peak, and when computers generate and objectify knowledge, scholars, foundations and cultural organizations, and the general public are reviving genealogy and the oral tradition—the tools of transmission of collective memory in nontechnological societies. Among scholars, this revival represents a revolt against "objective" social science and a shift from an emphasis on strictly formal knowledge to existential process. Oral history and the search for roots also fit into the effort of recent scholarship to integrate the experience of large segments of the population into the historical and sociological record. On a more popular level, the oral history revival is connected with an effort to authenticate the experiences of different ethnic groups in American culture. It thus represents a commitment to pluralism and expresses the reemergence of ethnicity and its acceptance as a vital aspect of American culture.

The current search is also prompted by a realization that the traditions which one is trying to record are about to become extinct. *The World of Our Fathers, The Godfather,* and many other ethnic monuments were generated at the moment when the last living links with the world are about to disappear.[16] Most of these efforts to capture ethnic traditions do not bring back the heritage from the old country, but rather the experience of the first generation of immigrants in America.

The search for roots in our time is not entirely new. An earlier centralized effort of this sort took place in the 1930s in the midst of the Great Depression. Current popular oral history projects are minuscule by comparison to the undertakings of the Works Progress Administration's Federal Writer's Project in most American communities. Some of its achievements include the American Guide Project, which generated a massive collection of local guides, the recording of over 2,000 narratives of former slaves, the compilation of numerous volumes of local oral histories, and the assembling of a number of major collections of folklore. The national folklore project under the direction of John Lomax was intended to capture the surviving oral traditions and folkways. It produced a national volume entitled *American Folk Stuff,* designed as a collection of readable tales. "All stories must be narrated as told by an informant or as they might be told orally with all the flavor of talk and all the native art of casual narrative belonging to the natural story-teller," read the instructions of the national program director to all state directors.[17]

The folklore project stressed the collection of materials from *oral* sources with reference to the life of the community and the background of the informant. It captured urban and ethnic folklore as well as rural. "All types of forms of folk and story-telling and all minority groups—ethnic, regional and occupational—are to be represented for two reasons: first to give a comprehensive picture of the composite America—how it lives and works and plays as seen through its folk storytellers; second, by the richness of material and the variety of forms to prove that the art of story-telling is still alive and that story-telling is an art."[18] Under the auspices of the Farm Security Administration, some of that generation's master photographers, such as Dorothea Lange, James Agee, and Walker Evans, recorded the words and faces of sharecroppers, "Okies," migrants, and Appalachians, bringing the faces of rural America into the center of the nation's consciousness. Thus, through a concerted government effort, rural roots were exposed and recorded for posterity.

Much of the social documentation of rural life resulted from the recognition that that world was fast disappearing, and from the fear that some of its wholesome values would be swept out by a new industrialism. To a large extent, this passion to document rural life was stimulated by the discovery of chronic poverty and deprivation in the rural South and Midwest, which had been ignored while the "pathology" of cities had occupied the limelight during the first three decades of the twentieth century. While they conveyed the suffering and deprivation of their subjects, the photographs and narratives in *Let Us Now Praise Famous Men* and in other kindred documentaries also conveyed the resilience and wholesomeness of this group.[19] The faces of the "Sharecropper Madonna" and of the Okies also had a sobering effect on those who idealized the myth of self-reliance and frontier life. In addition to the strong humanistic empathy for the subjects and their ways of life, these projects also expressed the period's longing for a lost mythical past of innocence and wholesomeness. The very launching of these projects in the midst of a catastrophic depression resulting from the "industrial plant being overbuilt" was a reaction against "progress" and, with it, the destructive pace of modern, industrial life.

The 1930s was the era of the discovery of rural native American and black roots. The day of the immigrant was still to come. The WPA writers' project also attempted to record urban folklore. The New York City folklore project, for example, was intended to reveal "the epic of construction, excavation and wrecking, transportation . . . and the symphony of New York night life. . . ." Similarly, the social ethnic project which the WPA launched was intended to shift the emphasis from "the contribution of ethnic groups to American culture" to their participation in various aspects of community life. However, the definition of ethnicity which the WPA introduced was one very different from the ethnic revival today: "Immigrants and the children of immigrants are American people. Their culture is American culture."[20] Generally, the images and experiences which captured the imagination of the 1930s were the documentaries of rural life. The earlier documentation of life and poverty in immigrant slums in New York, Chicago, and Baltimore, which was carried out in the late nineteenth and early twentieth centuries by Jacob Riis, the Russell Sage Foundation and the Survey,[21] and Lewis Hine's prolific photographic record of child labor, was documenting the plight of urban immigrants and the deterioration of social and economic life as part of a social protest movement, not in order to capture ethnic "roots." Immigrants who had flooded American cities between the 1880s and World War I were still too recent and still represented undigested alien masses.

The current quest for roots holds in common with that of the 1930s a genuine concern for recovering the historical experience as it was viewed and perceived by participants. As in the 1930s, the search emerged from a crisis in values, and from a questioning of the very foundations of American society. Both in the 1930s and in the 1960s, the search for roots came in response to a disillusionment with technology, industrialism, and materialism. In the 1930s the effort led to a reaffirmation of the qualities and strengths of American folk culture. Alfred Kazin, one of the unemployed writers in the WPA project, described the interview experience as "A significant experience in national self-discovery—a living record of contemporary American experience."[22] The current search is aimed more specifically at the recovery of ethnic group identities. In the 1960s and 1970s the search for roots has been individual as well as group oriented. Unlike in the 1930s when the effort was organized and supported by the government, in the current decade it represents a more spontaneous movement. Its very emergence is part of an aftermath of the Civil Rights and Black Power movements and as part of the recent acceptance of ethnicity as part of American culture.

Ironically, we are now engaged in recovering generational memory, after much of it had been wiped out in a century-long effort to assimilate immigrants. As Lloyd Warner pointed out, the symbols which dominated the historical rituals and pageants of Yankee City's Tricentenary were those of the colonial period and the era of the American Revolution.[23] An entire century of Yankee City's history had been almost completely ignored. Despite the fact that they already comprised a significant element of the city's population, the ethnic groups were expected to choose themes from the colonial and revolutionary era for the floats which they sponsored in the historical pageant (the Jews choosing an episode in the life of Benedict Arnold). Even in 1976, during the Bicentennial celebration in one of the historic mill buildings in Lowell, Massachusetts, the majority of the participants from the community (who were of different ethnic origins) were wearing revolutionary era costume, though Lowell was founded in 1820 and symbolized the beginning of the new industrial order. Similarly, a recent follow-up study on Yankee City in the 1970s find that the new owners of the Federalist houses in Newburyport are reconstructing the genealogies of these houses, rather than their own family histories.[24]

The current return to ethnicity in American culture is possible precisely because so much has been forgotten already and because of the distance in time between the current generation and the two generations of immigrants who came to the United States between 1880 and 1920. Before ethnicity could be recognized as a permanent feature in American culture, the different ethnic subcultures had to go the full cycle of assimilation and come close to extinction.

In some ways we are now witnessing the final consequences of the closing of the gates in the 1920s. The end of immigration at that point facilitated the absorption of immigrants who had arrived earlier into the United States. Had there been a continuous influx of new immigrants, it is doubtful whether ethnic diversity would have been accepted today as a genuine part of American culture. The current search for ethnic roots is in itself a rebellion against the concept of the melting pot; it is an effort to salvage what has survived homogenization. In the process, it is also likely to create new identities, new heritages, and new myths. Part of this process represents an effort to counteract alienation and to seek comfort and reassurance in memories of close family ties and community solidarity which are generally attributed to the lost ethnic past. For most ethnic groups this past represents the world of the first generation of immigrants in the United States, rather than the old country. The search for an ethnic past becomes especially significant for our times because of the generational watershed which we are currently experiencing: the two generations of European immigrants which had come here from the old country in the late nineteenth and early twentieth centuries are now dying out, while the generation which is now reaching the prime of its adulthood has no personal memory of World War II. What this would mean for the generational memory of the children of this age group is an interesting question in itself.

In assessing the significance of the current search for roots from a historical point of view, we must ask where this all leads. In 1911, confronting the DAR, Jane Addams warned them: "We know full well that the patriotism of common descent is the mere patriotism of the clan—the early patriotism of the tribe—and that, while the possession of like territory is an advance upon that first conception, both of them are unworthy to be the patriotism of a great cosmopolitan nation. . . . To seek our patriotism in some age rather than our own is to accept a code that is totally inadequate to help us through the problems which current life develops."[25]

It would be a historical irony, of course, if the groups which had been excluded for so long from the official cultural record would fall into a similar trap of exclusiveness and separatism when recreating their own history. Some of that danger would be present if the reclamation is particularistic and parochial. Is the current individualism and ethnocentrism going to result in a retreat and withdrawal from a common culture and common social goals? Will it eventually lead to fragmentation rather than a balanced pluralism? Whatever the outcome might be, the current search inevitably has to take place first within the subcultural compartments, since until very recently, the larger society has tried to mold the identity of different ethnic groups in its own image.

Notes

In the process of writing this essay, I have benefited from a number of enlightened conversations and from the insights of the following people: Randolph Langenbach, Richard Brown, Ronald Grele, Nancy Chudacoff, John Modell, Frank Fustenberg, and Carol Stack and Robert Levine. I am indebted to Stephen Graubard for valuable comments, to Howard Litwak for editorial assistance, and to Bernice Neugarten and Gunhild Hagestadt for their insights.

1. Quoted in M. I. Finley, "Myth, Memory, and History," in *History and Theory,* ed. George H. Nadel (New York: Harper, 1965), pp. 281–302.

2. Alex Haley, *Roots* (Garden City, N.Y.: Doubleday, 1976).

3. Margaret Gibbs, *The DAR* (New York: Holt, Rinehart and Winston, 1969), p. 21.

4. Erik Erikson, *Identity: Youth and Crisis* (New York: Norton, 1968); Erickson, *Life History and the Historical Moment* (New York: Norton, 1975).

5. Malcolm X, *Autobiography of Malcolm X,* with the assistance of Alex Haley (New York: Grove Press, 1965).

6. Theodore Rosengarten, *All God's Dangers: The Life of Nate Shaw* (New York: Knopf, 1974).

7. John Dollard, *Criteria for the Life History* (New Haven: Yale University Press, 1935); Gordon Allport, *The Use of Personal Documents in Psychological Science* (New York: Social Science Research Council, 1942); Robert White, *Lives in Progress* (New York: Dryden Press, 1952).

8. See Robert Coles, *Children of Crisis,* particularly "Migrants, Sharecroppers, Mountaineers" (Boston: Little, Brown, 1967); Oscar Lewis, *Five Families: Mexican Case Studies in the Culture of Poverty* (New York: Basic, 1959); Lewis, *La Vida: A Puerto Rican Family in the Culture of Poverty—San Juan and New York* (New York: Random House, 1966).

9. Lewis, *La Vida,* p. 2.

10. This project involved extensive and repeated interviews of approximately 300 former workers in the Amoskeag Mills in Manchester, New Hampshire (once the world's largest textile company). The people we interviewed represented all levels of skills and came from different ethnic groups. In addition to the workers, we also interviewed people from management, as well as people from different programs, including the clergy, and in the community. This oral history project grew out of extensive research in historical records. The reconstruction of most of each interviewee's work history and family history preceded the interview itself. Edited selections from this project were published in Tamara K. Hareven and Randolph Langenbach, *Amoskeag: Life and Work in an American Factory City* (New York: Pantheon, 1978).

11. Jan Vansina, *The Oral Tradition: A Study in Historical Methodology* (Chicago: Aldine, 1965; also see chapter 8 of the present volume).

12. Ronald Blythe, *Akenfield: Portrait of an English Village* (London: Allen Lane, 1969); Studs Terkel, *Hard Times: An Oral History of the Great Depression* (New York: Pantheon, 1970).

13. Cullom Davis et al., *Oral History: From Tape to Type* (Chicago: American Library Association, 1977).

14. Vansina, *Oral Tradition,* p. 77.

15. The exhibit, funded by the National Endowment for the Arts and by local foundations, was created and produced by Randolph Langenbach at the Currier Gallery of Art in Manchester, New Hampshire. It documented the development of the architectural design and the urban plan of Manchester, New Hampshire, by the corporation which founded the city and continued to control it until the corporation's shutdown in 1936. Through 80 mural-size photographic panels by Langenbach, as well as historic photographs, the exhibit documented the

connection between the architectural environment, corporate paternalism, and the experience of work. Unexpectedly, 12,000 people came to see the exhibit during its five weeks. Most of them were former mill workers.

16. Irving Howe, *The World of Our Fathers* (New York: Harcourt Brace Jovanovich, 1976).

17. Instructions from Henry Alsberg, director of the writer's project to all state directors, quoted in William F. McDonald, *Federal Relief Administration and the Arts* (Columbus: Ohio State University Press, 1969), p. 7.

18. McDonald, *Federal Relief Administration,* p. 11.

19. James Agee and Walker Evans, *Let Us Now Praise Famous Men* (Boston: Houghton Mifflin, 1941). For slave narratives see George P. Rawick, ed., *The American Slave: A Composite Autobiography,* 19 vols. (Westport, Conn.: Greenwood, 1972). On local oral history projects, see, for example: *These Are Our Lives: As Told by the People and Written by Members of the Federal Writers' Project of the Works Progress Administration in North Carolina, Tennessee, and Georgia* (Chapel Hill, N.C., 1939).

20. On the ethnic program see McDonald, *Federal Relief Administration,* p. 725.

21. Jacob Riis, *How the Other Half Lives* (New York: Scribner's, 1890); *The Children of the Poor* (New York: Scribner's, 1892). The Russell Sage Foundation sponsored and published studies of poor and working people; its most notable publication was Paul Kellogg, ed., *The Pittsburgh Survey,* 6 vols. (New York: Charities Publication Committee, 1909–14). *The Survey* was the best of a number of social reform journals.

22. Alfred Kazin, *On Native Grounds: An Interpretation of Modern Literature* (New York: Reynal and Hitchcock, 1942), p. 378.

23. Lloyd Warner, *The Living and the Dead* (New Haven: Yale University Press, 1959).

24. Personal communication, Prof. Milton Singer, Department of Anthropology, University of Chicago.

25. Jane Addams, quoted in Gibbs, *The DAR,* p. 2.

20

Black History, Oral History, and Genealogy

Alex Haley

Our final article on applying oral sources to family history describes a remarkable adventure in historical writing: Alex Haley's Roots. *Four years before the record-breaking broadcast of the televised film—now seen by hundreds of millions of people around the world—Haley gave the following account of his research during a colloquium of the Oral History Association.*

While this is no ordinary how-to story of family history, his article illustrates the excitement of research with living oral sources. Haley investigated oral traditional history, the historical narratives that passed from generation to generation by word of mouth. The final links in the historical saga uniting the author with his African ancestors of two centuries earlier was the Griot, or local history reciter, at one time common in tribal cultures.

Critics of Haley's research have charged that the documentation he provides to link his African and American families is more emotional than scientifically sound. Yet for the study—and inspiration—of black and ethnic history based on oral sources, this piece remains a classic. The late Alex Haley was the coauthor of The Autobiography of Malcolm X *(1965) and the author of* Roots: The Saga of an American Family *(1976).*

"Black History, Oral History, and Genealogy" by Alex Haley was first published in *Oral History Review* 1 (1973), pp. 1–25, and is reprinted by permission of the author and the Oral History Association.

W hen I was a little boy I lived in a little town which you probably never heard of called Henning, Tennessee, about 50 miles north of Memphis. And I lived there with my parents in the home of my mother's mother. And my grandmother and I were very, very close. Every summer that I can remember growing up there in Henning, my grandmother would have, as visitors, members of the family who were always women, always of her general age range, the late 40s, early 50s. They came from places that sounded pretty exotic to me—Dyersburg, Tennessee; Inkster, Michigan—places like that, St. Louis, Kansas City. They were like Cousin Georgia, Aunt Plus, Aunt Liz, so forth. And every evening, after the supper dishes were washed, they would go out on the front porch and sit in cane-bottomed rocking chairs, and I would always sit behind grandma's chair. And every single evening of those summers, unless there was some particular hot gossip that would overrule it, they would talk about otherwise the self same thing. It was bits and pieces and patches of what I later would learn was a long narrative history of the family which had been passed down literally across generations.

As a little boy I didn't have the orientation to understand most of what they talked about. Sometimes they would talk about individuals, and I didn't know what these individuals were often; I didn't know what an old massa was, I didn't know what an old missus was. They would talk about locales; I didn't know what a plantation was. And then at other times, interspersed with these, they'd talk about anecdotes, incidents which had happened to these people or these places. The furthest-back person that they ever talked about was someone whom they would call "The African." And I know that the first time I ever heard the word Africa or African was from their mouths, there on the front porch in Henning.

I think that my first impression that these things they spoke of went a long way back, came from the fact that they were wrinkled, greying, or completely grey in some cases, and I was a little boy, three, four, five, and now and then when some of them would get animatedly talking about something, they would fling their finger or hand down toward me and say something like "I wasn't any bigger than this young 'un here." And the very idea that someone as old and wrinkled as she had at one time been no older than I was just blew my mind. I knew it must be way, way back that they were talking about.

When they were speaking of this African, the furthest-back person of all, they would tell how he was brought on a ship to this country to a place they pronounced as "Naplis." And he was bought off this ship by a man whose name was John Waller, who had a plantation in a place called Spotsylvania County, Virginia. And then they would tell how he was on this plantation and he kept trying to escape. The first three times he escaped he was caught and given a worse beating than previously as his punishment. And then the fourth time he escaped he had the misfortune to be caught by a professional slave catcher. And I grew up hearing how this slave catcher decided to make an example of him. And I grew up hearing how he gave the African the choice either to be castrated or to have a foot cut off. And the African chose the foot. And I grew up hearing how his foot was put against a stump, and with an ax was cut off across the arch. It was a very hideous act. But as it turned out that act was to play a very major role in the keeping of a narrative down across a family for a long time.

The reasons were two. One of them was that in the middle 1700s in Virginia, almost all slaves were sold at auction. A male slave in good condition would bring on the average about $750. At the end of every slave auction they would have what they called the scrap sale, and those who were incapacitated, ill, or otherwise not so valuable for market, would be sold generally for amounts of $100 or less in cash. And this particular African managed to survive and then to convalesce, and he posed then to his master an economic question. And his master decided that he was crippled and he hobbled about, but he still could do limited work. And the master decided that he would be worth more kept on that plantation than he would be worth sold away for cash of less than $100. And that was how it happened that this particular African was kept on one plantation for quite a long period of time.

Now that came at a time when, if there was any single thing that probably characterizes slaves, it was that they had almost no sense of what we today know and value and revere as family continuity. And the reason simply was that slaves were sold back and forth so much. Characteristically slave children would grow up without an awareness of who their parents were, and particularly male parents. This African, now kept on the plantation by his master's decision, hobbling about and doing the limited work he could, finally met and mated with another slave on that plantation, and her name (in the stories told by my grandmother and the others on the front porch in Henning) was Bell the big house cook. And of that union was born a little girl who was given the name Kizzy. As Kizzy got to be four or five or so, this African would take that little girl by the hand, and he would take her around and point out to her various natural objects, and he would tell her the name for that thing—tree, rock, cow, sky, so forth. The names that he told her were instinctively in his native tongue, and to the girl they were strange phonetic sounds which in time, with repetitive hearing, the girl could repeat. He would point at a guitar and he would make a single sound as if it were spelled *ko*. And she came in time to know that ko was guitar in his terms. There were other strange phonetic sounds for other objects. Perhaps the most involved of them was that contiguous to the plantation there was a river, and whenever this African would point out this river to his daughter Kizzy he would say to her *"Kamby Bolongo."* And she came to know that *Kamby Bolongo* in his terms meant river.

There was another thing about this African which is in the background of all the Black people in this country, and that was that whoever bought them off the slave ship, when they got them to a plantation, about their first act was giving them an Anglicized name. For all practical purposes that was the first step in the psychic dehumanization of an individual or collectively of a people. And in the case of this particular African his master gave him the name Toby. But whenever any of the other adult slaves would address him as Toby, this African would strenuously rebuff and reject it and he would tell them his name was *"Kin-tay,"* a sharp, angular two-syllabic sound that the little girl Kizzy came to know her father said was his name.

And there was yet another thing about this African characteristic of all those original Africans in our background, and that was that they had been brought from a place where they spoke whatever was their native tongue, and brought to this place where it became necessary to learn English for sheer survival's sake. And gradually, haltingly, all those original Africans learned a word here, a phrase there, of the new tongue—English. As this process began to happen with this African, and he began to be able to express himself in more detailed ways, he began to tell his little daughter Kizzy little vignettes about himself. He told her, for instance, how he had been captured. He said that he had been not far away from his village chopping wood to make himself a drum when he had been set upon by four men, overwhelmed, and taken thusly into slavery. And she came to know along with many other stories the story of how he was chopping wood when he was captured.

To compress what would happen over the next decade, the girl Kizzy stayed on the plantation in Spotsylvania County directly exposed to her father who had come directly from Africa, and to his stories, until she had a considerable repertoire of knowledge about him from his own mouth. When the girl Kizzy was 16 years of age, she was sold away to a new master whose name was Tom Lea and he had a much smaller plantation in North Carolina. And it was on this plantation that after a while the girl Kizzy gave birth to her first child, a boy who was given the name George. The father was the new master Tom Lea. And as George got to be four or five or so, now it was his mother Kizzy who began to tell him the stories that she heard from her father. And the boy began to discover the rather common phenomenon that slave children rarely knew who their fathers were, let alone a grandfather. He had something which made him rather singular. And so it was with considerable pride the boy began to tell his peers the story of his grandfather; this African who said his name was *Kin-tay*, who called a river *Kamby Bolongo*, and called a guitar *ko* and other sounds for other things, and who said that he had been chopping wood when he was set upon and captured and brought into slavery.

When the boy George got to be about 12, he was apprenticed to an old slave to learn handling the master's fighting gamecocks. And this boy had innate, green thumb ability for fighting gamecocks. By the time he was in his mid-teens he had been given (for his local and regional renown as an expert slave handler and pitter of fighting gamecocks) the nickname he would take to his grave decades later—Chicken George.

When Chicken George was about 18 he met and mated with a slave girl. And her name was Matilda, and in time Matilda gave birth to seven children. Now for the first time that story which had come down from this African began to fan out within the breadth of a family. The stories as they would be told on the front porch in Henning by grandma and the others were those of the winter evenings after the harvest when families would entertain themselves by sitting together and the elders would talk and the young would listen. Now Chicken George would sit with his seven children around the hearth. The story was that they would roast sweet potatoes in the hot ashes, and night after night after night across the winters, Chicken George would tell his seven children a story unusual among slaves, and that was direct knowledge of a great-grandfather; this same African who said his name was *Kin-tay*, who called the river *Kamby Bolongo*, and a guitar *ko*, and who said that he was chopping wood when he was captured.

Those children grew up, took mates and had children. One of them was named Tom. And Tom became an apprenticed blacksmith. He was sold in his mid-teens to a man named Murray who had a tobacco plantation in Alamance County, North Carolina. And it was on this plantation that Tom, who became that plantation's blacksmith, met and mated with a slave girl whose name was Irene and who was the plantation weaver. And Irene also in time bore seven children. Now it was yet another generation, another section of the state of North Carolina and another set of seven children who would sit in yet another cabin, around the hearth in the winter evenings with the sweet potatoes in the hot ashes. And now the father was Tom telling his children about something virtually unique in the knowledge of slaves, direct knowledge of a great-great-grandfather, this same African, who said his name was *Kin-tay*, who called the river *Kamby Bolongo*, who said he was chopping wood when he was captured, and the other parts of the story that had come down in that way.

Of that second set of seven children, in Alamance County, North Carolina, the youngest was a little girl whose name was Cynthia, and Cynthia was my maternal grandmother. And I grew up in her home in Henning, Tennessee, and grandma pumped that story into me as if it were plasma. It was by all odds the most precious thing in her life—the story which had come down across the generations about the family going back to that original African.

I stayed at grandma's home until I was in my mid-teens. By that time I had two younger brothers, George and Julius. Our father was a teacher at small black land grant colleges about the South and we began now to move around wherever he was teaching. And thus I went to school through two years of college. When World War II came along I was one of the many people who thought that if I could hurry and get into an organization of which I recently heard called the U.S. Coast Guard, that maybe I could spend the war walking the coast. And I got into the service and to my great shock rather suddenly found myself on an ammunition ship in the Southwest Pacific, which was not at all what I had in mind. But when I look back upon it now, it was the first of a series of what seemed to be accidental things, but now seem to be part of a pattern of many things that were just meant to be, to make a certain book possible, in time. On the ships in the Coast Guard, totally by accident, I stumbled into the long road to becoming a writer. It was something I had never have dreamed of.

I became a writer in the time when if you were black and you went into the naval services you automatically went into what was called the steward's department. And first you were a mess boy, and that meant that you would shine shoes and wait on tables, clean the toilets, make up the beds, things like that. And if you did these things sufficiently well and long, you would advance to cook. And I became a cook on this ammunition ship in the Southwest Pacific. My most precious possession on the ship was a portable typewriter. Every night, when I would finish my pots and pans, I would go down in the hold of the ship, and I'd type letters to everybody I could think of—ex-schoolmates, friends, even teachers, anybody that I could think of. Other ships would take mail ashore.

With us out there, far from home as we were and for as long at sea we would stay (sometimes two, three months before we would get ashore in places like Australia and New Zealand), mail call was a very epochal event for us. And when I got things going pretty well, I would get on the average 30 to 40 letters every mail call. And ships have swift grapevines, and it quickly circulated about this ship that I was the ship's most prolific writer and receiver of mail.

Concurrently, after we would be at sea two or three months and finally got ashore somewhere in Australia or New Zealand, our topmost priority was to fall in love with somebody as quick as possible. And we would do the best we could and then we'd go back out to sea. And now there would be maybe a hundred young guys on the ship as I was, 17 or so, who was just smitten with some girl he had left ashore, and girls have a way of getting prettier in your mind the longer you're at sea, and some of my buddies who were not as articulate on paper as they were verbally, began to come around and in a covert way they began to suggest that since I wrote so many letters that maybe I would be willing to help them compose a letter to some girl. And I began to do this. I would sit at a mess table with a stack of three by five index cards. And my clients would line up and as they got to me I would just interview them. I'd say, "now, what does she look like—hair, eyes, nose, so forth?" And they would tell me. And I'd say, "what did you want to tell her, where did you go, was there anything you want to say in the way of details?" And then I would take each card, put her name and his name on it, and then later as I got a chance, I'd write, for him to copy later in his own handwriting, a rather personalized love letter utilizing that specific information about that girl.

The girls in Australia and New Zealand were not used to these kinds of missives. And I will never forget one day and night that were to prove most motivational and pivotal in my becoming a writer by accident. We had been at sea for three months, during which time three batches of mail had been taken off our ship, so that each of my client's girls had these many letters. We got into Brisbane, Australia about noon. Liberty was declared at six in the afternoon and everyone who had liberty just flew ashore. Around midnight most of those came back wobbling and stumbling, having accomplished the most they'd been able, which was to get very drunk. And then it was almost as if a script had been written. Around one in the morning my "clients" started coming back, individually. Before a steadily enlarging and increasingly awestruck audience, they were describing, in the graphic way that only sailors can, how when they in person got to that girl behind these letters, they met just incredible results, sometimes practically on the spot. I became heroic on that ship that night and for the rest of World War II, I never fought a soul. All I did was write love letters.

Writing love letters led me secretly to begin trying to write stories for modern romances and true confessions. I would write these stories making out I was a girl and this lout had done this, that or another to me and I was trying to resolve my problem, and I would send out those manuscripts and they would come back just as fast as wartime mails would permit. I wrote every single day, 7 days a week for 8 years, before the first story was bought by a magazine. And I stayed on in the service, shipping on whenever my hitch was up, until lo and behold I was 37 years of age and I had 20 years of service and retired. I came out of the service in San Francisco determined, because I had sold by now to *Atlantic Monthly*, *Harper's*, *Reader's Digest*, and a good number of stories to men's adventure magazines, mostly sea adventure stories because that was the material I had accessible to me in the service, I was going to find for myself a career as a free-lance writer. My first assignment was from *Reader's Digest* to do an article about the then-newly emerging social phenomenon called the Nation of Islam, or colloquially, the Black Muslims. I now met Malcolm X, I worked with him in writing that article. Then I worked with him and another writer writing a piece for the *Saturday Evening Post,* and in the interim I had happened to begin the feature called "Playboy Interviews," and *Playboy* asked me if I would interview Malcolm X, which I did. The interviews are very in-depth and intensive. I worked now with Malcolm very, very intensively for about three weeks. And when that interview was published, Doubleday asked Malcolm if he would be willing to tell his life in book-length detail. After some demurring Malcolm finally agreed. Because I had happened to be the black writer who worked with him on most of the major magazine stories which had been done about him, he asked me if I would be willing to work with him on the book. I was, of course, pleased and honored and flattered to do so.

I had a place in Greenwich Village and Malcolm X, after his extremely busy days, would come to my place about nine in the evening and stay generally until about one or two the following morning. And he would do this about four nights a week. And each of these nights I would just interview him, picking out of this man's memory every thread, every fiber of everything he could remember across the whole of his life. And that went across a calendar year. At the end of that time I had a great volume of notes of his memories. I spent a second year arranging those notes and vicariously, as if I were Malcolm, writing in the first person, putting onto paper, and with all the rewrites and the drafts, what hopefully would sound to a reader as if Malcolm X had just sat down and told that reader, from his memory, from earliest memory to the time he was talking. When the *Autobiography of Malcolm X* manuscript was finished I got in touch with Malcolm and we went into a hotel, and he went across the whole manuscript. I can see his red ball point pen, changing the name of someone whom he said he didn't wish to embarrass, and things of that nature. And finally when he was finished, he said: "Brother, I don't think I'm going to live to read this in print. So I'd like to read it again." And he spent three days in the New York Hilton Hotel, reading again that manuscript. And it was then sent to the publisher.

Malcolm proved very prophetic, because it was two weeks later he was shot to death on a Sunday afternoon in the Audubon Ballroom. And as much as Malcolm had talked matter-of-factly about the imminence of violent death, it just seemed to me impossible. And it was a very, very rocky, traumatic kind of night for me. The following morning I sat down at the typewriter, just dropping blank white sheets in that machine and drumming on the keyboard for the space of maybe 30 or 40 minutes, sit, stare at the keyboard, drum again. This is the only thing I've written in my life in that manner. And over a period of three days was written that part which appears now at the end of the book called "The Epilogue." And it was just a tumbling out of the memory of the reminiscence of having met and worked with this man, and anecdotes and insights into him. Then that was sent to the publisher.

Now there happened one of the things when I look back upon it, like the first of a series of miracles that were subsequently to make it possible for me to pull together a book that aspires to be the first of its kind in having to do with black history, black heritage, black pride, just blackness in general. The first thing that happened here in this series of miracles was *Playboy* magazine called and asked if I would fly over to England and interview the actress Julie Christie. So I flew over there. Julie Christie was involved in the making of a motion picture called *Far from the Madding Crowd*. The weather was terrible. They had to move the set from one side of England to the other and Julie Christie was so uptight she was scarcely speaking to the director, let alone some interviewer who had appeared from this country. I had to get in touch with *Playboy* and tell them this. And they sent me a cable and said, "Well, you're over there so stand by and see what develops." And that was how I, who always innately had loved history and had been steeped in history by grandma and others from the time I was a little boy, found myself plunked in one of the places on earth that had probably more history per square foot than anywhere I know—London. I was all over the place. There was scarcely a tour guide in London that didn't have me on the next several days.

One morning I was in the British Museum and I came upon something, I had vaguely heard of it, the Rosetta Stone. It just really entranced me. I read about it, and I found how, when this stone was discovered in 1799, it seemed to have three sets of texts chiseled into the stone: one of them in Greek characters, which Greek scholars could read, the second in a then-unknown set of characters, the third in the ancient hieroglyphics which it was assumed no one would ever translate. Then I read how a French scholar, Jean Champollion, had come along and had taken that second unknown set of script, character for character, matched it with the Greek and finally had come up with a thesis he could prove—that the text was the same as the Greek. And then in a superhuman feat of scholarship he had taken the terribly intricate characters of the hieroglyphics and cross-matched them with the preceding two in almost geometric progression, and had proved that too was the same text. That was what opened up to the whole world of scholarship, all that hitherto had been hidden behind the mystery of the allegedly undecipherable hieroglyphics.

And that thing just fascinated me. I would find myself going around London doing all sorts of other things and at odd times I would see in my mind's eye, almost as if it were projected in my head, the Rosetta Stone. And to me, it just had some kind of special significance, but I couldn't make head or tail of what it might be. Finally I was on a plane coming back to this country, when an idea hit me. It was rough, raw, crude, but it got me to thinking. Now what this scholar worked with was language chiseled into the stone. And what he did was to take that which had been unknown and match it with that which was known, and thus found out the meaning of what hitherto had been unknown. And then I got to thinking of an analogy; that story always told in our family that I had heard on the front porch in Henning. The unknown quotient was those strange phonetic sounds. And I got to thinking, now maybe I could find out where these sounds came from. Obviously these strange sounds are threads of some African tongue. And my whole thing was to see if maybe I could find out, just in curiosity, what tongue did they represent. It seemed obvious to me what I had to do was try to get in touch with as wide a range of Africans as I could, simply because there were many, many tongues spoken in Africa. I lived in New York, so I began doing what seemed to me logical. I began going up to the United Nations lobby about quitting time. I wasn't hard to spot Africans, and every time I could I'd stop one. And I would say to him my little sounds. In a couple of weeks I stopped a couple of dozen Africans, each and every one of which took a quick look, quick listen to me, and took off. Which I well understand; me with a Tennessee accent trying to tell them some African sounds, I wasn't going to get it.

I have a friend, a master researcher, George Sims, who knew what I was trying to do and he came to me with a listing of about a dozen people renowned for their knowledge of African linguistics. And one who intrigued me right off the bat was not an African at all, but a Belgian. Educated at England, much of it at the School of Oriental and African Studies, he had done his early work living in African villages, studying the language or the tongue as spoken in those villages. He had finally written a book called, in French, *La Tradition Orale*.[1] His name: Dr. Jan Vansina, University of Wisconsin. I phoned Dr. Vansina. He very graciously said I could see him. I got on a plane and flew to Madison, Wisconsin, with no dream what was about to happen. In the living room of the Vansinas' that evening I told Dr. Vansina every little bit I could remember of what I'd heard as a little boy on the front porch in Henning. And Dr. Vansina listened most intently. And then he began to question me. Being himself an oral historian, he was particularly interested in the physical transmission of the story down across the generations. And I would answer everything I could. I couldn't answer most of what he asked. Around midnight, Dr. Vansina said, "I wonder if you'd spend the night at our home," and I did stay there. The following morning, before breakfast, Dr. Vansina came down with a very serious expression on his face; I was later to learn that he had already been on the phone with colleagues, and he said to me: "The ramifications of what you have brought here could be enormous." He and his colleagues felt almost certain that the collective sounds that I had been able to bring there, which had been passed down across the family in the manner I had described to him, represented the Mandinka tongue. I'd never heard the word. He told me that that was the tongue spoken by the Mandingo people. He began then to guess translate certain of the sounds. There was a sound that probably meant cow or cattle; another probably meant the bow-bow tree, generic in West Africa. I had told him that from the time I was knee-high I'd heard about how this African would point to a guitar and say *ko*. Now he told me that almost surely this would refer to one of the oldest of the stringed instruments among the Mandingo people, an instrument made of a gourd covered with goat skin, a long neck, 21 strings, called the *kora*. He came finally to the most involved of the sounds that I had heard and had brought to him—*Kamby Bolongo*. He said without question in Mandinka, *bolongo* meant river; preceded by *Kamby* it probably would mean Gambia River. I'd never heard of that river.

It was Thursday morning when I heard those words; Monday morning I was in Africa. I just had to go. There was no sense in messing around. On Friday I found that of the numerous African students in this country, there were a few from that very, very small country called Gambia. And the one who physically was closest to me was a fellow in Hamilton College, Clinton, New York. And I hit that campus about 3:30 Friday afternoon and practically snatched Ebou Manga out of an economics class and got us on Pan American that night. We flew through the night to Dakar, Senegal, and there we got a light plane that flew over to a little airstrip called Yundum—they literally had to run monkeys off the runway to get in there. And then we got a van and we went into the small city of Bathurst, the capital of Gambia. Ebou Manga, his father Alhaji Manga (it's a predominantly Moslem culture there), assembled a group of about eight men, members of the government, who came into the patio of the Atlantic Hotel, and they sat in kind of a semi-circle as I told them the history that had come down across the family to my grandmother and thence to me; told them everything I could remember.

And when I finished, the Africans irritated me considerably because *Kamby Bolongo*, the sounds which had gotten me specifically to them, they tended almost to pooh-pooh. They said, "Well, of course *Kamby Bolongo* would mean Gambia River; anyone would know that." What these Africans reacted to was another sound: a mere two syllables that I had brought them without the slightest comprehension that it had any particular significance. They said, "There may be some significance in that your forefather stated his name was *Kin-tay*." I said, "Well, there was nothing more explicit in the story than the pronunciation of his name, *Kin-tay*." They said, "Our oldest villages tend to be named for those families which founded those villages centuries ago." And then they sent for a little map and they said, "Look, here is the village of Kinte-Kundah. And not too far from it is the village of Kinte-Kundah-janneh-Ya." And then they told me about something I never had any concept existed in this world. They told me that in the back country, and particularly in the older villages of the back country, there were old men called *griots,* who are in effect walking, living archives of oral history. They are the old men who, from the time they had been in their teen-ages, have been part of a line of men who tell the stories as they have been told since the time of their forefathers, literally down across centuries. The incumbent *griot* will be a man usually in his late 60s, early 70s, and underneath him will be men separated by about decade intervals, 60, 50, 40, 30, 20, and a teen-age boy, and each line of *griots* will be the experts in the story of a major family clan; another line of *griots* another clan; and so on for dozens of major clans. Another line of *griots* would be the experts in the history of a group of villages. Another would go into the history of the empires which had preceded it, and so forth. And the stories were told in a narrative, oral history way, not verbatim, but the essential same way they had been told down across the time since the forefathers. And the way they were trained was that the teen-age boy was exposed to that story for 40 or 50 years before he would become the oral historian incumbent.

It astounds us now to realize that men like these, in not only Africa but other cultures, can literally talk for days, telling a story and not repeating themselves, and telling the details in the most explicit detail. The reason it astounds us is because in our culture we have become so conditioned to the crush of print that most people in our culture have almost forgotten what the human memory is capable of if it is trained to keep things in it. These men, I was told, existed in the back country. And the men there told me that since my forefather had said his name was *Kin-tay* they would see what they could do to help me.

I came back to this country enormously bewildered. I didn't know what to do. It embarrasses me to say that up to that time I really hadn't thought all that much about Africa. I knew where it was and I had the standard cliché images of it, the Tarzan Africa and stuff like that. Well, now it was almost as if some religious zealotry came into me. I just began to devour everything I could lay eyes on about Africa, particularly slavery. I can remember after reading all day I'd sit on the edge of a bed at night with a map of Africa, studying the positions of the countries, one with relation with the other.

It was about six weeks later when an innocuous looking letter came to me which suggested that when it was possible I should come back. I was back over there as quickly as I possibly could make it. The same men, with whom I had previously talked rather matter-of-factly, told me that the word had been put out in the back country and that there had indeed been found a *griot* of the Kinte clan. His name, they said, was Kebba Kanga Fofana. When I heard there was such a man I was ready to have a fit. Where is he? I figured from my experience as an American magazine writer, the government should have had him there with a public relations man for me to talk to. And they looked at me oddly and they said, he's in his village.

I discovered at that point that if I was to see this man, I was going to have to do something I'd never dreamed before: I would have to organize a safari. It took me three days to rent a launch to get up the river, lorry, Land Rover to take supplies by the back route, to hire finally a total of 14 people, including 3 interpreters, 4 musicians (they told me in the back country these old oral historians would not talk without music in the background), bearers and so forth. And on the fourth day we went vibrating in this launch up the Gambia River. I was very uncomfortable. I had the feeling of being alien. I had the queasy feeling of what do they see me as, another pith-helmet? We got on up the river to a little village called Albreda on the left bank. And then we went ashore. And now our destination by foot was a village called Juffure where this man was said to live.

There's an expression called "the peak experience." It is that which emotionally nothing in your life ever can transcend. And I know I have had mine that first day in the back country in black West Africa. When we got up within sight of the village of Juffure the children who had inevitably been playing outside African villages, gave the word and the people came flocking out of their huts. It's a rather small village, only about 70 people. And villages in the back country are very much today as they were 200 years ago, circular mud huts with conical thatched roofs. And from a distance I could see this small man with a pillbox hat and an off-white robe, and even from a distance there was an aura of "somebodiness" about him. I just knew that was the man we had come to see. And when we got closer the interpreters left our party and went straight to him. And I had stepped unwittingly into a sequence of emotional events that always I feel awkward trying to describe, simply because I never ever verbally could convey the power, the physical power, of emotional occurrences.

These people quickly filtered closely around me in kind of a horseshoe design with me at the base. If I had put up my hands I would have touched the nearest ones on either side. There were about three, four deep all around. And the first thing that hit me was the intensity of the way they were staring at me. The eyes just raped. The foreheads were forward in the intensity of the staring. And it was an uncomfortable feeling. And while this was happening there began to occur inside me a kind of feeling as if something was turgid, rolling, surging around. And I had this eerie feeling that I knew inside me why it was happening and what it was about, but consciously I could not identify what had me so upset inside. And after a while it began to roll in: it was rather like a gale force wind that you couldn't see but it just rolled in and hit you—bam! It was enough to knock you down. I suddenly realized what so upset me was that I was looking at a crowd of people and for the first time in my life every one of them was jet black. And I was standing there rather rocked by that, and in the way that we tend to do if we are discomforted we drop our glance. And I remember dropping my glance, and my glance falling on my own hand, my own complexion, in context with their complexion. And now there came rolling in another surging gale force thing that hit me perhaps harder than the first one. A feeling of guilt, a feeling rather of being hybrid, a feeling of being the impure among the pure.

And the old man suddenly left the interpreters, walked away, and the people as quickly filtered away from me and to the old man. And they began a very animated talking, high metallic Mandinka tongue. One of the interpreters, his name was A. B. C. Salla, whispered in my ear and the significance of what he whispered probably got me as much as all the rest of it collectively. He said, "They stare at you so because they have never seen a black American." And what hit me was they were not looking at Alex Haley, writer, they didn't know who he was, they could care less. But what they saw me as was a symbol of 25 millions of us over here whom they had never seen. And it was just an awesome thing to realize that someone had thrust that kind of symbolism upon me. And there's a language that's universal. It's a language of gestures, noises, inflections, expressions. Somehow looking at them, hearing them, though I couldn't understand a syllable, I knew what they were talking about. I somehow knew they were trying to arrive at a consensus of how did they collectively feel about me as a symbol for them of all the millions of us over here whom they never had seen. And there came a time when the old man quickly turned. He walked right through the people, he walked right past three interpreters, he walked right up to me, looked piercingly into my eyes and spoke in Mandinka, as instinctively he felt I should be able to understand it. And the translation came from the side. And the way they collectively saw me, the symbol of all the millions of us black people here whom they never had seen was, "Yes, we have been told by the forefathers that there are many of us from this place who are in exile in that place called America and in other places." And that was the way they saw it.

The old man, the *griot*, the oral historian, Kebba Kanga Fofana, 73 rains of age (their way of saying 73 years, one rainy season a year), began now to tell me the ancestral history of the Kinte clan as it had been told down across the centuries, from the times of the forefathers. It was as if a scroll was being read. It wasn't just talk as we talk. It was a very formal occasion. The people became mouse quiet, rigid. The old man sat in a chair and when he would speak he would come up forward, his body would grow rigid, the cords in his neck stood out and he spoke words as though they were physical objects coming out of his mouth. He'd speak a sentence or so, he would go limp, relax, and the translation would come. Out of this man's head came spilling lineage details incredible to behold. Two, three centuries back. Who married whom, who had what children, what children married whom and their children, and so forth, just unbelievable. I was struck not only by the profusion of details, but also by the biblical pattern of the way they expressed it. It would be something like: "and so and so took as a wife so and so and begat and begat and begat," and he'd name their mates and their children, and so forth. When they would date things it was not with calendar dates, but they would date things with physical events, such as, "in the year of the big water he slew a water buffalo," the year of the big water referring to a flood. And if you wanted to know the date calendar-wise you had to find when that flood occurred.

I can strip out of the hours that I heard of the history of the Kinte clan (my forefather had said his name was *Kin-tay),* the immediate vertical essence of it, leaving out all the details of the brothers and the cousins and the other marriages and so forth. The *griot* Kebba Kanga Fofana said that the Kinte clan had been begun in a country called Old Mali. Traditionally the Kinte men were blacksmiths who had conquered fire. The women were potters and weavers. A branch of the clan had moved into the country called Mauretania. It was from the country of Mauretania that a son of the clan, whose name was Kairaba Kunta Kinte (he was *amarabout,* which is to say a holy man of the Moslem faith), came down into the country called the Gambia. He went first to a village called Pakali n'Ding. He stayed there for a while. He went next to a village called Jiffarong; thence he went to a village called Juffure. In the village of Juffure the young *Marabout* Kairaba Kunta Kinte took his first wife, a Mandinka maiden whose name was Sireng. And by her he begot two sons whose names were Janneh and Saloum. Then he took a second wife; her name, Yaisa. And by Yaisa he begot a son whose name was Omoro. Those three sons grew up in the village of Juffure until they came of age. The elder two, Janneh and Saloum, went away and started a new village called Kinte-Kundah janneh-Ya. It is there today. Literally translated it means "The Home of janneh Kinte." The youngest son, Omoro, stayed in the village until he had 30 rains, and then he took a wife, a Mandinka maiden, her name Binta Kebba. And by Binta Kebba, roughly between 1750 and 1760, Omoro Kinte begat four sons, whose names were Kunta, Lamin, Suwadu, and Madi.

By the time he got down to that level of the family, the griot had talked for probably five hours. He had stopped maybe 50 times in the course of that narrative and a translation came into me. And then a translation came as all the others had come, calmly, and it began, "About the time the king's soldiers came." That was one of those time-fixing references. Later in England, in British Parliamentary records, I went feverishly searching to find out what he was talking about, because I had to have the calendar date. But now in back country Africa, the *griot* Kebba Kanga Fofana, the oral historian, was telling the story as it had come down for centuries from the time of the forefathers of the Kinte clan. "About the time the king's soldiers came, the eldest of these four sons, Kunta, went away from this village to chop wood and was seen never again." And he went on with his story.

I sat there as if I was carved of rock. Goose-pimples came out on me I guess the size of marbles. He just had no way in the world to know that he had told me that which meshed with what I'd heard on the front porch in Henning, Tennessee, from grandma, from Cousin Georgia, from Aunt Liz, from Cousin Plus, all the other old ladies who sat there on that porch. I managed to get myself together enough to pull out my notebook, which had in it what grandma had always said. And I got the interpreter Salla and showed it to him and he got rather agitated, and he went to the old man, and he got agitated, and the old man went to the people and they got agitated.

I don't remember it actually happening. I don't remember anyone giving an order, but those 70 people formed a ring around me, moving counter-clockwise, chanting, loudly, softly, loudly, softly, their bodies were so close together, the physical action was like drum majorettes with their high knee action. You got the feeling they were an undulating mass of people moving around. I'm standing in the middle like an Adam in the desert. I don't know how I felt; how could you feel a thing like that? And I remember looking at the first lady who broke from that circle (there were about a dozen ladies who had little infant children slung across their backs), and she with a scowl on this jet black face, broke from that circle, her bare feet slapping against the hard earth, came charging in towards me. And she took her baby and roughly thrust it out. The gesture said, "Take it!" and I took the baby and I clasped it, at which point she snatched it away and another lady, another baby, and I guess I had clasped about a dozen babies in about two minutes. I would be almost two years later at Harvard when Dr. Jerome Bruner told me, you were participating in one of the oldest ceremonies of human kind called "the laying on of hands"; that in their way they were saying to you, "through this flesh which is us, we are you, and you are us." There were many, many other things that happened in that village that day, but I was particularly struck with the enormity of the fact that they were dealing with me and seeing me in the perspective of, for them, the symbol of 25 millions of us black people in this country whom they never had seen. They took me into their mosque. They prayed in Arabic which I couldn't understand. Later the crux of the prayer was translated, "Praise be to Allah for one long lost from us whom Allah has returned." And that was the way they saw that.

When it was possible to leave, since we'd come by water, I wanted to go out over the land. My five senses had become muted, truncated. They didn't work right. If I wanted to feel something I would have to squeeze to register the sense of feeling. Things were misty. I didn't hear well. I would become aware the driver sitting right by me was almost shouting something and I just hadn't heard him up to that point. I began now, as we drove out over the back country road, with drums distantly heard around, to see in my mind's eye, as if it were being projected somehow on a film, a screen almost, rough, ragged, out of focus, almost a portrayal of what I had studied so, so much about: the background of us as a people, the way that ancestrally we who are in this country were brought out of Africa.

The impression prevails that most of the slaves were taken from coastal Africa. Not so. Coastal Africa's population never could have begun to satisfy the voracious maw of two centuries of slavery. By far most of us came from those interior villages. And I was seeing the way so many, many times I'd read about it, many, many different accounts, that the people would come screaming awake at night in the villages with the thatched roofs aflame falling in on them. And they'd dash out into the dark, into the very arms of the people who fired the villages, and the element of surprise and the arms were on one side and the slaughter was relatively brief, and the people who survived, those who were left whole enough, were linked neck by neck with thongs into what were called "coffles." It is said that some of the coffles were a mile long. And then there would come the torturous march, down towards the sea where the ships were. Many, many died hideously along the way, or were left to die when they were too weak to go on. And finally those who survived would get to the beach area, and down on the beaches were what they would call "barracoons," low structures of bamboo lashed together with thongs. And it would be in here that they would be put, rested, washed, fed better for a period of time, greased, their heads would be shaved, and so forth, and when it was felt that they were in condition, they would be sent out into the small yards in front of the barracoons for inspection by those who came from the ships for the purpose of purchase. And those who were finally selected for purchase after the most incredible examinations of every orifice in the human body would be branded and marched out to the ships.

It seemed to me, seeing all this riding along there, that the Africans really hadn't up to this time comprehended the enormity of what was about to happen to them. And the reason being that there was precedent up to now for everything that had happened. Cruelty was nothing new to them. The Africans were hideously cruel one to the other. Slavery, as such, was nothing new to Africans. Over half the people in Africa were slaves of other Africans. The difference being that there was no concept in Africa of what western type slavery would be. Slavery in Africa would equate with what we call share cropping. It was only when, it seemed to me, these Africans were being moved from barracoon, freshly branded, across that strip of sandy beach, and they could see for the first time those cockle shell canoes at the water's edge and out further on the water the larger things that they thought were flying houses. I had read, and now was seeing it in my mind's eye, how when the Africans were being moved across that beach, many of them would scream, they would go into paroxisms of shouting, fall flat, go clawing as deep as they could with their heads down into the sand, and taking great gulping choking mouthfuls of sand trying to get one last hold on the land which had been their home. And they were beaten up from that and taken into the canoes and thus they went into the holds of those ships which are utterly undescribable. And it was in that manner that every single one of our forebears came over, with no exceptions. And I was full of this.

When we got to the first village, it was with a great, great shock I realized that the drums I'd been dimly hearing were the talking drums that still work in back country Africa. They told what had happened behind us in the village of Juffure. Now as the driver slowed down, I could see the people in the village ahead of us packed on either side of the road and they were waving and there was this cacophony of sound coming out of them, growing louder as we came closer. And when we got to the edge of the village, I stood up in the Land Rover and looking

down on these people, jet black people waving up, dimly I could see them. And I
heard the noise coming from them. And the first thought, that just overwhelmed
me, was that they were down there having never left Africa and I-we (symbolic of
we here in this country) were standing up there in the Land Rover, and it was
only caprice, which of our forefathers had been taken out. That was the only
thing that made the difference of where we were, one place or the other. And I
was just full of the realization of that. And I guess we'd gotten about a third of the
way in the village when it finally registered upon my brain what it was they were
all crying out. I hadn't understood it, I think, because they were all crying out the
same thing, tightly packed, tightly massed, wizened old black elders, little naked
tar black children all crying out in mass, "Mister Kinte, Mister Kinte." And let me
tell you. I'm a man, but a sob hit me at ankle level and just rolled up. I just began
crying as I have never cried in my life. It just seemed to me that if you really
knew the ancestral history of blacks, we blacks, if you really knew the way every
single one of us had come here, that no matter what ever else might later be your
reaction, that you first had to weep. And that's all I could do. I remember being
aware of people staring as if to say, "What's wrong?" And I didn't care. That was
all I could do.

    We got out of the village, we got to where I could get a taxi to Dakar. I got
there, I got a plane, got back to this country. It took me about a week to get
myself emotionally together enough to go back to the publisher. I went to Doubleday and I told them what had happened. I told them it isn't the story of a family; it's the saga of a people passed down in this oral history way. And the reason
it was a saga of people is because we black people—probably more than any
other people on the face of earth in as large a number—have the most common
generic background; that every single one of us without exception ancestrally
goes back to some one of those villages, belonged to some one of those tribes,
was captured in some way, was put on some one of those slave ships, across the
same ocean into some succession of plantations up to the Civil War, the emancipation, and ever since then a struggle for freedom. So this book had to be the
saga of a people. And since it was such, it was up to me to give it every possible
thing that I, as a symbol of us, who happened to be a writer, could bring to that
book. I had to do everything, to find every thread that could have any bearing on
the history, the saga, of us as a people. They said they understood, and they gave
me time to go.

    When I look back over the whole of my life it seems so many things hap-
pened from the time I was a little boy that would prepare me for something that
this book would demand. By accident I had gone to the Coast Guard. By accident
I had become a writer in the Coast Guard. When I began to write seriously the
material available to me had been old maritime records. I had spent years
combing in old records of the old U.S. Maritime Service, of the old Lighthouse

Service. Not a lot of people generally know a lot about old maritime records and in particular few black people happen to have been exposed to this simply because it's not something in our average background. But I did know a great deal about them.

From the time I was a little boy grandma always said that ship came to what they call "Naplis." Now I knew they had to be talking about Annapolis, Maryland. Now also I knew specifically where that slave came from; so obviously some ship had come from that area of the Gambia River and sailed to Annapolis, Maryland. And what I wanted now was the symbolic ship that brought over, it is said, 15 million of our forebears alive to this country, and in order to be the proper symbolic ship it had to be the specific ship that had brought Kunta Kinte. And I went now on a search for that ship. The *griot* had set a time reference in his oral history dating way: "About the time the king's soldiers came." And it was now when I found that he was talking about this group called Colonel O'Hare's forces who had come to the Gambia River in 1767 to guard the Fort James slave fort. So that gave me a calendar date. Now I went to work to find that ship. This was still colonies at the time; the mother country was England. So I got on a plane now and went to London. I began to search in records. I went to Lloyd's of London and got to a man named Mr. R. C. E. Landers. And I got in his office and I just poured out what I was trying to do, and after a while he said to me, "Young man, Lloyd's of London will do all we can to help you." And it was Lloyd's of London who began to open doors for me to get to the source of the records in England.

I began to search for the records of ships that had moved from Africa to this country. There are cartons of records of slave ships, of ships in general, but also of slave ships, that moved two centuries ago that have never been opened, nobody ever had occasion to go in them since. There are just stacks of records. Slavery was an industry; it was not viewed as anything pejorative at all. It was just a business at the time. In the seventh week of an almost traumatizing searching, one afternoon about 2:30 I was in the 1,023rd set of slave ship records and pulled up a sheet that had the movements of 30 ships on it, and my eye ran down it and I saw number 18, and my eyes went out to the right and something just said to me, that might be the ship. The essential things were there. My reaction was a very dull one. I wrote down on an envelope the information, turned it in at the desk and walked out. Around the corner from there on Castle Lane was a little tea shop. I went in there and I had tea and a cruller, and I'm sitting up there and sipping the tea, and swinging my foot like it's all in a day's work, when it suddenly did hit me that maybe I'd found that ship. I still owe that lady for that tea and cruller.

I got a taxi; I didn't even stop at the hotel to get a toothbrush. I told that taxi, "Heathrow!" In my mind's eye I was seeing the book I had to get my hands on. I'd had the book in my hands. The taxi got me to Heathrow in time to get the

6:00 Pan American to New York, and I flew that ocean that night and didn't sleep a wink. I could see that book, it had a dark brown leather cover, *Shipping in the Port of Annapolis* by Vaughan W. Brown. I got to New York, shuttled to Washington, the Library of Congress, got the book. One line in agate type tended to support that it was indeed the ship, and I just about went berserk. I got on the phone, got finally to the author Vaughan Brown, a broker in Baltimore. I got to that man's office, went by his secretary, just as if she wasn't there, and went in his office. Here was a man who probably had never exchanged a social syllable with a black person in his life. He was raised in Virginia, Maryland, and so forth, his background was that. But when I could, man to man, communicate the fervor, the drive, the passion of trying to pull together the history of a people based on an oral history, married by now with documented history, people would literally quit what they were doing, quit their jobs, temporarily, to help *me*. That man left his brokerage office, drove to Annapolis, to help me pin down that that was the ship.

I crossed the Atlantic Ocean round trip three times in the next ten days. In the next several weeks I was all over New England, Peabody Museum, the Widener at Harvard, various other places, looking for every thread, everything of any kind I could find about this ship, the symbolic ship that brought the 15 million, the specific ship that brought Kunta Kinte.

Finally, from one or another source, I knew that she was by name the ship the *Lord Ligonier*. She was built in 1765; this was her maiden voyage. Her captain was Captain Thomas Davies. She had sailed in 1765 with a cargo of rum to Gravesend, England. She had sold the rum, used the proceeds to buy the slaving hardware (the chains, the shackles, the other restraining objects) to put on the extra foodstuffs a slave ship needed, to put on the extra crew a slave ship needed, and then she had set out up the English Channel. There were look-out points at intervals along the waterways. And the records are still there for those look-out points. I would get the records from this one and sift wildly through them until I found the *Lord Ligonier* had passed and I'd run to these records, sift through them until she passed. It became almost like running along the beach looking at her. I knew what that ship looked like. I knew her timbers. She was made of loblolly pine planking. I knew that her beams were made of hackmatack cedar. I knew the nails that held her together were not really nails, they were "treenails." They were made of black locust split in the top with a wedge of oak. I knew the flax that made her sails had been grown in New Jersey. I knew everything about her. I knew the rig of her sails. And visually I could see her. I could read the captain's mind. I knew he had a new ship, maiden voyage, and everything in him was driving to get as fast as he could to the source of the black gold, to load and get back by the quickest passage which would make him look good to the owners. And I followed her from look-out point to look-out point and then she came along to a place called the Downs, and for God's sakes I found she dropped her anchor. And I nearly had a fit. Why in the world would she drop the anchor? I knew he was driving to make a great trip, and it just flipped me. I couldn't bear not to know why she stopped. And I began to think and it finally arrived upon me that ships then had no engines. The only thing that moved the ship was wind in the sails, so if I was going to find out why this ship moved or stopped, obviously what I had to know was more than I knew about weather. And I dropped everything. I found out the British meteorological headquarters was in a city called Bracknell. I got on a train, went over there, and told some people, look, I have got to have the weather for the fall of 1766. And they looked at me as if I was crazy.

And I went back that night to London as near suicide as I have ever been in my life. I was obviously just a total failure if I couldn't find that. It was three days before I was functioning again. And I came out of that stupor thinking there had to be a way. And now again the previous training came into play. I hadn't been 20 years in the U.S. Coast Guard for nothing. I went and got me a big blank meteorological chart. I got my little dividers and tools and figured the band of ocean through which any ship would have to sail to get from the mouth of the English Channel to the Gambia River on the mid–West African coast. Then I figured that what I had to do by any means I could possibly do it was to collect all possible documented weather data that I could for that particular band of ocean between the months of April and September, 1766. I began to go to every city in England that had in the 1760s been a major sea port—Liverpool, Hull, the others. And every time I'd get to one of these towns I'd go to everything that looked like a library.

And I knew one thing as an old sailor from the Coast Guard, that every time a sailing ship has the watch changed they record the weather and the longitude and latitude in the log. And whenever I'd find any ship that had been anywhere in any direction in that band of ocean between April and September, 1766, I would pluck out the weather readings and take the longitude-latitude figures to pin point where she was when she made that weather reading and date it.

I went back to Bracknell about three weeks later with 411 weather readings scattered over that band of ocean. I found two lieutenant-commanders, Royal Navy, professional meteorological people and they called in colleagues, and for them it was like a double acrostic puzzle. It took them about two days to re-create the weather in which the *Lord Ligonier* had sailed. I found out why at first she stopped: the wind had shifted on her. She had been coming around the Channel and in a place where she had to have easterly winds to keep progressing she'd met southwesterly winds, and all she could do was tack back and forth between the English and French coasts. So she had dropped the anchor in a place called the Downs, not too far from where Caesar's oared galleys had brought Britain into the Empire. She had had to lay in anchor there in about eight fathoms for about two weeks until the wind changed southeasterly. That was Tuesday morning, May 15th, 1766. The physical weather was about 66° temperature, the millibar reading was 10-10, the weather was a drizzle becoming fair. And that was the day she ran up the sails. She went out down past the white cliffs of Dover, Shakespeare Cliffs, Dungeness, Berry Head on down the Channel to Lizard Head. She went into the open sea southeast of the Bay of Biscay, southerly down past the Cape Verdes, the Canaries, and finally into the mouth of the Gambia River. She would spend the next 10 months slaving in the Gambia River area. At the end of 10 months she got a cargo: 3,265 elephants' teeth as they called tusks, 3,700 pounds of beeswax, 800 pounds of raw cotton, 32 ounces of gold, 140 slaves. And with that cargo she set sail July 5, 1767. It was a Sunday.

One of the most perverse things I was to run across was that the people who might be described as a hierarchy of slaving, the owners, the agents, the captains of those ships, strove in every possible way to manifest that they were functioning in a Christian context. If at all possible a slave ship when loaded would leave, as this one did, on the Sabbath. There was a popular saying at the time, "God will bless the journey." The *Lord Ligonier* sailed directly from the Gambia River to Annapolis, Maryland. She arrived the morning of September 29, 1767. September 29, 1967, I was standing on the pier at Annapolis drenched with tears.

I went to the Maryland Hall of Records (in the one set of records you can generally find back to the time of Christ: tax records) to find out what had she come in with and declared for tax. And I found she declared for tax the same cargo she declared leaving Africa, except that the original 140 slaves had become 98 who had survived that crossing. She crossed from the Gambia in two months, three weeks and two days, a voyage of about 5,000 miles.

I knew that when you had a cargo as valuable as slaves that then, as today, they advertised. And I went to the records of *The Maryland Gazette*. In the issue of October 1st, 1767, page 3, far left column, third head down was the *Lord Ligonier*'s ad. She had just arrived from the River Gambia "with fresh slaves for sale" to be sold the following Wednesday at Meg's Wharf. I trusted oral history now better than I trusted the printed page and I knew Grandma always said that Mas' John Waller had bought that slave had named him Toby but later Mas' John had sold him to Mas' William, his brother. And I knew that most transactions involving slaves, even among families, were legal matters. And I went to Richmond, Virginia, searching the legal deeds, and found a deed dated September 5, 1768, between the two brothers John and William Waller, Spotsylvania County, Virginia, transferring goods between them. And on the second page in this fairly long deed were the words "and also one Negro man slave named Toby."

I could stand up here six hours and talk about this. I'm obviously obsessed with it. I've been almost eight years now working on it. One of the spin-offs is that my brothers and I have begun a Kinte Foundation with numerous purposes. One of them is to establish this country's first black genealogical library. Wendell [Wray] and Courtney [Brown] and others of us have begun this work. There will be a staff of about 15 all told in time, of people who are beginning the early work of collecting the documentation for the creation of the Kinte Black Genealogical Library which will projectively open its doors in Washington, D.C., in bicentennial 1976. The library will collect everything that we can lay hands on that documents slaves, free blacks, any blacks, preceding 1900.

Since so much of our material is derivative, which is to say that you can find many of the black records in what are surfacely white records, it is most important that we try and communicate this to you. You in your work may come upon things that we would love to have that you would, I know, be happy to let us have. I feel that, hopefully, the book, the motion picture (motion picture rights have already been negotiated), the library, the foundation, the whole thing will project a tremendous new emphasis and public awareness of and public image—worldwide—of oral history. We also hope to be able to project worldwide a correction of something that plagues not just black history, but all history for everybody, and that is that history had predominantly been written by the winners, which messes it up from the very beginning. Here now is a vehicle that I hope will be able to spread an awareness that black history is not just some euphemistic cry on the part of a people trying to make some spurious case for themselves, but that it does happen to be a matter of disciplined documented dedicated truth.

Notes

1. Vansina, Jan. *De la traditional orale: Essai de méthode historique* (Tervuren, Belgique, 1961). The English translation is *Oral Tradition: A Study in Historical Methodology* (Chicago: Aldine, 1965; see chapter 8 of the present volume).

PART FOUR

*Oral History and
Related Disciplines:
Folklore, Anthropology,
Media, and Libriarianship*

21

The Oral
Historian and the Folklorist

Richard Dorson

Oral historians sometimes consider themselves pioneers, working with nontraditional sources, outside the mainstream of the historical profession. But this view overlooks our kinship with other researchers who rely on oral sources in their work, including folklorists, anthropologists, and others. In Part Four of our book we present important writings which have attempted to bridge the boundaries separating some other disciplines from oral history.

It is fitting that we begin with the writing of the late Richard Dorson, the Harvard-educated folklorist whose training included the disciplines of history and American studies. In this, Dorson's address to the Sixth Colloquium on Oral History, he suggests some fundamental differences between the oral historian, who interviews on the basis of prior research, and the folklorist, who collects often from chance encounters. The historian primarily researches national structures, in Dorson's view: laws, politics, battles, social trends; the folklorist seeks out traditions and what Dorson calls "people's history." The author suggests that oral historians widen their scope to include "oral folk history," which includes oral personal history (first-person narratives) and oral traditional history (sagas and local legends).

Richard Dorson, Professor of Folklore and History at the University of Indiana, was one of the most influential folklore scholars of the twentieth century. His publications comprised two dozen books, some 200 articles, and countless reviews and introductions. He was awarded numerous fellowships and grants, including an unusual third renewal of his Guggenheim Fellowship. A number of his other essays on oral history and folklore appear in Folklore and the American Historian *(1971).*

"The Oral Historian and the Folklorist" by Richard Dorson appeared in *Selections of the Fifth and Sixth National Colloquia on Oral History* (New York: Oral History Association, 1972). It is reprinted by permission of the Oral History Association.

*I*n the United States students of history and students of folklore have shared little common ground. This is less true in Europe, where history lies enshrouded in a traditional past and folkloristics is recognized as an authoritative branch of learning. If American history has not yet been extended back in time to embrace a mythical Indian past, its boundaries are being stretched to include large sectors—blacks, ethnics, mountain whites, city folk—whose stories must be sought through oral and traditional rather than through printed and written sources. And folklore as a scholarly discipline has made spectacular gains in American universities in the 1960s. Consequently the old rigid polarization between history as scrupulously documented fact, and folklore as unverified rumor, falsehood, hearsay, old wives' tale—often equated with myth and legend in similar senses—is beginning to break down. Historians are moving closer to the methods of the folklorist through the new departure of oral history, and folklorists are becoming more history-minded as their discipline solidifies. . . .

Folklorists by and large have not been very history-minded. Most of them lean toward literature on the humanities side and toward anthropology on the social science side. Since my own doctorate was in History of American Civilization, I have always supported the synthesis of folklore and history, and have found some response among our graduate students, notably Lynwood Montell, who in the dissertation eventually published as *The Saga of Coe Ridge* combined the two methodologies. . . .

A few historians could in turn be cited as having sympathy toward the folklore approach, notably Theodore Blegen in his too neglected *Grass Roots History,* but only with the advent of oral history is the historical profession making a turn toward the methods of the folklorist. Up until the new oral history, a sharp line always divided the documentary record that served the historian from the oral flotsam that he scorned but which, for some curious reason, the folklorist devoured. Wresting himself from the library and archives, the retooled oral historian now marches forth with tape recorder to interview live people face to face. And to his astonishment he discovers, at some point, that this technique of obtaining information is the particular speciality of the folklorist. Some of my history colleagues, bent on establishing an oral history archives on campus, were surprised when I told them that there already existed at the university an extensive folklore archives for the depositing of tape-recorded interviews. These tapes, as well as separately housed manuscript collections, contained chiefly songs, tales, and other folkloric genres, but they held their share of oral history.

Before the oral historian and the folklorist can compare notes over the tape recorder about interview techniques and archival systems, they need to consider large divergences in their concepts and methods.

In respect to method, the oral historian *interviews* while the folklorist in the field *collects*. It would never occur to a practitioner of oral history to set out in the morning toting his Sony or Wollensak or Uher with little or no idea as to whom he will meet and record. Such action would appear to be not historical research but some species of madness. Yet this is exactly the way the folklorist operates. He follows up one lead after another, frequently stumbling down blind alleys and reaching dead ends, in his search for articulate bearers of verbal traditions or savvy expositors of traditional life styles. On locating a good informant—the technical term for the folk narrator or folk singer—he may of course revisit him frequently. Yet he must continually be ferreting out new informants in the [effort] to cast his net as widely as possible, in his search for a broad tradition.

Collecting techniques vary according to the personality of the collector. Two of the most successful fieldworkers in the United States used quite opposite techniques. Cecil Sharp, the Englishman prospecting for old English and Scottish ballads in the southern Appalachians, employed the pointblank approach; climbing to the mountain cabin, he asked the surprised family if they knew old songs and if they did promptly wrote down words and music. Vance Randolph, lifelong resident of the Ozark hills, adopted the participant-observer strategy on his home grounds, never posed the frontal question, but hung around a likely informant waiting till he uttered items of folklore, then excused himself and surreptitiously wrote them down in his notebook. Recently a retired Episcopal clergyman, Harry M. Hyatt, had produced an extraordinary two-volume taperecorded collection of esoteric Negro magical beliefs, *Hoodoo, Witchcraft, Rootwork, Conjuration*, which he obtained by chasing down and directly interrogating Negro hoodoo doctors and their clients throughout the Southeast.

As a compromise between the two field strategies, some folklorists are now proposing what they call the "induced natural context" to create so far as possible a spontaneous storytelling or folksinging situation without waiting indefinitely for it to arise. All this is far removed from the interview situation in which the oral historian poses questions in the living room to a political or business or labor leader about his personal career.

Besides the schism in their methodology, the oral historian and the folklorist differ appreciably on their basic concepts. The one seeks personal data of contemporary history, the other hunts for folk traditions. The small number of history-minded folklorists will keep their ears open for folk history, that is, the versions of past events that have remained in folk memory and folk tradition. This folk history has little in common with the elitist history that prevails in professional historical circles. The guild of American historians operates within the conceptual framework of a national political structure, which determines the chronology, the cast of characters, the issues and topics that bore history students from primary school through graduate school. Students run on a treadmill that never takes them beyond the federal government, presidents and senators, the national economy, international diplomacy, reform legislation. Of the people's history, they hear nothing.

In an essay oft-cited but never followed, "Everyman His Own Historian" (1931), Carl Becker spoke for a personal rather than a national view of history. The guild praised it, but anyone looking at the flood of historiographical works on American history over the past decade—by Higham, Garraty, Cunliffe and Winks, Noble, Hofstadter, Eisenstadt, Schlatter, Skotheim, and others—can very quickly recognize the overwhelming force of national, elitist history as practiced by all leading American historians. While revisionism is much in evidence, it is revisionism of the research methods, interpretations, and judgments of Frederick Jackson Turner, Charles Beard, Carl Becker (who never pursued the injunctions of his own essay) and other giants of the profession, national historians all. Revision of their subject matter is not broached. Oral history faithfully follows the elitist emphases of the guild, naturally enough, for the broad outlines of nationalist, federal government-structured history are clear and familiar, and those of folk history are fuzzy and obscure. For until someone records folk history, we do not even know its shape and content.

One encouraging sign for the development of interest in oral folk history can be seen in occasional expressions by the professional historians of disaffection with elitist history. A. S. Eisenstadt comments on the concentration of American history writing on a narrative of well-known events in political history dominated by major American presidents, as in Allan Nevins' *Ordeal of the Union* and Arthur Schlesinger's *The Age of Franklin D. Roosevelt*. Yet Nevins himself declares that the most fascinating part of history, and the most difficult to obtain, is the story of how plain men and women lived and were affected by the economic, social, and cultural changes of their times. Samuel P. Hays asks for a shift from "presidential history" and "top-level affairs" to "grass-roots happenings." Speaking on the colonial period, Jack P. Greene rues that historians have spent so much time studying the elite and thereby ignoring other elements.

One school of American historians has in the past few years expressly called for a rejection of elite history and a revolution in historiographical attitudes that will bring about concern with the inarticulate mass of the people. These are the historians of the New Left—Staughton Lynd, Eugene Genovese, Jesse Lemisch, Barton J. Bernstein—and they scoff at pretended revisionists who merely swap heroes of business for heroes of politics. Yet they themselves fall into the same nationalist trap and attempt to write about history from the bottom up using the same old tired categories of the American Revolution, Jacksonian democracy, the Civil War, the rise of industrialism, and so down to the New Deal and the New Frontier. Valiantly attempting to make dead men who have left no records tell their stories, they bemoan the difficulty of getting at ordinary folk. Now here is where the folklorist can aid, for he does make dead men tell their tales—through the lips of their living descendants, who relay family and local history passed orally across the generations.

One New Left historian, John J. Williams, did discover the folklorists and presented a paper in the radical historians panel at the December 1970 meeting of the American Historical Association, on "The Establishment and the Tape Recorder: Radicalism and Professionalism in Folklore Studies, 1933–1968." Looking into the folklore scholarship of the past three decades, Williams perceived a watershed dividing the nonacademic Old Left folklorists of the 1930s and '40s, notably represented by the Almanac Singers, and the academic establishment folklorists of the 1950s and '60s, ignobly epitomized by myself, and he quoted various statements of mine to illustrate my establishment tendencies. Now the New Left historians and folklorists in general do share a common premise, that the folk, the mass of the people, possess a culture and a history well worthy of study. But as a folklorist I do not correlate my interest in the folk with a radical ideology—or with a liberal or conservative or any other ideology. The folk fall into all these camps, and outside them, and I listen to what they have to say without prejudgment. In Negro folklore you can find bitterness against whites, certainly, but you can also find tales preferring the southern white man to the northern white man, and you can find traditions aplenty that are shared by both blacks and whites.

How then is the oral historian to benefit from the techniques and concepts of the folklorist? The view of *oral history* must be enlarged to embrace *oral folk history*. Oral history as currently practiced is still elitist history, and so misses the opportunity to document the lives of anonymous Americans. Writing in the Oral History Association *Newsletter* of July 1971, on the Texas Oral History Project devoted to the life and times of Lyndon B. Johnson, Paige Mulhollan stated that "oral history testimony . . . is intended to supplement, not to replace, traditional documentary research." This is indeed the case. Oral traditional history, on the other hand, seeks out the topics and themes that the folk wish to talk about, the personal and immediate history with which they are concerned. We have no way of knowing in advance what are the contours of this history, except that they will bear no resemblance to federal government–structured elitist history. Local personalities are the actors, local events form the chapters, but this is not state history following state political boundaries, nor local history embalmed in township records, but folk history preserved in tradition. The incident that engages the attention of the folk may appear ludicrous, trivial, bizarre, and grotesque to the documentary historian. The anthropologist Robert Lowie roundly asserted that Indians possessed no ability to distinguish the sublime from the ridiculous in their historical records. Near the top of their list of memorable events, for example, they placed titanic drinking orgies. Scarcely of the same noteworthy character as the Wilson-Gorman Tariff or the Webster-Ashburton Treaty!

But it is not for the historian of the people to prejudge what the people consider important. On a field trip to the Upper Peninsula of Michigan I heard talk of several events celebrated in community remembrance: the lynching of the McDonald boys at Memoninee; the "stealing" of the courthouse at Iron River by the men of Crystal Falls; the highfalutin speech Pat Sheridan delivered to the iron ore trimmers of Escanaba; the incendiary Italian Hall fire in Calumet.

Each one of these episodes has a base in historical fact thickly coated over with legendary accretions, but otherwise they possess little in common. One involved a scene in a brothel, a killing, and a grisly lynch party; another is a comic saga of political rivalry between townships competing for the county seat; a third centers on a piece of unintentionally humorous rhetoric; a fourth deals with a disaster that led to charges and countercharges between striking copper miners and mine operators. The folk historian is as keenly interested in the legendary growth surrounding these happenings of six to nine decades ago as in the solid nub of fact, could he establish it, for the play of tradition upon the events leads us into the folk mind and the folk conception of the meaningful past.

Any folklorist engaged in fieldwork will stumble upon this folk history, whether he is looking for it or not—and most often he is not. While collecting Negro folktales I continually encountered historical traditions, usually obscure to me and removed from any familiar context. James D. Suggs told in close detail of the Ku Klux Klan killing a Negro brakemen on southern railroads in 1914, and of the public burning in Mississippi in 1904 of a colored man who confessed to killing two white men. E. L. Smith recounted exploits of his slave grandfather, Romey Howard, who outwitted and outran "patterollers" and bloodhounds. Mary Richardson related brutalities she had observed on a "colored prisoner farm" near Clarksdale, Mississippi where she worked as cook's helper:

> I seen them whip one man to death. He was a slim, skinny man, and they whipped him 'cause he couldn't pick 200 pounds—that was his task and he couldn't never get it. So they whipped him morning and night until he couldn't work at all, just lay in his cage. The prisoners all slept in one room with double-deck beds 'side the walls. He couldn't even get out of bed to get his food. The feeder wasn't allowed to unlock the door, and each man had to come and get his pan; so he'd leave the sick man's in the window. I'd take the bread and roll it up in a piece of paper and throw it to his bunk, like a puppy. They told me I'd get prison for life if they found that out.

> He died and they buried him in the farm cemetery, just like he was; didn't wash or change him. 'Cause the hole was too short they stomped on him, mashed, tramped, bent him down in there, and threw dirt on him.

Here is black experience from a black source, and because so few black sources are written, this and many sources equally informative are oral. Suggs, Smith, and Mary Richardson were all deft storytellers of traditional tales, but they were also all expert transmitters of oral history, precise with names, dates, places, settings, fluent and yet unemotional in their narratives, telling their grim narratives factually and without editorializing. The recollections at first-hand of Suggs and Mary Richardson we can call *oral personal history* of the nonelite, or the folk; the saga of Romey Howard as told across the generations by Smith, as well as accounts I was given of slave escapes on the Underground Railroad, fall under *oral traditional history*. Together they comprise *oral folk history*.

The oral folk historian will search out articulate members of the folk community and interview them for their personal and traditional history. Rewards obtainable from this kind of quest can be seen in the books of the skillful radio and television interviewer, Studs Terkel, who in *Division Street America* and *Hard Times, an Oral History of the Great Depression*, printed his taped interrogations of a number of people from different backgrounds concerning their own lives and outlooks. In the first work he confined himself to Chicago and eschewed celebrities, while in the second he cast a broader net, geographically and socially, for his speakers, and directed his questions more specifically to their recollections of the depression and its impact on them personally. *Hard Times* is consciously history-oriented, but in the national sense, so that *Division Street America,* centered on a Chicago neighborhood, conveys more the sense of personal folk history. While each Chicagoan possesses his own *gestalt*, he often shares certain common, traditional attitudes with his fellow residents on Division Street: one theme that echoes throughout the confessionals is the nostalgia for the good old days, when people walked, a true neighborhood existed, and the races interacted peaceably.

There are also sharp conflicts of attitude disclosed in these retrospective statements, and here lies a key aspect of oral folk history: the traditions collide. Or to put it another way, more than one folk exists, and each folk group regards events and personalities of the past through its own particular lens. Jesse James and Billy the Kid are hero-villains, depending on whether you talk with Midwestern farmers or southwestern cowpunchers. As a Robin Hood, Jesse held up banks and trains, the agencies of big business, and gave their tainted money to widows and the impoverished. As a desperado, he shot helpless cashiers and trainmen in cold blood and stole the widows' money they guarded. Billy the Kid as Sir Galahad protected the open range and the freedom of the grazing cattle from encroachers who would fence in nature's bounty, but as a badman he slaughtered in the manner of a sadistic gunman and moronic punk.

Examine local-history traditions and see how often they splinter into two or three reenactments. Legends of Beanie Short, a guerrilla leader in the Cumberland Mountains of northern Tennessee during the Civil War, portray him both as a rebel renegade and as a freedom fighter, with a blending of the two roles; some Cumberland families boast that Beanie stole supplies from their grandparents. Did the McDonald Boys kill their man only in self-defense, and were the lynch leaders who denied them a fair trial the real murderers, as the ballad made out? And whose blood permanently stained the jail cell wall from which they were removed by the mob, the blood of a McDonald or the blood of a lyncher? Or was there ever any bloodstain? Folklore consistently notes an ineradicable blood stain where murder has occurred. Men and women in Crystal Falls and Iron River agree that residents in the first town "stole" the courthouse (i.e., its blueprints, or building fund, or the county papers) from the second town, but where a native of Crystal Falls regards the deed as high derring-do, the property owner in Iron River thinks of it as the worst skullduggery. Was Pat Sheridan who defied the ore-boat owners for his nascent ore-trimmers union an heroic workman finding his voice or an inept buffoon tongue-tied when he tried to rise above his station? These ambiguities permeate folk history.

If there are such differences of opinion in the folk memory, how then can the folk memory ever be trusted to transmit a consistent historical record? The question of the trustworthiness of oral traditional history has been endlessly debated in a variety of scholarly disciplines, with judgments ranging the whole spectrum from complete rejection of verbally relayed testimony to its acceptance as gospel. Every folklorist knows how floating motifs creep into any orally repeated report, no matter how firmly grounded in historical fact—the Icelandic sagas are a case in point.

Yet, under given conditions, the historic kernels endure and are identifiable. These conditions, in brief, involve such matters as continuity of residence in the area of the tradition; reinforcement of the tradition with reference to surrounding landmarks; and the training, formal or informal, of oral chroniclers within the society.

Folk memory may prove surprisingly reliable. In collecting oral accounts of the lynching of the McDonald Boys I was puzzled by two variant descriptions as to where the bodies were strung up, one saying on a railroad crossing sign, the other on a pine tree; but ultimately I learned they had been lowered from the railroad sign, dragged to the tree, and hoisted up again. What the oral folk historian wishes to record is not the plain unvarnished fact but all the motions, biases, and reactions aroused by the supposed fact, for in them lie the historical perspectives of the folk.

A word should be said about the divisions or classifications of oral folk history. The commonest terms here, as employed by the folklorist, are legend, anecdote, memorat, family saga. *Legend* signifies a tradition of an historical happening shared by a group of people. *Anecdote* refers to an historical incident befalling an individual, whether a local eccentric or a popular hero. *Memorat* is the term introduced by the Swedish folklorist Carl von Sydow to describe a re-markable or unusual personal experience related by the person to whom it happened. *Family saga* covers the miscellany of reminiscences about pioneer times, immigrant crossings and culture shock, black sheep characters, and ancestral ups and downs that the family unit treasures as its own unwritten—and hitherto unsought—history. These are some of the kinds of spoken narratives for which the oral folk historian will cast his net.

In so doing, he will be recording fresh and valuable information for what now becomes his oral folk history archives. Into such an archives will go tape recordings of community, neighborhood, ethnic, black, Indian, occupational and other orally transmitted history. The interviewer will become a collector, or will add a collector to his staff, and he will plan ways of tuning in on the folk history of his area. An anthropologist on the American Universities Field Staff who spends much of his time in Afghanistan, Louis Dupree, became interested in planning an oral folk history project after visiting our Folklore Institute one year, and on returning to the field retraced the route of the British army's retreat in 1848 from Kabul to Jalalabad, carrying his tape recorder with him and collecting traditions of the battle all along the way. His findings, published in an article in the *Journal of the Folklore Institute*, and developed into a book, present the Afghan folk view of the war previously known almost entirely from British documentary sources. In the United States we have plenty of our own Kabuls and Jalalabads to keep us occupied.

22

Oral History as Communicative Event

Charles Joyner

Our second article on folklore and oral history is from Charles Joyner, who holds doctoral degrees in both history and folklore. On the basis of his readings in these fields, Joyner suggests that folklorists should emulate historians' concern with time and change, while oral historians should explore folklorists' emphasis on the telling of a story (or history) as a communicative event in a context of social interaction.

Joyner further urges oral historians to include in their interview histories the performance and sociolinguistic elements of the interview situation—"a full description of the context in which the testimony was taken, including the mannerisms and gestures of the informant and the reactions of the audience." A narrator's way of telling his history itself reveals a truth, one at times truer than the historical facts described. Joyner's extensive notes suggest readings in folklore of interest to historians. His article is an invitation to oral historians to view their work from the standpoint of its basic unit: the words used to communicate.

Charles Joyner is Professor of History and Anthropology at the University of South Carolina, Coastal Carolina College. His writings include Folk Song in South Carolina *(1971) and* Slave Folklife: Cultural Change in a South Carolina Slave Community *(1985). He had done extensive folklore field work in Scotland, Northern Ireland, Newfoundland, and the United States.*

"Oral History as Communicative Event" by Charles Joyner was first published in *Oral History Review* 7 (1979), pp. 47–52. It is reprinted by permission of the Oral History Association.

*H*ow do we honestly and carefully study the large proportion of the population who left behind few if any written records? At least part of the reason for the long neglect of Afro-American history, Native American history, the history of women and of various ethnic groups was an historical methodology which failed to provide us with sufficient usable data on such subjects. The great challenge is to develop a more adequate methodology for studying history "from the bottom up."[1] I believe that folkloristics (a term folklorists use to distinguish the discipline from the material studied) has much to contribute to the development of that methodology and the theory upon which it must stand. Because oral history makes possible the gathering of historical evidence on people who would otherwise be left out of historical study (or treated only statistically), and because oral communication reveals more than written documents, I believe oral history is the most important single method of historical research and should be part of the methodological training of every historian. The historian who is ignorant of oral history, like the historian who still does not comprehend quantification, is only partly trained.

But note that I refer to oral history as a method, not as a separate field of history. Oral history should be used in conjunction with other methods of historical inquiry, appropriate to the historical problem under consideration. Studies in oral history, like all historical studies, should begin with statement and analysis of the historical problem to determine what are the relevant data and what are the most effective means of obtaining them.[2] Not all historical problems are susceptible to oral research, but more of them are than many historians might think. It is not a sign of health in our discipline that most historians do not "do" oral history, and that most oral historians do not "do" any other kind of history.

I think we oral historians must accept an important part of the blame for this lack of health in the discipline. Oral history, as practiced by far too many of us, is stuck back at the stage where the study of folklore was 50 years ago, when so-called folklorists collected and published lore and made little or no attempt to comprehend the life of the "folk" who supplied it. Too many oral historians are content to interview and transcribe, making little effort to comprehend more than the literal referential meaning of the words.

It is not enough to proceed directly from problem statement to interview. To enter an interview without analyzing the problem is to invite a simple-minded and arbitrary collection of data. It is not enough to publish raw collections of testimonies. What is necessary is a full description of the context in which the testimony was taken, including the mannerisms and gestures of the informant and the reactions of the audience. What is necessary, and long overdue, is that publication be based upon meaningful interpretation of what those testimonies mean to the people who transmitted them.

The oral historian who would undertake to interpret the history of the folk is confronted with numerous problems. We must begin with careful ethnographic description. Anthony F. C. Wallace's dictum that "all of the comparative and theoretical work of cultural anthropology depends upon a thorough and precise ethnographic description" would seem to be no less true for the oral history of the folk.[3]

Merely to recognize the importance of careful ethnographic description, however, does not guarantee its attainment. The first problem is cultural comprehension. Too often historians interpreted their subject only in terms of their own customs and interests.

The riddle for us is how much our perceptions convey an accurate picture of the culture we are trying to interpret. The nearer we are culturally to the group we are trying to interpret, the more difficult it is for us to explain it to others; the nearer we are culturally to our audience, the greater our difficulty in understanding the subject.[4]

In the study of folk history, not only must the usual historical standards of internal and external criticism of sources be rigorously applied, but we need to be proficient in semiotics, structural analysis, sociolinguistics, and functional analysis as well. Since most historical training does not include work in these areas, historians have understandably shied away from the history of the folk.[5]

If we have shied away from oral folk history, we have shunned folklore proper like the plague. Folklore materials are not readily susceptible to the kinds of analysis with which we are most comfortable. Internal criticism seems irrelevant to a folktale which does not even purport to be true. And what is the historian to make of a proverb, or a riddle? And songs—even if the historian can find some semblance of meaning in the words, what is the historical meaning of the tunes? Those few historians who have tried to use folklore materials, such as John Blassingame and Eugene Genovese, have not plowed very deeply because their modes of analysis were irrelevant to the materials, and they were unable or unwilling to make use of folkloristic analysis.[6]

Furthermore, many of the large folklore collections of the past are so divorced from their social and cultural context as to be inadequate for our purposes. As an historian interested in folk culture, I have been led to fieldwork as much by necessity as by choice. Linda Degh states that collectors of folktales "should consider the close relationship between the text and the individual and should record the general atmosphere in which the text is transmitted."[7] Her injunction would seem to be applicable to all forms of oral tradition if they are to be of any value to the cultural historian.

I have not hesitated to complain about the historian's neglect of folk culture. I have elsewhere complained to folklorists of their neglect of history. A considerable sociological richness has been achieved in contemporary folklore studies through borrowings from the social sciences, but that achievement has been at the expense of historical richness. The pervasively static quality of much current folklore scholarship is the result of what M. G. Smith calls "the fallacy of the ethnographic present." Stephan Thernstrom observes, "Ahistorical social science is as often narrow and superficial as sociologically primitive history, and it is certainly no less common."[8]

Folklorists would do well to emulate the historian's concern with change and time, but oral historians have much to learn from folklorists as well, especially from their emphasis on folklore as a communicative process in a context of social interaction. An oral history interview is a communicative event, not comprehensible apart from social interaction, and intimately bound up with the changing values and institutions of a changing society.[9] Analysis of the interview as a communicative event offers oral historians who are willing to adopt folkloristic means an unusual opportunity to achieve unprecedented historical ends.

Such an analysis depends upon a conception of language as a part of social life and a deeper sense of the social patterning of language use. The concept of "performance" has come into increasing prominence in recent folklore scholarship. In particular three folklorists, Dan Ben-Amos, Roger Abrahams, and Alan Dundes, offer theories of performance which challenge us to integrate the communicative elements and the historical elements of oral history. Ben-Amos emphasizes that "the performance situation, in the final analysis, is the crucial context for the available text." Dundes distinguishes between knowing folklore and knowing how to use folklore, thus pointing toward analysis of communicative events in terms of cultural rules of communication—what is communicated to whom at what times and at what places. Abrahams links the concept of performance as a structured event and the concept of performance as stylized behavior. The communicative event involves reciprocity between performer and audience. The common element in their approaches is the emphasis on the communicative event, not the text, as the analytical focus.[10]

Such elements of an oral history testimony as the degree of explicitness, the use of conventional phrases and formulations, the use of direct vs. indirect speech, modes of addressing and referring to other persons, the means of issuing commands and requests, means of indicating politeness or rudeness, and the means of opening and closing conversations are not accidental. They have both linguistic and social meaning and are analyzable for historical meaning in ways that written documents are not.[11]

Thus the folkloristic analysis of the interview as a communicative event offers an approach to historical truth not previously available to scholars. I want to emphasize that the approach I am recommending is not limited to studies of the history of the folk. It is as applicable to the politician, the business executive, and the scientist as it is to the migrant farmer, the factory worker, the suffragette, or the ex-slave.

Seen from this perspective, the familiar complaint of orthodox historians that oral history is unreliable (because interviewees will attempt to present themselves in as favorable a light as possible) is irrelevant.[12] Of course they attempt to put themselves in a favorable light in interviews, as well as in correspondence, memoranda, and other written artifacts. Therefore what? I contend that informants never lie to a good historian (although they may try to); they just reveal the truth in some unique ways. Even if the informant consciously attempts to lie to the interviewer, he cannot help but reveal evidence of his deepest value system—that elusive "why?" of his motivation that historians have so long sought. The "lie" may reveal more truth than the mere fact.[13]

Truth, after all, is not precisely the same thing as a collection of facts, as any comparison of historical interpretations of the same event demonstrates. But what is an historical "event"? When people share an historical experience, did they remember or experience the "same" event? And if a society's perceived truth is "known" to the investigator to be an error, is it any less influential upon that society's behavior? Lies and errors may be a society's motivation for otherwise inexplicable actions.

The testimony that emerges from an interview may be fact or fantasy. We need not apologize for the method if we discover, not merely the straightforward truth of history, but also some of the more subtle truths of fiction and poetry. It is our responsibility as historians to ascertain which is which.

Notes

1. The idea of studying history "from the bottom up" seems to have been first advanced by folklorist Benjamin A. Botkin, in his *Lay My Burden Down: A Folk History of Slavery* (Chicago: University of Chicago Press, 1945), p. ix. It has been popularized in recent years, without attribution to Botkin, by Jesse Lemisch, in "The American Revolution Seen from the Bottom Up," *Towards a New Past: Dissenting Essays in American History,* ed. Barton J. Bernstein (New York: Pantheon, 1968), pp. 3–45.

2. See F. S. C. Northrop, *The Logic of the Sciences and the Humanities* (New York: Meriden, 1959).

3. Anthony F. C. Wallace, "Culture and Cognition," *Science* 135 (1962), p. 351. See also Herbert Halpert, "American Regional Folklore," *Journal of American Folklore* 60 (1947), pp. 355–56; Herbert Halpert, "The Functional Approach," *Journal of American Folklore* 54 (1946), pp. 510–12; Richard M. Dorson, "Standards of Collecting and Publishing American Folktales," *Journal of American Folklore* 80 (1957), p. 54; Kenneth S. Goldstein, *A Guide for Field Workers in Folklore* (1964; reprint ed., Detroit: Gale, 1974), p. 7.

4. Alfred Kroeber and Clyde Kluckhohn, *Culture: A Critical Review of Concepts and Definitions* (Cambridge, Mass.: Harvard University Press, 1952), p. 182; William P. McEwen, *The Problem of Social Scientific Knowledge* (Totowa, N.J.: Bedminster Press, 1963), pp. 34–35; Benjamin N. Colby, "Ethnographic Semantics: A Preliminary Survey," *Current Anthropologist* 7 (1966), pp. 3–32.

5. There are two notable exceptions to this generalization, both written by folklorists. W. Lynwood Montell's *The Saga of Coe Ridge: A Study in Oral History* (Knoxville: University of Tennessee Press, 1970; see chapter 14 of the present volume) reconstructs 90 years in the life of a black community in the foothills of the Cumberland mountains through extensive tape-recorded interviews with former residents, their descendants, and their neighbors. As a folklorist, Montell is able to identify with unusual accuracy the universal folklore motifs in his informants' testimonies and to penetrate the embellishments of his sources. Gladys-Marie Fry's *Night Riders in Black Folk History* (Knoxville: University of Tennessee Press, 1975) focuses on the theme of how whites used black folk as a means of social control of blacks during and after slavery. Fry combines analysis of interviews from the W.P.A. Slave Narratives Project with numerous interviews of her own.

6. John W. Blassingame, *The Slave Community: Plantation Life in the Ante-Bellum South* (New York: Oxford University Press, 1972); Eugene D. Genovese, *Roll, Jordan, Roll: The World the Slaves Made* (New York: Pantheon, 1974). A more satisfactory treatment is Lawrence W. Levine, *Black Culture and Black Consciousness: Afro-American Folk Thought from Slavery to Freedom* (New York: Oxford University Press, 1977). None of these studies, however, involves fieldwork, or folkloristic analysis of the kind I am calling for.

7. Linda Degh, *Folktales and Society: Storytelling in a Hungarian Peasant Community* (Bloomington: University of Indiana Press, 1969), p. vii.

8. Charles W. Joyner, "A Model for the Analysis of Folklore Performance in Historical Context," *Journal of American Folklore* 88 (1975), pp. 254–65; M. G. Smith, "History and Social Anthropology," *Journal of the Royal Anthropological Institute* 92 (1962), p. 77; Stephan Thernstrom, *Poverty and Progress: Social Mobility in a Nineteenth Century City* (Cambridge, Mass.: Harvard University Press, 1964), pp. 225–26.

9. Roger D. Abrahams, "Introductory Remarks to a Rhetorical Theory of Folklore," *Journal of American Folklore* 81 (1968), p. 157; Clyde Kluckhohn, "Parts and Wholes in Cultural Analysis," in *Parts and Wholes*, ed. Daniel Lerner (New York: Free Press of Glencoe, 1963), p. 121; John Gumperz, Introduction, *Directions in Sociolinguistics: The Ethnography of Communication*, ed. John J. Gumperz and Dell Hymes (New York: Holt, Rinehart and Winston, 1972), p. 26; Pier Paolo Giglioli, *Language and Social Context* (Harmondsworth, Middlesex, England: Penguin, 1972), p. 13.

10. Dell Hymes, *Foundations in Sociolinguistics: An Ethnographic Approach* (Philadelphia: University of Pennsylvania Press, 1974), pp. 3–66; Dan Ben-Amos, "Towards a Definition of Folklore in Context," *Journal of American Folklore* 84 (1971), pp. 3–15; Alan Dundes, "Texture, Text, and Context," *Southern Folklore Quarterly* 28 (1964), pp. 251–65; Roger D. Abrahams, "Introductory Remarks to a Rhetorical Theory of Folklore," pp. 144–45; Roger D. Abrahams, "Rapping and Capping: Black Talk as Art," in *Black America*, ed. John F. Szwed (New York: Basic, 1970), pp. 132–42; Roger D. Abrahams, "The Training of the Man of Words in Talking Sweet," *Language in Society* 1 (1972), pp. 15–30.

11. Dell Hymes, "Models of the Interaction of Language and Social Life," in *Directions in Sociolinguistics*, ed. Gumperz and Hymes, pp. 35–71. See also Joel Sherzer and Regna Darnell, "Outline Guide for the Ethnographic Study of Speech Use," in *Directions in Sociolinguistics*, ed. Gumperz and Hymes, pp. 548–54.

12. For a review of the long-standing controversy over the historical reliability of oral traditions, see Charles W. Joyner, *Folklore and History: The Tangled Relationship*, Newberry Papers in Family and Community History No. 78–2 (Chicago: University of Chicago Press, 1978).

13. Kay Cothran, "The Truth as a Lie—The Lie as Truth: A View of Oral History," *Journal of the Folklore Society of Greater Washington* 3 (Summer 1972), pp. 3–6. ⬎

23

The Anthropological
Interview and
the Life History

Sidney Mintz

Turning now to the interface of anthropology and oral history, we note that anthropologists and ethnographers share techniques with their colleagues in history, though they search out different information. In the anthropological "life history," the researcher "must have a conception of how people are at once products and makers of the social and cultural systems within which they are lodged," according to experienced field worker Sidney Mintz.

The anthropologist, unlike the oral historian, records interviews to learn the structure and patterns of a society as exhibited by a representative individual's world view, cultural traits, and traditions. The culture's internal perceptions of a specific activity's meaning may thus be more useful than an external appraisal. This discussion of the ethnographic interview provides useful insights in interviewing individuals not as historical witnesses but as culture-bearers.

Sidney Mintz is Professor of Anthropology at Johns Hopkins University; he has taught at Columbia and Yale universities and has conducted field work in Puerto Rico, Jamaica, Haiti, Iran, and other countries. He has served as a fellow to the American Anthropological Association and the Guggenheim and Rockefeller foundations. His books include Worker in Cane: Plantation Systems of the New World *(1959),* Caribbean Transformations *(1974),* An Anthropological Approach to the Study of Afro-American History *(1976), and* Esclave—facteur de production *(1981).*

"The Anthropological Interview and the Life History" by Sidney Mintz appeared in *Oral History Review* 7 (1979), pp. 18–26. It is reprinted by permission of the author and the Oral History Association.

*I*t is not entirely certain that the anthropological interview differs significantly from interviews by specialists in other disciplines, but it may be useful to explore this possibility from the vantage-point of ethnography. There is probably no better place to start than a fine essay by Harold C. Conklin, entitled "Ethnography," which appeared in the *International Encyclopedia of the Social Sciences:*

> The data of cultural anthropology derive ultimately from the direct observation of customary behavior in particular societies. Making, reporting, and evaluating such observations are the task of ethnography. . . . An ethnographer is an anthropologist who attempts—at least in part of his professional work—to record and describe the *culturally significant behaviors* of a particular society. Ideally, this description, an ethnography, requires a long period of intimate study and residence in a small, well-defined community, knowledge of the spoken language, and the employment of a wide range of observational techniques including prolonged face-to-face contacts with members of the local group, direct participation in some of that group's activities, and *a greater emphasis on intensive work with informants than on the use of documentary or survey data.*[1] (Italics added.)

Much of this concise statement would need discussion if we intended to examine the ethnographic undertaking in general, but I shall restrict my comments to the anthropological or ethnographic interview as used in collecting the life history. For this purpose, two of Conklin's emphases deserve special attention: the stress put upon "intensive work with informants," and the reference to "culturally significant behaviors."[2]

Even if fieldwork is confined at some point to dealing with a single informant, there is great benefit in being able at least to observe that informant interacting with other members of the group. Though there is no way of proving it, I suspect that a good deal of the confidence an anthropologist may feel in a particular informant arises from his or her judgments of how *others* regard that informant, as manifested in their interactive behavior. Even in confining my emphasis to interviewing for the life history, I would certainly not argue that verbal communication between informant and biographer can or should be the sole source of relevant information. Elsewhere, I have suggested the opposite, contending that many life histories lose some of their value because the fieldworker lacks sufficient knowledge of the community and culture within which the informant lives, and which he or she expresses, in one way or another, in nearly everything he or she says or does.[3] Thus, for the life history, while intensive work with one informant (or several) is of course absolutely essential, it must not preclude broader interviewing, or the study of the community within which the principal informant lives and works.

Conklin's reference to "culturally significant behaviors" addresses an important disciplinary premise. Anthropology is concerned with the range and variation of behavior in any given society, but it is also concerned with behaviors that are "culturally significant," which is to say other than random or unique. Thus, while a *life history* might be elicited precisely because the informant was so far from the apparent "norm" for his or her group in one or another regard, *anthropology* assumes that any individual, in some fundamental and inalterable ways, gives expression to, incarnates, the culture, and cannot do otherwise. David Aberle has argued:

> The individual of the life-history is only one of many comparable members occupying the positions in a social system. Every individual in a society is oriented to a set of explanatory beliefs, most of which he shares with others, and to social norms, felt both as facilitations and as constraints. Every action of his—conforming, individualistic, or revolutionary—is oriented to the fact of those norms, the existence of which he recognizes and knows that other people recognize.[4]

Aberle goes even further, in clarifying the irreducible nature of culture as something much more than personality writ large:

> Although it remains true that within a culture individuals differ because of biological inheritance, social positions and idiosyncratic experience, it is a central fact of social science . . . that experience is patterned and that the patterns are limited in any society. The reactions to culturally established situations, though varied, are also limited. The history of any individual's reactions affords considerable understanding of the relationship of motivation and institution. Where the individual grossly deviates—even to the point of being psychotic, deluded, and hallucinated—his experiences, interpreted with sufficient care against a background of the society, would still give us insights and valid knowledge.[5]

The relationship between culture and personality has never been articulated fully to the satisfaction of anyone. But I am sympathetic to those anthropologists who believe personality can only manifest itself in a cultural guise, and that no psychological interpretation, no matter how ambitious, can avoid dealing with the cultural encapsulation of personality. Coarse though such a view may seem in these days of psychohistory and sociobiology, it may at least keep us from trying to explain war as the consequence of aggressive drives, politics as the consequence of aggressive drives, politics as the consequence of an instinct for power, or good works as the inevitable outcome of the right genes.

If this viewpoint is accepted, then the ethnographic life history interview must deal with distinctions between the personal, unique or idiosyncratic, on the one hand, and the culturally typical or normative on the other. The distinction between these categories is not sharp; I tried elsewhere to specify the difficulty, when I wrote: "The goal of such an undertaking would not be to de-emphasize individual uniqueness or to eliminate the significance of personality in the study of change, but rather to specify with more confidence the way individuality plays itself out against terms set by sociocultural forces."[6] When one seeks to interpret a radical change in individual world-view—the acceptance of a new religion, in this case—as reflecting the convergence of different and superindividual forces, how can one weigh the relative importance of individual character in affecting this outcome? Presumably, not everyone in the culture, exposed to precisely the same forces, would react in the same way. But who would? To attempt to find out, one might consider collecting a number of life histories of converts who share some of the fundamental class, age, sex, occupational and familial characteristics of the first informant, in order to try to weigh the possible significance of each of these features, as against the importance of distinctive individual traits.

While the ethnographic interview as part of the life history can proceed primarily on the basis of simple question-and-answer exchanges, it will be profitable to return to Conklin's article once more, for the enumeration he provides of elicitation procedures:

> . . . [R]ecording and using natural question-response sequences and implications; testing by intentional substitution of acceptable and incongruent references; testing by paraphrase; testing by reference to hypothetical situations; testing by experimental extensions of reference; and testing by switching styles, channels, code signals, message content, and roles (by reference or impersonation). . . .

Because ethnographers interact personally and socially with informants, they find themselves carrying on a unique type of natural history, in which the observer becomes a part of (and an active participant in) the observed universe. The extent of this involvement and its importance for ethnographic recording depend on many situational considerations, including the personalities of the ethnographer and his informants. In some types of field inquiry the ethnographer's practical success or failure may depend as much on those impressions he makes locally as on the cultural events being observed. . . . Especially where long-term investigation of intimate personal relationships is concerned, most anthropologists would agree with Condominas (1965: 35) in stressing the *"nécessité d'ethnographier les ethnographes."*[7]

Such assertions underline the highly personal nature of the ethnographic interview in which, for most purposes, the ethnographer and his or her informant are interrogating each other. It is of course absolutely true that such confrontations are most frequently not only between members of two different cultures, but between those whose access to wealth and power is radically different. While it is conceded that, until the interview relationship is firmly established, the ethnographer may be figuratively at the mercy of the informant, quite the opposite is likely to be the case thereafter. It is one thing for a reporter to request and be granted an interview with a Begin or a Sadat, and quite another for an ethnographer to record the life history of a Hopi, or a Puerto Rican cane worker. The prerogatives available to the ethnographer, while they must be used with some restraint, strengthen his or her investigative powers immensely. How those powers will be used is, of course, a different matter.

I have already implied that life history studies must grapple with the problem of typicality or representativeness. One may expect a life history to reveal to the reader what is typical in that culture, but not how representative that life is within it. Indeed, many who have recorded life histories have consciously rejected the use of the life history for this purpose. If anything, the stress is usually on trying to "make sense" of the life itself. I say "if anything" because many anthropological life histories are, for the most part, descriptive accounts intended to speak for themselves. But they would be much more useful if the recorder would try to say who he or she is, and why the life history was recorded in the first place. Some of what are intrinsically the most interesting anthropological life histories—those by Oscar Lewis, or Leo Simmons' *Sun Chief,* or Michael Smith's *Dark Puritan,* or Waler Dyk's *Son of Old Man Hat*—seem to be pushed out in front of the reader at the end of a long stick, while the character of the collector and the relationship between him or her and the collected remain largely obscure. In such instances, the issue of the possible representativeness of the protagonist is as dormant as the nature of the rapport.

These assertions are consistent with the fictitious Trapnel's complaints: "The biographer, even at his highest and best, can only be tentative, empirical. The autobiographer, for his part, is imprisoned in his own egotism." But while Trapnel is entitled to conclude that only a novel can "imply certain truths impossible to state by exact definition," historically-oriented scholars disposed to use the spoken word as data are not thereby obligated to become novelists—even if some have tried. The choice ought not to be between a disembodied individual who floats outside and above the culture and society, on the one hand, and a culture and society which imprison and make irrelevant the individuality of the informant, on the other. The biographer-ethnographer must have a conception of how people are at once products and makers of the social and cultural systems within which they are lodged. He or she must also make an honest effort, at least after the materials have been collected, to address the issue of how the informant and the fieldworker were interacting, why they were drawn together, what developing concerns for (or against) each other influenced the rhythm and nature of the enterprise. In short, he or she must respond to Conklin's observation that ethnographers carry on "a unique type of natural history, in which the observer becomes a part of (and an active participant in) the observed universe."

There are really two contentions here. The first is that the ethnographer try to define his or her place between the informant and the reader. The second is that the ethnographer help the reader to see the informant within the culture and society. Perhaps a little more can be said about this second assertion. Many social scientists have grappled with the supposed distinctions between the concepts of "society" and "culture," and some have even referred to "personality" as a kind of third or middle term. It may be useful to add to this view with particular reference to the life history. In his illuminating essay on the study of life history, Mandelbaum distinguishes between the cultural and social dimensions in a satisfactory fashion. The cultural dimension provides a scenario or chart, with the attendant understandings and behaviors, for the individual life; while the social dimension comprises the real-life interactions in which individuals make choices, and even shift cultural definitions. To these, Mandelbaum adds a psychosocial dimension; in general, his treatment corresponds to that offered by Parsons, Geertz, and Wolf.[8] Though such conceptual schemata are never entirely satisfying, they do enable us to think usefully about our research.

An institution, a cuisine, a complex of belief and behavior traditional within some society, can be traced backward in time, and its elements or features isolated and examined. Whether it be pants-wearing, handshaking, or choosing godparents, the social historian is often able to provide us with historical guidelines of a kind. Such materials are "cultural." But at any point in time, in any specific society, the particular ways people wear pants, shake hands, or choose godparents, and the ways they start doing them differently, will depend on numerous considerations that are immediately relevant, and that cannot be explained simply by reference to the past. Such maneuverings are "social." They are the reflections of both the composition and structure of the social group at that point in time, and the manifestations of individual variation within the group. It is in this sense that the elusive phenomenon we dub "personality" reveals itself at the boundary between social and cultural perspectives on behavior. To be specific about the life of an informant, in order to illustrate this assertion, would require too much narration. Perhaps it is sufficient to say that we make our decisions, as individuals, under conditions laid down by forces over which we have unspecified control, and that our perceptions of such conditions clearly influence our sense of autonomy. In getting at the life-profiles of others by collecting data on their experiences, we may examine, within limits, the extent to which such profiles are isomorphic with each other, or with some aggregate profile of the culture as a whole—if we know enough about the culture to make such comparisons possible. Differences among individuals are revealed not only by difference in the decisions made, but also by differential perceptions of alternatives.

But there are only two immediately apprehendable ways to get at the range of variation within one or more cultural norms or values. One must either find out from a large number of people, by observing their behavior or by asking them about it; or one must pose to one or more informants who have acted in accordance with such norms or values the possibility of alternatives, to which such informants may then respond with word or deed. Since the ability of people to explain their behavior *post hoc* appears to be very widely distributed, there are tangible benefits to be gained from studying decisions that are being made while one observes them, together with the collection of data on past decisions of a similar kind. For instance, while allowing for the many possible sources of difference, I found it useful to ask older informants about their first marital unions, and, at the same time, collect information on how their children were entering into comparable unions in the present. Among other things, such subject matters naturally provoke considerable discussion about how things are not what they used to be. Although a good deal of phony piety may enter, so do moral judgments, moral prescriptions, and active comparisons. It is within such terms that culture, conceived of as a repository of prescribed opportunities, and society, conceived of as an arena of maneuver, may be highlighted by the opinions of a single informant silhouetting his or her distinctive experience against the backdrop of our knowledge of the group.

There is no high road to insights of this sort. But since there seems to be no way to learn about the culture without learning about the informant, or vice-versa, there are good reasons for making the life history interview the last kind of ethnographic undertaking, rather than the first. The questions we learn to ask may not be the better psychologically, but they should, at least, serve us well in coaxing the individual, the distinctive, and the idiosyncratic into clearer view.

Notes

1. Harold C. Conklin, s. v. "Ethnography," *International Encyclopedia of the Social Sciences* (New York: Macmillan, 1968).

2. I will not deal with the question of the observation of behavior, except insofar as it concerns the immediate behavior of informants, even though, from the ethnographic perspective, this is rather like forsaking sight in order to benefit from the simplicity of reading Braille. Cf. Sidney Mintz, "Comments: Participant-Observation and the Collection of Data," *Boston Studies in the Philosophy of Science, 1966–68,* vol. 4 (Dordrecht, Holland: D. Reidel, 1969), pp. 341–49.

3. I believe that this is true even for informants who have migrated elsewhere. Of course many factors can affect, reduce, trivialize, or romanticize the way the community and culture are expressed by an informant remote in space or time from his or her past. But past experience does continue to manifest itself in perception and articulation—only how much or how little is open to argument. Cf. Sidney W. Mintz, "Comments" on Mandelbaum: "The Study of Life History: Gandhi," *Current Anthropology* 14 (1973), p. 200.

4. David Aberle, *The Psychosocial Analysis of a Hopi Life-History,* Comparative Psychology Monographs, 21:1, serial no. 107 (Berkeley: University of California Press, 1951), p. 2.

5. Aberle, *Psychosocial Analysis,* p. 4.

6. Mintz, "Comments," p. 200.

7. Conklin, "Ethnography," p. 172; George Condominas, *L'Exotique est quotidien: San Luk, Vietnam Central* (Paris: Plon, 1965), p. 35,

8. David G. Mandelbaum, "The Study of Life History: Gandhi," *Current Anthropology* 14 (1973), pp. 177–206; Talcott Parsons, *The Social System* (Glencoe, Ill.: Free Press, 1951); Clifford Geertz, "Ritual and Social Change: A Javanese Example," *American Anthropologist* 55 (1957), pp. 32–54; Eric R. Wolf, "Specific Aspects of Plantation Systems in the New World: Community Sub-Cultures and Social Class," *Plantation Systems of the New World,* Social Science Monographs No. 7 (Washington, D.C.: Pan American Union, 1959), pp. 136–46.

24

Radio and the Public Use of Oral History

David K. Dunaway

Our penultimate essay on fields related to oral history brings us to the subject of broadcast media, an area where professional oral historians are increasingly active.

As historians reach out to the public, they often find themselves involved in publishing and broadcasting their interviews. This article examines radio, one medium for bringing oral narratives to wide audiences. As the costs of film and television rise, and as the public's interest in oral history grows, the relatively inexpensive medium of radio offers continuing possibilities for public programs. With patience, the right equipment, and the right guidance, any oral or community history group can produce its own programs. David Dunaway, this volume's co-editor, explores the advantages and disadvantages of radio production based on oral sources.

David Dunaway teaches folklore and oral history at the University of New Mexico. He is author of award-winning biographies based on oral interviews, How Can I Keep From Singing: Pete Seeger *(1981),* Huxley in Hollywood *(1989),* Aldous Huxley Recollected: An Oral History *(1995), and* Writing the Southwest *(1995). He has spent the last decade working as a producer and consultant on two dozen radio and television documentaries, including "Pie in the Sky," a historical radio series funded by the National Endowment for the Arts, and "Writing the Southwest."*

*R*adio broadcasting and oral history interviewing seem, at first glance, made for one another. Radio producers search constantly for thoughtful, provocative interviews; oral historians seek an audience beyond library stacks, a public for their work. Documentarians, academic and public-sector historians, community organizers, local history groups, educators, interested citizens—all could benefit from a marriage between history and radio.

Oral history archives can provide, when broadcast, an open window into history, one custom built for radio and rich with the color and pacing of real speech. Many interviews are of gem quality, though considerable mining and polishing may be required before the jewels are extracted. They carry greater depth than for-radio interviews; they are usually transcribed (and transcription makes for easy editing and assembling of programs); and they involve not certified experts but us regular folks, the narrators and the listeners, in the making and the transmission of history.

Why, then, aren't radio producers courting oral history archives? Before any wedding between the two fields can take place, radio and oral history producers must understand each other far better than they do today. Nevertheless, such an event will be worth waiting for, because radio broadcasting may be the medium of choice for the public use of oral history.

To understand the relationship between oral history and radio, we will explore the advantages and disadvantages of combining the two fields, the differing aims of producers of radio and oral history, and the production of a radio program based on oral history interviews.

This survey is addressed to three audiences: oral historians who wish to make their tapes available for public use through media presentation; historians who wish to produce radio programs themselves, basing them on oral history interviews; and radio producers considering oral history archives as a source for programs on historical subjects. While our subject is radio, many of the observations apply to film or video use of oral historical sources and to the related fields in the humanities which rely on oral sources (folklore, anthropology, and so forth).

History and Radio

Since the early days of radio broadcasting, theoreticians have realized the medium's power to use voices to connect a people with their past.[1] Pioneer radio productions such as "History Highlights" and "March of Time" used interviews and dramatic reconstructions to effect intimacy and create an understanding of an epoch.[2] The beginnings of radio drama employed actual interviews alongside researched and scripted historical treatments.[3] And since radio began, social scientists interested in cultural preservation have speculated on how the medium links isolated communities with their traditions.[4] Broadcasting has always relied on language and sound; thus the same words which individuals use to fashion history as they saw it can be recorded by either the oral historian or the radio producer. Old radio broadcasts have themselves become valuable documents for historians of the recent past, as English historian Paul Thompson has noted.[5]

Oral history has been used most effectively by radio in Europe and Canada, where sound archives are often associated with publicly supported broadcasting systems. Thus the British Broadcasting Corporation (BBC) produces some 60 programs per *week* which take material from archival sources, and the Foundation for Film Science in Utrecht, The Netherlands, is actively involved in media production using historical interviews. One of the leading groups in this effort has been the European Broadcast Union's Radio Programme Committee. Founded in 1967, this group takes as part of its mandate "the programme possibilities of sound archives." To this day, sound archivists have an edge over oral historians in using radio to promote public consciousness of the sound environment; this advantage to a great extent results from the work of professional organizations such as the International Association of Sound Archives and the U.S. Association for Recorded Sound Collections.[6]

In Canada, broadcasters interested in oral history have found a home in the Canadian Broadcasting Corporation (CBC).[7] Starting in the early 1960s, Imbert Orchard, the Cambridge-trained dramatist and radio producer, recorded almost 1,000 interviews for the CBC, "drawing from them the basis of some 200 radio programs."[8] In his work and writings, Orchard has developed the most sophisticated analyses of radio's use of historical interviews; he coined the term "aural history," referring to historical recordings of sounds. Others in the CBC have helped make it a world center for radio use of history, particularly at the CBC Archives in Toronto and the Sound and Moving Image Division of British Columbia's Provincial Archives.[9]

In the United States in the 1970s, the National Endowment for the Humanities and regional/state organizations have funded a number of award-winning radio series based on oral historical sources, though televised history programs have far outnumbered radio history projects.[10]

Advantages in Combining Radio and Oral History

Though radio and oral history involve distinct production operations, they can be joined, to their mutual benefit. As a medium of communication, radio has several inherent advantages for communicating the results and process of history.

Consider the nature of radio: the medium relies on sound, rather than on televised images, to achieve its effects. Listeners absorb the content without having to stop what they're doing; radio travels to where people are, in their cars, backyards, or kitchens. Listening does not disrupt the normal tempo of life. Americans already consume, on the average, three hours of radio daily. Using this popular medium avoids the difficulty of persuading the public to pick up a book and stop doing something else (much less read an unedited transcript). Furthermore radio, with its immediacy and speed, is a natural environment for sharing the voices of history. Unlike television or film, which require a suitable illustration for each sound, radio allows our minds to populate history from our own surroundings and to imagine the personalities behind the voices.

Radio production remains far less expensive than other broadcast media and also far less capital-intensive. Whereas professionally produced film or television documentaries cost from $5,000 to $25,000 per minute of finished product, radio's costs range around an eighth of that amount. This makes the medium particularly suitable for programs of less than national interest—local history and specialized topics. Instead of costly cameras, monitors, and editing bays (home video formats are more economical) radio can proceed with the equipment which an oral historian may already own: a microphone, two tape recorders, an inexpensive editing block, a razor blade. For sophisticated productions, more equipment will naturally be required, particularly computers and software, but it will still cost a fraction of the equipment for television or film production.

Radio is also less complex to master, in part because the creative elements are limited to sound. Complete mastery of the process of radio production naturally demands a good deal of practice—as any art does. But the beginning oral historian, who already knows how to work a microphone and a recorder, could probably learn the elements and basic procedures of audio production in a matter of months or even weeks, if he or she was fiercely determined. With the assistance of a trained technician (and a consultant to supervise the balance between technical and content elements), an oral historian might assemble an informative documentary about a community's history in several months, using existing interviews. By comparison, a filmed documentary, involving costly and time-consuming laboratory work, can take years to finish. Funding sources understand these differences in cost and effort; state humanities councils, for example, are increasingly relying on radio grants to widen public understanding of the humanities.[11]

One of the spin-off advantages of using radio for oral history projects is that the broadcasting and production studios are widely distributed, and can be found even in the most rural locations. Commercial television, with its sizable capital investment, tends to produce air-quality material only in the largest communities, with smaller stations serving as broadcast outlets. Virtually every radio station now operating, on the other hand, *could* be used to produce oral history programs. And since radio stations have a legal obligation to produce local programs in the public interest, oral history project workers may discover that their local stations are enthusiastic about programs which beam a community's history back into that community. There are many precedents for locally produced, locally sponsored programs of public affairs; the oral historian with carefully recorded topical interviews might find a radio station willing to include them in a weekly hour-long slot. (One way to begin is to write the station's program director and propose selected topics.)

Radio producers would likewise benefit from the resources of oral history, for there is a chronic shortage of thoughtfully produced public affairs materials for radio. As large corporate chains control more and more broadcast outlets, they may need locally produced material to balance the networked feeds from Los Angeles or New York.

The Different Aims and Methods of History and Radio

To date, oral history and radio production have rarely melded in the United States; one obvious reason is that they represent entirely different disciplines, showing virtually no overlap in training, employment, and professional communities. (Interestingly enough, in countries with a national broadcasting service which customarily employs liberal arts graduates, such as the famed BBC, the ties between the two fields are stronger.)

Radio producers are trained most often as journalists in departments of journalism, communication, or speech. Their education emphasizes not content but technique: how to record, edit, conceptualize, and finally produce a radio program, regardless of subject. Even in areas where the training of radio professionals might be expected to overlap an oral historian's—such as the basic techniques of interviewing—different ends demand different procedures. The radio producer is taught to conduct an interview on a moment's notice, under adverse circumstances, and to ferret out a story, overcoming the reluctance of the subject with a combination of bravado, cunning, and persistence. He or she reaches the controversial points fast, evokes a show of emotion, and presents the material all in a short time frame.

The professional oral historian, on the other hand, is most likely educated in departments of history, literature, or a specialized field such as medicine or physics. As researchers, they regard the content as the whole; the complex and subtle requirements of media production sometimes prove intimidating or frustrating. No matter how anxious university-trained oral historians may be to have their inquiry reach a wide audience, most leave the academy with only a smattering of knowledge on the audio-technical side of their profession; few oral history classes, for instance, discuss microphone placement at any length. Rarer still is the technical education which would allow scholars to use up-to-date equipment and evaluate sound environments for extraneous noises.

Unlike the radio producer, the oral historian seeks historical detail in interviews, not emotional reactions; relying on the subject's cooperation and on lengthy research, the interview proceeds at a more gradual pace. The historical interviewer gathers source materials, whose significance may be accurately determined only after years of further study.

In this context I will discuss some fundamental differences between radio and oral history, and I hope neither radio producer nor oral historian will take offense at the following general remarks. From the standpoint of a practitioner in both fields, the major differences concern time pressures, legal questions and authorship, and differing end products.

The production of radio works by deadline. Rarely, if ever, does time permit the producer to explore the nuances he or she sees, to find all their interview subjects at home or office, to take follow-up trips to the library to check and double-check facts. Historians, in contrast, proceed with extreme patience and caution. A single oral history project may continue for several years; by that time a radio producer or documentarian would have been sacked more than once.

There are several reasons for this different pace; one is the different legal considerations in each field. Radio producers are less concerned with questions of copyright, ownership, review, and storage of materials, matters over which full-time oral historians lose sleep. I do not mean to imply that radio producers are casual about their work—by no means! But a main concern of a media producer (and his boss) is not to violate laws of libel or invasion of privacy. The interviewer for radio assumes legal ownership (or at least broadcast privileges) for interviews and considers review of the interviewer by the subject not only impractical, but a violation of the producer's independence. By contrast, legal issues in oral history are sufficiently complex that few lawyers have had the patience even to survey the problems.[12]

Copyright and authorship may also be less complicated for the radio producer. While oral history is a joint, coauthored process, few radio producers would willingly share their byline with the government official interviewed for their program. Such sharing would open producers to charges of collusion with their sources, which challenges prevailing notions of an objective press and media. (In fact, in most productions sources "feed" information to the media in a state of mutual dependency.) Radio interviewing leans toward an adversary or investigative role, while oral history favors the collaborative, "as told to" approach. The for-radio interview relies on personalities to hold the audience's ear; some documentation may be lost in the press for entertainment.

These different approaches stem from differing end products and concerns. The final product of a thorough oral history session will be a narrator-approved transcript, deposited in a publicly accessible library or institution. This transcript and tape will be preserved whole, as a resource for future generations (though in the United States, the transcript, rather than the tape, will circulate).

In radio the end product is also a tape, but one composed of a series of interviews, edited, encapsulated, rearranged, and mixed together with sound effects, music, and sound ambience. (It is not unusual to use only a minute of an hour's interview in the final production.) This highly crafted tape is often all that is preserved—the original recording may lie on the floor of the editing room or may be erased for recycling. The program is the fruit of the producer's labors, and it is judged by immediate audience response and by the production values demonstrated—not by its value to future generations of scholars. Thus different documents emerge from the differing goals of the historian and the producer—and each answers (or inspires) different questions. Radio producers work with action, sensation, emotion, and audio presence in their palette; the oral historian, with objectivity and verisimilitude. Both pursue truth, on different roads.

In recent years, these distinct approaches have begun to coalesce. Radio producers, particularly on the network level, spend increasing time on research and on clearing legal issues through counsel. Similarly the oral history profession may be shifting its attention from exclusively collecting raw data to analyzing, editing, and evaluating their sources—in short, to making history (based on transcripts as well as other sources).

For this confluence to become a collaboration, producers of oral history and radio can begin with a few simple steps. Oral historians, whatever their intentions for later use of their materials, should: (1) produce high-quality recordings; (2) flag, in some fashion, the most striking statements in their interview; (3) use release forms which provide for the possibility of broadcast; (4) guide radio producers in the historical frame and main themes covered by the interview. They should encourage public use and access beyond print or tape circulation of interviews. This may require expanding the scope of collecting efforts to anticipate multiple use, such as collecting ambient sound during interviews—the sounds of a steel mill operation complementing an interview on steelworking, for instance.

Ultimately, this process will involve the archivist in initiating contacts with the local broadcast community, as discussed earlier. Even where interviews were originally done on substandard equipment, an oral historian can guide a producer to the best narrators and the best questions so that the interview can be redone, where possible, quickly and effectively.

On the part of radio producers, a collaboration might involve: (1) duplicating interviews in their entirety *before* editing, and making arrangements to donate this copy to a local archive; (2) obtaining permissions from interviewees which would allow these tapes to be deposited; (3) learning about existing interviews already stored in archives (such interviews would only enhance the producer's own efforts); and (4) making more time available for historical programming.

Disadvantages of Combining Oral History and Radio

Before describing the assembly of a radio program from oral history interviews, we should consider the disadvantages and difficulties of combining radio and oral history from the standpoint of the historian. These might be summarized as getting permission, getting audiences, and getting quality.

Without a proper release from all narrators, no one should broadcast an interview; to do so invites legal and ethical dilemmas. The information confided in an interview might not be appropriate for public distribution; the speaker might harm or libel or embarrass. Oral historians are not investigative reporters, and, as mentioned above, they work in different, more collaborative traditions. Radio broadcast constitutes "publication" in the legal sense of the term; information should not be published without the express consent of the interviewee.

Getting audiences for interviews involves publicizing the archives' holdings and making sure that use of the interviews will not present radio producers with headache-ridden, time-engulfing labor. Streamline the forms to be filled out, eliminate lengthy correspondence, routinely obtain clearance for broadcast. Provide high-quality duplications if at all possible (second- or third-generation copies are unacceptable for broadcast purposes). While some archivists may recoil at the thought of an edited interview, most realize that broadcasting a four-hour interview in its entirety would tax any listener.

Getting quality means obtaining, from the beginning, the very best recording which circumstances permit, and then handling and assembling the material with care and skill. Well-maintained equipment, skillfully manipulated, can add immeasurably to the potential of an oral history interview.

Bear in mind that not all oral history projects may be suited for adaptation to radio. Some historians may find, in the words of one archivist, that "the limitations of programme length, the producers' duty to entertain, the tendency of programme themes to become overly generalized or simplistic can be in contrast to the qualified or precise statements that historians are more accustomed to make."[13]

From the radio producer's standpoint, there may likewise be disadvantages to working with historians. Immersion in their subject may prevent historians from understanding how their findings would sound to an interested but uninitiated mass audience. Frequently the individualistic work patterns of historians make for a difficult transition into a collaborative production-team mode. And finally, using radio requires far more than rewriting an interview history so that it can be read aloud. Radio, like any medium of communication, has its own aesthetic boundaries which historians might profitably understand, even if they themselves do not intend to go into radio production.

Aesthetics of Radio Production

Radio, according to Marshall McLuhan's *Understanding Media,* "is that extension of the human nervous system which is matched only by human speech itself."[14] It is intimate and personal, carried from car to house to backyard. Ultimately, its aesthetic boundaries derive from its imitation of speech and its ability to paint images and emotions in sound. Some characteristics which the oral historian will want to consider in using the medium are the ways in which radio portrays the presence, pacing, clarity, and unity of sound.

The precisely trained ear can listen to a few bars of music or a minute of interview and can guess the room in which it was recorded: its height, wall and floor coverings, the size of the space. This is because a tape recorder captures not only the sound source—a speaker or event—but the sound *environment* or soundscape: the collection of echoes, low-flying airplanes, refrigerator hums, and so forth. If you doubt this, try splicing together two interviews, one recorded in a large roomy hall, such as a church, and the other in a small book- and carpet-lined study. The first will sound boomy, hollow, and live; the second flat, more intimate. No sound environment is best for all purposes, and a producer may choose to enhance or neutralize background noise to suit his or her ends. An interview with a retired whaler might be effectively recorded outside, by the ocean. Imbert Orchard at the CBC successfully juxtaposed readings from the journals of early explorers with sounds recorded on a contemporary canoe trip down their route.[15]

Since all media production involves telescoping life, compressing into minutes events which might have taken years, pacing is critical in TV and radio. This constraint presents special problems for oral historians. Some interviewees, no matter how crucial their words, will not broadcast successfully. They may talk too slowly, "um" and "er" with distracting frequency, or vary their volume from one sentence to another. While editing can slice out pauses or digressions, there are limits to even the best sound surgery. Preparing a program for the general public involves a constant battle between historical content and its presentation in an effective, moving manner; nowadays best done via computer.

The clarity and fidelity of sound is of course maximally important in broadcasting recordings. Radio cannot portray the gestures which may make a point clear in the interview situation. Listeners depend on clear, crisp recordings to fill in the lost visual information. Thus high-quality microphones and recorders, intelligently positioned, should be used to catch the speech flow. Such equipment requires more funds and more training than many amateurs currently have for oral history recording, but much equipment can be borrowed or rented. Clarity comes from paying as close attention to the quality of the sound as to the content of the interview itself. The advice of folklorist Kenneth Goldstein is useful on this point:

> Too many field workers treat their equipment as troublesome adjuncts to field work, and care little for the quality of their recordings as long as they are audible and transcriptions can be made from them. Yet these same collectors work extremely hard to insure the fidelity and exactness of their handwritten notes. Essentially there is no difference between the two forms of data-collecting. Both should be treated with equal care.[16]

Though sound enhancement techniques can help improve existing recordings (equalization, filtering, and panning sounds from one channel to another), these are costly, time-consuming processes which should ideally be used with recordings which are already well made.

By "unity of sound," I mean the whole that the ear receives from a well-crafted radio program. The essence is montage, the superimposition of sounds, interviews, and narration to create an aural effect. The craft of radio production rises to art in the hands of someone fashioning a program from disparate interviews, ambient noise, and historical recordings such as speeches and old radio broadcasts. By juxtaposing these elements, the expert producer creates a textured tapestry of sound, complete with the built in punctuation of pauses and music.

How to Produce a Radio Program from Oral History Interviews

The production of radio programs from oral history interviews can be long and demanding. The studio and editing time required for a short production (3 to 10 minutes) can vary from 10 to 25 hours per minute. As we explore all the steps involved, the reason will become clear. It is impossible to outline in detail all the steps and techniques of radio production in a few pages; in my brief discussion, I will ignore more technical issues in order to break the process down into preproduction, production, and postproduction phases.

Two important terms in radio production are *actuality* and *continuity*. Actuality refers to the interviews and sounds (ambient noise and special effects) incorporated into a production. Continuity is the narration, scripted beforehand, which ties the voices, sounds, and music together. Obviously music and special effects are also needed to create a pleasing texture of sound. The remarks that follow refer to both tape- and computer-based productions.

PREPRODUCTION

1. Reflect upon and plan your project. What is the overriding purpose of the program? Who is the audience? What special skills or knowledge do you bring—or must you obtain?

2. Survey existing materials on your subject. This includes previous broadcasts, interviews in your collection, interviews in other collections, holdings in national archives. Consider, in your survey, the success of other similar projects—who funded them, how were they received and distributed?

3. Design your project. What effect do you hope to produce? What will you include and omit? What will be the best length? How will it be distributed? Who will do the work, who will help? Where and when will the actual production take place?

4. Assemble your resources. Find funds and time to meet the objectives outlined above. Obtain the necessary hardware (such as microphones, tape recorders, an editing block, a studio for additional recording, if possible); software (reel-to-reel tape, cassettes, splicing tape, razor blades, equipment for labeling tapes, and the like) and technical assistance (consultants or colleagues to help review content and technical standards). Schedule production.

5. Practice using the microphones and recorder with a friend, paying particular attention to mike placement (ideally within one foot from the speaker, unless a clip-on or lavalier type is used). Practice changing tapes (prenumbered). Make recordings at different levels to find the best recording volume.

6. Prepare a rough script. This should include the overall framework of the program and the production elements (continuity, actuality, music if desired, sound effects). Decide what your story is and how you will present it, keeping in mind your specific audience.

PRODUCTION

1. Conduct your interviews. Listen attentively and take good notes. If the interviews are not yet transcribed, begin with selected passages which you are sure of using. Decide which supplemental interviews are needed to fill in the holes in what you already have. Check that you have all necessary permissions to broadcast materials.

2. Revise the script.

3. Duplicate (dub) the interviews on a reel-to-reel recorder for editing; this should be done at high speed (7 or 15 inches per second) to make editing easy. *Never* cut into an original recording. Make arrangements to deposit your original tape in an archive. Label everything clearly, reels and boxes.

Edit the passages you would like to include, reducing them considerably in size and length. Remember that selection is the heart of art.

4. Assemble your other production elements (music for interludes or dramatic effect, ambient noise, sound effects) on separate reels, or transfer them to a hard drive, using a computer's sound card.

5. Polish and record your continuity (narration); if possible, find a trained voice among the local broadcast or acting community. Divide the narration into numbered sections, so that each piece can be integrated later with interviews and effects in the final mix; record the names of your interviewees, so that these too can be intermixed. Include an introduction and an "outroduction" (the graceful closing, wrap-up remarks).

6. Mix the production elements into a smooth program—more easily said than done. This can be the most complex and time-consuming process of the project and the one in which craft is most evident and necessary.

7. Time your finished tape carefully.

POSTPRODUCTION

1. Put your program aside for a period so that it begins to mature in your mind's ear and heart, and then listen to it and begin cutting it to a distributable length.

2. Begin distribution; hire an assistant, if necessary, to handle the many phone calls and letters. Prepare a brochure or mailing to let the world know of your work. Be patient, organized, and persistent.

3. Duplicate several copies and circulate them to interested parties and authorities on your subject. (Note that high-speed tape duplication is usually inaccurate, and the best copies are made one-to-one, on the machines originally used for the program.)

Producing radio programs involves learning not only about radio production but about radio distribution—how to get programs aired once they are completed. (This is a long and complex process, and without including funds and time for distribution in a budget, no one may hear the results of your labor.) Professionals in radio production—like those in history—spend many hours in professional gatherings (such as the annual U.S. Public Radio Conference), read up on the latest equipment, carry on a professional correspondence with many in the industry, constantly write proposals for funding, and so forth. Above all they listen to work done by others under similar circumstances. Close attention to the finer productions heard on National Public Radio or the CBC will ease many beginners into a new field.

Conclusion

The future of oral history radio programs depends to a great extent upon future funding. Professional historians interested in radio believed as early as 1934 that the medium could be put to great public service for relatively little cost. Instead of broadcasting university lectures, the History Committee of the National Advisory Council on Radio in Education suggested "reasons for broadcasting to the man in the street in order to develop 'historical mindedness' and plans for intriguing 'by starting with what is on his mind.' "[17] To extend this process to oral history, "to what is on his tongue," would be simple, mostly a matter of national and regional funding.

One comprehensive study of the public's understanding of humanities concluded that collaborations between scholarship and public TV and radio offered "a promising model for increasing understanding."[18] Organizations such as the National Endowment for the Humanities could set up summer sessions for historians, folklorists, and other humanists interested in working in radio and other media. Such training sessions could include not only the basics of production but the subtleties of media presentation (such as those mentioned above in connection with aesthetic concerns). State and regional humanities councils could set up residencies for scholars in radio and TV stations and could encourage the development of curricula and programs joining the production of oral history and radio.

Recent developments in oral history suggest an increasing professionalization of the field, though oral history continues to rely on dedicated volunteers at a grassroots level. Perhaps training sessions for oral history volunteers could include a component on media production. Qualified consultants can be found among the few professionals trained in both fields. Local oral history projects might consider contacting their local media with an eye (or ear) to collaborating on a public affairs program of high community interest. Individual oral historians could participate in a summer seminar such as those outlined above or could themselves enroll in media production courses at local colleges.

From these steps could come not only more interesting and illuminating radio and television, but also the beginnings of a historically educated citizenry. In an electronic, media-laden culture, it may be too much to expect more than the smallest percentage of a population to read history. But by taking historical materials to the forms of media people use in these declining years of book reading, we can enfranchise and empower people with their own past.

Notes

1. See, for example, Frank Stanton, "Psychological Research in the Field of Radio Listening," *Educational Broadcasting 1936* (Chicago: University of Chicago Press, 1936), pp. 1–12; and Levering Tyson, ed., *Proceedings of the Fourth Annual Assembly of the National Advisory Council on Radio in Education: Report of the History Committee* (Chicago: University of Chicago Press, 1935).

2. Lawrence Lichty and Thomas Bohn, "Radio's 'March of Time': Dramatized News," *Journalism Quarterly* 51 (Autumn 1974), pp. 458–62, reprinted in *American Broadcasting,* ed. Lichty and Topping (New York: Hastings, 1975).

3. Max Wylie, *Radio Writing* (New York: Rinehart, 1939), pp. 297–308; most historical radio was at this time called educational or children's radio.

4. Stephen Reda, "Ramah Navajo Radio and Cultural Preservation," *Journal of Broadcasting* 22 (Summer 1978), pp. 361–71.

5. Paul Thompson, *The Voice of the Past: Oral History* (New York: Oxford University Press, 1978), pp. 12–14.

6. *Proceedings of International Association of Sound Archives in Lisbon, Portugal* (London, 1978); Rolf Schuursma, "The Sound Archive of the Film and Science Foundation and the Dutch Radio Organization" and Paul Thompson, "The B.B.C. Archives," *Oral History* 1 (Summer, 1971), pp. 23–26, 11–18.

7. Dennis Duffy and David Mitchell, *Bulletin of the Association for the Study of Canadian Radio and Television* 6 (November 1979), pp. 5–7. Another Canadian radio-historian is Barbara Diggins, author of "Designing Sound Documents," *Canadian Oral History Association Journal* 3 (1978), pp. 23–25.

8. Imbert Orchard, "Tape Recordings into Radio Documentaries," *Sound Heritage* 3 (1974), pp. 28–40; a more comprehensive draft is his unpublished "The Documentary in Sound." For the history of the coining of the term "aural history," see Orchard's interview with Dennis Duffy, July 6, 1978, Accession No. 990:6, pp. 11–12, Provincial Archives of British Columbia. Orchard told the author that his first public use of "aural history" came in 1968, in one of his pioneering "People in Landscape" series.

9. Robin Woods, *Canadian Oral History Association Journal* 5 (1980), pp. 41–42.

10. Some NEH-funded radio history productions are "Banks of Barre," "First Person America," and "Living Atlanta," referred to in *Medialog,* ed. L. Jimenez, M. Mayo, and V. Schofield (New York: Film Fund, 1982). See also the review of the Appalachian media production group, Appalshop, in *In These Times* (Chicago, Ill.) October 20, 1982.

11. See Richard Hinchcliffe, "The Sound of the Humanities," *Federation Reports* 4 (September 1981), pp. 12–15, and David Dunaway, "Media and the State Humanities Council," *Federation Reports,* 12 (April 1986), pp. 38–46.

12. The best review-articles are Joseph Romney, "Oral History, Law and Libraries," *Drexel Library Quarterly* 15 (October 1979), pp. 40–49, and Truman Eustis III, "Get It in Writing: Oral History and the Law," *Oral History Review* 4 (1976), pp. 6–18.

13. David Lance, "Dissemination of Radio Resource Materials," *Journal of the International Association of Sound Archives* 7 (December 1978), pp. 29–34.

14. Marshall McLuhan, *Understanding Media* (New York: McGraw-Hill, 1964), p. 264.

15. Imbert Orchard, "Tape Recordings."

16. Kenneth Goldstein, *A Guide for Fieldworkers in Folklore* (1964; reprint ed., Detroit: Gale, 1974), p. 45.

17. Levering, Tyson, ed., *Proceedings of the Fourth Annual Assembly of the National Advisory Council on Radio in Education* (Chicago: University of Chicago Press, 1935).

18. National Commission on the Humanities, *The Humanities in American Life* (Berkeley: University of California Press, 1981).

25

The Expanding
Role of the Librarian
in Oral History

Willa K. Baum

In our final article on disciplines related to oral history, Willa K. Baum, co-editor of this volume and author of two classic manuals on oral history, discusses the responsibilities of librarians in creating, curating, consuming, and counseling with respect to oral history. She explores the special problems libraries face in caring for and publicizing oral history holdings, and then points out how the library, through setting standards of acceptance, can play a part in encouraging well-researched oral history.

Willa K. Baum, head of the Regional Oral History Office of the Bancroft Library, University of California, Berkeley, served on the first and subsequent councils of the Oral History Association. Active in the field since 1954, she has played a major role in developing the technique of oral history through her two guidebooks, Oral History for the Local Historical Society *(1987) and* Transcribing and Editing Oral History *(1991), as well as through her many journal articles and lectures.*

"The Expanding Role of the Librarian in Oral History" is adapted from a 1976 lecture at the Louisiana State University Library School, published in *Library Lectures* 6 (1978), pp. 33–43. Copyrighted and reprinted by permission of the author.

*I*t appears to me that the greatest need in oral history is to engage the knowledgeable participation of librarians in oral history, especially librarians in the smaller local and regional libraries. Two things especially concern me:

1. the preservation and use of oral history tapes after they are produced and
2. the quality of the interviews being produced—I refer to the content of the interviews, not the quality of the sound recording, although that matter also requires attention.

I have recently been working with a library school student who has chosen as her field study assignment the compilation of a directory of all the oral history tapes in the San Francisco Bay Area. She has been discovering, and I think the San Francisco area is in this respect fairly representative of other regions, that oral history tapes are being produced by a myriad of individuals and temporary groups, that the tapes are getting into local libraries, and that there they are lost. They are not irretrievably lost, but lost to use—uncataloged or inadequately cataloged, often unshelved, undescribed as to subjects discussed on the tapes or how they came to be there at all, and with no information regarding access and restrictions on their use.

Another problem is that while the oral history tapes being recorded are often very good in terms of documenting local landmarks, the community's colorful characters, both praiseworthy and notorious, and major events, such as the earthquake and fire, the flood, and the opening of the bridge, the tapes are neglecting less dramatic but possibly more significant material. An interview with the town's chief of police for 40 years, for example, includes no discussion of changes in law enforcement problems or police methods during those four decades.

It seems to me imperative that librarians play a greater role in oral history if oral history is to fulfill its promise of providing a medium whereby all of the people and the regions and the occupations of this diverse nation are to be documented and their stories preserved and used in the telling of our nation's history. I mean to limit my remarks here to defining that role.

The Three Steps of Oral History

There are three major steps to oral history, the "three Cs," you might call them. In chronological order they are "creating," "curating," and "consuming." To this I will add a fourth, "counseling." By counseling I mean providing the advice, the readings and background material, and the ongoing supervision that will aid the creators of oral history in producing acceptable interviews that elicit the most useful information from the narrators.

Creating is not essentially a library function, though in fact many oral history projects emanate from a library, our own office included. But the counseling component of creating, although it could be done by another agency such as the history department of a college, will probably fall to the local library. Therefore I will discuss that function in some detail, and I include a bibliography of manuals on oral history that the librarian can provide for prospective interviewers.

The "consuming" of oral history materials is a laissez-faire situation, with librarians as welcome to participate as anyone else. It is not unknown for librarians to moonlight as writers of historical articles and editors of historical books. Librarians appear in the rolls of writers of historical fiction and even more so among the authors of children's books. The new breed of audio-visually trained librarians is even appearing in the ranks of the producers of radio and television programs and educational AV materials. In all of these areas, oral history materials provide a source of fresh, lively material. The librarian can make a vital difference in the quantity and quality of use of oral history materials by serving as a broker between creator and consumer of oral history.

But it is in the area of "curating" that the librarian is essential; at least, if we accept as part of the definition of oral history that it must, now or later, be available for research use, then it must be accessioned, preserved, made available by information retrieval tools, and serviced.

Definition of Oral History

Before I use the term "oral history" again, I should define it. Or perhaps I would be wiser *not* to define it, for among oral historians there is no agreement as to precisely what oral history includes and excludes. At the first gathering of persons doing what they called oral history, a meeting called by UCLA in 1966, the definition was hotly debated. Did it include tape-recorded folk tales and songs; surveys on tape of all the inhabitants of South Dakota more than 80 years old on "badmen I have seen"; taped interviews with farm families on why they decided to plant the south 40 in wheat instead of rye; intimate probing by a psychoanalyst historian into the dreams of a great leader; or the neatly typed transcripts of much-rewritten interviews, the tapes from which they were prepared having been erased? We could not agree then (we cannot wholly agree now), but we did applaud the late Dr. Philip C. Brooks, then director of the Truman Library, when he said, "I do have a naive feeling that oral history ought to be *oral*, and it ought to be history."

Yet recent events have caused us to discard even Brooks's vague definition. The Watergate tapes are without a doubt oral and without a doubt *history*, yet there is no oral historian who would accept them as oral history. They fail in the most basic tenet of oral history—that the parties being recorded know they are being recorded and that they agree to make the information they convey available for research.

Without trying to delineate any exact boundaries, let me define oral history as:

1. a tape-recorded interview, or interviews, in question-and-answer format;

2. conducted by an interviewer who has some, and preferably the more the better, knowledge of the subject to be discussed;

3. with a knowledgeable interviewee, someone who knows whereof he or she speaks from personal participation or observation (sometimes we allow a second-hand account);

4. on subjects of historical interest (one researcher's history could be everyone else's trivia);

5. accessible, eventually, in tapes and/or transcripts to a broad spectrum of researchers.

It is this fifth qualification that differentiates oral history from the time-honored method used by a researcher who asks the people who witnessed an event what happened. It presupposes a certain degree of selflessness, first, in asking questions which may not be of special interest to the interviewer but which are designed to provide information for many users, both present and future, and second, in depositing the product in a library or archive for use by others. And it is in this second step that the librarian becomes key to the value of oral history.

The Popularization of Oral History

The first oral history projects were aimed at the "movers and shakers of society." The presidential libraries sought the chief lieutenants and, sometimes, the chief opponents of their particular president. Special projects such as the John Foster Dulles Project or the General George Marshall Project likewise documented a great man, while multipurpose projects like Columbia's recorded the distinguished citizens of a given region. Our own office, the Regional Oral History Office of the University of California (Berkeley), came into being in 1954, charged by the regents with "tape recording the memoirs of persons who have contributed significantly to the development of the West and of the nation." But in the past decades the trend has been more to "people's history," to collecting the self-told tales of Indians, migrant workers, coal miners, mountain dwellers, sharecroppers, groups which would otherwise never be documented except by a few brief public records as birth, marriage, death, welfare rolls, or social security rolls.

The scholarly books drawing on oral history have multiplied geometrically with each year following 1960, the first year Columbia University issued a report of its holdings. Books drawing heavily on oral history include T. Harry Williams's biography, *Huey Long* (1969); Vivian Perlis's *Charles Ives Remembered: An Oral History* (1974); Fawn Brodie's *Richard Nixon: The Shaping of His Character* (1981); David Dunaway's *How Can I Keep from Singing: Pete Seeger* (1981); G. Edward White's *Earl Warren: A Public Life* (1982); and, for librarians, Guy R. Lyle's *The Librarian Speaking: Interviews with University Librarians* (1970).

Oral historians had always aimed for such use, although we initially assumed it would be future use, and we continue to be startled at the rapidity with which our materials are snapped up by current researchers. We did not anticipate the tremendous popularity of lay volumes based on "people's history" such as Studs Terkel's *Hard Times* (1970) and his *Working* (1974); Theodore Rosengarten's *All God's Dangers: The Life of Nate Shaw* (1974); Al Santoli's *Everything We Had: An Oral History of the Vietnam War* (1981); and Eliot Wigginton's *Foxfire,* ten volumes of interviews with Georgia folk done by his high school students.

The popularization and profitability of books derived from oral history may indeed prove damaging to the original concept of oral history's purpose, which was the obtaining of very candid remarks on historical events (to be seen only by a limited group of qualified scholars). Certainly the response has increased the problems of librarians, who must now worry about literary rights, royalties, libel, and invasion of privacy far more than in the early days of oral history.

Curating Oral History

Whether they be accounts of "movers and shakers" or of "the people," oral history tapes and transcripts must find their way into a library or an archive if they are to serve any purpose at all. This need brings us to the essential library function of curating.

Let me illustrate with an example. A professor from a nearby university deposited in the Donated Oral Histories Collection of the Bancroft Library the best tapes produced by students in her course in women's history. One tape recorded a woman who was and is an active trade unionist, first in Idaho and for the past 35 years in the San Francisco area. She is one of the prime movers in the founding of Union WAGE (Women's Alliance to Gain Equality), an alliance of trade union women to fight discrimination on the job, in unions, and in society. On the tape she tells of her first unionizing experience in 1933 when, as a waitress in a small cafe in Idaho serving CCC (Civilian Conservation Corps) boys, she refused to work seven days a week. Later in the tape she tells how she managed to support her children in a man's world and describes the ins and outs of union politics. In a very personal and understandable way, she takes the listener back in time to the beginnings of mass unionization in the Depression era, to the CCC days, to the mobilization of all man and woman power during World War II.

What a teaching resource this tape would be if the secondary teachers knew of its existence! Surely a librarian would be delighted to participate in bringing this sort of interview into being by working with the teachers, the volunteer oral historians, and the students who would be recording the interviews. Now, consider the problems raised by the donation of this tape:

1. Who owns it?
2. Who can grant permission to reproduce it in tape or transcript for scholarly use, perhaps for commercial publication?
3. How should it be cataloged? Must the librarian listen to a tape for the full hour and a half to determine the major subjects? Suppose that with the tape comes a file of photographs, a scrapbook of newspaper clippings about the narrator, and many official documents relating to the trade union struggles she was involved in. How shall these be cataloged? How shelved?
4. The narrator was at the time of the recording involved in a bitter struggle within her union, and she insisted on stating her case. Could the library be held actionable for slander if one of the opposing union officials learned of the tape?

Headaches? Challenges? Maybe entertainment for the librarian bored with dealing with books that come with LC numbers, catalog cards, and neatly excerpted book reviews on their jackets. There are no accepted solutions to these problems. Nonetheless, I will plunge in and give you my own suggestions.

ACCEPTING THE TAPES AND TRANSCRIPTS

Be prepared to cope with some of the problems of ownership, provenance, and cataloging at the time the oral history materials are offered to the library.

Gift Forms. Ownership of the tapes should be signed over to the library, unless the group that produced them is an ongoing organization that will be able to administer the interviews in perpetuity. Ownership can be established by having the interviewer and the narrator sign a gift form. The wording of the simple donor form used by the Bancroft Library is as follows:

> We, _____ (narrator)
> and _____ (interviewer)
> do hereby give to the Bancroft Library for such scholarly and educational uses as the director of the Bancroft Library shall determine the following tape-recorded interview(s) recorded on ____ (date[s]) as an unrestricted gift and transfer to the University of California legal title and all literary property rights including copyright. This gift does not preclude any use which we may want to make of the information in the recordings ourselves. (Signed by narrator and interviewer and accepted by the librarian)

To this gift form can be added any special restrictions the narrator or interviewer may request, such as:

> *Closed:* The entire tape and transcript shall be closed to all users until 1999. (Do not use vague expressions like "until the death of the narrator" unless one librarian will be permanently assigned to obituary watching.)

> *Some pages closed:* The following transcript pages and the tape relating hereto shall be closed to all users until_____(date) except with the written permission of_____(narrator). Transcript pages:_____.

> *Open for research, requires permission to quote:* The tape and transcript are open for research but may not be quoted for publication except with the written permission of___ _____(narrator or interviewer) until 1999 (in the event the narrator or interviewer are preparing a publication that will draw on the interview).

Insistent as the library should be on accepting only interviews with gift forms signed by narrator and interviewer, the occasion will arise when a collection is offered for which there are no signed gift forms and the narrators are dead or have dispersed. Should it be accepted? Yes, with prudence. Obtain a signed gift form from the interviewer on the assumption that the narrators gave their accounts to the interviewer and the material is now his or her property to donate. Try to obtain some evidence that the narrators intended to make the recordings available. Perhaps the letter asking them to participate in the recording program said it was for historic preservation. Perhaps the uses of the material are discussed on the tape.

Then, depending on the nature of the material, make the recordings available with care. For example, researchers may be required to identify the source of a quotation as anonymous if the material is personal or to draw general conclusions without providing specific, identified examples. Since the object of library oral history collecting is to make the material as widely useful and easily accessible as possible, the fewer limitations on use, the better.

PROVENANCE AND TOPIC SUMMARY
The library should request a written description of the major topics covered in the interview, who the narrator is, who did the interviews, and why. Obtaining this information will greatly reduce the time required by the cataloger, who otherwise might have to listen to all the tapes to establish subjects. The information about the narrator and interviewer will enhance the value of the tapes to the user as well as aiding the cataloger.

This information also can most easily be obtained by having a blank ready for the donor to fill out. Sample forms are available in the manuals listed in the bibliography. Be sure to ask for collateral material such as photographs, scrap-books, and so forth if they seem appropriate.

SHELVING AND CATALOGING OF TAPES AND COLLATERAL MATERIAL

Tapes, photographs, and papers all survive well under the same housing conditions, that is, in a clean environment (no smoking, no eating) with stable humidity (40–60 percent) and stable temperature (60–70 degrees Fahrenheit). They could all be stored together in closed manuscript boxes. But for purposes of more compact storage, tapes are often separated from papers. This separation is no problem as long as they are so cataloged that all the elements of one collection can be reassembled.

The card catalog determines whether the oral history materials will prove an exciting new resource or will be lost on some dusty shelf. Whatever catalog system you use, the most important thing about an oral history collection is the information it contains, not the fact that it is on tape. Do not bury oral history in an audio-visual materials catalog; file the catalog cards in your main subject/author catalog. The entries should relate to:

1. the narrator (author);
2. major subjects discussed;
3. the producing group (i.e., Baton Rouge Architectural Heritage Committee);
4. the subject "oral history" so that the material will be retrievable as an audio resource as well.

A sample of catalog cards for a transcript with tapes from the manuscript catalog of the Bancroft Library appears in Figure 25.1. Note that the transcripts catalog card indicates that there is a tape available; that there is a legal restriction; and that there are supporting materials. The tracings indicate cross-referenced subject catalog entries. In this instance, the interviewee's name is the major entry; it is a 184-page transcript with a well-known person. In other projects, the interviewees may not be well known and the major entry would relate to the topic; for example, "San Francisco Earthquake and Fire, 1906, recollections of."

SERVICING

Oral history materials are like other manuscript materials: they are unique and for safety's sake cannot be permitted to leave the library. In addition, the tapes require a tape recorder and headphones that may be used by patrons. And the library that receives tapes all in one format is lucky; more likely they will come on cassettes and on mono and stereo reels at all speeds from $1\frac{7}{8}$ to $7\frac{1}{2}$ inches per second, making necessary several playback machines or a way of duplicating tapes for patron use. Ideally, the archival or master copy of the recording will be held on reel-to-reel tapes, with copies duplicated on cassettes for patron use.

Partial phonotape also available
Please inquire at Desk

72/105   Rinder, Rose (Perlmutter)
     C   Music, Prayer and Religious Leadership, Temple Emanu-El,
          1913-1969. Berkeley, Calif. 1971.
              [44], 1841. Ms. 28 cm.
              Photocopy of typed transcript of tape-recorded interviews conducted
          1968-1969 by Malca Chall for Bancroft Library Regional Oral History
          Office. Introduction by Rabbi Louis I. Newman, Photographs inserted.
              SEALED UNTIL JANUARY 1973 EXCEPT WITH
          MRS. RINDER'S WRITTEN PERMISSION.

CONTINUED ON NEXT CARD

Notation: Phonotape available
Notation: Interview sealed until specified date

72/105   Rinder, Rose, P. Music, Prayer . . . (card 2)
     C   Recollection of the years she and her husband Cantor Rueben Rinder were
          associated with Temple Emanu-El in San Francisco; their participation in
          musical life in the Bay area; their friendship with many musicians includ-
          ing Ernest Bloch, Yehudi Menuhin, Isaac Stern and others.
              Copies of letters, programs, and other documentary material inserted.

(OVER)

1. Rinder, Reuben, 1887–1966   2. Jews in California   3. San Francisco, Temple
Emanu-El x-3. Templ-El. San Francisco   4. Music—San Francisco   5. Musicians—
Correspondence, reminiscences, etc.   6. Bloch, Ernest, 1880–1959.   7. Menuhin,
Yehudi, 1916–   8. Stern, Isaac, 1920–   I. Bancroft Library. Regional Oral History
Office   II. Newman, Louis Israel, 1893–

Tracings—Rinder, Rose. Cards crossfiled under these entries.

Figure 25.1 Sample oral history manuscript catalog cards.

If patrons use the master tape, be sure the playback machine has a lock on the
"record" button so that the tapes cannot be accidentally erased.

    If there are restrictions on the use of tapes or transcripts, they must be clearly
marked on both the catalog cards and the tapes or transcripts so that the librarian
cannot bring them to a patron without noting the restrictions.

LEGAL CONSIDERATIONS

We have now reached the question of restricted use and the possibility of libel or invasion-of-privacy lawsuits. Restrictions requested by the narrator or the donor are necessarily involved in oral history. If we are going to ask narrators to give a candid account, then we must have a way to protect them or the people they discuss. We therefore offer "seal privileges"—the opportunity to close the manuscript for a specified number of years, usually until the date when it may reasonably be expected that all the participants in an event will have died. Then, too, the donor may be a researcher who is willing to donate the tapes now but would like to reserve the exclusive right to publish from them for a specified number of years. Such a stipulation is fair enough. These situations can be covered by the above-mentioned clauses on the gift forms. But what about a case involving a narrator who was very outspoken about other persons in her union and did not accept the offer of seal privileges? The library may occasionally find itself in possession of unrestricted accounts of long-forgotten tales of scandal or incompetence or sharp business practices that could be actionable as slander, libel, or invasion of privacy or could reactivate old community feuds.

Legal considerations that relate to the ownership and use of oral history tapes and transcripts are many and complex. I will skirt the issue by providing a bibliography of articles on legal considerations of oral history, none of which can provide definitive answers.

Legal problems are a danger more in principle than in practice. There seems to be a well-established conspiracy by which both interviewers and narrators seek to clothe the past in rosy hues, to people the "good old days" only with heroes and heroines, and never to say anything bad about the dead. The problem is likely to be how to get a realistic picture of the past.

But though the danger of libel suits is rather remote, there may be some danger of "social injury," especially at the local or family level. Therefore, the wise librarian will always be alert to the content of the tapes and will exercise prudence in making them available. I recommend retaining in principle the right to place library-imposed restrictions on oral history materials. This right should be exercised only in the interest of preventing social injury, never to give some preferred scholar or group priority rights on use (unless, of course, they are the producers of the tapes and the restrictions form part of the gift agreement). In practice, all libraries have a backlog of cataloging, and the prudent librarian may just shift sensitive tapes to the bottom of the cataloging priorities and may simply avoid giving them the extra publicity that brings the users in.

PUBLICIZING

While the card catalog essentially determines the retrievability of oral history materials, cards alone are not enough.

Data Bases. Oral history collections should be reported to suitable data bases. Some states have a central reporting agency for oral history: they include Alaska, Colorado, Idaho, Illinois, Louisiana, New Jersey, and Washington, with more to come. If the collection numbers ten or more transcripts, it should be reported to the Library of Congress for inclusion in the National Union Catalog of Manuscript Collections (NUCMC will not report tapes), so that it enters the mainstream of primary source retrieval.

Public Use. Beyond library channels, full use of oral history materials requires that their existence be made known to the local community of prospective users, and this could involve some hustling for publicity on the part of the librarian who has a talent for it. A printed catalog of the library's oral history holdings could be circulated among libraries and in the community. The accession of a group of oral history materials could be announced in the local newspaper, the library newsletter, local or state historical newsletters, and journals in the field of the materials. If the materials are rich in local history, the librarian might call or send a note to the elementary school curriculum adviser, to high school or junior college teachers who include local history in their courses, and to the local radio station. A list of the most topical, famous, notorious, or otherwise enticing interviews could be sent to all local broadcasting stations, with a call to the public affairs or program directors thereafter to discuss how the interviews could be incorporated into radio programs. It is this final push that can involve the library in an active way with the community (for better or for worse, depending on the limitations imposed by the workload of the library staff).

Citing Oral Histories. Oral history is very often used as a source of quotations for publication in books, journals, newspapers, museum catalogs, exhibits, and so forth. Once an interview has been cited in a publication, its uses will multiply. Future users become aware of its existence and content if the citations are clear.

Footnote and bibliography manuals do not yet give an accepted form for oral history citations. The librarian can increase access to the oral history collections by, at the time of granting permission to quote for publication, recommending a citation form. The form recommended by the Bancroft Library is as follows:

> Paul, Alice, "Conversations with Alice Paul: Woman Suffrage and the Equal Rights Amendment," typescript of an oral history conducted 1972, 1973 by Amelia Fry, Regional Oral History Office, The Bancroft Library, University of California, Berkeley, 1976, 674 pages.

Counseling: The Librarian's Role in Creating Oral Histories

Having considered the essential library functions of curating oral history—accepting, cataloging, servicing, publicizing—let us return to creating, that first step of oral history. I have described creating as "not essentially a library function." Most of us find the idea of creating something more exciting than the idea of tending it properly after it has been created.

Or is there some self-selection factor among librarians that makes "tending" an equally satisfying function? I doubt it, for over the years I have met with many librarians, and usually their chief interest lies in "getting oral history going" in their communities. To the extent that they have channeled this drive into prodding some other group to initiate a project with the advice and guidance of the library, they have been successful; and to the extent that they have tried to sandwich oral history interviewing and processing in with their own too many other duties, adding to the burdens of their own overworked clerical staffs and their own overstretched library budgets, they have been disappointed. But even if the oral history program does not emanate directly from the library (and of course, many programs do), the librarian can and must taken an active part in its creation. The degree of creative participation by the librarian will often spell the difference between excellent oral history and mere tape recordings of conversations.

The creation of well-done oral history memoirs requires a knowledge of oral history methods, of historical background, and of current research trends and findings as well as continual monitoring of feedback from users. Colleges and universities or historical societies can offer some counseling, but they, too, will depend on their institutions' librarians for materials. And in the absence of faculty guidance, the librarian may stand alone as chief consultant. Such vicarious creating I have called counseling, and it is almost as essential as curating in the role librarians must play in oral history. What sorts of counseling aids, then, can the librarian be expected to provide?

RESEARCH MATERIALS

Let us assume that an organized group is already eager to do oral history, perhaps a committee of the local historical society, and comes to the library for help. First, the library should be able to provide several different manuals on how to do oral history. The more manuals the group can see, the better. Every oral history project has different goals, different capabilities, and different situations in which to work, and access to a number of manuals will enable people to select the procedures best fitted to their needs. A full set of all the oral history manuals listed in the bibliography will cost less than a few popular hardbacks.

Next, the oral history group will need assistance in finding materials on the locality and on the persons and subjects on which the interviews will focus. A librarian could compile a list of items in the library's collection—county histories, old "mug books," a run of the local newspaper, a collection of pamphlets issued by the chamber of commerce, genealogy materials, state histories, and general American histories. Such holdings can be outlined, first, in a general way as the oral history group defines topics and starts to select narrators. Once the project is under way, the librarian can help find background material for specific interviews.

As an example of such cooperation between librarian and oral history committee, I mention the recent visit to our office of a two-woman oral history committee (one of the women was past 70 and a member of a pioneer family) and the librarian of the county public library with whom the women work. The two oral historians had in one year tape-recorded 65 old-time residents of the county, an incredible feat, considering the amount of time required to research and then to arrange appointments for one interview. They could not have accomplished the task without having worked very closely with the librarian, who assembled family history and background materials on each narrator before the interview.

In addition to specific topics, a creative librarian can recommend reading in more general fields which will broaden the oral history interview. For example, "The American Family in Past Time" by John Demos, an article published in the summer 1974 issue of the *American Scholar,* raises many questions about the actual rather than apocryphal habits, the real life, of American families. Historians are studying them using demographic methods, census studies, court records on marriage, divorce, desertion, and so forth. Oral history could produce much information about the twentieth century family if the interviewer is alerted to the pertinent questions.

THE LIBRARIAN'S ON GOING SUPERVISION

Let us assume next that the finished oral history tapes and collateral materials have been promised to the library. The librarian should immediately indicate the need for a legal release, should help the oral history committee select a suitable form from the samples in the manuals, and should have blank forms prepared. The interviewer should discuss the legal release with the narrator before the interview, and the release could be signed by the narrator at the close of the interview session. At each step the fact that the form has been, first, discussed and, second, signed will keep the narrator and the interviewer aware of the fact that the tape recording is intended for permanent retention and historical use. The reinforcement of that fact alone will help keep the interview from deteriorating into a rambling conversation, and it will also help minimize casual attacks on other members of the community, thereby reducing the possibility of libel or slander.

The librarian will also want to work with the oral history committee to devise a set of procedures for describing the interview-provenance, major subject headings, and a subject-name index to the interviews. A blank interview description form provided by the library will list interviewee and interviewer with some information on each, the project title (if this is one of a series on a particular theme), and major topics, this information to be used for subject and cross-reference cataloging. Establishing the main subject headings will require thought. They should be coordinated with subject headings used by the library for other books and materials.

The form can then provide space for an interview index, a listing of the names and subjects discussed in the order they occur on the tape. This interview index will be useful to the transcriber and the cataloger; it can also serve as a summary of the interview if the transcript is not indexed. It may, in fact, be the only guide to the interview if the oral history project is not able to prepare transcripts and users must find their information on the tape. The librarian will want to work with the committee in establishing subject entries for the index.

Developing description procedures and subject entries is a useful exercise for the oral history committee. Even more instructive to the interviewer is the experience of listening to his or her completed interview for the purpose of completing the interview description form. In preparing the list of topics covered, a task which may initially seem routine, the interviewer will be forced to assess his or her own interviewing techniques and to distill from the chatter the subject headings that are most applicable. (Listening is often a sobering experience—the most common shock is to find that one's own voice is heard a greater proportion of time than the narrator's.)

Thus the library's requirement that the forms be filled out will, in effect, force the oral history committee to listen to its own tapes and thereby to learn from them and to consider the topics on which information is being collected. The librarian should be a party to this process as the work progresses—do not wait until the project is completed. The librarian's involvement could, for example, include examination of the interview description forms to see whether the topic entries conform to the topic entries used in the library's subject catalog.

SPONSORSHIP

So far we have been assuming that an organized group is ready to commit oral history and that the librarian becomes a key adviser to that group and is eventually the recipient and curator of the collection—probably an overoptimistic assumption. More likely someone, and that someone may well be the librarian, sees the need and value of such a program and tries to organize a small number of interested persons to create an oral history program. What can the library do to aid such a group?

It is nearly impossible for a group to find any support or to establish credibility unless it has some institutional affiliation. Funding agencies regard temporary groups with suspicion. What will happen to the equipment they purchase? Will the entire project collapse half-finished if the volunteers shift their enthusiasm elsewhere? Narrators may likewise wonder what will become of their historical accounts. Who will be around to see that no one quotes from their accounts without permission?

For such an unaffiliated group, library sponsorship could mean the difference between success and failure. Sponsorship might involve use of the library's letterhead for official correspondence, a permanent address and telephone number, a cabinet in which the group's tape recorders and supplies can be stored, a definite depository for the tapes with permanent housing and staff to administer any agreements with narrators, and the continuity of one permanent, paid staff librarian. That librarian might have no other responsibility to the oral history program than that of keeping loose track of what the group is doing and of referring calls and mail to the proper group member, but such continuity is essential. With library sponsorship, the group can apply for funds from local and state agencies or from private donors. (Tax deductibility becomes important if the group seeks private funding.)

PUBLIC PRESENTATIONS

From time to time the library can provide exhibit space for the oral history group's products or facilities for a demonstration program. An annual reception held in the library on a Sunday afternoon to honor oral history narrators and their families is a splendid way to bring the younger generations into contact with the older, linking the present with the past and the library with the community—depending on the selection of narrators, perhaps a segment of the community that is unfamiliar with the library. Radio, television, or tape-slide programs produced from the oral history collection offer a means of reaching an even broader segment of the community.

Collecting Oral History from Elsewhere

The library can perform another service as well by making oral histories produced elsewhere available to its patrons, either by collecting bibliographies and catalogs of oral history collections or by acquiring copies of oral history interviews which are especially pertinent to the library's own collections or to the interests of its patrons. Many collections are available for purchase in photocopy from the originating program or on microfiche from the Microfilming Corporation of America. The question of permission to quote from such secondary holdings may arise. As with holdings of microfilm or photocopies of manuscripts, requests for permission should be referred to the original holders of the materials.

Conclusion

As I come to the end of this exhortation, I hope I have not frightened anyone away from oral history. Many tasks are involved in the proper care and feeding of oral history, and I know that most libraries are understaffed and underbudgeted, with overworked staffs. Nonetheless, oral history, even the curating and especially the counseling, can offer to the librarian the sort of community involvement and one-to-one relationships with both the older actors in their communities' ongoing history and the younger teachers and learners of that history for which he or she may have hoped when selecting librarianship as a profession. To be sure, oral history is fun, and we all need a little fun in our workday lives. And it can be personally satisfying to serve as a catalyst to the preservation of the oral literature of one's region.

Through oral history, every library in the country can hold special and unique materials especially related to the community it serves and can provide services and satisfactions to a non-book-using clientele. And every library, by careful preservation, by developing an adequate information retrieval system, and by serving as a creative agent between creator and user of oral history can play a part in the writing of this nation's history.

In closing, I would like to relate an anecdote from one of our oral memoirs. It indicates the sort of human insight that oral history can add to the cold facts of history. The speaker is Clara Shirpser, Democratic national committeewoman for California, describing a whistle-stop campaign trip with President Harry Truman in 1952. She had joined the train at Eureka, where she met Truman for the first time, and the party was then staying overnight in San Francisco:

> So early this morning there was a knock on my door, and I answered it—I think I was in the middle of eating breakfast in my room, but I was dressed. (I usually had breakfast sent up, because it was quicker, if I ordered it the night before, and I'd be ready in time.) You had to be packed and have your luggage in the lobby at a given early hour, too, so it meant getting up very early. There stood a Secret Service man, and he said, "President Truman wants to see you in his suite." Immediately I thought, "Oh, I've done something that is wrong. What have I done? The President of the United States is calling me at this hour of the morning. Something must be wrong."
>
> With some fear I walked to President Truman's suite. Mr. Truman was walking up and down, in the central room, looking agitated, and he turned to me. I said, "Good morning, Mr. President. Is something wrong?" He said, "Am I President of the United States or am I not, Mrs. Shirpser?" I said, "Well, of course you're

President of the United States, Mr. Truman." This was my first president, too, the first President of the United States whom I knew, and I was in awe of him. He said, "Would you go into Margaret's room, and would you tell her that the President of the United States says that she has been late in starting every time, every place we have been so far, and that the President of the United States says he is going to leave this room in ten minutes, whether she's ready or not." So I said, "Are you sure you want me to tell her this? She'd pay much more attention if you told her that." He said, "Like hell she would."[1]

Notes

1. Clara Shirpser, "One Woman's Role in Democratic Party Politics: National, State, and Local, 1950–1973," an oral history conducted 1972–1973 by Malca Chall, Regional Oral History Office, Bancroft Library, University of California, Berkeley, 1975, p. 174.

Bibliography

Selected Oral History Manuals

Allen, Barbara, and Lynwood Montell. *From Memory to History: Using Oral Sources in Local Historical Research.* Nashville: American Association for State and Local History, 1981.

Baum, Willa K. *Oral History for the Local Historical Society.* Nashville: American Association for State and Local History, 1974.

———*Transcribing and Editing Oral History.* Nashville: American Association for State and Local History, 1977.

Cash, Joseph, Ramon Harris, et al. *The Practice of Oral History: A Handbook.* Glen Rock, N.J.: Microfilming Corporation of America, 1975.

Cutting-Baker, Holly, et al. *Family Folklore Interviewing Guide and Questionnaire.* Washington, D.C.: U.S. Government Printing Office, 1978.

Davis, Cullom, Kathryn Buck, and Kay MacLean. *Oral History: From Tape to Type.* Chicago: American Library Association, 1977.

Deering, Maryjo. *Transcribing without Tears: A Guide to Transcribing and Editing Oral History Interviews.* Washington, D.C.: George Washington University Library, 1976.

Epstein, Ellen Robinson, and Rona Mendelsohn. *Record and Remember: Tracing Your Roots through Oral History.* Washington, D.C.: Center for Oral History, 1978.

Ericson, Stacy, comp. *A Field Notebook for Oral History.* Boise: Idaho State Historical Society, Oral History Center, 1981.

Handfield, F. Gerald. *History on Tape: A Guide for Oral History in Indiana.* Indianapolis: Indiana State Library, 1979.

Hoopes, James. *Oral History: An Introduction for Students.* Chapel Hill: University of North Carolina Press, 1979.

Ives, Edward D. *The Tape Recorded Interview: A Manual for Field Workers in Folklore and Oral History.* Knoxville: University of Tennessee Press, 1980.

Jenkins, Sara. *Past, Present: Recording Life Stories of Older People.* Washington, D.C.: St. Albans Parish, n.d. (Order from National Council on Aging, 600 Maryland Avenue, S.W., Washington, D.C. 20036)

Key, Betty McKeever. *Maryland Manual of Oral History.* Baltimore: Maryland Historical Society, 1979.

Kornbluh, Joyce, and M. Brady Mikusko, ed. *Working Womenroots: An Oral History Primer.* Detroit: University of Michigan-Wayne State University, Institute of Labor and Industrial Relations, Program on Women and Work, 1979.

Lance, David. *An Archives Approach to Oral History.* London: Imperial War Museum, and the International Association of Sound Archives, 1978. (See chapter 10 of the present volume.)

Moss, William W. *Oral History Program Manual.* New York: Praeger, 1974. (See chapter 7 of the present volume.)

Neuenschwander, John A. *Oral History as a Teaching Approach.* Washington, D.C.: National Education Association, 1975.

Oblinger, Carl. *Interviewing the People of Pennsylvania: A Conceptual Guide to Oral History.* Harrisburg: Pennsylvania Historical and Museum Commission, 1978.

Shopes, Linda. "Using Oral History for a Family History Project." Technical Leaflet 123. Nashville: American Association for State and Local History, 1980. (See chapter 18 of the present volume.)

Shumway, Gary L., and William G. Hartley. *An Oral History Primer.* Salt Lake City: Primer Publications, 1973.

Whistler, Nancy. *Oral History Workshop Guide.* Denver: Denver Public Library, Colorado Center for Oral History, 1979.

Selected Works Addressing Legal Considerations

Eustis, Truman W. "Getting It in Writing: Oral History and the Law." *Oral History Review* 4 (1976), pp. 6–18.

Hamilton, Douglas E. "Oral History and the Law of Libel." In *The Second National Colloquium on Oral History,* ed. Louis M. Starr. New York: Oral History Association, 1968. (See pp. 41–56.)

Horn, David E. *Copyright, Literary Rights, and Ownership: A Guide for Archivists.* Indianapolis: Society of Indianapolis Archivists, 1978.

Moss, William W. *Oral History Program Manual.* New York: Praeger, 1974. (Discusses legal considerations on pp. 14–18, 55–57,104–107.) (See chapter 7 of the present volume.)

Neuenschwander, John. *Oral History and the Law.* Oral History Association, 1994, Second Edition.

Romney, Joseph. "Legal Considerations in Oral History." *Oral History Review* 3 (1975), pp. 66–76.

————"Oral History: Law and Libraries." *Drexel Library Quarterly* 15 (October 1979), pp. 34–49.

Society of American Archivists. *Forms Manual.* Chicago, 1973. (Contains sample legal agreements.)

Welch, Mason. "A Lawyer Looks at Oral History." In *The Fourth National Colloquium on Oral History,* ed. Gould P. Colman. New York: Oral History Association, 1970. (See pp. 182–95.)

Selected Works on Oral History and Libraries

Baum, Willa K. "Building Community Identity through Oral History—A New Role for the Local Library." *California Librarian* 31 (October 1970), pp. 271–84.

Catholic Library World 47 (October 1975).

Cullom Davis. "Tapeworms and Bookworms—Oral History in the Library," pp. 102–103.

Sister John Christine Wolkerstorfer. "Oral History—A New Look at Local History," pp. 104–107.

Betty McKeever Key. "Telling It Like It Was in 1968," pp. 106–109.

John W. Orton. "Oral History and the Genealogical Society," pp. 110–12.

Willa Baum. "The Librarian as Guardian of Oral History Materials: An Example from Berkeley," pp. 112–17.

William W. Moss. "Oral History: A New Role for the Library," pp. 118–19.

Drexel Library Quarterly 15 (October 1979). Ed. M. Patricia Freeman. Issue on "Managing Oral History Collections in the Library."

Carroll Hart. "The New Documentation: Oral History and Photography," pp. 1–11.

Mary Jo Pugh. "Oral History in the Library: Levels of Commitment," pp. 12–28.

F. Gerald Handfield, Jr. "The Importance of Video History in Libraries," pp. 29–34.

Ernest J. Dick. "Selection and Preservation of Oral History Interviews, " pp. 35–38.

Joseph B. Romney. "Oral History, Law, and Libraries," pp. 39–49.

Peggy Ann Kusnerz. "Oral History: A Selective Bibliography," pp. 50–75.

Dale E. Treleven. "A Brief Description of the TAPE System" [alternative to transcribing tapes], pp. 76–81.

Filipelli, R. L. "Oral History and the Archives." *American Archivist* 39 (October 1976), pp. 479–83.

Horn, David E. *Copyright, Literary Rights, and Ownership: A Guide for Archivists.* Indianapolis: Society of Indianapolis Archivists, 1978.

Key, Betty McKeever. "Oral History in the Library." *Catholic Library World* 49 (April 1978), pp. 380–84.

Lance, David. *An Archive Approach to Oral History.* London: Imperial War Museum and the International Association of Sound Archives, 1978. (See chapter 10 of the present volume.)

McWilliams, Jerry. *The Preservation and Restoration of Sound Recordings.* Nashville: American Association for State and Local History, 1980.

Morrissey, Charles T. "Oral History: More than Tapes Spinning." *Library Journal* 105 (April 15, 1980), pp. 932–33.

O'Hanlon, Sister Elizabeth. "Oral History and the Library." *Catholic Library* World 51 (July-August 1979), pp. 26–28.

Pfaff, Eugene, Jr. "Oral History: A New Challenge for Public Libraries." *Wilson Library Bulletin* 54 (May 1980), pp. 568–71.

Society of American Archivists. *Forms Manual.* Chicago, 1973.

Stewart, John F., and the Committee on Oral History of the Society of American Archivists. "Oral History and Archivists: Some Questions to Ask." *American Archivist* 36 (1973), pp. 361–65.

Zachert, Martha Jane K. "The Implications of Oral History for Librarians." *College and Research Libraries* 29 (March 1968), pp. 101–103.

Directories, Collection Guides, and Bibliographies

Cook, Patsy A., ed. *Directory of Oral History Programs in the United States.* Sanford, N.C.: Microfilming Corporation of America, 1982.

Fox, John. "Bibliographic Update." In *Oral History Review* (1977).

Mason, Elizabeth, and Louis M. Starr. *The Oral History Collection of Columbia University.* New York: Oral History Research Office, 1979.

Meckler, Alan M., and Ruth Mullin, eds. *Oral History Collections.* New York: Bowker, 1975.

New York Times. Oral History Program. *Columbia University Collection.* New York: New York Times, Library Information Services Division, 1972.

Oral History Guide No. 1. Glen Rock, N.J.: Microfilming Corporation of America, 1976.

Oral History Guide No. 2. Sanford, N.C.: Microfilming Corporation of America, 1979,

Oral History Guide No. 3. Sanford, N.C.: Microfilming Corporation of America, 1983.
(The New York Times Oral History Program guides list oral histories available on microfiche and microfilm from oral history offices nationwide.)

Riess, Suzanne, and Willa K. Baum, eds. *Catalogue of the Regional Oral History Office, 1954–1979.* Berkeley: University of California, Berkeley, Bancroft Library, 1980.

Shumway, Gary L. *Oral History in the United States: A Directory.* New York: Oral History Association, 1971.

Stenberg, Henry G. "Selected Bibliography, 1977–1981." *Oral History Review* 10 (1982), pp. 119–32.

Waserman, Manfred, comp. *Bibliography on Oral History.* Oral History Association, 1975.

PART FIVE

Oral History
and Regional Studies

26

Oral History in
Mexico and the Caribbean

Eugenia Meyer

This survey, by one of Latin America's most prominent oral historians, reminds us that in her context, the instinct to tell a story is very similar to that which creates history. Meyer surveys oral historical resources in Mexico, where she teaches, but also recent conferences and activities throughout the Americas and the Caribbean. She finds two primary directions in the 1990s: the preparation of books based on oral testimony, ranging from history of cinema to that of small communities; and museology and other public programs where oral historical content communicates history for public access. Throughout these tendencies, the orientation in Latin America has been away from interviewing social elites in favor of incorporating the testimony of the disinherited. Meyer's essay reminds us of the increasingly international context of oral history— pan-American, pan-Caribbean—which the editors of this volume hope to stimulate.

Professor Meyer teaches oral history at UNAM in Mexico City and works there with the National Council for Culture and the Arts; she is the author and editor of several book-length studies of Mexican history, including the classic, Historical Understanding of the Mexican Revolution of 1910 *(1970) and* Mexico: An Open Book *(1992).*

This article originally appeared in a special issue of Bios (1990). Used by permission of editor and author.

*F*or our peoples, the testimonial rescue runs parallel to our histories—whether by means of the oral tradition which Prehispanic cultures preserved from generation to generation until our days, reminding us of the magic magnitude of our inherited past; or whether due to the commendable and untiring task of the conquest chroniclers who, beginning with Fray Bernadino de Sahagun, in the territory that today is Mexico, took upon themselves to write about and understand the natives. From that former inheritance which has gone through the Spanish colonial effort (seventeenth and nineteenth centuries) of memoirs, diaries, and volumes of letters, right at the end of the twentieth century a need reaches our times: a need to rescue and preserve experiences, both of the mind and of the expression of daily happening which, put into tape and eventually transcribed, strengthens and consolidates our sense of belonging and identity.

As happened in the past with oral tradition, the concern of Latin American and Caribbean oral history seems to center on the scope of that which is social. This is because it rescues that which is the everyday thing, the transcendental, the historical fact expressed by word of mouth, in the style of its various protagonists—the very universe that builds diverse histories, finally integrating them into only one, in which its makers, plain men and women, are recognized.

It is worth insisting that from a methodological perspective, the social scientists, on reconstructing our two Americas' history, have not limited themselves to traditional materials and documents, but have resorted also to the testimony obtained through interviews, surveys, questionnaires, life histories after the style of anthropological works or, more formally, through oral history. At times the social scientists have looked for the unknown, or have corroborated already-known information. They have verified or amended history when weaving the yarn of the social process, beginning with those who have lived, known, or meditated over them.

Perhaps oral history development in our part of the North American continent is more identified with that which is performed by the Europeans (Italians and English), who clearly tend to channel the rescue of life histories toward the purpose of writing social history.

Paradoxically, we did not echo that which is nearer to us, and that to whose influence we should supposedly be more susceptible—that of the United States of America. It is in an oral history—which may be more mechanistic, more utilitarian, more on the road to the creation, preservation, and accumulation of testimonial archives—that an interviewer's know-how acquires outstanding dimensions. From a bird's eye view, we can observe in the works carried out in the United States trends that fluctuate between projects on eminent political figures and the rescue of personal experiences of minority communities: Blacks, Hispanics, Jews, Poles, and many others. On countless occasions, the interview becomes an end in itself, perhaps part of a larger project to repose in some foundation or presidential library or university files.

A truly multinational effort to modernize the ancient custom of the chroniclers was generated in the 1960s, and it is possible that Mexico may have been the pioneer country, although not the only one.[1] Groups and institutions there propounded the use of oral history as central to the task of the social sciences. It was not easy to penetrate fields that had been almost taken over by the anthropologists.

It took the oral history interview a long time to become understood, respected, and taken full advantage of. Today it is commonplace in courses, seminars, projects, and institutions, testifying to what we insisted upon defining as a methodology and not a mere technique. It deals with one element, a cultural output that may help analysis and interpretation.[2]

Likewise, and probably due first to the nature of our Latin American realities, then to the comings and goings of "caudillos," the military coups, the dictatorships, and the constant violation of human rights, finally the work and products of oral history acquire a fundamental dimension—that of "the great denouncer." There are many untold or destroyed histories that must be told and reconstructed of so many Latin American peoples, committed to democracy and social justice, whose recollections must not be forgotten in the distortions of political history.

Also, each one of our countries has a different and unique past to be preserved; undoubtedly the peculiarities of the oral history of Latin America are due to these.

We have pointed out Mexico's pioneering efforts in the 1960s, besides those accomplished here by North Americans such as the well-known Oscar Lewis. Mexico in 1972 organized the first formal project with the "Archivo de la Palabra" of the Instituto Nacional de Antropologia e Historia. Systematically, work was begun on the revolutionaries of 1910, on the development of public education (emphasizing the experiment of the socialist education of the 1930s), on the growth of the film industry; also on the history of medicine, of the Spanish refugees, and on regional history projects in the Northwest, the West, and the Southeast.[3]

After some time, those who founded the "Archivo de la Palabra" began to question and formulate thoughts of methodological order. They initiated seminars. They stimulated a real flow of private and institutional projects: worker's movement history, farmers' struggles, indigenous uprisings, religious movements, regional development, oil workers, fishermen, electricity workers, urban movements, and so on.

One might conclude that oral history is common practice and an essential instrument in all social science work in Mexico. There is not enough space here to reference the enormous quantity of publications that are the product of oral history—articles, essays, books—whether by using the transcriptions *per se*, or by integrating them in analytical and interpretative forms—but above all, as a way of rescuing and reappraising them in the popular mind. It is in this last possibility that even today one mines the most important vein. There is a resurgence of interest in the everyday event—the ordinary, the processes facing the ancient elitist trends, more concerned with political history and the remembrances of events.

But beyond its academic scope, oral history has a popular function with two fundamental streams. On the one hand, it is the production of testimonial books such as those of Elena Poniatowska: *La noche de Tlatelolco* and *Hasta no verte Jesús mío*.[4] And on the other hand, social history series such as *Testimonios para la historia del cine mexicano*[5] and that of *Palabras del exilio: Contribución a la historia de los refugiados españoles en México*.[6] Oral history provides fundamental matter for the assemblage of historical museums, assuming they must "communicate." The information provided in the interviews of oral history has significantly served in the reconstructions of historical processes and in the illustration of life styles from different times and circumstances.[7]

The beginning of the discipline in the academic field was difficult and had multiple slip-ups as historians faced and confronted the traditional orthodoxy of universities and research centers. Perhaps from this confrontation comes the interest that was soon manifested by other countries, with the consequent intellectual exchange, the proliferation of methodology seminars, and the emergence of countless institutional and private projects.

After two workshops, one in Brazil and another one in Venezuela in 1976 and 1977 respectively, we started to gather materials for a project catalogue of oral history in Latin America and the Caribbean that, with the sponsorship of UNESCO, it was possible to bring to completion in 1984.[8]

This first listing gives an account of the work accomplished in Argentina, Bolivia, Brazil, Cuba, Guatemala, Mexico, Nicaragua, Peru, Puerto Rico, and Venezuela; also, mention is made of the worlds of "Chicanos" and those of North Americans in Latin America. This forerunner effort has already been overtaken by an enormous number of new works from the abovementioned countries and from Costa Rica, Colombia, Uruguay, Chile, El Salvador, and Honduras.

The trend markedly inclined toward the disinherited, toward the marginal populations in the rural areas and the cities except in cases like that of Brazil where Aspasia Camargo[9] and her team have carried out a project on political elites. Consequently, oral history identifies itself, to a great extent, as an instrument of social struggle—such as in the case of Puerto Rico, where one must take into account the ingredients of separatism and nationalism, as well as in Nicaragua, where the project of oral history ran parallel to the literacy campaign, soon after the Sandinista triumph. Likewise in Cuba, where, besides various official projects, competences and prizes have been established, such as the international one for the testimony of the "Casa de las Américas." The resulting oral history literature travels roads that go from the *Biografía del cimarrón*[10] by Cuban Miguel Barnet, passing through the works of the Venezuelan Agustín Blanco Munoz on political movements,[11] continuing through the stimulating medley of texts and images of the Argentinians Elizabeth Jelin, Pablo Vila, and Alicia D'Amico[12] in their analysis of the populous urban sectors of Argentina. Also we must consider the first results of the Nicaraguan effort in its Instituto de Estudio des Sandinismo ("y se armó la runga. . . !")[13] until reaching the studies on exiled Latin Americans such as the Brazilians and Uruguayans. In brief, the work of oral history has provided a large group of testimonies that in fact constitute the essence of the historical study of our times.[14]

In countries such as Mexico, Brazil, and Costa Rica,[15] journals, seminar proceedings, and articles have been produced that tend to direct and enrich a particular bibliography on oral history. Most significant is the effort put forth by the Mexican journal *Secuencia*[16] as well as that of the UNESCO regional office of culture for Latin America and the Caribbean with headquarters in Havana, Cuba, which has edited *Oralidad*,[17] in which articles appear of Venezuelan, Jamaican, Puerto Rican, Cuban, Guatemalan, Peruvian, and Colombian authors.

In the fall of 1988, Mexico hosted the Primer Encuentro de Historiadores Orales de América Latina y Espana (First encounter of oral historians from Latin America and Spain), as the result of the Spanish-speaking participants' collective concern, expressed at the international meeting in Oxford in 1987, of having their own forum. Entitled De cara a la historia popular[18] (Facing popular history), the Encuentro held three simultaneous sessions: "Fuentes orales e historia popular" (Oral sources and popular history), "De la gente sin historia" (Of people without history), and "Metodología y pràctica de la historia oral" (Oral history methods and practice). About 150 researchers attended from 11 countries and 1 commonwealth—Argentina, Brazil, Costa Rica, Cuba, Spain, United States, Guatemala, Japan, Monaco, Venezuela, Uruguay, and Puerto Rico. Papers were presented in the "Fuentes orales e historia popular" session on different topics, providing a sampling of the diverse interests of Latin social scientists in oral testimony. Their analyses allowed for reaching consensus, created controversy, and also left doubts open for discussion.

The participants concluded that oral history is both source and method for learning the point of view of the actors of history in their ethnic, cultural, and linguistic diversity. This is because the channels of expression available to the marginal groups, the "people without history," are fundamentally oral. Therefore, saving them in testimonial form avoids the irreparable loss of such information and, at the same time, humanizes history, making it alive, social, and dynamic.

There was talk, too, about the interrelation between oral sources and written ones, which complement each other and allow for the scientific usage of testimonies through dialogue between the two sources, in which one creates richness and the other reveals its inadequacies.

For the most part, the papers in this session presented concrete results of oral history chores, which permit giving their history back to the people. There was talk, for example, of establishing a program on agrarian history and popular education; on oral sources linked to the creation of a new type of dynamic museum; of popular education and concientization [in the tradition of Paulo Friere], which involves society in the rescue and conservation of its cultural patrimony. Other papers dealt with the production of documentaries on different agrarian struggles and their diffusion through video-testimony; the kinds of documents that gather the social experience of different areas, when the only source isoral testimony; and the types of illiterate peoples' literature, concretely in the case of Chiapas' tzotzil groups, who "learned to read by learning to write books." In general, at the sessions there grew a concern for making a *means* and not an *end* of oral history, for making it become a valuable mechanism within its wider applications that respond to the needs of popular history. In the four panels that integrated the sessions "De la gente sin historia," the fundamental topics were: *minorities* (Puerto Ricans in Boston, Jews in Mexico City, and indigenous groups in Mexico); *women* (of diverse occupation and class—farmers, homemakers, professionals, upperclass, middle-class, lower-class); *workers* of different nationalities (Brazilians, Uruguayans, Mexicans), of different trades (textiles, rubber, mining, meat workers); and finally *the popular imagination*, that is, the oral tradition in Veracruz, Yucatan, and the "cristera" zone.

Gaps that had been forgotten by traditional historiography were covered. The resource of oral history allowed for the listing of the Chiapas indigenous voices that told of the "pain of poverty," or the voice of the Guanajuato miner who gathered courage to go down into the mine by getting himself drunk, or that of the women of the revolutionaries of Morelos, disdained by their spouses who learned that, during their absence, their wives had been raped.

Many matters surfaced that referred to the daily life of man and society, in the family, at work, in the neighborhood, at school, in recreation, in union activities, in times of health and in times of illness, in revolutionary times and in peacetime. In short, oral history placed us in direct contact with individuals and social sectors that had been ignored for a long time. At the same time, it gave "flesh and blood" to a history that can be rigid, cardboard-stiff and—let's say it—boring. Problems were discussed to which, at the moment, no definite solution could be found. One was what to do so as not to propagate or reinforce the speeches or attitudes of the dominating groups. Another was related to the difference between tradition and oral history; there was discussion on whether one term incorporates the other one, and whether each one has different themes and objectives. The last problem was in relation to the aim of oral history: Is it done for pleasure? For rescuing the unknown? For giving facts another approach? For giving known figures a new color? For helping with the democratization of a group or society? Perhaps it deals with all the preceding, but it also clarifies and understands past events. The "hidden" makers of history may thus acquire conscience of their reality and improve it. Thus they stop being "the people without history" or, better yet, as was suggested at the end of the debate, the "people without authenticity."

Several general conclusions were reached in the third session "Metodología y pràctica de la historia oral." Oral history can be established in all population sectors, beginning with the illiterate and ending with the elites: intellectuals, politicians, businesspeople, university folk. It was shown how oral history can be applied to social groups or specific individuals, and what limitations, failures, or successes it may present. The importance of topic selection was pointed out, and it was noted that there were very different economic, social, and political aspects, whose common denominator is the eagerness to rebuild the past, beginning with its very protagonists. Also, the significance of the questionnaire used to carry out the oral history interviews was touched upon, and discussion followed on how to formulate it better so that, without being rigid, it may make allowance for guiding the interviewee. It was considered that, though oral testimony has an intrinsic value, it must face, analyze, compare, and criticize itself against other written or oral sources so that it can acquire a new magnitude. Last, theoretical aspects emerged; for example, the relation between oral history and other disciplines, or the uses and abuses that have been made of oral history.

Perhaps the struggle to obtain a place and a space for oral history has been won in other countries. Yet because of the very verbal nature of our peoples, the idea of rescuing, safeguarding, and conserving oral testimony becomes, as a last resort, a task of strengthening a historical memory which, in spite of circumstances, catastrophes, and myths, remains present at all times, in all circumstances.

Notes

1. Eugenia Meyer, "Oral History in Mexico and Latin America," *Oral History Review* (New York: Oral History Association, July 1965). "Oral History in Latin America," *International Journal of Oral History* 1:1 (Connecticut: Meckler Publishing, 1980).

2. Eugenia Meyer, "Communicación y liberación tareas de la historia," *Revista Santiago* 52 (Santiago, Cuba: December 1983), pp. 6167.

3. See *Catálogo del Archivo de la Palabra* (México: Instituto Nacional de Antropologia e Historia, Instituto de Investigaciones Dr. José María Luis Mora).

4. Elena Paniatowska, *La noche de Tlatelolco* (México: Ediciones Era, 1971). *Hasta no verte Jesús mío* (México: Ediciones Era, 1978).

5. Eugenia Meyer, et al. "Testimonios para la historia del cine mexicano" (México: Instituto Nacional de Antropologia e Historia, Direción General de Cinematografía, 1975–1976, Cuadernos de la Cineteca, vols. I–VII).

6. María Soledad Alonso, et al., *Palabras del Exilio: Contribución a la historia de los refugiados en México* (México: Instituto Nacional de Antropologia e Historia, Secretaría de Educación Pública, Librería Madero, [4 vols.], 1980, 1982, 1985, 1988).

7. Eugenia Meyer, ed., *La lucha obrera en Cananea, 1906* (México: Secretaría de Educación Pública, Instituto National de Antropologia e Historia, 1980). *Museo histórico de la Revolución en el estado de Chihuahua* (México: Secretaría de la Defensa Nacional, Secretaría de Educación Pública, Instituto Nacional de Antropologia e Historia, 1982). *Y nos fuimos a la Revolución* (Mexico: Departamento des Distrito Federal, Instituto de Investigaciones Dr. José María Luis Mora, 1985).

8. See Eugenia Meyer and Ximena Sepúlveda, *Catàlogos de Proyectos de historia Oral en América Latina y el Caribe* (México: Instituto de Investigaciones Dr. José María Luis Mora, 1988) (manuscrito).

9. See *Programa de Historia Oral. Catàlogo de Departamentos, Centro de Pesquisa e Documentacao de História Contemporanea de Brasil* (Instituto de Directo Publico e Ciencia Política Fundacao Getulio Vargas, Editora Fundacao Getulio Vargas, 1981).

10. Miguel Barnet, *Biografía de un Cimarrón* (México: Siglo XXI, 1974).

11. Agustín Blanco Munoz, *La lucha armada; hablan 5 jefes* (Caracas: Universidad de Venezuela, Expediente, 1980). *La Conspiración Cívico Militar, Habla el "Guairazo," "Barcelonazo," "Caruparuzo y Portenazo"* (Caracas: Universidad Central de Venezuela, Expediente, 1981).

12. Elizabeth Jelín et al., *Podría ser yo: Los sectores populares urbanos en imagen y palabra* (Buenos Aires: Ediciones de la Flor, SRL, CEDES, 1987).

13. Instituto de Estudio del Sandinismo, *Y se armó la runga . . . ! Testimonios de la iresurrección Popular Sandinista en Masaya* (Nicaragua: Editorial Nueva Nuropea, 1982).

14. Elizabeth Burgos Debray, *Mi nombre es Rigoberta Menchu* (México: Siglo XXI, Editores 1983). Albertina de Olivera, Costa, et al., *Memorias do exílio, Depoimentos* vol. II (Rio de Janeiro: Paz e Terra, 1980). Ana Gutiérrez, *Se necesita muchacha* (México: Fondo de Cultura Económica, 1983). Hugo Neira Samarez, *Huillca, habla un campesino peruano* (Havana: Premio Testimonio Casa de las Américas, 1979).

15. See Juan Rafael Quesada Camacho, ed., *Primer Seminario de Tradición e historia Oral* (San José, Costa Rica: Universidad de Costa Rica, 1988).

16. See Eva Salgado, *Fragmentos de historia popular, Seminario: Revista Americana de Ciencias Sociales* vols. 2, 3, 4 (Mexico: Instituto de Investigaciones Dr. José María Luis Mora, 1985).

17. *Oralidad, Anuario para el Rescate de la tradición oral de América Latina* (Havana: ORCALC, 1988).

18. All the first encounter materials can be found for consultation at the Biblioteca del Instituto de Investigaciones Dr. José María Luis Mora, México. ⌇

27

The Development
of Oral History in Britain

Paul Thompson

*Next, Paul Thompson's survey of the oral history movement in Britain (through the
1980s) provides a useful overview of trends in which he himself has played a significant
role. Thompson traces the prehistory of oral history in Britain and documents how oral
sources lost their prominence and privilege in the work of historians in the last two centuries. Only in 1988 did Oxford University incorporate oral history into its degree
course in historical methodology.*

*Starting in the 1960s, the interdisciplinarity of newly established universities in Brit-
ain fostered a collaboration between sociology, history, folklore, and cultural studies.
Out of this conjunction have come new applications for oral history in Britain: in health
(particularly reminiscence therapy); in primary education; in labor and local history
groups; in community theater; and in broadcasting. Thompson discerns three notable
directions of the contemporary oral history movement in his country: in promoting
working-class consciousness; in revitalizing the community history of urban and immigrant communities; and in promoting a deeper understanding of family and work environments.*

*Paul Thompson is the founder and director of the National Life Story Collection at
the National Sound Archives. A Professor of Sociology at Essex University, through
whose influential seminars many British oral historians have passed, he is the author of a
half-dozen volumes, including* The Voice of the Past: Oral History *(1978, 1988) and a
volume on the transition in oral history from objective to subjective perspectives,* The
Myths We Live By *(1990) (with Raphael Samuel). He also has written widely on British
history, including* The Edwardians *(1975) and* I Don't Feel Old: Later Life Then and
Now *(1992). He organized the first International Oral History conference in 1992.*

This article originally appeared in *Bios* (1990) in Germany. Used by permission of the editor
and author.

Oral History in Britain, as in other European countries, has a long prehistory. The earliest British historians drew extensively on oral traditions, and even those like Bede whose *History of the English Church and People* of the Early Eighth Century was notable for his use of written records, were surest of evidence from direct witness. This high valuation of oral testimony, at least for recent history, continued into the eighteenth century, when we find the first explicit mention of oral history. The context of this is interesting because, in contrast to the contemporary situation of distinctive and often antagonistic disciplines, during the age of Enlightenment history and social science were not seen as separate but advanced hand in hand. Historians interpreted a continuous past which culminated in the present, while the founder of modern economic theory, Adam Smith, combined history and theory in his classic writing. Especially in Scotland there was a group of scholars who were at the same time philosophers, historians, anthropologists, and sociologists: besides Smith, there were David Hume, John Miller, William Robertson, and others. And it was with this group that the first mention of oral history in Britain occurs. In 1773 the famous Londoner Samuel Johnson (author of the *Dictionary*) found himself in Edinburgh on his return from a journey to the Scottish islands in search of a primitive culture. His biographer, James Boswell, has described (*Journal of a Tour of the Hebredes*, 1785, pages 45–46) how while he was breakfasting with Robertson, and discussing the 1745 rebellion of the Jacobites, Johnson said that this would be the moment to collect memories of the rebellion because those who had participated were now dying, but many of them were now willing to talk reflectively. He recommended the example of Voltaire in collecting evidence in this way. "You are to consider," he declared, "all history was at first oral."

Unfortunately during the nineteenth century the situation was radically changed by the development of separate specialist disciplines, above all because each chose a particular method as its hallmark: historians the document, sociologists the interview, and anthropologists the field journey to a distant territory—as Johnson had been making. At the same time the focus of history shifted backward to the more distant medieval past. It therefore became impossible for both reasons for historians to use interviews. There were only a few exceptions, for example in political biography, to a lesser extent in local history, and most notably with the rise of labour history. It is significant that the pioneers of British labour history, Sidney and Beatrice Webb, were not academic historians, but active sociologists who were engaged in politics, also founders of social science in Britain. In writing the first major history of British trade unionism they combined the use of documents with interviews throughout Britain, which now constitute a major historical archive.

It was only following the Second World War that the situation changed. Although Britain did not experience a military occupation or a resistance, so that documentary sources for the war period itself are adequate, it was followed by radical social and political changes. The first was the liberation of the colonial countries. Here English historians had until then written historical accounts in terms of the story of colonisation and subsequent administration by the British. They now found the need to construct a history of the indigenous people; and although the collecting of oral traditions had begun earlier, it was only at this point that they became extensively used for historical research. This tardiness in recognizing their value partly reflects the lack of strong oral traditions in England itself; the absence of peasant regions in which important traditions of popular culture and folk-lore could be maintained. These have only survived extensively in the Scottish north and west, in Wales, and in Northern Ireland, and despite the recording activities of the School of Scottish Studies and elsewhere they have been neglected by historians. Also—perhaps as an imperial nation—the English have tended to take their own popular culture for granted. Certainly the systematic use of oral traditions by historians only begins in the post-war period, which saw the translation of Jan Vansina's *Oral Tradition* (1965) and subsequently, in close contact with him, the development of an increasingly sophisticated Anglo-American school developing the use of oral sources for the history of Africa. (Recent notable British contributors include Beinart, Lamphear, Roberts and Willis.)

The second change, the 1945 electoral victory of the Labour Party which brought a new presence of the labour movement at the centre of power, made a profound and widespread impression. Radio, the press, and later television began to take a much greater interest in ordinary working-class life and increasingly to use life-story interviews as part of this. At the same time there was a shift in the character of published autobiography. This had developed exceptionally early in England and had already become a popular form of book during the 19th century, growing with the labour movement; but after the war the typical theme shifted from the labour movement leader, or perhaps that of a picturesque underdog, to serious autobiographies of ordinary workers including women domestic servants. A parallel influence can be seen in the academic world. It began within sociology, which had earlier studied the working-class primarily in terms of problems such as poverty and health, but now investigated ordinary working-class culture in, for example, the work of Jackson and Marsden, using sensitive in-depth interviewing (*Education and the Working Class*, 1962) the London studies at Bethnal Green by the Institute of Community Studies (Michael Young and Peter Wilmott, *Family and Kinship in East London*, 1957) and Richard Hoggart's exceptional early study of working-class oral culture (*The Uses of Literacy*, 1957). This influence reached history with *The Making of the English Working Class* (1963) by E.P. Thompson. Although focusing on the early 19th century,

Thompson in his introduction announces that his purpose is "to rescue the poor stockinger, the Luddite cropper, the obsolete hand-loom weaver, the Utopian artisan, and even the deluded failure of Joanna Southcott from the enormous condescension of posterity," seeing their ideas instead as "valued in terms of their own experience" (pages 12–13): almost a call for oral history.

Nevertheless a formidable obstruction remained to impede the revival of the historical use of oral sources: the gap between academic disciplines. Historians remained very suspicious of sociological concepts, and rarely interested themselves in contemporary history, while sociologists had concentrated almost exclusively on investigations of present-day society. During the 1960s a group of new universities—including Essex and Lancaster, to be the two most persistent centres of academic oral history research—were founded in which the barriers between the disciplines were less strong than in the older universities: indeed, on the contrary, interdisciplinary courses were strongly encouraged. This rapprochement undoubtedly provided a crucial stimulus through mutual exchange. In the social sciences we have seen the growth of a strong new interest in studying the past, while among historians a much more sympathetic acceptance of aspects of the theories and methods of the social sciences, including particularly those of anthropology, statistical analysis, and the interview. The gap undoubtedly remains, however, partly because neither historians nor social scientists have concentrated on the recent past; so that there is a continuing lack of studies from both fields in the last 50 years—that is to say, the prime period of living memory.

Oral history, therefore, in itself has provided an important bridge between the two disciplines: a stimulating if not always comfortable position. Formal academic support remains relatively reluctant. On the one hand, sociologists such as Ken Plummer who undertake oral history work are likely to define themselves in terms of "life stories" rather than oral history, and the funding of such qualitative studies remains notoriously less generous than those for conventionally quantitative survey work. On the other hand, historians have only slowly begun to incorporate the oral history methodology in their teaching: for example, it was finally introduced to the Oxford degree course only in 1988. There has been a similar official tardiness in the response of archives. Most archivists remain uncomfortable with nondocumentary sources. The lead here was taken early by the Imperial War Museum, but it is only during the last few years that principal county archives such as the Essex Record Office have set up oral history sections. Worse still, no serious attempt was made by the National Sound Archive to establish an oral history collection until the National Life Story Collection was started through my initiative in 1988. We have now set about remedying this deficiency and establishing a collection which ranges from leaders of national life to ordinary men and women.

It is partly because of this official neglect that oral history has made its most striking contributions in Britain through community work. These took various forms. The most recent and in many ways most important has been the use of oral history in reminiscence therapy. Following the pioneering work of Joanna Bornat (at Help the Aged, and as an editor of *Oral History*), during the 1980s there has been a strong and growing movement among social workers and health professionals working with older people for the use of memories of the past in group work. Stimulated by tape recordings, music, photographs, and slides, chosen from the period of their childhood and youth and concentrating on themes such as work, the family, or leisure, group discussions sharing memories can rekindle the spirit and restore an active interest in life to older people who have given up hope. Remarkable results have been observed: mute old people, for example, begin to talk; and often in each group a new spirit is generated, an opening of communication through the discovery of mutual interest. The method has been already adopted in over 1,000 centres, including not only old people's day centres and residential homes but also geriatric hospital wards.

Another area of community work with great potential is the school, but British work here has been less noteworthy. Although there has been excellent work with pupils of 8 to 12 years, stimulated in particular through the work of Sallie Purkis, the subsequent rigidity of the examination system has made work with older pupils difficult. Nothing in Britain has emerged to compare with the remarkable work of Eliot Wigginton's *Foxfire* project in the United States, which has so successfully stimulated older pupils on an interdisciplinary basis through focusing on the publication of a school journal. Nor has there been any notable group work at the graduate level: oral history research here remains an individual choice.

There has been some oral history work with trade unions, of which the most notable has been at the South Wales Miners Library in Swansea, but a much more successful link with working-class life stories at a community level has resulted from the availability until recently of government funds for community work for the unemployed. In these community projects young people have been taught to interview, transcribe, catalogue, and edit at the same time as writing community histories. The leading example here was Manchester Studies, directed by Bill Williams from the city's polytechnic, which developed a long series of projects collecting both oral recordings and photographs, which were used for local exhibitions as well as to build up a permanent archives. Another notable regional instance has been the Bradford Heritage Recording Unit (founded by Rob Perks, now Curator in Oral History at the National Sound Archive and active in the Oral History Society); and in Scotland the Dundee Oral History project. In London the Greater London Council for some years (until its own abolition by the Government) supported a major exhibition where up to 90 local history projects were shown in the Royal Festival Hall visited by 10,000 people of all ages. Often such community history programmes have included a musical dimension. Thus at Coventry the local museum held an exhibition on "Jazz in the 1930s," not only using retrospective interviews, but creating a living exhibition: staged in a room decorated in pink and green, three times weekly an elderly jazz band played music of the period to coach-loads of old citizens who came to talk, dance, and drink a cup of tea. It is very unfortunate that the abolition of the community programme in 1990 has suddenly brought to an end what has been in many ways the liveliest aspect of British oral history in recent years.

Another important area has been radio and television work, in which many excellent programmes continue to be based on oral history interviews, whether consciously or not. One successful television series on the Spanish Civil War was inspired by Ronald Fraser's book *Blood of Spain* (1979). A particularly popular series, "The Making of Modern London," was directed by Stephen Humphries, then Secretary of the Oral History Society, which ran for four years in the mid-1980s. It was combined with a competition for oral history project work which brought in many interesting entries, from groups of old people, schools, and individuals. In 1989, the National Life Story Collection collaborated with BBC radio in an oral history course which again leads to a competition. Unfortunately such experiments in the wide-spread involvement of popular interests through the media have been rare in Britain. We do not have a cultural tradition like that of autobiographical competitions in Poland, nor the linking of programmes with study circles as in the Scandinavian countries.

Another more original type of British community work has been reminiscence theatre. There have been a considerable number of theatre groups using life story material as the basis for dramatic productions, most notably by Elyse Dodgson of the Royal Court Young People's Theatre and Pam Schweizer of the Age Exchange Theatre, both in London. This type of work undoubtedly has great power to engage an audience. One of the best-known oral history books in Britain has been *The Dillen* (1981): the story of George Hewins, an impoverished unskilled labourer, brought up by his grandmother in a common lodging house, who lived in Shakespeare's town of Stratford-upon-Avon. The publication of his life inspired the world-famous Royal Shakespeare Company to mount a dramatic version of his life with the help of local people. Twelve professional actors were supported by 150 others from local families, and also the town band; and the production was staged not only in the theatre but went out into the town streets and parks, a building site, and an abandoned railway station. Each evening the audience soon found themselves surrounded by many spectators who had not bought tickets. The drama culminated in a terrifying scene representing the First World War when George had been seriously wounded and permanently mutilated; and after it the crowd, now at least 700 strong, would be given candles to light and return together into the town as a great procession, a silent demonstration against the horrors of war. This was indeed a new way of making, or at least revivifying, history.

Despite these examples, the commonest form of presentation of oral history, whether popular or academic, has remained the book. Essentially there have been two types of publication. The first is the straightforward testimony or collection of testimonies. The earliest English examples, as in many other countries, were based on the countryside, although of agricultural workers rather than peasants: Ronald Blythe's *Akenfield* (1969) and Mary Chamberlain's *Fenwomen* (1975). Although the American work of Oscar Lewis and Studs Terkel on city culture made a strong impression, it was only later that British examples followed: for example, Amrit Wilson's *Finding a Voice: Asian Women in Britain* (1978) and Raphael Samuel's *East End Underworld* (1981), an autobiographical portrayal of the criminal subculture of inner London.

The second type of book is interpretive. In many cases their contribution to historical understanding is not dissimilar to that of the edited testimony, for it is primarily empirical and ethnographic. The most important examples of this type include George Ewart Evans' studies of work, Stephen Humphries' of childhood, youth culture, courtship, and sex, and Elizabeth Roberts' of the family and working-class women in the Lancaster region—although all certainly go well beyond description, as we shall see. As a whole it is noteworthy that the strength is in social rather than political history: the rare exceptions are the work of Seabrook and also of Fraser—but in this case on Spain.

The dominance of this empirical tradition is characteristic of British historical work, even if less so of British sociology. Nevertheless, there has been a growing interest in the nature of memory and its subjectivity, partly influenced by the work of Luisa Passerini in Italy. A sharply critical approach to empirical oral history has been recently developed by the popular memory group at the Centre for Contemporary Cultural Studies in Birmingham. Another example has been Ronald Fraser's highly original *In Search of a Past* (1984), a new form of autobiography which is a reflection on the different levels of memory. Fraser, who was the son of a rich family and had been brought up in the 1930s with a nanny and servants, returned to make recordings with them about the daily life of his childhood home and family. Struck by the discrepancies between his memories and those of others, he almost abandoned the research. But eventually he made a totally different kind of history. His book presents three perspectives, intertwined, but kept distinct and intentionally unresolved: first his conversations with his father, now an old man with his memory almost disintegrated, second with the servants, and lastly with his own psychoanalyst. With his father dialogue is no longer possible, but between the other two there are important exchanges of interpretation. Fraser says that before writing his book he had never realised that he had two mothers and two fathers, his real parents and two of the servants, the gardener and the nurse. It is possible to see especially in his bonding to this second working-class father one of the pulls which led to his radicalism as an adult. Fraser's book not only offers a suggestive study of the nature of memory, but a new kind of autobiography.

In a very different way English work has explored another methodological problem of oral history, that is to say the possible use of systematic analysis in sample-based research projects. In our own research projects at Essex we have used a variety of sample bases varying from a representative quota sample of over 400, to smaller samples, both random and strategic, and we have combined qualitative analysis with simple qualification. We have been helped conceptually by our link with British sociologists using the systematic analysis of life story interviews. An outstanding example is the work of George Brown and Tirril Harris on *The Social Origins of Depressions* among married women with children, which have used life stories to identify critical "life events," such as the loss of a mother in infancy or social isolation, which increase vulnerability to depression. Another interesting approach is offered by the family systems approach developed by family therapy. In our own most recent project on "Families and Social Mobility" we have used a random sample base for interviews with two or three generations in *each* of 100 families. The first outcome was our book *I Don't Feel Old,* which presents a multi-generational perspective on the experience of ageing, both past and present.

Among the many areas in which British oral history has enabled advances of historical interpretation, three have been particularly significant: forms of working-class consciousness; urban communities and space; and the family and work. In practice they are not easy to separate. It is a problem and also a strength of oral history that the thread of each life story crosses the boundaries between the areas of life which are normally also accepted by historians. Because of this, historical generalization can only be made by exacting fragments of interviews from their context within each individual life story. But this difficulty is also a strength, for it allows original historical analysis to break across these boundaries and explore relationships which are normally invisible.

With regard to working-class consciousness for example, oral history has contributed less to the history of trade unionism itself, than to exploring its context within a wider culture of often unorganised workers. George Ewart Evans's vindication of the skills of East Anglian horsemen was an early instance. A particularly interesting book on the influence of religion among northern miners, *Pitmen, Preachers and Politics* (1974), was written by the leading sociologist Robert Moore—another instance of interdisciplinary influence in method and theory. Other studies have explored the consciousness of working-class women and children. Elizabeth Roberts' work on working-class women has effectively disproved the earlier theory of Michael Anderson that family help for old people was essentially "calculative," while Humphries has reinterpreted children's stealing as a form of family aid. Diana Gittins has shown how the dynamic for family limitation was transmitted within the working classes rather than as previously believed from middle-class influence, and how it was shaped above all by women's experience at work outside the home.

A second area in which oral history has made a special contribution concerns the relationships of family and work. There are many instances of this. Joanna Bornat, for example, showed, in her study of a northern textile union, how the difficulties of organising women and of their becoming active trade-unionists originated not from the nature of women or their youth but from the relationships between family and work, home, and factory. For the women were taken on at the factory through family recommendation, were trained there by their own kin, on payment would present their wages to their mothers, and were expected to ask their father whether or not to join the union; indeed the union dues were collected at their homes rather than on the factory floor. It is hardly surprising that in a community whose family culture remained patriarchal and where women were unwelcome in the pubs where the union met, it remained difficult to enroll them as union members and few were inspired to become militant trade unionists.

Our own research has also revealed important links between family and the economy. In my studies of Scottish communities (*Living the Fishing,* 1983) I found that family culture was a vital link in the continuation of the fishing economy itself. Because fishing is a difficult and dangerous job, it would not be chosen by young men without a strong sense of continued solidarity. But solidarity alone does not suffice. The fishing industry is particularly open to changes, and each generation has to adapt to different markets, different fishing stocks, and different technologies. Fishing communities, particularly when fishermen own their own boats as is normal in Scotland, therefore require a culture which also encourages individuality and adaptability. I found remarkable differences in family forms which resulted in equally various economic fortunes in different regions of Scotland. In the northwest, the patriarchal and authoritarian family culture had brought up men to follow their elders rather than to take their own decisions, and the fishing here had withered. In other regions like the north-east, children were much more included in social life, encouraged to talk with adults, and disciplined through reasoning rather than beating; and in this region the fishing industry continued to flourish on the basis of a continuously inventive local technology and active local investment. More recently we have explored similar issues in a comparative study of car workers in Coventry and Turin, and again found strong links between forms of family culture and economic adaptability and creativity. These are fundamental issues, both historical and contemporary, to which oral history can make a unique contribution.

Last, oral history has offered a new inspiration to urban history. A fundamental problem has been the sheer size of modern cities, making it difficult to construct convincing studies combining the dimensions of politics, housing, work, or leisure, all of which might be carried out in different geographical zones. But Jerry White's book *Rothschild Buildings* (1980) shows how a new form of urban history is possible through oral sources. White is both a London historian and housing officer, and his book concentrates on a single tenement block of flats, built for the families of Jewish immigrants: but through their stories he reconstructs not only the history of this particular block of flats, but also the history of the inhabitants' family lives and work, and thus of the local economy, the education system, and the development of relationships between classes and ethnic groups in the process of immigration and assimilation; in short, a microcosm of the processes of economic and social change in the metropolis.

It would be possible to continue with many other examples of oral history work in Britain. Let me finish by going back 20 years to the moment at which we began our own research and edited the first issue of our journal *Oral History*. We were then unaware of the long prehistory of the use of oral sources and had only recently discovered that we were, by analogy with the Americans who had started before us, indeed "oral historians." We have still a long way to go, but we have come a long way since then.

Selected Bibliography

Books about Oral History

Flurkis, S. *Oral History in Schools.* Oral History Society, 1980. A good overview of setting up and using oral history in schools.

Humphries, S. *The Handbook of Oral History—Recording Life Stories.* Inter Action, 1984. A clear and practical handbook on how to set up an oral history project, especially useful for community work.

Lance, D. *An Archive Approach to Oral History.* Imperial War Museum, 1978. Excellent on the archiving and documentation of oral history.

Lummis, T. *Listening to History: The Authenticity of Oral Evidence.* Hutchinson, 1978. Focuses on analysing oral history, including quantification.

Norris, A. *Reminiscence with Elderly People.* Winslow, 1986. A brief practical introduction to reminiscence therapy.

Plummer, K. *Documents of Life: An Introduction to the Problems and Literature of a Humanistic Method,* 1983. A valuable sociological discussion of life stories and other personal documents.

Popular Memory Group, "Popular Memory—Theory, Politics, Method" in Johnson, R. *Making Histories.* Hutchinson, 1982.

Seldon, A. and Pappworth, J. *By Word of Mouth: Elite Oral History*. Methuen, 1983. Using oral history research methods with elites.

Thompson, P. *The Voice of the Past: Oral History*. Oxford University Press, 1978 and 1988. Combines a historical and theoretical overview with practical advice, including model questions and a bibliography.

Journals

Oral History—the Journal of the Oral History Society. Published twice a year. News, reviews, and articles on all aspects of oral history. Subscription details from: The Oral History Society, Department of Sociology, University of Essex, Colchester C04 3SQ.

Directory of Recorded Sound Collections in the United Kingdom, British Library National Sound Archive, 1989. Lists nearly 500 private and public sound collections, including their addresses, access details, and contents. The Directory forms the basis of a national oral history database, to which details of oral history work can be sent c/o Curator of Oral History, National Sound Archive, 29 Exhibition Road, London SW7 2AS.

Books Using Oral History

Single lives:

Fraser, R. *In Search of a Past*. Manor House, Amnersfield, 1933–45, verso 1984.

Hewins, A. *The Dillen*. Oxford University Press, 1982.

Samuel, R. *East End Underworld: Chapters in the Life of Arthur Harding*. Routledge, 1981.

Collections of testimonies:

Bragg, M. *Speak for England*. Sceptre, 1987.

Chamberlain, M. *Fenwomen: A Portrait of Women in an English Village*. Routledge, 1975.

Fraser, R. *Blood of Spain: The Experience of Civil War 1936–9*. Penguin, 1979.

Kay, B. *Odyssey—Voices from Scotland's Recent Past*, vol. 1. Polygon, 1980.

Thompson, T. *Edwardian Childhoods*. Routledge, 1981.

Wilson, A. *Finding a Voice: Asian Women in Britain*. Virago, 1978.

Interpretations:

Bornat, J. "Home and Work," *Oral History* 5·2 (1977)

Davidoff, L. and Westover, B., eds. *Our Work, Our Lives: Women's History and Women's Work*. Hutchinson, 1988.

Evans, G. E. *Where Beards Wag All: The Relevance of Oral Tradition*. Faber, 1977.

Evans, G. E., and Thompson, G. *The Leaping Hare*. Faber, 1972.

Gittins, D. *Fair Sex: Family Size and Structure 1900–39*. Hutchinson, 1982.

Hoggart, R. *The Uses of Literacy*. Penguin, 1957.

Humphries, S. *Hooligans or Rebels: An Oral History of Working Class Childhood and Youth 1889–1939*. Blackwell, 1983.

Humphries, S. *A Secret World of Sex: Forbidden Fruit—The British Experience 1900–1950*. Sidgwick and Jackson, 1988.

Humphries, S., et al. *A Century of Childhood*. Sidgwick and Jackson, 1988.

Moore, R. *Pitmen, Preachers and Politics: The Effects of Methodism on a Durham Mining Community*. Cambridge University Press, 1974.

Roberts, E. *A Woman's Place: An Oral History of Working Class Women*. Blackwell, 1984.

Samuel, R. "Quarry Roughs," in *Village Life and Labour*. Routledge, 1975.

Seabrook, J. *What Went Wrong? Working People and the Ideals of the Labour Movement*. Gollancz, 1978.

Thompson, P. *The Edwardians: The Remaking of British Society*. Wiedenfeld, 1975.
Thompson, P., et al. *Living the Fishing*. Routledge, 1983.
Thompson, P., et al. *I Don't Feel Old: Later Life Then and Now*. Oxford University Press, 1990.
White, J. *Rothschild Buildings: Life in an East End Tenement Block, 1887–1920*. Routledge, 1980.

Oral tradition and oral history in Africa:
Beinart, W. *The Political Economy of Pondoland*. Cambridge, 1982.
Lamphear, J. *The Traditional History of Tbetie of Uganda*. Oxford, 1976.
Ranger, T. *Peasant Consciousness and Guerrilla Resistance in Zimbabwe*. Oxford, 1985.
Roberts, A. *A History of Bemba*. Madison, 1973.
Willis, R. *A State in the Making: Myth, History and Social Transformation in Pre-Colonial Ufipa*. Bloomington, 1981.

International collections:
Thompson, P., ed. *Our Common History: The Transformation of Europe*. Pluto, 1982.
Thompson, P. and Samuel, R., eds. *The Myths We Live By*. Routledge, 1990. Papers from the Second and Sixth International Oral History Conferences.

28

Oral History
in Germany
Karin Hartewig

According to this essay, oral history developed more slowly in Germany than in the United Kingdom, United States, and Scandinavia. This may have occurred because of the empiricist, quantitative tradition in German history and sociology, which impeded acceptance of history based on oral sources—a trajectory similar to that noted by Paul Thompson in the United Kingdom and Alessandro Portelli in Italy. Today the field is very much in the public eye, and widest acceptance has been won for research in biography, on World War II and its origins, and on immigrant and refugee populations. Karin Hartewig traces the arrival of the historically disenfranchised into public consciousness in West Germany. This development in German historiography paralleled a movement by which history was increasingly seen as constructed and subjective; this in turn led to a preoccupation with memory as a source, and, overall, a kind of small-is-beautiful ethos for oral history in both Germanies. Today we find at the top of the research agenda for German oral history the following fields: emigration, ecology, identity-formation, childhood and education, and women's concerns. By the beginning of the 1990s, a series of new German journals on oral history and biography had documented a growing interest in this field. Though this essay surveys western Germany, its points may be applicable to other German-speaking regions.

Karin Hartewig has been a lecturer at Fernuniversitat Hagen and is the author of Coal Miners and their Families in the Ruhr *(1988) and* Antifascism and the SED in the Buchenwald Concentration Camps *(1994). She has been a prominent figure at international oral history conferences since the 1980s.*

This article appeared in *Bios* (special issue, 1990). Used by permission of the editor and author.

Some Prehistory

Ten years ago, when the International Oral History Association first met, those few Germans who attended the meeting in Colchester in March 1979 were amazed at the state of a well-established tradition of oral history practice in Britain and America. At a time when we were still trying to figure out how this method could be introduced into our culture, the Anglo Saxon countries were able to display a well-rooted tradition of leftist and people's history among which oral history was steadily growing

For West Germany this was especially interesting, as in our culture leftist traditions had been broken by fascism, and the people ("Volk") had become a distrusted mass, evoking Nazi associations as in "völkische Bewegung" Volksgenossen, Volksempfänger, or even Volkswagen. To refer to the "people" with the meaning of "folk," "folklore," and "popular culture" for a long time carried a double meaning, or at least an allusion to this predominant image of "Volk"—since in German there is no linguistic differentiation between "people" and "folk." In postwar Germany, "Volk" lacked a popular tradition.

The ambivalence of this term derived not least from the active incorporation of "folklore," a sort of anthropology on "the Germans"—or "Volkskunde," as we used to call it—into the racial ideology of the Third Reich. With the rise of research on fascism in the mid-1960s this academic discipline, which is much more institutionalized in Germany than in other countries, was caught in the cross-fire of criticism. At that time it seemed very unlikely that there could be expected any inspiration toward research on popular culture from that side.

Another reason why oral history in western Germany was a late comer was the traditions of German academic historiography and sociology. Whereas in the nineteenth century historiography established itself in contradiction to the widespread popular culture of romanticism, early sociology showed a great deal of interest in empiricist and qualitative research and interviewing. But for academic sociology—as it was established around the turn of the century—positivistic concepts of the sciences and reflections at a very high level about societies' processes of modernization were much more important.

In close context with a stigmatized tradition of "popular culture" and oral history, asking people questions about their life experience and introducing the evidence of such interviews into contemporary history met with a good deal of suspicion. Was it not the same fallacy as the questioning before the tribunal of the infamous denazification in the early postwar years, where everybody denied having been among the people and the movement that had hailed the Führer? Was it not well established that people were lying about their past and that historians had to convict them of their *real* past instead of listening to their distorting voices? And again, had not the same historians some experience with the malleable memory even of the political elite, whose members they had interviewed in the 1960s and 1970s in good faith and very seldom had got anything resembling the facts on record, where they could be established from traditional sources?

It was not just because of narrowminded provincialism that oral history had such a late start in Germany. We rather thought we had learned our lesson in anthropological realism that warned us not to touch this taboo. Contemporary history as such, however, was booming in West Germany in the '60s and '70s, with more academic chairs established in this field than ever, and more than in any other part of the world—and when Germans say "contemporary history," they mean the history of the coexisting generations, as the great old man of the craft, Hans Rothfels, a Jewish conservative émigré from the United States, had already defined it in 1953. It was just because of this past and early spread of contemporary history in Germany and its anti-Nazi tendency that the country clung to the restoration of political history and methodological conservatism.

At the end of the past decade, however, the picture was obviously very different: anthropological research has not only been resurrected, but has become something of a bandwagon during the last couple of years, with much interest among both the public and academia; and with student populations flocking to it in vast numbers regardless of almost no job prospects at all. Oral history in the public perception is now dynamic, and even among academic historians (at least of the younger generation) it is more stimulating, if still thought of as a minor pursuit. In the German Society of Sociology, a section of biographical research has been established, and it has just published a bibliographical survey of articles and books with some 850 entries, most of them based on life cycle interviews or oriented toward methodological discussions, where the formerly well-established disciplinarian borders of history and anthropology often seem to fade away. In educational research, oral and biographical evidence has had a marked influence on a disintegrating discipline.

General Perspectives and Implications of Oral History

Even if oral history has only seen an upward trend and general interest in the public in the late '70s, there have been a couple of early and partly unsystematic attempts to conduct interviews with specific topics and to archive them. Several local, and a couple of private archives, questioned notables from local politics and business about regional history and politics from the '20s to the '60s, about "big politics" and the development of industrial enterprise. But also former activists from the working-class movement, and Jews who survived the Holocaust, were interviewed.[2] It has to be mentioned here that there is also a large collection of so called "Zeugenschriftentum," that is, written reports and transcripts of interviews with witnesses—of which the "Institut für Zeitgeschichte" has collected over 12,000.[3] Within a prehistory of oral history, the "Dokumentation der Vertreibung der Deutschen aus Ost und Mitteleuropa" has to be mentioned, which is the official—and massive as to volume and political suggestion—documentation of expulsion and refuge. It was started in the '50s and is based on 20,000 questionnaires about war and expulsion-experiences, plus 1,100 reports of refugees in manuscript.[4] As the topic "expulsion and refuge" was fast claimed by the political conservatives, of which the different groupings of refugees were prominent exponents, and as criticism of politics of occupation was a taboo to most of the leftist intellectuals up till the '70s, historians—who considered themselves critical and left-wing—distanced themselves from the topic and from that method of documenting the voice of the people. For some years the situation has eased. The interest of oral history and biography research in the life-history of expelled and refugees today has brought a new variety of questions.[5]

In general, it has to be said that the collections of the '50s and '60s in archives and documentation tend to manifest a fixation on political history, relying on material from the government instead of provoking changes of perspectives.

In the late '60s the historiographic social science challenged the conventional concept of politics and diplomacy as a few "great" (and many lesser) men. With an emancipatory attitude, they hoped to achieve a structural history of society, plus the histories of modernization, of industrialization, and of the working-class movement. All this had to be achieved by quantitative means. Still, the arguments against this approach were not easily set aside, and they damaged the leftist profile: the predominance of presumed structures in their research, an affirmative attitude toward progress, and participation in a kind of history writing by the victors, which tends to forget the nameless and nonorganized.[6]

When in the late '70s oral history was introduced into West Germany via the reception of research from the United States, England, and Sweden, it spread in a very fast manner. On the one hand, it offered a change of perspective and a way out of the uneasy feeling concerning the methodological conservatism of contemporary history and of the paradigm of modernization of social science in our country. On the other hand, it seemed to meet certain needs and feelings of society.[7]

The tableau of the past, displaying the great men of history or the inevitable process-structures, was shaken. The heroes from politics, diplomacy, political parties, and unions were cornered by the "supernumeraries of history," who politically never counted and who never had a lobby: the so-called "little people"—nonorganized workers, maids and petit bourgeois, peasants, unemployed women, Sinti, and Jews. The nameless and divided entered the public consciousness. In such an enlarged picture of history, not only did "new" groups of society have to be brought into focus, but also the underdogs of the society of the past had to reveal the social costs of progress, the processes of destruction, and the deficits in history. Against the fiction of a neutrality in historiography, the real subjectivity involved was brought to light. Partiality and scientific determinations were made transparent the moment history was perceived as a construction, resulting from subjective acts.

The acknowledgment of the "subjective factor" consequently expressed itself in the preferred method of oral history: life-history interviews advanced as the basic source of this new concept of history. Besides the possibility of a more down-to-earth form of an "everyday life history," this new method provoked questions about the individual ways of dealing with constructed and suffered experiences and about the structure of memory as such. This is obvious, as subjective memory only offers a rather fragile and hardly fixed testimony of the past, in which social relationships mix with political attitudes, feelings of happiness and helplessness, emotional highlights and depressions from the individual biographies—all that within a certain distance from "big" politics. From a methodological point of view, questions about the continuity of Germany from the years between the wars, through the "black box" of fascism up to the '60s, were once again asked, explicitly or only implicitly. Those questions formed the background for a lot of research done.

The political generation of '68—the major part of the middle-classes—believed by the '70s and '80s that it was suffering a severe crisis of identity. Under those circumstances, oral history—considered as a method of listening to social groupings and individuals not heard from in history before— freed fantasies about a supposedly strong leftwing culture of workers, even fantasies about the extreme resistance of women. In this fascination to explore unknown milieus of workers or even the petit bourgeois, there was also a tendency of hoping to appropriate this alternative for oneself. Both expectations vanished with the continuous work in oral history.

Oral history, understood as a critical assortment of life-histories and biographies, corresponds to a growing skepticism against society's macrostructures: the process of a continuous desensitization against an uncontrolled technological progress, the suspicion against giant development projects, the resistance against the erosion of social structures and milieus in urban and rural areas—all this stood for a culture of involvement with a kind of "local reasoning." This newly developed culture also signaled a strong desire for what in Germany is called "Heimat"—for small, easily surveyed surroundings, towns, neighborhoods, and streets, the idea of a fully developed community.[8]

Projects and Subjects of Research

One project, which cannot be overestimated in terms of its effect on the public understanding of history, is the pupils' contest, *"Deutsche Geschichte."* It was proposed by the former Bundespräsident (president of parliament) Gustav Heinemann and first opened in 1973. The idea was to guide historiographical interest of public school pupils toward understanding the democratic and partly hidden alternatives of German history. From the mid-1970s, the contest has been focused on everyday history. Counseled by their teachers, the contestants were asked to look at archives and libraries and even interview witnesses of the period in question. The results were in part to be published, to boost the public interest in history. Typical topics of this contest were "the working sphere," "living and leisure time," "foreigners," or "the environment." Two contests were held on the history of National Socialism. The publications from those two topics found a wide audience, especially because of the interviews those youths conducted.[9] The contests also encouraged the founding of history initiatives and workshops, which pushed local, regional, and commercial companies' involvement in history. The number of people dealing with and researching history outside of the university, tempered, for a short while, the flair of professional exclusivity from the history departments, even though—at second glance—more academically trained people got involved within this movement and those groups than initially was hoped for.

Within those workshops and initiatives, of which the "Berliner Geschichtswerkstatt," the "Arbeitskreis Regionalgeschichte in Konstanz," and the "Arbeitskreis des Deutschen Gewerkschaftsbundes 'Geschichte von unten'" are the most famous, a lot of local and regional history research was conducted, in which life-history interviews played a dominant methodological role. Rather typical projects were those like the one the West Berlin Geschichtswerkstatt conducted in 1987, dealing with living in the cooperative neighborhood "Lindenhof."[10] This was an integrated exhibition and book project. In the surroundings of the "Arbeitskreis für Regionalgeschichte" in Konstasz, some remarkable research was pursued into the personal and working lives of farmers and craftspeople in the Bodensee area, as well as a history of the town of Singen, in which the Maggi company has been pushing the standardization and industrialization of provisions for about 100 years.[11] The union initiative "Geschichte von unten," which was founded in 1985 in Hattingten, a steel town in the Valley of the Ruhr, existed for about two years and got about 90 projects on their feet. The general topics of this initiative were the local history of the unions, the relationship between local politics and unions, and the resistance of the working class movement against National Socialism.[12] A lot of research which did not directly evolve out of this context but was done by individuals or archives was published. This helped to found a new critical history of the habitat ("Heimatgeschichte"), which more often than not developed out of the history of National Socialism.[13] On the other hand this research was an attempt to critically discuss terms like milieu, class relationships, gender perspectives, and biographical epochs, in an attempt to form identities and traditions. Here, the earliest and longest interest is to be found in experiences of workers, traditionally rooted in the sociological biography research and industrial sociology, begun in the German empire.[14] This is especially the case for the industrial Valley of the Ruhr—a very hermetic proletarian milieu and an image of polarized classes, within which the petit bourgeoisie was very small for a long time—where you will find a lot of literature concerning working class history. One of the first projects was the "Hochlarmarker Lesebuch," which documents the miners' milieu in the area of Recklinghausen Hochlarmark in a very detailed way. Even on a methodological level, this project was very innovative, as the elderly people of this neighborhood collected memories, photos, and documents to tell "their" history about the history of this place—innovative even if they were counseled by a historian.[15]

A second, younger, and methodologically less sophisticated focus is on projects concerning the history of childhood, youth, and education. Beside general memories about the subjects' experiences in their childhood and youth (among greatly different social milieus and political settings), those projects deal particularly with youth protest, all forms of youth culture and organizations, plus left-wing educational institutions since the Weimar Republic. Still, what is true for a lot of historical projects has to be critically annotated: even though neutrally phrased, the history of childhood and youth amounts to a history of the male portion of this population.[16]

Two topics, even though one would not think they were two (considering the programmatic attitude of life history and everyday history), are histories about women and gender perspectives. Sometimes a female's perspective on life is so subsumed—rather one-dimensionally—under her social status that she is less a woman than a female worker. It is only just now that society's constructions of male worlds and female spheres and the perspectives men and women have of those domains, plus body experiences and sexuality in life-historical memories, form clear themes. Those questions have recently found some interest in academic women's studies.[17]

The transition between those projects and specific research in universities is a very smooth one. The differences between the "layperson" in the workshop and the "professional" at the university—differences that academic representatives from the historiographic social sciences very much expected to see—are not really to be found. Those so-called differences are quite likely to originate in one's fear of losing one's professional domain. Agreed, in most cases of the labyrinthical ways of historical tracking, the "layperson" does not prove to be a Sherlock

Holmes, for even among academic (social) historians one will always find a smokescreen.

For the academic oral history and everyday history, you will basically find the following topics:

- The history of the Third Reich and the postwar period by men and women from different peer and social groups;

- Discussions about the myth of the working class movement and women's history; and

- A stronger interest in the female biography, deviances, and a mentality of hidden resistance in politics and social relations.

In this context, the oral history project *"Lebensgeschichte und Sozialkultur im Ruhrgebiet, 1930–1960,"* which started in 1980 in Essen and went on to Hagen later on, led the path for oral history in Germany. The continuity of our people across political periods—1933, 1939, 1945, 1948; the dominance of economic over political questions, and the differentiation of "good" and "bad" times, resistance to the political history, in which the expectations of the economic boom of the '60s were preformatted in the '30s; the restricted forms of female emancipation and employment, which after the war was channeled from the public sphere into the upbringing of children; memories of the war, bombardment, and refuge, so far encapsulated in the ambivalence of something formerly thought private; the collaboration of the older HJ [Hitler Jungen] generation within the unions after 1945 as an entry and a new loyalty to the political fresh start, determined by a kind of pragmatism—all these were the most important topics of the project. Interviews were conducted with male and female workers, refugees and petit bourgeoisie.[18] A follow-up project with occupational groups, which generally are thought to belong to the middle class and to the elite of society, was planned. For that, interviews with journalists, female politicians, and industrialists were conducted.

In the context of the LUSIR project, a couple of individual research projects on the history of miners, and maids in urban housholds was conducted.[19] Lutz Niethammer, Alexander von Plato, and Dorothee Wierling also started a project about the history of experience in the German Democratic Republic, and the first results have been published.

Besides the study by Dorothee Wierling of maids in the first half of this century, several studies for the period between 1920 and 1950 about the history of women more or less based on oral history attempt to bring the whole female context of life into focus.[21]

Since oral history concentrates on the time of National Socialism and the postwar period, it is not only the goal to question the experiences of the willing (or unwilling) perpetrator, engaged or not engaged but still not resisting. In contrast to that, a number of projects focus on the perspectives of the surviving victims: political opponents to the regime, Sinti, Gypsies, Jews, who survived the Holocaust or Germans and Jews who fled Germany in exile.[22]

Some Methodological Questions

Since the 1980s, academic oral history—more than the free projects—has also been engaged in methodological reflections. These reflections circle around questions about the structure of memory in the situation of the interview. The question is whether the process of recollection is evoked and structured by chronological principles, by chains of association, in episodes or by known places in the life-story of the interviewee. Also some interest is focused on questions of interaction during the interview or on relations between the individual and collective memory.[23] A further methodological question—derived from the experience of fascism by the "normal" population—is also formed by reminders of images of foreigners and foes.[24] In Germany inquiries about the process of memory and recollection, and the concluding tests and analysis, are often more intense than questions about the possibility of combining different types of sources.

In the wide context of everyday history the ambivalent term "experience" is discussed heatedly. For a long time studies implicitly used the term in the sense of a primary self-perception and foreign perception and—at the same time—as its interpretation and integration by the interviewees within their biographies. Everyday research is also very undecided whether "experience" should be defined as showing tendencies of suffering and the resistance against it or as reaction to the contingencies of life and politics or as a more active construction within this life. Academic oral history understands the interviewed person more as an expert in one's private life, than as someone knowledgeable of political or public contexts.[25]

Most of the methods of oral history probably derived from its neighboring discipline, sociology. Concepts of peer group analysis (like that of political generations), reflections on gender specific, political, or class-determined socialization, models of industrial sociology, research about social habits, but most of all questions and approaches of the biographical method and of the life-cycle approach—all these important forces inspired oral history in West Germany. In particular, women's history within and without the realm of oral history gained a great deal of legitimacy.

Apart from all the efforts to interpret and conduct hermeneutical text-analysis of conducted interviews (still attempting to let the interviewee "speak" in the scientific text), unedited publications of interviews are rather widespread and popular among recipients. Most of the time these published sections form shorter or longer parts of the interviews, excluding the interviewer's presence and giving an impression of a monologue's being conducted (particularly with transcribed oral biographies). Presentations of "pure" interviews, being valuable for all groups of interviewees and topics, only mirror authentic experience. These are also used to show the fragmentary character of subjective experience and to expound patterns of individual explanations of the "world." On the other hand, people in a specific situation of being interviewed who tell the interviewer a part of or a version of their life story are—for both themselves and the reader—making their selected biography stand for their entire history. Probably the popularity of those publications have roots in loneliness and nosiness, which may otherwise not be experienced. The unedited "document" leaves much space for the reader's projections.[27]

Reviews and Bibliographies

For a long time German oral history and those interested in it had no printed forum for discussions or exchange of ideas (unlike in the United States, where it always had the *Oral History Review*); therefore one had to use the journals of neighboring disciplines like sociology or German studies. This was also partly the reason for a large numer of local publications and collections of articles in small publishing houses. A couple of articles were published in the *Kölner Zeitschrift für Soziologie und Sozialpychologie* or in *Fabula*. In 1982, there was even one volume of the journal *Literatur und Erfahrung* entirely devoted to oral history. The *Journal für Geschichte*, founded in 1979, which tries to show history from antiquity to modernity without using professional jargon, always documented the research done in the history workshops, but, with its wide orientation concerning topics and periods, was no journal for oral history.[28] The best one was *Geschichtswerkstatt*, founded in 1983, whose different volumes were always designed by different workshops.[29] It was only in summer 1988 that *BIOS—Zeitschrift für Biographieforschung und Oral History* appeared on the scene. Its concept was strictly interdisciplinary and offered a meeting ground for oral historians, sociologists, folklorists, and even literary critics. A large part of the journal was devoted to extensive bibliographies about biography research done in different countries. The first two volumes were devoted to the research done in western Germany.[30]

At this point let us cite a couple of other references, excluding those annexed bibliographies in journals and publications, which are well known:

First of all, the collection concerning oral history done by the *Fernuniversität Hagen*, which also includes a bibliography of publications done in the surroundings of the archives dealt with in this collection, has to be mentioned. Another very valuable source is the data presented by the *Informationszentrum*

Sozialwissenschaften in Bonn, which includes research projects and new publications between 1984 and 1986 from the areas of biograpical research and cohort analysis and which also presents life event data with short abstracts. This collection is prefaced by a very useful introduction into biography research and life-event analysis.[31] Bibliographies which are devoted to specific social groupings or specific topics are rather rare.[32]

ORAL HISTORY ARCHIVES

As a consequence of Germany's decentralized research praxis, you will find no central oral history archive or documentation center with the exception of collections in public archives. For the researchers willing to use such sources, this results, first, in a certain disorganization at the scene of archives and, second, in a certain closure of the material (which is welcomed by several oral historians, as it is not usual for us to draw on interviews you yourself did not conduct).

Closest to an archive of oral testimonies is the *Institut für Zeitgeschichte,* which stores not only transcripts of interviews done in the early years of the FRG (Federal Republic of Germany), but also started another rather conventional project of interviewing in Autumn 1988. It plans to conduct a series of interviews with journalists and politicians about political events in the '60s and '70s.[33] For work on life and political history—without too many local and regional connections—the archives of the different broadcasting stations are generally open to researchers and contain a great many interviews.[34]

Under the direction of Alexander von Plato, the *Fernuniversität Hagen* is right now building up an archive for biography research (*Dokumentations und Forschungsstelle Biographiches Material*), which will be an interdisciplinary joint venture between oral history and sociological biography research—possibly even, because of the methodological closeness between the disciplines, resulting in a life-cycle approach. This archive will try to bring written biographical and autobiographical material together with life-cycle interviews.

On the local and regional level, a multiplicity of medium-sized or small archive and documentation centers for spoken history exist, all willing to present their material to the public. One of the oldest and most enticing is the archive for biographical and local history interviews of the Berlin history workshop, called *Dezentrale.*[35]

Not unlike local alternative archives, museums and local cultural projects have recently started to use oral history on three levels: they encourage and conduct interview projects, they archive those memories, and they integrate passages from interviews into their exhibitions of objects and photos. It is here that oral history gains a new dimension as being right in the center of those exhibits. Passages from interviews offer the unshowable and unreadable to the visitor and listener, breaking through the evidence of objects. This is very much the case with exhibitions attempting a history of World War II, as the objects left by survivors and the heterogenous (and inherently ambivalent) experience of people caught up in the war create a remarkable tension.[36]

Conclusion

Oral history in western Germany—which has frozen itself around World War II and focused on fascism, but also on the destruction of former social milieus—can be interpreted as a struggle against a past without persons, without even traditions. Although the academic branch of oral history failed to install a *"history from below"* and although there is no oral history movement *per se*, this methodical approach had its impact on the culture of history in Germany and has gained some position within academic historiography. But oral history is rather a discreet if not hidden victor: By anthropologizing the historical social sciences, a certain success came via indirect channels. On the level of history workshops, however, a lot of local and regional documentary work in oral history, sometimes combined with other source material and presented in publications and exhibitions, helped bridge the gulf to this opening up of the German memory.

There is a strong interdisciplinary interest in historiography, in folklore, ethnology, and sociology and vice versa. Life-cycle, developmental, and biographical approaches, which are derived from a qualitative sociology, seem to be the only way to correspond to the dominant process of individualization in society. Perhaps one might say that the philosophy of history has come to an end and, with it, the link between macrohistory and the production of sense. Nevertheless, macrohistory remains essential for public and private orientation, though it begins to change its status from narrative doctrine to debatable theories. Starting from one's own life experience and the history of the smaller world around, a person can build a wider orientation and with it a sense of history's debatability.

We access history nowadays by starting out from individual experience and individual memory. Through this lens we view the dynamics of the subjective factors which interpret and reinterpret the rather complicated structures of our social surroundings. In this sense there might be a life for oral history after the end for history itself.[37]

Translated by Wulf R. Halbach

Notes

1. For many suggestions and comments I would like to thank Lutz Niethammer and Alexander von Plato.

2. For example: Interviews on political separatism after World Wars I and II and on the entry of American troops in 1945 in: Stadtarchiv Kaiserslautern. Interviews, conducted in 1960/1961 on the working class movement in Ludwigshafen between 1900 and 1933 and one interview (1963) on community politics between 1945 and 1948, both in Stadtarchiv Ludwigshafen. Numerous interviews with entrepreneurs on economics, industrial policy, and social policy (about 1,000 pages of manuscript conducted 1954), in: Institut der deutschen Wirtschaft, Köln. A survey on that kind of archives: Bernd Parisius, Franz-Josef Brüggemeier, Lutz Niethammer, Ingrid Klare, Ergebnisse einer Erhebung übver Bestände und laufende Projekte zur Oral History in der Bundesrepublik, (Hagen 1983).

3. Sammlung "Zeugenschrifttum," in: Institut für Zeitgeschichte, (München).

4. Dokumentation der Vertreibung der Deutschen aus Ost-und Mitteleuropa, hrsg. vom Bundesministerium für Vertriebene, Flüchtlinge und Kriegssachgeschädigte, 5 Bde. und 3 Beihefte, Bonn 1953–1963 (jetzt unveränderter Nachdruck München 1984). The State Archive of Hanover also has transcripts of 600 interviews on the "flight to the west," which were conducted between 1945 and 1950.

5. Alexander von Plato, Fremde Heimat. Zur Integration von Flüchtlingen und Einheimischen in die neue Zeit, in Wir kriegen jetzt andere Zeiten. Auf der Suche nach der Erfahrung des Volkes in nachfaschistischen Ländern, hg. von Lutz Niethammer und Alexander von Plato, Berlin/Bonn 1985, S. 172–219. Albrecht Lehmann, Flüchtlingserinnerungen im Erzählen zwischen den Generationen, in: BIOS. Zeitschrift für Biographieforschung und Oral History 2 (1989) S. 183–206. Rainer Schulze, "Die Flüchtlinge liegen uns alle schwer im Magen." Zum Verhältnis von Einheimischen und Flüchtlingen im ländlichen Raum, in: Geschichtswerkstatt 13 (1987) Thema: Nachkriegszeit, S. 35–45.

6. As key text to the debate about the German versions of historical social science and "everyday history," cf. Jürgen Kocka, Sozialgeschichte, Göttingen 1986. Alf Lüdtke (Hg.), Alltagsgeschichte, Frankfurt 1989.

7. Instrumental was an international collection of essays, edited by Lutz Niethammer, Lebenserfahrung und kollektives Gedächtnis. Die Praxis der Oral History, Frankfurt 1980 (with early literature on oral history). A title which has become almost a chiffre for oral history and for the history of everyday life is: "Dig, where you stand," which recently has been published in German. Sven Lindquist, Grabe, wo Du stehst—Handbuch zur Erforschung der eigenen Geschichte, Berlin/Bonn 1989.

8. For a survey comp. Hannes Heer/Volker Ulrich (Hg), Geschichte entdecken. Erfahrungen und Projekte der neuen Geschichtsbewegung, Hamburg 1985, especially the introductory essay of the editors. Gerhard Paul/Bernhard Schossig (Hg.), Die andere Geschichte. Geschichte von unten. Spurensicherung, ökologische Geschichte, Geschichtswerkstätten, Köln 1986. In the '80s the educational experiences and complicated attitudes of children of former Nazi activists has become a subject of interview documentation on its own, for example: Peter Sichrovski, Schuldig geboren. Kinder aus Nazifamilien, Köln 1987.

9. Cf.: Jahrbuch zum Schülerwettbewerb Deutsche Geschichte um den Preis des Bundespräsidenten 1980/1981. Alltag im Nationalsozialismus. Vom Ende der Weimarer Republik bis zum Zweiten Weltkrieg, hg. von Dieter Galinski und Ulla Lachauer, Braunschweig 1982. Ergebnisse und Anregungen aus dem Schülerwettbewerb Deutsche Geschichte um den Preis des

Bundespräsidenten 1982/83. Die Kriegsjahre in Deutschland 1939 bis 1945, hg. von Dieter Galinski und Wolf Schmidt, Hamburg 1985. Research done within this context: Michael Brenner, Am Beispiel Weiden. Jüdischer Alltag im Nationalsozialismus, Würzburg 1983 Der Krieg frißt eine Schule. Die Geschichte der Oberschule für Jungen am Wasserturm in Münster 1938–1945. Münster 1984.

10. Berliner Geschichtswerkstatt (Hg.), "Das war'ne ganz geschlossene Gesellschaft hier." Der Lindenhof: Eine Genossenschaftssiedlung in der Großstadt, Berlin 1987. Ein anderes Beispiel für die Geschichte von Berliner Stadtteilen im Jahr 1933: "Wer sich nicht erinnern will, ist gezwungen die Geschichte noch einmal zu erleben." Kiezgeschichte—Berlin 1933, hg. von der Arbeitsgruppe "Kiezgeschichte— Berlin 1933," Berlin 1983.

11. Cf.: Gert Zang, "Gedanken tausendmal gedacht, Gefühle tausendmal gefuhlt"? Versuche sich der Lebens und Gedankenwelt kleiner Gemeinden zu nähern: Mündliche Geschichte in der Bodenseeregion, in: Literatur und Erfahrung 10 (7/1982) S. 65–76. Gerd Zang, Die unaufhaltsame Annäherung an das Einzelne (Veröffentlichungen des Projektes Regionale Sozialgeschichte/Mündliche Geschichte, Nr. 12), Konstanz 1984. Alfred Frei (Hg.), Habermus und Suppenwürze. Singens Weg vom Bauerndorf zur Industriestadt, Konstanz 1987. Cf. also: Seegründe. Beiträge zur Geschichte des Bodenseeraumes, hg. von Dieter Schott und Werner Trapp, Weingarten 1984.

12. Besides a kind of methodological handbook on historical research within the unions, there are no publications of these projects. The interviews were given to the archives of the DGB. Manfred Scharrer, Macht Geschichte von unten. Handbuch für gewerkschaftliche Geschichte vor Ort, Köln 1988.

13. For example: Werner Freitag, Spenge 1900–1950. Lebenswelten in einer ländlich-industriellen Dorfgesellschaft, Bielefeld 1988. Lothar Steinbach, Erinnerungen aus einem halben Jahrhundert Sozialgeschichte der Industrie-, Handels- und Arbeiterstadt Mannheim zwischen Kaiserreich und Drittem Reich, Berlin/Bonn 1984. Gerhard Hoch, Zwölf wiedergefundene Jahre. Kaltenkirchen unter dem Hakenkreuz o.O., o.J. (1981). Jörg Kammler/Dietfried Krause-Vilmar/Siegfried Kujawski/Wolfgang Prinz/Robert Wilmsmeier, Volksgemeinschaft und Volksfeinde. Kassel 1933–1945. Eine Dokumentation, Fuldabrück 1984. Susanne Kauffels, Die Nationalsozialisitische Zeit (1933–1945) in Neuss. Zeitzeugenberichte (Dokumentationen des Stadtarchivs Neuss, Nr. 2), Neuss 1988.

14. Petra Frerichs, Bürgerliche Autobiographie und proletarische Selbstdarstellung, Frankfurt 1980. Wilfried Deppe, Arbeiterleben. Eine empirische Untersuchung über Lebensschicksale und lebensgeschichtliche Erfahrungen deutscher Industriearbeiter verschiedener Generationen, Diss. Göttingen 1978. Siegfried Reck, Arbeiter nach der Arbeit. Sozialhistorische Studie zu den Wandlungen des Arbeiteralltags, Lahn/Gießen 1977. Bernd Rabe, Der sozialdemokratische Charakter. Drei Generationen aktiver Parteimitglieder in einem Arbeiterviertel, Frankfrut 1978. Dietmar Brock/Hans-Rolf Vetter, Alltägliche Arbeiterexistenz. Soziologische Rekonstruktion des Zusammenhangs von Lohnarbeit und Biographie, Frankfurt 1982.

15. Hochlarmarker Lesebuch. Kohle war nicht alles. 100 Jahre Ruhrgebietsgeschichte. Bergarbeiter und ihre Frauen aus Recklinghausen-Hochlarmark haben in Zusammenarbeit mit dem kommunalen Kulturreferat ihre Geschichte aufgeschrieben, Oberhausen 1981. Cf. also: Bernhard Parisius, Lebenswege im Revier. Erlebnisse und Erfahrungen zwischen Jahrhundertwende und Kohlenkrise—erzähit von Frauen und Männern aus Borbeck, Essen 1984. Lutz Niethammer/Bodo Hombach/Tilman Fichter/Ulrich Borsdorf (Hg.), Die Menschen machen ihre Geschichte nicht aus freien Stücken, aber sie machen sie selbst. Einladung zu einer Geschichte des Volkes in NRW, Berun/Bonn 1984. As an example from another part of Germany: Stefan Bajohr, Vom bitteren Los der kleinen Leute. Protokolle über den Alltag Braunschweiger Arbeiterinnen und Arbeiter 1900 bis 1933, Köln 1984.

16. Cf.: Renate Wolter-Brandecker, Sie kamen aus der dumpfen Stadt. Arbeiterkindheit und Kinderfreundebewegung in Frankfurt am Main 1919–1933. Heidi Behrens-Cobet/Ernst Schmidt/Frank Bajohr, Freie Schulen. Eine vergessene Bildungsinitiative, Essen 1986. Heinz Hoffmann/Jochen Zimmer, Wir sind die grüne Garde. Geschichte der Naturfreundejugend, Essen 1986. Rolf Lindemann/Werner Schultz, Die Falken in Berlin. Geschichte und Erinnerung. Jugendopposition in den 50er Jahren, Berlin 1987. Land der Hoffnung—Land der Krise. Jugendkulturen im Ruhrgebiet 1900–1987 with some essays on the history of girls by Barbara Duka, Rosemarie Möhle-Buschmeier, and Dorothee Wierling. Cf. also the articles on the experiences of girls within the Nazi youth organizations by Nori Möding, in the third volume of the LUSIR Project, pp. 256–304 (cf. footnote 18).

17. For example: Ilse Kokula, Jahre des Glücks, Jahre des Leids. Gespräche mit älteren lesbischen Frauen, Kiel 1986. Anna-Elisabeth Freier/Annette Kuhn (Hg.), Frauen in der Geschichte, Bd. 5, Düsseldorf 1984; Kap. IV: Frauen erinnern sich—ein Beitrag zur Bewußtseinsgeschichte der Nachkriegszeit. Mit Beiträgen von Elke Nyssen/Sigrid Metz-Göckel, Sibylle Meier/Eva Schulze und Gudrun König, S. 312–409.

18. The results of this project are published in three volumes: Lutz Niethammer (Hg.), "Die Jahre weiß man nicht, wo man die heute hinsetzen soll." Faschismuserfahrungen im Ruhrgebiet. Lebensgeschichte und Sozialkultur im Ruhrgebiet (LUSIR). 1930 bis 1960, Bd. 1, Berlin/Bonn 1983 (2. Auflage 1986). Lutz Niethammer (Hg.), "Hinterher merkt man, daß es richtig war, daß es schiefgegangen ist." Nachkriegs-Erfahrungen im Ruhrgebiet (LUSIR), Bd. 2, Berlin/Bonn 1983. Lutz Niethammer/Alexander von Plato (Hg.), "Wir kriegen jetzt andere Zeiten. Auf der Suche nach der Erfahrung des Volkes in Nachfaschistischen Ländern (LUSIR)," Bd. 3, Berlin/Bonn 1985. As an instructive study on the generation of the "Flakhelfer," born between 1926 and 1930, comp: Heinz Bude, Deutsche Karrieren. Lebenskonstruktionen sozialer Aufsteiger aus der Flakhelfer-Generation, Frankfurt 1987.

19. Franz-Josef Brüggemeier, Leben vor Ort. Ruhrberglente und Ruhrbergbau 1889–1919, München 1983. Michael Zimmermann, Schachtanlage und Zechenkolonie. Leben, Arbeit und Politik in einer Arbeitersiedlung 1880–1980. Dorothee Wierling, Mädchen für alles. Arbeitsalltag und Lebensgeschichte der Dienstmädchen um die Jahrhundertwende, Berlin/Bonn 1987. Alexander von Plato, "Der Verlierer geht nicht leer aus." Betriebsräte geben zu Protokoll, Berlin/Bonn 1984.

20. Lutz Niethammer, Annäherung an den Wandel. Auf der Suche nach der volkseigenen Erfahrung in der Industrieprovinz der DDR, in: BIOS 1 (1988), S. 19-66.

21. Sibylle Meyer/Eva Schulze, Wie wir das alles geschafft haben. Alleinstehende Frauen berichten über ihr Leben nach 1945, München 1984. Sibylle Meyer/Eva Schulze, Von Liebe sprach damals keiner. Familienalltag in der Nachkriegszeit, München 1985. Inge Stolten (Hg.), Der Hunger nach Erfahrung, Frauen nach '45, Berlin/Bonn 1981. Gisela Dischner (Hg.), Eine stumme Generation berichtet. Frauen der dreißiger und vierziger Jahre, Frankfurt 1982. Annemarie Tröger (Hg.), Mutterkreuz und Arbeitsbuch. Frankfurt 1981. Karen Hagemann, Berlin, is working on Social Democratic working class women during the Weimar Republic in Hamburg, which will be published soon.

22. Bettina Wenke, Interviews mit Überlebenden. Verfolgung und Widerstand in Südwestdeutschland, Stuttgart 1980. Hajo Funke, Die andere Erinnerung. Gespräche mit jüdischen Wissenschaftlern im Exil, Frankfurt 1989.

23. Cf.: Dorothee Wierling, Franz-Josef Brüggemeier, Oral History. Kurseinheit 3: Auswertung und Interpretation (Studienbrief der Fernuniversität Hagen), Hagen 1986. Lutz Niethammer, Fragen, Antworten, Fragen. Methodische Erfahrungen und Erwägungen zur Oral History, in: Lutz Niethammer/Alexander von Plato (Hg.), "Wir kriegen jetzt andere Zeiten." Auf der Suche nach der Erfahrung des Volkes in nachfaschistischen Ländern. Lebensgeschichte und

Sozialkultur im Ruhrgebiet, Bd. 3, Berlin/Bonn 1985, S. 392–445 with further literature on methodological questions.

24. Comp. Lutz Niethammer, Juden und Russen im Gedächtnis der Deutschen, in: Walther Pehle (Hg.), Der Ort des Nationalsozialismus in der Geschichte. Frankfurt 1989, S. 114–34. Ulrich Herbert., Apartheit nebenan. Erinnerungen an die Fremdarbeiter im Ruhrgebiet, in, Niethammer, "Die Jahre weiß man nicht, . . .," LUSIR-Projekt Bd. 1, S. 233–66.

25. Ibid., Introduction, pp. 7–30. Niethammer, Fragen, Antworten, Fragen, in: Niethammer/Plato, LUSIR-Projekt Bd. 3, S. 427ff. Alf Lüdtke (Hg.), Alltagsgeschichte. Zur Rekonstruktion historischer Erfahrungen und Lebensweisen, Frankfurt 1989. Heide Gerstenberger/Dorothea Schmidt (Hg.), Normalität oder Normalisierung? Münster 1987. Cf. especially the articles of Alf Lüdtke and Heide Gerstenberger. Otto Grünmandel had put the contradictions between the political and private sphere so ironically into the title of his cabaret program: "Politisch bin ich ein Trottel, aber privat kenn' ich mich aus." ("Politically, I am an idiot, but about private life I know all.")

26. For example: The classical sociologist Karl Mannheim, Das Problem der Generationen, in: Kölner Vierteljahreshefte für Soziologie 7 (1928) S. 157–85; 309–30. Klaus Hurrelmann/D. Uhlich (Hg.), Handbuch der Sozialisationsforschung, Weinheim/Basel 1980 with numerous articles on several fields of education. Helmut Fogt, Politische Generationen. Empirische Bedeutung und theoretisches Modell, Opladen 1982. Martin Kohli, Die Institutionalisierung des Lebenslaufs. Historische Befunde und theoretische Argumente, in: Kölner Zeitschrift für Soziologie und Sozialpsyhcologie 37 (1985) H. 1, S. 1–29. Joachim Matthes/Arno Pfeifenberger/Manfred Stosberg (Hg.), Biographie in handlungswissenschaftlicher Perspektive, Nürnberg 1981. From the side of folklore: Albrecht Lehmann, Erzählen zwischen den Generationen. Über historische Dimensionen des Erzählens in der Bundesrepublik Deutschland, in Fabula 30 (1989) S. 1–25. Bernd Jürgen Warneken, Populare Autobiographik, Tübingen 1985. As to biographic and women's studies: "beiträge zur feministischen theorie und praxis" 7 (1982) Schwerpunktheft: Weibliche Biographien. An example for a strongly sociological research on the war-generation comp: Gabriele Rosenthal, ". . . Wenn alles in Scherben fällt . . . ." Von Leben und Sinnwelt der Kriegsgeneration, Opladen 1987.

27. Comp. such different persons and subjects like: Heinrich Galm, Ich war halt immer ein Rebell, Offenbach 1981. Michail Krausnick, Da wollten wir frei sein. Eine Sinti-Familie erzählt, Weinheim/Basel 1983. Peter Fleck, Aus der Schule geplaudert. Erinnerungen chemaliger Schuler und Lehrer aus Bensheim und heutigen Vororten, 1901–1973, Bensheim 1986. Lothar Steinbach, Ein Volk, ein Reich, ein Glaube. Ehemalige Nationalsozialisten und Zeitzeugen berichten über ihr Leben im Dritten Reich, Berlin/Bonn 1983. Bernt Engelmann, Im Gleichschritt marsch. Wie wir die Nazizeit erlebten, 1933–1939, Köln 1982. Bernt Engelmann, Bis alles in Scherben fällt. Win wir die Nazizeit erlebten, 1939–1945, Köln 1983.

28. "Kölner Zeitschrift für Soziologie und Sozialpsychologie" 1 (1948ff). "Fabula" 1 (1959ff). "Literatur und Erfahrung." Schwerpunkt: Oral History. Geschichte von unten. 10 (7/1982) u. a. mit Beiträgen von Ronald J. Grele, Gert Zang, Uli Herbert. "Journal für Geschichte" 1 (1979ff).

29. Von der Geschichtswerkstatt sind inzwischen 19 Hefte erschienen.

30. Cf. Charlotte Heinritz, BIOLIT. Literatur zur Biographieforschung und Oral History, Teil 1, in: BIOS 1 (1988) S. 121–67. Teil 2, in: BIOS 2 (1988) S. 103–32.

31. Cf. footnote 1. And: Analyse von Lebensverläufen. Biographieforschung, Kohortenanalyse, Life-Event-Daten. Forschungs und Literaturdokumentation 1984–1986. Bearbeitet von H. Peter Ohly und Aldo Legnaro, Bonn 1987. Cf. also: Frank Sygusch/Peter Engel/Marianne Peter/Hans-Jürgen Strack, Das Problem der sozialen Konstruktion dokumentierter Wirklichkeit. Eine Auswahlbibliographie zu einer Sozialwissenschaft der Interpretation unter besonderer

Berücksichtigung der Biographieforschung, Ethnomethodologie und Praxis der "Oral History" (Mündliche Geschichtsschreibung), Linden o.J. (1985). Werner Fuchs, Biographieforschung. Sammelrezension, in: Kölner Zeitschrift für Soziologie und Sozialpsychologie 39 (1987) S. 819–24.

32. Comp. Alexander von Plato, Die deutsche Arbeiterklasse in der Oral History der Bundesrepublik, Hagen 1989 (MS).

33. At the present moment this project, titled "Zeitzeugenbefragungen zur gegenwartsnahen Bundesrepublik-Geschichte" at the Institut für Zeitgeschichte, is only in an experimental phase (Pilotprojekt).

34. The West German Broadcasting Corporation, Cologne, holds interviews, reports, and statements, which were made for the radio program "Zeitfunk" in the years after World War II. Also the archive of the Southwest German Broadcasting Corporation preserves more than 3,000 interviews on politics and on everyday life (which were partly done for a program that is old-fashioned, called "the country and its people" which is a quotation of Wilhelm Heinrich Riehl, the grand old man of German folklore, in the middle nineteenth century).

35. Archiv für biographische und lokalgeschichtliche Interviews in der Berliner Geschichtswerkstatt e.V. (contact address: Frauke Bollow, Goltzstr. 49, 1000 Berlin 30). Other oral history and biographical archives: Archiv erzählter Geschichte und zeitgeschichtlicher Dokumentation in Frankfurt (contact address: Heide Wahrtich, Hallgartenstr).

36. The "Old Synagogue" in Essen, which is now a museum and memorial, is running an interview project with the Jewish survivors of the Nazi Holocaust from Essen. The Center of Industrial Culture, a communal museum project, in Nuremberg has a collection of interviews on industrial experiences. And an example for using interviews within an exhibition on World War II is: Über-Leben im Krieg 1939–1945, presented at the Ruhrlandmuseum in Essen in 1989/1990.

37. Cf. Lutz Niethammer, Posthistoire. Ist die Geschichte zu Ende? Reinbek 1989.

29

Oral History
in France

Danièle Voldman

Danièle Voldman's essay explores the diffusion (or return) of the insights of oral history back to the communities from which it arose. Her particular interests are in the work of archivists, teachers, and historians. Voldman is fascinated to see how constructs of family history, biography, and memory have entered popular discourse via research and educational projects in oral history. This analysis is based on the perspective of a key participant both in the French and international oral history movements, from Voldman's work with the Institute for Contemporary History in Paris and as a longtime researcher herself.

Danièle Voldman is the Regional Director of the famous National Center for Scientific Research (CNRS) for the French government. She is the author of a dozen articles on the role of oral sources in the writing of contemporary history.

This article appeared in French in *BIOS* in 1990. Used by permission of the author.

ince the last international meetings, in Barcelona in 1985, and then at Oxford in 1987, oral history in France has continued in its slow process of *banalisation*. There have been fewer battles to fight, more and more published works to consult. As Jean-Pierre Rioux has already stated in 1986, at the opening of the day-long meeting organized at the IHTP (*l'Institut d'Histoire du Temps Présent*) (and dedicated to the actual state of the field), "oral history has been making inroads into contemporary history for the past ten years. Be it the most clumsy of master's theses, or a DEA project in the making, it's no longer rare—or even indecorous—to hear students looking forward to actually reflecting one day on the interviews they're about to do. In some of the more respectable theses, some juries still pretend to be unshaken by [uncatalogued] words. The thesis writers, on the other hand, have counters on their recording machines, and flying hands to seize their tapes. They listen to narratives, said from memory, which ballast or unballast the most attractive collections of the regional archives. No collective investigation, be it a colloquium or seminar, can get away from reflecting precociously on the possibility of taking up another campaign of oral document gathering."[1]

Far from having a pejorative sense, the word *banalisation* is to be given here the connotation which it acquired at the end of the eighteenth century, signifying a current and common phenomenon of wide appeal. Even if one might object that this affirmation is somewhat optimistic in the strict, academic sense,[2] we would like to prove its validity through an analysis of the practices of three groups concerned with oral history: archivists, teachers, and historians.

Archivists and Oral Sources

In France, as in most other countries, the National Archives have been interested for several decades in the question of new archives generated by the contemporary escape from the world of Gutenberg and which are partly comprised of oral sources. The 1980s and 1990s have seen an intensification of this interest, as concretized in a series of measures. The first of these measures, the law of 3 January 1979, gives a new definition to the word "archives." In its first article it stipulates that "archives are the ensemble of documents, whatever their date, their form, or their material medium, produced or received by any person . . . and by any service . . . in the exercise of their functions." Tape recordings are thus legally considered henceforth as sources accessible to the historian.[3] The National Archives have adhered to this law as members of *Association française des archives sonores* (AFAS) [the French Association of Sound Archives]. The goal of this organization was "to study the problems inherent in the management of sound archives (conservation, cataloguing, transmission), to encourage research and publications relative to sound archives, in order to develop public and private sound archives to meet the needs of research."[4] The picture here becomes clearer: it is becoming more unusual in archivist circles to admit only paper and writing as fully recognized sources. Nevertheless, this evolution goes against the grain of a good many practitioners which years of academic training have formed uniquely around writing; and whose reticence is far from melting away like a snowball in the sun. Even so, the diffusion of new techniques (in particular, the widening acceptance of the computer and the omnipresence of audiovisual technology) continues the work of transforming the world of contemporary archives while posing new questions impossible to avoid.

This is why a group created in the heart of the Association of French Archivists [l'Association des archivistes français] has been working since 1982 specifically on the question of "oral archives"; productive work which—outside of reflections on methodology and technique—allowed active participation in the preparation of the 28th National Congress of French Archives [28° Congrès national des Archives de France] in October 1986—the theme of which had to do with new archives. This meeting served as a prologue to the Eleventh International Archives Congress [11° Congrès international des archives] in August 1988.[5] In the course of these two events, next to the sessions concerning fixed and animated images—as well as some workshops dedicated to computerized archives—a good deal of time was accorded to sound archives and oral history. Convinced of the importance of new media, methods, and areas of investigation, the archivists are thus preparing for the year 2000. As for oral archives, they have isolated three essential points.

First, the congress participants arrived at a definition of sound archives: "sound recording produced or received by any physical person and by any public or private organism in the exercise of their functions, oral archives constitute a sub-group of sound archives."[6] This definition has the effect of giving a near-legal status to archival documents, renders null and void certain discussions on the validity of taped recordings as documents, and opens the field to a vast project of reparation, collection, and conservation. Those regional archival centers which have been active for many years in the gathering of sound documents relating to folklore, ethnography, or history have seen compensation given to their pioneering undertakings: it is henceforth a matter of the daily task—banal, as I have said at the start—of archivists taking care of oral sources. Next to the better-known projects and investigations—which the last international conferences have taken into account[7]—the transmission project of the Essen Conference [Conférence d'Essen], presented by Gérard Noiriel, is indicative of the evolution described above. The author, a specialist in the history of emigration, begins with the fact that this form of history poses some delicate archival problems, since the written sources, very much dispersed, are largely insufficient—hence the necessity of a program of oral investigation. In close cooperation with the Administration of French Archives [*Direction des Archives de France*]—which seems to me even more signifi- cant from the point of view adopted here—it's now a matter of bringing up to date a guide to immigration archives, which would be collections from the mem- ory of immigrants and émigrés. This collection has become as a prerequisite for all large-scale research on this particular area of history.

Second, it is henceforth a given that archivists may eventually find them- selves working in cooperation with prospective users of the resources constituted by these collections. This has posed some real methodological and ontological questions. By definition, the archivist is someone who works for the future. His task is to keep from destruction a documentary mass which, if it is not in itself a form of memory, is at least a trace. Indeed, just as historians no longer believe in the absolute objectivity of research into the past, all archivists know just how much collection development depends on the personality of him or her in whose care that function is entrusted; just as it depends on the epoch and the context of its preparation. Nevertheless, the archivist is first and foremost at the service of distant times to come. In spite of this—and the archival project on French immi- gration between the two world wars is a striking example—the collaboration among archivists and historians, who have all become creators and inventors of archives, no longer seems such an aberration. Quite the contrary: it is something to be hoped for as a guarantee of both relevance and efficacity.

Third—and this is implied in all of the above—the collaboration going on between institutions of various kinds (teaching or research establishments; folk- lore and heritage societies; ministries and political administrations; radio and tele- vision; phono, video, and cinema libraries . . .) is now recognized as more and more necessary. This large opening-up of the archivist community—which usu- ally has a solid reputation for the opposite—is also to be attributed to the devel- opment of what we continue to call oral history.

Some Pedagogical Experiences

At the same time as a new public awareness of cultural heritage (which in France characterized the middle of the 1970s)[8] the idea of using life stories and oral tes- timonies to pedagogical ends was largely spread throughout the teaching circles of the 1980s. In tandem with post-1968 educational reform, putting into ques- tion content and modes of teaching, the opening-up of life stories came in the classroom as an incitement to look into the life of the family for traces of the same past being taught at school. Thus, from elementary school on up, students are currently asked to speak with grandparents and elders to help understand the direction of genealogies and chronologies. Everyone might thereby grasp the par- allelism between his own history and the more abstract and general teachings of his professors or teachers. The often collective construction of the genealogical tree of each student in the class or group teaches him the unfolding of time, the diversity of origins, the different trajectories which distinguish some families from others. Much later, for students between the ages of 11 and 15, the evolution of the techniques and modes of living becomes the goal of the research. In hearing their grandparents share their memories of school, the students grasp the transformations which have taken place in daily life with respect to running water, electricity, the telephone. . . . They also concentrate on the erosion of country life and the development of urbanization, a first approach to the phenomena of migration and mobility. Numerous studies have shown to what extent concentrated listening to one's relatives and kin enables the apprehension of time in the case of young adolescents.

Only the second-level high school courses, according to the pioneering work of Geneviève Joutard in Marseille, really take up the more strictly historical questions, in particular those involving the memory and current, world political events.[9] For this last category of students, oral history goes beyond an active pedagogical tool used to draw attention to a somewhat abandoned discipline—to showing the relationship between past and present, to the final goal of the method, to show how our present cannot be comprehended but through a knowledge of the past. The teachers who give themselves most to this exercise, not always very practical, belong for the most part to an active minority whose political sensibilities tend generally to the Left, and to whom all of us are actors in history. Geneviève Joutard adds to this an extra dimension: "It's also an occasion to initiate [students] into modern means of communication and to make them reflect upon the notion of bearing witness to history."[10]

The other area where oral history is applied to teaching is that of the life story, one of the more fecund genres in which the educational science has been interested for a long time.[11] Since it touches, as we know, upon many disciplines, it is not surprising to find it used for a variety of purposes in the diverse experiments thus far inventoried. On the one hand, it's a matter of language-learning, written and spoken, and reflection on the relation between these two forms of expression. This is how students are prepared to reflect on the subject of biography, beginning with their own. In this case, initiation into autobiography is conceived as a prelude to the handling of language as well as the awareness of self-identity.[12] On the other hand, the personal life story is used as an interviewing framework for a particular subject of study. With this technique, teachers have had success: the richness of the given account, its living and novel character once tied to the students' familiarity with audio-visual aids, the handling of recording and decoding techniques—the least dramatized emotional core of the whole material.[13] These experiments are no longer exceptional today, even if the youth of the users limits their import.

The distinction between eyewitness testimony and personal life story has been schematized for the convenience of this analysis. In the pedagogical experiments briefly related, it is not a question for either teachers or students of entering into sophistic debates on the difference between testimony and narrative—even where an essential investigation into the validity of the received word is intrinsic to the method used.

Geneviève Joutard, for example, insists greatly on learning the overall context of the period studied before gathering interviews, and on thus putting the narrative in historical perspective. These precautions are sometimes forgotten in the enthusiasm of listening to the other's speech. This no doubt explains the discrepancy felt here and there by certain teachers, thrown off by the suspicious arguments of their fellow researchers. So much so that the teacher, in a relatively pragmatic way, uses from the interviews gathered by the students whatever he can to guide their thoughts.[14] The result depends on the objectives of the work and takes on a historic, ethnological, or linguistic color according to the goal pursued and the formation of the teacher.

What one will retain from this diffusion of oral history in the schools, finally, is the great similarity between their preoccupations and those in basic research circles. Methodological works shrink somewhat before empirical research; general theories concede their place to a deepening of more centered and precise themes. This is how one discovers in the pedagogical experiments conducted in the elementary schools and high schools—beginning with oral history—a marked interest in the three most active poles of contemporary historiographic work: family lineage, biography, and memory, with each of these fields overlapping with its neighbors.[15]

The Objects of Oral History

Various authors have underlined the importance of returning to the biography as a compass charting the evolution of contemporary historiography, as it navigates between the individual and the masses.[16] As for what concerns us here, the use of oral sources, one can't overlook the accumulated body of works and the questions they have given rise to. All kinds of social actors have been touched by this; each has been able to find each his own biographer: politicians, most assuredly, such as Pétain, Laval, De Gaulle, to cite only the most well known; Jean Jardin or Léon Gingembre for the more specialized circles; but also artists, persons of letters, humble peasants and vicars. . . .[17] These biographical analyses, which appeal from a single voice to the spirit of history, make use of oral sources, among others; and this is what seems to me to best characterize *diffusion/banalisation*, the key concern of this paper.

The most literary, ethnographical, or sociological biography, on the contrary, produces its honey from the gathering of oral biography, without always avoiding the possible traps and inevitable consequences—positive or negative—of the method involved.[18] Thus, Pierre Bourdieu, in *Acts of Social Science Research*, was not afraid to affirm: "To try to view a life as a single series, sufficient in itself, of successive events without being tied or associated in any way to a 'subject' of which the constant is nothing more than a proper name, would be just about as absurd as trying to make sense out of a metro route without taking into account the structure of the network, in other words the matrix of objective relations between the different stations."[19]

Whatever be the precautions, "recounting one's life" for oneself and for others (which has been one of the first and most fertile objects of oral history) boldly provokes new studies and reflections.

Since the middle 1980s, one can observe a certain inflexibility, on the one hand, on the part of the humble toward the elite, and, on the other, an empirical as well as methodological effort to bring back the individual into the collectivity.[20] This displacement, however, does not alter the fundamental presuppositions of the principal users of the biographical method. In the article just cited, F. Elégoet, revolting against the Marxist interpretation which seems to make the peasants into a bunch of incapable miners, recalls that for him, the interest of the biographical method is to "meet the men at the heart of history and its constraints." By combining, he says, the economic, sociological and biographical approaches, "one will find that men can make their own history and are aware that they are doing just that."

From the individual, one passes easily and, one might say, naturally, to the family, this communal ensemble which tends to become in our contemporary world an aggregate of individuals.[21] Beyond analyses of the evolution of forms of family, two directions may be noted. The first, continuing the exploration of the relationship between the innate and the acquired, the individual and the social, involves the phenomena of geneology and transmission. One must cite the works of Daniel Bertaux-Wiame which for many years have taken up the histories of families as a fundamental aspect of their corresponding ethno-sociological studies.[22] These transmissions are above all transmitting modes of knowledge, culture, and *savoir-faire*—especially when it's a matter of families of workers—but also political attitudes involving political commitments and voting intentions.[23]

The second area, which overflows from the study of family in the strict sense, questions the notion of a "generation." Is this concept really operational in history? What does it bring to the study of groups and individuals? Is it possible to speak not only of biological families, but of intellectual, sociocultural, or political families, or even gather together individuals linked together by nothing else but some founding event? The two world wars and [the student protests of] May

1968 have thus given rise to works written from this "generational" angle.[24] In these approaches, it's a matter of exploring in what ways the different personal histories—which are quite parallel on both the national and international levels—differ from each other. In other words, we are dealing again with the problem of the relationship between the individual and the collectivity, a problem which remains—whatever one's fashion of addressing it—one of the strong points of oral history (or at least an area where the theoretical and methodological advancements have been greatest).[25]

Finally, the domain *par excellence* of oral history remains that of memory. Gone are the days when memory alone was able to suffice for historical speech: the works we see today fall directly into the line of the historiographic movement of the last several years, which explores the relationship between memory and history. These studies try to grasp the essence of the historical narrative in its difference with recollection or recited chronicles.[26] The most recent of these studies differ from the earlier ones in that they abandon both official and popular forms of memory (since the ensemble of recollection processes no longer leads to the memory, but to mémoirs). Beyond family memory, to which we have just alluded, it is especially World War II and Jewish memory which have mostly nourished these works. The exploration of war recollections, shattered memory, memory in movement—to use an expression of Robert Frank—is one of the traditional fields of oral history which continues to be explored.[27]

But these investigations on the subject of memory lead certain authors to conclusions which radically put into question historical practice. In this practice they see the destructive effects on the groups who submit to it. One may here recall the penetrating analysis by Yosef Hayim Yerushalmi on Jewish memory.[28] For this author, memory and history are mutually exclusive in Jewish thought. In short, while the faculty of recollection sifts, erases, and allows for a dynamic, imaginary reconstitution, history (which reconstitutes the community as an object of knowledge separated from the divine) escapes neither the shadowy zones nor the periods of little glory. The historical enterprise therefore represents a threat to an identity constructed from myth and religion. Such is also the conclusion drawn by Régine Robin, specialist of the *roman mémorial*, or the novel of rememberance. For her, the historical text of the positivist school leads to a certain dryness, the impossibility of a lived reconstitution, the loss of identity.[29]

History as threat: to the identity of beings and communities, to the inability of historical narrative to reconstitute the past, to the powerlessness of historians to put themselves to the test: is the process of history well-informed? Let us close with the admirable investigation by Nicole Lapierre on the Jews of Plock.[30] It's a study on the life of a community exterminated during World War II, the traces of which the author searches in the few survivors dispersed today over all the continents. The book is based on the play between historical reconstruction and identity reconstruction through memory. This allows for a comprehension of where and when memory fails, but especially for a sense of the urgent necessity of historical research, for, at the edge of a gulf represented by the death of the last survivors, "history is called upon to rescue memory, a rescue necessary for a refounding, before the human chain of remembrance is broken." Thus, in demonstrating how historical research might be heavy with perils for the community studied, the author underlines the important dynamic of a lively memory questioning history—which by its very danger is a positive source of movement.

Translated by Joseph-Charles MacKenzie

Notes

1. Jean-Pierre Rioux, "Six ans après." *Questions à l'histoire orale, Les Cahiers de l'IHTP*, n° 4, juin 1987.

2. See Michael Pollack's analysis "Pour un inventaire," *Questions.* . . .

3. Between 1980 and 1988, other laws have since updated the regulations concerning the conposition and the transmission of new archives: 29 July 1982, on audiovisual transmission; 3 July 1985, on the author's rights of artistic interpreters, producers of phonograms and videograms, and audiovisual communication companies; 25 March 1987 on the composition of judicial audiovisual archives (tied to the Klaus Barbie trial). . . . As for the regulation of audiovisual archives, see Jean-Pierre Defrance, "La production audiovisuelle des services centraux de l'État," *Sources,* n° 9–10, 1987.

4. Chantal de Tourtier-Bonazzi, "Les archives nationales et les sources orales," *Bulletin de l'Institut d'histoire du temps présent*, n° 20, June 1985.

5. Direction des Archives de France, "Les nouvelles archives, formation et collecte." *Actes du 28° Congrès national des archivistes français*, Paris, Archives nationales, 1987 et *Gazette des archives*, n° 141, 1988, numéro spécial; *Les archives françaises à l'horizon de l'an 2000: études rassemblées à l'occasion du 11° Congrès des archives*, Paris 22–26 August 1988.

6. Elisabeth Gautier-Devaux, "Synthèse des travaux de l'atelier archives sonores," *Les nouvelles archives.* . . .

7. For example, the work of gathering interviews with members of the Résistance or political officials of the Fourth Republic; the work done at the Regional Archives of Orne [*Archives départementales de l'Orne*]; that of the Municipal Archives of Metz [*Archives communales de Metz*] on World War II; that of the Territory of Belfort on the archivizing of sound documents from decentralized public radio stations; that of the Archival Commission of the Minister of Foreign Affairs [*Mission des archives au ministère des Affaires étrangères*]; the interviews gathered over the past ten years by the "Oral History" section of the Air Force Historical Service [*section "Histoire orale" du Service historique de l'armée de l'air*]. . . .

8. Numerous works bear witness; if we may point out from among a vast bibliography: the unpublished thesis by Gilles Jeannot, *Du monument historique au patrimoine local: l'évolution de la notion de patrimoine architectural à travers les publications des sociétés savantes et des associations de sauvegarde en France après 1945*, Institut d'urbanisme de Paris VIII, 1988; Jean-Pierre Rioux, "L'émoi patrimonial," *Le temps de la réflexion*, n° 6, Paris, Gallimard, 1985; Henri-Pierre Jeudy, *Mémoire du social*, Paris, PUF, 1986.

9. "Dis-moi grand-mère, Dis-moi grand-père." *Astapi*, n° 206, 15 May 1987 (guide for helping children to interview their grandparents to make them recount their lives); "La journée d'une écolière en 1914, ou comment mettre en scène avec un CM2 un récit vécu oral," *Le Français aujourd'hui*, supplément au n° 73, March 1986, pp. 8, 12; Claudie Richard et Jean-Claude Messier, "La mémoire retrouvée. L'écriture des récits de vie en LEP," *Le Colporteur*, revue de l'Association française des enseignants de français, Régionale de Basse Normandie, n° 2, 1987, pp. 11–12; "À la recherche du temps présent: Histoire orale et enseignement," study coordinated by A.J.M. Bernard, Amiens, C.R.D.P., 1987; Geneviève Joutard, *Le vent de l'exil*, film produced by a class of high school students of Marseilles during the 1985–1986 school year and presented first on regional television, then in Paris, March 1988.

10. Geneviève Joutard, "Pouvoir familial et puissance paternelle," *El poders a la societat*, V° Colloque international d'histoire orale, Barcelone, March 1985, mult. p. 276.

11. As for personal life stories, see the works of Philippe Lejeune, in particular the indispensable "Bibliographie des études en langue française sur la littérature personnelle et les récits de vie," which appeared in the *Cahiers de sémiotique textuelle*, Nanterre, Université de Paris X. (Number III, carrying the years 1986–1987, appeared in number 13 in 1988. The preceding issues are number 3 [1984] and 7 [1986].)

12. Denis Bertrand and Françoise Ploquin, "Moi je . . . Écrire à la première personne," *Le Français dans le monde*, n° 202, July 1986, pp. 57–59; "L'autobiographie," *L'école des lettres des collèges*, 1 March 1986, n° 10, pp. 17–18; Nicole Cellier, "Écriture autobiographique et expression dramatique en collège," *Le Colporteur*, n° 1, 1987, pp. 14–20.

13. This is not always the case, of course. In *Le vent de l'exil* [*The Wind of Exile*], for example, none of the Maghrebian students of the first or second generation agreed to testify before the camera.

14. One recalls the work accomplished in Toulouse by Rolande Trempé and her students, related in "Histoire orale et audiovisuel," *Colloque d'Aix-en-Provence*, 1982.

15. In a vast bibliography of often specialized works, we would like to point out here: André Burguière, Christiane Klapisch-Zuber, Martine Segalen, and Françoise Zonabend, *L'histoire de la famille*, Paris, A. Colin, 2 tomes, 1986; Actes du Colloque "Problèmes et méthodes de la biographie," Sources Paris, Publications de la Sorbonne, 1985; *Croire la mémoire? Approches critiques de la mémoire orale*, Aoste, Actes, 1988.

16. Among the various interpretations and very different points of view: Félix Torres, *Déjà vu. Post et néomodernisme: le retour du passé*, Paris, Ramsay, 1986, "Dossier Masses et individu," *Vingtième Siècle. Revue d'histoire*, n° 14, 1987. On the individual: contributions to the Colloque du Royaumont, 1985, Paris, Le Seuil, 1987.

17. To cite only the most significant from among many others: Jean Lacouture, *De Gaulle*, Paris, Le Seuil, 1986; Marc Ferro, *Pétain 1933–1954*, Paris, Balland, 1987; Assouline, *Jean Jardin* (this author is a specialist in biography and has recently published studies on the art dealer D. Kahnweiller, and another on the journalist A. Londres); James Steel, *Paul Nisan, un révolutionnaire conformiste?*, Paris, Presses de la Fondation nationale des sciences politiques, 1987; Sylvie Guillaume, "Léon Gingembre, défenseur des PME," *Vingtième Siècle. Revue d'histoire*, n° 15, 1987; also the collection "Récits, souvenirs," of La Pensée universelle.

18. "L'illusion biographique," Actes de la recherche en science sociales, n° 62/63, June 1986; "La biographie," *Diogène*, n° 139, July–September 1987.

19. Pierre Bourdieu, "L'illusion biographique," *Actes. . . .*

20. From this point of view, the study by Fanch Elégoet on the activities of the peasant leader Alexis Gouvennec is most significant since it joins these two tendencies. Fanch Elégoet, "Stratégies paysannes en Bretagne. L'action d'un leader: Alexis Gournennec," *Life stories / Récits de vie*, 3, 1987.

21. Antoine Prost and Gérard Vincent (dir.), *Histoire et la vie privée*, tome V, "De la première guerre mondiale à nos jours," Paris, Le Seuil, 1987.

22. Let us cite only the most recent publications which show the evolution of the thought and themes of these authors: "Le patrimoine et sa lignée: transmission et mobilité sociale sur cinq générations," *Life Stories / Récits de vie*, 4, 1988; not to forget the presentation and conclusion by Daniel Bertraux, in number 26 of the *Annales de Vaucresson*, 1987, "Histoires de vies. Histoires de familles. Trajectoires sociales," as well as the whole of the issue for questions relating to family.

23. Béatrix Le Vita, *Mémoire familiale et mémoire généalogique dans quelques familles de la bourgeoisie parisienne*, Ministère de la Culture, Mission du patrimoine ethnologique, 1987; Jean-Louis Beaucarnot, *Le livre d'or de votre famille*, Mengès, 1986; Florence Charpigny, "Généalogie et mémoire ouvrière," *Gé-Magazine*, n° 48, 1987; Michel Pincon, *Désarrois ouvriers. Familles de métallurgistes dans es mutations industrielles et sociales*, Paris, L'Harmattan, 1987; Anne Muxuel et Annick Percheron, "Histoires politiques de famille. Premières illustrations," *Life Stories / Récits de vie*, 4, 1988.

24. Dominique Boulier, "Récits d'adolescence: le traitement du changement selon Les générations," *Cahiers internationaux de sociologie*, January–June 1986; Jean-François Sirinelli (dir.), "Générations intellectuelles," *Les Cahiers de l'IHTP*, n° 6, 1987; Ronald Fraser and Daniel Bertraux, Bret Eynon, Ronald Grele, Béatrix Le Vita, Danièle Linhart, Luisa Passerini, Jochen Staat, Annemarie Tröger, *1968. A student generation in revolt*, London, Chatto and Windus, 1988.

25. Françoise Zonabend, "La mémoire familiale: de l'individuel au collectif," *Croire la mémoire*. . . .

26. For general questions, one might examine the *Lieux de mémoire*, series, edited by Pierre Nora, Paris, Gallimard, 1984–1988 (for the volumes which have thus far appeared); Jacques Le Goff, *Histoire et mémoire*, Paris, Gallimard, 1988.

27. One may recall the very important articles of Michael Pollak in the *Actes de la recherche en sciences sociales*. One might also cite Etienne Fouilloux and Dominique Veillon, "Mémoire du débarquement en Normandie," *Normandie 44: "Du débarquement à la libération,"* Paris, Albin Michel, 1987; Robert Frank, "Mémoires françaises de la deuxième guerre mondiale," *Bulletin de l'Institut d'histoire du temps présent*, n° 23, March 1986; Henry Rousso, *Le syndrome de Vichy, 1944–1949*, Paris, Le Seuil, 1987; Gérad Namer, *Mémoire et société*, Paris, Méridiens-Klinck-sieck, 1987; Dominique Veillon, "La seconde guerre mondiale à travers Les sources orales," *Questions à l'histoire*. . . .

28. Zakhor. *Histoire juive et mémoire juive*, translated from the English by Eric Vigne, Paris, La Découverte, 1984.

29. See the thesis on the *roman mémoriel*, "Récit de vie, discours social et parole vraie," *Revue d'histoire Vingtième Siècle*, n° 10, April–June 1986.

30. *Le silence de la mémoire. À la recherche des Juifs de Plock*, Paris, Plon, 1989.

30

Oral History
in Italy

Alessandro Portelli

In this essay, one of the only Italian professors publicly associated with oral history details its development in his country over the last 30 years.

Alessandro Portelli points out that oral history does not often find a home in the Italian academy and demonstrates how the field's precursors in Italy came from an independent, or activist, perspective. Instead, Italian oral history draws inspiration from related fields in the social sciences: ethnomusicology, anthropology, sociology— as much as it does from colleagues and movements within the historical profession. Thus some of the best oral history work of the 1970s and '80s emerged from literary biography, memory, and both gender-specific and class-specific studies of key historical epochs. In this work, and in its massive bibliography, we have a case study of what happens to a community of oral historians who offer social criticism and social activism from a platform outside the academy. Portelli's chronicle of Italian oral historians recapitulates the divisions and directions of oral history in developed nations.

Professor Alessandro Portelli holds a chair in American literature at the University of Rome. He is the author of seminal works on literature and oral history, including The Death of Luigi Trastulli: Form and Meaning in Oral History *(1991); and* The Practice of Oral History *(1996).*

*A*ny discussion of oral history in Italy must begin with a paradox. In a 1995 article, Alistair Thomson charged that, in the development of British oral history, "the tendency to defend and use oral history as just another source to discover 'how it really was' led to the neglect of other aspects and values of oral testimony." This positivistic approach was only later corrected, Thomson argues, also thanks to international influences, among which he lists primarily Italian contributions. In his response, Paul Thompson insisted that, to the contrary, Italian and other international "critical" oral history had been translated and made known in Britain at a very early date.[1]

Whatever the merits of this discussion,[2] the fact that it has taken place is an indication of the international relevance of Italian oral history and of its identification with methodological and theoretical sophistication, based on overcoming positivistic approaches through the study of subjectivity, of memory mechanisms, of narrative and linguistic aspects. Italian oral historians are amply represented in all international conferences, committees, journals, publications; they are invited to teach at international institutions, and their work is widely quoted, discussed, translated, and taught abroad.

On the other hand, Italian oral history is all but invisible in Italy. In the few cases in which notice has been taken of it, the work of Italian oral historians has been subjected precisely to the same charges from which it is supposed to have helped British oral history recover. In a recent survey, Pietro Clemente has claimed that Italian oral history is tainted with "naive realism in the use of sources" and "has been unable to completely overcome the image of naiveté and political or polemical utilization of sources" (his bibliographies, however, do not mention the Italian contributions over which British historians dispute).[3]

As a consequence of this neglect, younger Italian scholars who stumble onto oral sources are much less aware than oral historians abroad of the "critical" tradition of oral history in Italy, and the risk of methodological naiveté increases. As another consequence, not one person in Italy is gainfully employed in any capacity related to oral history.[4]

Some of the reasons for this paradox must be sought in the multiple and unorthodox origins of Italian oral history.[5] The influence of Benedetto Croce's high-minded historicism and philosophical idealism on the one hand, and the narrow-minded nationalistic cultural policies of Fascism on the other, both contributed to delaying the development of social sciences such as sociology and anthropology in Italy, and to giving Italian historiography a distinctly idealistic tinge that privileged the "ethical-political" level of elites and institutions. As a result, the historical presence and role of the nonhegemonic classes—let alone their memory and expression—was to a large extent ignored even by Left professional historians who transferred the "ethical-political" approach to the culture and leadership of the working-class parties.[6]

Thus, the awareness of oral sources developed primarily outside the university and on the margins of official organizations, often in antagonism with politically and academically established historians. The crucial role in this development was that of Gianni Bosio, as editor, publisher, cultural organizer, and a historian in his own right. Bosio's belief that the history of the working classes ought to not to be limited to the history of the leadership of the major unions and parties, but should rather include all their organized and spontaneous forms of expression (including nonpolitical and conservative ones) led him to work toward a synthesis of history with folklore and ethnology. His "praise of the tape recorder" can be considered the first articulated discussion of the role of oral sources in reconstructing the "alternative presence and critical study of the non-hegemonic classes."[7]

Bosio realized that the data for the interdisciplinary history from below he had in mind had to be created almost from scratch. He therefore constantly insisted on the primacy of fieldwork and insisted on the most rigorous, "philological" treatment of documentary evidence, written and oral. Although he was aware that fieldwork might be conducted at times in naive and uncritical fashion, Bosio believed that "inadequate" fieldwork is better than no fieldwork at all, inasmuch as it at least provides data for more sophisticated analysts. As an expression of this concern for sources, Bosio established Italy's first and possibly still most important archive of oral documents, in the Istituto Ernesto De Martino, founded in Milan and currently housed in Sesto San Giovanni, near Florence.[8] Responding to the oral form of the documents, Bosio also developed alternative ways of presenting the results of fieldwork, such as theater and concerts (he was one of the founders of the Italian folk revival) and long-playing records including songs, the spoken word, and other documents in sound in the series and label of the Archivi Sonori and Dischi del Sole which he also founded.[9]

The centrality of fieldwork remained a tenet for all the oral history tradition that harks back to Bosio. The interview was increasingly recognized not only as an essential information-gathering process, but also as a politically significant encounter, a learning situation and an "experiment in equality" for both the informant and the interviewer.[10] This may also be one reason for the lukewarm reception of oral history in academic circles where the idea that scholarly work could be conducted also outside the study and the library, the humility required to do the ordinary legwork of collecting oral sources, the listening attitude whereby a scholar can learn also from uneducated informants and from less established practitioners, penetrated slowly, if at all. Perhaps, rather than the alleged "anti-intellectualism" of oral historians, it was the worry that oral history might disrupt the practices and hierarchies of intellectual tradition that kept it safely out of the university.

Indeed, the fact that fieldwork can ultimately only be learned by doing is one reason why oral history practices, to an extent unknown to other disciplines, a constant dialogue between all levels and all endeavors. Experienced scholars and young independent researchers, including local enthusiasts and beginners, have met together at the same conferences, and have always had something to learn from one another. This was also true of the British experience and, to a large extent, of international conferences in Europe since their inception. As a statement of purpose for the journal *I Giorni Cantati* formulated it in 1981:

> Our project is to reveal, and to create, a continuum, a circulation of ideas and practices connecting the most advanced theoretical practices with the local experiences on the field. Clearly, the contributions of local groups cannot be measured on an abstract scale of academic competence, but must be interpreted in terms of the wealth of experience, work, collective knowledge, and potentiality that they reveal. They are, in a sense, both material *of* observation and material *for* observation. We want to ensure that his type of widespread and invisible work be known, confronted, discussed and, of course, also criticized. . . .[11]

Another voice that contributed to an awareness of oral, unofficial, rank-and-file, and marginal sources for an antagonistic history was that of Danilo Montaldi. While disagreeing with Bosio on several accounts of political strategy, and sharply critical of Bosio's "philologism" as mere uncritical adoption of the point of view of his sources, Montaldi shared Bosio's political tension (Bosio in turn found his treatment of documents somewhat cavalier). In his work on marginal and rank-and-file sectors of the nonhegemonic classes and the political Left, he used the life-story approach and laid the ground for the study of alternative subjectivity on the one hand and for the use of the life-story in qualitative social science research on the other. Like Bosio, Montaldi never held an academic position: both their politics and their cultural approach were too unconventional, and ultimately they were not much interested either. Both saw cultural work primarily as part of organizing and consciousness-raising.[12]

One of the major influences on Bosio, as on all of Italian anthropology, was Ernesto De Martino, an ethnologist and historian of religions who endeavored to combine his roots in Croce's historicism with Marxism and political concerns. Together with a generation of anthropologists and ethnomusicologists (primarily, Diego Carpitella, Alberto Mario Cirese, and Roberto Leydi) who were bent on documenting the multiple stratifications of Italian society negated or manipulated under Fascism,[13] Ernesto De Martino placed fieldwork at the center of his investigation of the ancient rural culture of Southern Italy and its relationship both with contemporary Italian society (the "Southern Question") and with the anticolonial insurgency in the Third World. De Martino seldom concerned himself directly with issues of modern and contemporary history, or with the collecting of historical testimony per se, and therefore his work cannot be directly associated with oral history; nevertheless, it remains an essential point of departure for oral history as well as for other disciplines, for a number of reasons: among them, his insistence on placing even the most apparently archaic cultural phenomena, from ritual possession to magic, in historical perspective and contemporary relevance; his constant awareness that he was collecting his information from contemporary people and citizens of his own country and society; and his indefatigable practice of fieldwork.[14]

As Cesare Bermani pointed out, De Martino was the first to practice "a way of doing research and being in the world at the same time that was shared in the 1950s and 1960s by Danilo Montaldi and Gianni Bosio—two 'activist researchers' motivated by quite different projects." To these names, we ought perhaps to add that of Rocco Scotellaro, a poet, political activist (as a leader in the struggle for land reform and the mayor of the small town of Tricarico, in Lucania, the South's then most depressed region), and rural sociologist, who began the first collection of life stories of Southern peasants.[15] As an example of this approach, Bermani quotes a famous passage in which De Martino describes his attitude while working in the field and seeking a mutual recognition with his "informants":

> Being together as "comrades," that is, meeting together in the endeavor to share a common history, was a totally new condition for ethnological research . . . only in this passion for changing the present into a reality more worthy of human beings could I conceive a passion for knowing the present also in those aspects that harked back to a recent, distant, or even primitive past.[16]

There is another, important aspect that Bosio, Montaldi, and de Martino shared: in different forms, they represented an anti-Stalinist, libertarian, rank-and-file Left that was in the minority in the 1950s but was to be the protagonist of the students and workers' movements of the following decade. Together with an alternative Marxist tradition (represented, in Bosio's case, by Rosa Luxemburg), and with the influence of Third World thinkers and leaders like Amilcar Cabral, an important influence was the rediscovery of Antonio Gramsci, beyond official interpretation of his Communist leadership. Gramsci's concept of folklore as a historical expression of the culture of nonhegemonic classes on the one hand, his practice of rank-and-file organization based on the consciousness of the working class in the workers' councils, and the inroads into subjectivity allowed by his concept of hegemony were to remain a lasting legacy to Italian oral history.[17]

The cultural-political organizational work launched by Bosio coalesced in the establishment of the Istituto Ernesto De Martino (1966), and in the work of Cesare Bermani, who combined Bosio's political and philological approach with a heightened attention to the realms of imagination and expression. Bermani's work, totaling over 1,000 titles, includes controversial historical reconstruction of episodes of the anti-Fascist and partisan struggle in the North, collections and analyses of musical oral traditions, and studies of magic in Central and Southern Italy. Perhaps no one more than Bermani carried out Bosio's strategy of tearing down the barriers between history and ethnology.[18]

The link between the work of the Istituto De Martino and the growing students' and workers' movements of the 1960s was reinforced by the establishment of "branch" organizations: the most long-lasting and active among them were the Lega di Cultura di Piadena (Cremona, Lombardy), established in the early 1960s by a group of rank-and-file working-class intellectuals and activists;[19] and the Circolo Gianni Bosio (Rome), a collective of activist musicians, folklorists, and oral historians founded in Rome in 1972, soon after Bosio's premature death. Throughout the 1970s and part of the 1980s, with the work of Susanna Cerboni,[20] Alfredo Martini, Marco Muller, myself, and others, the Circolo Gianni Bosio carried on oral history projects in Rome, Latium, Umbria, and Calabria. Its journal *I Giorni Cantati* (1973–1995), in many respects a precursor of the cultural studies approach, published oral history documents and essays along with folk music and popular culture.[21]

Other New Left publications between the late 1960s and the 1980s included oral history in the discussion of what was described as "militant history" and "antagonist subjectivity." *Il nuovo canzoniere italiano* presented the work done by or related to the Istituto De Martino. *Primo Maggio*, published also in Milan, combined militant documentation of contemporary working-class autonomy with in-depth historical analysis and theory; it published some of the first extended theoretical and methodological discussions of oral history, as well as the contribution of historians of the U.S. working class like Bruno Cartosio and Peppino Ortoleva.[22] *Ombre Rosse*, a journal dedicated primarily to politics, cinema, and literature, also published early discussions of oral history in the framework of "antagonist subjectivity."[23]

The relation of subjectivity and memory in working-class action was at the center of the debate. For a number of radical Left intellectuals, identified with the so-called "workers' autonomy area" (Autonomia Operaia), the cultural and political autonomy of the working class as a historical subject lay precisely in its lack of memory. Unencumbered by the burden of previous practices, organizations, traditions, the working class would act for itself, remaking its own composition directly on the grounds of production. On the other hand, the activist-historians gathered around the Istituto De Martino, *Primo Maggio*, and *I Giorni Cantati* insisted that memory was not a depository of dead information but an active process, and therefore the working class's capacity to generate and elaborate memory was a necessary part of any idea of subjectivity. Bosio's perception of how the urban working class was rooted in the history of preindustrial ways of life, struggle, and resistance allowed him to extend De Martino's and Gramsci's insights from the rural to the industrial world, thus identifying an "autonomous" (not separate, but linked in struggle) history of the working classes that rooted resistance and identity in a continuous antagonistic, or at least independent, memory. This approach was later reinforced by oral history contributions by Cesare Bermani and myself on the one hand, and (also drawing on the work of Herbert Gutman and George P. Rawick) by Bruno Cartosio.[24]

Toward the middle of the 1970s, some of the more established scholarly circles began to pay attention to oral history. The conference "Anthropology and History: Oral Sources" (Bologna, 1976) brought together a number of international scholars and several prominent Italian anthropologists. Established Italian historians were notable mainly for their absence (with the exception of Africanists) and the work of the Istituto De Martino was only marginally recognized. The conference stressed the interdisciplinary dimension of the work with oral sources, and attempted to create an epistemological basis for their use.[25] Ultimately, however, it failed to generate a significant follow-up in terms of historical research with oral sources and fieldwork. The academic circles that had promoted the conference soon lost most of their interest.

One of the reasons was that oral history had been introduced largely as a foreign, mainly British, import, ignoring or dismissing the 20-year old Italian tradition. A major contribution to an awareness of the British experience was Luisa Passerini's anthology *Storia orale* (1980).[26] While presenting samples of recent British and U.S. oral history, Passerini's introduction went beyond the themes of daily life and material culture that prevailed in her selection of essays, to lay the ground for concerns that were to become crucial to the specificity of Italian oral history in the future: the role of subjectivity, the use of psychological concepts and tools for the interpretation of narratives, and the study of the mechanisms of memory.

Passerini's work in the 1970s began in continuity with the Italian tradition of studies on the working class, enhanced by the workers' insurgency of the late 1960s and early 1970s. While studying the working-class communities of Italy's industrial capital, Turin, Passerini was from the beginning aware of the importance of subjective attitudes on the one hand and narrative form on the other. In an Italian historical tradition that was primarily concerned with the material relationship of workers to the machinery of production and with their political relationship to organizations, unions, and parties, Passerini focused on attitudes and ideologies concerning work, and on the expressions and silences of the less visible strata of the working-class community. Passerini's definition of subjectivity differed from that of the contemporary debate on workers' autonomy, in that it was concerned with the subjectivity of individuals as well as that of the working-class community, and therefore reached for a higher degree of complexity and contradiction. Subjectivity, she argued, may be an antagonistic stance but also the ground for subordination, manipulation, integration, and stereotypes. To establish canons by which "subjectivity may become object and source of scientific procedures," Passerini worked critically with concepts of history of mentality (Durkheim) and collective memory (Halbwachs), as well with concepts drawn from psychoanalysis (P. W. Winnicott) and from the history and theory of autobiography. In her later work, Passerini extended this "history and subjectivity" approach to the study of women's history and biography.[27]

Women's history was perhaps the only terrain in which political concerns and innovative scholarly practice were recognized to be, far from antagonistic, mutually necessary. The women's movement developed a generation of historians that were both academically sound and politically dedicated. Such themes as subjectivity, the relevance of the individual, and the history of private life were shared both by women's history and by oral history at large. The Women's Documentation Center in Bologna and the journal *Memoria* collected, published, and discussed oral sources for women's history and culture;[28] "Astrea," a series of books on women's narrative coordinated by Roberta Mazzanti, published several oral autobiographies of Italian and Third World women.[29] As Pietro Clemente notes, a genre-specific point of view and the general influence of feminist thinking permeate the best in Italian oral history of the 1970s and 1980s. Women's themes and contributions have prevailed in the Italian contributions to the international oral history conferences.

Another point of contact between scholarly and activist approaches is to be found in the Institutes for the History of Resistance, a nationally coordinated network of local research centers and archives dedicated to the history of anti-Fascism. In the Institutes, different types of researchers coalesced and worked together, including progressive academic historians, local historians, and activist researchers. It was not always a peaceful coexistence. As Cesare Bermani wrote, at the Institutes' conference on "History of Italy, History of the Resistance, and Local History" (Rimini, 1981), "the debate on oral sources was the occasion for taking sides for or against the demand of social history that had emerged after [the movements of] 1977, for or against the forms of radical historiography." Some of the more respected established historians at the conference responded by virtually equating oral history with complicity with terrorism and subversion.[30]

The Resistance Institutes, however, continued their concern with oral sources. In Turin, the local Resistance Institute and Gramsci Institute convened the first national meeting on oral history (Turin, 1981).[31] On this occasion, the bulletin *Fonti Orali* (1981–87) was established to coordinate local, rank-and-file, and academic work with oral sources in history, anthropology, and folklore. Finally, a conference on the use of oral sources in education ("Teaching

Anti-Fascism and the Resistance: Education and Oral Sources," Venice, 1982) brought together academics, researchers, and teachers. Although it failed to establish a middle ground of exchange between the scholarly requirements of historical research and the hands-on approach required in education, yet it signalled an interest in oral history among educators that, while hardly encouraged or recognized, continues to this day.[32]

The activist and academic strands of Italian oral history, however, remained by and large separate. Attempts to bring them together, such as the conference organized in Terni by *I Giorni Cantati* and *Fonti Orali*, failed, although the presentations included a number of excellent interdisciplinary contributions.[33] While some critics have attributed this failure to the excessive politicization and "anti-intellectual" attitude of oral historians,[34] others view it in the light of the reluctance of the academic world to make space for practices, ideas, and subjects that it could not control—as confirmed by the failure of the university to develop any significant contribution to the field ever since. The attempt to create a national society of oral historians (at a conference promoted by the Istituto De Martino in Mantova in 1984)[35] failed much for the same reasons, as well as for the increasing disintegration of the social movements to which some of the promoters looked for cultural and political reference.

Three themes dominated the discussion on oral history across these differences: reliability, representativity, and form. They can be connected, by and large, to three disciplinary areas: history, sociology, and literature (plus, more marginally, anthropology). Italian historiography was dominated to a large extent by the belief that archival, written, institutional sources were endowed with a degree of "objectivity" that made them more reliable than oral sources subjected to the vagaries of memory and subjectivity.[36] This approach recognized oral sources to at best function as a "subordinate and ancillary" medium for a "subsidiary" integration of "documentary evidence." Oral sources were, therefore, to be treated as "testimony" and used only for whatever referential value they might possess.[37] All possible precautions must be taken to keep oral sources from contaminating documentary evidence with their subjectivity.

The response of oral historians was two-fold. Cesare Bermani demonstrated that oral sources, when appropriately and critically treated, could yield as much reliable factual information as all other sources.[38] My own contribution began, on the other hand, with the assertion that oral sources had a "different" form of reliability that lay precisely in their subjectivity. By including error, imagination, and desire, oral sources reveal not only the history of what happened, but the history of what it meant; meaning (as revealed by narrative and linguistic form) rather than "fact" is what makes oral history different, and a necessary tool for the history of subjectivity.[39] From a different direction, Luisa Passerini was making the same suggestion at the same time, in her seminal studies of the "silences" in women's narratives of Fascism and in her criticism of the concept and structures of "collective" memory.[40]

Another naive criticism raised by established historians against the practice of oral history was that, as the formula goes, "you can't do history with oral sources alone." This objection was refuted both in practice and theory. In practice, all serious Italian oral history work—from Bosio to Bermani, from Passerini to Contini to myself and others—distinguished itself, if anything, for the extent to which archival, printed, and oral sources were investigated jointly and made to interact with one another in order to reveal their specificity and difference. Yet, at every conference and meeting, it was irritating to have to answer the same clichés from "scholars" who did not even bother to read what they criticized.[41]

What these scholars were resisting were less the (acknowledged) limits and shortcomings of oral history than the radical restructuring of the practice and the theory of history and the social sciences in general. As Nicola Gallerano (not an "oral historian" himself) noted, the "discovery" of oral sources raises questions of the formation and partiality of sources, of the role of the observer, of social and historical contextualization that deconstruct the pretense of inherent objectivity of *all* historical sources and that place the question of subjectivity (of the sources and of the historian) at the core of historiography. Indeed, the objection ought to be turned upon its head: when oral sources are available, it makes hardly any sense to continue, as most historians do, to do contemporary history using archival documents alone.[42]

It is no wonder, then, that the most intelligent use of oral sources by a "regular" historian is to be found in Claudio Pavone's definitive work on the Resistance.[43] A former partisan himself, Pavone came in contact with oral history through the Institutes for the History of Resistance. His book is dedicated less to a factual reconstruction of "what really happened" than to the exploration of the meaning and ethics, and therefore the subjective dimension of the partisan war. It makes ample and intelligent use of oral sources and of the work of oral historians.

Another promising sign was the involvement of oral historians and anthropologists, along with other historians, in the research project on the Nazi massacre at Civitella della Chiana (Tuscany, June 29, 1944) and in the final conference (Arezzo, June 1994). It was perhaps the first fruitful dialogue, on an equal footing of mutual respect, between "standard" and "oral" historians.[44]

Aside from these exceptions, therefore, a specifically historical use of oral sources is to be found mainly in "marginal" areas of historical research: local and regional history, including the study of rural and early-industrial society; labor and working-class history in the urban context, branching into material culture and political experiences (primarily, anti-Fascism and the Resistance); and women's history, including also the history of private life, of feelings, of the family. A book like Liliana Lanzardo's study of midwives in Veneto combines the three strands of locality, work, and gender.[45]

Perhaps the most remarkable example of an extensive and sensitive use of oral sources to reconstruct a specific local and rural culture is the work of Nuto Revelli on the impoverished Piedmont mountains in his native province of Cuneo. Revelli's work covers such themes as rural poverty, migrations, the memory and experience of war and Resistance, and the central role of women ("the strong link" in the fabric of society and the chain of memory). His work is representative of a number of oral history studies of rural and preindustrial cultures in Italy.[46]

The number of projects using oral history for themes related to work, unions, working-class parties, and politics is too ample (and too scattered in local publications) to be accounted for briefly. Among the most frequent thematic and structural approaches, are factory histories,[47] histories of industrial towns,[48] studies of political behavior and rank-and-file protagonism,[49] and studies of the processes and technology of work and attitudes toward it.[50]

While relatively few studies tapped the huge reservoir of tales about World War I (perhaps because it was thought to be too commonplace),[51] the history of Fascism and anti-Fascism was a major concern for oral historians. The question of "consent" has been crucial to the discussion of that era in Italian history, and oral history's approach to subjectivity was peculiarly suited to this field of inquiry, especially because it tapped into the memory and consciousness of silenced, politically invisible subjects, particularly women. Luisa Passerini, Bianca Guidetti Serra, Lidia Beccaria Rolfi, Anna Maria Bruzzone, and Laura Mariani explored the experience of women in the struggle against Fascism and in the Resistance, as well as in Fascist jails and Nazi concentration camps.[52] The testimony of 200 survivors of concentration camps, collected by a number of researchers in a project that lasted several years, and put together and edited by Anna Bravo and Daniele Jallà (*La vita offesa*), is one of the most moving products of Italian oral history.[53]

The antagonist origins of Italian oral history and the belief of Italian historians in the primacy of written documents also seriously limited the practice of elite oral history. An oral history society, established by major academic historians in the early 1980s produced a conference on the forms that an interview might take in journalism, folklore, and history, plus a few interviews with diplomats, and little else. None of the scholars and researchers whose work is described in this essay were ever invited to join (nor did they volunteer to). The growing interest toward the history of business, management, and entrepreneurs is behind Giampaolo Gallo's book-length oral autobiography of industrialist Bruno Buitoni.[54]

Perhaps the most systematic use of oral sources for historical research in the strict sense (though always with an interdisciplinary awareness and an eye to subjectivity) is the work of Alfredo Martini on the working class in southern Latium, and of Giovanni Contini on various aspects of working-class history and material culture in rural and urban Tuscany.[55] Martini and Contini collaborated in the first comprehensive and usable handbook of oral history published in Italy, *Verba Manent*,[56] and were also instrumental in the establishment and rationalization of oral archives and the recognition of oral sources by state historical archives.[57] Consistent with his concern with the actual processes and technologies involved in work, as evidenced by his earlier work on factory history, and with material culture in general, Contini has also been foremost in audio-visual approaches to oral history.[58] Needless to say, neither Contini nor Martini hold an academic position.

While historians were mainly concerned with reliability, sociologists concentrated on the question of the representativity of oral sources, the biographical method, and the relation of the individual to society. The use of oral sources toward a qualitative sociology was promoted primarily by Franco Ferrarotti, one of the founders of Italian sociology, who enriched the heritage of the Chicago school and the work of Thomas and Znaniecki on the one hand and the influence of Daniel Bertaux on the other, with an articulate awareness of the work of oral historians in Italy and abroad and a broad political perspective.[59] The sociological work that grew primarily around Ferrarotti in Rome, with scholars like Paola Bertelli, Enzo Campelli, Roberto Cipriani, Pietro Crespi, Maria Immacolata Macioti, and Enrico Pozzi, represented in the journal *La Critica Sociologica*, was characterized by a careful attention to the biographic method and the qualitative approach;[60] by an in-depth involvement in the study of urban marginal subjects and, more recently, immigration and multiculturalism;[61] and by the study of the sociological and anthropological aspects of the religious experience.[62]

Other sociological work, especially by Alessandro Cavalli and Gerardo Lutte, used the life-story method for the study of youth, and especially marginal youth. Youth culture and student movements have been the object also of a few, diversified attempts at historical reconstruction with oral sources.[63]

The contribution of anthropology to the discussion of oral sources must be sought mainly in epistemological criticism and commentary. However, perhaps because of the increasing abstraction and self-reflexivity of Italian anthropology, and the consequent weakening of De Martino's tradition of fieldwork and empirical research in favor of his more theoretical and philosophical side, the analytical and critical use of oral sources in actual anthropological studies of Italian society and culture has been very scant. Most contributions have taken the form of either theoretical articles (at times, unwarrantedly judgmental) or individual life stories.[64] Even such a question as the relationship of myth and history, which would appear to be the specific domain of cultural anthropology, has been treated instead by scholars with a historical or literary background.[65]

An original and fascinating blend of folklore and historical interpretation based on fieldwork is Aurora Milillo's study, *La vita e il suo racconto*, a comparative analysis of fairy tales and life-stories told by the same informants in Lucania, showing how folk motifs structure autobiographical narratives, while in turn autobiographical impulses are involved in the telling of fairy tales.[66] In fact, the work of folklorists on oral narratives and folk songs as historical documents[67] was a bridge between the practice of fieldwork in the social sciences and what was to be perhaps the most relevant Italian contribution to the study and interpretation of oral sources: the formal analysis of the narrative.[68] Linguists and literary theorists as well as critics who worked with oral materials drew attention to the fact that the oral quality of the sources is not a mere accident (to be dissolved by transcription), but rather the marrow of their meaning and relevance. In my own work, I repeatedly made the point that the meaning of the oral history narrative is to be found in its dialogic verbal form originating in the interview. The analysis of the narrative and symbolic structure and the variability and multiplicity of variants and versions are a key to implicit meanings in the tale; the use of socially shared genres and motifs bridges the gap between the individual and the collective, thus contributing to an answer to the question of representativity; the variability and multiplicity of variants and versions and the mutual interaction of fieldworker and informant, far from being a hindrance and an impurity, are the specific generic identity of the oral history interview. The experience of oral history, in turn, influenced the development of my work in literary criticism and history.[69]

The linguist Giorgio Cardona, in his studies on the anthropology and linguistics of writing, was inevitably drawn by contrast to the observation of orality in action, as demonstrated by fieldwork. Rejecting dualistic views of orality as opposed to writing, Cardona insisted on their mutual relationship, influence, and exchange.[70] Domenico Starnone did considerable work in oral history and the theory of oral expression as a second grade school teacher and member of the Circolo Gianni Bosio, before he went on to become one of the finest contemporary Italian writers, using the same oral history materials and experiences in some of his novels.[71] Finally, although Luisa Passerini's concern with the formal and narrative qualities of oral sources did not derive from a literary background, yet her intriguing *Autobiografia di gruppo* is a fascinating blend of autobiography, oral history, and self-reflective history of a research project that is also endowed with literary relevance.

Among the questions most heatedly debated by Italian oral historians are some of the following: what is the relationship of these voices with the voice of the historian? To what extent does the publication continue or represent the dialogue and the performance? What is, in each case, the balance between *oral* and *history*, the mode of transmission and factual reconstruction? I would like, therefore, to conclude with a brief survey of the formal and structural differences of some of the most influential works of Italian oral history in terms of the presentation of sources and of the interaction between the voices of the oral narrators and that of the historian.[72]

Nuto Revelli's books—*Il mondo dei vinti* (1977) and *L'anello forte* (1985)—are based on a rigorous distinction of voices: the historian writes rich, informative, sensitively self-reflective introductions, after which we read the edited testimony of the informants, one after the other, giving a sense of the shape of individual lives. The narrators are allowed to speak at length about themselves, and the interpretation is left to the reader, within the framework designed in the introduction. Documentary objectivity in the arrangement of voice is displayed in order to enhance the subjective pathos of each narrative.[73]

Luisa Passerini's *Torino operaia e il fascismo* (1984) is an example of how oral history can produce excellent history without adjectives. Passerini performs a sophisticated reading of the testimony as well as of written archival sources, framed in a tight historical narrative. The interviews are quoted very much in the same way as historical documents: textual verifications of a historical interpretation. The book's approach, however, is specific to oral history because it is centered on the reconstruction of subjectivity. While the orality of the sources is scarcely thematized, and little advantage is taken of the possibilities of narrative and linguistic analysis, the "oral" remains essential to the success of this book as "history," through the category of subjectivity.

In Maurizio Gribaudi's *Mondo operaio e mito operaio* (1987), the opposition between "world" and "myth," the effort to bring out factual reality and dispel ideological delusions, leads to an ancillary use of a limited number of oral sources as depositories of mainly factual information about economic strategies and demographic trajectories. The words of the interviewees are hardly quoted at all, and are interpreted rather cursorily, with scarcely any attention to the language, the narrative form, and their less explicit meanings. The balance between "oral" and "history" leans heavily toward the more conventional forms of the latter: this book has been described, in fact, as a case of "total devaluation of any significance of oral sources."[74]

My *Biografia di una città* (1985) is perhaps at the opposite end of the spectrum. An intense use of montage and bricolage of sources (including archival and printed ones) foregrounds polyphony and dialogue, while the historian ostensibly speaks as little as possible—providing connections and briefly suggesting ways of reading—yet is very much in control, and at key moments comes on stage to include the experience of the interview as a key to its meaning.[75] The minute fragmentation and recomposition of the voices (and their interaction with other sources) is re-created to convey the dialogic experience of a town's story told through many voices, less as objective reproduction than as creative representation. The models are derived less from history and sociology than from literature (Dos Passos, Conrad, Faulkner), cinema, music (the alternation of solos, arias, recitativo, choral and orchestral pieces of the baroque oratory). While factual events of history provide the skeleton of the narrative, its meaning lies almost entirely in the lower frequencies of the oral communication.

The most intense and self-reflective dialogue between the sources and the historian, finally, is presented in another work by Luisa Passerini, *Autoritratto di gruppo* (1988). Weaving oral histories of the student movement of 1968 with the history of her research and the analysis of the interviews, as well as with her own autobiography and psychoanalysis, Passerini creates an original synthesis of autobiography and historiography, psychoanalysis, social history, and literature, which is a new genre altogether. No wonder this book has inspired a form of presentation to which oral history seems to lend itself very successfully: a theater performance.

Now, the final question ought to be: is there such a thing as "Italian oral history"? As these examples indicated, individual practitioners have followed widely differing approaches to both the collection and presentation of sources. Indeed, any suggestions of a "school" or a "movement" of oral history in Italy have encountered lively resistance on many sides. Finally, the institutional weakness of the discipline, the fact that so much of it was done voluntarily, also favors fragmentation.

Yet, one cannot entirely discount the perception from abroad. Some shared traits become recognizable when seen from a distance: the focus of research on subjectivity rather than on factual reconstruction, on interpretation rather than collection and presentation of sources; the combination of active fieldwork, critical and methodological concerns, anti-authoritarian political horizons; the awareness of how social and individual mechanisms of memory, imagination, and desire influence the representations and projections of the past; the attention to narrative form as an expression of implicit meaning; the recognition of the dialogic nature of the field interview as a specific type of source formation; and the consciousness that oral history calls for a general reorganization of practice and theory in history and the social sciences at large. None of these traits are to be found in exactly the same way in all or even a majority of Italian oral history. Yet, they constitute the horizon of the debate and form the core of the Italian contribution to oral history in an international perspective.

We may therefore conclude with a quote from Luisa Passerini that summarizes most eloquently and concisely what makes Italian oral history different, and
what constitutes its challenge to history and social sciences at large:

> It is the concern of oral history to support and try to practice a historiography
> that shall be a conscious construction, from the standpoint of the present, of a
> past that is shaped by this reinterpretation but that, thanks to this effort of sub-
> jectivity, shall also return the object to what it really is and wants to be. A history
> that understands along which lines of real experience and power history—the
> intentional and unintentional activity of human and super-individual subjects—
> developed . . .
>
> Oral history is concerned with establishing a concept of memory as narrating act
> and symbolic mediation, to be studied in its diverse historical and social mani-
> festations. Discovering the discontinuities, contradictions, inertia, but also the
> creativity and fidelity of memory as an individual act in social contexts, may be a
> contribution toward broadening and humanizing the concept of historical
> truth.[76]

Notes

1. Alistair Thomson, "The Memory and History Debates: Some International Perspectives,"
Oral History (Autumn 1994), pp. 33–35; Paul Thompson, letter to the editors, *Oral History*
(Autumn, 1985), pp. 27–29. Luisa Passerini also confirms this version: "At the international
oral history conference at the University of Essex in 1979. . . the theme of memory had been
introduced, significantly, by the Italian contributions. But it was only the following year, at
Amsterdam, that a real discussion developed concerning the relationship of memory and for-
getting, narrative and silences. Until then, in fact, the factual approach of British oral history,
which sought primarily the contents of memory and merely claimed it as a legitimate source
along with traditional ones, had prevailed." "Il dibattito radiofonico come fonte," in *Storia e soggettività. Le fonti orali, la memoria* (Florence: La Nuova Italia, 1985), p. 167. At Amsterdam, it
was Luisa Passerini's opening paper that introduced the discussion on memory. For some of
the Italian contributions on memory at the Essex conference, see Paul Thompson, ed., *Our
Common History: The Transformation of Europe* (London, Pluto Press, 1982).
    2. Two influential Italian essays appeared quite early in *History Workshop*: Luisa Passerini,
"Work Ideology and Working Class Attitudes to Fascism, *History Workshop* 8 (1979); a shorter
version in Paul Thompson, ed., *Our Common History*, pp. 54–78; Alessandro Portelli, "On the
Peculiarities of Oral History," *History Workshop* 12 (1981), pp. 96–107; now in Alessandro
Portelli, *The Death of Luigi Trastulli and Other Stories. Form and Meaning in Oral History* (Albany,
N.Y.: State University of New York Press, 1991), pp. 45–58, as "What Makes Oral History Different" (originally published as "Sulla diversità della storia orale," *Primo Maggio* 13 (1979), pp.
54–60). Publication in *History Workshop* helped the international circulation and further trans-
lations: both articles are included in Dora Schwarzstein, ed., *La historia oral* (Buenos Aires:
Centro Editorial de América Latina, 1991): L. Passerini, "Ideología del trabajo y actitudes de la
clase trabajadora hacia el fascismo," pp. 142–72; A. Portelli, "Lo que hace diferente la historia

oral," ibid., pp. 36–52. The latter articles also appears as "La peculiaridades de la história oral," in *Tarea* [Perú] 11 (November 1984), pp. 21–29, and in *Cuadernos de Ciencias Sociales*, Facultad Latinoamericana de Ciencias Sociales, San José (Costarica), 1988.

3. Pietro Clemente, "Debate sobre las fuentes orales en Italia," *História y fuente oral* 14 (1995), pp. 81–94.

4. I am the only person identified with oral history who holds a chair in an Italian university—not, however, in history, but in American literature. Luisa Passerini was well known and respected internationally while she was still being refused associate professorships in history (she is currently at the European University in Florence, after several stints at U.S. universities). Of the historians mentioned later in this essay, Alfredo Martini works in public relations for an association of industrialists; Giovanni Contini works at the office for the cultural heritage in Tuscany (where he is allowed, but not required, to do oral history work); Nuto Revelli is a retired Army officer; Cesare Bermani, one of the founders and precursors of oral history in Italy, with over 1,000 books and articles to his credit, is unemployed: within one month, he was refused both an associate professorship in history in the university and a job as a janitor in his local elementary school. At least one member of the editorial board of *I Giorni Cantati*, a journal also associated with oral history, had to have her name removed from the list in order to be able to compete for a postgraduate fellowship in urban history.

5. Although an effort has been made to represent in the footnotes to this essay all significant trends and contributions in Italian oral history and related disciplines, yet no claim can be made for completeness. The very nature of the work with oral sources, scattered in a number of publications and publishers both national and local, scholarly, general, and activist, makes a truly complete listing all but impossible.

6. See Cesare Bermani, "Dieci anni di lavoro con le fonti orali," *Primo Maggio* 5 (1975), pp. 35–50.

7. Gianni Bosio, *Il trattore ad Acquanegra. Piccola e grande storia in una comunità contadina* (Bari: De Donato, 1981); *L'intellettuale rovesciato* (Milan: Bella Ciao, 1975); id. *Diario di un organizzatore di cultura* (Milan: Edizioni Avanti, 1962); *L'intellettuale rovesciato* (Milan: Bella Ciao, 1975). On Bosio, see Antonello Cuzzaniti and Cesare Bermani, "Biografia di un militante: Gianni Bosio," *Il Nuovo Canzoniere italiano* 4–5 (March 1977), pp. 37–59; Alfredo Martini, "Bosio, Gianni," in *Dizionario biografico degli italiani*, vol. XII (Rome: Enciclopedia Italiana, 1989); Alessandro Portelli, "Research as an Experiment in Equality," in *The Death of Luigi Trastulli and Other Stories. Form and Meaning in Oral History* (Albany, N.Y.: State University of New York Press, 1991), pp. 29–44; Cesare Bermani, "Gianni Bosio 'intellettuale rovesciato': l'organizzazione di cultura come supporto alla rifondazione politica," *Il de Martino*, bulletin of the Istituto Ernesto De Martino 1 (1992), pp. 10–28; Alessandro Portelli, "L'Elogio del magnetofono: alle origini della storia orale," ibid., pp. 29–43. All the reprints of Bosio's works listed above include ample introductions by Cesare Bermani.

8. On the Istituto De Martino, see Cesare Bermani, ed., *Il nuovo Canzoniere italiano dal 1962 al 1968* (Milan: Mazzotta, 1978), a reprint of the journal edited by Gianni Bosio and later by the Istituto Ernesto De Martino (a later series of *il nuovo Canzoniere italiano* was published until 1977). See also C. Bermani and Mimmo Boninelli, "L'attività dell'Istituto Ernesto De Martino," *I Giorni Cantati* 1 (1981), pp. 159–64; Franco Coggiola, "L'attività dell'Istituto Ernesto De Martino," in Diego Carpitella, ed., *L'etnomusicologia in Italia* (Palermo: Flaccovio, 1975), pp. 265–70; F. Coggiola, ed., *Fonti orali per la storia e l'antropologia: testimonianze e documenti del mondo contadino e operaio* (Urbino: Centro stampa dell'Università di Urbino, 1986). As of 1906, the Istituto held over 5,000 tapes in its collection. Currently, the Istituto publishes a bullettin, *il de Martino* (four issues, 1992–95)

9. P. Boccardo, G. Bosio, T. Savi, eds., *Addio padre. La guerra di Belochio, di Palma e di Badoglio* (Dischi del Sole, DS 304/6); Gianni Bosio, ed., *La Prima Internazionale* (Dischi del Sole DS 301/3/CP). For other examples of the l.p. record for the presentation of oral sources in the Dischi del Sole series, see A. Portelli, ed. *La borgata e la lotta per la casa* (SdL/AS/10); Franco Coggiola, ed., *Milano. Lotta operaia alla Crouzet* (SdL/As/11); Maria Luisa Betri and Annamaria Ciniselli, *Povero Matteotti* (DS/313/15); Maria Luisa Betri and Franco Coggiola, *Il sole si è fatto rosso. Giuseppe di Vittorio* (316/18).

10. Circolo Gianni Bosio, "Lavoro culturale e intervento politico. trasformazione di un rapporto," *I Giorni Cantati*, 4 1983), pp . 9–19.

11. Leaflet announcing the publication of the new series of *I Giorni Cantati*, a journal of the Circolo Gianni Bosio, Rome, 1981.

12. Danilo Montaldi, *Autobiografie della leggera* (Turin: Einaudi, 1961); id., *Militanti politici di base* (Turin: Einaudi, 1971). See Enzo Campelli, "Note sulla sociologia di Danilo Montaldi: alle origini di una proposta metodologica," *La critica sociologica* 49 (1977), pp. 26–50; Cesare Bermani, "Danilo Montaldi e Gianni Bosio," in *Bosio oggi: rilettura di un'esperienza* (Mantova: Comune di Mantova, 1986), pp. 153–61; Stefano Merli, *L'altra storia. Bosio, Montaldi e le origini della nuova sinistra* (Milan: Feltrinelli, 1977); Nicola Gallerano, "L'altra storia di Danilo Montaldi," in Istituto Ernesto De Martino, *Memoria operaia e nuova composizione di classe* (Rimini: Maggioli, 1986), pp. 197–204.

13. Diego Carpitella, "Profilo storico delle raccolte di musica popolare," *Studi e ricerche* 1948–1960 (Rome: CNSMP [Centro Nazionale di Studi sulla Musica Popolare of the Academy of Santa Cecilia], 1960); D. Carpitella, ed., *L'etnomusicologia in Italia* (Palermo: Flaccovio, 1975); Alberto M. Cirese, *Folklore e antropologia tra storicismo e marxismo* (Palermo: Palumbo, 1973); A. M. Cirese, *Cultura egemonica e culture subalterne* (Palermo: Palumbo, 1973); Roberto Leydi, *Canti sociali italiani* (Milano: Avanti!, 1963). For a collection of writings and documents on the political implications of postwar folklore and anthropology in Italy, see Pietro Clemente et al., eds., *Il dibattito sul folklore in Italia* (Milan: Edizioni di Cultura Popolare, 1976).

14. Ernesto De Martino, *Il mondo magico. Prolegomeni ad una storia del magismo* (Turin: Einaudi, 1948); *Morte e pianto rituale nel mondo antico* (Turin: Einaudi, 1958); *Sud e magia* (Milan: Saggiatore, 1959); *La terra del rimorso. Contributo ad una storia religiosa del Sud* (Milan: Saggiatore, 1961); *Furore, simbolo, valore* (Milan: Saggiatore, 1962).

15. Rocco Scotellaro, *Contadini del Sud* (Bari: Laterza, 1954); Vincenzo Padiglione, "Osservatore e osservato: problemi di conoscenza e rappresentazione. La vicenda Scotellaro," *Problemi del Socialismo* 20, 15 (1979), pp. 167–209; Alessandro Portelli, "Research as an Experiment in Equality" (also on the influence of De Martino and Gramsci).

16. Cesare Bermani, "Istituto Ernesto De Martino e Nuovo Canzoniere italiano. Quattordici punti di discussione con Glauco Sanga su un'esperienza di organizzazione della cultura emergente dal mondo popolare e proletario," in Istituto Ernesto De Martino, *Memoria operaia e nuova composizione di classe*, pp. 165–96; Ernesto de Martino, "Etnologia e cultura nazionale negli ultimi dieci anni," *Società*, 9:3 (September 1953), pp. 18–19.

17. Antonio Gramsci, "Osservazioni sul folklore," from *Quaderni dal carcere* vol. 3 (Turin: Einaudi, 1985), pp. 2309–17; Alberto M. Cirese, *Intellettuali, folklore e istinto di classe* (Turin: Einaudi, 1976); Cesare Bermani. "Gramsci operaista e la letteratura proletaria," *Primo Maggio* 14 (Winter 1980–81), pp. 11–25; id., "Breve storia del Prol'etkult italiano," *Primo Maggio* 16 (Winter–Fall, 1981–82), pp. 27–40. For oral history work on Gramsci, see C. Bermani., ed., *Gramsci raccontato* (Roma: Edizioni Associate, 1987); Collettivo di ricerca del Circolo Gianni Bosio, "Osservazioni del folklore su Gramsci," *I Giorni Cantati* 1 (1981), pp. 32–45; *Rereading Gramsci*, special issue of the bulletin *Il de Martino* 3 (September 1994).

18. Cesare Bermani, *L'altra cultura. Interventi, rassegne, ricerche. Riflessi culturali di una milizia politica* (Milan: Edizioni del Gallo, 1970); *Pagine di guerriglia* (Milan: Sapere, 1971); *La battaglia di Novara* (Milano: Sapere, 1972); *L'oro di Pestarena* (Milan: Sapere, 1973); "Dieci anni di lavoro con le fonti orali," *Il bambino è servito. Leggende metropolitane in Italia* (Bari: Dedalo, 1991).

19. *La Lega: dieci anni di attività delle leghe di cultura e dei gruppi del cremonese e del mantovano*, Lega di Cultura di Piadena (Cremona, 1975).

20. Susanna Cerboni, "Ruoli generazionali e cultura tradizionale a Guardavalle," *I Giorni Cantati* 13 (1979); id., "Guardavalle, Calabria. Trasformazioni di una ricerca," *I Giorni Cantati* 4 (1983), pp. 22–28.

21. *I Giorni Cantati* was published in different formats (mimeographed bulletin, research journal, mass magazine) from 1973 to 1995. Anthologies from this journal are in Circolo Gianni Bosio, *I Giorni Cantati. Vita quotidiana e cultura popolare a Roma e nel Lazio* (Milan: Mazzotta, 1983); Alfredo Martini and Alessandro Portelli, eds., *Memoria e resistenza umana. Vent'anni di Circolo Gianni Bosio* (Rome: Circolo Gianni Bosio, 1991). See also Alessandro Portelli, "Ricerca sul campo, intervento politico, organizzazione di classe: il lavoro del Circolo Gianni Bosio," in P. Angelini et al., *Studi antropologici e rapporti di classe* (Milan: Franco Angeli, 1980), pp. 190–200; id., "Memory and Human Resistance: For a History (and Celebration) of the Circolo Gianni Bosio," in *The Practice of Oral History: The Battle of Valle Giulia and Other Stories* (Madison: University of Wisconsin Press, forthcoming).

22. Beside titles already mentioned in these notes, some oral history and related contributions published in *Primo Maggio*: C. Bermani, "Dieci anni di lavoro con le fonti orali"; id., "La Volante rossa (Estate 1945–/febbraio 1949)" 9–10 (1977), pp. 81–106; A. Portelli, "Sulla diversità della storia orale"; Sergio Bologna, "Otto tesi per la storia militante" 11 (1977–78), pp. 60–65; Cesare Bermani and Bruno Cartosio, "Dieci anni di 'Primo Maggio'" 19–20 (Winter 1983–84), pp. 22–25.

23. Alessandro Triulzi, "Storia dell'Africa e fonti orali," *Quaderni storici* 35 (1977).

24. See Istituto Ernesto De Martino, *Memoria operaia e nuova composizione di classe. Problemi e metodi della storiografia sul proletariato* (Rimini: Maggioli, 1986), proceedings of a conference organized by the Istituto De Martino and *Primo Maggio* in Rimini, October 1981 (among the relevant papers, Sergio Bologna, "Memoria operaia e rifiuto della memoria operaia," pp. 459–64; Brunello Mantelli, "'Il dinosauro presbite.' Per una riflessione sul sapere storiografico degli anni '70 e la crisi attuale," pp. 419–27, and the transcripts of the discussions). See also Sergio Bologna, "Otto tesi sulla storia militante"; id., "Contro il revisionismo storiografico," *I Giorni Cantati* 13 (March 1990), pp. 44–46.

25. Bernardo Bernardi, Carlo Poni, Alessandro Triulzi, *Fonti orali. Antropologia e storia* (Milan: Franco Angeli, 1978); *Quaderni Storici*, special issue 20:35 (1977); Cesare Bermani and Sergio Bologna, "Soggettività e storia del movimento operaio," *Il Nuovo Canzoniere italiano* 4–5 (March 1977), pp. 7–36. For a commentary, see Alfredo Martini, "L'uso delle fonti orali negli studi antropologici e nella storiografia contemporanea," *Il Mulino* 249 (1977), pp. 125–32.

26. Luisa Passerini, *Storia orale. Vita quotidiana e cultura materiale delle classi subalterne* (Torino: Rosenberg e Sellier, 1978). The introduction is reprinted as "Conoscenza storica e fonti orali" in *Storia e soggettività. Le fonti orali, la memoria*, pp. 31–65.

27. Luisa Passerini, "Diritto all'autobiografia" in *Storia e soggettività*, pp. 2–30; "Per una critica ica storica dell'oralità," ibid., pp. 104–53 (first published in *Papers Presented to the International Oral History Conference*, Amsterdam, 22–24 October, 1980; *Torino operaia e fascismo. Una storia orale* (Bari: Laterza, 1984); "Italian Working Class Culture Between the Wars: Consensus to Fascism and Work Ideology," *International Journal of Oral History* 1 (1980); *Storie di donne e di femministe* (Turin: Rosenberg e Sellier, 1991). For a discussion of subjectivity in oral

history, with Italian contributions by Luisa Passerini and Alessandro Portelli, as well as by other European scholars, see *International Journal of Oral History* 1 (1985), pp. 3–46.

28. Anna Bravo, Luisa Passerini, Simonetta Piccone Stella, "Modi di raccontarsi e forme d'identità nelle storie di vita," *Memoria* 8 (1983), pp. 101–103; Franca Fossati, *Fonti orali e politica delle donne: storia, ricerca, racconto* (Centro di Documentazione, Ricerca e Iniziativa delle Donne: Bologna, 1983). See also Anna Bravo and Lucetta Scaraffia, "Ruolo femminile e identità delle contadine delle Langhe: un'ipotesi di storia orale," *Rivista di storia contemporanea* 1 (1979), pp. 21–55 ; Luisa Passerini, "Rappresentazioni del lavoro nella memoria delle donne e autorappresentazioni del lavoro di ricerca," and Lidia Piccioni, "L'intervista tra donne: similarità e differenza," both in *I Giorni Cantati* 4 (1983), pp. 29–35 and 36–41.

29. Elsa Joubert, *Il lungo viaggio di Poppie Nongena* (1987); Elisabetta Burgos, *Mi chiamo Rigoberta Menchú* (1987); Luisa Passerini, *Autoritratto di gruppo* (1988); Marcella Filippa and Giorgina Arian Levi, *Avrei capovolto le montagne* (1991); Carla Corso and Sandra Landi, *Ritratto a tinte forti* (1991); Salwa Salem, *Con il vento nei capelli* (1993); Bruna Payrot, *Oltre le nuvole. Storia di una curatrice d'anime* (1994); all published by Giunti (Florence).

30. Cesare Bermani, "Introduzione" to *Memoria operaia e nuova composizione di classe*, p. xxvii–xxviii. See the remarks of professors Giuliano Ventura and Giuliano Manacorda (in response to my report on the oral history workshop) as reported in the summary of the conference proceedings, *Italia contemporanea* (July–September 1979), pp. 100–26, and as quoted verbatim from the tape recording in Cesare Bermani's introduction. The official Communist press of the times also distinguished itself for a number of attacks on the intrinsic "contiguity" of the work of radical historians and oral historians to terrorism: see Bermani, pp. xx–xxi. Clemente's charge that Italian oral history is mainly characterized by a "political or polemical utilization of sources" is a late manifestation of this attitude.

31. *Atti del Convegno sulle fonti orali, Torino, 17 gennaio 1981*, mimeographed report by the Istituto Gramsci, Turin, 1981.

32. *La storia: fonti orali nella scuola* (Venice: Marsilio, 1982), introduction by Guido Quazza; Paola Falteri, G. Lazzarin, eds, *Tempo, memoria, identità. Orientamenti per la formazione storica di base raccolti e proposti dal Gruppo nazionale di Antropologia Culturale del Movimento di Cooperazione Educativa* (Florence: Nuova Italia, 1986). For a report on an education project using oral history with handicapped children, see Adriana Dondona and Mauro Marcelli, "Memoria e identità," *I Giorni Cantati* 21–22 (June 1994), pp. 43–44. Oral history was often used in projects generated by the so-called "150-hours courses" sponsored by the unions in the 1970s: see Lidia Piccioni and Alfredo Martini, "Autobiografia e oralità. Un intervento didattico a Roma," *I Giorni Cantati* 1 (1981), pp. 195–204. For an oral history project involving high school students in a history of their neighborhood, see Liceo Scientifico Statale Giambattista Morgagni, *Storia del quartiere di Donna Olimpia* (Roma: CISD, 1985).

33. Paola Bertelli, "Fra storia e fonti orali," *La Critica Sociologica* 66 (1983), pp. 148–50.

34. P. Clemente, "Debate sobre las fuentes orales en Italia."

35. Cesare Bermani et al., "Per una associazione di storici orali," *Fonti orali* 7:4 (1987).

36. Nicola Gallerano, "Fonti orali, fonti scritte e il mestiere di storico," *I Giorni Cantati* 21–22 (June 1994), pp. 40–42, describes and criticizes this attitude from the point of view of a professional historian.

37. A typical statement by a foremost historian is Renzo De Felice, preface to Sergio Zavoli, *Nascita di una dittatura* (Milan: Mondadori, 1983); see also the critical comments by Giuliana Bertacchi, "Esperienze didattiche degli istituti della Resistenza e uso delle fonti orali," in *La storia: fonti orali nella scuola*, p. 44. A more articulate, but ultimately dismissive, mention of interviews as historical sources is in Ernesto Ragionieri, "Considerazioni sugli studi locali," *Emilia* (December 1952), p. 32.

38. C. Bermani, "Dieci anni di lavoro con le fonti orali."

39. A. Portelli, "Sulla specificità della storia orale"; id., "L'assassinio di Luigi Trastulli. Terni 17 marzo 1949. La memoria e l'evento," *Segno critico* 4 (Perugia, 1980), pp. 115–42; id., "Una storia sbagliata: memoria operaia e mondi possibili," *I Giorni Cantati* 1 (1981), pp. 13–31; "The Time of My Life: Functions of Time in Oral History," *International Journal of Oral History* 2, 3 (November 1981), pp. 162–180; "Con inni e bandiere. Il conflitto culturale nello sciopero di Harlan," in R. Botta et al., *La cultura delle classi subalterne fra tradizione e innovazione* (Alessandria: Edizioni dell'Orso, 1988), pp. 151–68. All are included, in revised English versions, in *The Death of Luigi Trastulli*.

40. Luisa Passerini, "Soggettività operaia e fascismo: indicazioni di ricerca sulle fonti orali," *Annali della Fondazione Giangiacomo Feltrinelli*, 20 (1979–80), pp. 285–314; afterword to Maurice Halbwachs, *La memoria collettiva* (Milan: Unicopli, 1987)

41. See for an example the discussion at the conference on "Oral History and Life Stories" (Trieste, November 1985), in Liliana Lanzardo, *Storia orale e storie di vita* (Milan: Franco Angeli, 1988), p. 129–58; Alessandro Portelli, "'La verdad del corazón humano': los fines actuales de la história oral," *História y fuente oral* 2 (1989), pp. 91–97. Part of this attitude was generated by the misunderstanding that "oral history" meant the use of exclusively oral sources rather than, as it is understood worldwide and intended here, a type of historical research *based* on the systematic and critical, but not exclusive, use of oral sources. In this sense, "oral history" is a more restrictive term than, say, Bosio's formula, "the use of oral sources in historiography," inasmuch as the latter could also be applied to conventional history that makes a casual or ancillary use of a limited number of interviews. For a discussion of terminology, see also L. Passerini, "Fonti orali: utilità e cautele," *Storia e storie* 3 (1980), pp. 4–18.

42. Nicola Gallerano, "Fonti orali, fonti scritte e il mestiere di storico"; A. Portelli, "What Makes Oral History Different"; Luisa Passerini, "Conoscenza storica e fonti orali."

43. Claudio Pavone, *Una guerra civile. Saggio sulla moralità nella Resistenza* (Torino: Boringhieri, 1991).

44. A. Portelli, "Lutto, senso comune, mito e politica nella strage di Civitella Val di Chiana," in Leonardo Paggi, ed., *Storia di un massacro ordinario. Civitella della Chiana, 29 giugno 1944* (Roma: Manifestolibri, 1996), also in *The Practice of Oral History. The Battle of Valle Giulia and other Stories*. The conference proceedings, including other work by oral historians (Giovanni Contini) and anthropologists (Pietro Clemente, Valeria di Piazza and others), are also to be published shortly.

45. Liliana Lanzardo, *Il mestiere prezioso. Le ostetriche raccontano* (Torino: Forma, 1985).

46. Nuto Revelli, *Il mondo dei vinti. Testimonianze di vita contadina* (Turin: Einaudi, 1977); *L'anello forte. La donna: storie di vita contadina* (Turin: Einaudi, 1985). On oral history of rural society and forms of production, see Rocco Scotellaro, *Contadini del Sud*; Giovanni Rinaldi and Paola Sobrero, *La memoria che resta. Vissuto quotidiano, mito e storia dei braccianti del basso Tavoliere* (Naples: Amministrazione Provinciale di Capitanata, 1981); Marco Mietto and Maria Grazia Ruggerini, *Il proletariato invisibile. La manifattura della paglia nella Toscana mezzadrile* (Milan: Franco Angeli, 1991); Luciano Ardiccioni and Giovanni Contini, *Vivere di coltelli. Per una storia dell'artigianato dei ferri taglienti a Scarperia* (Florence: Centro Editoriale Toscano, 1989). On migrations, see Renato Cavallaro, *Storie senza storia. Indagine sull'emigrazione calabrese in Gran Bretagna* (Rome: Centro Studi Emigrazione, 1981).

47. Giovanni Contini, *Memoria e storia. Le officine Galileo nel racconto degli operai, dei tecnici, dei manager* (Milan: Franco Angeli, 1985); Dario Bigazzi, *Il Portello. Operai e dirigenti all'Alfa Romeo di Milano* (Milan: Franco Angeli, 1989); Liliana Lanzardo, *Classe operaia e partito comunista alla Fiat (1945–1948)* (Turin: Einaudi, 1971); id., "Fonti orali e storia della classe operaia: indagini sulla coscienza di classe alla Fiat," *Rivista di storia contemporanea* 2 (1981),

pp. 255–80; id., "Class Consciousness and the Fiat Workers of Turin since 1943," in P. Thompson, ed., *Our Common History*, pp. 79–89; Salvatore Ruju, *Via delle conce. Storia e memoria dell'industria del cuoio a Sassari* (Sassari: Libreria Dessì Editrice, 1990); Marco Mietto and Maria Grazia Ruggerini, *Storie di fabbrica. Operai metallurgici a Reggio Emilia negli anni '50* (Torino: Rosenberg e Sellier, 1988); Marcella Filippa, *Mia mamma mi raccontava che da giovane andavano a fare i mattoni* . . . (Alessandria: Edizioni dell'Orso, 1982); Maurizio Gribaudi, "Storia orale e struttura del racconto autobiografico," *Quaderni storici* 39 (1978), pp. 1131–46; id., *Mondo operaio e mito operaio. Spazi e percorsi sociali a Torino nel primo Novecento* (Turin: Einaudi, 1987); Daniele Jallà, "Perché mio papà era ferroviere . . . Una famiglia operaia torinese nei primi del Novecento," *Rivista di storia contemporanea* 1 (1980); *Fonti orali e cultura materiale*, special section in *Rassegne degli Archivi di Stato* 1–2 (January–August 1988), pp. 250–303. See also Coggiola, Grusso, Perotti, and Revelli, *Giorni della Fiat,* for a documentary use of oral history.

48. Alessandro Portelli, *Biografia di una città. Storia e racconto. Terni 1831–1984* (Turin: Einaudi, 1985); Lidia Piccioni, *San Lorenzo. Un quartiere romano durante il fascismo* (Rome: Edizioni di Storia e Letteratura, 1984); Alfredo Martini, *Biografia di una classe operaia. I cartai della Valle del Liri* (Rome: Bulzoni, 1994).

49. Maurizio Carbognin and Luigi Paganelli, *Il sindacato come esperienza* (Rome: Edizioni Lavoro, 1981); Arnaldo Nesti, *Anonimi compagni. Le classi subalterne sotto il fascismo* (Roma: Coines, 1976); L. Li Causi, *Il partito a noi ci ha dato! Antropologia politica di una sezione comunista senese nel dopoguerra* (Siena: Periccioli, 1993); Patrizia Ramondino, *Napoli: i disoccupati organizzati. I protagonisti raccontano* (Milan: Feltrinelli, 1977); Sesa Tatò, ed., *A voi cari compagni. La militanza sindacale ieri e oggi* (Bari: De Donato, 1981).

50. R. Botta, F. Castelli, B. Mantelli, eds., *La cultura delle classi subalterne fra tradizione e innovazione*; Giovanni Contini and Alfredo Martini, *Verba Manent. L'uso delle fonti orali per la storia contemporanea* (Roma: La Nuova Italia Scientifica, 1993), pp. 37–41; Annamaria Rivera, "Donne e lavoro contadino in Puglia," in Istituto De Martino, *Memoria operaia e composizione di classe*, pp. 111–20; Roberto Pincelli, Katia Sonetti, Silvano Taccola, "Coscienza e soggettività dentro una città fabbrica: Piombino 1944/1956," ibid., pp. 223–43; Alessandro Portelli, "Sport, lavoro e politica in una città industriale," ibid., pp. 263–92; Giovanni Boninelli, "Tecnici e operai di fronte all'informatica: l'esperienza di Dalmine," ibid., pp. 439–57; Roberto Botta, "L'operaio e la macchina. Aspetti della soggettività operaia all'Ilva di Novi Ligure: per un uso delle fonti orali," *Rassegna degli Archivi di Stato* 1–2 (1988), pp. 280–90.

51. Diego Leoni and Camillo Zadra, *La grande guerra* (Bologna: Il Mulino, 1989); Anna Bravo, "Italian Peasant Women and the First World War," in P. Thompson, ed., *Our Common History*, pp. 157–70. For pervasive memories of World War I, see Nuto Revelli's *Il mondo dei vinti.*

52. Bianca Guidetti Serra, *Compagne. Testimonianze di partecipazione politica femminile* (Turin: Einaudi, 1977); Lidia Beccaria Rolfi and Anna Maria Bruzzone, *Le donne di Ravensbruck* (Turin: Einaudi, 1978); Laura Mariani, *Quelle dell'idea. Storie di detenute politiche* (Bari: De Donato, 1982).

53. Anna Bravo and Daniele Jallà, eds., *La vita offesa. Storia e memoria dei lager nazisti nei racconti di duecento sopravvissuti* (Milan: Franco Angeli, 1986). See also A. Bravo, Lilia Davite, and D. Jallà, "Myth, impotence, and survival in the concentration camps," in Raphael Samuel and Paul Thompson, *The Myths We Live By* (London: Routledge, 1990), pp. 95–110; Ferruccio Cereja and Brunello Mantelli, *La deportazione nei campi di sterminio* (Milan: Franco Angeli, 1986).

54. Bruno Buitoni, *Pasta e cioccolato. Una storia imprenditoriale*, interview by Giampaolo Gallo (Perugia: Protagon, 1992). See also Giovanni Contini, *Santa Croce sull'Arno. Biografie di*

imprenditori (Empoli: Thesis, 1987). On the so-called Società Italiana di Storia orale, see the proceedings of the conference on *L'intervista strumento di documentazione*. *Giornalismo, antropologia, storia orale* (Rome: Ministero dei Beni Culturali e Ambientali, 1987); Maria G. Melchionni, *Istor. Colui che racconta in veste di testimone. Manualetto per praticare la storia orale* (Rome: Kappa, 1996). As of January, 1996, the Society also publishes a semestral newsletter. For a project of elite oral history, initiated by CENSIS (a social research organization based in Rome) in which the Society is also involved, see *Archivio delle fonti orali sugli anni '50. Memoria di un decennio di modernizzazione* special issue of *CENSIS. Note e commenti* 30:4 (Aprile 1994).

55. Alfredo Martini, *Biografia di una classe operaia;* id., "Operai e popolazione ad Isola del Liri nel secondo dopoguerra. Prime considerazioni su fonti e storia operaia," *I Giorni Cantati* 4 (1983), pp. 129–36; id., "Coloni e braccianti veneti nell'Agro romano. Maccarese negli anni Trenta," in Emilio Franzina and Antonio Parisella, eds., *La Merica in Piscinara. Emigrazione, bonifiche e colonizzazione veneta nell'Agro romano tra fascismo e post-fascismo* (Padova: Francisci, 1986), pp. 131–90; id., "Riflessioni sull'uso delle fonti orali nella ricerca storica," *Rassegna degli Archivi di Stato* 1–2 (January–August 1988), pp. 154–68; Giovanni Contini, "Fonti orali e fonti scritte: un confronto," *Classe* 18 (1980), pp. 285–328; id., "Fonti orali e storia delle identità individuali e collettive," *Rassegna degli Archivi di Stato* 1–2 (January–August 1988), pp. 136–43; id., *Memoria e storia. Le officine Galileo nel racconto degli operai, dei tecnici, dei manager;* id., "La história oral en Italia," *História y fuente oral* 5 (1989), pp. 131–38.

56. Giovanni Contini and Alfredo Martini, *Verba Manent. L'uso delle fonti orali per la storia contemporanea* (Roma: La Nuova Italia Scientifica, 1993).

57. On archives, see Paola Carucci and Giovanni Contini, eds., *Le fonti orali*, special issue of *Rassegna degli Archivi di Stato*, 48, 1–2, 1988; Alfredo Martini, Antonella Mulé, eds., *Fonti orali. Censimento degli istituti di conservazione* (Rome: Ministero per i Beni Culturali e ambientali, 1993).

58. See Giovanni Contini and Silvia Paggi, "La memoria divisa," video annexed to L. Paggi, ed., *Storia di un massacro ordinario*. A comprehensive catalogue of Italian visual archives in Luisa Arduini, ed., *Guida agli archivi audiovisivi in Italia* (Rome: Archivio audiovisivo del movimento operaio e democratico, 1996). The following possess significant amounts of oral history material: Archivio Audiovisivo del Movimento Operaio e Democratico (Rome); Archivio Etnostorico Nazionale (Catania); Archivio Nazionale Cinematografico della Resistenza (Turin); Biblioteca Civica Fonovideoteca "Antonio Tiraboschi" (Bergamo); Centro Etnografico Ferrarese (Ferrara); the Cooperativa Ricerca sul Territorio (Ostia, Rome); Multimediateca of the University of L'Aquila; Videoteca della Memoria of the Jewish Documentation Center (Milan).

59. Franco Ferrarotti, *La storia e il quotidiano* (Bari: Laterza, 1986).

60. Franco Ferrarotti, *Vite di periferia* (Milan: Mondadori, 1981); id., "Les biographies comme instrument analytique et interprétatif," *Cahiers Internationaux de Sociologie* 69 (1980), 227–48; id., "On the Autonomy of the Biographical Method," in Daniel Bertaux, ed., *Biography and Society. The Life History Approach in the Social Sciences* (London: Sage, 1981), pp. 19–27; Enzo Campelli, "Approccio biografico e inferenza scientifica," *Sociologia e ricerca sociale* 3, 9 (1982), pp. 71–94; Roberto Cipriani, Enrico Pozzi, Consuelo Corradi, "Histoires de vie familiale dans un contexte urbain," *Cahiers Internationaux de Sociologie* 79 (1985), pp. 253–62; Pietro Crespi, "Narrazione e ascolto. Aspetti e problemi dell'approccio orale in sociologia," *La Critica Sociologica* 70 (1984), pp. 41–52; Maria Immacolata Macioti, ed. *Biografia, storia e società. L'uso delle storie di vita nelle scienze sociali* (Naples: Liguori, 1985); M. I. Macioti and Consuelo Corradi, eds., special issue of *Biography and Society/Biographie et Societé* 9 (1987).

61. Paola Bertelli, "Da tanti canti furon pianti," *La Critica Sociologica*, n. 68 (1983–84), pp. 81–156; Roberto Cipriani, "Il caso di Valle Aurelia," *La critica Sociologica* 63–64 (1982–83), pp. 93–170 and 244–45; Maria Immacolata Macioti, "La Magliana nuova a Roma," *La Critica*

Sociologica 68 (1983–84), pp. 39–80; Roberto De Angelis, *Gli erranti. Nuove povertà e immigrazione nella metropoli* (Rome: Edizioni Kappa, 1991); Enrico Pozzi, "Marco Caruso e Aldo Moro. Ipotesi sulla degradazione dell'immaginario collettivo," *I Giorni Cantati* 1 (1981), pp. 98–108.

62. Pietro Crespi, *Prete operaio* (Roma: Edizioni Lavoro, 1985); Roberto Cipriani, *Il Cristo rosso. Riti e simboli, religione e politica nella cultura popolare* (Rome: Ianua, 1985); Enzo Campelli et al., "Religione e storie di vita familiare," *Idoc internazionale* 2–3 (1983), pp. 26–30; id. et al., eds., *Histoires de vie et groups primaires: une méthodologie pour l'analyse du phénomène religieux*, Actes de la XVIème C.I.S.R. (Conference of Religious Studies) (Lausanne, 1981); Franco Ferrarotti, "La iglesia católica y el problema de la convivencia intercultural," *História y fuente oral* 11 (1994), pp. 119–28. See also the anthropologist Clara Gallini's *Intervista a Maria* (Palermo: Sellerio, 1981); Alessandro Portelli, "La Ss. Trinità e la cassa integrazione," *I Giorni Cantati* 7 (1975), pp. 3–6.

63. For sociological approaches to youth culture using oral sources: Alessandro Cavalli, ed., *Il tempo dei giovani* (Bologna: Il Mulino, 1985); Gerardo Lutte, *Giovani invisibili: lavoro, disoccupazione e vita quotidiana in un quartiere proletario* (Rome: Edizioni Lavoro, 1981); M. Caccialanza, M. T. Torti, M. Di Massa, *L'officina dei sogni. Arte e vita nell'underground* (Genoa; Costa e Nolan, 1994); Alessandra Castellani, *Senza chioma né legge. Skins italiani* (Rome: Manifestolibri, 1994); Raffaele Rauty and Angelica Jacovino, *Giovani a Montefalcone* (Dipartimento di Sociologia dell'Università di Salerno, 1995). For more historically oriented oral history work on youth culture and history, see Micaela Arcidiacono, Francesca Battisti, et al., *L'aeroplano e le stelle. Storia orale di una realtà studentesca* (Rome: Manifestolibri, 1995); Marco Mietto and Maria Grazia Ruggerini, "Faber est quisque fortune suae. Gli studenti del Liceo Classico e dell'Istituto Magistrale a Reggio Emilia," *Contributi* (periodical of the Reggio Emilia city administration), 21–22 (1987), pp. 232–391; Rosanna Basso, "Myths in contemporary oral transmission: a children's strike," in R. Samuel and P. Thompson, eds., *Myths We Live By*, pp. 61–69; Cesare Bermani, "Novara, estate 1969: capelloni contro militari," *I Giorni Cantati* 10–11 (September 1989), pp. 4–15; Susanna Cerboni, "Ruoli generazionali e cultura tradizionale a Guardavalle"; Franco Coppoli, "Alcune divergenze fra il compagno Lama e noi: per una storia orale del '77 a Roma," ibid., pp. 38–42; Alessandro Portelli, "Intervistare il movimento: il '68 e la storia orale," ibid., pp. 67–72; id., "Cultura operaia, condizione giovanile, politicità del privato: ipotesi per una ricerca sul campo," *Rivista di storia contemporanea* 8:1 (January 1979), 56–83; id., "Conversations with the Panther. The Italian Student Movement of 1990," *International Annual of Oral History*, ed. by Ronald J. Grele (summer 1990 [publish. 1992]), pp. 145–166; Francesca Battisti and Alessandro Portelli, "The Apple and the Olive Tree: Tourists and Migrants in the University," *International Annual of Oral History and Life Stories* 3 (1994), pp. 35–52 (all to be included in the section on youth movements in *The Practice of Oral History*); Luisa Passerini, *Autobiografia di gruppo*. Passerini also contributed for the Italian parts of the project to Ronald Fraser, ed., *1968. A Student Generation in Revolt. An International Oral History* (New York: Pantheon, 1988).

64. Marisa Callari Galli, *Le storie di vita* (Roma: Edizioni Ricerche, 1966); Pietro Clemente, "L'oliva del tempo: frammenti di idee sulle fonti orali, sul passato e sul ricordo nella ricerca storica e demologica," *Uomo e cultura* 33–6 (1984–5), pp. 17–34; "Debate sobre las fuentes orales en Italia"; id., "Las fuentes orales en la história de los estudios demológicos en Italia. Apuntes," *Estudios sobre las cultural contemporáneas. Revista de investigación y análisis* 8–9 (Colima, Mexico, 1990); id., "Multiculturalismo, identità etnica," *Ossimori* 2 (1993, pp. 9–17); id., "Temps, mémoire et récits. Anthropologie et histoire," *Ethnologie française* 3 (1994); Valeria Di Piazza and A. Mugnaini, *Io sò nata a Santa Lucia* (Castelfiorentino, Arezzo: Società Storica Valdelsana, 1988); Amalia Signorelli, "Due storie di vita a confronto," *Scritti in memoria de Sebastiano Lo Negro* (Catania: Facoltà di Lettere e Filosofia, 1994), pp. 260–89. See also Cesare Bermani,

"Storia e antropologia. Appunti di lavoro," in R. Botta et al., eds., *La cultura delle classi subalterne*, pp. 17–42.

65. Luisa Passerini, "Mythbiography in oral history," and Alessandro Portelli, "Unchronic Dreams: Working-Class Memory and Possible Worlds," both in R. Samuel and P. Thompson, eds., *The Myths We Live By*, pp. 49–60, 143–60 (in the same volume, see also the articles by Rosanna Basso and Anna Bravo et al., cited elsewhere in this article); Cesare Bermani, *Il bambino è servito*.

66. Aurora Milillo, *La vita e il suo racconto. Tra favola e memoria storica* (Roma-Reggio Calabria: Casa del libro, 1983); see also *Fonti orali* 2–3 (1983), special issue on narrative and oral tradition, edited by Aurora Milillo.

67. Cesare Bermani, "Canti popolari e storie di vita," in L. Lanzardo, ed., *Storia orale e storie di vita*, pp. 91–118; Roberto Leydi, *La canzone popolare*, in *Storia d'Italia* (Turin: Einaudi, 1973), vol. V–II; id., *Canti sociali italiani*; A. Portelli, "Tipologia della canzone operaia," *Movimento operaio e socialista* 6:2 (May–August 1983), pp. 207–24 (now in *The Death of Luigi Trastulli*, pp. 161–92); Franco Castelli, "La 'storia adombrata': etnotesti e memoria orale," in R. Botta et al., eds., *La cultura delle classi subalterne*, pp. 265–81. An excellent series of publications bridging folklore, local history, and oral sources is the *Quaderni dell'Archivio della cultura di base* coordinated by Mimmo Boninelli (a musician and oral historian also connected to the Istituto De Martino) in Bergamo.

68. *Racconto: tra oralità e scrittura*, ed. by Irene Loffredo (Milan: Emme Edizioni, 1983), with contributions by Alessandro Portelli, Cristina Lavinio, and Domenico Starnone; C. Lavinio, Luisa Mulas, Giovanna Corina, *Oralità e scrittura nel sistema letterario* (Rome: Bulzoni, 1980).

69. *Il testo e la voce. Oralità, scrittura e democrazia nella letteratura americana* (Rome: Manifestolibri, 1992); Engl. trans , *The Text and the Voice. Speaking, Writing and Democracy in American Literature* (New York: Columbia University Press, 1994) See also "*Absalom, Absalom!*: Oral History and Literature," in *The Death of Luigi Trastulli*, pp. 270–82; "Oral History as Genre," in *The Practice of Oral History*.

70. Giorgio Cardona, "Oralità e scrittura," in Alberto Asor Rosa, ed., *Letteratura italiana* vol. 2 (Bari: Laterza, 1983). For a conversational linguistics approach to oral history, see Anna Scannavini, "Lingua orale e lingua scritta: lavori in corso," *I Giorni Cantati* 7 (1985); id., "Note preliminari sul discorso orale," *I Giorni Cantati* 25 (spring 1995), pp. 40–46.

71. Domenico Starnone, "L'eroe, la santa, le polveri: antinfortunistica sacra alla Snia di Colleferro," *I Giorni Cantati* 1 (1981), pp. 46–58; "Scuola, ricerca e teatro. Per riprendere la parola," *I Giorni Cantati* 4 (1983), pp. 52–65; Oralità subalterna e dominio della scrittura," in *Racconto: tra oralità e scrittura*, ed. by I. Loffredo, pp. 59–81. All three are based on a project later recounted in his novel, *Segni d'oro* (Milan: Feltrinelli, 1990).

72. This section is based on parts of a paper on "Oral History as Genre" presented at the conference on "Method and Methodology in Oral History and the Social Sciences," L'vov, Ukraine, September 1984, and included in *The Practice of Oral History*.

73. Revelli's use of "testimony" and "lives" in the subtitles ("testimonies of rural life," "stories of rural life") underlines the effect of objectivity; he goes so far as to incorporate his own questions into the informants' answers, so as not to appear to intrude: "Do I believe they sent a man to the moon?" Revelli uses a very different, dialogic, and self-reflective approach, in his recent *Il disperso di Marburg* (Torino: Einaudi, 1994), which focuses on the history of a research and on his own responses to the problems it raises.

74. Giovanni Contini and Alfredo Martini, *Verba Manent*, p. 47 n.

75. According to Luisa Passerini, the combination of montage and narrative contextualization in this book causes "a seeming disappearance of the subject, or, rather, an ambiguity as to

who is the subject in this game of rewriting and extrapolation—who plays which role in the piling up of quotations" ("Il programma radiofonico come fonte," *Storia e soggettività*, pp. 172–73). Ultimately, as the name on the cover clearly indicates, the speaking subject, responsible for the overall statement, is the historian himself or herself.

   76. L. Passerini, "Per una critica storica dell'oralità," pp. 116–17.

31

Oral History
in Latin America

Dora Schwarzstein

*As part of her research for the International Congress of Historical Sciences in Mont-
real in 1995, Dr. Dora Schwarzstein of Argentina surveyed her colleagues on oral history in Mexico, Costa Rica, Bolivia, Uruguay, Guatemala, Brazil, and Chile. What
emerged was this analysis of dynamic trends in Latin American oral history. The
author notes the different pace of development of archives, teaching, and interviewing
projects, according to country. Many factors have influenced the field's acceptance,
including university structures, intellectual and cultural traditions, and the ability to be
candid about a recent past which was tragically affected by counterinsurgent terrorism.
A key problem in many of these countries is how to elicit testimony without seeming to
interrogate, and how this testimony may be used to promote healing and critical historical consciousness.*

*Schwarzstein directs the program in oral history at the Institute of Argentine and
American History at the University of Buenos Aires. Her research interests include
migration, exile, the history of universities, and uses of oral history in social science.
She is the author of* Oral History *(1991),* Themes of Oral History *(1995), and* Luis
Santalo *(1995), all published in Buenos Aires.*

This article is a revised version of a paper presented at the IX International Congress of
Historical Sciences, Montreal, 1995, published in Spanish in *Historia y Fuente Oral* 14
(Barcelona, 1995). Used by permission of the author.

*T*he development of oral history in Latin America began much later than in Europe and the United States. Its origin in the region can be dated back to the 1970s. Since then, its development has been extremely slow and patchy. Furthermore, in some Latin American countries the field has not fully developed and it is only now that the very first experiences are taking place. Permanent political instability affected our countries until the mid-1980s, causing weak academic and university institutions. Therefore, all scientific disciplines faced major difficulties in creating and consolidating research groups.

During the 1970s several Latin American countries began their oral archives. Mexico, Brazil, and Argentina were the first. While the Mexican and Brazilian projects led to the creation of major institutions still in existence, the Argentine one was cut short in 1973. Those early experiences were influenced by the then prevailing styles in oral history in the United States. Their aim was the recovery of the testimonies of public figures to create archives open to public consultation.

Oral history was later developed, during the second half of the 1970s, in countries like Costa Rica, Mexico, and Ecuador, outside universities. It had political overtones and a strong emphasis on the recovery of the history of popular sectors. Peasants, members of Indian communities, urban workers, common men and women became the targets of oral history. A clear influence of the early British "history workshops," with their emphasis on political commitment and its close links with the labor movement and the new social movements, can be traced in many parts of Latin America. Oral history became then a major tool in the writing of history "from the bottom up." Its practitioners shared the hope of allowing the "voiceless" to speak.

It is only during the 1980s, with the end of both the military dictatorships and the dirty wars in the Southern Cone of South America, that oral history achieved a significant development in some Latin American countries. Associated with different environments, it has expanded its interests to include working class culture, the history of mentalities, rural-urban migration, Indian culture, issues of gender and identity, the history of organizations such as trade unions, the church, neighborhood communities, and even the history of elites.

Subjects and research styles vary in different national environments. While one can speak of a very important development of oral history in Latin America since the 1980s, it is also true that in many of our countries it is still marginalized from academic settings because it is not considered a "serious practice." That is the case in countries like Mexico, Argentina, and Uruguay where, in spite of its enormous developments during the last decades and the mushrooming of institutions with oral history projects, the links with the academic world are yet marginal. Probably the Latin American country where links between oral history and university institutions are better established is Costa Rica. The history department at the university has been working since the 1980s with popular organizations in research projects on the nonhegemonic classes.

In Mexico, there has been a transformation from the early empiricist attempts to build enormous oral archives to the development of specific research projects that create their own archives. In Brazil, the Oral History Program of the Getulio Vargas Foundation was created in 1975 with the purpose of interviewing national political leaders who had been active since the 1920s. At first, it was done primarily to keep a permanent and updated database. Another purpose for this archive was the recovery of the memory of processes prior to the military regime (1964–1985).[1] Starting in the early 1980s other oral history projects were created in universities and research institutions throughout Brazil. They mainly focused on the popular sectors. In the 1990s oral history has attained great development. As an expression of this growth, the Brazilian Association for Oral History was created in 1994. Today, several projects exist, covering topics as diverse as kids in the streets, the landless movements, and some on elite history. On an initiative from Columbia University, the first academic experience of oral history in Argentina was developed in Buenos Aires in 1970. It was the formation of an Oral Archive at the Instituto Di Tella, a private research center created in the 1950s. Influenced, promoted, and funded by Columbia University, it shared the same objectives as the New York–based projects at the time, that is, the collection of testimonies from politicians and trade unionists.[2] Nothing happened in the field of oral history for the next ten years. Since 1983, when the restoration of democracy opened a new cycle in the country's life, there has been a flourishing of oral history that seems likely to endure. The current work styles and themes are related in many ways to the political and cultural developments of the 1970s. The political upheavals and repression of that era originated a specific research agenda. Two national conferences confirmed the dynamism of the field in Argentina. The University of Buenos Aires, the largest one in the country, has created the first oral history program in the country, with the aim to promote research projects while simultaneously offering specific training in the field.

In Costa Rica there was also a start in the use of life stories during the late 1970s. Between 1976 and 1978, the Planning and Social Promotion School at the National University organized the First National Competition of Peasant Autobiographies, with the purpose of incorporating the peasants' viewpoint in the assessment of the country's agrarian processes. Research in Costa Rica using oral history interviews or life stories was focused on popular culture. Mainstream historians were not interested during the 1970s in the study of contemporary history. Oral history was thus seen as an nonacademic pursuit, mainly practiced outside universities.

This interest in popular history, associated to political militancy, was also to be found in Ecuador. During the 1970s the national government expanded its use of surveys of agrarian zones to better understand the working of community life: family organization, the income of the domestic unit, production patterns, and the like. In Ecuador the first experiences in the collection of oral testimonies took place in agrarian studies, in the mainly Indian regions of the highlands and the Amazons, under the influence of Mexican *indigenista* groups. More recently, in spite of the absence of a true trend of historical studies based on the recovery of oral testimonies, there have been in Ecuador isolated attempts to use oral history techniques in the research of the history, nature, and behavior of social movements, with special emphasis on the most marginal ones.[3]

Short after the victory of the Sandinistas, an oral history project was begun in Nicaragua in connection with the alphabetization campaign. The same had happened in Cuba, where the International "Casa de las Américas" Testimony Award has been created, and many official projects were begun. In Bolivia, in spite of early attempts during the late 1970s, it was only in the early 1980s that the encounter between a new generation of historians and several anthropologists of various nationalities created the conditions for the spread of oral interview techniques. The Andean Oral History Workshop (THOA) was created in the early 1980s as an interdisciplinary center reuniting historians, sociologists, anthropologists, and linguists. Their focus is on subaltern groups, mainly non-Spanish-speaking Indians. Thus, their work is partly conducted in Quechua and Aymara. Because of this bilingual characteristic of their work, they occupy a marginal place with regard to mainstream Bolivian social sciences. This position has begun to change, with a boom of new literature and experiences that incorporate oral history methodology. Since the late 1980s, when the Bolivian government began to emphasize the need to recover Indian cultures, this movement has been growing steadily. Because of this growth, Bolivian oral history has been split in two quite different varieties. One seems to worry about the recovery of an "essential" folklore, including disparate things ranging from indigenous contraceptive methods to cosmic philosophies of dubious origins. A second one, much more academic, has concentrated on social issues to be found in life stories and in the relationship between the individual and society, attempting to rebuild a "collective memory."

Developments in Uruguay began even later. Military dictatorship continued until 1985, leading to the quasi-destruction of the university and the exile of many social scientists. Some of the few who remained in the country found their place in private research centers with international funding. It was in those centers where new research orientations begun to emerge with an agenda very similar to the Argentine one, with the use of oral testimonies. Although some university courses on the methodology and techniques of historical research include references to oral sources, oral history is still marginal in Uruguay.

Research with systematic recourse to oral testimonies began in Chile also in the 1980s. Their subjects have included the struggle of urban sectors and their mobilization capacities, daily life and ideology among the mine-workers, and the Left under the Popular Unity.[4]

Guatemala and El Salvador are two countries where only recently have efforts been begun to develop projects that make use of oral testimonies. For Guatemala these are isolated cases with no influence on the community of historians. There is a project in a private research center to study the migrant population and to create an oral archive.[5] In El Salvador, where no history degree is offered, there have been various attempts in diverse settings. A course was offered in 1994 on "The use of oral sources in the historical research of the present," at the department of philosophy of the Universidad Centroamericana José Simeón Cañas.

In the whole of Latin America, although subjects are extremely varied, the main aim is the reconstruction of the historical experience of the popular sectors. In the cases of Costa Rica or Mexico, this implies an emphasis on peasant and small agrarian producers; in Argentina and Uruguay on workers, women, children and migrants; in Bolivia and Peru on research centers for those who regard themselves as Indians, exploited or marginalized both in rural and urban areas.

There is still much to be done to ensure that oral history is in a position to make important contributions to the development of the social sciences and the understanding of our societies. The last decade has seen the proliferation of projects to compile testimonies as means of letting the voiceless "speak." Many of those experiences are signaled by crude empiricism. The traditional task of historian all but disappears, as he or she is transformed into a mere compiler of testimonies. In such works one can observe an attachment to the description of isolated events, the absence of historical problems, and a strong predilection for sheer transcription of interviews. Some of these projects go as far as expressing their fear of the supposedly paralyzing effects that methodological debates can have on empirical research. These oral historians prefer nonacademic settings for their projects, such as social clubs, societies of various kinds, public libraries, museums, trade unions, and so on, with the aim of democratizing history through the voice and participation of anonymous protagonists. In such a way they attempt not only to recover collective memory but also to question history's social role, as well as to propose new places from which to produce nonacademic collective knowledge.

These trends are dominant in the field. They give priority to a certain type of use of oral testimonies. While allowing the voice of the "true" protagonists to be transmitted, there is no specific task for the historian to perform. All issues related to the production of the historical source, and the understanding and interpretation of the documents, are left outside the proposed research. The historian is thus denied room for critical activity. The feelings of identification and fascination experienced by the historian when confronted with his subject and his witness lead to distortions and a naive relationship with the sources produced in such a way. Sometimes, with a more political attitude, the case is made for a more organic relationship between intellectuals and the working class and popular sectors. The desideratum would be the full coincidence between the researcher and his subject matter. Those empiricist practices share the "naive realism" that characterized the early history workshop group. Raphael Samuel's autocritique about the risks of accepting the subjects' discourse as transparent could well be applied to them.[6]

Because of the instability of Latin American politics and the persistence of violence, many testimonies can be highly fascinating. Researchers will be tempted to integrate into a "community of equals," transferring the control of the historical operation to the interviewees. The specific work of our discipline is thus deprofessionalized.

Another trend is occurring in Latin America among those historians who use oral testimonies. These historians find their inspiration, as do many colleagues from other fields, in the set of practices, orientations, and reactions that Peter Burke has identified as those of the third generation of the Annales school.[7] For these historians the rapprochement with anthropology and the rehabilitation of the previously abhorred political history has been especially relevant. This last connection has been reinforced by strong developments in the field of intellectual and cultural history with points of reference in recent Anglo-Saxon historiography. In that general context, oral history becomes a specially apt road away from "structural determination" and into the apprehension of human agency, trajectories, representations, and subjectivity. For these historians, oral history is not only a technique, but also a historiographical field as defined by the international oral history movement, its research, and its methodological debates. These studies incorporate sophisticated perceptions regarding memory, ideology, and consciousness, with strong emphasis on the recovery of the subjective features of historical experience. Historians have a clear interest in discussing multiple methodological strategies to improve an approach seen as complex. The aim is to articulate the depth of the testimonies with analytical thoroughness. We historians need to be empirically faithful to the voices heard, but, simultaneously, to be analytically faithful to our task as historians. These historians share a lack of naivete when confronting oral testimonies, as with any other historical sources or regarding historical discourse itself.

Debates relate to the issue of how to use the oral source once it has been established. This is clearly the biggest challenge posed by oral sources, and significant progress is being made in many Latin American countries in this respect. The most common subjects are still the worlds of labor, migratory phenomena, the process of identity construction, and gender. Oral history is also used for elite history, as is the case of the projects on the history of the universities of Costa Rica and Buenos Aires, the oral history of medicine in Mexico, and on Mexican architects during the last half-century. It is possible to draw the conclusion that there is a great diversity of styles in the practice of oral history in Latin America, and it is that diversity that accounts for its strength and potential.

One should also take into account the current relationship between oral history and the social sciences in Latin America. In our continent there are many social scientists who show great interest in qualitative methodologies. Nonetheless, in many contemporary studies, the preferred field of political scientists, sociologists, and communication specialists—data offered by "key" informants—are taken noncritically. Their attitude is akin to the reverence shown by traditional historians when faced with old written documents at the archive. Very few among those planning to use interviews devote time and effort to train in specific techniques and to become aware of the many pitfalls involved.

On the contrary, anthropologists contribute to our field through their in-depth analysis of life stories, paying special attention to the relation between biography and social context. So do linguists, who offer many new and relevant insights for all those working with oral testimonies. In spite of the interest of these perspectives, interdisciplinary approaches benefitting oral history are not very common in Latin America. Nonetheless, oral historians seem very open to what neighboring disciplines can offer, and, in their interest in achieving a comprehensive understanding of actors and social life, they strive to integrate various approaches.

Oral history makes an important contribution to the historical discipline. It allows the recovery of experience in history. It allows history to gain in complexity and texture, to be inhabited by more actors, to include everyday life. Yet this is not enough. As happens with all types of historical sources, it is the way in which oral testimonies are used and interpreted that really matters. Oral history should integrate into a complex narrative both the witness's viewpoint and the historian's rhetoric, thus becoming a part of a larger effort toward a broader and more qualitative social history.

Notes

I wish to thank Jorge Acevez Lozano and Graciela De Garay in Mexico, Victor Acuña Ortega and Soili Buska in Costa Rica, Silvia Rivera Cusicanqui, Maria Eugenia Choque, and Rossana Barragán in Bolivia, Laura Bermúdez in Uruguay, Matilde González in Guatemala, and Julio Pinto Vallejos in Chile, who have generously provided me with information for this paper.

1. Aspasia Camargo, "Elaboración de la historia oral en Brasil. El proceso de transición visto a través de las historias de vida de los dirigentes políticos," *Secuencia* 4 (Mexico, January–April 1986), pp. 114–22.

2. The interviews are in the Oral History Archive of the Instituto Di Tella (Buenos Aires). Copies of those interviews can be found at the Oral History Archive, Columbia University (New York).

3. Ruth Moya, "Antropología e Historia Oral en Ecuador: balance y tendencias," paper presented at the "Coloquio de Historia y Antropología Andinas," Centro Bartolomé de las Casas (Cusco, 1988), mimeo.

4. Gonzalo Cáceres, "Historia oral o fuentes orales para la investigación histórica?: algunas relfexiones sobre la situación chilena," *SOLAR- Estudios Latinoamericanos* 3 (Santiago, 1993).

5. Matilde González, AVANCSO, "Historia Oral, una manera de acercarse a la población desplazada?," paper presented at the "II Congreso Centroamericano de Historia" (Guatemala, 1994), mimeo.

6. Raphael Samuel and Paul Thompson, eds., *The Myths We Live By* (London and New York, 1990), p. 2.

7. Peter Burke, *The French Historical Revolution. The Annales School, 1929–1989* (Cambridge, England, 1990).

INDEX

About the Editors

DAVID KING DUNAWAY attended the University of Aix-en-Provence, France and the University of Wisconsin, with graduate training at the University of California, Berkeley, where he received Berkeley's first Ph.D. in American Studies. At the University of New Mexico, Dr. Dunaway teaches biography, oral history, and media studies. He has served as a Fulbright lecturer at the University of Nairobi and the University of Copenhagen. For 20 years, he has written and produced documentaries based on history and literature.

His biography of Pete Seeger, *How Can I Keep From Singing?* (1981), won the Deems Taylor Award from the American Society of Composers, Authors and Publishers. His volumes of biography and oral history include *Huxley in Hollywood* (1989), *Aldous Huxley Recollected* (1995) and *Writing the Southwest* (1995), in Japenese, Spanish, and English editions. A past consultant to UNESCO, his articles about American culture appear in publications ranging from the *Virginia Quarterly* to the *New York Times*.

WILLA KLUG BAUM directs the Regional Oral History Office of the University of California, Berkeley. A graduate of Whittier College, Baum received her M.A. from Mills College, in American History and Political Science. At Berkeley, she continued her graduate studies, in California History, and since 1954 directed the third-oldest oral history collection in the United States, supervising 1500 bound volumes.

Baum has played a major role in developing oral history as a technique for local history and grassroots projects, with her classic guides, *Oral History for the Local Historical Society* (1974) and *Transcribing and Editing Oral History* (1977), both published by the American Association for State and Local History. She was a founding member of the Oral History Association and today lectures and contributes articles to library and history journals.